D1496374

Yours &c

Ira B, Peck

A Genealogical History

OF THE

Descendants

OF

Joseph Peck

WHO EMIGRATED WITH HIS FAMILY
TO THIS COUNTRY IN 1638;
AND RECORDS OF HIS FATHER'S AND
GRANDFATHER'S FAMILIES IN ENGLAND;
WITH THE PEDIGREE EXTENDING BACK
FROM SON TO FATHER FOR TWENTY GENERATIONS;
WITH THEIR COAT OF ARMS,
AND COPIES OF WILLS.
ALSO,

AN APPENDIX,

GIVING AN ACCOUNT OF
THE BOSTON AND HINGHAM PECKS,
THE DESCENDANTS OF JOHN PECK OF MENDON, MASS,
DEACON PAUL OF HARTFORD,
DEACONS WILLIAM AND HENRY OF NEW HAVEN,
AND JOSEPH OF MILFORD, CONN,
WITH PORTRAITS OF DISTINGUISHED PERSONS
FROM STEEL ENGRAVINGS.

Ira B. Peck

A Heritage Classic

Reprint 1868
Boston

A Facsimile Reprint
Published 2001 by

HERITAGE BOOKS, INC.
1540E Pointer Ridge Place
Bowie, Maryland 20716
1-800-398-7709
www.heritagebooks.com

ISBN 0-7884-1871-8

A Complete Catalog Listing Hundreds of Titles
On History, Genealogy, and Americana
Available Free Upon Request

INTRODUCTION.

I MAKE no apology for having devoted so much time, labor and expense to the genealogy and history of the Pecks. To such of my readers, if any such there should be, as have no taste for such subjects, — who never knew or wished to know so much as the name of their grandfather, or who their ancestors were, or where they came from, — who have no respect for their memories, and not love enough for their parents to erect gravestones to their memory, or care whether their remains are covered or above ground, apology would be of no use, or arguments to show the duties we owe them, or the good that may result from such works to future generations, of no avail.

To such of my readers as can appreciate the motives and feelings which led me to attempt the task, and such of my friends as have urged me to pursue the subject to the extent I have, there is no necessity for apology. To these, I hope the work may prove acceptable and pleasing.

No one of them will ever know the amount of labor and toil and money it has cost me, or the difficulties, perplexities and discouragements with which I have had to contend. The collection of the material, and the arrangement of it, has occupied much of my time for more than ten years. During the time, I have not only travelled much, but my correspondence has extended into nearly all the United States and Territories, the British Provinces, New Brunswick, Nova Scotia, the Canadas and England. I have written and sent out about 3,000 letters, and 1,000 printed circulars. Of these letters, I have preserved copies of over 2,700. In answer to them, I have on file received from my correspondents over 2,000, many of them of much interest, all of which, if published, would make a volume many times larger than this. The manuscript has all of it been written over twice, much of it three, and some of the appendix four times, to admit of additional families and different arrangements of its several branches.

I hope to have been the means of bringing to light and preserving much that would otherwise have been lost. I feel that the work contains, not only much that is valuable now, but that will be more so as time passes away, and the names and histories of those now living, as well as those now gone, shall have been forgotten. I have endeavored to make the records it contains as full and correct as possible; but, where information and records are collected from so many different individuals and such a variety of sources, the information from one often conflicting with that from another, without the means of determining which is correct, it is very difficult to avoid errors.

Those who have never attempted to collect genealogical information know little of the difficulties attendant upon such labors. I have found many obstacles to contend with, which, could I have foreseen, I never should have attempted the task I have endeavored to accomplish. It often occurs that members of the same families will disagree as to the intended orthography of their names, and in relation to the dates of the births and deaths in the family; and when an appeal from them to the family record is made, and from that to the town record, each will be found to disagree with the other. In such cases I must leave them out, or adopt the one in which I had the most confidence. Persons of the same name often insist upon spelling it differently. In writing the names, I have generally followed the usual orthography, unless varied by the parent or person themselves. In copying from tombstones and early records, I have intended to preserve the ancient orthography.

In collecting information by correspondence, it often occurs that letters received will be such as to render it impossible to determine what was intended by many of the names and dates. The authors of such letters, when written to for explanations, often refused or neglected to answer my letters, — perhaps offended because I could not read their letters, or uncertain themselves in relation to the names and information given. Sometimes information must be received from aged persons, the only source from which it can be obtained. They are liable in the presence of a stranger, approach them with all the care you can, to become confused, or, from the impaired condition of their memories, to give incorrect information. Some of my information has been received from town clerks; they are liable to errors in copying records, often old, worn and defaced.

After the work was arranged, it was carefully read through and compared with the letters, records and documents from which it was compiled; and where records given by different individuals and by the same individual at different times disagreed, or wherever errors of any kind were suspected, letters of inquiry were written. Some of these were promptly answered, and the corrections, when necessary, were made. Others were not answered until the work was in the press, too late for corrections or additions, except at the end of the book.

After the records and historical matter were printed, it was again read through, and such errors as were found, whether typographical or otherwise, however small or of little consequence, were pointed out. This was preferred, rather than leave them to the conjecture and query of the reader, as is sometimes done in such works.

Another source of much difficulty and unpleasant feeling in collecting this kind of information is the little interest felt in the subject by many. Some, when called upon, would appear to think it an imposition to be asked for a record of their families, or to be supposed to know their ages, or to know the name of their grandfather, or to care who their ancestors were, or where they came from. Such persons were generally anxious to know if there was any "*property* anywhere *coming* to the Pecks that I was *after*," evidently thinking more of counting their dollars than keeping records of their families. Others, when called upon, would express an interest in the subject, and a willingness to send me, at some *future* time, records of their families, if they could only know who their ancestors were, how far back I had traced them, etc., but, when given the information, which perhaps had cost me months or years of labor, would forget their promises, and it would be the last I should hear of them or their records.

But those who have done the most to delay and injure the work and me, are those who have expressed an interest in the subject they seem never to have felt, made promises only to break them, and those who, when written to with the return postage, etc., inclosed, have neglected or refused to answer my letters and return my circulars. I would forget these gentlemen, and the unkindness — to call it by no other name — which I have received from some of them, if I could.

Although there have been many things unpleasant and discouraging in the preparation of the work, it has not all been so. In my travels, as well as in my correspondence, I have found many friends, who have lent me their aid and assistance, and treated me with a kindness and generosity that can never be forgotten. Some have subscribed for a number of copies, and furnished me with engravings of their likenesses for the work To all such I return my sincere thanks, especially to those who have had them engraved especially for the work.

The book is larger than it was at first expected to be. When my circulars were issued for subscribers, it was supposed, as stated in them, that it would contain about 350 pages, and about 6,000 names, including those who had become allied with the Pecks by marriage, and others; but much was afterwards added, and it now contains, notwithstanding I have condensed it all I could, 440 pages and over 11,000 names.

It was at first designed to arrange the names of the children in single columns, but, by leaving out the surname Peck and substituting b. for born, and using smaller type, they have been put in double columns. This reduced the size of the work about one quarter, and improved its appearance. In the appendix the names of the children follow each other, like other matter. There were so large a number of children in these branches of the name whose births and deaths I could not obtain, that to arrange them in columns made the work too open and broken to look well.

In condensing the work, foreign matter only has been left out. I have endeavored to retain all the names and dates, places of residence, early settlements, and such wills, deeds and papers as were thought to be of interest and best worth preserving, with the references and *data* by which the persons contained in the work might be traced out, and a more extended history of them learned, if desired. Had the work been arranged and printed as open as such works sometimes are, the descendants of the female branches traced out, more history and biography of the different individuals given, and matter foreign to the subject admitted, it would have been so large and expensive as to be purchased by but a few. It is now within the reach of every one. It will be found to contain the descendants of Joseph Peck, who emigrated to this country with his family in 1638, now generally known as the Massachusetts Pecks; with an appendix containing an account of the Boston and Hingham Pecks, also of the descendants of John Peck of Mendon, Mass., Joseph of Milford, Conn., Henry of New Haven, Deacon Paul of Hartford, and an account of some of the descendants of Deacon William of New Haven.

When I commenced my investigations I supposed that all the Pecks of this country were the descendants of Joseph of Massachusetts, but afterwards found that there were others by the name who early emigrated to this country and became progenitors, leaving descendants.

The extensive race of Pecks from Connecticut, now mixed in their settlements with each other and with the Massachusetts Pecks throughout the country, are from other ancestors, who early settled there. To separate these different branches of the same patronymic has been a work of much labor and perplexity. It has been in tracing out the descendants of the different ancestors, separating them from each other, and placing them in their proper positions or families and generations that the most of my labor has been required, and the difficulties and perplexities encountered.

Had all the Pecks of this country been the descendants of one emigrant ancestor, my labors would have been little in comparison to what they now have. The reader will find on examination that the descendants of Joseph, John, Nicholas, Samuel, Nathaniel and Israel Peck, who settled in Rehoboth, and John of Mendon, Mass., Deacon Paul of Hartford, — Deacon William and Henry of New Haven, and Joseph of Milford, ancestors of the Connecticut Pecks, have been separated from each other and arranged under their respective heads as separate ancestors.

What the relationship between the ancestor of the Massachusetts Pecks and the ancestors of the Connecticut Pecks was, or where they came off from the main branch of the name, has not been learned; but it is hoped that some of their descendants will now follow them back, and learn the connecting link. I would have been glad to have attempted this; but to obtain information from the other side of the water requires much time, is very expensive, and none of them offered to assist me, although many of them are men of wealth. Among many of the descendants of these Connecticut Pecks I found a coldness and indifference to the subject that I did not anticipate, and which was very discouraging to me. Although I found some who lent me their aid and assistance, and treated me with a generous kindness that will long be remembered, I found others who I felt treated me with a lack of generosity and an unkindness that I shall try to forget.

In addition to the history in this country of the descendants of Joseph Peck, the ancestor of the Massachusett Pecks and records of their families, the work will be found to contain not only a pedigree giving a record of his own, his father's and grandfather's families, with the names of his ancestors back from him in regular ascent for twenty generations, with the coat of arms, but also a copy of his own, his father's, his brothers', and his uncles' wills. I think it will be found that but few have been more successful in connecting their name with their English ancestry, or who have done so with any more certainty of correctness. Others may have been more successful in tracing out their names in this country, but I think few have devoted more time and labor to the subject.

The work was not commenced as an enterprise by which to make money. The collection of the material was at first commenced from a love of the subject, and a desire to learn who my ancestors were, and where they came from. After having traced back my own branch of the name to Joseph Peck, the immigrant ancestor to this country, and learned that he was of English descent, I desired to connect him with the name there. This, after a long time, was accomplished, but with much expense. When my friends learned what I had done, they urged me to trace out their branches of the name, and arrange them into families and generations with their proper connections. This I should have never attempted, had I anticipated the great amount of labor and time it required, and the expense attendant upon it. After this was accomplished, and my friends learned the amount and character of the information and material collected, they desired its publication, and offered me their assistance by subscribing for the work, and otherwise, some generously offering to contribute their likenesses for it; and I consented to prepare it for the press.

Although the collection of the material for the work was commenced without the expectation of any assistance or remuneration, its publication was assented to and undertaken with the promise and expectation of the co-operation and assistance of those of the name, by subscribing for the work or otherwise, so far at least as that I should lose nothing by it more than my time and labor. But in this I fear I am to be disappointed. As a means of obtaining subscribers, I have sent out to those of the name circulars for signatures, each containing a request that they should be returned, that I might know whether the person to whom they were addressed received them or not, and whether they would become subscribers. With each was enclosed the postage or return envelope, making the person to whom they were addressed no expense to return them, and as little trouble as I could. Notwithstanding this, less than one half of them have been returned. Of those who returned them, many did not become subscribers. A few not only subscribed themselves, but with much kindness obtained other names. This want of interest in the subject, and unkindness in refusing to return my circulars, was not anticipated; had it been, they never would have been issued. I have obtained a less number of subscribers than was expected, and the work has cost me much more.

The price of the book is lower in proportion to the number of names, the amount of information, and the number and excellence of the engravings it contains, and the present price of publishing, than such works usually are, or than any one of the kind with which I am acquainted. The engravings, which are upon steel, the most of which were done expressly for the work, cost, with the prints, over one thousand dollars. The price, which was limited to four dollars, and the postage in the circulars sent out for subscribers, is too low for the expense of the work. It was fixed when it was supposed the work would contain only about three hundred and fifty pages and six thousand names, and a few engravings, which my friends at first proposed should be lithographs, — an inferior and much cheaper engraving, although such as are often used in books of the kind. It was at first designed to only give the ancient arms of the Pecks printed in black lines, as is usually done in such works, at an expense of eight or ten dollars ; but they are now given with the quarterings, crest and motto in colors, and the ancient arms embossed upon the cover, at an expense for both of over one hundred dollars.

Many of my friends have advised me to raise the price of the book in proportion to its increased size and cost; but I have preferred to let the price remain to my subscribers, as limited in the circulars sent out for subscriptions, at four dollars and the postage, and trust to their generosity and sense of justice to contribute towards its increased size and value or not, as they may feel disposed. The price to those not subscribers will be fixed at five dollars. Should any of my subscribers feel generous enough to forward that sum for their books, it will be thankfully received ; and, as I must rely upon the sale of other copies in addition to those subscribed for to meet the expenses of the work, I hope many of my friends of the name not subscribers, and others who may chance to become its readers, will purchase it. All who will do so at any time, and assist in its sale, will do me a kindness for which I shall be thankful. Its completion and publication, the collection and arrangement of the additional material and information, and the execution of the engravings, — the last of which was finished but a few days before the work was given to the binder, — occupied more time than was expected ; but it has all been to the advantage of the subscriber.

The arrangement of the book has been made plain and easy to be understood. The explanations which follow and those at the commencement of the Index will enable the reader to find the names of the different persons in the work, and trace them forward and find their descendants, or trace them back and find their ancestors, with ease and without confusion.

EXPLANATIONS AND ABBREVIATIONS.

As Joseph Peck, the ancestor whose descendants the work was designed to contain, had six sons, each of whom had families, it is divided into six parts, giving the descendants of each son separately.

The numerals or consecutive numbers at the left of the names represent the number of each person individually from the ancestor.

This + sign placed before a name indicates that the person becomes a parent, and refers forward to the number of that person inclosed in brackets, where he and his family may be found.

When the name is not carried forward to another place in the book, whatever is said of the person is said in connection with and immediately following his father's family.

The figures in brackets at the left of the name refer back to the numerals, where that person and his father's family may be found.

The small figure over the name and above the line indicates the number of the generation to which the person belongs.

b, is used for born; bap. for baptized; m. for married; and unm. for unmarried.

T. Rec., B. 8, p. 367, means Taunton records, book 8, page 367; R. stands for Rehoboth; S. for Swansey; B. for Bristol; Bar. for Barrington; St. for Scituate; W. for Warren; P. for Providence; C. for Cumberland; A. for Attleborough; and cht. for chart or pedigree.

NAME.

Pek, Peck or Pecke, Peke, Peak or Peake, found in the different works on heraldry, are supposed by some to have been originally the same; but Peck and Peak were doubtless distinct names.

During a portion of the fifteenth and sixteenth centuries, many of the Pecks added the final *e* to their names, as indeed did the English to almost every name that would admit of it. So far as I learn, the Pecks now universally drop it.

The name is of very ancient origin. There are various theories as to its original meaning or signification, and conjectures and speculations as to those who first bore it, as there are in relation to other names, frequently given by those who write genealogies, and those who furnish arms and pedigrees, to order. Of these a chapter might be given; but as I design to deal with facts, and not legends and conjectures, I leave them all out as not worth the space they would occupy.

The name is of great antiquity. They are found seated in England, in Belton, Yorkshire, at a very early date. From there they spread into other portions of Europe, and are now found scattered throughout every country where civilization has found its way.

A branch settled at Hesden and Wakefield, in Yorkshire, whose descendants removed to Beccles, Suffolk County, and were the ancestors of Joseph Peck, of Hingham, Norfolk County, who became the emigrant ancestor to this country.

It will be seen by the pedigree, to which the reader is referred, that he was a lineal descendant in the twenty-first generation from John Peck, Esq., of Belton, Yorkshire, and baptized April 30, 1587, being in the fiftieth year of his age when he emigrated to this country.

PEDIGREE OF PECK

John Peck, of Belton, in Yorkshire, Esq. — daughter of ____ Mulgrave.

Thomas Peck, of Belton, Esq. [2] — daughter of Middleton, of Middleton ____ Brompton.

Robert Peck, of Belton, Esq. [3] — daughter of ____ Tunstall.

Robert Peck, of Belton, Esq. [4] — daughter of ____ Musgrate.

John Peck, of Belton, Esq. [5] — daughter of ____ Watford.

Thomas Peck, of Belton, Esq. [6] — daughter of ____ Blaxton, of Blaxton.

Thomas Peck, of Belton, Esq. [7] — daughter of ____ Littleton

John Peck, 2d son, settled in Northamptonshire.

John Peck, of Belton, Esq. [8] — daughter of ____ Carre

John Peck, of Belton, Esq. [9] — daughter of ____ Flemming

John Peck, of Belton, Esq. [10] — daughter of ____ Wemborne.

John Peck, of Belton, Esq. — daughter of ____ Fennwike.

daughter and sole heir of John Peck — John Ratcliffe, of Tostnorton. By his wife he possessed Belton.

Richard Peck, 2d son. [11] — daughter and heir of ____ Brunnne.

Richard Peck, of Hesleu, Esq. [12] — daughter of ____ Savill.

Thomas Peck, of Hesslen, Esq. [13] — daughter of ____ Bradley.

Richard Peck, of Hesleu, Esq., and of Wakefield, in Yorkshire [14] — daughter and heir of ____ Hesselden.

John Peck 1st son, a lawyer [15] — Isabel, daughter of John Lacie, of Brombleton.

Richard Peck, 2d son, died young.

Thomas Peck, 3d son —

Richard Peck, of Wakefield, Esq. [16] — Joan, daughter of John Harrington, Esq.

John Peck, of Knoston, in Colchester —

Stephen Peck, of Knoston — Anne, dau. of Cave, of Peckwell.

Richard Peck, Esq. [17] — Alice, daughter of Sir Peter Middleton, knt.

William Peck — Martha, daughter of William Peck, of Spixwell, in Norfolk; Knoston. Second husband, Henry Allen, of Rutlandshire.

John Peck, of Wakefield, Esq. [18] — Joan, daughter of John Anne, of Treckey.

Robert.   Catherine, mar. Scargill.   Joan, mar. ... Morton.   Margaret.   Elizabeth.

Thomas.   Margaret.   Isabel.   Joan.   Judith.

Margaret.   Anne.   Elizabeth.   Isabel.

William Peck, of Knoston.

John Peck.

William Peck, of Knoston.

Richard Peck, = Anne, dau. and heir of Sr. John Hotham, of Scarboro', Knt.
of Wakefield.

Richard Peck, dau. = Katherine, of Sir Wm. Vavasour, of Wakefield. of Haselwood, Knt.

| John. | Thomas. | Ralph, mar. a dau. of Leake. | Nicholas = ... daughter of ... Tryant, of Bradford. | Francis. | Robert Peck, = ... daughter of ... of Nor-ton. | Katherine, mar. Jo. Lenke, of Normanton. | Margaret, mar. John Taylor. | Anne, mar. Robert Page. | Dorothy, mar. William Rouke. |

Thomas, died young.

John, died young.

Dorothy, m. Mathew Lenzh, of Delaroobs.

Elizabeth, mar. Ralph Vavasour.

Katherine, ob. without issue.

Jasper Peck = Anne, daughter of ... Hooper, of Co. Warwick.

Thomas. Richm. Nicholas. John.

Thomas Peck = Cecilia, daughter of Geo. aged 10 in 155-. Medcalfe, of S.

Elizabeth, mar. John Dravcott.

George Peck ... Anne, dau. of Wm. Clatton, of Carlbrook.

Alice. Richard. Avery.

Thomas aged 8 in 1611.

Godfrey. Richard. Francis. Faith. Catharine. Philip.

John Peck, died without issue.

Robert Peck = Helen, daughter of Nicho-of Beccles, d. his Bibbs, of Guilford. 1582, aged 17.

Thomas Peck, died without issue.

Anne Peck, died without issue.

Margaret Peck, died without issue.

John Peck, mar. Richard Wearman, of Beccles.

Olivia Peck, mar. Richard Nall, of Beccles.

Martha.

Samuel, ob. 1635.

Nicho. Peck, = Rachel, dau. aged 21 in and wife later 1605. of William Younge, mar. at Yarmouth, Feb. 16, 1626.

Robert Peck, aged 50 in 1644, took his degrees at Magdalen College Cambridge, A.B. in 1599, and A. M. in 1603; Institute to the parish of Hingham, Co. Norfolk, in 1605, January 2 ...

Richard Peck, died in 1614, aged 24 without issue.

Anne, buried at Hingham, in England, 30th August, 1648.

Joseph Peck, of Hingham, in Norfolk Co., bap. April 30, 1587. Second wife.

Rebecca Clark married at Hingham, 21st May, 1617. She was buried 24th October, 1637.

Anne Peck, bap. Mar. 12, 16-8; buried 24th July, 1636.

Rebecca Peck, bap. 20th May, 16-0.

Joseph Peck, bap. 6d Au. 22nd, 1623.

John. Nicholas, ap. 26th April, 1630.

Samuel, bap. 2d February, 1635-3.

Nathaniel, bap. 31st October, 1631.

Israel, bap. 4th March, 1641.

William Peck, bap. 11th Sept ...

Robert Peck, bap. ... Octo.; bur. 11th April, 1618.

Joseph Peck, bap. 23d April, 1620.

Benjamin Peck, bap. 29th September, 1628.

Samuel Peck, bap. 11th March, 16-2-3.

Nathaniel Peck, bap. 31st December, 1641.

Daniel Peck, buried 8th June 1641.

Thomas Peck, bap. 6th September, 1626.

Samuel Peck, bap. 1st March, 1647-8.

Samuel Peck, bap. 15th March, 16-6.

Anne Peck, bap. 15th November, 1645.

PEDIGREE.

The pedigree, as it is here given, may be found in the British Museum, London, England, excepting the two last families, those of Robert and Joseph, which are added to it.

The family of Robert, and the eldest children of Joseph, are from the parish records of Hingham, England. The three youngest children of Joseph are from the records at Hingham, Massachusetts, being born here.

It will be seen that the pedigree extends back from Joseph, twenty generations, to John Peck, Esq., of Belton, Yorkshire, and must be of interest to all who feel an interest in the subject.

The following is the certificate of the heralds accompanying the pedigree and arms in the British Museum.

20th Nov. 1620.

Visum agnitum et in munimenta Collegii Heraldorū relatum die et Anno suprascriptis.

Testamur hoc.

> Henry St. George, Richmond.
> Henry Chitting, Chester.
> John Philpott, Rogue Dragon.

It may be translated to mean that they had seen or examined it, acknowledged it true, and entered it upon record, or placed it in the archives of the Heralds' College on the day and year above written.

ARMS.

The arms, which are here given in colors, are in the British Museum, with the pedigree certified to by the heralds. The quartering is with the Brunning and Hesselden families, the heiresses of which the early Pecks married.

The first and fourth are the arms of Peck, the second of Brunning, and the third of Hesselden, and in heraldic language may be thus emblazoned or described:

Peck — Argent, on a chevron engrailed, Gules, three Crosses formée, of the first.

Brunning — Azure, two bars nebule, Argent.

Hesselden — Gules, a cross patonce, Or; on a chief, Azure; three round buckles of the second.

Crest — A cubit arm erect, habited, Azure; cuff, Argent; hand proper, holding on one stalk, enfiled with a scroll; three roses, Gules; leaves, Vert.

There are in the British Museum the arms of Peck, impaled with the arms of many families, into which they have married.

There is no motto recorded with the early arms of the family. The one given, "Probitatem quam divitias," "probity (or truth and honesty) rather than riches" has been added. Some of the Pecks in England who use the arm and rose for a crest, I am told, have added or adopted for a motto, "Crux Christi salus mea," or "the cross of Christ is my salvation."*

The arms upon the cover of the book, are the ancient arms of Peck before the crest or the arms of the Brunning and Hesselden families, or the motto, was added.

---

* A crest or a motto is not a part of a coat of arms, but they are added or adopted by those entitled to the arms who desire to do so.
The helmet is sometimes used without the crest, as it is upon the tombstone at page 34, and sometimes with the crest. It is used with the crest, on the arms of Peck, in the British Museum.

GENEALOGY.

JOSEPH PECK, THE ANCESTOR.

Joseph Peck, the emigrant ancestor of the Pecks in this country, known as the Massachusetts Pecks, now a numerous and extensive race scattered throughout the United States, its Territories, the British Provinces, and the Canadas, was baptized in Beccles, Suffolk County, England, April 30, 1587. *

He was the son of Robert Peck, as will be seen by a reference to the chart, being a descendant in the twenty-first generation from John Peck, of Belton, Yorkshire. He settled at Hingham, Norfolk County, England. In 1638, he and other puritans, with his brother Robert Peck, their pastor, fled from the persecutions of the church to this country. They came over in the ship Diligent of Ipswich, John Martin, master.

Daniel Cushing, then town clerk here at Hingham, Norfolk County, New England, in speaking of his arrival in this country says: "Mr. Joseph Peck and his wife with three sons and daughter and two men servants, and three maid servants, came from Old Hingham, and settled at New Hingham." His children were as follows:

Anna, baptized in Hingham, England, March 12, 1617–18, † and buried there, July 27, 1636. Rebecca, baptized in Hingham, England, May 25, 1620; and, as appears by her father's will, married a

---

* Upon early records, births and deaths are not often given. They were generally kept by Parish clerks, who only gave the baptisms and burials.

† For an explanation of this kind of dating, see birth of Ichabod Peck, No. 10, Part I.

2

Hubbert. Joseph, baptized in Hingham, England, August 23, 1623. For the history of him and his descendants, see Part I. John, baptized about 1626. For a history of him and his descendants, see Part II. Nicholas baptized in Hingham, England, April 9, 1630. For his history, see Part III. Samuel, baptized here at Hingham, in New England, February 3, 1638-9, see Part IV. Nathaniel, baptized here at Hingham, New England, October 31, 1641, Part V. Israel, baptized here, March 4, 1644, Part VI.

He was twice married. His first wife was Rebecca Clark. They were married at Hingham, England, May 21, 1617. She died and was buried there, October 24, 1637. The name of his second wife, and the baptism of his son John, was not found. It was not upon the records at Hingham, where his first marriage and the baptisms of his other children were recorded. It probably took place in another parish where the records were not preserved.

He seems to have belonged to that class in England known as gentlemen or the gentry entitled to coat-armor, etc., who ranked next to Baronets.[*]

Soon after his arrival here, he settled in Hingham, Mass. The records there in 1638 say:

Mr. Joseph Peck [†] received a grant of seven acres of land, for a house lot, next to Robert Peck his brother; he also received other grants of land.

---

[*] In relation to his political, public or private life in England, or that of his father, I did not attempt to learn anything. To have done so at this late day, now more than two hundred years since they lived, would have been attended with great expense and much uncertainty as to finding anything reliable in relation to them. My resources had been heavily drawn upon in tracing him back to England, connecting him with his ancestors there, and learning what I had in relation to them; and as none of my friends, although many of them were abundantly able, offered to contribute towards the expense, I was obliged to content myself with what I had already learned there, that I might devote my means to tracing out his descendants here.

[†] This prefix or title of Mr., which is found with his name wherever it appears upon record, indicates the position he occupied in society. It was of much more import and significance then than now. There were but a few of those who came over to whose name it was attached: they generally occupied a lower position in society.

He remained at Hingham about seven years, when he removed to Seekonk.

While he remained at Hingham, he was one of its leading men. He was Representative, or deputy to the General Court in 1639, 1640, 1641 and 1642. He took an active interest in the business of the town. He was one of the selectmen, justice of the peace, assessor, etc.

He was appointed by the court to grant summons and attachments, to see people joined in marriage, to keep the records, etc.

In 1641, he became one of the principal purchasers * of the indians of that tract of land called by them Seacunk or Seekonk, afterwards incorporated into a town since known as Rehoboth, Mass., at first called eight miles square, but afterwards found to be about ten. It comprised what is now Rehoboth, Seekonk, and Pawtucket. † He did not however remove there until 1645.

Upon the Rehoboth records is the following notice of an accident which befel him on his removal thither :

" Another strange accident happened by fire about this time. Mr. Joseph Peck, and three others of Hingham, being about to remove to Seacunk, (which was concluded by the Commissioners of the United colonies to belong to Plymouth,) riding thither they sheltered themselves and their horses in an indian wigwam, which by some occasion took fire, and (although there were four in it, and labored to their utmost) burnt three of their horses to death, and all their goods, to the value of fifty pounds."

---

* See confirmation deed from the colony to the town of Rehoboth, in 1685, (Plymouth Colony Records, B. 5 P. 341,) also quitclaim deed from William Bradford, in 1689.

† The proprietors of Rehoboth also purchased other lands of the indians. Their second purchase was a tract known as Wanamoiset, being what was afterwards a part of Swansey and Barrington.

Their third purchase was in 1661, from Wamsitta, brother of King Philip, called the north purchase, including what was afterwards Attleborough, Mass. and Cumberland, R. I. It was incorporated into a town, taking the name of Attleborough, in 1694. It remained Attleborough until the settlement of the line between the Plymouth and Rhode Island colony, when the part since Cumberland was set off to Rhode Island. It was incorporated into a town in 1746, taking its present name. It has since been divided, a portion of it taking the name of Woonsocket, the Indian name of the locality.

After his removal to Seekonk, his name continually appears upon the records of the town, in the management of its affairs, until his age precluded him from such duties.

His name also appears upon the Plymouth Colonial records, as it did upon those of Massachusetts.

He was appointed to assist in matters of controversy at court. In 1650, the court appointed him to administer marriage. In 1651, he was appointed to determine all controversies, not exceeding a certain amount. He was also appointed to administer oaths, issue warrants, etc.

He seems to have been one of the principal men here, as he had been at Hingham, as well as one of the wealthiest.

In the purchase of the town as in the appraisal of the purchaser's rights for the apportionment of a tax, there was but one who paid more or whose rights were prized more than his.

In addition to his interest in the first purchase of the town, he afterwards bought other rights which made him a large owner.

His rights in the common undivided lands at his decease were given to his sons, as well as those which had then been divided. In some instances, these lands still remain in the name and are owned and occupied by his descendants. The Pecks of Barrington (Ellis, Asa and others) now occupy lands given to his youngest sons, Nathaniel and Israel.

The proprietors of Rehoboth first settled upon what has since been known as Seekonk Plain,* a tract of cleared land which had been the planting grounds of the indians. The settlers appropriated it to the same purpose until its fertility became exhausted, when they were obliged to leave the plain and seek the smaller openings which were more productive, thus gradually penetrating the wilderness, and extending the settlements of their town.

The house of Joseph, which seems to have been of the better class, stood upon the plain in the northerly part of the " Ring of

---

* Bliss, in his history of Rehoboth, supposes this word to be composed of the indian words seaki, meaning black, and honk, goose — black goose being the indian name for the wild goose, and thinks the place received its name from the fact of great numbers of wild geese in their semi-annual migrations, alighting here in the river and cove adjacent.

the Town."* Its location was near the junction of the present Pawtucket with the old Boston and Bristol road, so called, westerly and not far from the present depot of the Boston and Providence Railroad as it crosses the plain.

It was here that he lived, and died December 23, 1663, in the seventy-seventh year of his age, far from the tombs of his fathers, the associations of his youth, and the scenes of his early life, but doubtless happy in the thought of having been able to worship God after the dictates of his own conscience, and of being surrounded by his children, in whose care his remains would be left to be buried where they would be surrounded by those of his descendants.

No stones, now more than two hundred years since, mark the spot of their interment, but the subsequent graves of his descendants indicate the place.†

The following is a copy of his will :

Know all men by these presents that I joseph Peck Sen[r] of Rehoboth do ordain and make this my last will and testament in manner and form following

Item — I give and bequeath unto my son joseph all my lands and medows lying and being near unto the River called Palmers River to him and his heirs forever

Item — I give unto him my old black mare and my great chist in the parlor

Item — I give unto my son john my house and lands which I purchased of joseph Torry and the half of the meddow betwixt Mr Newman and mee on the other side of the new meddow river to him and his heirs forever Also I give unto him my great chist in the hall.

Item — I give and bequeath unto my son Nicholas all my meddow at

---

* The proprietors first selected their lots and erected their dwellings in a semicircle, the circle opening towards the Pawtucket or Seekonk River, with their parsonage and meeting-house in the centre. The circle was called the ring of the town. It can still be seen in the present location of the houses there, in an eastern view from the church.

† The gravestones of his son Israel were still standing in a good state of preservation when I last visited the place, although he had then been deceased over one hundred and forty years. For the inscriptions, see Israel, Part VI.

2*

the hundred acres and the meddow called bushey meddow and all my medows on the north side of the town to him and his heirs forever

Item — I give and bequeath unto my son Samuell my house where I now dwell with all the houses standing there The outyards and all my house lott and all my land in the second Division and my Plaine lotts excepting half my furthest which I give unto my son Nicholas; and also I give unto him my meddow called cheesbrooks meddow and also my salt marsh att broad cove To him and his heirs forever Item — I give unto my sonns Nathaniel and Israel all my lands which I purchased of John Adams and Mr. Bradford with the meddow called the long beach which is betwixt Mr Newman and mee, and all my meddow at Squamquammett which is betwixt John Allin and mee; and olso my meddow at Papasquash betwixt John Allen and mee to them and their heirs forever.

Item — I give my use of the meddow att Kekemuett unto John Pecke my son and also all my lands att Wackemauquate I give unto my sonnes Joseph and Nicholas to be equally devided betwixt them Item — I give and bequeath unto my Daughter Hubbert thirty pounds in such pay as can be raised out of the goods I shall leave to be paid by my Executors within one year after my decease and also I give unto her my wifes best cloak and one fine Pillowbeer and my Damask Napkin

Item — I give unto my son Samuell my silver beaker and two silver spoons and one gould Ringe which was his mothers and also one paire of fine holland Sheets and one Diaper Tablecloth and six Diaper Napkins 2 fine pillow beares and the feather bed and bolster and pillow and two Blanketts whereon I now lye my second Rugg with some other small linnene in my Trunk in the parlor which I also give unto him and the other chist under the window in the parlor and my best curtains and curtain rodds Item — I give unto my son Nathaniel my biggest silver cupp and gould Ringe two silver spoons my best feather bed one bolster two Blanketts the Rugg that now lyeth upon mee my trunk in the parlour chamber my round table three Diapir napkins one long table cloth betwixt Israell and him

Item — I give unto Israell my son my silver salt 2 silver spoons my two bed teekes with the bolesters the old flocke bed two blanketts my best coverlid one bolster one pillow two pillowbears also unto Nathaniel one pillow 2 pillowbears. Item — I give unto Israell ten of my best ewes and my sorrelled mare two of my best cowes and my bull and my segg and three Diaper napkins Item — I give unto my son Joseph five ewes and to my son Samuel my two oxen called Bucke and Duke and two cowes my cart and one of my little Plowes one chain with the copses for the cart and I give unto Nathaniel two steeres and two cowes Item — I give unto my son Nicholas the feather bed which he hath alreaddy and my best Rugg and unto my son John I give the feather bed and bolster which he alreaddy hath and 40s to buy him a rugg and to Israell I give the two little chists in the chamber and his mothers little trunke and unto my son Samuel I give my Bedstead in the parlour chamber Item — I give unto my son Joseph my gould Ringe and unto John and Nicholas my two silver wine cupps — My mind is that my three younger sonnes should have each three platters and all the rest my pewter should be equally between my six sonnes and all my apparrel I give unto my three elder sonnes and all my wifes Apparrell I give unto my three youngest sonnes to bee equally divided betwixt them Item — I give and bequeath all the rest of my goods cattles & chattles my debts and legacies being payed and my body brought to the grave unto my six sonnes equally to be divided amongst them the youngest and weakest to have as good a share as the eldest and strongest dsireing Mr Newman and my brother Thomas Cooper to be the supervisors of this my Testament and last will and I do ordaine my son Nicholas and my son Samuell the executors of this my last will desiring the Lord to guide theire hartes to do all according unto my intent heer sett down

The last will & Testament of mee Joseph Pecke written with my own hand.

A further Amplyfication of our fathers will upon his death bed, which was not expressed in his written will. Item — hee gave to his son Joseph half his meddow that hee purchased of Mr Bradford lying on the further side of the new Meddow River: to his son John thirty-five pounds of comon: to his son Samuel two hundred and fifty pounds of comon to his son Nathaniel two hundred pounds of comon. These gifts were given to them and their heirs forever moreover our father added to his daughter hubbert ten pounds more than was sett downe in his written will Item — that Nathaniel and Israell shall have equal shares of the corne that shall be raised upon that ground which hee hath given to his son Samuel for this year ensuing they bestowing an equal share of labor with them upon the land. It was further expressed by him that seeing those oxen expressed in his will that was given to his three younger sons was disposed of before his

death that those younge oxen and steeres that are coming on in theire
romes should bee made choice of by them in manor as followeth his
son Samuel first choosing his son Israell next and Nathaniel last   It
was his will also that those two mares which were given to his sonnes
Joseph and Israel being not extant that Joseph should have his old
mare and Israell his young mare instead of the other — further
whereas our father gave to his sonnes Joseph five sheep and Israell
ten they also being sold before our fathers death wee have agreed that
they shall have in valuation as they were sould which was nine shillings a pieece.

This we own to be our fathers will expressed by him unto us when
he was in his perfect memory which we owne as his proper will and
desire.

In witness whereof wee have sett to our hands

Witness hiereof	
STEPHEN PAINE,	JOSEPH PECKE,
THOMAS COOPER	JOHN PECKE,
JOHN REED	NICHOLAS PECKE
	SAMUELL PECKE
	NATHANIELL PECKE
	ISRAELL PECKE

This will is recorded upon the old Plymouth Colony Records, Book
of Wills, 2d part, Vol. 2d, Folio 12.

ROBERT PECK.

ROBERT PECK, the father of Joseph the ancestor, was also the son
of Robert, as will be seen by the chart. He was of Beccles, Suffolk
County; born in 1546 and died in 1593, aged forty-seven. The
position which he occupied in society was that known in England
as gentleman or gentry entitled to coat-armor, etc., and at that
time, before the title of Baronet* was given, next to the nobility,
or the title honored.

---

* This order was instituted by James I. in 1611.

From all the information I obtained in relation to the name there, it is evident that this branch was one of much distinction. Among all the coats of arms, charts and records which I obtained in relation to other branches, there were none apparently so ancient or upon which the Heralds had bestowed so much labor as upon those of this branch of our patronymic.

It was not customary in the early days of heraldry to give the collateral branches; only the lineage from father to son.

He married Hellen Babbs, daughter of Nicholas Babbs, of Guilford.

His children were Richard, who died without issue; Nicholas, who married Rachel, daughter of William Young; Robert, Rector at Hingham; Joseph, the Ancestor here; Margaret, Martha and Samuel.

He was a man of wealth, consisting of lands, houses, etc. His will was found at Ipswich after a tedious search. It was written with his own hand.

The following is a copy:

In the name of God Amen The xxij day of March in the year of o^r Lord God according to the computation of the church of England 1592 and in the xxxvth yere of the Reigne of o^r moste gratious soveraigne Lady Elizabeth by the grace of god of England ffrance and Irelande Quene Defend o^r of the faith etc. I Robert Peck of Beccles in the countye of Suff hole of mynd and perfect of Remembrance thanks be to the maiestye of god therefore Although sick and weake of body at chemissfforde in the cowntye of Essex at this p^r sente of a pluresye not knowinge whither it will please god to take me awaye here or not, do for the better orderinge and dispocision of such goods cattels chattells plate lands tenements and other heriditaments with the appertences do make and dispose them as followeth ffirst I bequeath my sowle to the Infinite mercye of Almightye Gode trustinge assurealye to be saved by the meritts death and passion of Jesus christ his dere sonne, and my bodye to be buried where it shall please god to call me Item I give and bequeath to Hellen my welle loved wife (in consideration of the paiment of my debts the bringinge up of my children and the finishinge of the houses wch I am now in buildinge) All my houses Lands Tenements medowes pastures fedings as

well free hold as coppeholde and all other my leases plate goods and
cattles whatsoev' or wheresoev' ling wth in the townes of Beccles,
Barsh^m Ingate or else where to haue and to hold all and singular the
p^r mises wth the apprtens to the said Hellen or her assignes for and
duringe her natural life in concinderacion of the things above mentioned and also paienge such legacies unto my children as I shall
appointe or otherwise leave it for want of tyme to her godly consideration where in I desire her in gods behalf to provide for them accord-
inge to her abillitye.

And for the better accomplishinge here of I do give unto her full
power and authoritye to sell my woods in Barshm" or my medows in
Barshm" or both if neede shall so require   And I doe hartelye desire
my very good ffriends Mr Bartholomew Stiles and Mr John Talbot
to be aidinge and assistinge my said wife wth there good counsell
advice and labo^r about the execution of this my last will and Testament.

Item I give unto Richard Peck my sonne all that my houses where
in I dwell in Blibergate street my close at Ingate church. my pightill
in the same field to have and to hold to him and to his heres forever
And olso all the lease lands adioyinge to the said close for and duringe the numbers of yeres y^t to come yf his mother will vouchsafe
him such favo^r uppon condicon that he paye such legacies as his
mother shall think good to appoint him to doe

Item whereas Thomas Peck my brother deceased by his last will
and Tistament did give unto the said Richard my sonne two tennements inc Balligate street lately burnt and now againe one of
them builded upon the same grownde and the other upon pcell
of the said grownde and upon pcell of other free grownde w^ch
I purchased of mine uncle Wm Waters I will therefore that
the said Richard my sonne w^thin one month after that he
shall be of his age of xx j^th years shall make over astate in fee simple
to such of my sonnes and there heirs as I shall hereafter bequeath the
said tennements unto and also surrendo^r my coppeholde if it come to
his handes for want of surrendo^r.   And yf my saide sonne Richard
shall not pform theise things before assigned him I will that he shall
loose the benefit of such houses landes and leases as I have before
assigned unto him and the same to be to thoese of my twoe sonnes to
whoeme I shall geve the foresaide newe tenements and to there heires
and assignes forever   Item I give to Nicholas Peck my sonne my
newe tenement ptely builded uppon the Tenement late Wm Waters

and my medowes lienge in Barshm (if his mother shall spare the saide medowes) To have and To holde to him the said Nicholas and his heires for ev^r paienge out of the same such somes of money as his mother shall assigne him to doe. Item I geve unto Samuell Peck my sonne the other newe tenement and little coppiholde yard to have and to holde to him & his heires forev^r paienge out thereof to such of his brothers and sisters such money as his mother shall assigne him to doe

Item I will yf for the benefit of paienge my debtes bringinge up my children findinge my sone Robert* at Cambridge and providinge legacies for my twoe daughters and my sone Joseph That if my saide wife shall make a lease of all or any pcell of my sayde landes and Tenements That the same shall continue for so many years as she shall lease the same her saide death or any other legacies what soev^r before given or appointed to the contrary in any wise notw^th standinge. The Residewe of all my goodes and chattells whatsoever. I give them whoelye to the saide Hellen my wife whoeme I make my sole execu-trix desiringe her in godes behalf to have care of thoese my children whoese legacies I have lefte to her consideracon.

And also of Joane Babb & Elisabeth Babb and Robert Meriman & my sister Note as she may Item I ordain Mr Bartholomewe Stiles clerk, Mr Roger Peirson and Mr John Talbot supervisoer hartelie desiringe them to Aide my wief wth there beste helpe counsell and advice aboute the Execution hereof Written wth myne owne hande The day and yere above saide By me

Proved at Beccles Nov 10—1598

The following is a copy of the will of Thomas Pecke, uncle of Joseph the Ancestor.

In the name of god amen, The xvj^th daie of ffebruarie in the yere of o^r Lord god m^tcccccLxxiij^th I Thomas Pecke of Beccles in the countie of Suff and dioces of Norw^ch holl of mynde & in pfit helth of bodie thanks be gyven to Allmightie god intending by gods sufferance to

* Afterwards Rev. Robert, Minister at Hingham.

travell into farren cuntries and purposing before my departure to declare my mynde and set suche things as god hath sent me at steye least in my absence god doth call me sodenlie awaye do orden make and declare this my last will and testament in manner and forme followinge

ffirst I bequeath my soule to Allmightie god and my bodye to be buried where it shall please god to call me Item I gyve and bequeath unto Richard Pecke my Nephew the sone of Robert Pecke my brother all those my two tenements with theire Appurtenes situate lienge and beinge together in Beccles next unto a streete called Balligate to have & to holde unto hym the seid Richard and his heires forever upon condicon that he the said Richard his heires or Assignes do paic or cause to be paid unto Oleff the wief of Richard Note and Ane Pecke my sister to either of them at such tyme as he doth enioye the p^{r}misses the some of fyve marks of lawfull money of England. And if it shall fortune the said Richard to die before he come to his lawfull age and do enioye the p^{r}mises then I gyve and bequeath all and singular the p^{r}misses with the appurtennes to the abovenamed Robert Pecke my brother and his heirs forever upon condicon that he the seid Robert do paie unto the seid Olyff and Ane my sister to either of them the some of fyve marks at suche tyme as he doth enioye the same Item I gyve and bequeth unto said Richard and Robert or to which of them that shall happen to enioye my said tenements all that mye lease and terme of yeres wch I have of a certen ground adioyndge unto the p^{r}misses

All the residue of my goods whatsoever I gyve and bequeath them to my seid brother Robt Pecke whome with the said Richard my nephew I orden and make my executors

In witness where of I have sette my hand and seale the daie and yere above said in the p^{r}sence of Richard Crompton Simeon Smyth and others   Witnesses to the same by me

THOMAS PECKE	Teste me	RICHARD CROMPTON
	Teste me	SIMEON SMYTHE

REV. ROBERT PECK.

Rev. Robert Peck, the brother of Joseph the ancestor, was born at Beccles, Suffolk County, England, in 1580.   He was graduated at Magdalen College, Cambridge; the degree of A. B. was conferred upon him in 1599, and that of A. M., in 1603.   He was set apart to the ministry, and inducted over the church at Hingham, Norfolk County, England, January 8, 1605, where he remained until 1638, when he fled from the persecutions of the church to this country.

He was a talented and influential clergyman, a zealous preacher, and a nonconformist to the superstitious ceremonies and corruptions of the church, for which he was persecuted and driven from the country.   Brooks, in his lives of the puritans, gives many facts of interest in relation to him.   In particularizing some of the offences for which he and his followers were persecuted, he says, " for having catechised his family, and sung a psalm in his own house on a Lord's day evening, when some of his neighbors attended, his lordship (Bishop Harsnet) enjoined all who were present to do penance, requiring them to say, I confess my errors," etc.

Those who refused were immediately excommunicated, and required to pay heavy costs.   This, Mr. Brooks says, appears from the bishop's manuscripts under his own hands.   He says, " he was driven from his flock, deprived of his benefice, and forced to seek his bread in a foreign land."

Cotton Mather in speaking of him says, he was by the good providence of heaven fetched away into New England about the year 1638, when the good people of Hingham did rejoice in the light for a season; but within two or three years, the invitation of his friends of Hingham, England, persuaded him to return to them, where being though great in person for stature, yet greater for spirit, he was greatly serviceable for the good of the church.

He arrived here in 1638.   In relation to his arrival, the town clerk at Hingham here says: " Mr. Robert Peck, preacher of the gospel in the Town of Hingham, in the County of Norfolk, old England, with his wife and two children, and two servants, came over

3

the sea and settled in this town of Hingham, and he was a Teacher
of the Church." Mr. Hobart, of Hingham, says in his diary, that he
was ordained here teacher of the church, November 28, 1638. His
name frequently appears upon the records of the town. He had
lands granted him.

His family as seen upon the chart consisted of nine children.
His son Joseph and daughter Anne came over with him. He was
twice married. His first wife Anne, died at Hingham, England,
and was buried there August 30, 1648. His second wife was Mrs.
Martha Bacon, widow of James Bacon, Rector of Burgate.

He remained here until the long Parliament, or until the persecutions in England ceased, when he returned and resumed his Rec-
torship at Hingham.

Mr. Hobart says he returned October 27, 1641; and Mr. Cushing, the town clerk, says his wife and son Joseph returned with
him; his daughter Anne remaining here. She married Captain
John Mason, "the conqueror of the Pequots." *

He died at Hingham, England, and was buried in his church-
yard there. His funeral sermon was preached by Nathaniel Joslin
and published. †

His church (St. Andrews) at Hingham was a noble structure
with a lofty tower, containing eight musical bells.

The following is a copy of his will:

July the xxiiij[th] 1651

I Robert Pecke Minister of the word of God at Hingham in the
countye of Norff beinge in bodilye health and perfect memory knowinge the unccartainety of mans life, doe dispose of that worldly estate
God hath given me in manner and form followinge

Imprimus   I give and bequeath unto Thomas my Sonne and Samuel
my Sonne and their heirs forever   All that my messuage wherein I
now dwell situate and lyenge in Hingham a forsaid with all the edifi-
ces yards and orchards thereunto belonginge   As alsoe the Inclose

---

* Her children were, Priscilla, Samuel, John, Rachel, Ann, Daniel and Elizabeth. Samuel married for his second wife his second cousin Elizabeth Peck,
daughter of Joseph Peck, of Rehoboth, Mass.

† In Bloomfield's History of Norfolk is an allusion to Robert Peck, evidently prejudiced, and as incorrect in other respects as it is in its dates.

and Barnes adioyninge   As olso one Inclose now devided called The Lady close conteyninge about eight acres be it more or less   As olso one pightell at the end thereof conteyninge twoe acres and d,d uppon condicons followinge, and for the paiement of such legacies as are herein expressed

First   I will and bequeath unto Robert Pecke sonne of my sonne Robert deceased the sume of 20£ at his age of 23 years

Item   I give unto John Pecke sonne of the said Robert deceased 10^{Ls} To be paid to him at his age of 22 years

Item   I give unto Beniamin Pecke the youngest sonne of the said Robert deceased at his age of 22 years 20^{ls}

Item   I give to the children of Anne Mason my daughter wife of captain John Mason of Seabrooke on the river connecticut in new England the sume of Forty pounds to be devided equally unto them and to be sent to my sonne John Mason to dispose of it for their use within 2 years after my death

Item   I give to my sonne Joseph Dureinge his natural life the sume of 14^{ls} yearlie to be in the hands of my Sonnes Thomas and Samuel as it shall arise out of my houses lands and chattles for his maintenance with necessarie foode and apparrell duringe the terme of his naturall life And I doe wholie comitt my said Sonne Joseph to the care of my twoe sonnes Thomas and Samuell to provide for him in such a way as he may not want things necessary for his livelyhood

Item   I give to the children of Thomas and Samuell my sonnes which shall be liveinge at my decease the sume of Five pounds apiece at their severall ages of 21 years

Item   I give to my now wife Martha Pecke 40^{ls} To be paid wthin twoe months after my decease   Item   I give to the poore of Hingham 5^{ls} To be destrubted at the discrecon of my Executors Thomas Pecke and Samuel Pecke whome I do ordeyne and make Executors of this my last will and Testament confiding that they will faithfully fulfill and performe this my last will according to my trust reposed in them

All my other goods cattells debts moneys household stuffe or whatsoever ells belongeth unto me I give and bequeath to my said Executors toards payeinge of my legacies alrerdy bequeathed and towards the bringinge of my body to buriall which I desire if I depart this life in Hingham may be entered in the church yard near unto Anne my wife deceased

In witness whereof I have written this my last will and testament with my own hand the day and yeare above written

Robt Peck

This will was proved at London before the judges for probate of Wills and granting of Administrations the tenth day of April in the year of our Lord God One thousand six hundred fiftye and eight

PART FIRST.

THE DESCENDANTS OF JOSEPH PECK, JR,

ELDEST SON OF JOSEPH THE ANCESTOR.

JOSEPH PECK, JR.,[2] was born in England, and baptized there, August 23, 1623, and came over with his father in 1638, being then about 15 years of age. He removed with the family from Hingham Mass., to Seekonk, in 1645. He settled near his father at what was then called Seacunk since known as Seekonk plain. His house was located near, if not upon the exact spot where now stands the depot of the Boston and Providence Railroad, where it crosses this plain.

His name frequently appears upon the records of the town. In 1655, he was one of a committee to levy a tax or rate for the maintenance of the minister. His name appears among those who drew lots in the north purchase at different times. In 1661, he was appointed to view the damage in the Indian's corn upon Kickemuet neck, and Consumpsit neck, and give the town notice of it. He was one of those who advanced money for the prosecution of King Philip's war.

About 1660, he left the plain, and settled upon Palmer's river in the southwesterly part of Rehoboth. * The remains of his old

---

* He deeds, July 15, 1665, to Thomas Cooper, his house, orchards, yards and home lot, containing twelve acres. Bounded on the south by the town common, on the west by land of said Cooper, on the north by a highway, and land he bought of Edward Gillman, adjoining upon the aforesaid land to the west of the common, south of the land of Peter Hunt; east and north by land which he had possessed for fifteen years. Likewise twenty-five pounds state of town common with all the rights and privileges appertaining to said common.

The said Cooper was to enter upon said lands at the next Michaelmas or as soon as the said Peck had gathered and carried away his corn.

3*

cellar and well were still to be seen when I visited the place, which is about one mile northwest from the Orleans Factory so called, near the late residence of Mr. William Covel. He became the owner of a large amount of land, in addition to that given him by his father. Here he lived and died.

The following is a copy of his will:

In the name of God Amen, in the year of our Lord one thousand six hundred ninety & seven in the ninth year of his majiesties reigne the fifth day of the seventh month called July   I Joseph Peck of the town of Rehoboth of the county of Bristol within his Maj^{ties} province of Massachusetts Bay in New England sen^r yeoman being now aged and weak of body & in expectation of my change yet through the mercy of God I am whole and sound in my memory and understanding and of a disposing mind do make this my last will & Testament for the disposing & settling the things of this world which the Lord has entrusted me to & among my children in manner & form as followeth   And imprimis I bequeath my soul into the hands of our most blessed savior and dear redeemer & my body to the dust untill the resurrection day which I die in the firm belief & expectation of   Item 1sly   I give unto my daughter Patience wife of Richard Bowen & to her heirs forever twenty acres of land in the first division last agreed upon & twenty pounds

Item 2^{d}ly   I give unto my daughter Mary the wife of Benjamin Hunt & to her heirs forever half my lot in the north purchased lands belonging to Rehoboth purchase and twenty pounds

Item 3^{d}ly   I give unto my daughter Elizabeth wife of Capt Mason & to her heirs forever the other half of my lot in the aforsaid north purchase & twenty pounds

Item 4thly   I give unto my daughter Hannah wife of Daniel Reed & to her heirs forever all my medow in the north purchase & twenty pounds   And my mind & will is the abovesaid sums given to my daughters (each being named) be by my executor of this my last will & testament well & truly paid within the term of four years after my decease   Furthermore my mind & will is that if all or any of my daughters shall happen to die before the time prefixed by me for my executors paying the several sums before expressed unto them — then my mind & will is that each daughters legacy that shall happen to die shall be sold & truly paid to her children by an equal distribution

Item 5thly   I give unto my son Jathnall Peck as an addition to

what I have before given unto him the lot upon which his dwelling
house now stands containing twenty acres be it more or less which lot
I had of William Carpenter of Rehoboth in exchange and also one
parcel of land being a lot of twenty & six acres lying on the easterly
side of Palmers River in Rehoboth near the oak swamp be the same
more or less And also I give him my fresh meadow formerly purchased of William Bucklin late of Rehoboth and also six acres of upland, adjoining to the said meadow & also my upper meadow upon
Palmers River and also the great piece of meadow that lieth in the
meadow abutting upon the meadow of Joshua Smith on the one side
& the meadow of Preserved Abell on the other side and also that part
of my salt marsh lying on the southerly side of the creek bounded
from a pine tree unto a little creek upon a straight line & also half
my common rights in the town of Rehoboth and all my common in
the north purchased lands yet undivided —All and each of these lands
I give unto my said son Jethniel Peck & to his heirs forever. Item
6thly I give unto my son Samuel Peck & to his heirs forever my
dewelling house barn and out houses & all my lands wheresoever &
whatsoever which by deeds & grants their quantity & places being &
bounds will appear which in this my last will & testament are not
before by me given, with the residue of my common rights Item
7thly My mind & will is that after my debts and funeral charges be
paid out of my movabal estate, that then the whole & residue thereof
be equally divided amongst my children or those of their children that
survive if any of them be dead before that time shall come Item
8thly I do by this my last will & testament make null & void & of
none effect all other & former wills by me made
  Finally I do nominate constitute appoint & ordain my son Samuel
Peck my sole executor of this my last will & testament unto whom I
commit all power for the execution & performance thereof & for the
burrial of my body in decent & christian manner & for all other
things requsite unto him as my executor and in testimony this above
written is my true & last will & testament I the said Joseph Peck
have hereunto set my hand & seal the day & year first above written

                                             JOSEPH PECK

  Read, signed & sealed
in the presence of
  JOHN PECK
  WILLIAM DEAN
  JONAH PALMER

These presents may serve to declare to all whom it doth & may concern that whereas I Joseph Peck sn^r living at Palmers river within the township in the county of Bristol in the Province of Massachusetts Bay in New England have made my last will & testament bearing date the fifth day of July in the year of our Lord 1697 for the settleing of my estate upon my surviving children & for the preventing of trouble & difference after my decease do also now for the same end & cause make this declaration as an explanation of my said last will & testament unto which these presents are annexed. That is to say that all the lands that I have given & bequeathed to any of my children sons or daughters I give to them & to each of them & to each of their respective heirs & assigns forever without any design of entailment of the said lands or any of them   And further whereas I have given to my son Jathniel Peck that part of my meadow or salt marsh lying on the southerly side of the creek bounded from a pine tree to a little creek upon a straight line & it is to be understood of that part of my salt marsh lying & being on the southerly side of the creek bounded from the pine tree standing by the Indian graves & from said tree to the river   And to this declaration & explanation of my last will as above expressed I have set my hand & seal this eleventh day of March in the year of our Lord one thousand seven hundred & one in the eleventh year of his majesties reign William the third over England &c

JOSEPH PECK

Signed & sealed in the presence of us as an explanation of the last will & testament of the said Joseph Peck

THOMAS ORMSBEE
WILLIAM BLANDIN
HANNAH ORMSBEE

This will may be found upon record at Taunton, Mass.

CHILDREN. — THIRD GENERATION.

1.	Rebecka,[3] b. Nov. 6, 1650.	5.	Mary, b. Nov. 17, 1662.
2.	Hannah, b. March 25, 1653.	6.	Ichabod, b. Sept. 13, 1666.
3.	Elizabeth, b. Nov. 26, 1657.	7.	Patience, b. Oct. 11, 1669.
4.+	Jathniel, b. July 24, 1660.	8.+	Samuel, b. Oct. 11, 1672.

Hannah m. Daniel Read, Aug. 20, 1677.

Elizabeth m. Major Samuel Mason, of Stonington, the son of Major John Mason, the conqueror of the Pequots, being his second wife. Her children by him were Samuel, b. Aug. 26, 1695, and d. Nov. 28, 1701; Elizabeth, b. May

6, 1697, and m. Rev. William Worthington; Hannah, b. April 14, 1699, and d. Nov. 1724, unm.

Ichabod died upon the Island of Anticosti, about 1690, in the old French War, in the expedition of Sir William Phips to Canada.

Mary m. Benjamin Hunt.

Patience m. Richard Bowen.

[4.] JATHNIEL PECK,[3] son of JOSEPH,[2] settled near his father. The house in which he lived, and to which his father refers in his will, stood upon the plain or flat, northerly, and not far from the late residence of Gideon Peck, of Rehoboth, deceased. He became a man of wealth and influence. He was a representative to the General Court in 1721, 2, 3, 6, 7, 8, 9, 30 and 31. He also took an active part in the affairs of the church. He was one of those instrumental in organizing and building up the one at Palmer's River. He and Captain Samuel Peck gave each one acre of land for the site of the house which stood upon the hill, northerly, and not far from what is now known as the Orleans Factory.* They were members of the church. Jathniel and his wife were buried here. Their tombstones, when I last visited the place, were in a good state of preservation.

The following are the inscriptions upon them:

In Memory of Mr Jathniel Peck deceased April y[e] 5th 1742 in y[e] 82[d] year of his age   Rev 14.13 Blessed are y[e] ded w[ch] die in y[e] Lord &c

Here lies y[e] body of M[rs] Sarah Peck y[e] wife of M[r] Jathniel Peck dec[d] June y[e] 4th 1717 in y[e] 47th year of her age

> The sweet remembrance of y[e] just
> Shall flourish when they sleep in dust.   Psalm 112.6

He deeded his lands to his children. The deeds may be found upon the records at Taunton, Mass. He married Sarah Smith, February 28, 1688–9.

---

* This house was commenced in 1717, and completed about 1721. The church was organized in 1721, consisting at first of ten members. The house stood until about 1773.

CHILDREN. — FOURTH GENERATION.

9.+Daniel,[4] b. Jan. 30, 1689–90.

10.+Ichabod, b. March 9, 1690–1.*

11. Solomon, b. Sept. 20, 1692. Suppose died unm. Dec. 1728.

12. Esther, b. April 30, 1694. Suppose died Feb. 1729–30.

13.+Jathniel, b. Sept. 10, 1695.

14.+Ebenezer, b. Sept. 20, 1697. Baptized June 14, 1697.

15. Sarah, b. March 1, 1698–9.

16. Rebecka, b. Oct. 10, 1700. Baptized May 25, 1701.

17.+Joseph, b. April 18, 1702. Baptized June 14, 1702.

18. Ann, b. April 7, 1704. Baptized May 28, 1704.

19.+Benjamin, b. Jan. 18, 1705–6. Baptized —— 1706.

20. Elizabeth, b. Oct 31, 1707. Baptized April 17, 1709,

21.+Henry, b. Dec. 7, 1709.

22.+Nathaniel, b. Sept. 14, 1712.

Daniel, Ichabod, Solomon, and *Esther,* were baptized April 11, 1696.

Sarah married Ephraim Hunt, Nov. 8, 1822. (R. Rec., B. 1.) She left no issue. Mr. Hunt was a large landholder. He gave lands to the church in Rehoboth, for the better support of the ministry, which I am told they now hold

Rebecka married Edward Martin, and settled in the eastern part of Seekonk. The farm was the one recently owned and occupied by Capt. Jonathan Bowers. Her descendants were men of distinction. Simeon Martin, of Newport, a Lieut.-Governor of Rhode Island, and Philip Martin, of Providence, were her grandchildren.

Ann married Caleb Ormsbee. John H. Ormsbee, late of Providence, for

---

* This method of double dating was adopted to represent the old, or Julian, and the new, or Gregorian style of computing time.

By the old calendar of Julius Cæsar, the year was made to consist of three hundred and sixty-five days, and six hours. These six hours, amounting to one whole day in every four years, were added to February, making those years to consist of three hundred and sixty-six days, called leap years.

This computation made the year about eleven minutes longer than the true solar time, which in every one hundred and thirty-one years amounted to one whole day. In consequence of this, the 21st day of March, which should have been when the sun crossed the equinoctial line at the vernal equinox, had fallen back, so to speak, from the time of the Council of Nice, in the year 325 of the Christian Era, to the time of Pope Gregory XIII, ten days. He therefore ordered that ten days should be left out of the year 1582 to make the 21st day of March fall on the time when the sun crossed the vernal equinox; and to prevent a like occurrence, ordered that three days should be abated in every four centuries.

Although most countries adopted the new style long before, Great Britain and her colonies did not fully do so until 1751, when Parliament ordered that the year 1752 should commence on the first of January, and that the difference between old and new style, which then amounted to eleven days, should be

Here lies
Inter'd ye Body of
Capt. Samuel Peek.
Dec'd June ye 9th Anno
Domini 1736 in ye
64th Year of
his Age

To Me, t'was givn to DIE: to Thee tis givell
To LIVE: Alas! one Moment sets us even
Mark! how unpartial is ye Will of Heaven

many years Agent of the Hartford Insurance Company, I am told, was one of her descendants.

[8.] SAMUEL[3] PECK, son of JOSEPH,[2] settled upon his father's farm. He became a large landholder. He probably added to the homestead. He was entrusted with various offices in the town, and was a member of the church at Palmer's River. He died June 9, 1736, and was buried upon his own land. The graves of his family may be seen near the late residence of Mr. William Covel.

He died June the 9th, 1736, in the sixty-fourth year of his age.
She died November the 12th, 1756, in the eighty-first year of her age.

His will, dated May 1, 1736, is upon the Taunton Records, B. 8, p. 367.

He gives to his daughter Rachel, wife of Simon Dillis, the use of one room in his house at the south end of his farm, to dwell in during her natural life, and the keeping of a cow winter and summer, while she remains in said house, and also five pounds a year, annually, to be paid during her life, and his best bed and bedding, after the decease of his wife.

He also gives to her children four hundred pounds, to be equally divided amongst them when they become twenty-one years of age.

---

left out of the following month of September, or in other words, that the time should be set forward so much by calling the third day of that month the fourteenth.

For many years, during the change which was taking place in commencing the year, double dating was of frequent occurrence. By old style, the year commenced on the 25th of March, and by new style, on the first of January. These double dates, therefore, occur in the months of January, February, and to the 25th of March. By a moment's reflection it will be seen what was intended by them. Take, as an example, the above birth of Ichabod, which is recorded as occurring March 9, 1690, or 91. If old style was followed, and the year considered to commence on the 25th of March, he was born in 1690; but if new style was followed, and the year allowed to commence on the first of January, then the 9th of March would be in the year 1691, instead of 1690.

To change old style to new, previous to 1700, add ten days; between 1700 and 1800, add eleven days; and between 1800 and 1900, add twelve days.

The Russians still follow old style. To change their time to ours, add twelve days.

He gave to the children of his daughter Hannah, deceased, as follows: To her son Comfort, his heirs and assigns, all the houses, lands, and orchards, where his father, Nicholas Peck, then lived. To her daughter Elizabeth, one hundred pounds, and one bed and bedding, after the decease of his wife. Also to her daughter Hannah, and her heirs forever, one hundred pounds. Also to her daughter Margaret, and her heirs forever, one hundred pounds.

He gave to Rachel, his wife, one room in his house at the south end of his farm, a cow, and her keeping winter and summer, and all his indoor goods, and what more she might need, in sickness and health, during her natural life.

He gives to his son Abiezer, and his heirs forever, all his houses, lands, and orchards, with all his lands and meadows at the north end of his farm, and his salt meadow, near Miles bridge, and one hundred and twenty pounds of stock, which he had loaned to him, and twenty pounds which would be due, and a mare of three years old, and also one-half of his apparel and arms, and half of his land at Long Hill, and one-half his common rights in Rehoboth.

He gave to his son Samuel, and his heirs, his house and barn and orchard, on the south end of his farm, and all his lands adjoining to the dividing line, and half his lands at Long Hill, and all his meadows and lands in the ash swamp, joining to land of Nathan Bliss, and his land in the ox pasture; also his land on the north side of the way, and his land by Samuel Bullock's, and his land by Joseph Peck's land, and half his common right in Rehoboth, with all his lands and common rights in Attleborough; and if there should be any land forgotten in his will, it was to be divided equally between his two sons. If his wife did not dispose of what he had left for her use, it was to be equally divided between his four children. Abiezer was to be at the expense of supporting his mother, and was to pay the legacies to the children of Hannah. Samuel was to pay the legacies to his daughter Rachel and her children. He appoints Samuel his executor.

CHILDREN. — FOURTH GENERATION.

23. Hannah, b. July 21, 1697. Baptized Sept. 12, 1703.
24. Elizabeth, b. June 5, 1700. Died March 29, 1703.
25. Benjamin, b. May 26, 1702. Died March 27, 1703.
26. Rachel, b. Sept. 12, 1704. Baptized April 22, 1705.
27.+Samuel, b. Dec. 2, 1706. Baptized April 13, 1707.
28.+Abiezer, b. April 21, 1714.

Hannah married Nicholas Peck. No. 1506.
Rachel married Simon Dillis.

[9] DANIEL[4] PECK, son of JATHNIEL,[3] settled in that part of the Rehoboth North Purchase which was afterwards Attleborough, and now Cumberland, R. I., at an early date. He purchased lands there in 1715 and 18 (Taunton Records, B. 17, pp. 18 and 129), consisting of uplands, swamps and meadows, being in different allotments (Attleborough Proprietors' Records, pp. 49, 99 and 157). These, with the lands laid out to him upon his rights in the common land, made him an extensive landholder. His lands were bounded west by the Blackstone, or Pawtucket River, and extended so far east as to include what was afterwards known in the town as the Amesbury farm, being a part of the lands given in his will to his daughter Anna, adjoining those given to Sarah. His residence was upon that part of his lands afterwards long known in the vicinity as the Sessions farm. His lands here included several of the farms now in that vicinity. About three hundred acres descended to his grandson, Col. George Peck.

He was the town treasurer of Attleborough in 1724, and the town clerk of Cumberland after it was set off to Rhode Island. He held the office at the time of his decease.

His will is upon the Records of Cumberland, B. 1, pp. 46, 47 and 48.

The following is a copy:

In the name of God Amen, the sixth day of August one thousand seven hundred and forty eight; I Daniel Peck of Cumberland in the County of Providence, in the Colony of Rhode Island, in Providence Plantations in New England Yeoman; being weak in body but of perfect mind and memory thanks be given to Almighty God therefor; — therefore, calling to mind the mortality of my body, and knowing it is appointed for all men once to die, do make and ordain this my last will and Testament, that is to say, principally and first of all, I give and recommend my soul into the hands of God that gave it, and my body to the earth, to be buried in a decent christian burial, at the discretion of my Executrix, nothing doubting but at the General Reserrection, I shall receive the same again by the mighty power of God — and touching such worldly estates wherewith it hath pleased God to bless me in this life, I give, demise and dispose of the same in the following manner and form.

Imprimus, I give and bequeath to my well beloved son Daniel Peck,

4

his heirs and assigns fovever, all that part of my homestead which I have already given him a deed of gift of, and, as it is expressed in said deed, likewise I give unto my son Daniel his heirs and assigns forever, that right of land I purchased of James Wheeler Jun', lying near fort Dummer in a place called Gallops Town, with all the priveleges and appurtenances belonging to it, and likewise one whole right or share of common, in the purchase, called Rehoboth North Purchase and likewise I give unto my said son Daniel, his heirs and assigns for ever; (but after my wife Sarahs decease) that part of my homstead on the West side of mendon road, and on the East side of Pawtucket River, and also that part that lyeth between Stephen Brown's homestead and that which I gave to my said son Daniel in the deed above said, with all the priveleges and appurtenances belonging to it

Item. I give to my well beloved daughter Sarah, the wife of John Whipple, to her, and to her heirs and assigns forever, the whole of that tract of land lying upon Snecheteconet brook lying on the east side of mendon road, and between the land of Lieut Joseph Brown and Stephen Brown, containing several small allotments as may fully appear by the records of Attleborough land, alias Rehoboth north purchase lands, reference there to, being had; Likewise one quarter of a whole share of common in said Rehoboth North purchase, with all the priveleges and appurtenances belonging to both bequestments

Item. I give to my well beloved daughter Anne, the wife of Gideon Bishop, to her, and to her heirs and assigns forever: all that part of the situation, said Gideon Bishop liveth upon, which I have already given to my said daughter Anne a deed of gift of, as it is expressed in said deed of gift, with all the priveleges and appurtenances thereunto belonging, likewise, one quarter of a whole share in the common in the north purchase.

Item. I give to my grand daughter Molly Chapman, when she shall arrive at the age of eighteen years old, to her and to her heirs and assigns forever, that tract of land lying on the west side of Gideon Bishops homestead, containing by estimation, eighteen acres, be the same more or less, in two allotments, and as the same are bounded in the records of the Rehoboth North purchase land; likewise, that piece of land Thomas Alexander liveth upon, when said Thomas and his wife are dead.

Item. I give unto my grand children, that is to say, the children of my daughter Anne and Sarah, forever, in equal shares, to them and to their heirs and assigns for ever, my other right or share in the before mentioned Gallop's Town, with all the priveleges and appurtenances to the same.

Item. My mind and will is, that my son Daniel's right or share in said Gallop's Town, be that which said James Wheeler Jr purchased of said James's father, to wit, Mr James Wheeler; and likewise, my dwelling after my wifes decease, to be to his heirs and assigns for ever.

Item. I give to my dearly beloved wife Sarah, the improvments of the whole of my homstead during her natural life; likewise, I give to my said wife, all my movable estate within doors, and without, with all credits, to enable her to pay my Just debts; likewise I give to my wife Sarah and for her heirs an assigns for ever a certain piece of land partly improved and partly unimproved lying on the East side of Mendon road and South of that which I give to my said son Daniel by deed as above is said, likewise my mind and will is that my movable Estate above mentioned is my wife's, to dispose of as she pleases forever likewise I constitute make and ordain my said wife Sarah my sole Executrix of this my last will and testament and I do hereby utterly disallow revoke and annull all and every other form testaments wills legacies and bequests and Executors by me in any ways before named willed and bequeathed ratifying and confirming this and no other to be my last will and testament in witness where of I have here unto set my hand and seal the day and year above written

Signed sealed published pronounced and declared by the said Daniel Peck as his last will and testament

DANIEL PECK L S

In the presence of us the subscribers·

ICHABOD PECK
JOHN TOWER
JUDITH PECK

The following is the inscription upon his tombstone in the Attleborough City Burying Ground, so called·

In memory of Ensign Daniel Peck who departed this life ye 6th of November A D 1750 in ye 61th year of his age

He married Sarah Paine, daughter of Samuel Paine, who settled in Woodstock, Conn.

CHILDREN — FIFTH GENERATION.

29 Anna, b Oct 13, 1716.   31 +Daniel, b Nov 13, 1723.
30 Sarah, b Aug 6, 1720.

Anna married Gideon Bishop.
Sarah married John Whipple.

[10] ICHABOD PECK,[4] son of JATHNIEL,[3] settled in that part of Attleborough now Cumberland. He purchased lands there as early as October 23, 1721. He purchased of John Sweetland lands, with house, etc, lying at the north end of Red Earth Hill, on each side of the road to Diamond Hill. It appears from the records at Taunton, and the Proprietors' Records, of Attleborough, that he was the owner of large tracts of land, laid out to him upon his own, and upon the rights of his father and grandfather, in the common lands.

Ichabod Peck

He held different offices, at various times, in Attleborough and in Cumberland. His house was situated near the late residence of John Newell, Esq., upon the opposite side of the road.

I am told by those who remember to have seen it, that it was two stories in height, and large for those days. His old well, now upon the roadside, is still kept in repair, and noted for the purity of its water.

He married Judith Paine,* daughter of Samuel Paine. She died November 26, 1778. He July 8, 1773. His son Benjamin was administrator upon his estate (Cumberland Probate Records, Book 5, pp. 97 and 350).

CHILDREN — FIFTH GENERATION

32 Judith, b Sept 16, 1720	37. Rebecca, b May 18, 1731. Died March 28, 1732
33 +Ichabod, b Feb 4, 1721-2.	
34 Seth, b Feb 13, 1723-4.	38 +Solomon, b April 19, 1733
35 Mary, b June 18, 1726.	39 +Oliver, b. Feb 5, 1736-7
36 Joseph, b Sept 16, 1728.	40 +Benjamin, b. Sept 12, 1739.

Seth settled in Rumboot, Dutchess County, N Y, suppose left no issue

Judith married Peletiah Haws, April 15, 1740 (Wrentham Parish Records). They settled at Peekskill, N Y He died August 27, 1791 She died September 22, 1805. Their children were *Peletiah,[6] Seth,[6] Solomon,[6] Rebecca,[6] Mary,[6]* and *Judith [6]* Her grandsons, *James[7]* and *John C Haws,[7]* were residing in Peekskill in 1853 Her descendants are numerous

Mary, it is supposed, died unmarried, as I learn nothing of her.

---

* Upon the records at Worcester, Mass, Book 7, p. 124, may be found the agreement between her and her brothers and sisters in relation to her father's estate, December 28, 1728.

[13.] JATHNIEL PECK,[4] JR., son of JATHNIEL,[3] married for his wife Damaras Hunt, widow, October 19, 1719. She was appointed administratrix upon his estate, October 28, 1739 (Taunton Records, B. 9, p. 108). In the settlement of the account, he is called Lieut. Peck.

CHILDREN — FIFTH GENERATION (R Rec , B 2, p 21.)

41. Oliver, b Feb 1, 1719-20.   43 Sarah, b May 30, 1723.
42 Mary, b. Oct. 3, 1721.

I learn nothing of these children, they probably died young

[14.] EBENEZER[4] PECK, son of JATHNIEL,[3] settled in the northeasterly part of Rehoboth, near Great Meadow Hill, so called, upon a branch or tributary of Palmer's River, where he established a forge, at which he and his sons did an extensive business for many years. Connected with it was also a saw-mill and grist-mill. The place is still known as the forge privilege; little business is however now done there.*

Ebenezer was a man of much distinction. His descendants were numerous. His sons settled near him, mostly in the vicinity of the forge. They owned a large tract of land, at least, it is said, one mile square. The place was long known as the Peck neighborhood.

The will of Ebenezer is upon the Records at Taunton, dated August 6, 1760 (B. 17. p. 94).

He gives to his wife Margaret, his Negro man, named Toney ; & all his indoor and out door movables, including cattle, Sheep and swine ; with the improvment of his real estate, during her natural life. He divides his lands among his 4 sons, Jathniel, Shubael, Ebenezer and Philip ; including his interest in the saw Mill &c ; they paying legacies to his daughters, Margaret, wife of James Short, and Sarah, Mary, and Susa.

He married Margaret Whitaker, August 12, 1724 (R. Rec., B. 2).

---

* When I visited the place, in 1862, it was nearly deserted The water power, like that upon other small streams, when the lands become cleared, had failed The remains of the saw-mill and grist-mill were there, but the house of Ebenezer was gone, and in place of the forge was a small building containing cotton machinery.

4*

44 +Jathniel, b Nov 22, 1725
45   Margaret, b Jan 26, 1726-7.
46 +Shubael, b May 31, 1730
47 +Ebenezer, b Sept 17, 1732 ⎰
48. James, b Sept 17, 1732.   ⎱
       Twins , James d unm March
       7, 1754.

49. Hannah, b March 26, 1735.
       Suppose d unm
50. Sarah, b Jan 26 1737-8.
51   Elizabeth, b May 1, 1741.
52   Mary, b Sept 27, 1744
53 +Philip, b. April 25, 1747
54. Susa, b March 24, 1750.

Margaret married James Short, and settled in Seekonk. *Ebenezer,[6] Shubael,[6]* and *Simeon[6]* Short were her sons
  Sarah, I am told, married Rev. Elhanan Winchester
  Mary married Ichabod Wade   Settled in Seekonk. *Elhanan,[6] Lewis,[6] Ebenezer,[6]* and *Comfort[6]* were her sons.

[17.]   JOSEPH[4] PECK, son of JATHNIEL,[3] is supposed to have married Mary Bliss, July 13, 1731 (R. Rec., B. 2), and to have settled in Rehoboth, where Isaiah Lane afterwards resided.

His widow was appointed administratrix upon his estate, March 21, 1737-8 (T. Rec., B. 9, p. 45). It is supposed she afterwards married a Fuller, as a Mrs. Mary Fuller was appointed guardian of Joseph, Aaron and Prescilla Peck, children of Joseph Peck, February 19, 1739 (T. Rec., B. 9, p 332).

55. Joseph, b March 6, 1732.
56   Aaron, b Dec 7, 1733

57. Prescilla, b Oct 9, 1737.

Joseph, I am told, resided for some time in Rehoboth, upon the Lane farm, so called, in that vicinity , and from there removed and settled upon the Connecticut River, in the vicinity of Springfield, where he is supposed to have left descendants. I have been unable to find them
  Aaron resided with his brother Joseph while in Rehoboth   He is supposed to have afterwards settled in Richmond, N H , ard to have married, at an advanced age, a widow, Chloe Gurnsey, Sept. 16, 1798   He died about 1805, leaving no issue   A daughter of this widow was the wife of Calvin Peck (No 186), son of Daniel   By the records at Keene, N. H , it appears that Aaron purchased lands in Richmond, in 1794.

[19.]   BENJAMIN[4] PECK, son of JATHNIEL,[3] settled in the southwest part of Attleborough, in that part now Cumberland.*

---

* It will be seen that the three brothers, Daniel, Ichabod and Benjamin, left Rehoboth at an early date, and settled in Attleborough, at nearly an equal distance from each other, and about three miles apart, doubtless thinking themselves, at that time, quite near neighbors.

A part of the house which he is supposed to have built, and in which his son Solomon afterwards resided, was standing in 1852. It has since been taken down.

The cellar walls were still standing when I last visited the place. The location is about two miles northeast from Lonsdale Village, near the late residence of John Follett, Esq. Here Benjamin lived and died, August 10, 1749. His will is upon the Cumberland Records, B. 3, p. 22.

He gives to his son Solomon, sixty acres of land, to be set off from the south part of his farm. He gives to his wife Elizabeth, all the rest of his lands, buildings, houses, debts due him, and movable effects. He gives to his daughters Bebee and Anne Peck, five hundred pounds each. He makes his wife his executrix.

He was twice married: first, to Elizabeth Whitaker, February 13, 1728–9; second, to Elizabeth ———. His first wife died April 15, 1731; his second, September 4, 1756.

CHILDREN — FIFTH GENERATION

58 +Solomon, b May 11, 1730
59. Elizabeth, b June 22, 1734. Died Jan 21, 1747–8
60. Ichabod, b March 12, 1736–7. Died Oct 6, 1741.

61. Bebee, b March 27, 1740. Died April 30, 1743
62. Lydia, b Oct 13, 1742. Died Nov. 7, 1742
63. Bebee, b. Nov 6, 1743
64 Anne, b Feb 8, 1745–6.

Bebee married Daniel Read, Jr, of Attleborough, April 23, 1765.
Anne married Eliphalet Day, of Attleborough, March 2, 1769.

[21.] HENRY[4] PECK, son of JATHNIEL,[3] lived and died in Rehoboth, near what is now known as the Village, and I am told, upon the farm occupied in 1863 by Mrs. Hannah Allen, widow.

He married Rachel Whitaker, March 26, 1732 (R. Rec., B. 2). She died at the residence of her son Solomon, in Royalston, Mass., aged ninety-three years.

CHILDREN — FIFTH GENERATION · (R. Rec., B 2, p 114)

65 +John, b Feb. 4, 1734–5
66 +Henry, b Feb. 28, 1737–8.
67. Rebekah, b. Feb 11, 1739–40.

68 +Daniel, b. May 17, 1741   }
69. Benjamin, b May 17, 1741 }
Twins, Benjamin, unknown.

70. Oliver, b. Oct. 24, 1742. Died young

71. Rachel, b Feb 12, 1744-5. Died with the small-pox

72 Lydia, b Sept. 10, 1747. Died young.

73 +Solomon, b Oct 3, 1749

74 +Oliver, b Feb 26, 1751-2, or March 9, 1752 *

75. Lydia, b Feb. 1, 1755

Rebekah married Elisha Phiney, of Warren, R I. *Daniel* and *Elisha* Phiney, of Warren, are her descendants

Lydia married Samuel Turner, grandson of Rev. David Turner, and settled in Royalston, Mass.

[22.] NATHANIEL[4] PECK, son of JATHNIEL,[3] settled in Rehoboth, it is supposed near his father, upon the homestead or a part of it. I learn but little in relation to him. He died about 1762. Sylvanus Martin was appointed administrator upon his estate, August 3, 1762 (Taunton Records, B. 17, p. 624) The inventory names twenty acres of land and buildings. In 1777 a guardian was appointed over Mercy Peck, widow of Nathaniel, and daughter Rebecca.

CHILDREN — FIFTH GENERATION.

76 Rebecca, and it is supposed others.

[27.] REV. SAMUEL[4] PECK, son of SAMUEL,[3] resided upon a part of the homestead. He was a baptist clergyman, denominated at that time one of the new lights. The house in which he preached was located in that part of Rehoboth since Seekonk, near the late residence of Joshua Smith. It was taken down in 1815. He is said to have been a zealous preacher, much attached to his religious tenets. He married Hannah Allen.

The following is from their tombstones:

Samuel Peck who died Nov[r] 26, 1788 in y[e] 82 year of his age who was an Eld[r] of a church of christ in Rehoboth near 40 years Having served his generation by y[e] will of God fell asleep in Jesus — Ended his life with y[e] words of y[e] holly Apostle Sec[nt] Timothy 4 [chap] 7th verse

" With heavenly weapons I have fought the battle of the Lord Finish[t] my corse & kept y[e] faith and wate the sure reward

Hannah Peck, wife of Rev. Samuel, died August 13, 1778, aged 71 years.

---

* Upon the town records, it is February 26, and on the family records, March 9, one being in old, the other in new style.

77 +Samuel, b Feb. 27, 1734-5.   80. Benjamin, b Nov 18, 1741.
78 +Allen, b Feb 1, 1735-6.   81.+Lewis, b Feb 3, 1745.
79 +Josiah, b May 18, 1740.

Benjamin, I am told, settled, lived and died in Virginia, where he became wealthy, leaving descendants. I have been unable to find them He is supposed to have deeded his estates in Providence, August 18, 1784 (P Rec., B 21, p 131).

[28.] ABIEZER[4] PECK, son of SAMUEL,[3] resided upon a part of the homestead. He was twice married. First, I am told, to Submit Sawyer; second, to Naomi Allen, sister to the wife of Rev. Samuel Peck. His first wife died October 20, 1740. He died September 20, 1800. His second wife died July 2, 1801.

82 Submit, b Jan 14, 1738-9.   87 Hannah, b. April 13, 1749   Died
83. Abiezer, b. Feb 6, 1739-40.   Aug 6, 1754 (R Rec., B. 3)
     Died March 17, 1740-1.   88.+Elihu, b Jan 19, 1750-1
84 Naomi, b Feb 29, 1743-4, by   89. Isaac, b Nov 4, 1752   Died
     second wife.   Nov. 22, 1772.
85. Rebecca, b Sept. 13, 1745.   90. Ann, b. Dec 31, 1754   Died
86.+Perez, b Sept 9, 1747   Sept 28, 1778
                                     91. Rachel, b. Jan. 16, 1757.

Submit married Elder Jacob Hicks, left no issue.
Rebecca married Thomas Allen, of Rehoboth.
Rachel married Christopher Barney, of Swanzy.
Naomi married Henry Peck. No. 66.

[31.] DANIEL[5] PECK, son of DANIEL,[4] settled near his father. He died at an early age, a few days previous to the decease of his father. His will is upon the Cumberland Records, dated October 10, 1750.

He appoints his wife Hopestill his executrix. He gives her all his household goods; also his mare, and one cow, and the benefit and improvement of his farm until his son George should become of age. If she remained his widow until his son became of age, then she was to have her living out of his estate so long as she remained his widow, and no longer. He gave to his son George all his lands and buildings in Cumberland, and one-half of a share of a whole right of common in Attleborough; and to his daughter Sarah three hundred pounds, to be paid her by his son George, when twenty-one years of age.

He married Hopestill Dexter.   He died October 11, 1750.*

92.   Sarah, b. Feb 27, 1747–8   93.+George, b. Sept 3, 1749

[33]   ICHABOD[5] PECK, son of ICHABOD,[4] resided in Cumberland, R. I.   He enlisted in the war of the Revolution; was promoted to a Lieut.-Colonel, as I am told; was wounded, and died of his wounds.   He is said to have been a brave officer.

He married Lydia Walcott, of Cumberland, February 28, 1750 (Cumberland Records, B. 1, p. 4).

94 Mary, b Jan 14, 1752	98 +Ichabod, b Nov 26, 1761.
95 +Daniel, b May 4, 1754	99 +Jeremiah, b June 7, 1764
96 Seth, b. Feb 22, 1757. Died unm	100 Joseph, b Sept 16, 1767. Suppose left no family.
97. Lydia, b Feb. 17, 1759.	

Lydia married a —— Page, and settled in Marlborough, N H , where she left children.

[38.]   SOLOMON[5] PECK, son of ICHABOD,[4] settled, lived and died in the southwesterly part of Wrentham, Mass , where his son Royal, and his grandson, Joel F. Peck, have since lived and died, and where his great-grandson Royal now resides.

He is represented by those who knew him to have been a man of distinction, — a wealthy, industrious, and thrifty farmer.   He married Mercy Foster, daughter of Ebenezer Foster, of Cumberland, R. I., June 14, 1756.   She was born May 22, 1734.

From their tombstones :

In memory of Mr Soloman Peck who died Dec[r] 31st 1802 in y[e] 70th year of his Age	In memory of Mr[s] Marcy Peck relict of M[r] Soloman Peck who died July 25th 1806 in ye 73[d] year of her Age
Tis but a few, whose days amount To three score years and ten , And all beyond that short account, Is sorrow toil and paine.	Children, see as you pass by, Your parents here together lie. O dont forget, that soon you must Follow them here, and turn to dust.

---

* His widow married Joseph Brown, June 2, 1752.   Sarah, the daughter, married Dr David Brown, April 28, 1765.

CHILDREN — SIXTH GENERATION.

101 +Levi, b. April 14, 1757.
102 +Royal, b June 13, 1759
103 +Joel. b April 9, 1761
104 Mercy, b April 28, 1765. Died
    Sept. 4, 1775.

105. Lois, b. May 3, 1767 Died
    April 11, 1773
106 +Solomon, b July 28, 1769
107 Darius, b March 22, 1775.
    Died young.
108 +Jesse F , b April 2, 1777.

The following was found among his papers:

Augst 30th } THE UNITED STATES OF AMERICA to Solomon Peck Dr
1778

To sundry articles lost in the retreat from the Island of Rhode Island in passing Howlands Ferry so called viz

To one good great Coat	£15
To one large new blanket	6
To one new pair of tow cloth trowsers	1 10
To one pair of yarn stockings	1 4
To one Flannel shirt	3 10
To one knapsack	1 10
	£28 14

Solomon Peck

STATE OF RHODE ISLAND ss

In Cumberland 12th of November A D 1778 Mr Solomon Peck the above subscriber made solemn oath that the above articles by him lost and charged against said United States is just and true in all its parts

Before me

JOHN DEXTER Justice of Peace

[39.] OLIVER[5] PECK, son of ICHABOD,[4] settled at first at Fishkill, then at Norway, Herkimer County, N. Y., where he died June 1796.

Oliver Peck & Fear Foster both of Cumberland were married April ye 22 1759 by Job Bartlett Justice of Peace

Recorded Apr 3 1765

Witness JOHN DEXTER Town Clerk

CHILDREN — SIXTH GENERATION

109. Nancy, b Nov 25, 1759, m Stephen Ketchum.
110. Oliver, b Nov 22, 1761.*
111 +Joseph, b Nov 13, 1763.
112 +Foster, b Dec 20, 1765.
113.+Amos, b May 16, 1768.

114 +Ira, b Oct 15, 1771
115.+Lewis, b Dec 17, 1773.
116 +Eli, b Jan. 23, 1776
117. Polly, b. Jan 23, 1778, m. Silas Elsworth.

[40.] BENJAMIN[5] PECK, son of ICHABOD,[4] remained upon the homestead at first, then removed to Stoughton, Mass., where he died in 1795. He married Letisa Titus, June 15, 1768.

CHILDREN — FIFTH GENERATION (C Rec., B. 2, p, 18)

118 +Benjamin, b Aug. 20, 1769.
119.+James, b Dec 14, 1771.
120 Olive, b April 5, 1774.

121 +George, b. July 21, 1776
122 Chloe, b March 20, 1779.
123 Nancy, b July 3, 1781.

Olive married Enos Ray, October 3, 1796, and died leaving three girls, who died without issue.

Chloe married James Gillinore, December 15, 1796, no issue.

Nancy married Paul Clark, January 9, 1806.

[44.] JATHNIEL[5] PECK, son of EBENEZER,[4] occupied the forge of his father, continuing the business, in connection with his brothers. The house in which he resided, probably more than one hundred years old, was standing when I visited the place. He married for his first wife, Sybel Butterworth; for his second, Mrs. Sarah Michel, widow, formerly Miss Sarah Ingols; for his third, Mrs. Rebecca Martin, formerly Miss Rebecca Horton. His first wife died March 15, 1769. His second wife died August 9, 1798. He died March 23, 1812.

CHILDREN — SIXTH GENERATION (R. Rec., B. 2, p. 121)

124. Jathniel, b Feb. 24, 1747-8. Died unm
125 +Otis, b April 10, 1750
126 Esther, b April 21, 1752.
127.+James, b Aug 10, 1754.
128. Olive, b Nov. 20, 1756 Died unm
129 Sylvester, b July 9, 1759. Died in the army, unm.

130 Sybel, b Sept 24, 1761
131 +Shubael, b July — 1764
132 +Benoni, b Feb 8, 1769
133 +Edmund, b Sept 2, 1773
134. Sarah, b Oct 11, 1775, m Noah Carpenter.
135 +George W. b Nov 11, 1777.
136. Shubael, b Jan. 22, 1779

---

* *Oliver*, I am told, was residing at Cobleskill, Schoharie County, N Y , in 1814, and had two children, *Patty* and *Jane*, and perhaps others I have been unable to find them.

[46.] SHUBAEL[5] PECK, son of EBENEZER,[4] settled near his brothers. He was an active business man. He held a colonel's commission, represented his town in the State legislature, was justice of the peace, etc. He was twice married: first, to Huldah Hunt; second, to Molly Wade. He died from injuries received in the saw-mill.

CHILDREN — SIXTH GENERATION (R. Rec , B 3, p 63)

137. Huldah, b Feb 23, 1755.   138 Elizabeth, b. Jan. 31, 1757.
        Died young   Died young.

[47.] EBENEZER[5] PECK, son of EBENEZER,[4] remained upon the homestead, where he lived and died. He was a man of public influence and distinction. He married Mellison ———.

CHILDREN — SIXTH GENERATION (R Rec., B 3, p 126)

139 Calvin, b. June 11, 1759 Died   141 +Cromwell, b July 18, 1763
        in the army.   142. Huldah, b ——— ———.
140. Ebenezer, b June 8, 1761.
        Died in the army.

Huldah married Ephraim Goodwin, of Dighton, Mass

[53.] PHILIP[5] PECK, son of EBENEZER,[4] was a blacksmith by trade and occupation. His residence was near his brothers. His house, which was large, is still standing in good condition, and was occupied, in 1862, by his son Cyril C. Peck. He was very much respected. He held various public trusts. He was one of the selectmen of the town for many years, both political parties supporting him, in return for his honesty and fidelity.

He married Ruth Williams, July 5, 1768. He died April 6, 1805. She died January 12, 1830.

CHILDREN — SIXTH GENERATION (R. Rec , B. 3, p 197.)

143 +Williams, b July 3, 1770.   148. Polly, b Aug 2, 1780
144 +Lemuel, b April 2, 1772   149. Sally, b June 3, 1782
145   Clarina, b Oct. 16, 1774.   150 +Ebenezer, b. March 8, 1784.
146   Philip W , b Aug 2, 1776.   151   Ruth, b Dec 14, 1786
147 +James, b June 17, 1778.   152 +Cyril C , b Jan 31, 1789.

Clarina married Asahel Pierce, of Calais, Vt , a wealthy farmer. She left descendants, who are residing there.

Sally married Gideon Hicks , settled in Calais, Vt. He was a prominent man in the town, and left descendants, who are still residing there.

5

Polly married John Davis.

Ruth died unmarried, in 1862.

Philip W was a school-teacher, and a teacher of music and dancing in his early life. He afterwards settled in Virginia, where he became a leading member of the church. He died much respected

[58.] SOLOMAN[5] PECK, son of BENJAMIN,[4] settled upon the homestead, where he remained until 1784, when he moved to Sutton, Mass., where he resided until his decease, April 5, 1794.

He married Esther Wiswold, December 7, 1758, daughter of Ichabod Wiswold, of Attleborough, Mass. She was born July 1, 1740, and died December 31, 1816.

CHILDREN — SIXTH GENERATION.

153. Élizabeth, b. Sept. 19, 1759. Died May 10, 1831, unm.

154 Esther, b Sept. 8, 1761. Died Jan. 14, 1795, unm.

155. Lydia, b Dec. 7, 1764. Died May 9, 1788.

156 +Benjamin, b Aug 1, 1767, Died Oct 18, 1832.

157 +David, b Oct 10, 1769 Died Sept. 10, 1840.

158.+Solomon, b. Feb 19, 1773. Died Aug. 27, 1809.

159. Bebee, b May 25, 1775. Died May 11, 1831.

160. Anna, b. May 29, 1778. Died Oct. 10, 1798, unm

161. Mary, b Nov. 5, 1780. Died Aug. 12, 1798, unm

162. Ichabod, b Feb. 2, 1784. Died March 23, 1802, unm

Lydia married Dr Joseph Lee, of Cumberland, R. I Her children were *Newton*, *Galen*[7] and *Alfred*[7]

Bebee was twice married first, to Ezra Barrus, second, to Deacon Jacob Ide. *George*,[7] of Taunton, Mass, and *Ira Barrus*,[7] of Providence, R I., both physicians, are her sons.

[65.] JOHN[5] PECK, son of HENRY,[4] left Rehoboth, and settled in Royalston, Mass., about 1775. From there he removed to Montpelier, Vt., in 1806, where he died, March 4, 1812. He was a farmer; and while he resided in Royalston was one of the town officers many years. He devoted a portion of his time to school teaching, and, I am told, was quite a poet.* He married Mary Drown.

---

* A poem, in opposition to the doctrine of Universal Salvation, said to have been written by him, was published in pamphlet form in 1813, and reprinted by John P. Jewett & Co., Boston, in 1858.

CHILDREN — SIXTH GENERATION

163.+Joshua, b.
164　Oliver, b. d. 1786, unm.
165 +Hiram, b.
166.+Nathaniel, b.

167 +Squire, b.
168 +John, b.
169.　Rachel, b.
170.　Mary, b.

Rachel married William Drown.
Mary married a Hathaway, and settled in Vermont.　One of her sons is a merchant in Boston, of the firm of Hicks & Hathaway.

[66.] HENRY[5] PECK, son of HENRY,[4] settled in Seekonk, upon what has been known in that vicinity as the Dr. Brigham farm.

He married Naomi Peck (No. 84), daughter of Abiezer Peck, April 25, 1765.　She died June 8, 1824.　He August 8, 1839.

CHILDREN — SIXTH GENERATION

171　Gideon, b Nov 14, 1765.
172　Martha, b
173　Lucy, b.
174　Henry, b d unm.
175　Naomi, b

176 +William, b
177　Ezra, b was lost at sea.
178　Hannah, b. d. April 30, 1863.
179　Mary, b
180.　Sally, b.

Martha married Thomas Bullock.
Lucy married William Daggett.
Naomi married Simeon Read
Hannah married Thomas Bullock, who had been the husband of her sister Martha, deceased.
Sally married Drayton Carpenter.

[68.] DANIEL[5] PECK, son of HENRY,[4] removed from Rehoboth, and settled in Royalston, Mass., about 1775; an industrious and enterprising farmer.

He married Relief Joy, of Rehoboth, November 7, 1771.
He died in Royalston, in 1814.　She died in 1832.

CHILDREN — SIXTH GENERATION

181 +Daniel, b Feb 6, 1772
182 +Ichabod, b April 6, 1774
183.　Sally, b Nov 29, 1775.　Died
　　　　Sept 17, 1778
184 +Solomon, b. March 6, 1776
185.　Royal, b. March 7, 1778.　Died
　　　　Sept 19, 1778.
186.+Calvin, b. Oct. 16, 1779.

187　Sally, b Sept 9, 1781.
188 +Moses, b Dec 17, 1783.
189　Rebeckah, b Oct 16, 1785.
190.　Charlott, b Aug 4, 1787.
191.　Lydia, b. Nov 16, 1789.
192　Relief, b. Sept. 11, 1792. Died
　　　　unm.
193.　Huldah, b. Aug. 11, 1794.

Sally married Asa Gould, November 24, 1803, and settled in Warwick, Mass.

Rebeckah married Salma Algiers, for her first husband, and Eugene Baker, for her second. She was residing in Chelsea, Mass., in 1865. To her kindness I am indebted for my information.

Lydia married Rev. Joseph Hancock, of Montpelier, Vt.

Huldah married John Pierce, settled in Swanzey, N. H., where she died, leaving no issue.

[73] SOLOMON[5] PECK, son of HENRY,[4] left Rehoboth, Mass., and settled in Royalston, in 1779. He at first purchased about thirty acres of land, to which by enterprise and industry he afterwards added much. He died November 14, 1822.

His wife, before marriage, was Anna Wheeler. They were married July 1772. She died November 10, 1810.

CHILDREN — SIXTH GENERATION

194 Rachel, b Nov 15, 1773 Died Sept 19, 1794
195 Silvia, b Feb 17, 1775
196 Sally, b Jan 26, 1777
197 +Solomon, b May 4, 1779.
198 +James W, b July 7, 1781
199 +Benom, b July 27, 1783
200. Anna, b. July 12, 1785.
201 Polly, b. Nov 9, 1787 Died in 1807
202 Betsy, b June 25, 1790
203. Ambrose, b June 12, 1792 Died June 24, 1808
204 Harvey, b March 31, 1794. Died Dec 2, 1810
205. Martha, b Nov. 21, 1798.
206. Diana, b Aug 8, 1800.

Silvia married Ebenezer Chase, February 20, 1800, and settled at Athol, Mass

Sally married Comfort Fuller They and their children are deceased.

Anna married Amos Goff, September 5, 1805, no issue

Betsy married Samuel Goff, September 5, 1811, and settled in Ohio.

Martha married Ezra Baldwin, September 26, 1820, settled in Ohio

Diana married Daniel Boyce, January 1, 1818, and settled in Vermont.

[74] OLIVER[5] PECK, son of HENRY,[4] lived and died in the northerly part of Rehoboth, where his son now resides, an industrious and wealthy farmer. He married Hannah Bliss, October 25, 1774. He died January 26, 1839. She March 14, 1837.

CHILDREN — SIXTH GENERATION

207. Darius, b Jan. 20, 1776; left no family
208. Hannah, b June 5, 1778.
209. Lepha, b Jan 23, 1781. Died Sept 2, 1792.
210.+Oliver C., b. Feb. 9, 1784.
211.+Rufus, b June 17, 1786.
212 +Caleb, b. Jan. 10, 1789
213 +Samuel, b. Nov 24, 1791.
214. Royal, b May 11, 1794. Died April 29, 1815, unm.
215. Lepha B., b. Dec. 13, 1797.

Hannah married Leonard Hodges, of Norton   *Leonard, Earle, Andrew* and *Royal* Hodges, of Illinois, are her descendants.

Lepha B married Zeba Bliss, settled in Portland, Maine   *Zenas* and *Ziba* Bliss, now residing there, are her descendants.

[77] SAMUEL[5] PECK, son of Rev. SAMUEL,[4] settled upon the lands given him by his father. He was a wealthy farmer. The farm is the one recently owned and occupied by Mr. William Covel, of Rehoboth, now deceased.

He married Sarah Jencks, of Pawtucket, R. I.

CHILDREN — SIXTH GENERATION   (R Rec , B 3, p 116)

216   Susannah, b Feb 26, 1760
217   Hannah, b July 25, 1762
218. Sarah, b July 21, 1765
219 +George, b March 7, 1768.
220   Lydia, b. Sept 5, 1769.

221   John, b Sept 3, 1772   Died unm
222. Eve, b June 7, 1775.   Died May 16, 1804.

Susannah married Elnathan Lake, and resided in Rehoboth   Her daughter *Lydia* married William Covel, and settled upon the homestead of her grandfather   From her I received my information in relation to her connections

Sarah married Grindall Chase, and moved to Plainfield, Conn

Hannah married Gaicus Peck, No 2669.

[78.] ALLEN[5] PECK, son of Rev. SAMUEL,[4] resided for some years in Providence, then returned to Rehoboth, and lived and died upon the homestead.

He married the widow Elizabeth Dexter, of Providence.

CHILDREN — SIXTH GENERATION   (R Rec , B. 4, p 98)

223. Hannah, b Feb 5, 1777
224. Elizabeth, b Sept 20, 1779.

225 +Benjamin, b Dec 25, 1781
226   John R , b March 18, 1784, no children

Hannah married Oliver Allen, of Providence, where they lived and died.

Elizabeth married Sylvanus Martin, of Providence, where they lived and died.

[79.] JOSIAH[5] PECK, son of Rev. SAMUEL,[4] settled at first upon a part of the homestead, and then upon the farm, since occupied by the town of Seekonk as an Asylum. He married Patience Bosworth, September 14, 1764.

5*

CHILDREN — SIXTH GENERATION: (R Rec , B. 3, p. 178.)

227.+Joseph, b May 30, 1765
228 Samuel, b Feb 22, 1767. Died in Savannah, April 6, 1786.
229. Patience, b Dec 11, 1768.
230 Betsey, b March 30, 1771.
231.+Josiah, b April 18, 1773.
232. Anne, b June 6, 1775. Died Oct 22, 1794, unm.

233. Susannah, b Sept. 20, 1777. Died unm.
234 William, b. Oct 3, 1780. ⎫
235. Temperance, b Oct 3, 1780. ⎬ Twins, William died June 5, 1797, on a passage from Havana to Warren, R I

Temperance was twice married, first, to Dr —— Thompson, of Warren, second, to Major Allen Monroe, of Seekonk.

[81] LEWIS⁵ PECK, son of Rev. SAMUEL,⁴ settled in Providence, where he became wealthy. He was a merchant. He built and owned the wharf since known as Peck's Wharf.

He married Nancy Foster, daughter of John Foster, December 19, 1773. He died November 10, 1823. She March 6, 1847, aged 93 years, 5 months, and 16 days.

CHILDREN — SIXTH GENERATION

236 Ann, b Jan 1, 1775.
237. John, b May 25, 1777 Died unm.
238. James, b Jan. 14, 1780. Died unm
239 Clarissa, b April 16, 1782 Died April 13, 1849, unm
240 Horace, b Oct 22, 1784

Horace died, unmarried, March 27, 1817
Ann married Griffin Childs, of Providence, R I She died April 15, 1816 Lewis Peck Childs, Esq , of Providence, is their son To his kindness and generosity I am indebted for the likeness of the tombstone of his great-great maternal grandfather, Capt Samuel Peck This stone (see page 35) was procured in England The work upon it is a fine specimen of art

[86] PEREZ⁵ PECK, son of ABIEZER,⁴ settled at first upon the homestead; afterwards in Coventry, R. I , where he died.

He married Experience Smith. She died November 7, 1803. He October 13, 1825.

CHILDREN — SIXTH GENERATION

241. Isaac, b April 20, 1773. Died Sept 14, 1787
242.+Cromwell, b Sept 30, 1774
243. Noah, b Sept 17, 1776. Died Sept 16, 1778
244. Arnold, b May 5, 1778. Died Dec 21, 1784
245. Anna, b May 18, 1781. Died April 2, 1851.

246. Sebea, b Sept 18, 1783. Died Jan 4, 1803
247.+Perez, b Sept 14, 1786.
248 Cynthia, b May 13, 1789. Died Aug 25, 1854
249 Irena, b March 30, 1793. Died June 2, 1842.

Anna married Lewis Chafee, no issue.

[88.] ELIHU[5] PECK, son of ABIEZER,[4] settled in Providence. He was a house carpenter by trade and occupation. He married Rebecca Burlingame, daughter of Edmund Burlingame. He died June 23, 1806. She died December 20, 1824. She was the Executrix upon his estate, and presented the inventory to the court November 24, 1806.

CHILDREN — SIXTH GENERATION

250. Mary, b May 29, 1777. Died Aug 30, 1779
251. William, b Sept. 16, 1779. Died Nov 6, 1798, unm
252. Benjamin, b Oct 14, 1781. Died Jan 5, 1803, unm
253. Anne, b April 14, 1785.
254. Cyrus, b Oct 3, 1787.
255 Maria, b Oct 9, 1790
256 Elizabeth, b June 10, 1793. Died Oct 13, 1794
257 Elizabeth, b Dec 29, 1794. Died May 7, 1856.

Anne married Rev Luther Bailey, October 8, 1808. Mr Bailey settled in Medway, Mass , where he preached twenty-seven years He died December 1861

Cyrus married Ann Jackson, of New York City, and left one child by the name of *Mary Ann*

Maria was living, in 1863, unmarried

[93.] GEORGE[6] PECK, son of DANIEL,[5] resided upon the estates, in Cumberland, R. I., inherited from his father and grandfather. He was a man of much distinction in the town. He represented it in the General Assembly, and held various offices.

He held a colonel's commission during the war of the Revolution, in which he took an active interest.

He was twice married; first, to Phebe Whipple, daughter of Stephen Whipple, April 12, 1770. About 1782 he left Cumberland, and settled at Eastport, Me. He resided for several years upon the Island of Campobello. He drew a pension for several years previous to his decease. His second wife was Phebe Ballou, daughter of Elisha Ballou, of Cumberland.

CHILDREN BY FIRST WIFE — SEVENTH GENERATION (C Rec , B 1, p 128.)

258. Daniel, b Oct. 7, 1770. Died unm
259 Amey, b May 2, 1772.
260 Sally, b June 2, 1774
261. Anna, b May 2, 1776. Died unm.
262 George, b March 19, 1779
263. Anstel, b June 5, 1781. Died July 9, 1811, unm
264. Whipple, b. Aug 13, 1783. Died unm.

George died at sea on board the ship "Washington," March 1799.

265. John   268. Clarissa.
266. Henry.   269. Nancy.
267. George.   270. Alpha.

The sons died in early life without issue.

Amey married Richard Arnold, August 11, 1793.

Sally married Stephen Joslyn, of Cumberland, R. I., where she was residing a widow in 1863

Clarissa married Capt Henry Young, and settled in New Brunswick.

Nancy married Constantine Wilson, and settled at Falmouth, Nova Scotia.

Alpha married, and settled in New Brunswick.

[95.] DANIEL[6] PECK, son of ICHABOD,[5] enlisted in the war of the Revolution.   After its close, he settled in Marlborough, N. H. From there he moved to Sand Lake, Rensselaer County, N. Y., where he died, May 30, 1840.

He married Mehitable Harvey, of Marlborough, in 1780.   She died November 12, 1826.

CHILDREN — SEVENTH GENERATION

271 Philotte, b March 2, 1781.   275 +John, b Aug 24, 1792
272 +Joel, b Nov 6, 1782.   276 +Harvey, b Jan 2, 1795
273 +Daniel, b May 30, 1785   277 +Ichabod, b March 4, 1797   Died
274.+Bethuel, b June 16, 1788.   young.

Philotte married Moses Mowry, of Otsego County, N. Y.

[98.] ICHABOD[6] PECK, son of ICHABOD,[5] settled first in Marlborough. N. H , then in Fulton County, N. Y , near Johnstown, where he died, May 1, 1848.   He married Mary Dean in 1780. She died in Hadley, Saratoga County, in 1814.

CHILDREN — SEVENTH GENERATION (A. Rec , B 3, p 36)

278. Mary, b. Jan 15, 1782. Died   282 +George W , b Jan. 17, 1795.
          in 1833.   283 Samuel D , b 1797. Died in 1813.
279. Sarah, b. 1784   Died 1789   284 +Oliver D , b 1800
280 +Charles, b Jan. 14, 1786.   285 Sally Ann, b 1805   Died 1807.
281. Lydia, b 1788   286.+Alexander D , b 1808.

Mary married a man by the name of Carmittee, and left children.

Lydia married James Smith , died 1856.

[99.]   JEREMIAH[6] PECK, son of ICHABOD,[5] lived and died in Attleborough, Mass.   He married Elizabeth Gains, December 25, 1792.   He died April 26, 1846.   She died February 20, 1846.

CHILDREN — SEVENTH GENERATION ·

287 +George, b May 22, 1794.
288.+Lewis, b. April 1, 1796.
289 +Walcott, b March 4, 1798.
290   Margaret, b Oct. 21, 1799.

291.+Daniel, b Sept 3, 1802.
292.   John, b. March 22, 1805.
293.   Lydia, b. Jan. 22, 1811.

Margaret married Matthew Campbell, and settled in Attleborough, Mass.

John married Louisa Hall, March 20, 1833, and settled in East Attleborough, Mass, where he died, March 11, 1865, leaving no issue.   His wife survived him, and was residing there, a widow, in 1865

Lydia was residing in Attleborough, unmarried, in 1864.

[101]   LEVI[6] PECK, son of SOLOMON,[5] settled in Westminster, Vt, where he died September 17, 1835   He was a prominent man, and much respected.   He married Hannah Stodard, of Westminster, December 27, 1785.   She died February 18, 1842.

CHILDREN — SEVENTH GENERATION .

294 +Ara, b. Aug 2, 1787.
295 +Uri, b. Sept 21, 1789.
296 +Shubael, b April 21, 1794

297.   Rhoda, b March 27, 1798.
298.   Mira, b. Dec. 29, 1802.

Rhoda married Daniel Fisher, and settled in Hinsdale, N. H.

Mira was unmarried in 1863.

[102.]   ROYAL[6] PECK, son of SOLOMON,[5] at first settled in Cumberland, R. I.   From there he removed to Westminster, Vt., where he became one of the leading men of the town.   He remained in Westminster until about 1802, when he returned, and settled upon the paternal homestead, in Wrentham, Mass., where he lived and died, honored and respected, both in his public and private life.   He was one of the kindest of husbands, and most indulgent of parents.   Although possessed of more than usual energy and decision of character, he was always kind and courteous in all his relations in life.

Royal Peck

He married Abigail Ballou, daughter of Noah Ballou, January 23, 1780.   She was one of the best of women, the most affectionate of wives, and the kindest of mothers. She died June 6, 1846, in the eighty-fifth year of her age. He died September 20, 1849, in the ninety-first year of his age.

CHILDREN — SEVENTH GENERATION.

299. Celinda, b. Oct. 29, 1781, in Cumberland, R. I.

300.+William, b Jan. 14, 1785, in Cumberland, R. I.

301.+Joel F., b. May 20, 1797, in Westminster, Vt

302.+Ira B , b Feb. 12, 1805, in Wrentham, Mass.

Celinda married William Bishop, of Cumberland, R. I., by whom she had one child, a daughter, who married Gustavus Alexander, of Cumberland. She died January 24, 1862. Her daughter died June 23, 1853, leaving two children.

[103.] JOEL[6] PECK, son of SOLOMON,[5] settled in Cumberland, R. I. He was a mason by trade and occupation, an industrious and worthy man. He died November 24, 1794.

I hereby certify that Joel Peck son of Solomon Peck of Wrentham and Keziah Ballou daughter of Noah Ballou of Cumberland were lawfully joined to gether in marriage on the 15th day of February 1784 by me Abner Ballou Elder

Recd Feb 23 1784 & Recorded accordingly

Witness JOHN DEXTER Town Clerk

CHILDREN — SEVENTH GENERATION.

303. Asmah, b. March 8, 1785. Died Dec. 7, 1794.

304. Lois, b Dec. 24, 1786.

305 +Foster, b Nov. 11, 1789.

306 +Lewis, b Dec. 28, 1793.

Lois married Arnold W Jencks, of Cumberland She died October 23, 1833

Her children were *Joel P ,*[8] *Eliza,*[8] *Harriet,*[8] *Allen*[8] and *Lewis.*[8]

[106] SOLOMON[6] PECK, son of SOLOMON,[5] lived and died in Cumberland. He was an industrious and successful farmer; a man much respected.

He married Phila Whipple, daughter of Preserved Whipple, of Cumberland, R. I. He died August 29, 1850. She died March 9, 1864.

CHILDREN — SEVENTH GENERATION.

307.+Alfred, b. Nov. 12, 1791.

308. Lucy, b. Oct. 2, 1793.

309. Eunice, b. Sept 22, 1795.

310.+Whipple, b. Jan. 19, 1798.

311. Philina, b. July 2, 1801.

312. Olive, b. June 22, 1804.

313 +Stephen, b. April 10, 1807.

314.+George B., b. Oct. 26, 1810.

Lucy married Joel F. Peck (No. 301). He settled in Wrentham, Mass., upon the homestead

Eunice married Joseph Metcalf, of Cumberland, where they reside.* Their children are *Abby*,[8] who married Edward Harris, a wealthy and extensive manufacturer, of Woonsocket, and *Eunice*,[8] who married Stafford W. Razee, a merchant of Providence, R. I.

Philina married Alfred Whipple, of Cumberland, R. I , August 7, 1817.

Olive married Edward Ballou, also of Cumberland, August 21, 1825.

[108.] JESSE F. PECK,[6] son of SOLOMON,[5] resided in Pelham, Mass. He was a farmer by occupation. He was well educated, enterprising and intelligent. Much of his early life was spent in school teaching and public business. He became one of the leading men of the town.

He was twice married: first, to Anna Cole, daughter of Joseph Cole, of Cumberland; second, to Matilda Tingley, daughter of Samuel Tingley. He died November 26, 1822. His first wife died November 8, 1818; his second, October 15, 1821.

CHILDREN — SEVENTH GENERATION

315. Azel, b March 1800. Died May 23, 1817, unm.
316 +Kelly, b July 16, 1802.
317. Lyman, b March 13, 1805. Died Oct 26, 1828, unm
318. Lavonia, b. Aug 24, 1808.
319. Harriet, b March 23, 1811.
320. Adaline, b. July 23, 1814.

Harriet married Josiah Grout, and settled in Springfield, Otsego County, N. Y , where they reside.

Lavonia married Thornton Furgerson, and settled in Springfield, Otsego County, N Y , where they reside.

Adaline married Daniel Whipple, of Cumberland, R. I., where they reside.

[111.] JOSEPH[6] PECK, son of OLIVER,[5] married Phebe Vincent, daughter of Jeremiah Vincent, June 5, 1788. He died in 1840. She in 1849. He settled in Middletown, Saratoga County, N. Y.

CHILDREN — SEVENTH GENERATION

321.+John, b Jan 20, 1790.
322 Amos, b Dec. 16, 1791. Died young.
323 +Jeremiah, b April 1, 1794.
324. Elizabeth, b. Aug 1, 1796. Died unm.
325 +Ira, b Nov. 22, 1798.
326 +George, b. Dec 29, 1800.
327. Nancy, b March 16, 1803
328. Clarissa, b Aug. 10, 1805.
329.+Joseph F., b Oct. 8, 1807.
330 Mary, b May 11, 1810
331. Phebe, b Oct 4, 1812.

* He died December 27, 1867.

Nancy married David Cooper.
Clarissa married John Sampson.
Mary married John Warden.
Phebe married John Weatherwax.

[112] FOSTER[6] PECK, son of OLIVER,[5] I am told, settled at first at Fishkill, N. Y., and then in Dover, N. Y. He afterwards settled at Ithaca, where he died. He was twice married: first, to Rachel Willsee; and second, to Widow Patience Lodes. His first wife died in Dover, in 1808. His second wife died in Corning, in 1860. He died November 1849.

CHILDREN — SEVENTH GENERATION

John	Polly.
Nancy.	Willsee.
Ira.	Stephen.
Betsey.	Phebe.*

John was residing at East Toledo, Ohio, in 1865. He married Louisa Tuttle, September 26, 1823. She was born June 19, 1804 His children were· *Ebenezer*,[8] *William*,[8] *Rachel*,[8] *Jacob*,[8] *Louisa*,[8] *John*,[8] *Levi*,[8] *Sylvia*,[8] *James*,[8] *Charles*[8] and *Emma* [8]

Nancy married Joseph Finkle, and settled in the vicinity of Hudson, N. Y.

Ira died in Fishkill, N. Y , in 1816.

Betsy married, first, Jeremiah Cronk, who died in Newfield, Tompkins County, N. Y , second, John Woodin, and was residing in Newfield, N. Y., in 1865

Polly married George Cooper He died in 1855 She afterwards married Hiram Birdsell, and was residing in Maryville, Cayuga County, N Y , in 1865.

Willsee was residing in Hillsdale, Columbia County, N. Y., in 1865 He married Catharine Thompson Their children were *Nancy*,[8] *Mary Jane*,[8] *Charity*,[8] *Duncan*,[8] *Louisa*,[8] *Catharine M* ,[8] *George*[8] and *Ira* [8]

Stephen was residing in Gibson, Steuben County, N. Y., in 1865.

Phebe married Alonzo Gale

[113.] AMOS[6] PECK, son of OLIVER,[5] married Mary Wagman, daughter of Henry Wagman, March 12, 1793. He died in 1845. They resided in Saratoga, N. Y.

CHILDREN — SEVENTH GENERATION

332 Nancy, b June 1, 1795.	336 Lucinda, b June 26, 1804.
333. Elizabeth, b March 15, 1797.	337 Clarina, b. Dec. 19, 1806
334. Rachel, b July 7, 1799.	338 +Amos, Jr., b. Oct. 28, 1809.
335.+Henry W , b. Aug 28, 1801.	339. Mary, b March 31, 1812.

---

* The above family of Foster was received too late to be numbered and included in the index.

Nancy married Samuel Baird, March 10, 1825
Elizabeth married Simon P Clark, January 15, 1827.
Rachel married Horace Buel, May 8, 1835
Lucinda married Nathaniel Godard, May 20, 1835.
Clarina married Hiram Haight, January 5, 1830
Mary was residing at Richfield Springs, unmarried, in 1863.

[114] IRA[6] PECK, son of OLIVER,[5] married Lydia Palmer, daughter of Caleb Palmer, of West Stockbridge, Mass. He settled at Saratoga, N Y, where he resided for many years. From there he removed to Michigan. He died, May 4, 1864, at Owassa, Michigan.

CHILDREN — SEVENTH GENERATION :

340 +Oliver, b Dec 9, 1799.
341. Eliza, b June 30, 1802
342. Mary, b Nov 6, 1804. Died Sept 23, 1822.
343. Ann M, b July 9, 1807. Died July 12, 1843.
344. Sarah, b. Dec. 22, 1809. Died Dec 25, 1824
345 +Ira L, b Aug 18, 1812
346 Jane M, b. Dec. 24, 1814.
347.+Aruna C. T, b June 12, 1817
348. Louisa A, b. Dec. 28, 1819.

Eliza married Lorenzo Hunt, and settled at Fairport, Monroe County, N Y, where they were residing in 1864

Jane M married, for her first husband, George W Richards, May 15, 1854, and settled at New Michigan, where he died, October 26, 1855. For her second husband, she married Rev. John Booth, December 24, 1862, settled at Howell, Michigan, and afterwards at Owassa.

Louisa A married Amos Gould, and settled at Owassa, Michigan, where, I am told, Mr Gould has been Mayor, District Attorney and Judge of Probate.

[115.] LEWIS[6] PECK, son of OLIVER,[5] settled at Ellenville, Ulster County, N. Y., where he died, February 1853. He married Ann Maria Potter. She was living in 1855.

CHILDREN — SEVENTH GENERATION

349 +Stephen.
350 Catharine.
351 Uriah
352. Rebecca
353 John B
354 +Enoch
355 +Anquevine
356. Rachel

Catharine married John H Goodsire, of Ellenville, N Y.
Rachel married Thomas Butterworth, of Homowack, N. Y.

[116.] ELI[6] PECK, son of OLIVER,[5] at first settled in Schoharie County, N. Y. From there he removed to Tully, Onondaga

6

County, about 1794, where he resided for twenty-five years; when he removed to Pine Grove, Warren County, Pa., where he died in February 1854. He married Huldah Bailey, formerly Huldah Chase, daughter of Eleazer Chase, of Little Compton, R. I., May 1804. She survived him, and was residing in Russellburgh, Warren County, Pa., in 1865.

CHILDREN — SEVENTH GENERATION

Ann, b Sept 27, 1805.	Joseph L , b. Nov 7, 1812.
William, b Oct 6, 1807	Reuben, b Sept 16, 1815
Polly, b Sept 14, 1809	Alonzo, b. June 30, 1818

Ann married Jesse Patten, of Tully, Onondaga County, N. Y , where they were residing in 1865. Their children were *Harriet M.,*[8] *Fidelia H ,*[8] *Robert A ,*[8] *Frances P*[8] and *Rosalie E*[8]

William married Rhoda Brooks, and settled in Erie, Whiteside County, Ill., where he died. His children were *Huldah,*[8] *Reuben,*[8] *Mercy,*[8] *Ann*[8] and *Emeline.*[8]

Polly married Jeremiah Rueland, and was residing at Pine Grove, Warren County, Pa , in 1865. Their children were *Huldah,*[8] *Eli,*[8] *Learned*[8] and *Sylvester*[8]

Joseph L married Sarah Pearsall, daughter of John Pearsall, of Tully, Onondaga County, N. Y , January 1848 They resided in Camden, N. Y , in 1865 Their children were One died in infancy, and *Charles,*[8] who married Sarah Dimond, March 1861.

Reuben married Mary E Raynor, and was residing in Elk, Warren County, Pa , in 1865. Their children were *Mary J.,*[8] *Wesley,*[8] *Phebe A.,*[8] *Edwin D.,*[8] *Harriet L ,*[8] *Flora A.,*[8] *Benjamin E.,*[8] *Nancy E*[8] and *Emma G.*[8]

Alonzo married Fanny Palmer, September 18, 1842, and was residing in Farmington, Pa , in 1865. Their children were *Amos,*[8] *Huldah,*[8] *Zoar,*[8] *Eunice*[8] and *Robert A*[8]

The names of the above children were received too late to be numbered and included in the index.

[118.] BENJAMIN[6] PECK, son of BENJAMIN,[5] settled at South Adams, Mass., where he died, October 4, 1857, in his 89th year. He was a very benevolent, kind-hearted man, and much respected. While collecting the genealogy of his branch, I received many letters of interest from him. He took a deep interest in the subject until the close of his life. He married Patience Chase. She died May 27, 1866.

CHILDREN — SEVENTH GENERATION

357. Lucy, b June 20, 1793 ⎤
358. Polly, b June 20, 1793 ⎦ twins.
359   Chloe, b June 8, 1797.
360. Phebe, b. Oct 26, 1799.
361.+Jacob, b Dec 6, 1801.
362 +Cyrus, b Feb 21, 1804.

363 +Levi, b Aug 31, 1807.
364   Ruth, b Aug 4, 1809
365 +George, b Oct 11, 1811
366. Maria S , b. Dec. 9, 1813.
367.+Benjamin, b. Dec. 5, 1817.

Polly married Otis Sprague, and settled at Huron, Erie County, Ohio. Their children are   *John W ,[8] Asa,[8] Celia A ,[8] Lucy M.,[8] Martha P ,[8]* and *Almira B ,[8] Sprague.*

Chloe married Miles H Andrews, June 29, 1817. Their children are   *Eliza,[8] Lucy,[8] Harriet L ,[8] Cornelius D C ,[8]* and *Chloe P [8] Andrews*

Phebe married Henry Larkin, and settled at Troy, N Y   Their children were *Marie L ,[8] Samuel,[8] George H ,[8] Phebe A.,[8] H M ,[8]* and *Chloe A [8] Larkin.* He died July 27, 1837, and she July 22, 1839

Ruth married Benjamin T Hoxie, September 7, 1828, and settled in Iowa Their children were   *Herbert M ,[8] Melissa P ,[8] Melville B ,[8] Rose M ,[8] William H ,[8] George P ,[8]* and *Florence S [8] Hoxie*

Maria S married David Aldrich, May 31, 1838   Their children were *Daniel A.,[8] Phebe M ,[8] George H ,[8]* and *Newton R [8] Aldrich.*

[119] JAMES[6] PECK, son of BENJAMIN,[5] settled in Glenville, Schenectady County, N. Y., where he lived and died. He married Deborah Manchester. She was born December 1774, and died December 24, 1851.

CHILDREN — SEVENTH GENERATION

368. Ruby, b. Nov 9, 1798.
369. Patience, b Feb 9, 1800.
370   Sarah, b Feb 22, 1802
371 +George J , b Sept 28, 1803.
372   Lewis, b Feb 9, 1805.
373   Olive, b Oct 10, 1806. Died
      Aug 10, 1832.

374   Jefferson, b. Aug 25, 1808.
375. Hannah, b Nov. 19, 1809. Died
      Dec 31, 1856
376. Nancy, b Aug 18, 1811. Died
      July 10, 1860
377. Sebea, b. Aug 9, 1813
378. Clarissa, b. July 21, 1815.

Patience married Asa Lawrence.

Sarah married Pardon Angell.

Lewis married his cousin, Deborah Wing, of Greenfield, Saratoga County, N. Y , and emigrated to Oregon. No issue.

Olive married William T Benedict.

Nancy married Perry Yates, to whom I am indebted for a record of the family

Sebea located at Dundee, Kane County, where he engaged in mercantile pursuits   He married Melissa Kibby   His wife died in about eighteen months after their marriage, and he in about one year after her decease. No issue.

Clarissa married, first, a Mr. Hewitt , second, Philander Stuart.

[121] GEORGE[6] PECK, son of BENJAMIN,[5] resided for some time at Ballston, N. Y. He afterwards settled about two miles southwest from Saratoga Springs, where he owned a forge and carried on an extensive business. When I visited the place, the privilege was unoccupied; but several of the old buildings were still standing. He was a man of untiring energy and perseverance, and by his industry became wealthy. He married Elizabeth Ellis, daughter of Robert Ellis, of Saratoga, February 6, 1801.

CHILDREN — SEVENTH GENERATION

379   Robert E , b Dec. 7, 1801. Died   381. Elizabeth H , b.
        Oct 6, 1803.   382   Elenor E , b July 4, 1812.
380   James E , b ——. Died at   383.+George, b July 2, 1816.
        sea.

Elizabeth married Rockwell Putnam, and settled at Saratoga.
Elenor married William Kidd, and settled at Rochester, N. Y.

[125] OTIS[6] PECK, son of JATHNIEL,[5] settled in Rehoboth, near the homestead of his father, and carried on the business of the forge, which had been occupied by him. He was a man of extensive business. He was a justice of the peace, and held other public offices. He married Grace Carpenter. He died October 9, 1805.

CHILDREN — SEVENTH GENERATION   (R Rec , B 4, p 130)

384   Charlotte, b Jan 27, 1774   389.+Otis, b March 23, 1785.
385 +Jathniel, b April 22, 1775   390   Nancy, b Jan 9, 1787
386   Elizabeth, b Jan 8, 1777.   391.   Vashtia, b March 9, 1789.
387   Esther, b Oct 25, 1778   392.   Perla, b Nov 9, 1791. Died
388   Grace, b March 28, 1782. Died   April 11, 1792
        May 17, 1802, unm

Charlotte married George Williams, of Dighton, Mass.
Esther married Caleb Bliss, and settled in Vermont.
Elizabeth married Russell Smith, of Taunton, Mass
Vashtia married Ezra Perry.
Nancy married Darius Bowen.

[127.] JAMES[6] PECK, son of JATHNIEL,[5] settled in Rehoboth, upon the east side of Great Meadow Hill, so called. He was a soldier in the army of the Revolution. He married Lydia Pratt. He died April 3, 1834. She October 20, 1838, in her 73d year.

CHILDREN — SEVENTH GENERATION   (R. Rec , B 4, p 183)

393   Silda, b Jan 13, 1785   Died   397. Linda, b. June 29, 1798   Died
    unm   unm
394 +Bela, b Nov. 19, 1786.   398   Cynthia, b. Sept 21, 1800.
395 +Lyman, b July 28, 1792.   399.+Horatio, b April 21, 1806
396.+Oren, b Sept. 16, 1795

Cynthia married Leonard Nie, of Taunton, Mass.

[131.] SHUBAEL[6] PECK, son of JATHNIEL,[5] settled in the neighborhood of his brothers   He resided in what was known as the forge house.   He married Hannah Williams, of Dighton, Mass. She was born November 29, 1784.

CHILDREN — SEVENTH GENERATION

400. Clarissa, b Feb 1, 1808.   405. Olive B , b Dec 15, 1818
401 +George W , b Oct 30, 1810.   406. Edward J , b Jan 29, 1821.
402 +Jeremiah P , b March 9; 1812.   Died unm.
403 +William P , b Jan 17, 1814.   407. Henry W , b. Feb 23, 1824.
404. Sarah W , b. April 1, 1816

Clarissa married Rhodolphus G. White, of Taunton.
Sarah W married Newton Capron, of Smithfield, R I.
Olive married Asaph Bliss, of Rehoboth
Henry W went to California. Supposed died unmarried

[132.] BENONI[6] PECK, son of JATHNIEL,[5] settled near his father.   He married Mary Horton, daughter of William Horton, of Rehoboth, Mass.

CHILDREN — SEVENTH GENERATION

408. Esther B   412. Lucy Ann.
409 +William H   413   Mary
410 +Libbeus.   414   Julianna C.
411 Albert   415 +Sylvester.

There were two other children, who died in infancy
Esther married Jacob Green, of Thompson, Conn
Albert, when last heard from, was in Montpelier, Vt.   I have been unable to find him
Lucy Ann married William L. Bairus, of Warren, R. I. , they reside in Providence
Mary married Job B Crossman, of Taunton, Mass
Julianna C married Obed Ruggles, of Medway, Mass

[133.] EDMOND[6] PECK, son of JATHNIEL,[5] at first settled near Great Meadow Hill, so called, and afterwards lived and died

upon the farm occupied in 1862 by Lewis L. Hix. He married
Sybil Codding, of Dighton, Mass., daughter of William Codding.

CHILDREN — SEVENTH GENERATION   (R Rec , B 4, p 181)

416	George W , b Feb 4, 1795.	420	+Arnold J , b May 26, 1803.
417	Caleb M , b Oct 9, 1796	421	+Otis, b. April 24, 1808
418	+Edmond J , b Sept 5, 1798.	422.	Maria, b Sept 12, 1810.
419.	Sybil, b Aug 10, 1800	423	+Henry W , b. Jan 16, 1814.

*Caleb M married Tamma Stebbins, August 24, 1830, and settled at **Munson**,
Geauga County, Ohio, where he died August 24, 1855   His children were:
Henry W,[8] b May 23, 1831, and was residing in Iowa in 1866
Alroy E , b February 28, 1833, and was residing in Chardon, Ohio, in 1866.
Maria P , b February 26, 1836 , residing in Chardon in 1866
George C , b August 31, 1839 , residing in Chardon in 1866.
Louisa E , b April 15, 1846 , residing in Chardon in 1866
Oren C , b. April 26, 1849 , residing in Chardon in 1866
Sybil married Randall Haskins, of Rehoboth, Mass
Maria married Jotham Hicks, and was residing in East Bridgewater, **Mass.**,
in 1865.

[135] GEORGE W.[6] PECK, son of JATHNIEL,[5] settled, lived
and died upon the homestead. He was twice married : first, to
Martha Wheaton, daughter of Col. Joseph Wheaton, of Rehoboth ;
second, to Hannah Carpenter, daughter of Abial Carpenter, of
Rehoboth.

CHILDREN — SEVENTH GENERATION

424	Mary Ann, b. June 3, 1805.		By second wife
425.	Sarah W , b March 2, 1807. Died April 23, 1812	428.	George W , b Dec 4, 1817. Died unm.
426.	Martha W , b April 7, 1809	429.	Hannah C , b Sept 10, 1820.
427.	Catharine S , b July 22, 1811. Died young.	430	Handell D W , b Sept 14, 1826

Martha W married Christopher C Dean, of Taunton, Mass
Handell D W was residing in Boston, Mass , in 1863, unm †

[141.] CROMWELL[6] PECK, son of EBENEZER,[5] lived and
died upon the homestead. He married Peddy Cushman, March 6,
1796.

---

* This family was received too late to be numbered and entered in the
index
† Died suddenly, in a sleeping car, on his way from Boston to New York,
December 1, 1867.

CHILDREN — SEVENTH GENERATION

431.   Shubael, b Feb. 13, 1797. Died Nov 16, 1826, unm
432   Amanda, b. May 2, 1799.
433 +Billings, b May 11, 1801
434.+Parliamon, b March 24, 1803.

435.   Peddy, b. March 20, 1805.
436 +Nelson, b. April 4, 1807
437 +Bradford, b March 7, 1809.
438.   Laura A , b. March 10, 1811. Died unm., Dec. 14, 1833.

Amanda married Elnathan Jones, of Rehoboth. She died December 17, 1833

Peddy married first, Edmond J. Peck (No. 418), and then James Bliss; and was a widow, residing with her daughter, in 1862.

[143.]   WILLIAMS[6] PECK, son of PHILIP,[5] at first settled in Rehoboth. He was for a time interested in the factory now known as the Orleans Factory. He afterwards removed to East Bloomfield, Genesee County, N. Y., where he died July 12, 1843.

He married Sybel Short, January 12, 1800.

CHILDREN — SEVENTH GENERATION:

439   Serepta M., b. March 5, 1801.
440.   Ruth S , b July 13, 1803
441 +Parmenia W , b Sept 21, 1808.
442 +Ira R , b Dec 22, 1809.

443   Rufus B , b Jan 18, 1811. Died Nov. 12, 1825
444 +Horatio N , b July 24, 1813.
445   Delight G , b March 25, 1815.
446   Martha W., b July 11, 1817.

Serepta married Daniel S. Brambles. He died in Michigan She was living, in 1863, a widow

Ruth S married Stephen H. Lovejoy, settled in Ogden, Monroe County, N. Y

Delight G married Thomas Flagg; settled in Alabama, Genesee County, N. Y.

Martha married James Colby, settled in Ogden, Monroe County, N Y.

[144.]   LEMUEL[6] PECK, son of PHILIP,[5] resided in Rehoboth until his decease. He married Sally Jones, daughter of Ebenezer Jones, of Taunton, Mass., November 30, 1797. She died May 3, 1840. He April 11, 1848.

CHILDREN — SEVENTH GENERATION

447.+Josephus, b. Dec. 28, 1801.

448.   Philip, b Aug 4, 1804, and died April 20, 1840.

[147.]   JAMES[6] PECK, son of PHILIP,[5] settled at Montpelier, Vt., where he resided until 1816, when he removed to the French

Mills, where he died June 17, 1823. He was twice married · first, to Abigail Jones, October 2, 1803; second, to Hannah Sanborn, December 22, 1819. He was an enterprising business man, owned a nail factory, kept a dry goods store, dealt in lumber, etc.

CHILDREN — SEVENTH GENERATION

449. Rowena Toby, b Dec 18, 1805.

450.+Jonathan Jones, b. Aug 29, 1808

451 Celinda, b Nov 21, 1810 Died in Rehoboth, April 10, 1830

452. Philip Williams, b Nov. 4, 1813. Suppose unm

453. Orinda, b. Dec 3, 1815

454. Gideon Hicks, b. May 8, 1818. Died May 11, 1818.

455. Abigail J., b Aug 3, 1820.

Rowena T. married Silas Wheelock, and settled in Calais, Vt , where she was residing in 1863   To her kindness I am indebted for my information in relation to the family.

Orinda married Azariah Moor, of West Fairlee

Abigail J married Benjamin O'Donnell, settled at Jamaica, Long Island.

[150.] EBENEZER[6] PECK, son of PHILIP,[5] first settled in Rehoboth, afterwards in Lyndon, Vt. He died June 27, 1851.

He was twice married: first, to Nancy Horton, daughter of William Horton, of Swanzey, July 28, 1805; second, to Patience Short.

CHILDREN — SEVENTH GENERATION

456 +Martin H , b May 27, 1806

457 Ann Eliza, b Oct 7, 1807

458.+James M , b June 12, 1809.

459. Nancy F , b March 12, 1811.

460. Sally A , b May 30, 1814.

461 +Lucius W , b. March 28, 1821.

Ann Eliza married Lewis Gilson, of Danville, Vt , son of Samuel Gilson, November 25, 1835   Their children were *Henry M ,*[8] b November 16, 1836, *Mary N ,*[8] b July 12, 1840, *Edward P.,*[8] b January 4, 1844, and *Martha E ,*[8] b. November 20, 1852

Nancy F married Joseph Page, of Wentworth, N H. *Sarah J ,* their only child, married Robert Shelbourn, of Graves County, Ky., December 20, 1855, and died, May 22, 1856, in the twenty-fifth year of her age

Sally A married, for her first husband, Horatio Morrill, of Wheelock, Vt., September 9, 1833, by whom she had two children, *James P ,*[8] b. August 13, 1836, and *Luvai,*[8] b January 16, 1841   For her second husband, she married Eli Smith, of Graves County, Ky By him she had one child, *Martha,*[8] b. June 11, 1845   She died March 17, 1847

[152] CYREL C.[6] PECK, son of PHILIP,[5] settled upon the homestead, where he was residing when I visited him, in 1862. To him I am indebted for my information in relation to his branch of

the name. He, and his son near him, were the only ones left here to represent this branch of the Pecks, or who have continued to hold any of the great tract of land once owned by them in this vicinity. He owns a valuable farm, and has carried on with it the blacksmithing business. He married Cynthia Hicks, November 29, 1810.

CHILDREN — SEVENTH GENERATION

462.+Cyrel C. jr , b Feb. 8, 1812.
463 +Joseph S , b. Nov 22, 1813.
464 Abiah W , b Jan. 19, 1816
465 Cynthia H , b Oct. 23, 1817.
466 +Philip W , b Sept 21, 1819
467 Mason S , b Feb 26, 1822
468. Rhoda M., b March 4, 1824.

469. Cassandana W., b June 29, 1826.
470 +George G , b Sept. 22, 1830.
471 +Alfred R , b July 30, 1833
472 Ruth A , b Feb 26, 1836.
473. Sereptina A., b March 20, 1828.
  Died Aug 27, 1833.

Abiah W was in California, unmarried, in 1862.
Cynthia H married Jacob White.
Rhoda M married Nathaniel Thurber.
Cassandana W married Josiah Woodworth.
Mason S married Azuba Bagley. He was residing in Pawtucket, R. I., in 1863, no issue.

[156.] BENJAMIN PECK,[6] son of SOLOMON,[5] settled in Providence, R. I. He married Sarah Batchelor, July 4, 1797.

The following epitaphs are from their tombstones:

Benjamin Peck, born August 1, 1767, died October 18, 1832.

Sarah Peck, widow of Benjamin Peck, and daughter of Rev. William Batchelor, born March 21, 1776, died May 10, 1864.

"OUR MOTHER"

Upright with man, he had hope toward God only through Jesus Christ.

A believer in Christ from early years, she waited trustingly "all the days of her appointed time" for His salvation.

CHILDREN — SEVENTH GENERATION

474 +William, b April 6, 1798
475 +Solomon, b Jan 25, 1800.
476 Harriet, b Oct 5, 1801
477. Fanny, b June 9, 1804.

478 +George B , b Aug. 6, 1807.
479. Galen, b Sept 9, 1812. Died March 25, 1830.

Harriet was residing in Providence in 1864, unm.
Fanny died July 1857, unm.

[157.] DAVID[6] PECK, son of SOLOMON,[5] settled in Providence, R. I. I am told, he was for some time deacon of the Second Baptist Church. He married Elizabeth Hicks, of Sutton, Mass.

CHILDREN — SEVENTH GENERATION.

480. Lyman, b July 1, 1792. Died unm., Sept 23, 1817.
481 Lydia, b July 13, 1794.
482 +Lewis, b Sept 17, 1796.
483. David, b. Nov. 2, 1798. Died unm.
484. Anna, b Oct 26, 1800.
485. Elizabeth, b June 22, 1805.
486. Joseph C., b Aug 5, 1807.

Lydia married John Calder, of Providence, where they were residing in 1863.

Elizabeth married Joshua H. Fowler, January 31, 1836, and was a widow, residing in Providence, in 1863.

Joseph C. removed west, unknown where he is

[158] SOLOMON[6] PECK, son of SOLOMON,[5] settled in Providence, where he died August 27, 1809. He married Huldah Kinsley, of Providence.

CHILDREN — SEVENTH GENERATION:

487. Sally, b. Sept. 7, 1801.
488. Ann L., b June 1805

Sally married Elijah Bellows, and settled in Savanna, Ill, where she was residing, in 1863, a widow

Ann L. married James Temple; settled in Galena, Ill, where she died, leaving two daughters, one of whom married Rev William Bray, of Aurora, Ill.

[163.] JOSHUA[6] PECK, son of JOHN,[5] settled at first in Royalston, Mass., then in Montpelier, Vt., and afterwards in Clinton, Me., where he died. He was a soldier of the Revolution, and received a pension during the latter part of his life.

CHILDREN — SEVENTH GENERATION:

489. Sally
490 Esther

Sally married a man by the name of Quinly, for her first husband, and Michael Casey, for her second.

Esther married a man by the name of Bowler.

[165] HIRAM[6] PECK, son of JOHN,[5] settled, at an early date, at Montpelier, Vt. He took an active interest in the organization of the town, and was one of the first Selectmen. He moved

from Montpelier to Waterbury, where, I am told, he was a prominent man; from here he removed to Parishville, N. Y., where he died. He married Wealthy Kibburn, February 20, 1801. He died January 28, 1831, aged 67 years. She died March 16, 1836.

CHILDREN — SEVENTH GENERATION.

491. Albert, b. June 13, 1802. Died in infancy
492. Chauncey H , b Oct 4, 1804
493. Minerva, b. July 26, 1806. Died in infancy
494. Lucy, b Jan 18, 1809
495. Maiy, b April 1, 1811 ⎰
496. Sarah, b. April 1, 1811 ⎱
       Twins   Sarah drowned in childhood.

497. Minerva, b May 31, 1813. Died in childhood.
498.+Hiram H., b. Nov. 16, 1815.
499. Josiah K., b. Feb. 5, 1818. Died young
500.+John W , b Nov 7, 1819.
501.+Comer M., b March 18, 1822.

Chauncey H. has been twice married first, to Grace Spencer; second, to Susan Willaid He was residing at Prescott, Canada West, in 1863.

Lucy married H Christy, of Medina, N. Y.

Mary married J. T Gould, and died April 9, 1834.

[166.] NATHANIEL[6] PECK, son of JOHN,[5] settled in Montpelier at an early date, where he died April 10, 1827. He was a farmer. He was twice married: first, to Jane Toggett; second, to widow Phebe Carpenter, formerly Phebe Smith, daughter of Ezekiel Smith, of Rehoboth, Mass. She died October 30, 1844. He was a man much respected and honored in the community in which he resided.

CHILDREN — SEVENTH GENERATION:

502. Mary, b June 19, 1796.
503. Laura J., b. Dec. 15, 1804.

By his second wife
504.+Addison, b Sept. 6, 1807.
505.+Russell, b Nov. 10, 1809.
506. Sharlock, b March 27, 1812

There were other children by his first wife, who died young, viz Gustavus Adolphus, Flavious Josephus, and Laura; and two by his second wife, who died in infancy

Mary was residing in Montpelier in 1863, unm

Laura Jane married Stephen Wright, and settled in Berlin, Vt.

Sharlock married Margaret Clifford, and was residing in Montpelier, Vt., in 1862, no issue

[167.] SQUIRE[6] PECK, son of JOHN,[5] removed from Royalston, Mass., with his father, to Montpelier, about 1806, where he

died August 25, 1838. He married Elizabeth Godard. She died
October 4, 1834, aged 62 years.

507 +Nahum, b Oct 5, 1796

508. Josiah, b. July 16, 1798 Died
young

509. Myra, b Jan. 27, 1800.

510 Betsey, b Jan. 17, 1802.

511. Asahel, b. Sept. 1803

512. Tamar, b. March 1806 , is unm.

513. Jonas G , b. June 1808. Died
unm., aged about 30.

There were three others, who died young

Myra married Joseph R Waite; settled in Hinesburgh, Vt.

Betsey married Orlo Lockwood, and settled at St George's, Vt.

Asahel resides in Burlington, Vt   He is a man of distinction. He has been
a lawyer of extensive practice for many years, and one of the judges of the
Supreme Court of Vermont

Tamar is unmarried, and resides with her sister Myra.

[168] JOHN[6] PECK, son of JOHN,[5] settled in Waterbury,
Vt. He was known as General Peck; and, I am told, was a man
of much talent, although I have been able to learn little in relation
to him. He was for some time high sheriff, and held other important offices. He married Ann Benedict. He died in 1826.

514.+Lucius B , b 1804

515. Casius, b. 1806

Casius settled in New York City, engaged in mercantile business, and died
there, leaving no children.

[171.] GIDEON[6] PECK, son of HENRY,[5] lived and died in
Seekonk. He was a farmer. He married Keziah Lyon, daughter
of Samuel Lyon, May 29, 1791. She was born August 4, 1771,
and died January 30, 1834. He died March 31, 1839.

516. Nancy, b Sept 1, 1795.

517. Betsey, b Jan 29, 1798.

518. George A , b July 27, 1800.

519 Mary Ann, b. Aug 3, 1803.

520. Ezra, b. April 23, 1807.

521. Maria, b. Nov 4, 1815

Nancy was residing in Seekonk in 1863, unm.

Betsey was residing in Seekonk in 1863, unm.

George A , unknown where he is

Mary Ann married Edward Dodge , was residing with her daughter, wife
of Peleg Spooner, in 1863

Ezra, unknown where he is.

Maria was residing in Seekonk, unm., in 1863.

[176.] WILLIAM[6] PECK, son of HENRY,[5] I am told, married Susannah Graham, of Providence, and left one child.

522   William, whom I have been unable to find, probably died young.

The will of William Peck is upon the Providence records, dated December 23, 1812. He gives his clothing, excepting his uniform suit, to his brothers, Gideon and Henry. He gives to his wife, Susannah, his uniform suit, with all his personal and real estate, during her life, or so long as she remained his widow; directing his yoke of oxen, and horse and wagon, to be sold for the payment of his debts. He appoints his wife executrix.

[181.] DANIEL[6] PECK, son of DANIEL,[5] resided in Royalston, Mass., where he died, October 5, 1839. He was a farmer. He married Delia Gale, April 27, 1795.

CHILDREN — SEVENTH GENERATION

523   Rulina, b Feb 13, 1796
524.+Chauncey, b March 2, 1797.
525.+Pomroy, b Feb 16, 1799.
526. Harriet, b Sept 13, 1800.
527   Mary, b Oct 19, 1803
528 +Lyman, b Feb 11, 1804.
529 +Sullivan, b March 27, 1806.

530. Hannah F , b May 30, 1809.
531. Elvira, b May 14, 1811
532. Elsa S , b March 11, 1813.
533   Delia, b Jan. 14, 1815
534   Huldah C , b Feb 9, 1817
535   Augusta, b April 13, 1820.

Rulina married Hugh Foster, March 2, 1818
Harriet married Daniel Bliss, October 11, 1821.
Mary married Rev. Timothy Crosby, 1831.
Hannah F married Elisha M. Davis, June 14, 1829.
Elvira married George Batchelor, November 1837.
Delia married George Pierce, May 5, 1835.
Huldah married Emory ——, April 1846.
Augusta married George Gibson.

[182] ICHABOD[6] PECK, son of DANIEL,[5] removed from Royalston to Montpelier. He was a farmer. He married Polly Forbes, December 16, 1800, daughter of John Forbes, of Royalston.

CHILDREN — SEVENTH GENERATION

536   Emily, b Jan 1802
537   Clarissa, b 1805
538 +John Q A , b Nov 15, 1808.

539 +William N., b Sept. 22, 1811.
540   Caroline M , b. Sept. 30, 1813.

Emily married Silas Fisher. Settled in Phayson, Vt.
Clarissa married John Fulsom. Settled in Phayson, Vt.
Caroline M married Addison Page, of Montpelier, Vt.

7

[184.] SOLOMON[6] PECK, son of DANIEL,[5] at first settled with his father, in Royalston, Mass. After his decease, he removed to Orange, Franklin County, where he was residing in 1863, a farmer. He married Mercy Simmons, of Swansey, Mass , October 27, 1803 (S. Rec , B. 2).

CHILDREN — SEVENTH GENERATION

541   Louisa, b May 28, 1805.   545   James M , b Jan 10, 1814
542   Roby, b May 1, 1807   546 +Daniel, b Oct 31, 1816.
543   Delina, b Sept 19, 1809   547   Susan   Died unm
544   Mary Ann, b Dec 4, 1811.   548   John   Resides with his father.

[186.] CALVIN[6] PECK, son of DANIEL,[5] settled in Orange, Mass., where he resided until about 1852, when he removed to Medway, Mass., where he died, January 30, 1861. He was a bridge builder and house carpenter by trade, which business he carried on extensively. He was twice married · first, to Anna Gurnsey, of Montpelier, Vt., who died November 22, 1837; second, to Eliza Barton, of Leicester, Mass.

CHILDREN — SEVENTH GENERATION

549   Adaline, b Dec 4, 1808   553   Sephronia. Died Oct 19, 1831,
550   Villroy, b March 4, 1811.   unm
551   Emeline   Died Feb 11, 1823,   554   Lavinia, b March 24, 1822
     unm   555 +Napoleon B , b. June 20, 1827.
552.+Jerome B.

Adaline married Emory Barns, and resides in Wrentham, Mass.
Villroy married Prentis H. Pond, and resides in Woonsocket, R I
Lavinia married Jason B Reynolds, and resides in Wrentham, Mass.

[188.] MOSES[6] PECK, son of DANIEL,[5] resided first in Royalston, Mass. From there he removed to Montpelier, Vt., and from Montpelier to Middlesex. He married Polly Cass, daughter of John Cass, of Richmond, July 10, 1808. She was born May 20, 1786.

CHILDREN — SEVENTH GENERATION

556   Angeline, b April 15, 1809.   559 +Charles E , b Sept. 2, 1816
557 +Moses, b Jan 9, 1812.   560   Emeline M , b Jan 1, 1820
558 +John C , b June 14, 1814.

Angeline married Edwin C Lewis, of Montpelier, Vt.
Emeline M married Chester Briggs, of Rockford, Ill.

[197.] SOLOMON[6] PECK, son of SOLOMON,[5] settled first in Topsham, Vt., and then in Harlam, Ohio. He was three times married first, to Philoma Holbrook, in Townsend, Vt ; second, to Widow Laura Bishop, in Richmond, N. H.; third, to Elizabeth Nutt, in Topsham, Vt. He died at Harlam, Ohio, October 1844. His first wife died in 1805.

CHILDREN — SEVENTH GENERATION

561 +Horace M , b May 1801
562 +Sewel, b June 1803.
563. Philoma, b Dec 1805   Died
     in 1807.

By second wife

564. Lyman, b 1807   Died unm
565 Narcissa, b 1809
566 Mary, b 1811
567. Catharine, b 1813

By third wife

568   Philetta H , b Aug 31, 1821
569   Franklin, b June 2, 1823
570   Solomon. b March 2, 1825
571 +John N , b Nov 18, 1826
572 +William N , b June 22, 1828
573. Elizabeth Jane, b May 26, 1831.
574   Mary Ann, b May 26, 1831
575 +Dexter, b April 25, 1833.

Narcissa married Elijah Crocker
Mary married Samuel Clark, of Vernon, Vt.
Catharine married a Buffam
Philetta H married Cyrus Rogers
Franklin died, April 11, 1847, unmarried
Soloman died in the Mexican war, in 1849, unmarried.
Elizabeth Jane married William Rogers
Mary Ann married Stephen L Emerson

[198.] JAMES W.[6] PECK, son of SOLOMON,[5] settled in Topsham, Vt. He married Nellie Mann, of Richmond, N. H , October 10, 1805. He died September 21, 1825. She died June 1854, aged 64.

CHILDREN — SEVENTH GENERATION

576   Mahala, b March 29, 1806.
577   Vienna, b Oct 7, 1804
    Died young
578   Annie, b July 1809.
    Died young
579 +Horatio N , b Aug 4, 1812.
580 +Arnold M , b May 10, 1816

581. Alonzo, b. Jan 12, 1817   Died
    unm
582   Lydia A , b April 23, 1821   Died
    young
583   Horace, b May 4, 1824   Died
    Nov 18, 1855

Mahala was residing in Lowell, Mass , in 1863, unmarried

[199] BENONI PECK,[6] son of SOLOMON,[5] settled upon the homestead, where he resided until 1862, when he removed to Fitz-

william, N. H. He has been highly honored and respected. He
held a military commission, and was called into service in the war
of 1812. He has continually held some public office in his town
for many years, and has represented it in the State legislature. He
has been a justice of the peace for more than forty years, and
notwithstanding his advanced age still holds the office, transacting
business with the vigor of a middle age, and is still sought after
for council and advice. He has also devoted much of his time to
probate business, administering upon and settling the estates of
deceased persons. He has also taken an active interest in Free-
masonry, to which fraternity he has belonged for more than sixty
years. To him I am indebted for my information in relation to his
branch of the name.

He has been twice married; first, to Eunice Rogers, who is said
to have been a lineal descendant of John Rogers, who was burnt
at the stake,* second, to Malinda Richards. His first wife died
March 3, 1853.

CHILDREN — SEVENTH GENERATION

584. Caroline, b. June 16, 1809
585 +Philip, b Jan. 16, 1812.
586.+Levi, b Aug 31, 1814
587 +James W , b Oct 9, 1817
588. Benjamin, b. Feb 9, 1820 Died
June 1841
589   Eliphalet, b March 16, 1822.
590   Calista, b Nov. 7, 1824
591   Eunice, b June 6, 1827   Died
in 1846
592 +Henry, b Aug 2, 1829
593. Mary, b Oct. 6, 1831. Died in
1855.

Caroline married Josiah Parker, and settled in Ashland, Mass   She died in
1854, leaving six children.

Calista married Levi N. Fairbanks

Eliphalet was residing in Worcester in 1863. He married Nancy Smith; no
issue.

---

* The following is from the *Fitchburg Reveille*

"Mrs Peck was the daughter of Mr Eliphalet Rogers, late of Royalston,
and son of Mr Benjamin Rogers, who was son of Rev John Rogers, Pastor
of the First Church in Ipswich, and President of Harvard College, who died
July 2, 1684   This gentleman was eldest son of Rev Nathaniel Rogers, who
came from England in 1636, and settled at Ipswich, as colleague pastor with
Rev Nathaniel Ward, and died July 2, 1655, aged 57   Nathaniel Rogers was
a son of the Rev John Rogers, of Dedham, England, who died October 18,
1639, aged 67, and John was son of the Rev John Rogers, the Martyr, who
was burned at Smithfield, February 5, 1555."

[210.] OLIVER C.⁶ PECK, son of OLIVER,⁵ was residing upon the homestead, in Rehoboth, Mass., in 1860; an industrious and thrifty farmer, much respected.

He married Nancy Macomber, daughter of John Macomber, April 21, 1808.

CHILDREN — SEVENTH GENERATION

594. John M , b May 11, 1809.

595. Nancy S , b June 1, 1812. Died Feb 25, 1838.

596 +Royal C , b June 11, 1816

597 Adaline B , b Oct 12, 1822.

John M was residing at home in 1860, unm.
Adaline B. married Lindley Horton, of Rehoboth.

[211] RUFUS⁶ PECK, son of OLIVER,⁵ settled in New Providence, Clark County, Indiana, where he died, August 6, 1826. He married Naomi Alexander, daughter of Roger Alexander, of Cumberland, R. I., April 6, 1812.

CHILDREN — SEVENTH GENERATION

598 Hannah B , b May 20, 1813.

599 Rachel W , b Oct 25, 1815

600 Hannah H , b Oct 20, 1821.

601 +Rufus A , b March 30, 1825.

602 Anna H , b Oct 26, 1826.

Hannah H married James Gibson, and settled upon the homestead   Their children are *Royal M.,*⁸ *John B ,*⁸ *Richard M ,*⁸ *Melvina A.,*⁸ *James K ,*⁸ *Emily O ,*⁸ *Isaac A ,*⁸ *Thomas W , Rufus W ,*⁸ and *Emmet* ⁸

Anna married Washington Johnson, and resided in the town of New Providence, Ind   Her children were   *Theodore V.,*⁸ *Rufus P.,*⁸ *Jasper N.,*⁸ *Eli B.,*⁸ *Naomi E ,*⁸ and *Perry D* ⁸

[212] CALEB⁶ PECK, son of OLIVER,⁵ was residing in Seekonk, Mass., in 1860, a farmer. He married Polly Jacobs, daughter of Calvin Jacobs.

CHILDREN — SEVENTH GENERATION

603 +Calvin J , b Oct 28, 1812

604 Nancy C , b Nov 22, 1814. Died unm

605 Maria Louisa, b Feb. 3, 1817. Died Aug 13, 1821

606. Susan Ann, b. Aug 7, 1819. Died Aug. 21, 1821.

607. Susan M., b. Oct. 3, 1821 Died unm

608. Hannah C , b Aug 21, 1824. Died unm

609 +Henry R., b. June 17, 1827.

7*

[213]   SAMUEL PECK,[6] son of OLIVER,[5] settled in Salem, Washington County, Indiana.   He was, for several years, I am told, Judge of Probate, and held other offices.   He married Malinda Hide, April 20, 1820.   He died in Texas, June 13, 1843, while journeying there, in the hopes of improving his health.

CHILDREN — SEVENTH GENERATION

610   Harriet H , b Jan 30, 1821
611   Catharine L , b Jan 10, 1823
612 +Hiram A , b June 21, 1824
613. Samuel C , b June 28, 1826
       Died Nov 15, 1826
614   Samuel, b Nov 8, 1827

615   Lizzie P , b Nov. 13, 1829.
616   George W , b Oct 13, 1831.
617   Rufus H , b Nov 25, 1833.
618   Mary A , b June 15, 1836.
619   Daniel W , b July 29, 1839.

Harriet H married Dr Samuel Reid, of Salem, Indiana   She died January 20, 1863, leaving six children, four sons and two daughters

Catharine L married William S Townsend, of Greencastle, Indiana, and has five children, three sons and two daughters

Samuel was residing in Greencastle, Indiana, a merchant, unmarried, in 1863.

Lizzie married William H Butler, of Louisville, Kentucky, November 3, 1851   Mr Butler was a highly educated man, He was killed in his schoolroom, November 3, 1853, by Mat F Ward

George W settled at Robinson, Crawford County, Illinois   He was a lawyer.   He enlisted in the 21st Illinois Volunteer Infantry , was elected a Captain, and afterwards promoted to Lieut -Colonel   He was taken sick, came home, and died January 28, 1863.

Rufus H was residing at Salem, Indiana, unmarried, in 1863

Mary A married Robert Morris, of Salem, where they were residing in 1863   Their children were *Jessie*[8] and *Hattie* [8]

Daniel W was residing at Salem in 1863.   He married Lizzie Lockwood,[8] of Salem, November 11, 1862

[219.]   GEORGE[6] PECK, son of SAMUEL,[5] settled in Rehoboth, near his father.   He married Nancy Carpenter, daughter of Caleb Carpenter, of Reboboth.

CHILDREN — SEVENTH GENERATION

620. George. Died in infancy.
621   George   Died in infancy
622   George   Died in infancy

623   Ann   Died in infancy.
624   Susan

Susan married Philip Martin, of Guilford, Mass.

[225.] BENJAMIN[6] PECK, son of ALLEN,[5] settled in Providence, R. I., where he died in 1843. He was a merchant. He married Roby A. Ormsbee. She died in 1806.

CHILDREN — SEVENTH GENERATION

625 +Allen O , b Nov 17, 1804   626. Mary S , b May 19, 1806.

Mary S married Esek Aldrich, and settled in Providence.

[227.] JOSEPH[6] PECK, son of JOSIAH,[5] settled in Charlton, Mass., where he lived and died. He was a farmer. He married Sarah Whipple, daughter of Christopher Whipple, of Cumberland, R. I. He died August 28, 1824. She November 14, 1847, aged 77 years.

CHILDREN — SEVENTH GENERATION

627 Almira Died in infancy	632 Anna, b July 1, 1803
628 +Otis, b Sept 18, 1793	633 Joseph W , b Oct 26, 1806
629 +Arnold, b. Oct 21, 1796	Died at sea unm
630. William, b. July 21, 1799	634 Temperance, b. 1808 Died 1825
631 Harriet W , b Dec 17, 1801	

[231.] JOSIAH[6] PECK, son of JOSIAH,[5] settled in Eaton, Mass , where he was residing in 1853.

He married Elizabeth Barton, daughter of Hale Barton, August 30, 1798 (R. Rec., Book 4).

CHILDREN — SEVENTH GENERATION

635. Nelson, b Nov 13, 1798 , was killed by the falling of a tree, Aug 23, 1817	640 +Josiah, b May 15, 1809
	641 Elizabeth, b Dec 16, 1811. Died July 19, 1814
636 Louisa, b April 15, 1800	642 Ann R , b Feb 25, 1813 Died Oct 23, 1827
637 +Barton, b Feb 8, 1802	
638 Lydia B , b Feb 17, 1804	643 +Alonzo, b March 23, 1815
639 Patience B , b Sept 3, 1806. Died July 16, 1814	644. Samuel W , b Feb 16, 1817.

Louisa married Samuel Merritt.

Lydia married John J Doin

Samuel W is a physician He is settled at Washington, Davies County, Indiana He married Hannah B. Havens, daughter of Dr P B Havens, of Hamilton, N Y , no issue

[242.] CROMWELL[6] PECK, son of PEREZ,[5] settled in Coventry, R. I. He was a blacksmith and machinist by trade and occupation. He married Mary Cushing, of Providence, July 22, 1804. He died August 12, 1838, and his widow, August 1, 1851.

CHILDREN — SEVENTH GENERATION

645. Mary, b in Coventry, Nov 24, 1806.

646 Sabra, b in Coventry, April 9, 1808

647. Lydia, b in Coventry, Nov 17, 1810.

648 Ann, b. in Coventry, Aug. 6, 1813.

649. Eliza, b. in Providence, Sept. 4, 1816

Mary was twice married first, to James Davis, by whom she had two children, both of whom died in infancy Her second husband was Olney Windsor; by him she had three children, *Cromwell P*,[8] *Mary Caroline*,[8] and *Josephine*[8]

Sabra married William Morris, by whom she had one daughter, *Elizabeth*,[8] b Feb 3, 1827

Lydia married Charles S Lawrence; no issue She died November 2, 1860.

Ann married Joseph Whipple, by whom she had two children, *Ann E*,[8] and *George C*

Eliza married James Austin Her issue were *James*,[8] *Edward*,[8] and *Clara*[8] After the decease of her husband, she married James Chappell, with whom she was living in 1863

[247] PEREZ PECK,[6] son of PEREZ,[5] settled in Coventry, R. I., where he was residing in 1864. He is a machinist by trade, which business he carried on for many years. He commenced it in 1805. He has been considered one of the most trustworthy manufacturers in the country. He married Joanna Brown, December 9, 1813.

CHILDREN — SEVENTH GENERATION

650 Harriet, b April 19, 1815. Died May 23, 1840

651 Mary Ann, b July 15, 1816

652 Lydia H , b Dec 31, 1817

653 Sarah, b April 15, 1820. Died Dec 2, 1821

654 Joanna, b Sept 13, 1821.

655 +Isaac, b Oct 11, 1824.

Mary Ann married Asa Sisson, and resides in Coventry Their children are, *Harriet P*,[8] b May 25, 1845, and died August 10, 1846, *Charles*,[8] b. September 7, 1848, and *Emily*, b January 15, 1856

[272] JOEL[7] PECK, son of DANIEL,[6] settled in Greenbush, now Poestenkill, Rensselaer County, N. Y., where he remained until his decease, August 8, 1855.

He married Hannah Baldwin in 1811.

656   Mahala D , b Feb 22, 1812.
657. William H , b Dec 8, 1816.
658   Calista, b May 23, 1818
659. Joel C , b Aug 28, 1820

660   Marvin R , b July 16, 1822.
661   Mariette, b Nov 16, 1829.
662. Emily, b March 13, 1831   Died
        Nov. 20, 1847.

Mahala married Jacob Dingman, February 18, 1835, and settled in Poesten-kill, Rensselaer County, N Y., where they were residing in 1864   Their children are   *Charles N* ,[9] b October 4, 1838 , *Mary E* ,[9] b April 10, 1841 , *Joel B* ,[9] b September 25, 1843 , *Delia F* ,[9] b March 1, 1847 , *Mahala* ,[9] b June 18, 1850 ; *George W* ,[9] b February 5, 1853 , *Marcia L* , b July 14, 1855

Calista and *Marietta* were residing with their mother in Poestenkill in 1864, unmarried

William H was residing in the town of Sandy Creek, Oswego County, N. Y He married, for his 1st wife, Sally M Harger, and for his 2d, Lois Roberson His 1st wife died September 7, 1848   His children are   *George W* ,[9] *William G* ,[9] *Mary L* ,[9] *Emma J* ,[9] *Delia A* ,[9] *Maria* ,[9] *Clarence*[9] and *Charles* [9]

Joel C was residing in Troy, N Y , in 1864   He married Mary Lynd.[9] His children are   *Emily A* ,[9] *Ella F.* ,[9] and *Catharine L* [9]

The names of the above children were received too late to be numbered and entered in the index.

[273] DANIEL[7] PECK, son of DANIEL,[6] first settled, in 1808, at Sand Lake, Rensselaer County, N. Y. In 1830 he settled at East Pembroke, where he was residing in 1864. He married, for his first wife, Hannah Woodward, daughter of David Woodward, February 18, 1808. For his second wife, Bathsheba Gould, daughter of Reuben Gould, October 18, 1810. His first wife died January 15, 1809. His second, August 3, 1848.

663   David, b Jan 15, 1809   Died
        Jan 15, 1809
664   William, b Aug 19, 1811
665   Mehitable, b Nov 9,   1812.
        Died Oct 22, 1813
666. Emeline C , b April 22, 1814.
667. Daniel, b Feb 24, 1816   Died
        March 15, 1816
668   Bathsheba, b Jan. 13, 1817.
        Died Nov 5, 1843.
669. Daniel G., b. June 16, 1818

670   Edward, b Jan 9, 1820   Died
        Sept 14, 1846
671   Hannah, b March 24, 1821.
        Died April 30, 1834
672   Nathan, b. Nov 14, 1822.
673. Sophia, b May 29, 1825. Died
        May 10, 1826
674   Reuben, b Feb 22, 1827.
675   George, b Nov. 23, 1829   Died
        May 9, 1830.

William mained Celinda Ryckman March 5, 1837, was residing in East Pembroke in 1864   Their children were   (676) *Joel,*[9] b December 3, 1837, (677) *Lydia J,*[9] b March 6, 1839; (678) *Franklin,*[9] b February 12, 1845

Emeline married Charles Gorham and settled in Belvidere, Boon County, Ill

Bathsheba married Dexter Fales, no issue

Daniel G, of West Bergen, N Y, married Mary A Tompkins, December 15, 1847   His children are   (679) *Wealthy,*[9] b August 4, 1848, (680) *Francis,*[9] b May 13, 1850; (681) *George W,*[9] b October 26, 1853, (682) *Freemont J,*[9] b. March 16, 1856, (683) *Flora E,*[9] b March 4, 1858, (684) *Richmond O,*[9] b. August 24, 1860, and (685) *Elinor E,*[9] b September 10, 1862

Edward married Martha Ann Baker, and settled in East Pembroke   Their son is (686) *Charles Edward*[9]

Nathan married Selina Maria Peck (704) daughter of Harvey Peck, October 18, 1848   Their daughter, (687) *Mary Clara Ida,*[9] was born December 29, 1856

Reuben married Polly Wrightman, April 24, 1846, and was residing in Wisconsin in 1864   His children are   (688) *Ellen F,*[9] b January 19, 1847, (689) *David,*[9] b November 17, 1848, (690) *Estella E,*[9] b February 22, 1850; (691) *Arthur C,*[9] b August 29, 1852, (692) *Malvina, E A,*[9] b April 26, 1855, (693) *Eugene C,*[9] b July 12, 1859, (694) *Ernest C,*[9] b April 11, 1861, *Reuben;*[9] *Mary C;*[9] *Carrie M*[9]   These three last children were not at first received with the record of the family, therefore not numbered

[274.] DR BETHUEL[7] PECK, son of DANIEL,[6] married Jerusha Wiston.

He settled at Glens Falls, N. Y., where he was a physician for many years. He was a member of the State Legislature. He died July 11, 1862. His widow was residing in Chicago in 1864.

CHILDREN — EIGHTH GENERATION

695. Gloriannah, b in 1824   Died in 1827.

[275.] JOHN[7] PECK, son of DANIEL,[6] married Sarah Whyland, September 25, 1816. She was born in 1797.

CHILDREN — EIGHTH GENERATION

696 Agnes, b March 1, 1818	699 Maria, b Dec 18, 1823
697 Philotte, b Aug 16, 1819.	700. John, b Feb 28, 1826.
698 Barnard, b Aug 14, 1821	

Agnes married Ezra De Freest, November 13, 1836   They were residing in Troy, N Y, in 1864   Their children were. *Daniel W,*[9] *Mary F,*[9] *John W,*[9] *George E,*[9] and *Bethuel P.*[9]

Philotte married David Philips, June 8, 1847   They were residing in Brunswick, N Y , in 1864   Their children were *Frances P ,*[9] *Willard D.,*[9] and *Jennette* [9]

Barnard married Catharine Watson, October 1845   He died March 6, 1850. His son, (701) *Barnard,*[9] was born September 18, 1846, and died December 20, 1846

Maria married Henry W Danforth, January 14, 1823   They were residing in Troy, N Y , in 1864.   Their children were *Emma P ,*[9] *Henry W jr.,*[9] *Susan J ,*[9] *Mary A ,*[9] and *Harriett J*[9]

John was residing in Troy, N. Y , in 1864, unmarried.

[276]   HARVEY[7] PECK, son of DANIEL,[6] married Elenor McMellen, daughter of William McMellen.   They resided in Poestenkill, Rensselaer County, N. Y., in 1864.

CHILDREN — EIGHTH GENERATION

702   Mehitable, b April 4, 1817
703   Jane A , b July 27, 1820
704   Selina M , b March 28, 1822.
705.   Elenor, b Oct 18, 1824

706   Jerusha, b April 25, 1826.
707.   William H , b June 29, 1829.
708.   Bethuel, b Feb 5, 1833

Mehitable married Leonidas Harger, and died November 9, 1848.
Jane A * married Calvin F Waterman, April 26, 1840
Selina M married Nathan Peck.   No 672
Elenor is unmarried
Jerusha married Daniel Hovee, October 21, 1848

[280.]   CHARLES,[7] PECK, son of ICHABOD,[6] settled in Johnstown, Fulton County, N. Y., where he was residing in 1864.   He married Phebe Seley, daughter of Stephen Seley, of Hadley, Saratoga County, N. Y., December 10, 1815.

CHILDREN — EIGHTH GENERATION

709   Sally Jane, b Dec. 17, 1816
       Died 1848.
710   John, b April 21, 1818
711   Adaline, b Nov 20, 1819. ⎫
712   Emeline, b Nov. 20, 1819 ⎬
       Twins
713   Esther C , b June 20, 1821.

714.   Lydia A , b Sept 12, 1823. Died 1847.
715.   Charles J , b June 13, 1825. Died young
716.   Mary, b May 7, 1827 ⎫
717.   Mariem, b May 7, 1827. ⎬
       Twins , died young.

---

* Her eldest son enlisted as a soldier   He was one of Scott's 900, where he served two years, and re-enlisted into the N Y Cavalry, where he remained until his discharge, and died, March 6, 1866, from the effects of the hardships and exposures he suffered in the army

718. Charles J , b April 20, 1829
719. George W , b Aug. 3, 1831.
720. Philander W , b Jan 20, 1834.

721. Olivia E , b. April 13, 1837
　　　Died 1860.
722　Daniel A , b. Aug 8, 1839. Died young.

Adaline married Lambert Christyan
Sarah Jane married William Pool
Emeline married Benjamin Place
John married Phebe Taylor, daughter of David Taylor, August 1, 1840. He was residing in Johnstown, N. Y , in 1864, engaged in the leather and lumber business　His children were　(723) *Almenia H ,*[9] (724) *John F ,*[9] (725) *Anna M.,*[9] (726) *Albert T ,*[9] died April 8, 1850; (727) *Albert T ',*[9] (728) *Jerome A.,*[9] (729) *Arthur W ,*[9] (730) *Ellenor J ,*[9] (731) *Esther J* [9]
Esther C married Leonard M Curtis, and was residing in California in 1864.
Charles J married Susan M Harris. His children are　(732) *Charles A ,*[9] (733) *Emma,*[9] (734) *George W ,*[9] and (735) *Eugene W.*[9]
Lydia A married William A Emory
Olivia E married John T Hill
George W married Charlott Vanthusen　His children are　(736) *James M.,*[9] (737) *George,*[9] (738) *Anna,*[9] and (739) *Octavee* [9]
Philander married, for his first wife, Lodusky Wilde, and for his second, Sybil Plaisted　His child is, (740) *Eugene W* [9]　He was residing in Johnstown in 1864

[282.]　GEORGE W.[7] PECK, son of ICHABOD,[6] settled in West Troy, N. Y , where he died, in 1852, from injuries, as I am told, received in a saw mill.

He married Isabella Sturtevant at Fort Edward, Washington County, N. Y., where she died.

CHILDREN — EIGHTH GENERATION

741. Mahala was residing at Saratoga Springs in 1864.

742. Louisa was residing at Saratoga Springs in 1864.

[284.]　OLIVER O.[7] PECK, son of ICHABOD,[6] settled in Johnstown, Fulton County, N. Y., where he was residing in 1864.

He married Judith Ayers, daughter of Jedidiel Ayers, March 17, 1827.

CHILDREN — EIGHTH GENERATION

743　George W , b. Jan 23, 1828. Died Sept 6, 1829
744　Harvy J , b Nov 1, 1829
745　Lydia M , b Jan 13, 1832
746　Caroline A , b Aug 23, 1833 Died April 4, 1859

747. Mary E , b April 6, 1835. Died Nov 12, 1855
748　William H , b. Nov 12, 1839. Died Feb 17, 1841.
749. Judith A , b Jan 21, 1842
750　Dyer O , b Aug 8, 1844. Died Aug 1863.

Harvy J was residing near Alexandria, Va , unmarried, in 1864.

Lydia M married Orange R Lawrence, and was residing in Johnstown in 1864.

Caroline A married Bradley Vanderburg, and resided in Bleeker, Fulton County, N Y., in 1864

Mary E. married Ames Smith, and was residing near Alexandria, Va., in 1864.

Judith A. married Victor Stricker, and was residing at Alexandria, Va , in 1864.

[286.] ALEXANDER[7] PECK, son of ICHABOD,[6] settled in Alexandria, Jefferson County, where he was residing in 1864. He is a carpenter and joiner by trade and occupation. He married Elizabeth Hollet, daughter of Joseph Hollet, November 4, 1830. She was born August 21, 1805.

CHILDREN — EIGHTH GENERATION

751. George A., b Sept 29, 1832.
752   Joseph, b July 25, 1834   Died March 5, 1835
753. Charles, b Nov. 7, 1835. Died July 12, 1847.
754. Elizabeth, b Dec 15, 1837.
755. Sarah J , b April 14, 1839.
756. Martha, b. April 1, 1841.
757   John, b. Aug 26, 1843.
758. Daniel, b. Jan. 5, 1847.

George A married Catharine Merrill, daughter of James Merrill. His children were *George M* [9], b September 21, 1858 , *John H* ,[9] b. June 5, 1864 , and *Mary*,[9] b. June 17, 1862 , resided in Alexandria, Jefferson County, N. Y., in 1864.*

Elizabeth married George Taylor

Sarah Jane married John Overoker.

Martha was unmarried in 1864.

[287.] GEORGE[7] PECK, son of JEREMIAH,[6] married Phebe Sweet, of Johnston, R. I. He was a stone-cutter by trade, and resided in different places.

CHILDREN — EIGHTH GENERATION

759   Amanda
760   Cyril.
761. Harriet.
762   Daniel.
763   ——. Died young.

[288] LEWIS[7] PECK, son of JEREMIAH,[6] settled at Mount Tabor, Vt , where he died. He married Abigail.

---

* His children were received too late to be numbered and entered in the index

764. Abigail

[289.] WALCOTT[7] PECK, son of JEREMIAH,[6] married Rachel
Dodge, daughter of John and Rachel Dodge, of Amherst, N. H.
She was born July 1795, and died in Blissfield, Lenawee County,
Michigan, April 21, 1837.   He was residing in Keene, N. H., in
1864, with his daughter.

CHILDREN — EIGHTH GENERATION

765   Sarah Margaret, b. April 25,   766   ——, died young.
      1831

Sarah Margaret married John Robinson, of Acworth, N. H , January 5,
1859
There were also other children, who died in infancy.

[291.] DANIEL[7] PECK, son of JEREMIAH,[6] married Sarah
Green, daughter of Elisha Green, of Plainfield, Conn.   They first
resided at Poughkeepsie, N. Y.   In 1840, they moved to Troy, and
in 1842 removed to Sand Lake, where he settled.   In April 1850,
he died, leaving his widow with seven children.   In February 1851,
their house was burned, with all they had in it.   In 1852, the
widow removed with her little children to Pawtucket, R. I., where
she found employment in the cotton mills, and by her industry and
frugality has supported herself and family.
  She was residing at Valley Falls in 1863, when I learned from
her the above.

CHILDREN — EIGHTH GENERATION

767. Daniel, b. May 2, 1838.   771. Sarah, b. Sept. 27, 1847.
768   Margaret, b May 13, 1840.   772. Olive, b. June 14, 1849.
769   Lydia, b June 4, 1842.   773. Elisha, b. Sept. 24, 1850
770. Hiram, b. March 4, 1845.

There were three children who died in infancy

[294.] ARA[7] PECK, son of LEVI,[6] first settled in Westmoreland, N. H , and afterwards at Salina, N. Y., where he died, August
31, 1862.   He was twice married; first, to Phebe Mitchel, of Westmoreland, N. H., by whom he had one daughter: second, to Mary
Pierce, August 2, 1820, daughter of John Pierce, of Westmoreland,
N. H.   She died November 17, 1854.

774. Mary
775. Amoret, b. May 25, 1821. Died
       April 15, 1849
776. Sarah Lucelia, b. Nov. 29, 1822.
       Died Aug. 22, 1842.

777. Prusia Cozelia, b Jan 17, 1825
       Died Feb 17, 1857.
778 John Alfred, b Feb 22, 1827.
779. Mira, b. Jan 12, 1830   Died
       Sept 25, 1831

Mary married Charles Burns, and settled in Troy, N. Y.
Prusia C married Charles H Dunback, of St Johns, New Brunswick.
John A married Elizabeth Nichols, daughter of Isaac L Nichols, of Cohasset, Mass. He was residing at Newton, Mass , in 1864   His children were (780) *Charles Alfred,*[9] b. December 3, 1856, and (781) *Mary Abby*, b November 7, 1860

[295.]   URI[7] PECK, son of Levi,[6] settled in Westminster, Vt., where he was residing in 1863. He married Asenath Powers, December 6, 1812.

782. William, b Dec 23, 1813. Died
       Jan. 7, 1814.
783 Levi S., b Oct 19, 1814.
784 Susan, b. Dec 7, 1817
785 Wealthy A , b Oct. 31, 1819
       Died July 28, 1841
786. Solomon, b Sept 4, 1821.
787. Warren, b. Oct 30, 1823

788. Uri L , b Oct. 22, 1825
789. Irena, b Sept. 16, 1828   Died
       Feb. 27, 1829
790. Melinda, b Nov 30, 1830   Resided at home, unm , in 1864.
791. James, b Oct 5, 1833   Died
       May 5, 1835.

Levi S married Clarinda Chipman, of Westminster, Vt., and was residing in Fulton, Wis , in 1864   Their children were   (792) *Ella C ,*[9] (793) *Alonzo,*[9] (794) *Mary E ,*[9] (795) *Kirk*, (796) *Sophronia,*[9] and (797) *Leonora B* [9]
Susan married Warren Baker, and settled in Leicester, Conn
Solomon was supposed to be in Cincinnati, in 1864, unmarried.
Uri L. was in the United States Army, no family in 1864.
Warren was residing at home, unmarried.

[296.]   SHUBAEL PECK,[7] son of Levi,[6] settled in Westminster, Vt., where he was residing in 1863.
He married Thurza Wheeler, daughter of Jonas Wheeler, December 18, 1821. She died October 25, 1867, in her 69th year.

798. Sanford L , b. July 13, 1823.
799 Clarissa A , b April 26, 1825.
800. Orestes F , b Aug 22, 1826.
801 Charles C., b. Dec 6, 1827.

802. Hannah E , b Dec 3, 1835
       Died March 29, 1850
803 Ellen J , b. April 21, 1840.

Sanford L. married Mary Stodard, daughter of Joshua Stodard, of Sutton, Vt , September 12, 1849, for his first wife, and Sarah E Sanford, daughter of Seth Sanford, of Ohio, for his second   He settled at McGregor, Clayton County, Iowa, and then at Clayton   He is an attorney at law   His children in 1864, were   (804) *Sanford K.,*⁹ born January 18, 1857 , (805) *Laura J.,*⁹ born August 19, 1859 , and (806) *Mary Ellen,*⁹ born September 18, 1863   Died February 23, 1864.

Clarissa A married Lester Woodford, of Bloomfield, Conn , January 12, 1850.

Orestes F married Mary M. Pierce, May 1, 1850   Their children are   (807) *Olive,*⁹ born April 9, 1853, and (808) *Orestes E ,*⁹ born April 7, 1859

Charles C married Adaline Keech, September 12, 1854   She died December 19, 1862, leaving three children   (809) *Ella M ,*⁹ born October 24, 1855 · (810) *Charles A* ⁹, born September 25, 1857 , (811) *William L* ⁹, born June 1859, and died August 22, 1860; (812) *Sanford Ariel,*⁹ born July 13, 1860.

Ella J was residing at home, unmarried, in 1863

[300.]   WILLIAM⁷ PECK, son of ROYAL,⁶ settled at first in Wrentham, Mass., where he resided for many years, and from there removed to Franklin, Mass.   He has been what may well be called a model farmer,— industrious and successful,— a man of excellent judgment and fine natural ability.

Although he has kept aloof from party politics, neither seeking or accepting office, he has usually taken an interest in the affairs of his town, giving his advice or expressing his views upon matters of interest; and at public meetings few have been able to command more respect.   In his younger days, he was fond of military tactics, and for a long time commanded a military company.   He was often urged to accept higher positions; but he chose to remain a captain.   He was an excellent disciplinarian, and took much pride, as well as his men, in their being known as one of the best drilled companies.   He is still known, and called among his early associates, by the to them familiar name of Capt. Peck; although in his 84th year, he still retains his faculties.

He married Sarah Arnold, daughter of Rufus Arnold.   She died March 24, 1852.

CHILDREN — EIGHTH GENERATION

813. Mary Ann, b July 9, 1805 *   814   Naomi, b April 26, 1807

---

* *Mary Ann,* the eldest child in the family of William, had two grandmothers, four great-grandmothers, and one great-great-grandmother, making seven grandmothers, all living at the time of her birth

Yours as ever
William E. Peck

815   Abigail, b April 6, 1810.   818.   Sarah Maria, b. Aug 1, 1815
        Died Aug 21, 1811   819.   Rufus Arnold, b April 16, 1818.
816   Abigail, b June 10, 1811   820   William Edward, b Oct 13,
817   Ann Janett, b. May 25, 1813.   1821.

Mary Ann married Fennah Grant, of Cumberland, R I
Naomi married Richard Crowninshield, also of Cumberland
Ann Janett married Albert Ballou, of Franklin, Mass
Sarah Maria married Abijah Rockwood, also of Franklin, Mass
Abigail is a school teacher, and is unmarried
Rufus Arnold married Abby S Thurber, and settled in Providence, R I
His children are (821)   *Anna A*,[9] (822), *Horace G*,[9] (823), and *Helen A*[9]

William Edward prepared himself for a profession, and chose that of a lawyer He entered the office of Richard W Green, of Providence, R I, late judge of the Supreme Court, as a student, in 1847 He was admitted to the bar in 1850, and settled in Providence, where he entered into practice He was elected a Representative from the city to the State Legislature, in 1852 He was also one of the judges of the Court of Magistrates In 1855, he removed with his family to Greenwich, R I, but continued his office in Providence He was elected a Senator from Greenwich in 1857 He continued his practice, both in Providence and Greenwich, until the war, in which he took a deep interest His patriotism did not allow him to remain neutral, or a spectator to the noble effort the State made to assist in subduing the rebellion

He not only lent his aid and influence in raising soldiers, but set the example of being one himself He loved his country, and knew too well how to prize its government and laws to remain passive during her struggle He gave his life in their defence He enlisted in the Rhode Island cavalry, where he received a commission as first lieutenant

After joining his regiment in Louisiana, he was appointed judge advocate, which position he held until his decease, which occurred at Napoleonville, August 13, 1865 He was taken sick at Thibodeaux while attending the duties of his office. He remained there until the adjournment of the commission, when he returned to Napoleonville, was seized with a congestive chill, and died in about two hours

He was buried with military honors His body was placed in a metallic coffin, and then enclosed in a brick vault

---

The following is the inscription from the tombstone of her great-great-grandmother

" In memory of Mrs Desire Allen, Relict of Mr John Allen (formerly the wife of Mr Ebenezer Foster), who died November 27, 1810, aged 100 years 1 month and 28 days.

       ' Blessed are the dead who die in the Lord, for they
         rest from their labors and their works do follow them "

Her name before marriage was Desire Cushman She married Ebenezer Foster, September 17, 1730 Their daughter, Mercy Foster, married Solomon Peck, the great-grandfather of Mary Ann.

8*

His name, with the name of others like him, will be remembered and honored, while the Northern traitors and Southern sympathizers he left behind will be forgotten, or remembered only to be despised

Mr Peck married Harriet E Newell, daughter of Nelson Newell, Esq , of Franklin, Mass. His children are (824) *Hattie A* ,⁹ and (825) *William E* ⁹

[301.]   JOEL F. PECK, son of ROYAL, married Lucy Peck, daughter of Solomon Peck, of Cumberland, R. I., December 1820, and settled upon the homestead, where he died, July 17, 1866.

CHILDREN — EIGHTH GENERATION

826. Phila Amanda, b. Dec 15, 1823.   828. Royal Jackson, b. Dec 14, 1831.
      Died Aug. 13, 1826
827. Abby Selina, b. Nov 29, 1827.
      Died Feb. 13, 1848.

Royal Jackson married Ellen E Follett, daughter of Ellis Follett, of Cumberland, R I   Their children are (829)   *Charles H* , born November 1854; (830) *Abby J.*, born September 15, 1856 , (831) *Joel E* , born March 15, 1859 , (832) *Ides E* , born December 20, 1860. He resides upon the homestead which has now been in the name more than 150 years.

[302.]   IRA B.⁷ PECK, son of ROYAL,⁶ married Mary Blackinton, daughter of Ellis Blackinton, of Attleborough, Mass., June 19, 1834.   He resides at Woonsocket, R. I.

CHILD — EIGHTH GENERATION

833. Ira E , b Aug. 24, 1846

[305.]   FOSTER⁷ PECK, son of JOEL,⁶ resides in North Providence.   He married Susan Arnold.

CHILDREN — EIGHTH GENERATION

834. Susan.   835. Foster

Susan married John Barnes, of North Providence, R. I

[306]   LEWIS⁷ PECK, son of JOEL,⁶ resided in Cumberland, R. I., where he died, October 25, 1827.   He was a carpenter by trade, enterprising and industrious.   He married Permelia Carpenter, daughter of William Carpenter, of Uxbridge, Mass., March 24, 1816.   She resided at Valley Falls, R. I., in 1863.

CHILDREN — EIGHTH GENERATION

836. Lucena, b. June 26, 1818.   838   Maria C , b Dec. 14, 1823.
837. Edward, b May 17, 1821.

Lucena married Leonard Cumstock, of Providence, R I
Edward married Abba Woodward, of Taunton, Mass   He died August
1852, leaving two sons, (839) *Lewis*,⁹ and (840) *Henry*,ᵃ who were residing
with their mother in Taunton in 1863.
Maria C. married Jesse Moffett. They reside in Pawtucket, R I

[307] ALFRED⁷ PECK, son of SOLOMON,⁶ resided in Cumberland, R. I , where he died.

" I here by certify that Alfred Peck of Cumberland son of Solomon
Peck and Huldah Ballou daughter of Edward Ballou of Cumberland
were lawfully joined together in marriage on the 26th day of September A D 1810 by me
          BENJAMIN WILKINSON *Justice of Peace.*

CHILDREN — EIGHTH GENERATION

841. Welcom Riley, b. Nov. 21, 1818.   842. Mary Adaline, b Dec 7, 1827.

Welcom R. married Nancy M Whipple, daughter of Daniel Whipple. He
died April 30, 1840, leaving no issue
Mary A. married Barton Follett, of Cumberland, R I , where they reside.

[310.] WHIPPLE⁷ PECK, son of SOLOMON,⁶ resided in Franklin, Mass., where he died.
He married Roxana Harris, daughter of Oliver Harris, of Cumberland, R. I., November 17, 1815. His widow was residing in
Franklin in 1863.

CHILDREN — EIGHTH GENERATION ·

843. Eunice A , b. March 13, 1816.   849   Leland T , b Dec 7, 1828.
        Died Oct 2, 1819.   Died Feb 28, 1834
844. Nancy S., b Nov. 4, 1817.   850   Oliver H , b Feb 15, 1831.
        Died Sept. 26, 1819   Died Jan 25, 1842
845. Phebe, b Dec 14, 1819   851   Whipple, b Feb 20, 1834.
846. Russell, b. Dec 2, 1821.   852   Henry C , b. June 27, 1837.
        Died Dec 11, 1866   853. Francis, b Nov 28, 1839.
847   Philina, b Oct 13, 1823.   Died Oct. 19, 1867.
848. Eliab H , b. Feb. 10, 1826.
        Died May 8, 1846.

Phebe married Barton Ballou, and resides in Franklin, Mass.

Russell married Olive Ann Whipple, daughter of Simon Whipple, of Cumberland, R I   Their daughter (854), *Emma Jane,*[9] was born October 23, 1847.

Philina married James Greenwood, and was residing in Chelsea, Mass., in 1864

Eliab H. married Jane Bishop

Whipple married Marion Burr, and settled in Richmond, Vt.   Their son is (855) *Edwin* [9]

Henry C was residing with his mother, in 1863, unmarried

Francis was residing in Boston, unmarried, in 1864.

[313.]   STEPHEN[7] PECK, son of SOLOMON,[6] married Eliza Tingley, March 25, 1834, daughter of Columbia Tingley, of Cumberland, R. I.   They resided in Smithfield, R. I, where he died, December 1, 1859.   His widow resides at Central Falls, R I.

CHILDREN — EIGHTH GENERATION

856.   Amoret, b July 12, 1835.

857   Crawford, b March 19, 1837

858.   William, b Aug 6, 1839.   Died Aug 17, 1839

859   Laura A , b Oct 26, 1840

860   Mahala A , b Nov 22, 1842

861   Hiram L , b Sept 13, 1844   Died July 26, 1851

862   Stephen A , b Nov 5, 1846.

863.   Eliza J , b Nov 17, 1848   Died July 29, 1851

864.   Wilbour M , b Aug 29, 1852.   Died Sept 26, 1852

865.   Walter B , b Aug 2, 1853.

[314.]   GEORGE B [7] PECK, son of SOLOMON,[6] married Mary Ann Franklin, daughter of Ebenezer Franklin.   He died in Cumberland, R I.

CHILD — EIGHTH GENERATION

866   George Andrew , resides in Boston, Mass

[316]   DR. KELLY [7] PECK, son of JESSE,[6] settled in Cumberland, R. I., where he died, February 14, 1840.   He married Amey Ann Arnold, November 17, 1831, daughter of Eleazer Arnold, of Cumberland, R. I.

CHILDREN — EIGHTH GENERATION :

867   Menzo W., b. Aug 28, 1832

868.   Eliza A., b April 16, 1834.

869   Imogene, b July 3, 1837.

870.   Conrad M , b. April 8, 1839.   Died September 8, 1840.

Menzo married Ellen Marsh, February 24, 1860   Their daughter, (871) *Amey Ann,*[9] was born January 30, 1862.

[321.]   JOHN PECK,[7] son of JOSEPH,[6] married Sally Blacket, daughter of John Blacket, of New York City, October 3, 1818. He died July 21, 1835.   She died February 5, 1846.

CHILDREN — EIGHTH GENERATION

872.   Jane M., b. Aug 17, 1819.   874.   Phebe V , b Jan 6, 1828.
873   John B , b. Jan 20, 1822
         There were other children who died young
     Jane M married John W. Broderick, and settled in New York City, where she died, March 9, 1849.
     John B. married Maria Azlee Landry, and was residing in New Orleans in 1865.
     Phebe V married John H. Wood, and was residing in New York City in 1865.

[323.]   JEREMIAH [7] PECK, son of JOSEPH,[6] married Sally Houghtalin, daughter of James Houghtalin, of Half Moon, Saratoga County, N. Y., October 28, 1815.   She was born May 9, 1796.   He resided at Adrian, Mich., where he died March 27, 1864.

CHILDREN — EIGHTH GENERATION ·

875.   Caroline, b. Aug 22, 1816   880.   Harriet N , b Oct 19, 1825.
876   Benjamin F , b Dec 28, 1817.   881.   Abijah, b Dec 4, 1827.
877.   James H , b Oct 7, 1819.   882.   Lydia E , b April 16, 1829.
878   Louisa, b April 19, 1821.   883   Jeremiah, b Nov 20, 1833.
879   Mary J , b Oct. 16, 1823.

     Caroline married Allen Armstrong, and resides in Butler, Wayne County, N. Y.
     Their children are   *Sally,*[9] *Samantha,*[9] *Thomas,*[9] *George,* and *James* [9]
     Benjamin F has been twice married   1st, to Margaret Congor; 2d, to Abigail H Dudley.   He resides in Walcott, Wayne County, N Y   His children in 1864 were
         (884) *Eron J.,*[9] born May 12, 1844, and (885) *John W ,*[9] born December 8, 1846, and one died in infancy.
     James is unmarried, he is a physician.   He was residing, for the restoration of his health, upon one of the Chincha Islands, near the coast of Peru, South America, in 1864.   *Louisa* [9] married John Conger   They reside at Adrian, Mich   Their children are   *Charlotte,*[9] *Albine,*[9] *Clarence G ,*[9] *Louisa,*[9] and *Frances* [9]
     Mary J married Leander Spring, of Mass. Resides at Medina, Mich. Their children are   *James Henry,*[9] *Jeremiah,*[9] *Arthur Almirin,*[9] *Mary,*[9] *Charlotte* [9] and *Charles* [9]
     Harriet N married Frederick Irish, and resides at Adrian.   Their children are . *Ellwood*[9] and *Hattie Louisa.*[9]

Abijah married Elizabeth Fleek. They reside in Hart, Mich, Their children are *Charles* [9] and *Harriet* [9]

Lydia E married Amos Letcher. They resided in Hudson, Mich Their child is *Herbert* [9]

Jeremiah was 2d lieutenant in the 1st Michigan Infantry, and was wounded at the battle of Stone River, Tenn, December. 1862, taken prisoner; left in the hands of the rebels, and died January 1, 1863   He married Adelaide ——. His children are   (886) *William H.* [9] and (887) *Elmer J.* [9]

[325.]   IRA [7] PECK, son of JOSEPH, [6] married Nancy Guild, January 29, 1823.   She was born in Lansingburg, Rensselaer County, N. Y., June 16, 1801.   They resided in the town of Halfmoon, Saratoga County, N. Y.

He died December 1862.   She December 3, 1846.

CHILDREN — EIGHTH GENERATION

888   Horatio Guild, b Oct 31, 1823.

889.   Nathan Henry, b Oct. 10, 1825.

890.   John Naphthalia, b. Feb. 4, 1834.

891   Hiram A , b Nov 15, 1836

Horatio G married Sarah Edmonds, October 14, 1847.   She was born in Stillwater, Saratoga County, May 25, 1822.   Their children are   (892) *Caroline M,* [9] b in Wilton, September 23, 1848 , (893) *Jane,* [9] b. October 17, 1851, in Colesville; and (894) *Elizabeth,* [9] b May 28, 1861, in Stillwater

Nathan H married Maria Elizabeth Riley, August 30, 1851   She was born June 21, 1837.   They reside at Saratoga   Their children are   (895) *George A ,* [9] b. February 23, 1853 , (896) *Charles Henry,* [9] b October 11, 1856 , (897) *Harriet Augusta,* [9] b August 4, 1859 , *Hiram A* enlisted into the army, and *John N* is supposed to have gone to Pike's Peak.

[326.]   GEORGE [7] PECK, son of JOSEPH, [6] settled in Canton, Io., where he was residing in 1864.   He has been twice married: first, to Ann Eliza Ide, January 7, 1821; second, to Mrs. Margaret Hunter, formerly Miss Margaret Lyle, October 15, 1854.   His first wife died June 27, 1854.

CHILDREN — EIGHTH GENERATION ·

898   Gilbert I , b. Feb 13, 1822

899.   Sarah J , b June 13, 1824. Died Aug 25, 1841

900   George W , b Jan 10, 1827. Died in infancy

901.   William H , b Jan 25, 1828

902.   John I , b June 21, 1830; unm. in 1864.

903.   George, b Feb 25, 1833.

904   Lewis J , b Nov 5, 1835

905.   Phebe L , b Jan 6, 1838. Died April 29, 1838.

906.   Samuel E , b July 28, 1840.

907.   Eliza J , b March 14, 1843.

Gilbert married, first, Sarah J Barber; second, Almira Shumway. His children are (908) *Oscar,*[9] (909) *Anthe Jane,*[9] and (910) *Ann Eliza.*[9] He was residing at Dowagiac, Mich, in 1864

William H married Rachel Lake. His children are (911) *Milo D*[9] and (912) *Zilpha G*[9]

George married Harriet Allen, and settled in California

Lewis J. died unmarried

Samuel E married Mary E Widel. His children are (913) *Devillo*[9] and (914) *Eliza J*[9]

Eliza J married George W. Gibson. She was a widow, residing in Canton, Mich, in 1864.

[329.] JOSEPH F.[7] PECK, son of JOSEPH,[6] married, for his first wife, Catharine A. Gow, daughter of Cornelius Gow; for his second, Elizabeth Staly, daughter of Abraham Staly; and for his third, Mary E. Kimball. His first wife died April 4, 1837. His second wife died February 22, 1849. He was residing at Kalamazoo, Mich., in 1864.

CHILDREN — EIGHTH GENERATION

915. Perrin, b. May 26, 1830
916. Ephraim K., b. Jan 16, 1832
    Drowned July 16, 1834.
917. Daniel W, b April 3, 1835.
    Killed at Fayette, Missouri, March 29, 1862
918. Hellen M, b. Feb. 19, 1837.
919. Flavious J., b. Feb. 22, 1839.
    Died Aug 19, 1839.

920. Clarissa T, b May 7, 1840.
921. Phebe P, b. March 29, 1842.
922. Mary E., b Oct. 28, 1843.
    Died Aug 27, 1846.
923. Henry C., b Jan. 12, 1845
924. Caroline A., b Jan. 14, 1847.
925. ——, b, Feb 16, 1849. Died in infancy, unnamed.
926. Adeliza, b. Feb. 19, 1851.

[335.] HENRY W.[7] PECK, son of AMOS,[6] married Melinda Vanderworker, daughter of Sovereign Vanderworker, of Northumberland, Saratoga County, N. Y., October 6, 1830. She was born November 3, 1807. They reside in Northumberland. He is a farmer.

CHILDREN — EIGHTH GENERATION :

927. Mary Ann, b March 9, 1832.
928. George Henry, b. Jan. 20, 1835.
929. Reed, b. Feb. 11, 1841.

[338.] AMOS[7] PECK, son of AMOS,[6] married Elizabeth Ann Nelson, daughter of Gilbert Nelson, of Saratoga Springs, May 13, 1846. He resides upon the homestead, a farmer.

930. Mary Frances, b Feb. 12, 1847.
931 Charles Nelson, b. Nov. 17, 1854.

932. Carrie Elizabeth, b. April 13, 1861.
933. One died in infancy, unnamed.

[340.] OLIVER[7] PECK, son of IRA,[6] resided in Saratoga, where he died, November 14, 1832. He married Sarah Patrick, October 14, 1830.

934. Isaac L., b. Dec. 14, 1831.

935 Oliver, b March 14, 1833.

[345.] IRA L.[7] PECK, son of IRA,[6] settled at Farm Ridge, Lasalle County, Illinois. He has been twice married: first, to Louisa Allen, December 28, 1834; second, Elizabeth Vanantwerp, April 18, 1844. His first wife died May 23, 1843.

936. Mary L , b. Sept 23, 1836.
937 Ira S , b Dec 4, 1845.
938. Lydia Jane, b. Sept 27, 1847.

939. Francis Wayland, b Aug. 23, 1850.
940. Julia Ella, b May 20, 1855.

Mary L. married Henry L. Cummings, Nov. 23, 1854.

[347.] ARUNA C. T.[7] PECK, son of IRA,[6] resided at Saratoga Lake in 1863. He married Ellen A. Abel, daughter of David Abel, February 17, 1842.

941 Carrie L., b. June 22, 1843.
942 John W , b Aug 31, 1847
943. Hannah C., b. July 25, 1850.

944. Ella J., b Jan. 24, 1853.
945. Jesse B , b March 4, 1863.

[349.] STEPHEN[7] PECK, son of LEWIS,[6] married Isabella Bains, January 12, 1827. He resides at Denning, Ulster County, N. Y., a farmer.

946 Mary E , b Dec 14, 1832.
947. Sarah, b Nov 27, 1834
948 Alexander H , b April 25, 1837.
     Mary Jane, b June 21, 1839.

950 Ann, b. Dec. 18, 1840
951. Louisa, b. Nov 4, 1843.
952 Laura, b June 7, 1845
953 Cornelia, b. Aug 22, 1848.

[354.] ENOCH[7] PECK, son of LEWIS,[6] resides at Homowack, N. Y. He married Sarah Rogers, November 16, 1844. She was born March 2, 1825.

CHILD — EIGHTH GENERATION.

954. George W , b Oct 8, 1848.

[355.] ANQUEVINE[7] PECK, son of LEWIS,[6] resided at Homowack, N. Y., where he died, November 1854. He married Deborah Polhamus. She survived him, and married again.

CHILDREN — EIGHTH GENERATION

955. William
956. Mary Catherine.
957. John
958. Isaac Henry.
959. Anna Maria

960. Ellen Jane
961. Lena Catherine.
962. Thomas
963. Mary.

[361.] JACOB[7] PECK, son of BENJAMIN,[6] married Amey Bowen, December 15, 1828, daughter of Samuel Bowen He was residing in Mobile, Ala., in 1863.

CHILDREN — EIGHTH GENERATION.

964. Mary B , b Oct 25, 1831.
965. Sarah M , b Feb 1, 1835
    Died April 1, 1836.

966. Albert B., b May 29, 1837.

[362.] CYRUS[7] PECK, son of BENJAMIN,[6] married for his first wife, Melissa Ryan, daughter of Zarks Ryan; for his second, Ruth Hoxie, August 1833, daughter of Cornelius Hoxie, for his third, Fanny Hoxie, daughter of Cornelius Hoxie; for his fourth, Ruth Davis, October 21, 1841, daughter of Isaac Davis. His first wife died July 3, 1831. His second wife died October 22, 1835. His third wife died in 1839. He died in Sonora, Illinois, November 12, 1859.

CHILDREN — EIGHTH GENERATION.

967. Melissa R., b June 25, 1831.
968. Eliza A., b June 11, 1835
969. Morris, b. Oct 21, 1842.
970. Cyrus D Died young.

971. Jacob C. Died young
972. Zack, b Oct 10, 1848 Died May 1855.

9

Melissa R. married Edwin J Aldrich, January 31, 1849.

Eliza A married Robert S Owen, November 5, 1856

Morris married Elizabeth Willson, April 13, 1862 His daughter, *Elizabeth,*[9] was born April 3, 1864. They were all residing in Montrose, Iowa, in 1864

[363.] LEVI[7] PECK, son of BENJAMIN,[6] married Orelia G. Flower, daughter of Orman Flower, September 29, 1832. She was born August 17, 1812. They reside in Huron, Ohio.

CHILDREN — EIGHTH GENERATION

973 Ruth O , b. March 10, 1834
974 Harriet L , b July 7, 1835 Died Aug 24, 1849
975 William W , b Oct 19, 1839
976 Bertha L , b July 28, 1841. Died April 5, 1859.
977 Henry L , b Aug 20, 1842
978 Edward F , b Sept 25, 1844
979 Patience, b Oct 20, 1846
980 Sophronia, b. Aug 5, 1850

Ruth O. married William Bardshar, May 20, 1855, and settled in Castalia Village, Ohio.

[365.] GEORGE[7] PECK, son of BENJAMIN,[6] married Catharine Stearns, daughter of Joseph Stearns, of Middleborough, Vt. Her mother, before marriage, was Betsey Hager, of Waltham, Mass. They reside at Jonesville, Michigan.

CHILDREN — EIGHTH GENERATION.

981. George Franklin, b July 1846
982 Herbert Jacob, b. Sept 28, 1848.
983. Sylvia Maria, b Nov 3, 1853. Died July 11, 1857.
984. Harriet Catherine, b. Sept. 25, 1858.

[367.] BENJAMIN[7] PECK, JR , son of BENJAMIN,[6] married Clara Loomis, March 24, 1844. He resided in Mobile, Ala., where he died with the yellow fever, October 17, 1853.

CHILDREN — EIGHTH GENERATION

985 Phebe Ellen, b Dec 20, 1844
986 Caroline Patience, b. July 8, 1847.
987. Clarence B , b March 21, 1853.

[371.] GEORGE J.[7] PECK, son of JAMES,[6] married Marett Mansfield, of Schenectady, March 1, 1837. He resides in Dundee, Kane County, Ill.

CHILDREN — EIGHTH GENERATION

988 Cordelia U., b May 10, 1838, at St Charles, Ill

989 Permelia Eliza, b April 6, 1841, at Elgin, Ill.

990. George M , b Aug 14, 1843, at Dundee, Ill

991. Sanford James, b Dec 24, 1847, at Dundee, Ill

992 William Alston, b Jan 27, 1859, at Dundee, Ill

Cordelia U married William Alston, of Chicago, October 6, 1857 He died in California, December 9, 1858 She was again married to Sanford Wilcox, October 8, 1862 Their daughter, *Isabella*,[9] was born January 16, 1864

[383.] GEORGE[7] PECK, son of GEORGE,[6] settled at Rochester, N. Y , where he engaged in mercantile business. He married Harriet Prindle, October 1840, daughter of Harvey Prindle, one of the pioneers of Western New York.

CHILD — EIGHTH GENERATION

993. George Prindle, b Aug 1841

[385.] JATHNIEL[7] PECK, son of OTIS,[6] settled upon the homestead. He married Sybil Horton, daughter of Shubael Horton, of Rehoboth, Mass. She was born October 18, 1788. He died July 13, 1840.

CHILDREN — EIGHTH GENERATION

994 Otis C , b March 15, 1812 Died March 9, 1853

995 Joanna B , b June 24, 1815.

996 Sybil M , b July 13, 1819 Died Jan 24, 1840

997 George H., b Oct 1, 1821

998 Jathniel A , b Jan 8, 1829

Otis C married Mary Ann Goff His children are (999) *James O ,*[9] b September 13, 1823 , (1000) *Jathniel C ,*[9] b October 15, 1846 , (1001) *Sybil*,[9] b February 22 1849 , (1002) *Thomas B ,*[9] b January 29, 1851

Joanna married Jacob H Horton

George H married Sarah W. Hersey His children are (1003) *Sarah J ,*[9] b March 9, 1843 , (1004) *George W ,*[9] b October 7, 1845 , (1005) *Jacob H ,*[9] b December 22, 1846 , (1006) *Joanna B ,*[9] b January 17, 1849 , (1007) *Mary E ,*[9] b July 19, 1851 , (1008) *Grace*,[9] b December 25, 1855 , (1009) *Emma J ,*[9] b October 29, 1857 , (1010) *Albert C ,*[9] b November 28, 1858

Jathniel A , married Abbie L White His children are (1011) *Herbert L ,*[9] b January 21, 1850; (1012) *Clerince A ,*[9] b January 22, 1853 , (1013) *Frank Otis ,*[9] b December 28, 1860.

[389] OTIS[7] PECK, son of OTIS,[6] married Cynthia W. Bliss, daughter of Abadial Bliss, of Rehoboth, Mass., April 10, 1810. He resided in different places. He died October 10, 1842.

1014   Grace C., b Feb 29, 1812   1017   Harriet N , b July 23, 1818
1015   George Otis, b Sept 15, 1814.   1018   William H , b Sept 19, 1820
         Died Aug 27, 1815   was in California in 1864.
1016. George Otis, b Jan 20, 1816.   1019   James W., b. Nov 18, 1824.
         Died in 1817

Grace C. married Willard Pierce.
Harriet N. married William H. Barney

[394.]   BELA[7] PECK, son of JAMES,[6] married Roba Wheeler. He lived and died in Attleborough, Mass.

1020   Orvilla.   1024   Orvilla
1021. Harriet   1025   Nancy
1022   Fanny.   1026   Henry
1023. Marrett.

[395.]   LYMAN[7] PECK, son of JAMES,[6] married Mercy Wheeler.

1027   Harrison Gray Otis, b. Nov 9,   1028   Hyleman Julius, b Oct 1818.
         1811

[396]   ORIN[7] PECK, of Boston, son of JAMES,[6] married Eliza Williams, daughter of Samuel Williams, of Milton, Mass , December 6, 1821. He was located at the Boylston market for many years. He was much respected by all with whom he did business for his kindness, honesty and integrity. He died May 7, 1865. His wife died April 26, 1858.

1029   Lydia Adaline, b July 23, 1825   1032. Oren Henry, b Aug 7, 1832
1030. Helen A. Williams, b Nov. 24,   1033. Martha Anna, b Aug 30, 1834
         1827.   1034   George Williams, b April 16,
1031   Emily Belinda, b. Feb. 11, 1830   1837.

Lydia married Jeremiah Richards
Helen married Joseph N Wheeler
Oren H and *George W* are married, and reside in Boston.
Oren H married Julia S Emery. Their children are   *Emily W ,*[9] *Henry S*[9] and *Herbert*[9]
George W married H. Eliza Pratt Their children are *Arthur E ,*[9] b December 28, 1862, died March 1, 1863, and *Oscar Tyler,*[9] b September 2, 1867

[399.] HORATIO⁷ PECK, son of James,⁶ married Sally
Bliss, daughter of Abadial Bliss, May 17, 1834.

CHILDREN — EIGHTH GENERATION

1035. Charles Warren, b April 9, 1836
1036 Sarah Amelia, b Oct 28, 1838
1037 Justin Abadial, b. Nov. 17, 1842.

1038. Saraphina Prat, b July 12, 1846
1039. Josephine Bliss, b July 12, 1846

Twins.

[401.] GEORGE W.⁷ PECK, son of Shubael,⁶ died in Providence, March 14, 1860.   He married Ann Eliza Coggshall, daughter of John Coggshall, of Pawtucket, R I.

CHILDREN — EIGHTH GENERATION

1040. George W.
1041 Sarah
1042 William F
1043. Andrew J

1044 Thomas H.
1045 Mary.
1046. ——
1047 Charles

George W. married Ann Armstrong. He resided in Providence, R I , in
1863 His children were (1048) *Mary A* ,⁹ (1049) *James*,⁹ (1050) *Henry*,⁹
(1051) *Ella Jane*,⁹ (1052) *Margaret*,⁹ (1053) *Elizabeth Ann*,⁹ and (1054) *George
W* ⁹

[402.] JEREMIAH⁷ PECK, son of Shubael,⁶ resided in
Taunton, Mass , in 1863   A machinist by trade and occupation.
He married Ann A. Wilbor, of Taunton.

CHILDREN — EIGHTH GENERATION

1055. Hannah W , b May 3, 1838.
1056. Mary E., b Jan 2, 1840
1057. William E , b Sept. 21, 1842.
1058 Charles H , b Jan 29, 1843
1059. George A , b. May 4, 1845.
      Died young.

1060 Sarah F , b. Dec 2, 1846
      Died young.
1061. George F , b. Sept 25, 1849.
1062 Thomas E , b Dec 27, 1853
1063 Adaline U , b Sept 27, 1855
1064 Alonzo M , b. April 10, 1857

[403] WILLIAM P.⁷ PECK, son of Shubael,⁶ married Mary
A. Philips He died October 29, 1857. She survived him, and
was residing in North Dartmouth in 1863.

CHILDREN — EIGHTH GENERATION

1065 William B , b March 9, 1842
1066 Henry A , b. Feb 3, 1847.
      Died Sept 24, 1848.

1067 Charles H , b Sept. 27, 1848

9*

William B. married Ellen Thomas, and was residing in North Dartmouth in 1863.

[409.] WILLIAM H.[7] PECK, son of BENONI,[6] married Hannah Tolman, of Dorchester, daughter of Lemuel Tolman. She was born May 20, 1808, and died June 29. 1855. He was residing in Roxbury, Mass., in 1862, a mechanic.

CHILDREN — EIGHTH GENERATION

1068	William, b Jan 18, 1832	1073	Harriet, b April 3, 1840
1069	Mary E T , b June 18, 1833	1074	Otis, b Nov 7, 1841
1070	Albert, b Oct 3, 1834. Died	1075	Angeline, b Dec 1, 1845
	Nov 11, 1834	1076	Julia M , b Aug 1, 1848
1071.	Sarah H , b Jan 27, 1836.	1077	Charles F , b July 28, 1850
	Died April 10, 1862		Died Aug 5, 1850
1072	Lucy Ann, b Oct 6, 1838		

William married Cabrilla Kemp, and settled at Mount Pleasant, Saratoga County, N Y. His children are (1078) *Willie,*[9] (1079) *Eddie,*[9] and (1080) *Charles* [9]

Mary married Edward W Murry, of Roxbury, July 4, 1852.

Lucy married David G. Hovey, of Willimanton, Vt

[410.] LIBBEUS[7] PECK, son of BENONI,[6] married Emeline Flint, of Ashford, Conn , daughter of Aaron Flint, November 24, 1831. They reside in Providence, R. I.

CHILDREN — EIGHTH GENERATION

1081	Emeline, b Oct 15, 1833	1086	Lucy Adaline, b Oct 14, 1844
1082	Edward Flint, b July 10, 1835.		Died Feb 26, 1849
	Died Oct 18, 1836	1087	George Libbeus, b Dec 19,
1083	Eliza Ann, b Sept 20, 1837		1846 Died June 29, 1847
1084	Frances Emeline, b Feb 14,	1088	George Libbeus, b Jan 22,
	1840		1848 Died Feb 19, 1849
1085	Edward Kimball, b Jan. 1,		
	1843		

[415.] SYLVESTER[7] PECK, son of BENONI,[6] married Elenor Baird, of New York city, April 29, 1841. His family were residing at Bridgeport, Conn , in 1863.

CHILDREN — EIGHTH GENERATION

1089	William C , b Feb 10, 1842.	1092	Elenor Jane, b Feb 19, 1847
1090	Sarah A , b Aug 21, 1843	1093.	Lucy Ann, b Sept 28, 1853
1091	Oscar, b. May 27, 1845		

[418] EDMOND J.[7] PECK, son of EDMOND,[6] married Peddy Peck, No. 435, daughter of Cromwell Peck, of Rehoboth, Mass., October 28, 1822. He died March 10, 1829. She survived him, and married James Bliss, by whom she had five children. She was residing in Attleborough, Mass., in 1863.

CHILDREN — EIGHTH GENERATION

1094   Catharin A , b Sept 1, 1823
1095   Caleb S , b Feb 5, 1825
1096   Phebe A , b Dec 3, 1826
  Died Feb 17, 1849.

1097. Edmond E , b Oct 3, 1828.
  Died Aug 10, 1829

[420] ARNOLD[7] PECK, son of Edmond,[6] married Betsey Hicks. He was a sea-faring man, and has not been heard from for many years.

CHILDREN — EIGHTH GENERATION

1098   Alice N , b April 15, 1825
  Died May 26, 1857
1099   Cyrus F , b Dec 22, 1826
  Died July 12, 1858.
1100. Martha M , b Aug. 1828.
  Died Sept 15, 1859.

1101   Adaline, b July 1830
1102   Charles, b July 3, 1838   Died Aug 20, 1860
1103   George, b June 20, 1840.

[421.] OTIS T.[7] PECK, son of EDMOND,[6] settled in Waterbury, Conn., where he died, in 1851. He married Laura Ann Kilbourn. She died in 1860, aged 49 years.

CHILDREN — EIGHTH GENERATION

1104   Fidelia A.
1105   Wellington
1106   Hollister
1107   Maria Louisa
1108   Frank C

1109   Erwin H
1110   Edward L
1111. Thomas J
1112   Emogene
1113   Mary J

Fidelia A married, first, Cyrus P. Morrill, second, Luther Fuller; and was residing in Boston in 1864

[423.] HENRY W.[7] PECK, son of EDMOND,[6] married Anna Maria Pettee. They resided in East Taunton, Mass., in 1864.

CHILDREN — EIGHTH GENERATION

1114   Mary Muncrief, b May 18, 1846
1115   Deborah Austin, b Nov. 11, 1847

1116   Walter Henry, b April 25, 1849
1117   James Edmond, b June 21, 1851
1118   Frank Wheaton, b Oct 7, 1853.

Mary M married George A. Hall, of North Bridgewater, September 1862.

[433.]   BILLINGS[7] PECK, son of CROMWELL,[6] married Delila Goff, daughter of Charles Goff, January 9, 1825.   She was born February 24, 1807.   They reside in Rehoboth, Mass.

CHILDREN — EIGHTH GENERATION

1119   Francis H , b March 10, 1826   1121   Hattie A , b June 15, 1845
1120   Caroline P , b July 28, 1837

Francis H married Harriet Goff, daughter of Shubael Goff, of Rehoboth, Mass   Then children are   (1122) *Billings,*[9] b October 18, 1849 , (1123) *Harriet E ,*[9] b March 11, 1851, (1124) *Emma F ,*[9] b. March 7, 1852 , (1125) *George B ,*[9] b. February 26, 1854 , (1126) *Cora J ,*[9] b. September 11, 1856 , and (1127) *George H ,*[9] b October 18, 1858

Caroline married Daniel B Clement, of Norwich, Vt.

Hattie was residing at home, unmarried, in 1863

[434.]   PARLEAMON[7] PECK, son of CROMWELL,[6] married Polly L. Green, widow of John Davis Green, of Rehoboth, Mass., March 10, 1833.   He at first settled in Rehoboth, and afterwards in Illinois.   He died at Joliet, Will County, March 28, 1857.

CHILD — EIGHTH GENERATION

1128   Shubael H , b July 29, 1836.

He resided at Bristol, Kendall County, Ill , in 1863

He married Lucia M Wheeler, December 21, 1862   Their children are (1129) *Parker A ,*[9] b. October 1, 1863, and *Julia Emma,*[9] b January 14, 1866. The last name was not received until after the arrangement of the work, too late to be numbered and entered in the index.

[436.]   NELSON[7] PECK, son of CROMWELL,[6] married Polly Cole, daughter of George Cole, of Rehoboth, Mass., September 12, 1830.   They were residing in Monroe, Wisconsin, in 1863

CHILDREN — EIGHTH GENERATION

1130.   Andros, b Sept 13, 1833   1132.   Arthur, b June 25, 1846
1131.   Everett, b March 3, 1838

Andros married Lucinda Humphrey.   He was in the Union Army, Wisconsin Volunteers, 22d Regiment, in 1863.   Their children were   (1133) *Otis C ,*[9] *Everett E*[9] and (1134) *Willard H*[9]

Everett married Mary E Cameron   He was residing in Green County, Wis , in 1863.   Their child was   (1135) *Sarah E*[9]

Arthur was attending the Wisconsin University, in 1863, unm.

[437.]   BRADFORD W.[7] PECK, son of CROMWELL,[6] resides in the southwesterly part of Attleborough, Mass.   He married

Lucretia A. Horton, daughter of Wheeler Horton, December 17, 1835. She was born August 25, 1809.

CHILDREN — EIGHTH GENERATION

1136. Amanda A , b Jan. 6, 1837.
1137 John B , b Oct 4, 1842.
1138. A daughter, b April 12, 1846.
       Died in infancy

Amanda married Ebenezer Short, February 20, 1856
John B was serving his country, in the Army of the Potomac, in 1863.

[441.] PARMENIO W.[7] PECK, son of WILLIAMS,[6] married Abigail Gauss, daughter of Benjamin Gauss, of East Bloomfield, N. Y., a revolutionary soldier, and one of the first settlers of the town. They resided at East Bloomfield, N. Y., in 1860. He is a farmer.

CHILDREN — EIGHTH GENERATION

1139 Elias C , b March 13, 1836
1140 Abigail G , b Dec 22, 1839.
1141 Benjamin, b April 1, 1842
1142. Sarah C , b May 26, 1844.
1143. Phebe E , b. April 5, 1851.

Elias C. is a farmer, settled at East Bloomfield, N. Y
Abigail, Sarah and *Phebe* were residing at home, in 1863
Benjamin enlisted in the 85th Regiment, Company A , New York Volunteers, August 1861, and died in the Douglass Hospital, at Washington, of the typhoid fever, June 8, 1862

[442] IRA R.[7] PECK, son of WILLIAMS,[6] resides in East Bloomfield. He is a farmer. He married Clarissa Hamlin, daughter of William Hamlin. She died May 1833.

CHILDREN — EIGHTH GENERATION

1144   Herman J , b Sept 7, 1832.

Herman J married Helen Root. He resides at East Bloomfield , a farmer.

[444] HORATIO N.[7] PECK, son of WILLIAMS,[6] resides at Rochester, N. Y., where he is extensively engaged in the milling business. He married Hannah M. Colby, daughter of Col. Eastman Colby, of Ogden, Monroe County, N. Y., August 13, 1851.

CHILDREN — EIGHTH GENERATION

1145. Eastman C , b. May 6, 1853.
1146. Horatio N , b Aug 26, 1854.
1147. Lucy H , b May 9, 1856
1148 Lewis R , b Sept 30, 1857.
       Died July 10, 1864
1149 William M , b June 9, 1859.
       Died Feb 8, 1860

[447.] JOSEPHUS[7] PECK, son of LEMUEL,[6] married Lemyra Salsbury, daughter of Levi Salsbury, of Rehoboth, Mass., July 3, 1825. She was born July 18, 1802.

CHILDREN — EIGHTH GENERATION

1150. Sally A , b June 9, 1826.   1151 Floia E , b April 27, 1841

There were three other children in this family, who died young.

Sally A. married Israel Dean, November 27, 1845, and settled at Taunton, Mass.

Flora E. married Charles R Burt, May 14, 1862, and settled in Nevada.

[450] JONATHAN J.[7] PECK, son of JAMES,[6] resides in Barre, Vt. He is a farmer. He has been twice married: first, to Mira Jane Tucker, daughter of Jonas Tucker, Esq , of Newbury, N. H.; second, to Roxanna Lowell, daughter of David Lowell, of Salsbury, N. H. His first wife died January 30, 1846.

CHILDREN — EIGHTH GENERATION

1152 Jonas Oramele, b Sept 4, 1836	1156 Clara Jones, b Jan 15, 1856.
1153 Abbie Jane, b Feb 12, 1838	1157 Effie Lowell, b May 18, 1857 Died Nov 19, 1861
1154 Eugene Chase, b May 29, 1840	1158 Jonathan Jones, b Dec 20, 1859 Died Jan 16, 1862
By second wife	1159. George Herbert, b Aug 29, 1861 Died Nov 17, 1861.
1155 Flora May, b July 15, 1854.	

Jonas O is a Methodist clergyman , was settled in Chelsea, Mass , in 1863.

Abbie married Dr Joseph L Perkins, November 6, 1862   They were residing in St Johnsbury, Vt , in 1863

Eugene C was in the Navy Yard, at Boston, unm , in 1863

[456] MARTIN H.[7] PECK, son of EBENEZER,[6] first settled in Vermont, and then in Ohio. He afterwards moved to Nauvoo, Ill., and from there to Salt Lake, U. T. He married, for his first wife, Susan C Clough, of Danville, Vt , June 18, 1827. She died in West Milton, Ohio, November 6, 1843. For his second wife, he married Mary Thorne, at Nauvoo, Ill., March 28, 1844.

CHILDREN — EIGHTH GENERATION

Edwin M , b July 24, 1828	Hezekiah H , b March 19, 1845
Joseph A , b April 4, 1830	Susan, b Nov 28, 1848
James E , b March 7, 1832.	Mary A , b Oct 11, 1850
William P , b April 15, 1834	Sarah E , b Sept 7, 1852 Died Sept. 29, 1853
Eugene H , b May 25, 1837.	
Hiram, b Nov 25, 1840	Horton T , b Aug 20, 1854 Died Oct 24, 1855
Henry, b. Nov. 25, 1840	

The record of the above family was received after the arrangement of the work, too late to be numbered and entered in the index

[458.] JAMES M.[7] PECK, son of EBENEZER,[6] settled in Kentucky. He married Melinda James, daughter of Thomas James, of Graves County, Ky., January 22, 1839.

CHILDREN — EIGHTH GENERATION

1160	Lucius, b. Oct 13, 1839	1165	Rodman P , b Sept 20, 1850.
1161	Luvertia, b April 25, 1841	1166	Mary F , b Feb 16, 1853
1162	Julia A . b Jan 16, 1843.	1167	Emma H , b Dec 19, 1855
1163	Edward A , b. July 8, 1845	1168	James M , b Oct 23, 1857
1164	Melinda, b Sept 24, 1847		

Julia A married David Stubblefield, of Graves County, Ky , December 17, 1861

[461.] LUCIUS W.[7] PECK, son of EBENEZER,[6] married Elizabeth Vore, October 26, 1842. They settled at West Milton, Miami County, Ohio, where he resided until 1863, when, as his wife writes, he migrated to Salt Lake City, leaving her and her children at Milton

CHILDREN — EIGHTH GENERATION

1169	Susan Vore, b Sept 2, 1843	1174	Nancy Ellen, b. Aug. 1, 1854
1170	Rebecca Ann, b Feb 14, 1846.	1175	Emma Caroline, b June 23, 1857
1171	Mary Parolee, b Feb 24, 1848		
1172	Sarah Elizabeth, b. July 22, 1850	1176	Eliza Alice, b Nov 12, 1860.
1173	Martha Jane, b Oct 14, 1852 Died Aug 23, 1853.	1177.	Eldora Bell, b. July 4, 1862

Susan V married Adam D Leckrone, August 21, 1862 They reside in Monroe, Miami County, Ohio. Their son, *William Henry,*[9] was born May 25, 1863

[462] CYRIL C [7] PECK, son of CYRIL C.,[6] married Hannah W. Bliss, daughter of Cyrus Bliss, of Rehoboth, January 25, 1843. They reside in North Rehoboth, where he is engaged in trade.

CHILDREN — EIGHTH GENERATION

1178.	Edwin A , b Nov. 2, 1843.	1182	William H , b. Aug 23, 1850
1179	Hannah M , b March 2, 1845	1183	Charles H , b July 18, 1853. Died April 14, 1861
1180	Sarah, b April 1846 Died in infancy		
1181	Henry M , b. Sept 27, 1848 Died July 17, 1853.	1184.	Charles E., b May 27, 1861

[463]   JOSEPH S.[7] PECK, son of CYRIL C.,[6] married Lucinda Woodward, daughter of David Woodward, of Norton, Mass. He was wrecked at sea, between November 4 and 11, 1846.

CHILDREN — EIGHTH GENERATION

1185   Lorinda R , b 1839   Died in   1187.   Mary A., b. Nov 1842
           infancy   1188   Sarah W , b June 1844   Died
1186   Marcus R., b Nov 1840   Aug 8, 1861.

[466]   PHILIP W.[7] PECK, son of CYRIL C.,[6] married Fanny J. Barney, of Swansey, Mass. They reside in South Rehoboth, Mass , where he is engaged in trade.

CHILDREN — EIGHTH GENERATION

1189   Thomas D , b Aug 20, 1844   1192   Josephine M , b March 3, 1851
1190   Cassandana F , b Sept 9, 1846 1193   May E , b July 7, 1853
1191   Cyril C , b April 17, 1849   1194   Cynthia H , b July 2, 1858

[470]   GEORGE G.[7] PECK, son of CYRIL C.,[6] married Susan Gifford, for his first wife, and Sarah Harris, for his second. He resides in Mattapoisett, Mass.

CHILD — EIGHTH GENERATION

1195   Sarah G , b April 1857.

[471]   ALFRED R.[7] PECK, son of CYRIL C.,[6] married Mary Easterbrooks, of Swansey, daughter of Joseph Easterbrooks. They reside in Rehoboth, Mass.

CHILDREN — EIGHTH GENERATION

1196   James W , b Aug 27, 1855.   1197.   Mary F , b Dec 29, 1858

[474]   WILLIAM[7] PECK, son of BENJAMIN,[6] was a physician, and settled at Cincinnati, Ohio. He died June 2, 1857. He married Jane Thane, daughter of Dr. Samuel Thane, of Hillsdale, Columbia County, N. Y.

CHILDREN — EIGHTH GENERATION

1198   Ann Thane, b March 1, 1824   1201   William Henry, b April 20,
           Died Nov 21, 1842   1830.
1199   Susan Jane, b Dec 10, 1825   1202   George Bachelor, b. Sept. 14,
           Died Feb 26, 1826   1833.
1200   Mary Gano, b March 11, 1828. 1203.   Harriet Jane, b Oct 19, 1835.
                                      1204.   Edwin Tyler, b. Jan 9, 1839.

Yours truly
Solomon Peck.

[475.] REV. SOLOMON[7] PECK, son of BENJAMIN,[6] was graduated at Brown University, at the age of 16 years, and afterwards became one of the teachers. At 20, he entered the Theological Institution, at Andover, Mass.; was ordained to the ministry of the gospel at 23, became Professor of Latin and Hebrew at Amherst College at 25; at 32, was appointed missionary to France by the American Baptist Board of Foreign Missions, and subsequently was their Foreign Secretary at Boston, Mass, more than twenty years; within which period he visited their missions in France, Germany and Greece, and in 1852–3–4, those in Hither India, Assam and Burmah. In 1861, on the reduction of Port Royal, S. C, he went to the front, and became pastor of the Beaufort (colored) church, remaining till the close of the war. In 1866, he became chaplain of the "Disabled Soldiers' Home," in Boston, Mass. He received the honorary degree of Doctor of Divinity from Waterville College, Me., and from his *Alma Mater*. He was highly distinguished in all the offices he held, performing his various duties with signal ability. He is a fine scholar, an elegant and chaste writer, and noted for his high moral and religious character. He married Elizabeth R. Hooker, daughter of Rev. Asahel Hooker, and great-granddaughter of President Jonathan Edwards, May 11, 1826. His residence is in Roxbury, Mass.

CHILDREN — EIGHTH GENERATION

1205 Elizabeth Hooker, b March 17, 1840

1206. Sarah Edwards, b. April 2, 1842

[478] GEORGE B.[7] PECK, son of BENJAMIN,[6] resides in Providence, R I He graduated at Brown University in 1826. He was admitted to the Bar in 1830. He relinquished the profession in a few years for mercantile pursuits, in which he is still engaged. He married Ann P. Smith, daughter of John K. Smith.

CHILDREN — EIGHTH GENERATION

1207. George B, jr, b Aug 12, 1843

1208. John B., b June 30, 1845.

1209. Emily S, b Feb. 2, 1847 Died Feb 2, 1847

1210. William T, b July 25, 1848.

1211. Annie S., b. Oct. 17, 1850.

George B , jr , graduated at Brown University in 1864   He was elected 2d Lieutenant in the 2d Regt R. I Volunteers, December 13, 1864 , was wounded at Sailors' Creek, Va., April 6, 1865 , resigned his commission, and was honorably discharged, June 30, 1865

John B graduated at Brown University in 1866   He was appointed acting third assistant engineer in the U. S Navy, November 20, 1866, and ordered to the Naval Academy for a professional course of study   He was promoted to full third assistant, June 1868 , and assigned to active duty on the U. S Ship Mohongo, of the North Pacific Squadron

William T. is a member of the class to graduate in 1870, Brown University

[482.]   LEWIS[7] PECK, son of DAVID,[6] married, for his first wife, Mary Ann Fowler, of Yonkers, Westchester County, N. Y., daughter of Benjamin Fowler.   For his second wife, Eliza Bunker, of New York city.

CHILDREN — EIGHTH GENERATION

1212	Benjamin, left no issue.	1216.	Lewis. Died young.
1213	Ann Eliza	1217	Esther. Died unmarried.
1214	Susan Jane	1218	Harriet Louisa
1215	Aaron, no issue.	1219.	Lewis Died young.

Ann E. married William Sawin, of New York city.
Susan J married John Rich, of New York city.
Harriet L married Henry K Potter, of Providence, R. I

[498.]   HIRAM H.[7] PECK, son of HIRAM,[6] was residing at Potsdam, N. Y., in 1863.   He married Cornelia Harmon, August 16, 1843.

CHILDREN — EIGHTH GENERATION

1220	Charles Kibburn, b. June 15, 1845. Died Oct. 17, 1851.	1222.	Arthur, b. Feb. 23, 1853. Died Aug 28, 1854.
1221	Hiram Harper, b. June 6, 1849.	1223.	Anna Cornelia, b. July 12, 1855

[500.]   JOHN W.[7] PECK, son of HIRAM,[6] was residing in Cynthiana, Ky., in 1863.   He married Nancy J. Veach, March 2, 1843, daughter of David Veach, Esq.   He was born in Harrison County, where he resided until his decease.

CHILDREN — EIGHTH GENERATION

1224	Hiram D , b March 23, 1844.	1227.	Lydia W., b. Aug. 7, 1855. Died June 7, 1859.
1225	Mary K , b March 25, 1848		
1226.	Lucy W., b. April 19, 1853.		

[501] COMER M.[7] PECK, son of HIRAM,[6] was residing at Potsdam, N. Y., in 1863. He married Sarah Minerva Hoit, May 23, 1848.

CHILDREN — EIGHTH GENERATION

1228   Mary Emma, b. June 19, 1852
1229.   Fred Hoit, b May 10, 1856

1230   Edward Mason, b March 4, 1858   Died April 7, 1859.
1231.   Frank Mason, b Jan 9, 1860

[504.] ADDISON PECK, son of NATHANIEL, resides upon the homestead in East Montpelier, Vt., where he is a prominent man. He devotes much of his time, I am told, to public business, settling estates, acting as guardian, etc. He has been honored with various offices and public trusts. He has represented his town in the General Assembly, and has also been a member of the Senate. He has also been High Sheriff. He married Mary Dodge, May 14, 1837, daughter of Solomon Dodge, of Calais, Vt. She was born December 20, 1811.

CHILDREN — EIGHTH GENERATION

1232   Marietta, b April 18, 1841
1233   John Howard, b March 8, 1843

1234.   Ellen Ortensa, b Jan. 8, 1847.
1235.   Martha Orlana, b March 25, 1849.

[505.] RUSSELL[7] PECK, son of NATHANIEL,[6] resides, in East Montpelier, near the homestead, an industrious and thrifty farmer. He married Olive Hedges, daughter of Elijah Hedges.

CHILD — EIGHTH GENERATION

1236.   Charles M , b Dec 1843

[507] NAHUM[7] PECK, son of SQUIRE,[6] resides in Hinesburg, Vt. He is a lawyer of extensive practice. He has been a member of the Vermont Legislature, and held other honorable positions. He has been twice married · first, to Lucinda Wheeler, of Montpelier, Vt., October 1825; second, to Marcia Wood, of Keesville, N. Y., May 12, 1857. His first wife died January 17, 1854.

CHILD — EIGHTH GENERATION

1237.   Cicero Godard, b. Feb 17, 1827.

He married Maria C Coleman, daughter of Maj -Gen Coleman, of Williston, Vt , March 1854. They reside in Hinesburg

[514.]　LUCIUS B.[7] PECK, of Montpelier, Vt., son of JOHN,[6] is an attorney-at-law of much distinction.　He has been a member of Congress.

He married Martha Day, daughter of Ira Day, of Barre, Vt., May 10, 1832.*

CHILD — EIGHTH GENERATION

1238.　Ann, married William M. Mallory, of Corning, N Y.

[524]　CHAUNCEY[7] PECK, son of DANIEL,[6] resides in Boston, Mass.　He married Jemima Bush, daughter of Ephraim Bush, of Templeton, Mass., June 13, 1824.

CHILDREN — EIGHTH GENERATION

1239　Alfred P , b Aug 16, 1825
1240　Charles L , b Dec 16, 1827
1241.　Chauncey L , b Aug 15, 1828.
1242　Georgianna E , b Jan 29, 1830.
1243　Frederick C , b. March 7, 1832.

Two children, who were twins, died in infancy, unnamed.

Alfred was residing at home in 1863

Charles L died in California, March 30, 1852.

Chauncey L died in the army, August 30, 1862.

Georgianna married Charles C Littlefield, of Boston　She died September 4, 1854

Frederick died March 4, 1850

[525.]　POMROY[7] PECK, son of DANIEL,[6] married Amanda Searls, of Sutton, Mass., where they settled.　He died August 1854.　She was residing in Sutton in 1866.

CHILDREN — EIGHTH GENERATION

1244　Clarinda Amanda, b June 12, 1829
1245.　Elvira Maria, b. March 13, 1832
1246.　Daniel Pomroy, b July 15, 1836.
1247　Delia Gale, b March 27, 1838.
1248.　James Madison, b May 30, 1845. Died April 30, 1848.

[528.]　LYMAN[7] PECK, son of DANIEL,[6] settled in Royalston, Mass.　He married Lorina Davis, January 21, 1829, daughter of Joseph Davis, of Royalston, Mass., for his first wife, and Fanny Harrington, widow of Abraham Harrington, formerly Fanny Harwood, for his second wife, December 6, 1860.　His first wife died May 9, 1860.　He died December 2, 1862.

---

* He died December 28, 1866.

CHILDREN — EIGHTH GENERATION

1249	Wayland F , b Nov 2, 1830	1253.	Polina L , b April 12, 1838.
1250	Philander L , b May 1832	1254	Nelson F , b. July 1840
1251	Eugene F., b Dec 1833,	1255	Joseph W , b March 1842
1252	Willard, b Dec 1835 Died	1256.	Daniel W , b April 10, 1843.
	Dec 1835	1257	Lowell H , b Oct 1845.

Wayland F married Mary Burnett, resides in Athol, Mass. Their children are (1258) *Stella May*,[9] b July 1856, and (1259) *Mary Estella*,[9] b 1861 Stella May[9] died September 1857.

Philander L married Roxanna Lewis, resided in Royalston in 1864 Children were (1260) *Ella*,[9] b in 1856, (1261) *Edwin*,[9] b. in 1859, and (1262) *Lyman*, b January 8, 1864

Eugene F married Rosina Glaze, and settled in Ohio

Polina L married Noah Rankin, and settled in Erving, Mass

Joseph W. married Roxy Mayo, and settled in Orange, Mass

[529.] SULLIVAN[7] PECK. son of DANIEL,[6] resided in Royalston, Mass., in 1864. He married Czarina Davis, daughter of Joseph Davis, of Royalston, May 29, 1831. She was born August 7, 1808.

CHILDREN — EIGHTH GENERATION

1263	Martha J , b March 10, 1832.	1267.	Georgianna, b April 23, 1843
1264	Chauncey P , b April 5, 1834	1268.	Hamilton S , b Oct 22, 1845
1265	Warren D , b Feb 28, 1836	1269.	Hammond W , b Sept 28,
1266	Elsa J , b July 1, 1838		1847.

Martha J. married Stephen Gates, and was residing in Burlington, Vt , in 1863 Their children were *Walter B* [9] and *Nellie G* [9]

Chauncey C married Mary Collopy, was residing in Burlington, Vt , in 1863 Their child was (1270) *Warren L* ,[9] b August 10, 1861.

[538.] JOHN Q. A [7] PECK, son of ICHABOD,[6] married Fanny Cutler, June 6, 1832 He was residing at Montpelier, Vt , in 1864.

CHILDREN — EIGHTH GENERATION

1271.	Charles, b Jan 29, 1834.	1273	Alonzo T , b July 1, 1838
1272.	Frances M , b May 30, 1836	1274	Mary, b Oct 24, 1840

[539] WILLIAM N [7] PECK, son of ICHABOD,[6] married Julia Clark, January 16, 1838. He resided at Montpelier, Vt., in 1864.

CHILDREN — EIGHTH GENERATION

1275	James S , b Dec 6, 1838.	1277	Rawsel K , b March 26, 1850
1276.	George A , b July 10, 1842	1278.	John W., b April 29, 1853

10*

[546.] DANIEL[7] PECK, son of SOLOMON,[6] was residing in Charlestown, Mass., in 1864. He has been three times married: first, to —— Smith; second, to Lydia W. Moor; third, to Margaret Moor.

CHILDREN — EIGHTH GENERATION

1279. Georgia A E , b Nov 19, 1844.

1280 Chauncey W , b July 28, 1846.

1281. Daniel M , b. Dec 30, 1847

1282. Lydia W , b July 18, 1850.

1283. Bradford, b Feb 21, 1853.

1284. Charles H , b Jan. 9, 1855.

[552] JEROME B.[7] PECK, son of CALVIN,[6] settled in Medway, Mass., where he died January 22, 1861. He was twice married: first, to Harriet Hixon, October 24, 1837; she was born February 24, 1816, and died January 11, 1855; second, to Mary Ann Miggs (widow), February 14, 1856. She was born March 5, 1822.

CHILDREN — EIGHTH GENERATION

1285 William G , b. March 10, 1839.

1286. Sarah Jane, b March 5, 1847.

1287. George G , b Nov 19, 1856.

[555] NAPOLEON B.[7] PECK; son of CALVIN,[6] resides at Woonsocket, R. I. He married Ann Roberts, daughter of Adams Roberts, of Exeter, R. I.

CHILD — EIGHTH GENERATION

1288. Ann, b Feb 21, 1864

[557] MOSES[7] PECK, son of MOSES,[6] resides at Hyde Park. He married Julia A. White, daughter of Seth White, of Waterbury, Vt., October 22, 1844.

CHILDREN — EIGHTH GENERATION

1289. Jane, b Dec. 28, 1846

1290 Kate, b Feb 12, 1849 Died May 25, 1851

1291. John C , b March 25, 1851

1292 Willie B , b April 4, 1853.

1293 Lilly K , b June 23, 1855.

1294. James R L , b. Jan 14, 1858.

1295. Carrie S , b Oct 10, 1860

—— b. April 2, 1863

[558.] JOHN C.[7] PECK, son of MOSES,[6] resides in Waukegan, Ill. He married Hannah Tucker, November 2, 1853.

CHILDREN — EIGHTH GENERATION

1296. Charles E , b Aug 2, 1854.   1297. John C jr , b Feb. 12, 1857.
     Died Aug. 24, 1854.   Died Dec. 5, 1863

[559.] CHARLES E.[7] PECK, son of Moses,[6] resides at Win-
netka, Ill. He married Sarah M. Russ, October 21, 1841.

CHILDREN — EIGHTH GENERATION ·

1298. Marion A., b. Jan. 3, 1843.   1299 Helen M., b Nov. 25, 1844.

[561.] HORACE M.[7] PECK, son of Solomon,[6] married Rosilla Bourn, daughter of Joseph Bourn. He was residing in Liberty, Ohio, in 1863.

CHILDREN — EIGHTH GENERATION

1300. Almerine H , b May 1842.   1303. Harriet R , b May 1850
1301   Mary B , b Sept. 1843.   1304. Lucy L , b. July 1852.
1302   Joseph J., b. May 1846.

[562] SEWEL W.[7] PECK, son of Solomon,[6] married, for
his first wife, Chloe Melvin, daughter of Nathan Melvin, of Topsham, Vt.; and for his second wife, Mary A. Perrin, widow of William Perrin, formerly Mary A. Wheeler, daughter of Otis Wheeler.
His first wife died April 12, 1845.

CHILDREN — EIGHTH GENERATION

1305. Melvin R , b Oct 1830   1307. Martha D , b. May 1836.
1306. Narcissa A , b Oct 1833   1308   Henry H , b. Oct 1840
  Melvin R married Percy Curtiss, daughter of David Curtiss   Their chil-
dren are   (1309) *Leonora A.*,[9] (1310) *Martha C*,[9] (1311) *Jenette*[9] and (1312)
Henry W[9]
  Narcissa A married Elnathan Carpenter.
  Martha D married James Brown.

[571] JOHN N[7] PECK, son of Solomon,[6] married Lois
Blood, of Corinth, Vt. They reside in Gorham, Fulton County,
N. Y.

CHILDREN — EIGHTH GENERATION

1313. Laura J , b March 12, 1850   1315. Allen S , b. Sept. 19, 1860.
1314. Gillman D , b Dec. 29, 1853.

[572]   WILLIAM N.[7] PECK, son of SOLOMON,[6] married Sarah E. Wright, daughter of Alexander Wright, of Johnstown, Ohio. They resided in Johnstown, Ohio, where he died, September 28, 1863.

CHILDREN — EIGHTH GENERATION

1316. Victory, b Aug 1849
1317. George Willie, b. June 1855.
1318   Charles Grandville, b. Jan. 1859
1319. Maria Emma, b. July 1862.

[575.]   DEXTER[7] PECK, son of SOLOMON,[6] resided at Kerkersville, Ohio.   He married Comfort Parkinson, daughter of John Parkinson, June 1853.

CHILDREN — EIGHTH GENERATION

1320. Perry, b May 1854
1321. William F , b Aug. 1856. Died Sept 1857.
1322. Willis R , b Nov 1858
1323. Mary J , b. March 1860   Died Sept 20, 1863.

[579.]   HORATIO N.[7] PECK, son of JAMES,[6] resided in Kansas, in 1863.   He married Emily Carrier.

CHILDREN — EIGHTH GENERATION

1324. Emily
1325. Mary.

[580.]   ARNOLD M.[7] PECK, son of JAMES,[6] resided in Hatfield, Mass , in 1863.   He married, for his first wife, Annis Tower, of Chesterfield.   She died September 21, 1825.   For his second wife, he married Myra H. Stevens.

CHILDREN — EIGHTH GENERATION

1326. Jane J , b March 31, 1842. Died Sept 15, 1842.
1327. Hattie L , b in 1858.

[585]   PHILIP[7] PECK, son of BENONI,[6] settled in Walpole, N. H. ; a merchant, now retired from business.   He married Martha Ellen Bellows, daughter of Thomas Bellows, November 21, 1839.   She was born April 1, 1811.

CHILDREN — EIGHTH GENERATION

1328. Henry Philip, b Aug 31, 1840   Died July 13, 1852
1329   Thomas Bellows, b. Aug. 18, 1842.

[586.]   LEVI[7] PECK, son of BENONI,[6] resides in Chelsea, Mass.; is in mercantile business, in Boston.   He married Lucy M. Whitcomb, daughter of Mark Whitcomb, of Winchendon, Mass., December 2, 1844.

CHILDREN — EIGHTH GENERATION

1330. Charles Henry, b. June 4, 1847.   1331. Frederick Whitcomb, b Oct. 10, 1849.

[587.]   JAMES W[7] PECK, son of BENONI,[6] was a merchant, in Boston, for a number of years.   His health failed him, and he retired from business, and died in Winchendon, in April 1860. He married Caroline M. Ladd, of Boston.

CHILDREN — EIGHTH GENERATION '

1332. James Benjamin, b. March 21,   1333. George Walter, b. Jan 1849.
1847.

[592.]   HERNY[7] PECK, son of BENONI,[6] resides in Winchendon, Mass., where he is engaged in the marble business.   He married Mary Frances Cory, of Fitzwilliam.

CHILD — EIGHTH GENERATION '

1334. Henry Eddy, b. March 1862.

[596.]   ROYAL C.[7] PECK, son of OLIVER C.,[6] married Matilda Drown, daughter of Joshua Drown.   He resides upon the homestead, with his father.

CHILD — EIGHTH GENERATION

1335. Lepha, b. 1857.

[601.]   RUFUS A.[7] PECK, son of RUFUS,[6] resides in New Providence, Ind.   He married Lydia B. Dow.

CHILD — EIGHTH GENERATION.

1336. Theodore A., b. Sept 9, 1849.

[603.]   CALVIN J.[7] PECK, son of CALEB,[6] resides in Seekonk, Mass.   He married Emeline Lock, daughter of Thomas Lock, of Lexington, Mass., April 7, 1844.

1337. Thomas J , b Jan 15, 1845.   1341   Harriet E , b June 18, 1853
1338   Mary M , b Aug 18, 1846   1342   George G , b May 18, 1856.
1339   Hannah C , b Feb 1, 1849.   1343. Andrew R , b Aug 19, 1860.
1340. Henry C , b Jan 13, 1851.   1344. Fanny, b May 27, 1863.

[609.] HENRY R.[7] PECK, son of CALEB,[6] resided in Providence, R I. He married Abba Carr, daughter of Capt. Caleb Carr, of Warren, R. I. He died May 1857.

1345   Henry C , b May 1855   1346   Jesse Fremont, b 1857.

[612.] HIRAM A.[7] PECK, son of SAMUEL,[6] resides in Salem, Ind. He is a merchant. He married Ellen Cone, of Ohio, March 30, 1855. She died March 14, 1862.

1347   Mattie, b Jan 30, 1856   1349   George, b Sept 10, 1859.
1348. Nora, b Sept. 1, 1857.

[625.] ALLEN O.[7] PECK, son of ALLEN,[6] resides in Providence, R. I. He was for many years President of the American Insurance Company, and is now President of the Narraganset Fire and Marine Insurance Company. He married Mary Elizabeth Whitaker.

1350   Ellen Ormsbee, b Aug 8, 1856.   1353. Elizabeth Andrews, b Nov. 2,
1351   Mary Talbert, b. April 12, 1858.   1861.
1352. Maria Stores, b Dec. 3, 1859

[628.] OTIS[7] PECK, son of JOSEPH,[6] married Sarah Allen, of Barton, Vt. He died in Thompson, Conn., December 7, 1835.

1354. Emily W., b Nov. 10, 1822.   1356. Minerva A , b April 3, 1827.
1355. Lydia E , b Jan 10, 1825.   Died Aug 1848
           Died Sept 20, 1852.   1357. A son. Died in infancy.
  Emily W. married Samuel Butterfield.

[629.] ARNOLD[7] PECK, son of JOSEPH,[6] resides near Pawtucket, R. I. He has been twice married: first, to Content Stevens (widow), formerly Content Barney, daughter of Cyrenus Barney; second, to Sylvia Freeman, daughter of Daniel Freeman, of Attleborough, Mass. He was married to his first wife, October 2, 1832. She died September 27, 1846. He was married to his second wife May 3, 1849.

CHILDREN — EIGHTH GENERATION

1358. Samuel Arnold, b. Aug 4, 1833. Died Dec 17, 1834

1359 Sarah Temperance, b March 2, 1836. Died Dec 6, 1838.

1360 Susan, b May 22, 1838. Died May 26, 1840.

[637.] BARTON⁷ PECK, son of Josiah,⁶ settled, at first, in Indiana, where he remained about fifteen years. In 1836, he left, as captain of a company, for Texas, and after the battle of Jacinto remained in the State, and engaged in business there. He died at his residence, at Goliad, October 13, 1861. He married Frances O. Menefee, daughter of Thomas Menefee, Esq., of Texas.

CHILDREN — EIGHTH GENERATION :

1361   Lucina E
1362   Susan
1363   Frances
1364   Barton.
1365   Viola.
1366   Alonzo
1367   Samuel.
1368   Mary.
1369. George
1370. A son   Died in infancy.

[640.] JOSIAH⁷ PECK, son of Josiah,⁶ resides in Washington, Daviess County, Ind. He married Elizabeth P. Ladd, daughter of Dann Ladd, of Lebanon, Madison County, N. Y.

CHILDREN — EIGHTH GENERATION

1371   Ellen D, b April 25, 1835 Died Nov 3, 1841.
1372. Barton P, b April 18, 1837. Died June 3, 1842.
1373. Mary A, b Aug 20, 1839
1374. Josiah E, b April 9, 1842.
1375. Lewis J, b June 9, 1844.
1376. Samuel W, b Sept. 20, 1846. Died June 29, 1848.
1377. Henry, b. Aug 1, 1850.
1378. Hannah B., b Oct. 29, 1853.

Mary A married James R Clark, September 4, 1861 They reside in Washington, Daviess County, Ind. Their son, *Samuel C.*,⁹ was born January 5, 1863.

[643.] ALONZO⁷ PECK, son of Josiah,⁶ resides upon the homestead, at Eaton, N. Y. He is extensively engaged in the forwarding business, as well as in cheese making and farming. He married Maria A. Record, daughter of Darius Record, of Madison County, N. Y., January 1852.

CHILDREN — EIGHTH GENERATION

1379. Hattie M., b July 17, 1858   1381. Lucy A , b. Oct 29, 1861.
1380. Sophia E., b. Dec. 20, 1859

[655.] ISAAC[7] PECK, son of PEREZ,[6] resides in Coventry, R. I. He is a machinist by trade and occupation. He married Lucy Cordelia Brayton, December 9, 1845.

CHILDREN — EIGHTH GENERATION .

1382   Perez Lindley, b. April 25,   1384. Harriet Augusta, b. Aug. 1,
          1849   1858.
1383   Edgar Brayton, b Jan 7, 1855.

PART SECOND.

THE DESCENDANTS OF JOHN[2] PECK,

SECOND SON OF JOSEPH[1] THE ANCESTOR.

JOHN PECK was born in England, and came over to this country with his father, in 1638, being then about eleven years of age. He moved with the family from Hingham, Mass., to Seekonk, in 16 15. He settled in the southeast part of Seekonk, near what is now known as Luther's Corners. He was accepted as a freeman of the town in 1658, and drew his proportion in the meadows on the north side of the town. He was chosen one of the townsmen in 1680, and representative to the General Court of Massachusetts in 1700. He died in 1713. The inventory of his property was presented to the court, October 1713. His will is recorded upon the Records at Taunton, Mass., B. 3, p. 163.

The following is a copy:

In the name of God Amen. In the year one thousand seven hundred and eight, in the seventh year of her Majesties Reign, on ye twenty six day of May; I John Peck of Rehoboth in the county of Bristol in her Majesties Provinces of the Massachusetts Bay in New England , Being aged & weak of body, & in expectation of my change, yet through the mircy of God I am whole & sound in my memory & understanding, & of a disposing mind , do make this my last will & testament, for the disposing & settleing the things of this world wth which the Lord hath intrusted me, to & amongst my wife and children in manner and form as followeth.

And Imprimis. I bequeath my soul into the hands of my blessed Savior and Deer Redeemer, & my body to the Dust, to be decently buried by my executor here in after named.

Item I give and bequeath to my daughter Esther Wilmarth, in

11

addition to what her grand father gave her, wch was my proper Estate ; all that my lot of land in the Easterly side of ye grand division, to her, & her heirs and assigns for ever.

Item   I give and bequeath to my daughter Dorothy Glover, & her husband Edward Glover, my house lot and all my buildings there on, provided ; he pay over to my executor here in after named, ten pounds money & the barn there on or, as many boards & nails as will build such a barn, and ten acres of undivided lands in Rehoboth already drawn for ; being part of my first alotment ; & one bed after my wive's decease, and fifteen pounds of commonage in said Rehoboth ; to be, and remain to them & their heirs & assigns forever.

Item   I give and bequeath to my daughter Anne Peck, thirty acres of land, lying on the easterly side of the white Oak hill, near Samuel Fullers. — likewise, fifteen pounds estate of commonage in Rehoboth, & one acre of salt marsh, and a cow or the value there of, at her marriage ; to be and remain to her, and to her heirs & assigns for ever.

Item   I give and bequeath to my daughter Abigail Peck, fifty three acres of land, lying adjoining to seargent John Wilmarths house lot near Palmers River ; and one acre of salt marsh &, fifteen pounds estate of commonage, in Rehoboth , and a bed after my wive's decease ; to her, & her heirs and assigns for ever.

Item   I give and bequeath unto my son Nathan Peck, all the rest and residue of my lands and meadows, with their quantitis & qualities, both undivided and divided, in Rehoboth and Attleborough or where soever, & one yoke of oxen, with my yokes, carts, ploughs, chains & tools ; and the bed on which I lodge, with the furniture, after my wives decease, hereby obliging him to take care, maintain & provide for my wife Rebecca Peck, in sickness and in health, for and during her natural life, with honorable full maintainance. I do hereby make my son Nathan Peck, my sole executor, of this, my last will and testament ; hereby revoking all other wills by me heretofore made.

In testimony whereof, I have here unto set my hand and seal, this day & year, first above written.

Signed sealed and published in the presence of us witnesses

    JOHN BUTTERWORTH
    SAMUEL COOPER   JOHN PECK
    DANIEL SMITH

It appears from the records of Rehoboth, and from his will, that he was three times married. The records (book first) say, " Elizabeth his wife was burried December 9, 1667"; and also afterwards, that "Elizabeth his wife was burried April 21, 1687"; and in his will he makes provision for his wife Rebecca.

CHILDREN — THIRD GENERATION ·

1385 Elizabeth, b. Nov. 27, 1657. Burried Dec. 18, 1657.

1386. Esther, b. Jan. 7, 1658.

1387. Anne, b Oct. 6, 1661. Burried Feb 26, 1662

1388. John, b Oct. 7, 1664. Burried Dec. 18, 1666.

1389 Elizabeth, b Nov 13, 1669 Burried July 29, 1687

1390. Dorothy, b June 28, 1671

1391 Rebecca, b April 8, 1674.

1392 Anne, b July 17, 1677.

1393 +Nathan, b July 6, 1680.

1394 Abigail, b March 16, 1682-3

Esther married a —— Wilmarth.
Dorothy married Edward Glover, April 3, 1707 (R Rec , B 1)

[1393.] NATHAN[3] PECK, son of JOHN,[2] it is supposed, settled upon the lands given him by his father, where he lived and died. He married Patience Carpenter, January 11, 1719. He died April 12, 1734 (T. Rec., B. 2). His widow was appointed administratrix upon his estate, June 18, 1734 (T. Rec., B. 8, p. 128). The estate was divided between the widow and children, April 4, 1749 (T. Rec., B. 11, p. 688).

CHILDREN — FOURTH GENERATION (T Rec , B 2, p 28)

1395 John, b Oct 5, 1721

1396 +Nathan, b Dec 31, 1722

1397 +Charles, b Jan 5, 1724-5.

1398. Elizabeth, b Aug 6, 1726.

1399 Patience, b Jan. 5, 1727-8.

1400. Ann, b July 30, 1732. Died June 27, 1733.

John left no descendants His estate, left him by his father, was divided between his brother Nathan and sisters, December 20, 1773, after his decease (T. Rec , B 23, p 154)

Patience married Enos Walker.

Elizabeth married —— Arnold, was deceased at the time of the division of her father's estate, leaving a son, *Daniel*,[5] and daughter, *Elizabeth*[5] Arnold.

[1396] NATHAN[4] PECK, son of NATHAN,[3] resided upon the homestead. The house was a short distance south from Luther's Corners, now so called, upon the east side of the old Bristol and Boston road. It was taken down many years since, by Joseph West, into whose possession it came from his wife, the daughter of Nathan. Its location was pointed out to me by his son, from whom I obtained my information. The remains of the old cellar were to be seen when I visited the place. Nathan was twice married:

first, to Martha Carpenter, May 11, 1749; second, to Rhoda Luther, of Swansey.

His will is upon record at Taunton, B. 33, p. 500, dated June
13, 1793.

He gives his wife Rhoda her dower in his estate, the improvement
of his new dwelling-house, barn, and fifteen acres of land.   He divides
his property among his children : *Martha, Susannah Weaver*, the wife
of James Weaver, *Dorothy, Ann Emerson*, wife of Ephraim Emerson,
and *Patience West*, the wife of Joseph West, whom he makes the executor of his will.

CHILDREN — FIFTH GENERATION

1401   Martha, b Oct 13, 1749
1402   Susannah, b Dec 25, 1751.
1403.+Nathan, b April 11, 1755.

1404.   Dorothy, b. May 11, 1760 Died
        unm.
1405.   Patience, b. April 11, 1763.
1406   Ann, b. May 9, 1770.

Susannah married James Weaver.

Patience married Joseph West, of Seekonk. *Joseph[6]* and *Nathan[6] West* are
her sons.

Ann married Ephraim Emerson. Her children were *Ezekiel,[6] John[6]* and
Jerold [6]

[1397.]   CHARLES[4] PECK, son of NATHAN,[3] resided near
his brother, upon what has since been known in that vicinity as the
Sweeting farm, where he died, April 15, 1799.   He was twice
married: first, to Rachel Sweeting, December 7, 1749 ; second, to
Lydia Fry, daughter of Stephen Fry.   His first wife died February
20, 1774, and his second wife, July 20, 1797.

CHILDREN — FIFTH GENERATION

1407.   Abigail, b April 29, 1750
1408   Susannah, b. Nov. 5, 1752.
        Died Oct. 6, 1778.
1409 +Charles, b Feb 17, 1755
1410.   Rachel, b Aug 15, 1757
1411 +John, b. Feb 19, 1760
1412 +Thomas S , b. July 11, 1762.
1413.   Sarah, b Nov 7, 1764
1414   James, b   March 5, 1767.
        Died, unm , Jan 22, 1787.

1415 +Peter, b. June 15, 1769.
1416   Lucy, b Nov 8, 1771
1417   Lydia, b. May 8, 1775, by 2d
       wife
1418   Stephen, b Sept 18, 1775.
1419. Asa, b Feb 13, 1780   Died
       unm , Dec 24, 1797.
1420. Mary, b June 18, 1782.

Abigail married Ebenezer Fuller   Her children were *Charles,[6] Shubael,[6]*
and *Nancy,[6]* who married Col —— Shorey, a Revolutionary soldier, and *Lucy,[6]*
who married Asa Armington, of Providence.   These two girls were living in
1862.

Rachel married Robinson Chafee and Ebenezer Short

Sarah married Henry West, had no issue

Lucy married Darius Peck (No 2714).

Lydia married Sanford Ross. Her son, Jeremiah[6] Ross, was residing in Providence in 1862

Mary married Levi Fuller   He died April 13, 1861   She was residing, in 1862, with her son-in-law, Hermon A Peck, of Providence   *Stephen P Fuller*,[6] of Seekonk, and *Calvin S*,[6] of Providence, are her sons.

Stephen was a physician   He settled and practised medicine in Provincetown, Mass, where he died.   He married Bethiah Nickerson.   They had one child   It died in infancy.

[1405.]   NATHAN[5] PECK, son of NATHAN,[4] lived and died near the residence of his father, upon the lands he had given him. The old house was taken down several years since.   The place in 1862 was owned by the heirs of Ebenezer Miller.   He married Anna Thurber, December 3, 1772.

CHILDREN — SIXTH GENERATION

1421   Nathan, b Aug 10, 1777.   1423.   Ann, b. March 12, 1789.
1422 +Otis, b. Dec 27, 1780.

Nathan resided for several years upon the homestead, then settled in Attleborough, Mass, near what is now known as Dodgeville, where he died about 1854   He married Abigail Fuller, daughter of Ebenezer Fuller.   She died in 1858.   He left no issue.

[1409.]   CHARLES[5] PECK, son of CHARLES,[4] remained upon the homestead.   He was a deacon of the Baptist church.   He married Chloe Bliss, daughter of Deacon Jacob Bliss, of Rehoboth.

CHILDREN — SIXTH GENERATION

1424.   Phebe, b Aug 8, 1780.   Died   1426 +Obed, b Dec 27, 1784.
          July 29, 1781   1427   Susan.
1425.   Roxalana, b June 15, 1782.   1428 +Sylvester, b Nov 2, 1798.
          Died May 8, 1784

Susan was residing in Seekonk in 1862, unmarried.

[1411.]   JOHN[5] PECK, son of CHARLES,[4] remained upon the homestead with his brother Charles, where he died, December 28, 1828.   He married Rachel Bliss, daughter of Deacon Jacob Bliss. She died March 18, 1854, in her 85th year.

CHILDREN — SIXTH GENERATION

1429.   Rachel, b. July 11, 1806.   1430.   Louisa, b Feb 12, 1814   Married Rev. Welcome Leonard.

11*

Rachel married Perry Barney, January 5, 1842, of Seekonk, now East Providence, where they reside Their children are *Rachel E*,[7] b November 16, 1842, *Eliza K*,[7] b March 12, 1848, who died May 10, 1848, and *John P.*,[7] b. September 17, 1851.

[1412.]   THOMAS[5] PECK, son of CHARLES,[4] settled in Seekonk, upon the farm recently occupied by Levi Fuller. He married Rebecca Chafee, daughter of Nathaniel Chafee, of Seekonk, May 7, 1789.

CHILDREN — SIXTH GENERATION

1431. Huldah, b July 5, 1791

1432. James, b Nov 9, 1792. Died May 25, 1822, unm

1433 +Thomas, b Sept. 2, 1794

1434. Rebecca, b Jan 15, 1796

1435 Susannah, b Sept 20, 1797.

1436 +Asa, b Feb 6, 1799.

1437. Ruth, b Dec. 25, 1800

1438. Nancy A , b. May 1, 1802.

1439. Daniel, b Nov 11, 1803. Died July 12, 1804, unm.

1440. Mary Ann, b Nov 28, 1804.

1441 Hannah C , b Dec 20, 1806.

1442 Charlott, b. July 31, 1810

1443. Darius, b June 19, 1812. Died in infancy.

Huldah married Nathaniel Millard, was residing in Rehoboth in 1862, a widow.

Rebecca married Philip Millard, was residing in Rehoboth in 1862, a widow

Susannah married Jonathan Monroe, of Swansey She died in 1852. *Albert*[7] and *James*[7] Monroe, of Brighton, Mass., are her sons

Ruth died young

Nancy A married Ira Medbury She died February 16, 1815

Mary Ann died December 2, 1814

Hannah married Robert Tripp, of Little Compton, where they resided in 1862

Charlott married Ira Mason, of Seekonk.

[1415.]   PETER[5] PECK, son of CHARLES,[4] settled in Danville, Vt, where he lived and died, August 8, 1835. He married Diana Peck (No. 1684), daughter of Peleg Peck. She was living in 1853.

CHILDREN — SIXTH GENERATION

1444. James, b Feb. 18, 1797 Died unm

1445. Sally, b May 29, 1801. Died unm.

1446. Charles, b Aug. 17, 1803. Died unm

1447 +Elisha, b. Nov 9, 1805.

1448 Phebe, b. July 3, 1807.

1449. Mary, b. July 18, 1811. Died unm

1450 Sophia, b. Feb 8, 1815. Died unm.

1451 +Simon, b April 13, 1816.

1452. John, b June 6, 1820. Died unm.

[1422.] OTIS[6] PECK, son of NATHAN,[5] resided upon the homestead with his brother for several years; then in different places. I have been able to learn little in relation to him. He married Polly Miller. He died about 1822. He was then settled near his brother Nathan.

CHILDREN — SEVENTH GENERATION

1453. John   Resided in Rehoboth   1454. Otis   Died at sea.
and other places.

[1426.] OBED[6] PECK, son of CHARLES,[5] married, for his first wife, Lydia Allen, March 24, 1811, and settled in Rowe, Mass. She died February 26, 1835. He married, for his second wife, Phidelia Payne, August 23, 1835.

CHILDREN — SEVENTH GENERATION

1455. Lydia, b. Dec 13, 1811.
1456. Mary, b Jan 24, 1814.
1457. Chloe, b Feb. 24, 1816.
1458. Nancy, b Aug 5, 1818; unm. in 1862
1459. Margaret, b Dec 25, 1820.
1460. Martha, b. Dec 25, 1820.
1461. +Obed, jr , b Aug 9, 1826.
1462. James, b. Aug 27, 1836. Died July 16, 1842.
1463. Allen, b. March 12, 1838.

Lydia married Timothy King; settled in Rowe, Mass
Mary married John Christie; settled in Monroe, Mass
Chloe married Ephraim Tinsdell, settled in Rowe, Mass.
Margaret married Samuel Merriam, settled in Coleram.
Martha married David R. Stanford, settled in Rowe.
Allen was residing in Rowe in 1862, with his father and mother, unmarried.

[1428] SYLVESTER[6] PECK, son of CHARLES,[5] moved from Seekonk about 1822 to the town of Rowe, Mass.; from there he afterwards removed to Charlemont, where he died, November 6, 1861. He married Sally Potter, daughter of John Potter, of Barrington, R. I., June 6, 1821. She was born May 5, 1799.

CHILDREN — SEVENTH GENERATION

1464. +Charles, b March 4, 1822
1465. William H , b. Feb. 8, 1826. Died June 24, 1827.
1466. William H , b Jan 30, 1828. Died Sept 25, 1829.
1467. Ann E , b. Sept. 23, 1830. Died July 10, 1835.
1468. Sarah M , b May 23, 1834.
1469. George S , b. Nov. 10, 1838

George S was residing in Charlemont in 1863, unmarried
Sarah M. married Rev. C. S. Hartwell, of Charlemont, June 20, 1863.

[1433.]   THOMAS[6] PECK, son of THOMAS S.,[5] married Elmira Cole, daughter of Aaron Cole, of Swansey, Mass., March 24,
1825, where they were residing in 1862; a wealthy farmer.

CHILDREN — SEVENTH GENERATION

1470 +William H , b Dec 29, 1825   1472 +James C , b Dec. 27, 1829.
1471. Elizabeth B , b Dec 27, 1827.   1473 +Benjamin T , b. June 22, 1832.

Elizabeth B married William H. Sherman, of Swansey, Mass. Their children are *Ellen Frances*,[8] b. August 8, 1858 , *Herbert Lester*,[8] b. August 24,
1863.

[1436.]   ASA[6] PECK, son of THOMAS,[5] resides in East Providence; is a mason by trade.   He married Betsey Hale, daughter
of Daniel Hale, of Swansey.

CHILDREN — SEVENTH GENERATION

1474 +Daniel S., b Sept 26, 1827.   1476. Mary Ann, b. Nov. 29, 1831.
1475 +Luther B., b. Dec 4, 1829.

Mary Ann married Charles F. Bowen, of Rehoboth, Mass. They were
residing in East Providence in 1865.

[1447]   ELISHA[6] PECK, of St Johnsbury, Vt., son of PETER,[5]
married Elizabeth Warden, March 17, 1842.   She was born June
28, 1811.

CHILDREN — SEVENTH GENERATION

1477. Mary Ann E , b May 19, 1845.   1479. George H., b Dec. 18, 1849.
       Died June 13, 1845   Died Sept 1, 1852.
1478. Emeline E , b Feb 27, 1847.   * Azro M., b. Sept. 28, 1854.
       Died June 9, 1847.

[1451.]   SIMON[6] PECK, of St. Johnsbury, Vt., son of PETER,[5]
married Emily Chickering.

CHILDREN — SEVENTH GENERATION

1480. Helen, b Aug 27, 1848.   1482. Lilis, b. Jan. 5, 1852
1481. Charles, b. March 17, 1850.

[1461]   OBED[7] PECK, son of OBED,[6] settled in Windsor,
Vt. He married Sarah Hendricson.

CHILDREN — EIGHTH GENERATION .

1483. Clara.   1484. Mary.

---

* This name was not received until after the names were numbered and
arranged.

[1464] CHARLES[7] PECK, son of SYLVESTER,[6] married Rosetta H. Dix, May 19, 1848, and was residing in Charlemont, N. H., in 1863.

CHILDREN — EIGHTH GENERATION

1485. Charles A.   1487. Frank F.
1486. Sarah E.

[1470.] WILLIAM H.[7] PECK, son of THOMAS,[6] married Sarah A. Marble, of Somerset, Mass, and settled in Providence, R. I., where he was residing in 1863.

CHILDREN — EIGHTH GENERATION ·

1488. Josephine E., b Jan 15, 1856.   1489 Sarah J , b Sept 7, 1860.
        Died June 14, 1863.   1490 Josephine, b Aug 5, 1864.

[1472.] JAMES C.[7] PECK, son of THOMAS,[6] settled in Providence, R. I., where he was residing in 1863. He married Mary A. Kinsley, of Swansey.

CHILDREN — EIGHTH GENERATION

1491. Hattie B , b Feb. 26, 1860.   1492   Allen K , b June 14, 1863.
        Died Dec. 11, 1864.

[1473.] BENJAMIN T.[7] PECK, son of THOMAS,[6] married Louisa J. Davis, of Somerset, Mass. They were residing in Assonet, Mass., in 1863.

CHILD — EIGHTH GENERATION ·

1493. Louisa Adelaide, b. April 12, 1860.

[1474.] DANIEL S.[7] PECK, son of ASA,[6] married Mary J. Sutton; was residing in East Providence in 1865.

CHILD — EIGHTH GENERATION .

1494. One child.

[1475.] LUTHER B.[7] PECK, son of ASA,[6] married Ann F. Wilcox, daughter of George G. Wilcox, and was residing in Providence, R. I , in 1865.

CHILD — EIGHTH GENERATION

1495. Luther F., b. Feb. 27, 1864.

PART THIRD.

THE DESCENDANTS OF NICHOLAS[2] PECK,

THIRD SON OF JOSEPH[1] THE ANCESTOR.

NICHOLAS PECK was born in England, and baptized there, April 9, 1630, and came over to this country with his father, in 1638, being then about eight years of age. He removed with the family from Hingham, Mass., to Seekonk, since known as Seekonk Plain, in 1645.

After his marriage, Nicholas settled in the southeastern part of Seekonk, near the place now known in that vicinity as Major Monroe's, where he lived and died.

From the records, it appears that he took an active part in public affairs. He was frequently one of the raters (assessors) and select-men of the town. He was elected Deputy to the Court at Plymouth, in 1669. He was also elected Deputy for each successive year, from 1677 to 1690, except in the years 1687 and 1688, when the town elected no deputies. From 1677 to 1684, he is called Ensign Nicholas Peck; after that, Lieutenant, and then Captain.

He died May 27, 1710. His will may be found recorded at Taunton, Mass., B. 3, p. 3.

The following is a copy:

In the name of God Amen I Nicholas Peck of the town of Reho-both in the County of Bristol in her Majesties Provinces of the Massachusetts Bay in New England being aged & infirm of body yet having perfect memory & understanding blessed be God for it Do make this my last will and Testament for the disposing the things of this world with which the Lord hath entrusted me to and amongst my children in manner and form as followeth

Item I give and bequeath to my son Joseph Peck two acres & half of salt marsh at the hundred acres begining at that end of my meadow next to the swamp & so to run from the ditch to Jeremiah Wheatons bounds Likewise the one half of my lot of land lying on the east side of the mill river near Nathaniel Reads and my swoid wch I commonly wear said lands and meadows to be and remain to him and his heirs and assigns for ever

Item I give unto my son Hezekiah Peck half my meadow and swamp at bushy meadow and my sixth allotment drawn in the Rehoboth North purchased lands which appears by record to be & remain to him & his heirs and assigns for ever

Item I give to my son Jonathan Peck half a hundred pounds Estate of commonage in the town of Rehoboth and also my second allotment drawn in Rehoboth north purchased lands as appears by record to be and to remain to him his heirs and assigns for ever

Item I give unto my son Elisha Peck my home lot with ye housing and orchard there on, but not the corn, if any there be on it and my lands in the second division and my wood lot near the forty acres & the other half of my meadow and swamp at bushy meadow & the other half of my lot near Natha^l Reads & my lands on the great plain and half a hundred pounds estate of commonage in Rehoboth; also my share of meadow in the north purchased lands to be and remain unto him his heirs and assigns forever hereby obliging him not to sell mortgage convey or any ways to alienate any of ye above s^d parcels of land or meadows or any part of them without the consent of two of his brothers if living Also I give to my son Elisha Peck my cart plough and yokes

Item I give the remaining part of my salt meadow at ye hundred acres and my undivided right in the North purchased lands equally to be divided amongst my four sons to them and their heirs and assigns forever

Item I give unto my daughter Mary Smith wife to Ensign Joshua Smith the bed on which I lodge & the rugg & two blankets bolster and pillow & cubbard * . . . platters that stand on it & my chest with . . . likewise I give her mothers wearing apparrel . . . and woolen . . .

Item I give to my daughter Martha wife of . . . feather bed in the bed room th . . .

Item My lawful debts being paid by my Executors here in after

---

* Illegible — the leaves worn and crumbled away.

named and my body being deacently burried funeral charges defrayed my will is that the rest and residue of my estate be equally divided amongst my five children

Item   I do appoint ordain & constitute my son Joseph Peck & my son Jonathan Peck to be executors of this my last will & testament hereby revoking all other wills by me before made

In testimony where of I have here unto set my hand and seal this second day of October in the year of our Lord God One thousand and seven hundred and seven & in the sixth year of her Majesties Reign

Signed sealed and published In the presence of us witnesses

SAMUEL PECK
JOHN BUTTERWORTH   NICHOLAS PECK
DANIEL SMITH

His inventory was presented to the judge October 25, 1710.

Nicholas was twice married. His first wife, Mary, died November 6, 1657. His second wife, Rebecah, died November 2, 1704 (Rehoboth Rec, B. 1).

His first wife was Mary Winchester, eldest daughter of Alexander Winchester (Plymouth Colony Rec., vol. 3, p. 120). The name of his second wife is unknown.

CHILDREN — THIRD GENERATION:

1496 +Joseph, b Oct 27, 1650
1497. John, b. Aug 8, 1660   Died
         Aug 16, 1660
1498 +Hezekiah, b April 1, 1662
1499 Mary, b Sept 15, 1664

1500 +Jonathan, b Nov 5, 1666.
1501   Nicholas, b June 6, 1669. Died
         Jan 1690-1
1502.+Elisha, b April 11, 1673.

Mary married Ensign Joshua Smith.

Nicholas died January 1690-1 He was a corporal under Capt Gallup, in the expedition against Canada, in the old French war His cousin, Ichabod, died in the same expedition, upon the island of Anticosti

[1496]   JOSEPH[3] PECK, son of NICHOLAS,[2] settled near his father. His wife was Martha ——.

CHILDREN — FOURTH GENERATION (R Rec., B 1, p 63)

1503   Mary, b July 27, 1686
1504   Joseph, b May 2, 1689. Died
         May 14, 1689.
1505 +Joseph, b May 27, 1690
1506 +Nicholas, b Aug 10, 1693.
1507. Elizabeth, b Sept 4, 1695 Died
         Dec 27, 1707.

1508   Israel, b. Nov. 18, 1697. Unknown.
1509 +Stephen, b Jan 1, 1701 2.
         Baptized June 14, 1702.
1510. Lydia, b Nov 8, 1704. Baptized June 17, 1705
1511. Margaret, b Sept 28, 1706.
         Baptized Oct 13, 1706.

John Butterworth was appointed guardian for Margaret, and Peter Hunt, for Lydia, February 1722   Joseph and Nicholas were appointed administrators.   The inventory was presented to the court, October 8, 1720.

[1498.]   HEZEKIAH³ PECK, son of NICHOLAS,² at first settled near his father.   He sold his lands here to Ephraim May, July 16, 1705.   After this he resided for some time in Swansey, and then removed to Attleborough, Mass., and settled where his son, his grandson, and his great-grandson have since lived and died.

The farm is now owned by Mr. Capron Peck, his great-great-grandson, having now been in the name more than one hundred and fifty years.   Its location is about one-half mile northwest from the depot of the Boston and Providence Railroad, as it passes through the town.   He married Deborah Cooper.   They were buried near his residence, the place afterwards becoming the family burial ground.

The following are the inscriptions upon their tombstones.

Here lies yᵉ Body of Mʳ Hezekiah Peck who departed this life August yᵉ 9ᵗʰ 1723 in yᵉ 62ⁿᵈ year of his age

Here lies yᵉ Body of Mʳˢ Deborah Peck Relict of Mʳ Hezekiah Peck decᵈ March yᵉ 5ᵗʰ 1730 in yᵉ 72ⁿᵈ year of her age

CHILDREN — FOURTH GENERATION

1512   Deborah, b Sept 18, 1687.
1513   Judith, b Aug 13, 1690.
1514   Hannah, b Oct 20, 1692
1515 +Hezekiah, b Feb 22, 1695-6.
        Baptized April 5, 1696
1516   Rachel, b April 18, 1698 Baptized June 19, 1698
1517 +John, b * —— Baptized Oct. 13, 1700
1518.   Patronella,† b April 8, 1707   Baptized April 17, 1709
1519   Perthenia, b July 10, 1711.

Hannah, it is supposed, married John Sweet, January 22, 1718–19 (A. Rec , B 2, p. 46)

Rachel, it is supposed, married Benjamin Freeman, July 3, 1718 (A. Rec., B. 2, p 60)

---

* Probably born in Swansey, and for that reason not recorded with the rest of the family in Rehoboth and Attleborough   That he was one of the family, may be seen upon the Taunton Records, B 20, p 281, and B. 6, p. 384   His tombstone may be found in the family burying ground

† The orthography of these two last names is different as they occur in various places upon record

Patronella married Ebenezer Blake, December 11, 1729 (A. Rec , B 2, p 88)

Perthenia married Jonathan Willard, October 29, 1734 (A Rec , B 2, p 113)

Hezekiah was appointed guardian for Paterneile and Parthenia, June 25, 1725 (T. Rec , B. 5, p 106).

[1500.] JONATHAN[3] PECK, son of NICHOLAS,[2] settled upon what has since been known as Peck's Hill, a rise of ground on the present road from Bristol to Warren, R. I., and about two miles from the former place. He became possessed of large tracts of land, extending, as I am told, from the summit of the hill southwardly, including what has since become the estate of William D. Wolf; and from Peck's Rock, across the Neck, so called, to Little's Narrows, a tract of superior land, and beautifully situated. This land has now mostly been disposed of by his descendants, and comprises valuable farms. The homestead, however, remained in the name until about 1838. The old house has recently been taken down.

He married Elizabeth Throop She presented the inventory of his estate to the Judge of Probate, July 3, 1717 (T. Rec , B. 3, p. 160).

CHILDREN * — FOURTH GENERATION

1520 +Jonathan, b Sept 12, 1698.　1522 +William, b. Nov 1702
1521 　Nicholas, b Nov 11, 1700　1523 　Isaac, b 1703 Died young
　　　　Died Sept 20, 1730, unm　1524 　Elizabeth, b. 1707
　　　　(B. Rec , B 2, p. 8)　　　1525 +Thomas, b 1711

Elizabeth sold her interest in her father's estate to her brother Jonathan, December 16, 1728 (T Rec , B 18, p 333).

A guardian was appointed for Thomas, February 23, 1728 (T Rec , B 6, p 69)

[1502] ELISHA[3] PECK, son of NICHOLAS,[2] is supposed to have at first settled upon the homestead. He afterwards moved to Attleborough, and from there he is supposed to have removed to Providence, R I. He married Martha Lake, February 1703–4.

---

* There were other children in this family, who died young. (See Bristol Records.)

1526   Martha, b Oct 13, 1705
1527. Jaiel, b June 1, 1707 Baptized July 13, 1707.
1528. Jerusha, b Jan 1, 1708-9
1529. Eunice, b March 12, 1710-11.
1530   Inspertion, b. Feb 22, 1712-13

1531 +Constantine, b May 26, 1715
1532   Martha, b April 8, 1717
1533 +Nicholas, b April 30, 1719
1534. May, b Aug 31, 1724
1535. Elijah, b. Sept 7, 1729   Unknown.

This family mostly died young   The four last children were born in Attleborough.

[1505.] JOSEPH[4] PECK, son of JOSEPH,[3] resided in the southeasterly part of Rehoboth. He was twice married : first, to Rebecca Brown, daughter of Jabez Brown ; second, to Hannah ——. He died January 6, 1741–2. Hannah, his widow, was appointed administratrix upon his estate, April 20, 1742, and guardian for his daughter Mary, March 20, 1743–4 (T. Rec., B. 10, p. 407). A guardian was appointed for Jerusha and Winchester, they being above the age of fourteen years, May 1742 (T. Rec , B. 10, p. 155). A division of the estate between the widow and children was made October 1745 (T. Rec., B. 11, p. 65).

1536   Jerusha, b. Nov 18, 1724
1537 +Winchester, b Oct 31, 1726.
1538   Mary, b May 17, 1737

1539. Jabez, b Aug 20, 1738   Died 1743

Jerusha married Rev Peleg Heath, of Barrington, December 8, 1743 (Bar Rec , B. 1, p 172). She afterwards married Joshua Bicknell, father of Joshua Bicknell, Judge of the Supreme Court of R. I.

Mary died unm.

[1506.] NICHOLAS[4] PECK, son of JOSEPH,[3] resided in the westerly part of Rehoboth. He married Hannah, daughter of Samuel Peck. See the will of Samuel (T. Rec., B. 8, p. 367).

1540. Joseph, b April 30, 1723. Unknown
1541. Elizabeth, b Aug 22, 1724
1542. Hannah, b. March 10, 1726

1543. Comfort, b Aug 15, 1728. Unknown
1544. Margaret, b. May 18, 1730.

[1509.] STEPHEN[4] PECK, son of JOSEPH,[3] settled near his father. His wife, before marriage, was Rebecca Sweetland, of Attleborough, Mass.

CHILDREN — FIFTH GENERATION

1545 +Nicholas.	1549 Rebecca.
1546 Joseph	1550 Anna.
1547 Betty	1551 Molly
1548 Lydia	

Joseph died at sea, unm
Betty, it is supposed, married a Toogood, of Barrington
Lydia married a Jackson, settled in Cornish, N H.
Rebecca married Caleb Fuller; settled in Pomfret, Conn
Anna married John Greenwood, son of Parson Greenwood, of Seekonk
Molly married Simeon Bowen, of Seekonk.

[1515.] HEZEKIAH[4] PECK, son of HEZEKIAH,[3] settled upon the homestead, where he lived and died. His wife, before marriage, was Elizabeth Carder

The following is from his tombstone:

Mr Hezekiah Peck died in ye year 1753 in ye 58th year of his age
Blessed are the dead that die in ye Lord

His son Hezekiah was appointed administrator, September 3, 1753 (T Rec, B. 13, p. 466).

CHILDREN — FIFTH GENERATION (A Rec, B 2, p 89)

1552 Mary, b Aug 1, 17— Died 23d of same month	1557 Jonathan, b June 21, 1737, no issue
1553 Mary, b July 15, 1728	1558 +Joseph, b Dec 30, 1741
1554 +Hezekiah, b May 7, 1732	1559 Hannah, b Oct 13, 1744 Died unm, Jan 6, 1826.
1555. Jonathan, b April 6, 1734 Died young	1560 Nicholas, b Aug 21, 1747 Died March 29, 1751
1556. Elizabeth, b June 15, 1736 Died unm, Nov 1809	1561 Nicholas, b Sept 11, 1751. Suppose died young

Mary married Daniel Shepherdson.

[1517.] JOHN[4] PECK, son of HEZEKIAH,[3] remained upon the homestead with his brother Hezekiah. A division of the lands left them by their father was made March 14, 1729–30 (T Rec., B. 19, p. 343). His will is dated March 14, 1729–30 (T. Rec., B. 6, p. 384).

He gives to Rebecca his wife, whom he makes his executrix, all his outlands and common rights, with all his household goods and mov-

12*

ables, to enable her to provide for his child or children. He gives to his beloved son John, two-thirds of his homestead lands, and house, and the other third part to his child, then unborn, freely to possess, enjoy, etc. (T. Rec., B. 6, p. 384).

The following is from his tombstone:

In Memory of Mr John Peck who De^{cd} March ye 22^d 1730 in ye 30th year of his Age

He married Rebecca Richardson, May 26, 1724. She survived him, and afterwards, I am told, married a man by the name of Jones.*

CHILDREN — FIFTH GENERATION (A. Rec., B 2, p 67)

1562 +John, b June 13, 1725
1563. Hannah, b Feb 10, 1726 Died
　　　Aug 9th following.
1564   Rebecah, b Feb. 6, 1727 Died
　　　21st of same month.
1565.+Abial, b May 19, 1730.

[1520.] JONATHAN⁴ PECK, son of JONATHAN,³ remained upon the homestead. He became wealthy. He was twice married · first, to Hannah Wood, of Little Compton; and second, to Hannah Lam. His first wife died June 11, 1730. His second wife died August 11, 1756, in the 50th year of her age. He died February 25, 1757.

CHILDREN — FIFTH GENERATION (B Rec , B 2, p 153)

1566. Rebecca, b. Sept 26, 1721
1567   John, b April 24, 1723   Died young
568 +Jonathan, b Jan 4, 1724–5
1569   Nicholas, b March 14, 1726–7. Died young
1570   Hannah, b Feb 20, 1728–9.
1571   Deborah, b Feb 23, 1732–3
1572   Elizabeth, b 1734
1573 +Thomas, b June 24, 1736
1574   Sarah, b Feb 11, 1737–8
1575   Lydia, b March 16, 1739–40
1576   Mary, b Dec 30, 1741
1577   Abigail, b May 11, 1743 Died unm
1578 +Loring, b Jan 19, 1744–5
1579   Nathaniel, b Dec 3, 1746. Died Oct 22, 1756

* She deeded her interest in the common lands in Attleborough, to Hezekiah Peck   The deed is now in the possession of Caption Peck, the great-grandchild of Hezekiah, dated the nineteenth day of May, in the year of our Lord one thousand seven hundred and thirty-one, and in the fourth year of the reign of our Sovereign Lord George the 2d, by the grace of God King of Great Britain, France and Ireland, Defender of the faith, etc.

Hannah married Jonathan Fales, of Bristol.
Deborah Married Samuel Gray, October 25, 1750.
Elizabeth married Samuel Bosworth.
Sarah married Simon Martindale.
Lydia married Nathaniel Peckham and Nathaniel Pierce.
Mary married Benjamin Simons.

[1522.] WILLIAM[4] PECK, son of JONATHAN,[3] settled in New Haven, Conn., where he remained for some time. He returned to Bristol, R. I., and from there removed to Dighton, Mass. I learn but little in relation to him. By the records, he appears to have been three times married: first, to Elizabeth Throop, who died April 18, 1731; second, to Elizabeth ———, who died November 12, 1740; third, to Rebecca Talbott.

CHILDREN — FIFTH GENERATION.

Elizabeth, b Sept 15, 1726.
Mary, b Dec 3, 1727.
Martha, b Feb 1, 1730
Nicholas, b. March 23, 1731-2.

*Benjamin, b. Sept. 13, 1740.
1580 Seth
1581. Chloe.

Seth married Elizabeth Peck (No 1588), daughter of Deacon Thomas, and settled in Northern Massachusetts He died in Northfield His daughter *Chloe*[6] and the widow afterwards resided at Brattleborough, Vt.

[1525.] DEACON THOMAS[4] PECK, son of JONATHAN,[3] settled in Swansey. He married Mary Kinsley, only daughter of Jonathan Kinsley, of Rehoboth. He died February 9, 1770. She survived him about thirty-four years, and died, May 27, 1804, in her 92d year. She was a very noted and celebrated midwife, to which profession she devoted many years. Her practice was very extensive. The following is from her tombstone:

Here lies the remains of that reliegeous and most faithful Midwife Mary wife of Dean Thos Peck died May 27 1804 Aged 91 years

His tombstone bears the following inscription:

In Memory of Deacon Thomas Peck, who Decd Febry the 9th. ADom. 1770. In the 59th. Year of his Age.
>   Stand still kind reader, spend a Tear
>   Upon the dust that slumbers hear,
>   And whilst you read, the fate of me
>   Think on the Glass that runs for The

---

* The above children were found too late to be numbered and entered in the index.

1582 +Jonathan, b Jan 17, 1734.
1583 +Peleg, b March 6, 1736
1584 May, b Oct 20, 1738
1585 +Thomas, b March 21, 1740-1.
1586 +Aaron, b Jan 20, 1743-4
1587 +Ambrose, b Nov 17, 1747
1588. Elizabeth.

Elizabeth married her cousin, Seth Peck, the son of William, November 15, 1780.

Mary married Zepheniah Carpenter

[1531.] CONSTANTINE⁴ PECK, son of ELISHA,³ it is supposed, settled in Attleborough. He married Prescilla ———. I have been able to learn but little in relation to him or his family.

CHILDREN — FIFTH GENERATION (R Rec , B 2, p 150)

1589 Jael, b Sept 1, 1737.
1590 Susannah, b May 13, 1738
1591. Benoni, b Nov. 25, 1739. Died young
1592 Abraham, b May 30, 1742 Died June 7, 1747
1593. Inspersion, b July 6, 1745. Died young
1594. Nicholas, b Oct 2, 1746 Died Nov 7, 1747
1595 Elisha, b Nov 25, 1747
1596 Eleazer, b March 7, 1750
1597 Martha, b Aug 8, 1752
1598.+Abiah, b Dec 18, 1755
1599 Mary, b May 19, 1758
1600 Gersham, b July 20, 1760
1601 Anne, b June 10, 1762

Elisha is supposed to have settled in Providence, R I , and married Freelove Knight, of Cranston, March 11, 1773 (P Rec , B 2, p 39)
Eleazer is supposed to have resided in Providence, and to have married Elizabeth Tift, of Cranston, October 20, 1771 (P Rec , B 2, p 39).

[1533.] NICHOLAS⁵ PECK, son of ELISHA.⁴ I learn but little in relation to him. He is supposed to have married Hannah Sprague, of Smithfield, R. I., June 1, 1739.

CHILDREN — SIXTH GENERATION

1602. Jerusha, b Feb 11, 1741
1603 Hannah, b Sept 4, 1739.
Hannah married Nathaniel Jillson, of Cumberland, R I

[1537.] WINCHESTER⁵ PECK, son of JOSEPH,⁴ is supposed to have settled upon the homestead in the southeasterly part of Seekonk. He married Mary Michels, daughter of James Michels, who, it is said, emigrated to this country from France. She was born August 20, 1731. After the decease of Winchester, she married Nathaniel Peck (No. 3385).

CHILDREN — SIXTH GENERATION .

1604 +Joseph, b. Dec. 11, 1750
1605 Mary.

[1545.] NICHOLAS[5] PECK, son of STEPHEN,[4] settled in the southeasterly part of Seekonk. He married Jerusha ——.

CHILDREN — SIXTH GENERATION (P. Rec , B 3, p 242)

1606	Anna, b April 18, 1760. Died young	
1607.	Stephen, b July 18, 1762. No issue.	
1608	+Nicholas, b June 24, 1764.	
1609	Deborah, b March 2, 1767.	
1610	+James, b Aug 20, 1769	
1611	Betty, b Dec 18, 1771.	
1612	+Joseph, b Aug 16, 1775	
1613	+Joshua, b Feb 28, 1777.	
1614.	+Winchester, b Oct. 1781	

Deborah[5] married Daniel Maxwell.

[1554.] HEZEKIAH[5] PECK, son of HEZEKIAH,[4] remained upon the homestead, where he lived and died. He married Ann Skinner, daughter of Thomas Skinner, of Mansfield, Mass. He died October 14, 1775. She June 14, 1822, in her 89th year.

CHILDREN — SIXTH GENERATION (A Rec , B 2, p 77)

1615	+Hezekiah, b May 22, 1755.	1617 Anna, b Dec 7, 1761
1616	+Henry, b Dec 10, 1756	1618 +Jonathan, b July 29, 1769.

Anna married Manassah Short, of Rehoboth, Mass , where they lived and died Her children were *Manasseh, Jr.,*[7] *Anna,*[7] *Josiah,*[7] *Rhoda,*[7] *Hezekiah P.,*[7] and *Philip* [7]

[1558.] JOSEPH[5] PECK, son of HEZEKIAH,[4] left Attleborough at an early date, and resided for some time in the western part of Massachusetts. I have been unable to find him or his descendants. He moved, I am told, into the State of New York. He married Elizabeth Read, daughter of Deacon Read.

CHILD — SIXTH GENERATION

1619. Esther, b July 10, 1776, in Attleborough

He probably had other children after he left Attleborough

[1562.] JOHN[5] PECK, son of JOHN,[4] at first resided in Attleborough, Mass. He afterwards settled at Pawtucket, R. I., where he owned a forge, and from there removed to New Brunswick, and settled at Shepody, now Hopewell, Albert County, where he remained for several years. He afterwards returned to Attleborough. He was twice married: first, to Hannah Walker, of Seekonk, Mass.; second, to a widow Paddlefoot; and resided near Taunton, where he died, May 19, 1807. His first wife died October 2, 1804.

1620	John Died unmarried.	1623	Hannah
1621	——; was drowned at Paw-	1624	Chloe
	tucket, when young	1625	Polly.
1622	Peter Died unmarried		

Hannah married William Cole, of Seekonk, Mass , and settled in Sterling, Conn

Chloe married Simeon Goff, of Seekonk, Mass , and settled in Surry, Mass.

Polly married Andrew Davison, of New Brunswick, from there they removed to Attleborough, Mass She died at Bethany, aged 74 years To the kindness of her son, *John K Davison,*[7] of Aldenville, Pa , I am indebted for my information in relation to the family.

[1565.]   ABIEL[5] PECK, son of JOHN,[4] married Ruth Skinner, of Attleborough, Mass.   He left Attleborough at an early date, and settled at Cumberland, Nova Scotia   After residing there for some time, he removed to Shepody, now Hopewell, Albert County, New Brunswick, where he obtained a large and extensive grant of land from the government, said to have been about six thousand acres. This land was much of it marsh land, or alluvial soil, overflowed periodically by the spring or high tides.   It is now reclaimed and improved, and is the best and most productive aggricultural part of that country, some of it still remaining in the possession of his descendants, who are wealthy farmers.

Upon the northern bank of the Shepody River, on a kind of promontory that juts out and forms a bend of the river (from which the prospect is very picturesque and beautiful), is the old family or private burial ground.   On one of the tombstones is the following inscription ·

Here lies interred the body of Abiel Peck, a native of Boston,* and one of the first settlers of this place, who, on the 16th day of December, 1802, unfortunately perished in a boat, in the 73d year of his age, leaving upwards of threescore descendants to lament his melancholy fate.

During his life the country was comparatively a wilderness, with no roads or means of communicating with the different settlements

* The father of Abiel died in Attleborough about three months before Abiel was born The widow may have removed to Boston. She afterwards married a Jones.

upon the shores except by water, in boats. It was upon one of these occasions, while attempting to cross the Bay from Cumberland to his own place in an open boat, at that inclement season of the year, that he lost his life. He is represented to have been a man of large stature, great physical strength, and much energy of character.

CHILLDREN — SIXTH GENERATION

1626	Ezra, b Jan 12, 1752	Died	1631	Ruth, b Feb 14, 1761.	
	Jan 13, 1752		1632	Lois, b 1762	
1627	Abiel, b Jan. 1, 1753	Died	1633	+Elisha, b 1763	
	Dec 8, 1754		1634	+Thomas, b 1767	
1628	Rachel, b May 6, 1754		1635	Rhoda, b June 1769	
1329	+Abiel, b May 15, 1756		1636	Nancy, b 1772	
1630	Rebecca, b Aug 7, 1758				

The first six children were born in Attleborough, Mass

Rachel was twice married For her first husband she married Thomas Calhoun, by whom she had two sons *George Calhoun,*[7] *Esq* , Register of Deeds and Wills, and Judge of the Court of Common Pleas for the County of Albert is a grandson For her second husband she married Robert Dickson, by whom she had two sons and eight daughters She died November 5, 1803.

Rebecca married Oliver Stiles, by whom she had five sons and three daughters *Reuben Stiles, Esq* ,[7] for many years a member of the Provincial Parliament of New Brunswick, is a grandson She died in 1850, in Hopewell, Albert County

Ruth died unmarried, aged about 20 years

Lois married Joel Edgett, by whom she had sons and daughters She died in 1826

Rhoda married John Edgett, by whom she had sons and daughters She died in 1857

Nancy married Nicholas Pearson, by whom she had sons and daughters. She died in Hopewell, Albert County.

[1568.] JONATHAN[5] PECK, son of JONATHAN,[4] resided upon the homestead. He was an active and industrious farmer. He accumulated a large landed interest in addition to that left him by his father. He married Mary Throop, of Bristol, R. I , June 2, 1757 (B. Rec., B. 2, p. 70 and 81). He died October 7, 1797. She November 6, 1803, aged 66 years.

CHILDREN — SIXTH GENERATION (B Rec , P 2, p. 36)

1637	Abigail, b Aug 14, 1758.	1644	Lydia, b March 16, 1771.	
1638	+Jonathan, b June 5, 1760	1645	Hannah, b Feb 8, 1773.	
1639	+Nicholas, b May 6, 1762.	1646	Elizabeth, b Dec 26, 1774.	
1640	+John, b March 2, 1764.	1647	Anna, b Aug 1, 1777. Died	
1641	Sarah, b Feb 19, 1766		Sept 1778	
1642	+Mary, b Sept 28, 1767.	1648.	Nancy, b Aug 29, 1799.	
1643.	William, b March 15, 1769.			
	Died Sept. 8, 1803 , no issue.			

Abigail married George Reynolds, and settled in Amenia, Dutchess County, N Y. Her sons, I am told, are wealthy

Mary married Jonathan Reynolds, and settled in Bristol, R. I   *Samuel Reynolds,*[7] of Boston, and *Jonathan,*[7] of Bristol, are her sons

Sarah married George Ingraham, and settled in Amenia. *George*[7] and *William*[7] are her sons

Lydia married Thomas Richmond   They had but one son, now deceased.

Hannah married Nathaniel Howland. ·*Nathaniel,*[7] near Grand Rapids, and *Frederick,*[7] who settled at Cleveland, O , are her sons.

Elizabeth married William Reynolds, son of Judge Reynolds, and settled in Bristol, R I   She left one son, *George,*[7] (who was for a long time collector of customs,) and three daughters, *Lydia,*[7] *Mary*[7] and *Betsey* [7]

Nancy married Capt Nathaniel Gladding, and settled at Bristol, R I. *Nathaniel,*[7] and *John,*[7] who settled in Philadelphia, and *Josiah,*[7] of Bristol, were her sons.

[1573] THOMAS[5] PECK, son of JONATHAN,[4] I am told, resided at Bristol, R. I., upon what is known as Popposquash, where he died, August 10, 1795. He married Mary Richmond, December 2, 1762. I learn but little in relation to him.

CHILDREN — SIXTH GENERATION (R Rec , B 2, p 63)

1649 +Samuel Vial, b Oct 22, 1763.
1650 Hannah, b May 29, 1765 Died Sept 28, 1795
1651 +Nathaniel, b March 20, 1767.
1652. Rogers Richmond, b Sept. 19, 1771 Died Oct 20, 1772

[1578.] LORING[5] PECK, son of JONATHAN,[4] resided in Bristol, R. I., until May 1798, when he settled in Amenia, Dutchess County, N. Y. In 1811, he removed to the town of Lake Pleasant, Hamilton County, where he continued to reside until his decease He died at an advanced age.

He was a zealous patriot, and a prominent man during the war of the Revolution, in which, I am told, he held a Colonel's commission. He was a member of the State Legislature many years.

He was twice married: first, to Sarah Richmond, June 4, 1769 ; second, to Jane Burk. His first wife died April 20, 1774. His second wife died in 1824. He died July 29, 1833.

CHILDREN — SIXTH GENERATION

1653 Henry Died young
1654 Richmond Died young
1655 +William B , b Aug 27, 1788, he was by second wife
1656 Loring, b March 17, 1782. Died unm May 5, 1861.
1657. Sarah, b Dec 24, 1784
1658 Frances, b July 16, 1786.
1659 +George, b Feb 13, 1788.
1660 +Henry, b April 2, 1791
1661.+Richard, b Oct 9, 1792

Sarah was residing at Sharon Springs in 1866, a widow She has been twice married first to Harry Hutchinson, second, to Barnabas Eldredge She has no issue living She is a lady of superior intellect and attainments She is a member of the church, much beloved and respected

Frances married Rev William Swayze She died at McConnelsville, O., a widow, in 1864.

[1582.] JONATHAN[5] PECK, son of THOMAS,[4] resided in the south part of Rehoboth, where he kept a public house many years. He married Ruth Wheeler, February 22, 1759 (R. Rec., B. 3).

CHILDREN — SIXTH GENERATION (R Rec , B 3, p 108)

1662 +Jonathan, b Sept 19, 1759
1663 +Rufus, b Nov 11, 1761
1664   Candice, b March 25, 1764.
1665 +Gideon, b Aug 2, 1766.
1666 +Ambros, b Jan 31, 1769.
1667 +Philip, b. Oct. 3, 1771

1668   Ruth, b Dec 10, 1776. Died Nov 3, 1778
1669. Noah, b April 27, 1774. Died at sea, no issue
1670   Ruth, b Sept 15, 1778
1671 +William, b Dec 31, 1780.
1672 +Sylvanus, b April 21, 1784.

Candice married Capt. Richard Pierce, and settled in Sudbury, Vt.
Ruth married Amos Wright, of Warren, R I.

[1583.] PELEG[5] PECK, son of THOMAS,[4] resided in Swansey, where he was one of the leading men of the town. He early took an active interest in military affairs. He held a commission under the Colonial Government, issued by Thomas Hutchinson, Esq., "Captain General and Governor in Chief in and over His Majesties Provinces of Massachusetts Bay, and vice Admiral of the same, dated September 4th in the 12 year of the Reign of his Majestie King George the third. Annoque Domini 1772."

This commission was in the possession of his son, Deacon Benjamin Peck, of Rehoboth, Mass., in 1863.

After the commencement of the Revolutionary War, he was a zealous patriot, acting as agent in raising soldiers, etc. He held a Captain's commission of one of the military companies of Swansey.

The following is a copy which I was permitted to make of one of his orders·

SWANSEY, July 8, 1778.
To the Sergents and Corporals of the 2d Foot Company in Swansey.

You are hereby required forthwith to examine the arms and other equipments of both the training band and alarm list within your di-
13

trict, and if there be any delinquents, you are to return their names to me, that they may be returned to General Sullivan, agreeable to express orders from him bearing date the 7th inst. Here of faile not and make return of this with your doings, as you will answer it at your peril.

Peleg Peck Cpt

He entered the army, where he is said to have been an active and brave officer. He was twice married : first, to Phebe Mason, daughter of Hezekiah Mason, of Swansey ; second, to Mary Thornton, widow of Stephen Thornton, formerly Mary Salsbury, daughter of Martin Salsbury, of Cranston, R. I. His first wife died July 23, 1778. He died June 1807. His second wife died April 11, 1841.

CHILDREN — SIXTH GENERATION

1673 Hannah, b March 17, 1757. Died unm
1674 William, b Oct 30, 1758. Died in the army a lieutenant, unm
1675 Mary, b May 5, 1760
1676 +Nicholas, b Jan 9, 1762.
1677 Betsy, b. Aug 12, 1763 } twins
1678 Phebe, b Aug 12, 1763 }
1679 Rebecah, b Aug 19, 1765
1680 +Thomas, b. Feb 12, 1767
1681 +Hezekiah, b Oct 27, 1768
1682 +Seth, b. June 13, 1770.
1683 Sarah, b Feb 21, 1772
1684 Diana, b Dec 26, 1774.
1685 +Peleg, b. May 5, 1776
1686. Ruth, b April 29, 1778
1687 Abigail, b July 22, 1782, by 2d wife Died young.
1688 Olive, b Feb 2, 1784
1689. Cranston, b Jan. 2, 1786.
1690 +Salsbury, b Feb 19, 1788.
1691 +Benjamin, b June 3, 1790.

Mary married William Davis, settled in Rehoboth
Betsy married Aaron Peckham, settled in Rehoboth
Phebe married Salsbury Wheeler, of Bristol, removed to N H
Rebecah married Lewis Wade, of Rehoboth
Sarah married Daniel Newman, of Rehoboth.
Diana married Peter Peck (No 1415), and settled at St Johnsbury, Vt.
Ruth married Stephen Martain, of Warren, R 1
Olive married David Kinsley, of Rehoboth, September 22, 1811

[1585.] THOMAS[5] PECK, son of THOMAS,[4] settled first in Swansey, then in Bristol, where he lived and died. He married Elizabeth Sanford. She died July 12, 1798. He February 29, 1812.

1692   Ruth, b. Oct. 17, 1767. Died young.

1693.   Waite, b March 25, 1769 Died unm.

1694.   Martha, b Oct 4, 1771, married E. Monroe, of Bristol.

1695 +George B , b. Feb. 16, 1778

[1586.] AARON[5] PECK, son of THOMAS,[4] settled in Providence, R. I. He was a merchant. The store which he occupied was on North Main Street. The house where he resided was standing, opposite the court house, upon Benefit Street, in 1862. He was married three times: first, to Alsey Arnold, June 18, 1767, daughter of Jeremiah Arnold, of Smithfield, born April 4, 1747; second, to Amey Spencer, of North Kingston (P. Rec , B. 2, pp. 31 and 188); third, to Widow Rachel Chase.

1696   David, b Sept 27, 1767. Can learn little in relation to him.

1697.   Lydia, b Oct 29, 1769.

1698   Amey, b. Aug 6, 1772

1699   Nancy, b. April 12, 1775.

1700   Candice, b. Sept. 14, 1777. Died young

1701 +Aaron, b June 5, 1779

1702.   Alsey, b Jan 20, 1784. Died unm

1703.   Benjamin, b June 27, 1785. Died unm.

1704.   Mary, b. Oct. 15, 1786   Died young

1705.   John S , b. Feb 26, 1789. Died at sea unm.

1706   Samuel, b March 29, 1790. Died young

1707   Elizabeth, b Sept 25, 1791. Died young.

Amey married Edward Knowles, of Providence, March 24, 1793, where she died, October 24, 1838. He died January 11, 1811. Their children were *Joseph B* ,[7] who resides in Nashville, Tenn , *James D* ,[7] who died in Newton, Mass , a Professor in the Baptist Theological Seminary, *Henry*,[7] *Edward P* ,[7] and *John P* ,[7] of Providence, and *Amey Ann*,[7] who married William S Humphrey

There were also two children who died in infancy.

Nancy married James Davis, and settled in Watertown, Mass.

[1587.] AMBROS[5] PECK, son of THOMAS,[4] lived and died in the westerly part of Swansey. He was a cabinet-maker by trade. He married Polly Lindley.

1708 +Robert, b Jan 10, 1782

1709.   Betsey, b Nov 13, 1785

1710   Erasmus, b Aug 28, 1786.

1711 +Danforth L , b. June 11, 1789.

1712   Nancy, b Aug 27, 1791   }

1713.   Polly, b Aug. 27, 1791   }

        Twins

1714.   Abby, b Sept 2, 1792. Died young.

148   PECK GENEALOGY, — PART THIRD.

Betsey married Samuel Luther.
Nancy married John Davis.
Polly died unmarried.

[1598.] ABIAH⁵ PECK, son of CONSTANTINE ⁴ I have been unable to learn anything of him, excepting what I find upon the town records. His wife was Hannah ———,

CHILDREN — SIXTH GENERATION

1715   Joel, b Dec. 4, 1775   1716. Joseph, b. Feb. 1787

[1604.] JOSEPH⁶ PECK, son of WINCHESTER,⁵ settled in Providence, R. I, where he became engaged in trade, and where he lived and died. During the great fire in 1800, his store, and much other property, was burned. He afterwards erected upon the same ground, the brick building now standing on the east side of South Main Street, between Star and Power Streets.

He married Sarah Hacker, daughter of Joshua Hacker, of Newport, R. I.

CHILDREN — SEVENTH GENERATION

1717   Sarah, b. May 6, 1784.   1719   Ann, b. Sept 1, 1790
1718   Maria H , b June 11, 1788   1720   William, b. Dec 6, 1796

Sarah was residing in Providence in 1864, unmarried
Ann died unmarried.
William died unmarried.
Maria H married John P Jones, of Providence, where she was residing, a widow, with her daughter, the wife of C N. Caswell, in 1864.

[1608.] NICHOLAS⁶ PECK, son of NICHOLAS,⁵ married Molly Maxwell, of Bristol, R. I. He left Rhode Island, and settled at Pharsalia, Chenango County, N. Y., and from there removed to Trout Creek, Delaware County, where he died. I have been able to learn little in relation to him.

CHILDREN — SEVENTH GENERATION

1721. Daniel   1725   Lydia
1722. William.   1726   Polly
1723   Nicholas.   1727. Thursa.
1724   Jerusha.

Polly married Joseph Dare, and was residing a widow near Trout Creek in 1866   *S G Peck*, a grandson of *Nicholas*, was also residing there, but neither of them would give me any information in relation to the family   Whether there was anything that they were unwilling to have known I do not know. I could get nothing from them.

[1610] JAMES[6] PECK, son of NICHOLAS,[5] married Olive Armington, daughter of John Armington, of Seekonk.

CHILDREN — SEVENTH GENERATION

1728 +Israel, b Oct 22, 1794
1729 Rebecca, b Feb 13, 1798
1730 +William, b. April 1, 1800
1731 Prudence, b Sept 26, 1801
1732 +John, b Jan 1, 1805
1733 Almira, b April 8, 1807.
1734. Betsey, b June 21, 1810.
1735 +Joseph, b Oct 9, 1813.
1736 Sarah, b Oct 23, 1817.
1737 Polly.
1738 Samuel

I am told that *Polly* and *Samuel* died in infancy
The members of the family disagreed as to the time of each others' births
I have given the most of them as furnished me by Mrs Almira Barney.
Rebecca married Joseph Maxwell
Prudence married first, Joseph Barney, second, Samuel Potter
Almira married Jonathan Barney
Betsey married first, John Elliott, and second, William Pearsons.
Sarah married Charles Barney.

[1612.] JOSEPH[6] PECK, son of NICHOLAS,[5] settled in Bristol, R I, where he lived and died. He was married: first, to Abigail Maxwell, daughter of David Maxwell, of Bristol, second, to Esther Goff, daughter of James Goff, of Bristol, third, to Mary Bosworth, of Barrington.

CHILDREN — SEVENTH GENERATION

1739 +Stephen, b Nov 16, 1804
1740 Abby, b. 1812.
Abby married Benjamin Usher, of Bristol

[1613] JOSHUA[6] PECK, son of NICHOLAS,[5] resided for some time in Bristol. From there he removed to Smithfield, R. I., where he died. He was married: first, to Hannah Bowen; second, to Nancy Briggs; third, to Sarah Drown. His first wife died April 12, 1806. His second wife died May 17, 1807. His third wife died August 12, 1863. He died October 25, 1849.

CHILDREN — SEVENTH GENERATION

1741 Ann. Died Dec 20, 1806, aged 18 months
1742 +Benjamin D , b April 1813
1743 +Samuel D , b Feb 17, 1818
1744 +Nicholas T , b March 23, 1821.
1745 Jerusha T , b Sept 16, 1815.
1746 Rebecca J., b March 7, 1824.
Jerusha married Albert Sweet, of Smithfield, R I
Rebecca married Abel Hobert, of East Douglas, Mass.

13*

[1614.] WINCHESTER[6] PECK, son of NICHOLAS,[5] married Thressay W. Maxwell, of Bristol, R. I., daughter of David Maxwell. He died May 8, 1859. She died April 8, 1847.

CHILDREN — SEVENTH GENERATION

1747. Hannah B , b Jan 25, 1811.
      Died Feb 7, 1849
1748 Thressay M , b Nov. 15, 1813.
      Died Sept 12, 1844
1749 +Hezekiah M , b Sept 4, 1816

1750 Ann B , b Jan 10, 1820
1751. Betsey M , b July 13, 1822.
1752 Anne E , b May 18, 1830
1753. Isabella M., b May 7, 1832.

Hannah B married Horace Viol, of Warren, R I.
Thressay M married Joseph Furna, of Warren, R I.
Ann B married Henry Butts, October 12, 1840
Betsey M married Joseph Sawfell, November 25, 1847
Anne E married Charles S Sisson, October 2, 1856
Isabella M married William H Surgens, January 23, 1853

[1615.] HEZEKIAH[6] PECK, son of HEZEKIAH,[5] left Attleborough, Mass , at an early date, and settled in Newport, N. H. He and his brother purchased lands there of Phineas Willcox, May 1, 1779. (See Records at Keene, N H., B. 22, p. 614.) He married Hepsibah Dryer, of Rehoboth, Mass. He died at Newport, aged 57 years.

CHILD — SEVENTH GENERATION

1754 Esther
      She married Daniel Nettleton, and died, leaving one daughter *Esther*

[1616.] HENRY[6] PECK, son of HEZEKIAH,[5] left Attleborough, Mass , at an early date, and settled near his brother at Newport, N. H. From here he removed to Lowville, Lewis County, N. Y., where he died, June 11, 1838. He married Ann Richardson, daughter of Seth Richardson, of Attleborough, January 18, 1781. She was born April 1, 1760, and died August 26, 1840.

CHILDREN — SEVENTH GENERATION

1755 +Henry, b Nov 12, 1781.
1756 +Dexter, b July 10, 1783
1757 +Seth, b April 10, 1785
1758 +Calvin, b May 14, 1787.
1759 +Hezekiah, b. May 28, 1790

1760. Nancy, b June 11, 1793
1761 Abigail, b June 1, 1795
1762 Hannah, b Nov 13, 1798
1763 Elioenor, b Oct 8, 1801.
1764 +Silas, b. Dec 6, 1803

Abigail married a Thomas, and settled in St Lawrence County, N. Y.
Nancy was residing in Harrisburgh, N Y , in 1864, unmarried
Hannah married Joseph Chadwick, and settled at West Lowville, N Y.
Elioenor married Lester Weller, and settled at Harrisburgh, N Y. To her kindness I am indebted for my information in relation to the family.

[1618.] JONATHAN[6] PECK, son of HEZEKIAH,[5] remained upon the homestead of his ancestors, where he lived and died much respected. He married Sabra Capron, daughter of Joseph Capron. He died February 9, 1850. She November 2, 1853.

CHILDREN — SEVENTH GENERATION ·

1765. Capron, b. Feb 4, 1797.
1766. Willard, b Feb 19, 1801. Died young.

1767 Hezekiah, b. July 11, 1807. Died young
1768 Lattimer, b. Dec. 4, 1815. Died young

[1629.] ABIEL[6] PECK, son of ABIEL,[5] resided in Shepody, now Hopewell, Albert County, New Brunswick, where he died, October 28, 1814. He married Lois Esterbrooks. He was a wealthy farmer. He settled upon a part of the extensive tract of land owned by his father. He held a captaincy in the militia, and is always alluded to by the old settlers as Captain Peck.

CHILDREN — SEVENTH GENERATION

1769 +William, b Sept 12, 1781.
1770. Abiel, b. March 24, 1784
1771 Valentine, b May 5, 1786 Died Oct 5, 1786
1772 Lois, b Feb 27, 1788.
1773 Ezra, b Dec 28, 1790.

1774 Anna, b. July 29, 1793. Died Sept 13, 1793
1775 Ruth, b Jan 5, 1795
1776 Sarah, b May 10, 1797.
1777 +James, b Nov 5, 1800
1778 Caroline, b Nov. 26, 1802.
1779 Amy, b Nov 21, 1806.

Abiel was drowned November 28, 1804. He left no issue

Lois was three times married first, to Elijah Calkins, her issue by him being a daughter He died April 29, 1813, in his 30th year. Second, to Thomas Wilbur Her issue by him was a son. After the decease of her second husband, she married Duncan Shaw, by whom she had two sons and one daughter. She died at Hopewell, Albert County, N. B.

Ezra married Margaret Rogers, April 28, 1813, no issue He was residing in the parish of Moncton, Westmoreland County, in 1865.

Ruth married William Hamilton, June 3, 1817, by whom she had three sons and two daughters

Sarah married Stephen Smith, October 17, 1813, by whom she has nine sons and five daughters They were residing in Hopewell in 1865.

Caroline married Johiel Peck, October 17, 1822 They reside in Hopewell (see his record)

Amey married Eben Wilbur, May 3, 1824 They have issue, and resided in Hopewell in 1865

1633.] ELISHA[6] PECK, son of ABIEL,[5] resided in Shepody, since Hopewell, Albert County, New Brunswick. He settled upon a portion of the lands owned by his father. He was a wealthy farmer.　He married Sarah Akerly, a native of the State of New York.　He died December 29, 1846.　He was born in Cumberland, Nova Scotia.

CHILDREN — SEVENTH GENERATION

1780　Elizabeth, b Nov 18, 1787.
1781　Nancy, b June 9, 1789.
1782 +Reuben, b Oct 1790.
1783 +Elisha, b May 11, 1793.
1784 +Elias, b July 5, 1796.
1785　Susannah, b Jan 11, 1798.
1786 +Johiel, b Nov 23, 1799.
1787　Sarah, b Jan 23, 1801
1788 +Abiel, b Jan 11, 1804
1789.　Amey, b Oct 23, 1805.
　　　A son b 1764. Died in infancy.

Elizabeth married John Bennett, January 1808, by whom she had six sons and five daughters　He was a farmer, and died some years since in Hopewell　She was residing there in 1865

Nancy married Joseph Turner, December 9, 1813　Her issue was four sons and four daughters　He is deceased　She was residing in 1865 upon the homestead

Susannah married James Wallace, January 12, 1821, by whom she had three sons and six daughters　He was ordained a Baptist minister in 1825.　He retired in 1864 in consequence of bodily infirmities　He was living in 1865.　Their eldest son, *Isaiah Wallace*,[8] took the degree of A B at Acadia College, Nova Scotia, in June 1855, and was ordained a Baptist minister in 1856.　He was married in 1857　In 1859 the degree of A M was conferred upon him by the college.　Since his ordination he has been actively engaged in the cause of education, pastoral and missionary labors.　He was filling the pastorate of the Baptist church at Lower Granville, Nova Scotia, in 1865

Sarah married first, Duncan Reed, June 1819, by whom she had two sons and two daughters, second, Levi Elliott, June 1830, by whom she also had two sons and two daughters, third, Robert Hoppen, March 17, 1841, by whom she had a son and daughter　*Elisha*,[8] the son by her last husband, graduated " A B " at Acadia College, N S , June 1862.　He then pursued in London, England, a course of Theological studies, after which he returned, and in 1865 was settled as pastor of a Baptist church in Westmoreland County, N. B , in the Parish of Shediac

Amey married Edward Duffy, October 30, 1833, by whom she has six sons and two daughters　He is a farmer, and resides in Coverdale, Albert County, N. B.

[1634.]　THOMAS[6] PECK, son of ABIEL,[5] settled, as did his brothers, in what is now Hopewell, Albert County, New Brunswick, upon the lands given him by his father, where he lived and died a wealthy farmer.　He married Anna Brewster.　He died October 16, 1825.

CHILDREN — SEVENTH GENERATION.

1790　Harriet, b March 24, 1796
1791 +Joseph, b Dec 4, 1798.
1792.　Cynthia, b Jan. 30, 1800. Died in her 18th year.
1793.　Ann, b. Nov. 9, 1801.
1794　Margaret, b Feb 17, 1803.
1795 +Thomas, b Sept 5, 1806.
1796.+William, b. Jan 1, 1808.
1797.　Mary Ann, b. May 5, 1810.

Harriet married E. Bishop.
Ann married David Akerly.
Margaret married Andrew Bishop
Mary Ann married Reuben Stiles.

[1638] JONATHAN⁶ PECK, son of JONATHAN,⁵ settled at first in Bristol, R. I.   He moved from there to Dutchess County, N. Y., in June 1793.   He married Nancy Wardwell, November 2, 1782.   She died September 20, 1803, aged 41 years.   He died in the town of Alexandria, Jefferson County, July 30, 1836, aged 76 years.

CHILDREN — SEVENTH GENERATION.

1798. Lydia, b Oct 5, 1784.   Died Dec 9, 1804, unm
1799   Charlotte, b Oct 5, 1785
1800 +Jonathan, b Feb 2, 1787.
1801 +Henry, b. Feb 24, 1789.
1802. Abigail, b. Nov 18, 1790 Died Sept. 7, 1817, unm.
1803 +George, b Aug 29, 1792
1804   Nancy, b. Dec 8, 1793
1805.+Allen, b July 20, 1795
1806   Harriet, b Dec 10, 1797
1807. William, b Jan 7, 1802
1808.+Nathaniel W , b Aug 24, 1803

Charlotte married Dr Jonathan Buck, was residing, in 1853, in West Lowville, Lewis County, N Y, with a second husband
Nancy married Jervis Pierce, of Bristol, R I, and settled in Bradford County, Pa   She was accidentally shot by her husband
Harriet married Mr Joseph Wood, and settled in Montezuma, where they were residing in 1863
William died at an early age in Bristol, R. I.

[1639.] NICHOLAS⁶ PECK, son of JONATHAN,⁵ resided in Bristol, R. I., where he became wealthy.   He was a merchant, a man of much energy and perseverance.   He died June 1847.   He married, for his first wife, Elizabeth Smith, daughter of Stephen Smith, of Bristol, October 2, 1785.   For his second wife, he married Jemima Gorham, daughter of Capt. Isaac Gorham, October 1, 1797; and for his third, Sally Gorham, sister of Jemima, October 5, 1799.   His first wife died May 1796, in her 30th year.   His second wife died November 7, 1798, in her 24th year.   His third wife survived him, and was residing a widow upon the homestead in 1863.   To her kindness, and that of her son Isaac, I am indebted for my information in relation to the family.

1809 Mary, b June 28, 1787
1810 +Nicholas, b July 13, 1789
1811 John, b. Sept. 26, 1791. Died
  in Maryland in 1804, unm
1812 Francis, b May 30, 1794 Died
  June 6, 1796
1813. Elizabeth, b. May 20, 1796.
  Died Sept. 30, 1796.
1814. Jemima G , b. Oct. 12, 1798
  By 2d wife.

1815 Isaac G , b. July 15, 1800 By
  3d wife
1816. Elizabeth, b Sept 14, 1802
1817 Susan, b March 30, 1809. Died
  April 21, 1810.
1818.+Francis, b May 2, 1811
1819. Veites G , b Feb 18, 1814
1820. Susan, b March 29, 1818. Died
  Aug 1, 1830

Mary married Dr. Lemuel W. Briggs. Her children were *Abby P ,*[8] *Lemuel W.,*[8] and *Walter D* [8] Lemuel W is a physician, and Walter D. was a merchant, of the house of Page, Briggs, & Babbitt, Boston, in 1863

Jemima married Capt Benjamin W. Bradford, was a widow in 1863 Her children were *Henry Felix,*[8] *Elizabeth*[8] and *Mary.*[8]

Elizabeth married Randal H Moale, of Baltimore, a counsellor-at-law. They have a large family of children.

Veites was residing upon the homestead unmarried in 1864.

[1640.] JOHN[6] PECK, son of JONATHAN,[5] settled in Bristol near the homestead of his ancestors, where he died, March 1, 1821. He held a Judgeship in the Court of Common Pleas for several years. He was twice married: first, to Patience Turner, daughter of Dr. John Turner, April 9, 1795. She died July 12, 1801, aged 36 years. Second, to Ann Reynolds, daughter of Joseph Reynolds, of Bristol, May 16, 1802. She was residing with her daughter, Mrs. Benjamin Smith, in 1863.

1821. Emma, b. May 21, 1796. Died
  Dec 3, 1858, unm.
1822 +Jonathan, b Feb 24, 1798.
1823 Susan, b Aug 25, 1799.
1824 +John T , b July 10, 1801

1825 +William, b June 16, 1803.
1826 +Henry, b Dec 4, 1804
1827 +Horace, b July 1, 1806.
1828 +George R , b April 20, 1808.
1829 Ann, b Jan. 25, 1810.

Susan married Marke A Smith, of Bristol, R I
Ann married Capt. Benjamin Smith, and settled in Galesburg, Ill.

[1649] SAMUEL[6] VIAL PECK, son of THOMAS,[5] resided in Bristol, R. I., upon what is known by the name of Popposquash, where he died, February 21, 1804. He is represented to have been kind-hearted and benevolent.

He erected the house, as I am told, owned and occupied in 1863

by Stephen T. Church. He married Joanna Lincoln for his first
wife, and for his second, Martha Howland. His first wife died
November 16, 1796, aged 37 years. His second wife died January 14, 1849, aged 82 years. She was appointed administratrix
upon his estate, April 7, 1804.

CHILDREN — SEVENTH GENERATION :

1830. Ashbel Harrick Died Oct. 21, 1796, aged 13 years.
1831 Mary Richmond, b. Dec. 26, 1787. Died Nov. 9, 1822
1832 Samuel Vial Died Nov. 12, 1796, aged 8 years.
1833 Joanna. Died Nov. 10, 1796, aged 5 years.
1834. Medberry Lincoln. Died Sept. 3, 1795, aged 9 months and 2 days.
1835. An infant son. Died Oct 22, 1796, aged 7 days.
1836 Martha Howland, b. April 1, 1798 Died young.
1837. Eliza Ann, b March 14, 1800.
1838. Martha Vial, b March 20, 1804.

Mary Richmond married Philip M Topham. *Robert C* [8] and *William* [8] Topham, of New Bedford, are her sons

Eliza Ann was residing in Bristol in 1863, unmarried

Martha Vial married Nathaniel Fales, and was residing in Bristol in 1863

The first six children in this family were those of the first wife, four of whom with their mother died with the yellow fever.

The tombstones of these children may be found at Bristol. They have been removed from the ancient burying-ground (now converted into a common) to the grounds adjoining * Near the tombstones of these children, when I visited the place, lay upon the ground that of the mother, once a fine stone, then apparently uncared for. That of the father had been removed to the North burying-ground. The following is the inscription from that of the mother

In memory of Mrs. Joanna the amiable Consort of Samuel Vial
Peck who departed this life Nov. 16–1796 in the 37th year of her age.

[1651.] NATHANIEL[6] PECK, son of THOMAS,[5] left Bristol,
R. I., about 1793, and settled in Amenia, Dutchess County, N. Y.,
where he resided for many years. He removed to Chenango County,
and afterwards to La Salle, Michigan, where he died, September 20,
1836. He married Mary Wilson, daughter of John Wilson, of
Taunton, Mass. She died May 27, 1856, aged 86.

---

* Upon the stones of these children, or upon that of the mother, is a singular error. Upon the stone of the mother the name is Joanna. Upon that of the children she is called Hannah.

1839   Thomas, b. Dec 30, 1792 Died unm , Sept. 13, 1836

1840 +Samuel V., b Nov 22, 1794

1841 +Nathaniel B , b Feb. 8, 1797.

1842   Hannah, b Aug 15, 1799.

1843   Maria, b Aug. 27, 1801.

1844   John, b Nov 28, 1803 Died June 2, 1804.

1845   William L , b March 7, 1806. Died at St Jago, Cuba, Feb. 20, 1836, unm.

1846   Betsy, b July 9, 1808   Died March 5, 1811.

1847. Betsy W., b. Dec. 31, 1810.

Hannah married John M. Wheeler, of Amenia, September 15, 1819, where they settled. She died September 23, 1862.

Maria married Geoge J Barker, of Amenia, August 24, 1823. Settled at Grand Rapids, Mich , where she died, August 23, 1852

Betsy W married William Bosworth, of Pharsalia, January 15, 1829, and died at Amenia, October 1857.

[1655.] WILLIAM B.[6] PECK, son of Loring,[5] married Elizabeth Keese, daughter of Samuel Keese, of Keeseville, N. Y., January 22, 1811, and settled at Lake Pleasant, Hamilton County, N. Y.

I am told that he was early possessed of much physical ability, energy and decision of character, which fitted him for the active life he afterwards lived.   He held various public offices during his life, both civil and military.   In 1812, '13, '14 and '15, he held a commission, and was in service upon the frontier or Canada line.

He was supervisor of his town and Justice of the Peace for many years, and in 1822 was appointed one of the judges of his county, which office he held during his residence there.

In 1826, he removed to Stuyvesant Landing, upon the Hudson River, and engaged in the commission freighting and grain business   From here he removed to Chomahon, Will County, Ill., where he was again intrusted with various public offices.   In 1837, he was appointed by the President Indian Agent to settle claims; and in 1840, Assistant United States Marshal.   He held minor public offices, as Justice of the Peace, Post Master, etc., until the close of his life.

In speaking of his private life, his son, Samuel K., to whom I am indebted for my information, says: " My father will be long remembered as one of the most pleasing companions, and the most charitable and beneficent of men."

He was accustomed to take an active part in political matters, and was a pleasing and popular public speaker.

He died June 22, 1849. His wife in 1845.

CHILDREN — SEVENTH GENERATION

1848.	Harriet S , b 1812	1852	Robert H , b Jan 1824 Died
1849	Ellen, b 1815		Oct 26, 1852, unm
1850	Samuel K , b March 27, 1818.	1853	Phebe F , b March 29, 1826.
1851	Jane, b 1820 Died 1824	1854	+Philip S , b March 27, 1829.

Harriet married in 1836, settled in Illinois, and died in 1846

Ellen married Elisha C Fellows, was a widow residing at Joliet, Ill , in 1863

Samuel K was residing at Clinton Corners, N Y , in 1864, unmarried

Phebe F married George W Washington, of Mount Vernon, grand-nephew of General George Washington   She died September 1849

[1659]   DR GEORGE[6] PECK, son of Col LORING,[5] married Elizabeth Dunning, of Lake Pleasant, Hamilton County, N. Y., where he resided until about 1817, when he removed to Western New York. He resided for some time at Monroe. From there he removed to Niagara, where he remained for several years. He was educated for a profession, and chose that of medicine and surgery, which he afterwards practised. He was surgeon in the war of 1812. He was also a surveyor and engineer, in the practice of which he sometimes engaged.

In 1836, he removed to the West, and settled in Iowa, upon the west bank of the Mississippi River, where he afterwards laid out and founded the city of Camanche. He remained here until his decease.

His son, Franklin K , to whom I am indebted for my information, in speaking of his decease, says · " He now lies buried near the city, in a place of his own selection. Upon his tombstone is the following inscription :

Doct George Peck founder of Camanche died Oct 13, 1838 Aged 51 years

His wife lies buried by his side. She died May 10, 1844, aged 48 years.

14

CHILDREN — SEVENTH GENERATION

1855 +Franklin K , b May 10, 1812
1856 Mary Ann, b Feb 22, 1814.
      Died July 19, 1848
1857 John R , b Jan 8, 1816
1858 Elizabeth, b Dec 22, 1818
1859 Loring D , b Aug 6, 1820.
      Died April 14, 1848

1860 Sarah, b Dec 20, 1822
1861 Jane, b Jan 1826
1862 Frances C , b Dec 11, 1827
      Died June 2, 1861.
1863 +George, b Feb 4, 1830

Mary Ann married Charles Harrison, September 1, 1837 Her children were *Norman*,[8] *Daniel*,[8] *Henry*[8] and *John* [8]

John R married Nancy Bucon, May 1840; resides in California, no issue.

Jane married Charles Harrison, the former husband of her deceased sister, November 30, 1848   Her child, *Sarah Harrison*,[8] was born March 13, 1850

Sarah married Ira Stockwell, March 30, 1843   Her children are *George H*,[8] *Edwin E* [8] and *Nellie* [8]

Elizabeth married first, Jonathan M Warner, June 19, 1836 , second, Eli S Boice, July 12, 1840   Mr Warner died August 20, 1839, and Mr Boice August 16, 1862   Her children by them are *George Warner*,[8] *William*,[8] *Mary J*,[8] *Caroline E*,[8] and *David E* [8] *Boice*

Frances C married Francis K Bennett, September 11, 1849   Her children were *Frances*, *jr* ,[8] *Rodolphus*,[8] and *George* [8]

[1660.]   HENRY[6] PECK, son of Loring,[5] is a wealthy farmer, and resides at Bangall, Dutchess County, N. Y   He married Nancy Conger, October 19, 1811, daughter of Benjamin Conger, of Milan, Dutchess County, N. Y.

CHILDREN — SEVENTH GENERATION

1864 George, b April 8, 1813
1865. Richard, b May 5, 1815
1866 Jane A , b Nov 15, 1819

1867. Alfred, b Jan 1, 1822   Died
      Sept 1837

Jane A married Charles H. Smith, and settled at Hartsville, Dutchess County, N. Y

George is a physician, was unm. in 1863

Richard is a lawyer; was unm in 1863

[1661.]   RICHARD[6] PECK, son of Loring,[5] settled at Lake Pleasant, and from there removed to Wells, Hamilton County, N. Y., where he was residing in 1864.   He has been a judge, member of the State Legislature, etc.   He married Lavinia Kasson, daughter of Robert Kasson.

CHILDREN — SEVENTH GENERATION

1868 Caroline, b Dec 28, 1819
1869 +William B , b Sept 24, 1822.
1870 Nancy, b. March 29, 1825.

1871 Maria Louisa, b Aug 28, 1828.
1872 +Charles H , b. June 14, 1832.
1873 Walter B , b. Feb. 28, 1834.

Caroline married David Brown, resides in Northampton, Fulton County, N. Y. Their children are *Albert*,[8] b September 5, 1846, *Charles*,[8] b December 20, 1847, *Dewitt*,[8] b June 5, 1849, *Maria*,[8] b March 10, 1856, *Ella*,[8] b October 27, 1862, and *Lavinia*,[8] b September 28, 1852

Nancy married Ulyssis H Cowles Their children are *Sarah Jane*,[8] b. April 15, 1845, *Richard P*,[8] b April 2, 1847, *Luna*,[8] b. February 19, 1849, *James H*,[8] b July 11, 1851, *Mary*,[8] b April 10, 1853, *Ida*,[8] b May 15, 1859, *Alfred Ulysis*,[8] b in 1860

Walter B was in the army, in 1864, unm.

[1662]   JONATHAN[6] PECK, son of JONATHAN,[5] resided, at first, in Rehoboth, Mass, afterwards in other places in that vicinity. He married Betty Ormsbe, October 21, 1782 (R. Rec., B. 3). He died in Cumberland, August 1846. She died in Providence, May 1849.

CHILDREN — SEVENTH GENERATION   (R. Rec , B 3, p 296)

1874+	Cyrus, b March 3, 1784	1878	Sarah, b July 18, 1794
1875	Cynthia, b Oct 3, 1786. Died April 17, 1864	1879.	Betty, b April 20, 1796
1876 +	Jonathan, b April 7, 1789.	1880.	Lucy, b Sept 15, 1798 Died unm
1877 +	Caleb, b Jan 14, 1792	1881	Ruth Ann, b Oct. 25, 1801.

Cynthia resided in Providence, in 1863, unm
Sarah married John King; resided in Providence, in 1863, a widow
Betty married John Draper, of Providence
Ruth Ann married Wilbor Wheaton, of Providence, was a widow, residing there, in 1863.

[1663]   RUFUS[6] PECK, son of JONATHAN,[5] settled in Providence, R I. He was a merchant. He married Lydia Lyon.

CHILDREN — SEVENTH GENERATION   (P Rec , B 2, p 111)

1882	Bethia, b Nov 14, 1793 Died young	1884.	Rufus, b March 11, 1798 Died young
1883	Ruth, b Oct 18, 1795 Died young	1885	Philip L , b. Nov 9, 1799
		1886.	Amos L , b June 10, 1802. Suppose died young.

Ruth married Rev Wilbor Fisk He was a Methodist clergyman, at one time principal of the Methodist school at Wilbraham, and afterwards of the college

[1665.]   GIDEON[6] PECK, son of JONATHAN,[5] settled in Rehoboth, Mass., near what was known in that vicinity as the Governor Martin estate, where he lived and died.

He married Lydia Bullock, daughter of Judge Stephen Bullock,

of Rehoboth, March 17, 1791. She was born March 23, 1765.
He died December 20, 1843. She died November 30, 1846.

CHILDREN — SEVENTH GENERATION (R Rec , B 4, p 17)

1887	Belinda, b Dec 23, 1791	1891	Lydia B , b Maich 23, 1799
1888	Patsey, b, Feb 9, 1794	1892	Candice, b Jan. 21, 1801
1889 +Edwin, b Dec 3, 1795		1893	Mary, b Apiil 4, 1803
1890 +Noah, b Sept 19, 1797		1894	Rosalie, b March 5, 1805.

Patsey married Aaron T Mason, of Swansey   Their childien are *Gideon
P ,*[8] *Mary B ,*[8] *William E ,*[8] *Horace D ,*[8] *James A.*[8] and *Aaron T*[8]

Lydia married Autil Luther; settled in Pawtucket, R I   Their children
were *Chailes Autil,*[8] *William Thompson,*[8] *Abby P*[8] and *Samuel*[8]

Belinda mained Sullivan Maitin, of Bairington   Then children were
Anna D ,[8] *Edwin L.,*[8] *George S ,*[8] *Stephen B*[8] and *Nathaniel F*[8]

Candice resides in Seekonk, unm

Mary mained Gaidnei Luther, of Seekonk, no issue

Rosalie married Capt Henry R Howland, of New Bedfoid   They reside in
Seekonk, Mass   Their childien weie *Florence* and *Lydia.* Floience died
Januaiy 17, 1864, aged 20 years and 13 days.*

[1666.] AMBROS[6] PECK, son of JONATHAN,[5] resided in Rehoboth, where he died. He was a cooper by trade.

He married Amey Mason, daughter of John Mason, of Rehoboth,
Mass.

CHILDREN — SEVENTH GENERATION

1895	Mary Died young.	1898	Eliza Died young
1896	Nancy. Died young	1899.	Lemma, b 1801.
1897.	Amie. Died young		

Lemua mained Bela Peck (No. 2686).

[1667.] PHILIP[6] PECK, son of JONATHAN,[5] resided in Providence. He was a merchant. He was twice married: first, to
Sally Chase, December 8, 1799, daughter of Amos Chase; second,
to Abigail Chase, January 25, 1807, sister to his first wife. His
first wife died December 1, 1804. He died April 7, 1824. His
second wife died October 14, 1834.

---

* To her excellent letteis I am indebted for much of my information in
relation to the family

CHILDREN — SEVENTH GENERATION (P Rec , B 2, p 206)

1900. John A , b Oct 17, 1801 Died unm

1901 William K , b Jan 8, 1803 Died unm

By second wife ·

1902 Sally C , b Oct 31, 1807

1903 +Philip F W , b Jan 16, 1809

1904 +Henry C , b Feb 1, 1811 }

1905 +Charles M , b Feb 1, 1811. }

Twins

1906 Abby Ann, b Sept 30, 1812

1907. Henry, b April 12, 1819.

Sally C married Benjamin T Church, of Providence.

Abby Ann resides in Providence, unm

[1671.] WILLIAM[6] PECK, son of JONATHAN,[5] settled in Rehoboth, near his father. He married Hannah Pierce, daughter of Isaac Pierce, of Rehoboth.

CHILDREN — SEVENTH GENERATION

1908 +William, b Nov 19, 1804

1909 Martha W , b June 5, 1807

1910 Mary P , b Nov 8, 1809

1911 +Josephus, b Sept 22, 1811

1912 +Noah L , b Nov 20, 1816

1913 Hannah, b June 21, 1818.

Martha married Obadiah Ross, of Thompson, Conn

Mary P married first, Jerome Westcott, and second, David Horton, of Providence

Hannah married Philip Mowry, of Woonsocket, R I

[1672.] SYLVANUS[6] PECK, son of JONATHAN,[5] resided in Rehoboth, not far from the Orleans Factory, so called. He married Charlotte Wright, daughter of Joseph Wright.

CHILDREN — SEVENTH GENERATION

1914 +Albert G , b Oct 29, 1805

1915 Charlotte W , b. March 15, 1808

1916 +Cyrus, b Nov 24, 1809.

1917 +James M , b July 11, 1818.

1918 Ruth W , b Feb 25, 1815

1919 +Sylvanus, b March 18, 1822

1920 Frances A , b Sept 1832

Charlotte W married E A Brown

Ruth and *Frances* married John C Marvel

[1676.] NICHOLAS[6] PECK, son of PELEG,[5] was early apprenticed to Seth Peck, who married his aunt, and removed with him to Northern Massachusetts, where his uncle died. He afterwards married and settled in Ashfield, Mass. From there he removed to Oblong, Dutchess County, N. Y , where he remained until about 1795, when he settled on Grand Island, in Lake Champlain He remained here until 1804, when he removed into the State of New York. In 1812, he returned to Grand Isle, where

14*

he resided until 1819, when he removed to Clinton, Clinton County, N. Y, where he died in 1837.*

He was twice married· first, to a Miss Merrick; and second, to Mrs. Eunice Barney, formerly Miss Eunice Clark. She died in 1842.

CHILDREN — SEVENTH GENERATION

1921 Phebe	1925 +Peleg
	1926 Eunice
By second wife	1927 +Seth, b Dec 28, 1800
1922 +William, b March 24, 1789	1928 Nicholas
1923 Polly, b Nov 3, 1790	1929 Lydia
1924 +Charles, b Nov 6, 1794	1930 Rosilla †

Phebe married Nathan Hill, for her first husband, and James Hinds, for her second

Polly married Stephen Martin, and settled in St Lawrence County, N Y, where she died in 1863

Eunice married Norman Starks, and was residing in Dellona, Sauk County, Wis, in 1864

Nicholas was unm in 1864, and residing in Monona, Iowa

Lydia married Doras Martin, and was residing in Clinton County, N Y, in 1864

Rosilla married Ira B Smith, and was residing at Eau Claire, Wisconsin, in 1864

[1680.]   THOMAS⁶ PECK, son of PELEG,⁵ settled in Swansey, Mass. The following was communicated by his son, at my request, to whose kindness and generosity I am also indebted for the likeness of himself and of his father:

Thomas Peck, son of Peleg, was born in Swansey, Mass., February 12, 1767. He was brought up. and at his majority commenced life a farmer. His father and eldest brother held commissions in the war of the Revolution, and my father experienced some of the privations so

---

* He left his native town at so early a date that his relatives had lost all knowledge of him   It was with much difficulty that he was traced out, and his descendants found   His children, when found, though already aged themselves, knew nothing of their ancestors, or of their father's connections, and seemed surprised and rejoiced to learn that they had many relatives, and an uncle still living; and what was still more singular, these children had become so separated in their settlements, that they did not know where each other resided, each having to be traced out separate, requiring much time and labor

† I am told that there was a son by the name of Ambros in the above family, who died young, being killed by the falling of a tree.

Thomas Peck

common during the war. Six weeks comprised his entire school advantages. I find among his papers several commissions, viz: one Ensign, dated 1791; Lieutenant, 1792, Captain, 1803; and Justice of the Peace, in 1805.

For several years he was a selectman of the town, and appears to have taken considerable interest in public affairs. It was, however, chiefly in his office of Justice of the Peace, that he became known and appreciated by the public.

Misdemeanors and crimes of a deeper shade seem to me to have been more frequent then than now, and the spirit of litigation more common. But his principal business was the collection of debts. His attention and scrupulous regard for the interest of the creditor, soon attracted from a large circle most of the business in this line. In identifying himself with the interests of the creditor, he did not overlook what was due to the debtor, and usually secured the esteem of both.

So large was his legal business of various kinds, that he required almost the entire time of a sheriff to serve the numerous papers he issued. Justices then made writs returnable before themselves. He necessarily had his regular court days. These were often numerously attended, and sometimes parties appeared by eminent advocates, making these days of great interest to me.

How long his business continued so large, I do not recollect; but at length, from changes in the laws and the usages of society, it diminished. As his business from these sources decreased, he extended it in other directions. He surveyed lands and wrote deeds, wrote wills and administered on numerous estates, and became a sort of general counsellor and legal adviser and assistant for a large circle of acquaintances.

In his more private relations, as in those already mentioned, he was the same man of mind, of principle, of a moral sense rarely in fault, to which sentiment and passion, were subjected to reason; and the highest good, rather than the greatest gratification, had prominence.

The above is a very inadequate expression of a life so full of earnest and various occupations. I have mentioned those acts and features which seemed to me most likely to be of some general interest to our numerous relatives, known and unknown.

That your work may become a medium to the widely scattered members of the *Peck family*, and like the telegraph wire, bring us nearer together, and into more interesting relations, is the desire and confident hope of yours,

Respectfully,

G. M. PECK.

He married Elizabeth Mason, daughter of Job Mason, of Swansey, Mass. He died October 1851. She November 24, 1844.

CHILDREN — SEVENTH GENERATION

1931 +William, b April 12, 1795
1932 +Gardiner M , b Feb 8, 1797
1933 Lebanon, b Sept 18, 1798.
    Died in 1798.
1934 +George, b. Oct 7, 1799

1935. Adaline, b Dec 16, 1801. Died
    in 1803
1936 Seth, b March 24, 1803
1937. Eliza S , b May 29, 1806

Eliza married John Bailey, of Swansey.

[1681.] HEZEKIAH[6] PECK, son of PELEG,[5] settled at first in Bristol, R. I., and then in Smithfield, Bradford County, Pa He was twice married: first, to Abby Gray; second, to Mrs Abigail Brigham, formerly Abigail Mason. His first wife died May 31, 1833. He died October 29, 1854. His second wife June 1857.

CHILDREN — SEVENTH GENERATION

1938 Sarah G , b April 23, 1792, in
    Rehoboth, Mass.
1939.+William, b. May 15, 1794, in
    Warren, R I.

1940.+Hezekiah M , b Aug 23, 1796,
    in Warren, R I
1941 +Peleg, b Dec 11, 1798, in Warren, R I

Sarah G. married Eleazer Waldron, and settled in Fall River, Mass

[1682.] SETH[6] PECK, son of PELEG,[5] settled in Warren, R. I. He was widely known as a public man, and very popular. He was elected to some public office in the town for more than forty years. He was weigher and gauger of the port of Warren many years. He held a colonel's commission. He was also a distinguished Mason, and was for a long time Master of the Grand Lodge.

He was three times married: first, to Lillis Child; second, to Widow Sally Chase, third, to Widow Sarah Cole, who survived him, and was residing in Warren, in 1863.

CHILDREN — SEVENTH GENERATION

1942. Patience, b Aug. 25, 1792
    Died unm
1943. Seth, b Feb 22, 1798. Died
    June 24, 1799

1944 John G , b Sept 7, 1800 Died
    at sea, unm

[1685.] PELEG[6] PECK, son of PELEG,[5] remained upon the homestead. He was a farmer. He married Abigail Fairbanks,

Beryn Peck

October 14, 1798, daughter of Jonathan Fairbanks, of Rehoboth, Mass. She died July 3, 1846. He, March 12, 1809.

CHILDREN — SEVENTH GENERATION

1945. Angeline, b May 12, 1800.　　1947　Henry, b Nov 23, 1806　Died

1946　Abigail, b June 7, 1804　　　　　　at Cape Good Hope, unm.

　　　　　　　　　　　　　　　　　　　1948　Freelove, b. Oct 23, 1808.

Angeline married Thomas Russell, of Swansey, Mass.

Abigail married James Peckham, of Swansey, Mass

Freelove married N K Weaver, of Rehoboth, Mass

[1690.] SALSBURY⁶ PECK, son of PELEG,⁵ followed the seas. He died in Havana, in 1818, master of a vessel. He married Eliza Barney, daughter of Cyrenus Barney, of Swansey, September 16, 1815.

CHILDREN — SEVENTH GENERATION

1949 +Salsbury, b Oct. 11, 1818.　　1950　Amey Ann, b. Feb. 24, 1817.

[1691] DEACON BENJAMIN⁶ PECK, son of PELEG,⁵ resides in Rehoboth, Mass. He has been a mechanic. During a portion of his early life, he was a millwright by occupation; an ingenious and excellent workman, being one of the pioneers and leading men in the business. He built, in 1813, the two first water wheels that operated cotton machinery in Fall River, now one of the largest manufacturing cities in the country.

Coming upon the stage of active life at the commencement of improvements in mechanics and manufactures, he contributed much to their advancement. He early entered into the business of manufacturing. He has been one of the owners, and the manager of a cotton mill, for more than forty years, enjoying the confidence of those with whom he has been associated, and the community in which he has resided. Notwithstanding his age, — now in his 77th year, — he has but recently retired from business.

Although of decided political opinions, he has had no aspirations for political preferments. He has kept aloof from the corruptions of party politics, exercising in the community what was more congenial to his nature and feelings, a moral and religious influence.

He is deacon of the ancient Baptist church of Swansey, Mass., of which he has been a leading member for many years, the same church of which his grandfather was the deacon more than one hundred years before him.* He was early the subject of religious impressions. He was baptized while residing in Providence, in 1820, by Dr. Stephen Gano, and united with his church. When he settled in Rehoboth, he removed his relations with this church to that in Swansey, where he still continues to worship.

Deacon Peck early took an interest in whatever related to his ancestry, and watched with much interest and kind feelings my efforts in tracing back our progenitors, and following out their descendants, often lending me his helping hand. To his assistance in tracing out the Rehoboth Pecks, I am more indebted than to any other one. For his kindness and for his generosity in contributing his likeness for the history, I am under many obligations.

He married Mary Luther, daughter of Martin Luther, of Swansey, Mass. She died September 23, 1825.

CHILDREN — SEVENTH GENERATION

1951 +Peleg, b. Feb. 19, 1817.   1953   Mary L., b Aug 11, 1822.
1952.   Martha D , b. Oct. 13, 1820.

Mary L. married William A King   They reside in Rehoboth   Their children are *Benjamin P ,[8] Rufina M E ,[8] Mary H [8]* and *William L [8]*

Mr. King is a machinist, an ingenious and excellent workman   He also takes an active interest in public matters.   He has held different offices.   He now represents his town in the State Legislature.

---

* This church was organized in 1663, by the Rev John Myles, from Swansey, in Wales (England), from which place he fled to escape persecution for his religious opinions, and nonconformity to the doctrines of the church. Mr Miles and his adherents for some time encountered the same intolerant sentiment here   The organization of the church was offensive to the congregational church at Rehoboth, and other churches, and the interposition of the court at Plymouth was sought to arrest the growth of the new doctrine Each member of this church, at one time, was fined five pounds, and prohibited from worship for the space of one month

They removed out of Rehoboth, and erected a house for worship at Wannamoiset, a neck of land now in Barrington   They afterwards removed to near where their present house stands.

The opposition they met with seemed only to bring them into notice.   Mr. Myles was an able and learned man, and the church soon became the centre of a widespread influence, receiving members from the surrounding towns In 1667, these Baptists were incorporated into a town, taking the name of Swansey, which it still retains.

[1695.]   GEORGE B.[6] PECK, son of THOMAS,[5] settled first in Bristol, then in Rehoboth, where he lived and died.   He was a hatter by trade   He married Rachel Carpenter, daughter of Peter Carpenter, of Rehoboth.

CHILDREN — SEVENTH GENERATION

1954   Elizabeth S , b Sept 29, 1817   1956   Patience C , b April 22, 1822
1955   George M , b   1819. Died   Died in 1815
      young   1957 +George B , b. March 13, 1824

Elizabeth married George B Bliss, of Rehoboth, Mass

[1701]   AARON[6] PECK, son of AARON,[5] married Mary Barnard, of the city of New York.   She was born in Hudson, N. Y., August 27, 1784, and died in Providence, R. I., May 1, 1819.   He died in the State of New York.

CHILDREN — SEVENTH GENERATION

1958   Alice Ann, b Aug 6, 1805   1961   Ann Barnard, b Dec 1814.
1959   William Edgar, b July 20,   1962   Phebe Barnard, b March 29,
      1807   Died Nov 1827   1819. Died May 19, 1819.
1960   Josephine Coffin, b   July 3,
      1809

Alice Ann married Jacob T Burgen, of New York City, where they were residing in 1864

Josephine C married William S Dori, and died in New York City, April 16, 1836

Ann B married, for her first husband, John B Hunt, June 24, 1833   He died at East Douglas, Mass , May 3, 1852   For her second husband, she married N G Whiting, August 28, 1855   They were residing at Worcester, Mass , in 1864.

[1708]   ROBERT[6] PECK, son of AMBROS,[5] resided in Swansey, Mass.   He was a cabinet-maker by trade.   He married Polly Millard, daughter of Aaron Millard.   He died February 1830. She died August 14, 1859, aged 76.

CHILDREN — SEVENTH GENERATION

1963 +Horace M , b July 10, 1806.   1967   Mary L., b. Oct 31, 1816
1964 +Isaac L , b April 24, 1808   1968 +Robert A , b Aug 9, 1818
1965. Adaline, b Jan. 21, 1810   1969   Antil L , b. May 22, 1821
1966 +Josias L , b July 17, 1813   1970   Nancy D , b Nov 14, 1823

Adaline married Thomas Luther, of Swansey   Her children are   *Ruth Ann,*[8] *Henry,*[8] now of Swansey, and *Adaline* [8]

Mary married Sheldon Young, of South Providence , is a widow, and has several children.

Antil L married Joanna F. Tabor, July 2, 1846, daughter of S M Tabor, of Swanville, Mass

Nancy D married Daniel Briggs. They were residing in Pawtuxet in 1863

[1711.]   DANFORTH L⁶ PECK, son of Ambros,⁵ resides in Pawtucket, R. I.   He is a pattern-maker by trade and occupation. He married Susan Peckham, daughter of Aaron Peckham, August 13, 1815.

CHILDREN — SEVENTH GENERATION

1971   Abby W , b March 29, 1818.   1972   Irene B , b May 6, 1822

[1728.]   ISRAEL⁷ PECK, son of James,⁶ resided in Swansey, where he died, January 4, 1850.   He married Lydia Newman, daughter of Daniel Newman, of Rehoboth, Mass.

CHILDREN — EIGHTH GENERATION

1973   Lucinda B , b. Dec 14, 1820.   1978   Theodore, b April 5, 1832
      Died June 18, 1834   1979   Lydia N , b March 31, 1834
1974   Mary A., b Feb 8, 1823   1980   Josephus F , b Oct 4, 1835
1975. Ann Janett, b Feb 8, 1825.   1981   Horace S , b Jan 20, 1837.
1976   Almira A , b Dec 14, 1827.   Died Oct 5, 1853
1977   James J , b April 17, 1829

Mary A married Elish Tabor, and resided in Fairhaven in 1865
Ann Janett married Peter M Levitt, of Turner, Maine
Almira A married William Gardner, of Taunton, Mass
James J and *Theodore* were residing in Rehoboth, Mass , in 1863, unm
Lydia married John L West, of Bristol, where they resided in 1864
Josephus married Julia A Weldon, of Rehoboth, Mass   Died in the hospital, at Washington, D C , July 17, 1862.

[1730.]   WILLIAM⁷ PECK, son of James,⁶ resides in Warren, R. I.   He married Sarah T. Hatch, daughter of Solomon Hatch, of Connecticut, October 17, 1827.

CHILDREN — EIGHTH GENERATION

1982. Sarah Throop, b Sept 25,   1987   Hannah Tabor, b June 9, 1840.
    1828   Died Sept 29, 1828.   1988   Isabella Hatch, b Dec 23,
1983   Anna Frances, b Jan 4, 1830   1842   Unm in 1863
1984. William Frederick, b March 6,   1989   George Edward, b. Aug 22,
    1834   1845
1985. Isabella, b March 1836   Died   1990   Sarah Throop, b May 28, 1848.
    in 1838   Died March 25, 1849.
1986. Elizabeth Northrop, b. Oct 17,
    1838.

Anna F married George L. Murdock, and resides in West Boylston, Mass.
William married Sarah Phinney Davis, no issue
Elizabeth N married James Macumber, and resides in Providence.
Hannah T. married William Kies, of West Boylston, Mass

[1732.] JOHN[7] PECK, son of JAMES,[6] resides in New Bedford, Mass. He married Lydia Tabor, daughter of Elisha Tabor, of Fairhaven.

CHILDREN — EIGHTH GENERATION

1991 John Edward, b April 6, 1837
1992 Timothy T , b April 7, 1841
1993. Sarah T , b Sept 21, 1845
1994 Albert F., b Jan 28, 1846
1995. Georgianna T , b Aug 30, 1848
1996 Arthur L , b Oct. 18, 1850

John E married Sarah A Barney, daughter of Jonathan P Barney, of East Providence, R. I

[1735.] JOSEPH[7] PECK, son of JAMES,[6] resides in Fairhaven, Mass. He married Lydia Blaisdale, daughter of William Blaisdale, of Bucksport, Maine.

CHILDREN — EIGHTH GENERATION :

1997 Olive A , b, Feb 23, 1842
1998 James N., b March 12, 1844
1999 Alphonso T , b Aug 16, 1846
2000 Joseph B , b Sept 25, 1848
2001 Eliza M , b July 1, 1851
2002 Wallace H , b Dec 17, 1853.
2003 Harriet H , b May 8, 1857.

[1739.] STEPHEN[7] PECK, son of JOSEPH,[6] resides in Bristol, R I. He married Mary A. Sylvester.

CHILDREN — EIGHTH GENERATION

2004 Joseph S , b March 19, 1827
2005 Mahala, b Feb 15, 1829
2006. Newell S , b Sept 16, 1831
2007 Phebe, b Aug 7, 1835
2008 Ellen M , b June 26, 1839

[1742.] BENJAMIN D.[7] PECK, son of JOSHUA,[6] was residing in Washington, D. C., in 1863 He married Nancy Miller, daughter of Russell Miller, of Cumberland, R. I., August 1839.

CHILDREN — EIGHTH GENERATION

2009 Mary J., b March 27, 1840
2010 Lloyd G , b Nov 7, 1841
2011 Eugenia A , b June 28, 1843
2012 Benjamin B , b Dec. 16, 1844.
2013. Edward F , b Dec 12, 1847

[1743] SAMUEL[7] PECK, son of JOSHUA,[6] was residing in Providence, R I., in 1864. He married Violeta Chappell, daughter of James Chappell, of Sutton, Mass., December 17, 1840.

15

CHILDREN — EIGHTH GENERATION

2014	Samuel D , b. Feb 17, 1818	2017	Saiah D , b Sept 12, 1843
2015	Violeta C , b Feb 1, 1815.	2018	Samuel C., b June 8, 1848
2016	William J., b. June 7, 1842	2019.	George H , b Aug 14, 1854

[1744.] NICHOLAS[7] PECK, son of JOSHUA,[6] was supposed to be residing in California, in 1863. He married Celinda Latham, daughter of Thomas Latham, of Smithfield, R. I.

CHILDREN — EIGHTH GENERATION

2020	John Angell, b Dec 24, 1844. Died Aug 1846	2021	Laura Maiia, b March 17, 1846

Laura Maria was residing in East Douglas, in 1863

[1749] HEZEKIAH[7] PECK, of Warren, R I., son of WINCHESTER,[6] was married to Adaline B. Sawtell, June 25, 1843, by Isaac Bonney.

CHILDREN — EIGHTH GENERATION

2022	Allen Pitman, b Oct. 11, 1844	2025	Rosabella Thressa, b Feb. 16, 1852 Died Nov 9, 1853
2023	James Edward, b. Oct 17, 1846	2026.	Walter Biadfoid, b Nov 1, 1856 Died Aug 19, 1857
2024.	Lucina Sawtell, b. Maich 3, 1848		

James Edwaid died in Newbern, N C , October 29, 1862, in the Union Aimy, Company A., 5th Regiment R. I Volunteers.

[1755] HENRY[7] PECK, son of HENRY,[6] settled in Harrisburgn, Lewis County, N. Y., in 1807, where he died, December 20, 1840. He married Hepzibeth Kelsey, of Newport, N. H., daughter of Roswel Kelsey.

CHILDREN — EIGHTH GENERATION

2027.	Louisa	2031	Willard
2028	Jonathan	2032	Ira.
2029	Nelson	2033.	Frederick.
2030	Lois.		

Louisa married Allen Parker, and left seven children, who settled at Copenhagen, Lewis County, N Y.

Ira was living near Cannon Falls, Min , in 1863

Fiederick was living at Beaver Dam, Wis., in 1863, the others at Harrisburgh, Lewis County, N. Y.

[1756] DEXTER[7] PECK, son of HENRY,[6] settled at Harrisburgh, Lewis County, N. Y., in 1807, where he died, January 29, 1841.

He married Polly Peck, daughter of Azeriah Peck, who was from Lime, Conn.

CHILDREN — EIGHTH GENERATION

2034 Monroe, b Feb 1818
2035. Francis, b June 11, 1821
2036. Emma A , b Sept. 21, 1829

2037. Sarah A., b Sept 21, 1832
2038. One child, b 1824. Died in infancy

Monroe married Mary A Dickins, and was residing at Oak Grove, Wis , in 1863 His children were (2039) *Rosina,*[9] (2040) *Eugene,*[9] (2041) *George,*[9] and (2042) *Mary* [9]

Francis married Lydia Jane Millard, and was residing at Beaver Dam, Wis , in 1863 His children were (2043) *Ellen,*[9] (2044) *Jane,*[9] (2045) *Alice,*[9] (2046) *Lelia,*[9] (2047) *Velma,*[9] (2048) *Wayne,*[9] and (2049) *Addison* [9]

Emma A married Ninde Thomas, of Adams, Jefferson County, N Y

Sarah A. married Frederick Denio, and settled at Sanford Corners, Jefferson County, N Y.

[1757] SETH[7] PECK, son of HENRY,[6] first settled in New Hampshire; from there he moved to Harrisburgh, Lewis County, N. Y., where he died, March 23, 1832.

He married Anna Clapp, of Wendall, N. H., in 1808, where she was born, July 24, 1788. She was the daughter o Job Clapp

CHILDREN — EIGHTH GENERATION

2050 Laura, b Nov 7, 1809
2051. Plooma, b March 1, 1812.
2052 Savilla, b Nov 11, 1815
2053. Abigail, b Sept 3, 1821
2054. Polly, b Jan 13, 1819. Died Aug. 12, 1822.

2055 Polly, b Nov 3, 1823
2056. Lucy, b Sept 16, 1827   Died Sept. 13, 1828
2057. Lucy, b July 28, 1834.

Plooma married Benjamin Shults She died July 1837
Laura married first, Bonepart Strader; second, William Millard
Savilla married Ira Strader
Abigail married Charles Turner.
Polly married D. Gordon

[1758] CALVIN[7] PECK, son of HENRY,[6] settled in Claremont, N. H., where he was residing in 1863.

He married Lois Kelsey, daughter of Roswell Kelsey, of Newport, N. H., May 13, 1809.

CHILDREN — EIGHTH GENERATION

2058. Hepsibeth K , b March 5, 1811
2059 Cynthia, b June 13, 1813. Died Sept 17, 1830
2060. Philena, b. Feb 28, 1815.

2061 Hiram H , b June 10, 1816
2062 Elias S , b Sept 17, 1821
2063. Lois K , b. Sept 14, 1824

Hepsibeth K. married John B Hardy, of Acworth, N H , June 29, 1833
Philena married Willard Hardy, of Acworth, N H , November 10, 1840
Hiram H married Maria Rumrill, daughter of John L Rumrill, March 1, 1843 They were residing in Londonderry, Vt , in 1864 Their children were (2064) *Henry H*,[9] b. April 5, 1844, (2065) *Lurilla J*,[9] b March 18, 1847 , (2066) *John L*,[9] b April 25, 1850 (2067) *Charles E* ,[9] b April 12, 1854 , and (2068) *Nellie M*,[9] b October 10, 1860.

Elias S married Harriet S Hale, daughter of Stephen Hale, of Rutland, Vt His child. (2069) *Elmer*,[9] was born May 14, 1861

Lois K married Thomas A Hardy, of Acworth, May 21, 1845

[1759.] HEZEKIAH[7] PECK, son of HENRY,[6] resided at Beaver Dam, Dodge County, Wis., in 1863. He married Ruth Cram, October 1814.

CHILDREN — EIGHTH GENERATION

2070   Abigail, b Jan 19, 1817
2071. Hezekiah,b May 9, 1820. Died April 3, 1856

2072   Mary, b Dec 15, 1821   Died Aug 6, 1827
2073. Sylvester, b Aug 9, 1830.

Abigail married John Ellis.

Hezekiah married Lucinda Ellis, April 3, 1842, and died April 3, 1856, leaving five children (2074) *Smith*,[9] (2075) *Mary Ann*,[9] (2076) *Oscar Adelbert*,[9] (2077) *Hannah Sylista*,[9] and (2078) *Hezekiah Seth* [9]

Sylvester married Caroline Edwards, March 13, 1851

[1764] SILAS[7] PECK, son of HENRY,[6] settled at Copenhagen, N. Y. He married Jerusha Cobb, daughter of Ezra Cobb.

CHILDREN — EIGHTH GENERATION

2079   Mehitable, b Feb 26, 1835.
2080   George J , b April 26, 1836
2081   Hannah, b July 7, 1840.

2082. Miles, b Feb 2, 1843
2083. Jason, b Dec 18, 1844

Mehitable married Henry Thomas. They had two children *Lydia D.*[9] and *Carson H.*,[9] in 1864.

[1765] CAPRON[7] PECK, of Attleborough, Mass., son of JONATHAN,[6] married Lydia Daggett, daughter of Ebenezer Daggett, of Attleborough, Mass., June 21, 1824.

CHILDREN — EIGHTH GENERATION

2084. Sabra, b April 4, 1825
2085   Sally Maxcy, b Oct 12, 1826.
2086. Joseph Capron, b April 12, 1828 Died Feb 3, 1829.
2087. Jonathan Maxcy, b. Nov. 25, 1829
2088. Lydia Daggett, b Feb 2, 1833. Died Feb 23, 1834
2089. A son, b Feb 17, 1834. Died the same day.

2090. Ebenezer Daggett, b May 22, 1835 Died Dec. 26, 1841.
2091. John McClellan, b May 28, 1837 Died Aug 14, 1838
2092. John Daggett, b July 12, 1838 Died Sept 2, 1839
2093. George Capron, b Oct 21, 1840 Died Feb 21, 1841
2094. Mary Isadora, b April 15, 1842. Died May 10, 1852.
2095. Lydia Daggett,b Feb 3, 1844.

Sabra,[9] *Sally M.,*[9] *Jonathan M ,*[9] and *Lydia*[9] were residing in Attleborough, unmarried, in 1863.

[1769.] WILLIAM[7] PECK, son of ABIEL,[6] resided at Shepody, now Hopewell, Albert County, New Brunswick. He was drowned, November 28, 1804, with his younger brother Abiel, while attempting to cross the mouth of Shepody River in an open boat, which the high winds and a heavy sea caused to founder. He married Elizabeth Reed.

CHILD — EIGHTH GENERATION :

2096. William A , b May 5, 1805.

He was residing in Rockland, Me , in 1865 He married Ruth Rogers, November 9, 1826 Their children are (2097) *Lucy,*[9] who married Rev. Thomas B Tupper; (2098) *Elizabeth,*[9] who married Charles Tupper; (2099) *George R ,*[9] (2100) *Eunice,*[9] (2101) *Amanda,*[9] (2102) *Edward C ,*[9] (2103) *Christopher J ,*[9] and (2104) *Mary S*[9] A full record of this family was received, but too late.

[1777.] JAMES[7] PECK, son of ABIEL,[6] was residing in Hopewell, Albert County, New Brunswick, in 1865 He has been three times married . first, to Sabina Pearson, July 11, 1821 ; second, to Mary Mills ; third, to Zylphia Briggs.

CHILDREN — EIGHTH GENERATION

2105	Sabina, b March 1, 1822	2110	William A , b April 18, 1851
2106.	Rufus, b Jan 1, 1827	2111	Martin C , b April 1851
2107.	James E , b March 5, 1829	2112.	Rachel R , b Sept 20, 1852.
	Died Dec. 25, 1858, unm	2113	Joshua V , b Aug 17, 1854.
2108	Samuel, b May 17, 1832 Died	2114	Caroline, b Aug 28, 1856
	March 15, 1859	2115.	James M , b Sept 4, 1858.
2109.	Ezra, b Feb. 24, 1835		

There were three sons and one daughter who died in infancy

[1782.] REUBEN[7] PECK, son of ELISHA,[6] settled in Hopewell, Albert County, New Brunswick, where he died, March 15, 1855. He was an active, energetic and a prosperous farmer. He married Elizabeth Brewster.

CHILDREN — EIGHTH GENERATION

2116	Abiel, b Feb 26, 1815	2120	William, b Nov 13, 1823
2117.	Lavinia, b Aug 2, 1817		Died Jan 10, 1848
2118	Nathaniel, b Aug 21, 1818	2121	Jane, b Aug 6, 1826
2119.	John, b April 29, 1820		

Abiel was residing in Hopewell in 1865. He married first, Lydia Hunt, who died without issue, second, Nancy Reed, December 22, 1842 Their

15*

children are   (2122) *Nancy J*,[9] (2123) *William R.*,[9] (2124) *Amey E*,[9] (2125) *Sarah J*,[9] (2126) *Ruth E*,[9] and (2127) *Alberta M*[9]

Lavinia married George Calhoun, by whom she has three sons and two daughters   Her husband is Register of Deeds and Judge of the Court of Common Pleas for the County of Albert

Nathaniel is a farmer, and resided in Hopewell in 1865. He married Margaret Calhoun, November 16, 1858. Their children were   (2128) *Edson E*,[9] (2129) *Reuben L*,[9] and (2130) *Budd D*[9]

John has been twice married, first, to Eliza Steeves, second, to Ruth S Calhoun   His children are   (2131) *Mary C.*,[9] (2132) *Martha E*,[9] (2133) *Nathaniel S*,[9] (2134) *Francelia*,[9] and (2135) *William F*[9] He is a farmer, and was residing in Hopewell in 1865

Jane M married Rev. William D Fitch, a Baptist clergyman, by whom she had a son, who died December 20, 1860. Her husband died January 17, 1861. She died May 1864.

[1783.]   ELISHA[7] PECK, son of ELISHA,[6] resides in the Parish of Hopewell, Albert County, N. B. He is an extensive farmer, owning one of the best farms in the county. He has been a Justice of the Peace for many years. He married Sarah Brewster, June 21, 1817.

CHILDREN — EIGHTH GENERATION

2136. Nancy, b March 9, 1818 Died aged about 12 years.	2142 Alexander, b July 15, 1832 Died young
2137. Anne, b Jan 18, 1820.	2143 Reuben, b Oct 20, 1834 Died Nov 14, 1859
2138. Cynthia, b Oct 5, 1822.	2144. Judson N , b Dec 9, 1836
2139 Elisha, b. Oct 13, 1825.	2145 A twin, b Dec 9, 1836. Died in infancy
2140 Miles, b Dec 9, 1827.	2146. Charles A , b Aug 20, 1839.
2141 Joseph B., b Jan. 28, 1830.	

Anne married Winthrop Robinson. Their issue is two sons and three daughters   They were residing in the Parish of Harvey, Albert County, in 1865   He is an extensive farmer

Cynthia married Daniel M Clark, by whom she had three sons and two daughters. He died January 22, 1865. She survived him, and was residing in Hopewell in 1865

Elisha resides in Hopewell, where he has a fine farm. He married Rebecca Lewis, December 28, 1854   His children are   (2147) *Lavinia Alice*,[9] (2148) *John Lewis*,[9] (2149) *Charles Le Baron*,[9] and (2150) *William Lyell*[9]

Miles was residing in Hopewell in 1865, a merchant and farmer He married Rebecca C Rogers   Their children are   (2151) *Isabella*,[9] (2152) *Alexander Lyell*,[9] (2153) *Miles*,[9] and (2154) *Elisha*,[9] who died in infancy.

Joseph B is a barrister and attorney-at-law of extensive practice   He resides at Dorchester, Westmoreland County, N B   To his kindness I am indebted for much of my information in relation to the descendants of Abiel Peck, his ancestor

Judson was residing in Hopewell in 1865, a farmer   He married Anna Turner, July 30, 1862. Their son, (2155) *Egbert*,[9] was born August 9, 1863.

Charles A. is a barrister and attorney-at-law at Hopewell, Albert County, N. B He married Amelia Nichols, February 17, 1864.

[1784.] ELIAS[7] PECK, son of ELISHA,[6] settled in Hopewell, Albert County, N. B., where he was residing in 1865. He is a farmer. He married Rachel E. Calhoun, November 24, 1831. She died February 1865.

CHILDREN — EIGHTH GENERATION

2156. Rebecca, b. Aug. 26, 1832.
2157. Sarah, b. July 17, 1834. Died Feb. 12, 1835.
2158. John E , b. Jan. 29, 1836.
2159. Samuel C., b. March 29, 1838.
2160 Mary E , b March 17, 1840.
2161. Sarah J , b Jan. 23, 1842.
2162 Elias J , b Jan. 20, 1844.
2163 Harris B , b March 9, 1846.
2164 George W., b. Sept. 2, 1849.

[1786. [JOHIEL[7] PECK, son of ELISHA,[6] was residing in Hopewell in 1865, a farmer. He married 'Caroline Peck, daughter of Abiel, October 17, 1822.

CHILDREN — EIGHTH GENERATION .

2165. James V , b. May 30, 1823 Died Jan 6, 1843
2166. Abiel, b Oct 1, 1825
2167 Susan, b April 29, 1828.
2168. Almira E , b Sept 19, 1830.
2169 Johiel E , b July 12, 1836.
2170. Amy C , b Feb 13, 1839 Died Feb 26, 1862.
2171 Sarah L , b June 1, 1841
2172 Abner V., b June 8, 1848.

Amy C. married Michael Keiver, October 27, 1858.
Sarah L. married Capt. Douglass Nichol, May 26, 1864.

[1788.] ABIEL[7] PECK, son of ELISHA,[6] resided in Hopewell, Albert County, N. B., in 1865, where he owned a fine farm. He married Lois Hunt, January 27, 1825.

CHILDREN — EIGHTH GENERATION

2173. Ruth M A., b. April 12, 1826. Died June 17, 1854.
2174 Alfred H , b April 19, 1831
2175. Warren D , b. Sept 1, 1833
2176. Alonzo B , b. March 16, 1836.
2177. Lydia, b. March 11, 1839
2178. Valentine T , b June 11, 1842 Died Sept. 11, 1846
2179. Gilbert M., b. June 15, 1844)
2180 Guilford R , b June 15, 1844. } Died Sept. 7, 1846) Twins
2181. Valentine G., b Aug 26, 1846.
2182. Eliza D , b June 20, 1852.

Alfred H married Kate Dickie, of Philadelphia, August 1, 1839 He is a physician and graduate of the University of Pennsylvania He was settled in Hopewell, Albert County, N B , in 1865 His daughter, (2183) *Alida Cornelia*,[9] was born March 14, 1860

Warren D resided in Hopewell, where he died, October 10, 1863. He married Ruxby E Reed in 1860 Their children are (2184) *Arthur S* [9] and (2185) *Ema E.*[9]

[1791.]   JOSEPH[7] PECK, son of Thomas,[6] settled in Hopewell, Albert County, N. B., where he was residing in 1865.   He married Melissa Akerly, September 30, 1824.   He is a farmer.

CHILDREN — EIGHTH GENERATION ·

2186 Thomas, b. Aug 9, 1825	2190 Mary, b April 6, 1833
2187. Wesley, b June 18, 1827.	2191. Asahel W , b. Dec 20, 1834.
2188. Seraphina, b July 24, 1829	2192 Harriet, b. March 16, 1837.
2189. Amy, b. March 16, 1832.	

One died in infancy
Thomas married Catharine Kenne.
Wesley married Mary Rogers.
Amy married Pierce Kenne
Harriet married Hiram Edgett.
Mary married Judson Pearson.

[1795.]   THOMAS[7] PECK, son of Thomas,[6] was residing in the Parish of Hopewell, Albert County, N. B , in 1865, a farmer. He married Rachel Dixon, September 14, 1827.

CHILDREN — EIGHTH GENERATION

2193 Edward, b July 5, 1828	2199 Allen, b April 16, 1840
2194. Mary Ann, b Dec 3, 1829	2200 Elizabeth, b May 7, 1842
2195. Lavinia, b Dec 11, 1831	2201 Ruth, b Jan 13, 1846
2196. Margaret, b Oct 28, 1833.	2202. Rachel, b Oct 1, 1848
2197. James, b. Nov 29, 1835	2203 Drusilla, b Dec 19, 1850
2198. Thomas W , b. April 13, 1838	2204. Robert C , b Sept. 11, 1856.

One died young
Edward married Ann Rogers.
Mary Ann married Edward McLellan.
Lavinia married Joel Bray
Margaret married Lewis Crossman.
Thomas married Ann Marshall

[1796.]   WILLIAM[7] PECK, son of Thomas,[6] settled in Hopewell, Albert County, N. B.   He was a .farmer.   He also occasionally engaged in the lumber business.   He was killed in 1846 by falling over a precipice, from the brow of which he was rolling logs.   He married Elizabeth Stevens, February 9, 1832.

CHILDREN — EIGHTH GENERATION

2205. Rebecca, b June 13, 1834.	2207 Sarah, b. April 28, 1838.
2206 Anna, b May 10, 1836	2208. Solomon, b Aug 9, 1841.

Two or more died in infancy, unnamed
Rebecca married Daniel Stewart.
Anna married George Stiles
Sarah married William Kinne.

[1800.] JONATHAN[7] PECK, son of JONATHAN,[6] settled at Denmark, Lewis County, N. Y., and afterwards at Alexandria, where he was residing in 1864.

He married, for his first wife, Abby Nye, daughter of Holland Nye, of Bristol, Dutchess County, N. Y., June 5, 1808. She was born December 25, 1789, and died August 25, 1831. For his second, he married Malinda Burbank, formerly Malinda Gilbert, December 17, 1832

CHILDREN — EIGHTH GENERATION

2209	Lydia, b Nov 13, 1809		2217.	Alexander H , b Oct 26, 1825.
2210	Hollan N , b June 24, 1811		2118	Philander G , b Jan 29, 1828
2211	Malinda, b Aug 15, 1813			Died May 25, 1852, unm.
2212	Joanna, b July 22, 1815.		2219	Julia Ann, b Aug 4, 1831.
2213.	Abby, b March 2, 1817		2220	Charles E , b Feb 7, 1834
2214.	Woolsey, b April 25, 1819			By 2d wife
2215	Jonathan, b Feb 26, 1822		2221	Horace G , b Nov 20, 1835.
2216	William R , b Sept 3, 1823		2222	Harriet M , b Jan 30, 1838.
			2223	Wesley W., b May 3, 1840

Lydia married Solomon Bowen, June 16, 1831, settled in Marquette, Wis.

Hallon N married Alvira S Freeman, February 5, 1837 He first settled in Alexandria, Jefferson County, N. Y , and from there he moved to Hammond, Wis , where he was residing in 1864. His children were (2224) *Franklin*,[9] (2225) *William W*,[9] (2226) *Henry H*,[9] (2227) *Alexander*,[9] (2228) *Sidney*,[9] and (2229) *Mary E*[9]

Malinda married Elias Lacy, August 21, 1835, and settled in Lowville, where she died

Joanna married Amaziah P Ellis, January 5, 1837, and was residing at Plessis, Jefferson County, N Y , in 1864

Abby was residing at home unmarried in 1864.

Woolsey married Catharine McAlister, December 17, 1845, and settled, first, at Alexandria, afterwards at Orleans , no children in 1864

Jonathan married Caroline Burbank, April 10, 1846, and was settled at Hammond, St Croix County, Wis , in 1864 His children were (2230) *Franklin*,[9] (2231) *Alzina*,[9] (2232) *Elvin*,[9] (2233) *Elbert*,[9] (2234) *Melona*,[9] and (2235) *Adelbert*[9]

William R. settled in California supposed unmarried in 1864

Alexander married, for his first wife, Laura Cooper, daughter of Allen Cooper, and was residing at Westfield, Marquette County, Wis., in 1864. His children were (2236) *Lucina S*,[9] (2237) *Cecelia L*,[9] (2238) *William R*,[9] and (2239) *Wilbert F*.[9] His second wife was Melissa L. Brown, daughter of Harris Brown.

Charles E married Merrilla A Shumway, October 31, 1857, and settled at Alexandria, Jefferson County, N. Y Had one child, (2240) *Ida*,[9] in 1864

Horace G married Harriet Beckwith, October 4, 1860, and settled in Alexandria , no issue in 1864

Wesley W. was in the army and unmarried in 1864.

Harriet was residing at home unmarried in 1864.

[18^1.] REV. HENRY[7] PECK, son of JONATHAN,[6] is an Episcopal clergyman, settled in the town of Guilford, Chenango County, N. Y. To his kindness and assistance I am much indebted. He married Nancy Price, December 16, 1810, daughter of Samuel Price.

CHILDREN — EIGHTH GENERATION :

2241. Benjamin P , b Jan 1, 1812   June 9, 1834
2242. Lorenzo, b April 1, 1813 Died   2243. Francis H., b Sept 20, 1815.

Benjamin married Caroline Chamberlayne, October 29, 1834   He was residing at Mount Upton, Chenango County, N. Y , in 1864   Their children were (2244) *Harriet Maria,*[9] b July 29, 1836 , (2245) *Nancy Amelia,*[9] b June 16, 1843 , and (2246) *Henry Calvin,*[9] b December 19, 1853.

Francis Horatio married Mary Jane Haight, February 28, 1844. He was residing at Morris, Otsego County, N Y., in 1864   Their children were (2247) *Clarissa Anna,*[9] b. September 11, 1846 , (2248) *Amelia Jane,*[9] b. January 23, 1851 , (2249) *Amanda Maria,*[9] b. February 8, 1853 , (2250) *Francis Augusta,*[9] b June 13, 1855 , (2251) *Henry Seth,*[9] b. September 15, 1863, and died November 18, 1863.

[1803.] GEORGE[7] PECK, son of JONATHAN,[6] settled at first at Rome, Oneida County, N. Y.; afterwards at Sterlingville, Jefferson County, where he died, May 27, 1854. He married Fanny Reynolds, daughter of Solomon Reynolds, of Rome, Oneida County, November 4, 1812. She survived him, and was residing with her son Dewane in 1864. She was born July 6, 1792.

CHILDREN — EIGHTH GENERATION

2252. Nancy, b Oct. 25, 1815   2256. William R., b Dec 13, 1825. ⎫
2253. Henry, b April 26, 1817. Died   2257 Lavinia, b Dec. 13, 1825.   ⎬
　　　　April 26, 1851   Twins
2254 George, b. May 13, 1819   2258 Julia Ann. b. Dec 29, 1830.
2255. Angeline, b April 6, 1822   2259. Dewane, b June 25, 1833.

Nancy married Ira Ward, and was residing in Sterlingville, in 1864.

Henry married Eunice Tifft, of Lewisburgh, N. Y., where he died, April 26, 1851. His children are   (2260) *George,*[9] (2261) *Fanny,*[9] (2262) *Andrew,*[9] (2263) *Amelia*[9] and (2264) *Alice* [9]

George married Lavinia Caldwell, of Carthage, N. Y., and settled in Russell, N. Y. His children are   (2265) *Balinda,*[9] (2266) *Alpheus,*[9] (2267) *Chandler*[9] and (2268) *Lodence* [9]

Angeline married Sylvanus Glasby, of St Lawrence County, N. Y.

William R. married Lucretia Tooly, April 25, 1845, and was residing in Plesses, N. Y , in 1864. His children were   (2269) *Dewane,*[9] (2270) *Josephine,* (2271) *Adelbert,*[9] (2272) *William L* [9] and (2273) *Carie.*[9]

Lavinia married Marques Bacon, of Sterlingville, N Y

Julia Ann married Joseph Pliner, of Sterlingville, N. Y.

Dewane married Clarinda Barns, February 28, 1856, and was residing at Lafargeville, N Y , in 1864. His children were   (2274) *Armetee*,⁹ (2275) *Mary J* ⁹ and (2276) *Willie*.⁹

[1805]   ALLEN⁷ PECK, son of JONATHAN,⁶ settled at Carthage, Jefferson County, N. Y., where he lived and died.   He was twice married · first, to Ann Gilbert, daughter of Moses Gilbert, of Putney, Vt., November 4, 1820; second, to Cynthia Dean, daughter of Samuel Dean, of Westfield, Mass., May 21, 1829.   His first wife died August 23, 1828.   He died April 14, 1853.

CHILDREN — EIGHTH GENERATION

2277   Harriet, b Aug 15, 1821 Died   2279   Harriet A , b April 8, 1830
           Nov 24, 1822   Died Nov 10, 1859
2278   William A , b Oct 28, 1823   2280   Leonard G , b Sept 3, 1832
           Died Nov 18, 1863

William A married Susannah C. Budd, October 22, 1850   Their children were   (2281) *William A* ,⁹ b August 2, 1851, and (2282) *Allen G* ,⁹ b. December 8, 1858

Leonard G married Helen F Bellinger, July 7, 1858, and was residing at Carthage, N. Y , in 1864   Their child   (2283) *Harriet L* ,⁹ was born January 27, 1862

[1808]   NATHANIEL W.⁷ PECK, son of JONATHAN,⁶ resides in Hammond, St. Croix County, Wis.

He married Julia Nye, daughter of Holland Nye, of Poughkeepsie, N. Y.

CHILDREN — EIGHTH GENERATION

2284   Ophelia A., b Feb. 15, 1825.   2285   Dempster, b Dec 22, 1838
Ophelia married S D Broadshaw, a farmer, of Hammond, St Croix County, Wis.

Dempster is a farmer, residing also at Hammond, in 1864   He married Catharine M Cross   Their children were   (2286) *Francis N* ,⁹ (2287) *Richard W*.⁹ and (2288) *Dempster* ⁹

[1810.]   NICHOLAS⁷. PECK, son of NICHOLAS,⁶ married Nancy D. W. Bradford, October 2, 1815.   She was born August 16, 1795.   He settled in Bristol, R. I.   He afterwards removed to Texas, where he died January 28, 1838.

CHILDREN — EIGHTH GENERATION

2289.   John Bradford, b July 21,   2293   Henry Wardwell, b Feb 21,
           1816   Died April 8, 1817   1830.
2290   Benjamin Bradford, b May 9,   2294   William D. Wolf, b. Feb 21,
           1818   Died May 8, 1863   1832
2291   John Nicholas, b March 15,   2295   Elizabeth Smith, b May 19,
           1821   1837.   Died Sept 20, 1838.
2292.   Nancy Bradford, b. Sept. 26,
           1823.

John N settled in Bristol, R I. He married Mary Rimears, of Bristol; no issue.

Nancy B. was residing in Bristol, in 1863, unm

Benjamin B married Elizabeth Morrison, of Gonzales, Texas, for his first wife, and the widow of Dr Broddast, of Texas, for his second.

Henry W. was residing in Bristol, unm , in 1863

William D. Wolf was residing in Texas, unm , in 1863

[1818.] REV. FRANCIS[7] PECK, son of NICHOLAS,[6] settled at Brookline, L. I., as pastor of St. Mark's Episcopal church.

He has been twice married. first, to Mary Bowen, daughter of Capt. Ephraim Bowen, of Providence, R. I., second, to Augustine Felix, daughter of Henry Felix, of Cuba, W. I., formerly from the United States.

CHILDREN — EIGHTH GENERATION

By first wife

2296 Frances Eugene, b Aug 17, 1851

2297. Herbert Lewis, b March 2, 1854.

2298 Cecil Russell, b July 26, 1856

2299 Ernest Felix, b Jan 24, 1859

2300 Adele Fernen, b June 24, 1861.

[1822.] JONATHAN[7] PECK, son of JOHN,[6] resides in Columbia, Bradford County, Pa.

He married Fanny Waldron, daughter of Newton Waldron, of Bristol, R. I., May 30, 1824.

CHILDREN — EIGHTH GENERATION

2301. John Newton, b March 28, 1825

2302 George Leonard, b June 28, 1832

John N died August 12, 1848

George L resides in Troy, Bradford County, Pa He married Abbie Peck, daughter of Peleg Peck, of Sylvania, Bradford County, Pa. Their child, (2303) *Fannie W*,[9] was born October 30, 1858. Their great-great-great-grandfather was one and the same person

[1824.] JOHN T.[7] PECK, son of JOHN,[6] settled, lived and died in Troy, Bradford County, Pa.

He married Laura Sanford, of Candor, Tioga County, N. Y., May 6, 1835. He died April 20, 1856.

CHILDREN — EIGHTH GENERATION

2304 Horace N., b Oct 23, 1836

2305 Emma A., b Feb. 6, 1844.

Horace died October 19, 1847

Emma was residing in Mainsburgh, Tioga County, Pa., in 1863

[1825.]   WILLIAM[7] PECK, son of JOHN,[6] resides in Columbia, Bradford County, Pa.

He married Lucy Ann Coggshall, daughter of John Coggshall, of Bristol, R. I., June 9, 1833.

CHILD — EIGHTH GENERATION

2306.   Ann Sophia, b. Nov 9, 1834

Ann Sophia married Orin McCalum, of Troy, Bradford County, Pa.

[1826.]   HENRY[7] PECK, of Fall River, R. I., son of JOHN,[6] married Mary B. Talbot, daughter of William Talbot, of Dighton, Mass., September 30, 1829.

CHILDREN — EIGHTH GENERATION

2307   Rev John Milton, b June 13, 1830.   2308.   Mary Baylies, b June 14, 1834

Rev John M. is an Episcopal minister; was settled in Claremont, N H., in 1864   His children were   (2309) *Cornelia T*[9] and (2310) *Robert H*[9]   He married Catharine J Turnbull, daughter of John Turnbull, of Paisley, Scotland

[1827.]   HORACE[7] PECK, of Bristol, R. I., son of JOHN,[6] married Eliza Cole, May 16, 1838, daughter of Luther Cole, of Bristol.   He is a wealthy farmer.

CHILDREN — EIGHTH GENERATION

2311   Eliza T Cole, b Aug 11, 1839
2312   Helen Louisa, b Feb 3, 1842
2313.   Susan Emma, b. July 27, 1844
2314.   Ann Smith, b Nov 20, 1846.
2315.   Abbie Elizabeth, b. May 17, 1852
2316.   Clara Wheaton, b Jan. 6, 1858.

[1828.]   GEORGE R.[7] PECK, son of JOHN,[6] resides in Galesburg, Ill.   He has been twice married: first, to Margaret Caldwell Smith, daughter of Barnard Smith, of Warren, R. I., July 24, 1844; second, to Lavinia Alice Hathaway, June 24, 1858.   His first wife died December 1855.

CHILDREN — EIGHTH GENERATION

2317.   Barnard Smith, b. May 24, 1845.
2318.   George Francis, b July 18, 1847.
2319.   William Smith, b Sept 4, 1849
2320   Walter Everett, b Jan 2, 1852

[1840.]   SAMUEL V.[7] PECK, son of NATHANIEL,[6] settled at first at Amenia, Dutchess County, N. Y.   He died at Poughkeep-

16

sie, November 11, 1830.   He married Phebe Maria Peabody, September 30, 1817.

CHILDREN — EIGHTH GENERATION

2321   Caroline A., b. Aug. 1818.
2322. William H , b. June 1820   Died 1858.
2323. Horatio A., b. 1822.
2324. Frederick A , b. 1824.
2325   Mary, b 1826 Died in infancy.
2326. Dewit C., b. 1828. Died 1838.

Caroline A. married Hamilton Broadshaw, and settled in Brooklyn, N Y
Horatio A. married Phebe D. Laird, settled at Grand Rapids, Mich.
Frederick A married Mary Peck, daughter of Nathaniel B. Peck, of Pharsalia. He settled in New York City.

[1841.]   NATHANIEL B.[7] PECK, son of NATHANIEL,[6] settled at Pharsalia, N. Y., where he was residing in 1863.   To his kindness I am indebted for my information in relation to his father's family.   He married Nancy Babcock, September 14, 1828.

CHILDREN — EIGHTH GENERATION

2327. Byfield, b. Nov. 7, 1830. Died   Jan 30, 1847.
2328. Mary, b. May 9, 1837

Mary married Frederick A. Peck, February 6, 1856.

[1854.]   PHILIP S.[7] PECK, son of WILLIAM B.,[6] settled first in Illinois, and from there removed to California in May 1862.   He married Sarah A. Ward, of Illinois, May 1855.

CHILD — EIGHTH GENERATION

2329. Harvey, b. Aug. 1857.

[55]   FRANKLIN K.[7] PECK, son of DR. GEORGE,[6] resides at Clinton, Iowa, a wealthy farmer.   To him I am indebted for the interest he has taken in my work, and his kindness in furnishing me with information.   He married Frances E. Brown, daughter of William Brown, March 20, 1838.   She was born April 10, 1818.

CHILDREN — EIGHTH GENERATION .

2330   Jane M., b. Oct 13, 1839
2331. William B , b. Feb. 10, 1841.
2332. John R , b. Sept. 1, 1843. Died young
2333   Marriett, b Sept. 24, 1844.
2334. Frances, b Nov. 11, 1846.
2335. Ellen, b Sept 16, 1848. Died Nov. 20, 1858.
2336. Sarah, b. Jan 26, 1850. Died Dec. 2, 1858.
2237. Elizabeth, b. Oct 20, 1851.
2338. David, b. Jan 18, 1854. Died young.
2339. Franklin K. Jr , b. Feb. 17, 1855. Died Dec 8, 1858
2340. Minerva, b Nov 9, 1856. Died Sept 24, 1857.
2341. George, b. April 29, 1858.
2342. Frank, b Aug. 22, 1860.
2343. Wesley, b. June 11, 1863.

Jane M married John W. Brindle, of Clinton, Iowa, May 20, 1859. He died June 14, 1860 Their child, *Mary L.*, was born May 10, 1860, and died August 30, 1861. She then married William Ehrhart, at Dubuque, Iowa, February 23, 1862

Marriett married Francis Bennett, at Clinton, Iowa. Their child (2344) *Francis W.[9] Bennett*, was born November 14, 1863.

[1863.] GEORGE[7] PECK, son of Dr. George,[6] resides in California. He married Sarah Maynes, daughter of Andrew Maynes.

CHILDREN — EIGHTH GENERATION

2345   Loring, b 1850.
2346. Julia, b. 1856.

2347. Charles J , b. 1860
2348. John, b 1862

[1869.] WILLIAM B.[7] PECK, son of Richard,[6] settled at Wells, Hamilton County, N. Y., where he has been for many years clerk and county register. He has now, 1863, resigned his office and entered the army in the service of his country, as he writes me, " to hand down to his children the inheritance so nobly bequeathed to them by their honored grandsire." * He married Frances M. Craig.

CHILDREN — EIGHTH GENERATION ·

2349   Richard, b July 27, 1849.
2350   Jackson, b. Jan. 22, 1851
2351   Robert, b. Aug. 5, 1852
2352. Lavinia, b. March 22, 1854.

2353. Jay, b. June 12, 1856
2354. William B., b Oct 1, 1857
2355. Henry, b July 1, 1860.
2356. Frances, b Feb. 17, 1862.

[1872.] CHARES H.[7] PECK, son of Richard,[6] is now, 1864, in the army in the service of his country. His family reside at Providence, Saratoga County, N. Y. He married Ann Mandeville.

CHILDREN — EIGHTH GENERATION

2357. Louisa, b. Sept 12, 1859.

2358   Charles, b. Dec. 10, 1861

[1874] CYRUS[7] PECK, son of Jonathan,[6] married Nancy Pierce, daughter of Isaac Pierce.

CHILDREN — EIGHTH GENERATION :

2359. Mary Ann.

2360. Nancy.

Mary Ann, who married Reuben Emmerson, settled at Webster, where she died, leaving children

Nancy, who married a Mois, settled in the State of New York, where she died.

---

* He was killed at the battle of the Wilderness, May 8, 1864.

[1876.]   JONATHAN[7] PECK, son of JONATHAN,[6] married a Monroe.   He lived and died in Bristol, R. I.

CHILD — EIGHTH GENERATION

2361. Albert.

Albert also married, lived and died in Bristol, R I

[1877.]   CALEB[7] PECK, of Central Falls, R. I., son of JONATHAN,[6] married Betsey Kendall, daughter of Cheever Kendall, of Hope, Me., November 26, 1826.   They were residing at Central Falls, R. I., in 1863.

CHILDREN — EIGHTH GENERATION

2362 Betsey E , b Aug 21, 1830.	2365 Sarah Ann, b April 27, 1836 }
2363. Lucy E , b Feb 16, 1832	2366 Lydia Ann, b April 27, 1836 }
2364. Maria F., b. Feb. 8, 1835.	Twins

[1889.]   EDWIN[7] PECK, son of GIDEON,[6] was a sea-captain.   He died in Providence, R. I., September 13, 1840.

He married Martha W. Burr, daughter of Capt. Hazard Burr, of Rehoboth, Mass.   She died April 23, 1849.

CHILDREN — EIGHTH GENERATION

2367 Delight R , b Oct. 23, 1823.	2370 Julia Ann, b Jan 31, 1832.
2368 Edwin H , b Dec 22, 1824	2371 Martha W , b. April 25, 1833
2369 Henry Clay, b. Aug 13, 1828.	2372 Darius B , b. Oct 10, 1834.

Delight married Simeon C Hewett, a Universalist clergyman

Edwin H,[9] married Emma Cornell, of Swansey   He died in the U S Navy, August 1, 1863   His family were then residing in Providence, R I.   His children were   (2373) *Amey F*,[9] (2374) *Edgar H.*,[9] (2375) *Julia A*,[9] (2376) *Carrie L*,[9] (2377) *Everett H*,[9] and (2378) *Jemima.*[9]

Julia Ann married Samuel Anthony, and was residing at Olneyville, R. I., in 1863

Martha married James Bickford, of Boston, Mass , and afterwards a Wheelock, of New York City.

[1890.]   NOAH[7] PECK, son of GIDEON,[6] remained upon the homestead, where he died, January 7, 1856.

He was twice married: first, to Abby Maxwell, daughter of Squire Maxwell, of Rehoboth, Mass.; second, to Emma H. Luther, daughter of Gardiner Luther, of Dighton, Mass.

CHILDREN — EIGHTH GENERATION '

2379 William M , b. Jan. 14, 1826
      Died May 23, 1826.
2380. William M., b. May 11, 1827.
      Died Nov. 18, 1846.
2381. Noah A , b June 12, 1829.
      Died June 2, 1863
2382. Maria E , b Oct 16, 1832.
      Died Dec. 16, 1837.
2383. Abby H., b. Aug. 26, 1836.
      Died Sept. 15, 1836.

2384 Edwin L , b. Feb. 10, 1839, by
      2d wife.
2385. Jonathan W , b. Jan 17, 1841.
      Died July 24, 1842
2386. Abby M , b. Oct 10, 1843
2387 Emma H., b Jan. 31, 1846.
      Died Aug 31, 1847.
2388. Walter R , b Sept 16, 1850.
2389. William M , b. Aug 23, 1853.

[1903] PHILIP F. W.[7] PECK, of Chicago, son of PHILIP,[6] married Mary K. Wythe, of Philadelphia.

CHILDREN — EIGHTH GENERATION

2390. Walter Leslie, b. Sept. 19, 1839.
2391 Clarence Ives, b Aug 20, 1841.
2392. Harold Stoughton, b. Dec. 11,

1845.
2393. Ferdinand Wythe, b. July 15, 1848.

[1904.] HENRY P.[7] PECK, son of PHILIP,[6] resides in Bloom, Cooke County, Ill.

He has been twice married : first, to Caroline Lawton, daughter of Joseph Lawton ; second, to Helen Smith, daughter of Jerusha Smith.

CHILDREN — EIGHTH GENERATION

2394 Sarah C , b. Dec. 31, 1848
2395. Mary C , b April 22, 1851.
2396. Charles V , b. Aug 31, 1855.
2397. Anna A , b Aug. 2, 1856.

2398. Henry W., b Nov 5, 1857
2399. Oren B , b. June 14, 1859
2400 Philip A., b May 17, 1861.
2401. Ella C., b. Jan 29, 1863.

[1905.] CHARLES M.[7] PECK, son of PHILIP,[6] resides in Providence, R. I.

He married Adriana Fisher, daughter of Rufus Fisher, of Edgartown, Mass., September 16, 1838.

CHILDREN — EIGHTH GENERATION

2402. Mary Chase, b. July 15, 1839.
2403. Charles Edward, b. April 9, 1843.
2404. Edmond Burk, b. April 24, 1844

2405. Ella Frances, b. Jan. 16, 1847.
2406. Louis W., b. Oct. 18, 1851.
2407. William Frederick, b. Sept. 6, 1855.

[1908.] WILLIAM[7] PECK, son of WILLIAM,[6] married Lucinda Emerson, daughter of Willard Emerson, of Thompson, Conn.,

16*

in 1827. He died in Providence. She was residing in Worcester, Mass., in 1864.

CHILDREN — EIGHTH GENERATION

2408　Charles H , b March 11, 1829　　2409.　George F , b. July 30, 1831

George F. was residing in Milwaukee in 1864, unmarried.

Charles H. settled in Worcester, Mass., where he was residing in 1864　He married Harriet G　Holyoke, daughter of E Holyoke, of Brookline, Mass , January 1, 1854.　Their child (2410) *Florence E.*,[9] was born February 18, 1855.

[1911.] JOSEPHUS[7] PECK, son of WILLIAM,[6] married Louisa Taft, daughter of Adolphus Taft, March 9, 1837. She was born in Northbridge, April 3, 1815. He died in Georgia, October 24, 1842.

CHILD — EIGHTH GENERATION .

2411.　Edwin C., b　Feb. 3, 1840

Edwin C resides in Northbridge, Mass. He married Susan E　Butler, of Wilbraham, Mass., November 20, 1861　She was born May 8, 1845.　Their child (2412) *Emma Louisa*[9] was born November 28, 1862.

[1912.] NOAH L.[7] PECK, of Woonsocket, R. I., son of WILLIAM,[6] married Polly Brown, daughter of Capt. Walter Brown, of Webster, Mass., January 26, 1837.

CHILDREN — EIGHTH GENERATION :

2413.　Walter Brown, b. Oct. 18, 1837.
2414.　Emily Ann, b. Jan. 11, 1840.
2415.　Jonathan, b. June 24, 1841.
　　　　Died July 24, 1841.
2416.　Elizabeth, b.　April 3, 1843.
　　　　Died Oct 21, 1843
2417.　Leonard, b　May 18, 1847.
　　　　Died June 11, 1847

[1914.] ALBERT G.[7] PECK, son of SYLVANUS,[6] resides in Rehoboth, Mass. He has been twice married: first, to Abby M. Stephens, daughter of Joseph Stephens, of Providence, R. I., March 11, 1833; second, to Patience Davis, daughter of John Davis, of Rehoboth, Mass., October 12, 1857. His first wife died November 4, 1854. She was born June 15, 1812.

CHILDREN — EIGHTH GENERATION :

2418.　Albert M., b　Jan 12, 1834.
2419.　Abby R., b　Aug. 12, 1836.
2420.　Adelaide F , b　April 11, 1838.
2421.　William H , b. Nov. 11, 1841.
　　　　Died Feb. 3, 1844.
2422.　Ruth W , b. Aug　14, 1844.
2423.　Ann E , b. Dec. 6, 1846.
2424.　John D., b. Oct. 13, 1862 , by
　　　　2d wife.

Albert M. married Mary Abby Northup, of Central Falls, R. I.
Abby R. married John M. Davis, of Rehoboth, Mass.
Adelaide F. married Henry Grayham, of Swansey.
Ruth W married Wheaton Cole, of Pawtucket, R. I.
Ann Elizabeth was residing in Warren, R. I., unmarried, in 1864.

[1915.] CYRUS[7] PECK, son of SYLVANUS,[6] married Rebecca P. Sherman, daughter of Robert Sherman, of Newport, R. I., December 1830. She died in Newport, May 27, 1859.

They have had five children, four of whom died in infancy.

CHILD — EIGHTH GENERATION.

2425. Gustavus B , b Dec 31, 1832.

Gustavus B. resides in Rehoboth, Mass. He married Lydia Luther, daughter of Rodolphus Luther, of Rehoboth, January 4, 1858. Their child (2426) *Ella R.*,[9] was born September 10, 1858.

[1917.] JAMES M.[7] PECK, of Warren, R. I., son of SYLVANUS,[6] married Elizabeth Luther, daughter of Samuel Luther.

CHILDREN — EIGHTH GENERATION

2427. Samuel L., b Dec. 17, 1845.
2428. James C., b. Jan. 29, 1850.

A daughter, b. Feb. 22, 1857.
Died in infancy, unnamed.

[1919.] SYLVANUS[7] PECK, JR., of East Providence, son of SYLVANUS,[6] has been twice married. For his first wife he married Caroline Hicks, daughter of Capt. Nathaniel Hicks, of Rehoboth, Mass., April 25, 1843. For his second wife he married Mrs. Elizabeth Caruthers, widow, November 16, 1851, formerly Miss Elizabeth McKensy, daughter of Alexander McKensy. His first wife died December 8, 1850.

CHILDREN — EIGHTH GENERATION :

2429. Edwin C., b Aug 8, 1843.
2430. Caroline H., b. Nov. 15, 1850.

2431. Jane E., b. Dec. 17, 1855.

[1922.] WILLIAM[7] PECK, son of NICHOLAS,[6] settled at first upon Grand Isle, in Lake Champlain, Vt.; afterwards in Chateaugay, Franklin County, N. Y., where he died, September 18, 1864.

He married Mary Ann Martin, of Grand Isle. She was born October 8, 1790. She survived him, and was residing in Chateaugay in 1864.

CHILDREN — EIGHTH GENERATION :

2432. Lury, b. Nov. 10, 1810.

2433. William W., b. Aug. 17, 1812.

2434   Ambrose, b Jan. 5, 1815.

2435. Martin, b Feb. 8, 1817.

2436. Sarah, b July 23, 1819.

2437. Seth S., b Jan. 23, 1822.

2438. Mary Ann, b. Feb. 28, 1829.

2439. Guy, b. April 13, 1828

2440. Julia M., b March 23, 1832.

2441. Horace, b June 13, 1834.

Lury married Martin Smith. She died September 16, 1841. He died September 16, 1842. They left five children.. *Mary J.,*[9] *Lucy Ann,*[9] *Sarah Hannah,*[9] *Polly Amelia,*[9] and *Lucy Alzina* [9]

William W married Clarissa A. Smith, of Chateaugay, settled in Illinois, and from there removed to Iowa. His children are (2442) *Clarinda,*[9] (2443) *Willard W.,*[9] (2444) *Claretta E ,*[9] (2445) *George W.,*[9] (2446) *Charles W.,*[9] and *Oliver L* [9] *Clarinda* married Nicholas Stark.

Ambrose married Hannah Nichols, of Peru, N Y., and resided in Chateaugay in 1864. Their children were (2447) *Sarah Ann,*[9] (2448) *Harvey,*[9] (2449) *Eliza,*[9] (2450) *Henry,*[9] and (2451) *Ruamie.*[9]

Martin married Alice Cheeney. They were residing in Dellona, Sauk County, Wis., in 1864. Their children were (2452) *Harriet,*[9] (2453) *Decature,*[9] (2454) *Jackson,*[9] and (2455) *Nelson.*[9]

Sarah married William Woodward, of Chateaugay. Their children are *Ruth,*[9] *George,*[9] *Julia,*[9] and *Hiram.*[9] Mr. Woodward died November 14, 1858.

Seth S. married Jane Gale. They were residing in Iowa in 1864. Their children were (2456) *Calista,*[9] (2457) *Eugene,*[9] (2458) *Helen,*[9] (2459) *Sylvester,*[9] (2460) *Willard,*[9] and (2461) *Wolford,*[9] twins.

Mary Ann married R. S. Church, of Chateaugay, to whose kindness I am indebted for my information. Their children are. *Elmore,*[9] *Almon,*[9] *Nancy Ann,*[9] and *Sanford Reuben.*[9]

Guy was residing in Chateaugay in 1864, unmarried.

Julia M married Silas Colby, of Lowell, Mass. , was residing in Chateaugay in 1864 Their children were *Augustus,*[9] *Emma,*[9] *Walter,*[9] *Ady,*[9] *Frank,*[9] and *Henry,*[9]

Horace married Mary Muncil, and resided in Chateaugay in 1864. Their children were (2462) *Ida,*[9] (2463) *Chloe,*[9] and (2464) *Lilly.*[9]

[1924.] CHARLES[7] PECK, son of NICHOLAS,[6] married Polly Martin, daughter of Jonah Martin, November 15, 1815. He was residing in Camden, Lorain County, Ohio, in 1865. His wife died May 25, 1865.

CHILDREN — EIGHTH GENERATION

2465. Hardy, b. Aug 6, 1816.

2466. Hester, b. March 20, 1822.

2467. Hiram, b Feb 6, 1824.

2468. Hector, b July 30, 1826.

2469. Charles, b. Dec 8, 1831.

2470. Allen, b. June 22, 1864.

Hardy married Jane Dodd, April 15, 1838. He settled in Illinois, where he died, September 12, 1838

Hester married Marvin Mosher, October 12, 1859 ; was residing in Camden in 1865.

Hiram married Sarah Ann Griggs, November 10, 1848. He was residing in

Brighton, Lorain County, Ohio, in 1865. His children were (2471) *Merton*,[9] (2472) *Charles*,[9] and (2473) *Elizabeth* [9]

Hector married Angeline Laurence, August 20, 1853 He was residing in Waubec, Linn County, Iowa, in 1865. His children were (2474) *Franklin*,[9] (2475) *Sherman*,[9] and (2476) *Charles*.[9]

Allen was also residing in Waubec in 1865. He married Elizabeth Bliss, July 28, 1864

Charles was in Australia in 1861. He married Isabella Linton, April 6, 1854. His child (2477) is *Alice May*.[9]

[1925.] PELEG[7] PECK, son of NICHOLAS,[6] married Emily Gates. He settled in Thurlow, Canada West, where they both died, leaving five daughters and one son. He died January 3, 1838. She died February 20, 1852.

CHILDREN — EIGHTH GENERATION

2478. Sarah, b July 17, 1824.	2481 Eunice, b Oct 11, 1833.
2479 Isaac, b Sept 2, 1829.	2482. Alzina, b Dec 18, 1836.
2480. Angeline, b June 3, 1832	*Eliza Jane

Sarah married Aaron Lighthall, and settled in Michigan

Angeline married John Collins, was residing in Thurlow, Canada West, in 1865.

Eunice married Richard Brady, was residing in Huntington, Canada West, in 1865

Alzina married Gilbert McIntosh, was residing in Sidney, Canada West, in 1865

Eliza Jane was residing with her sister Angeline, unmarried, in 1865

Isaac was residing in Huntington, Canada West, in 1866 He married Martha Carson Their children were *William J*,[9] b. November 2, 1852, *Thomas B*,[9] b June 24, 1854, *Emily Jane*,[9] b February 22, 1857, *George*,[9] b. January 2, 1859, *Isaac*,[9] b June 22, 1861, *Margaret*,[9] b. 1865.

[1927.] SETH[7] PECK, son of NICHOLAS,[6] was residing at Dellona, Sauk County, Wis., in 1864. He married Cynthia Emmons, April 24, 1826.

CHILD — EIGHTH GENERATION :

2483. Seth, b. Jan. 1, 1827. Died Jan. 5, 1827.

[1931.] WILLIAM[7] PECK, son of THOMAS,[6] settled in Dighton, Mass., where he lived and died. He is said to have been a man of much talent. He was a Brigadier-General, and was president of the court-martial which tried Lieut.-Col. G. T. Winthrop for failing to properly do escort duty with his command in Boston on election day in 1832.

---

* This name was not received until after they were numbered and arranged.

He married Lemira Mason, daughter of Job Mason, of Swansey, Mass. He died May 25, 1839. She died November 12, 1856.

CHILDREN — EIGHTH GENERATION

2484. Betsey V., b. June 5, 1825
2485. Adaline G , b. Jan. 30, 1827
2486. Lemira M , b Nov 13, 1828.
2487. Martha E , b May 23, 1834

Betsey V has been twice married first, to Andrew J. Briggs, June 5, 1843; second, to Joseph Pitts, March 30, 1852. They settled in Illinois.

Adaline G married Denis Kenyon, August 20, 1854, and settled in Illinois.

Lemira married George K. Vinekum, and settled in Swansey, Mass.

Martha E married Jason Place, and settled in Connecticut.

[1932] DR. GARDNER M.[7] PECK, son of THOMAS.[6] His name appeared before the public in 1821 as a graduate of the degree of Doctor of Medicine at Brown University, Providence, R. I. He settled in Foxborough, Mass. He soon acquired a large measure of public confidence, and his practice became widely extended.

After a professional life of about fifteen years, the fatigues and privations of a country practice became intolerable, and he resolved to abandon it. He accordingly gave notice of his intentions, and at a time fixed discontinued his professional services, except in special cases.

He afterwards engaged in manufacturing business. In the autumn of 1838, he removed to the city of New York, and entered into mercantile business, in which he continued until his retirement in 1864.

Since then he has taken considerable interest in the mining business of the country, and is understood to be president of one or two New York Mining Companies.

He has been twice married. For his first wife, he married Elizabeth H. Mason, daughter of Job Mason, of Swansey, Mass. She died in 1840. For his second wife, he married Sarah Talbot, daughter of Capt. Seth Talbot, of Dighton, Mass.

CHILDREN — EIGHTH GENERATION

2488. Martha E , b. Jan. 14, 1822. Died Sept. 10, 1832.
2489 Gardner M., b. Jan. 29, 1825. Died April 4, 1825
2490. Thomas G , b Dec. 22, 1827. Died Sept. 10, 1832.
2491. Benjamin C., b. May 25, 1832.
2492. Joseph, b April 22, 1835. Died Feb 9, 1838
2493. Elizabeth M , b April 6, 1837.
2494. Helen G , b Sept. 8, 1846, by 2d wife
2495. Ella M , b. Dec. 29, 1853. Died March 24, 1857.

G. M. Peck

[1934.] GEORGE[7] PECK, son of THOMAS,[6] remained upon the homestead. He married Mary Davis. He died July 1, 1845. She December 26, 1838.

CHILDREN — EIGHTH GENERATION.

2496. George, b May 29, 1822. Died July 21, 1842, unm
2497. Eliza S., b May 25, 1827.
2498. Seth F , b Feb. 27, 1829.
2499. Mary D., b. Jan. 18, 1831.
2500. Martha G., b. Dec 8, 1833.
2501. Betsey G., b April 22, 1835
2502. Thomas, b Nov 17, 1837. Died Dec 8, 1837.

Eliza S. married Charles Mason, and settled in Warren, R. I.
Mary D. married John Hubbard, settled in Warren, R I.
Martha G married William Baker; settled in Warren, R. I.
Betsey G married John H. Bowen, settled in Warren, R I.

[1939.] WILLIAM[7] PECK, son of HEZEKIAH,[6] left Warren, R. I., September 17, 1818, and settled at first in Portsmouth, Sciota County, Ohio. He was residing at Xenia, Dallas County, Iowa, in 1863. He has been twice married: first, to Mary Ann Hickey, December 16, 1819; second, to Zidania Pettet, October 21, 1850. His first wife died at Muscatine, Iowa, May 1, 1849, with the cholera. He held the office of Justice of the Peace for several years at Portsmouth, and has also held the office where he resides.

CHILDREN — EIGHTH GENERATION

2503. William G., b Dec 25, 1820.
2504. Hezekiah M , b Oct. 23, 1823.
2505 Maria K , b Feb 21, 1826.
2506. John G., b. June 16, 1828. Died Jan. 9, 1829
2507. Lydia, b Jan. 11, 1830 Died Sept. 25, 1839.
2508. Daniel, b. Nov 15, 1832.
2509. Joseph, b. April 21, 1837. Died Sept. 22, 1839.
2510. John B , b. Sept 24, 1839.
2511. Turner M., b. Dec. 21, 1842.
2512. Charles W., b. June 24, 1845.

By second wife

2513. Abigail, b May 18, 1852.
2514. Sarah Ann, b July 2, 1854.
2515. Isabel L , b May 11, 1856
2516. George M , b. Dec 23, 1858.
2517. Mary E , b. Jan 21, 1861
2518. Frances V., b. Feb 23, 1863

William G. married Charlott Bennet, by whom he has had six children He was a Deputy Sheriff for some time at Muscatine. From there he removed to St Louis.

Hezekiah was a pilot upon the Mississippi River, where he died with the cholera, December 23, 1848.

Maria K. married Thomas Platt, and settled at Muscatine, Iowa

Daniel settled in Jackson, Ohio.

John B married Mary Hutchings. Their child was (2519) *William Lewis,*[9] b. August 19, 1862, and died October 1, 1862.

Turner M enlisted in the 11th Iowa Volunteers.

Charles W. enlisted in the army, was taken sick, and came back to Muscatine, and died.

[1940.]   HEZEKIAH[7] PECK, son of HEZEKIAH,[6] left Warren, R. I., about 1819, and settled in Smithfield, Bradford County,
Pa., where he remained until about 1857, when he removed to
Towanda, where he was residing in 1864.   I am told that he formerly took an active interest in military matters, and at one time
held a Colonel's commission.   He married Ruth Hale, at Smithfield, Bradford County, Pa , September 6, 1821.   She was born at
Warren, R. I., March 11, 1803.

CHILDREN — EIGHTH GENERATION ·

2520. Mary W., b May 13, 1823.   2522. Sophia C , b May 30, 1828.
2521   George S., b July 23, 1825.   2523   William A., b Jan 24, 1833.

Mary W married Clark M Stanley, February 14, 1848 , resided at Athens,
Bradford County, Pa , in 1864.

George S. married Calista M Salsbury, in 1848   They were residing at Towanda, Bradford County, Pa , in 1864 He was Captain of Co G, 57th Reg. P.
V. His children were (2524) *William,*[9] b in Smithfield, Bradford County, Pa ,
July 31, 1849, (2525) *George,*[9] b. May 31, 1852, (2526) *R* [9] ——, born in Towanda, September 18, 1855 , and (2527) *Clarence,*[9] b. January 16, 1858

Sophia C married George H. Estelle, October 30, 1845. They were residing
at Towanda in 1864.

William A married Jennie L Tracy, at Smithfield, Bradford County, Pa ,
November 26, 1862. They were residing at Towanda, Pa , in 1864   He was a
Physician and Surgeon, and had charge of 104th Regiment Pennsylvania Volunteers, afterwards Surgeon in charge of the 1st Brigade in Casey's Division,
through the Peninsular Campaign , then medical director of Perkins' Division,
4th Corps , and afterwards medical purveyor of the Department of Susquehan-
nah, on General Couch's Staff He was practising law at Towanda, Pa., in
1864.

[1941.]   PELEG[7] PECK, son of HEZEKIAH,[6] left Warren, R.
I., December 1819, and settled in Smithfield, Bradford County, Pa ,
where he remained until 1840, when he moved to Columbia. From
here he removed to Sylvania, where he was residing in 1864.   He
married Lydia C. Hunter, daughter of Daniel and Lydia Hunter, of
Bristol, R. I., November 23, 1821.

CHILDREN — EIGHTH GENERATION

2528. William H , b Feb 2, 1822.   2534. Emma A , b. Sept. 15, 1836
2529. Hannah, b May 9, 1824.   2535. Francis H., b. Feb. 2, 1839.
2530. Hezekiah, b Nov. 17, 1826.   2536. George M., b. July 2, 1841.
2531. Seth, b. April 17, 1829.   2537. Thomas, b. April 23, 1844.
2532   Peleg, b July 2, 1831.   2538. Josephine A , b. Oct 22, 1846.
2533   Abbie E., b Dec 6, 1833

William H commenced the study of law, February 1846, with Messrs.
Hazard and Pierce, in Troy, Bradford County, Pa , where he now resides, in

the practice of his profession He was admitted to the bar in 1847. He married Helen M Spaulding, of Troy, September 22, 1852 Their daughter (2539) *Florence*[9] was born April 16, 1854, and died August 6, 1860

Hannah married Lewis B. Robinson, January 1, 1843, and settled in Columbia He was killed by lightning, June 8, 1843. She died September 12, 1857, leaving one daughter *Hannah*,[9] born December 5, 1843

Hezekiah resides in Columbia, Bradford County, Pa. He married Jane Ballard, daughter of Myron Ballard, of Columbia, April 17, 1840 Their children are (2540) *Horace B*,[9] b August 27, 1851, (2541) *Edward Y*,[9] b June 27, 1853, (2542) *William*,[9] b June 7, 1858, and (2543) *Barton*,[9] b. November 10, 1862

Seth married Juliet Kieff, daughter of Andrew Kieff, November 7, 1855. Their son (2544) *Floyd*[9] was born March 13, 1860

Peleg resides in Smithfield, unmarried

Abbie married, September 19, 1855, George L Peck, son of Jonathan Peck, of Columbia, Bradford County, Pa , formerly of Bristol, R. I. He is a merchant They are settled in Troy. Their great-great-great-grandfather was one and the same person

Emma A died September 3, 1852.

Francis H was serving his country in the Union army in 1864.

George M was residing in Troy

Thomas was residing in Columbia

Josephine was residing in Sylvania, unmarried.

[1949] SALSBURY PECK,[7] son of SALSBURY,[6] married for his first wife, Ruth Peckham, daughter of Silas Peckham, of Providence, R. I., January 8, 1843. For his second, Margaret A. Robinson, August 21, 1854. His first wife died October 17, 1852.

CHILDREN — EIGHTH GENERATION

2545	Emory A , b Feb 15, 1846,	2548. Annah A , b July 13, 1856.
	Died Aug 2, 1846	2549 Laura R , b May 6, 1860.
2546	Francis E , b July 3, 1851	2550 Emma A , b November 1862
2547.	Alice M , b Aug. 24, 1852	

[1951] PELEG[7] PECK, of Rehoboth, son of BENJAMIN,[6] married Laura Thresher, daughter of Asahel Thresher, of Rehoboth.

CHILDREN — EIGHTH GENERATION ·

2551.	Laura W , b June 19, 1844.	2553 Lydia A , b Dec 9, 1851.
	Died Sept 23, 1847	2554 Susan M , b June 19, 1854
2552	Mary T , b Mar. 1, 1846.	2555 Imogene, b June 18, 1856

Mary T married Michael J Higgins Lieut Higgins enlisted in the 3d Rhode Island Regiment Heavy Artillery, soon after the breaking out of the Rebellion Notwithstanding his youth, he filled with much honor and credit, the positions of Private, Corporal, Sergeant, and first and second Lieutenant. He was in command for some time at Fort Pulaski, Tibee and Morris Islands,

17

filling for more than six months the position of Post Adjutant   He resigned his commission at the age of 19, after having been in the service three and one-half years.

[1957.]   GEORGE B.[7] PECK, son of George B.,[6] resides in Warren, R. I.   He married Cordelia J. Adams, daughter of Ira Adams, of East Smithfield, Pa., September 1, 1849.

CHILDREN — EIGHTH GENERATION

2556   Clara Aldelia, b. Mar. 25, 1851

2557.   William Howard, b Nov. 22, 1855.

2558.   Rachel Amelia, b Sept 5, 1861.

2559   George Ira, b Mch 24, 1863

[1963.]   HORACE M.[7] PECK, of Providence, son of Robert,[6] married Rachel Maxfield, daughter of David Maxfield, of Dartmouth, Mass., May 8, 1833

CHILDREN — EIGHTH GENERATION

2560   Susan Amanda, b. July 4, 1834

2561.   Horace Montraville, b Oct. 9, 1836

2562   Rachel Maxfield, b Mar 11, 1839   Died June 28, 1840

2563   Ambros Robert, b May 18, 1841.

2564   Allen Millard, b Dec 11, 1843

2565   Ednah Augusta, b May 8, 1846   Died Oct 2, 1847

2566.   Waldo Ames, b Sept 25, 1849

2567.   Frank Richardson, b Mar 23, 1852

2568.   Minnie Cowell, b Feb. 14, 1861

Horace M. married Mary E Allers, daughter of Capt John G Allers, November 16, 1859   He was residing in California in 1863 * *Sarah D*,[9] their child, was born May 12, 1864

Susan Amanda married Charles Henry Cowell, of Wrentham, Mass , January 24, 1861.   They were residing in Providence in 1863

[1964.]   ISAAC L.[7] PECK, of Warren, R. I., son of Robert,[6] married Jane D. Burrell, of Pawtucket, R. I., October 20, 1839, daughter of Benjamin Burrell.

CHILD — EIGHTH GENERATION

2569.   Sarah A , b Sept 15, 1840.

Sarah A married Henry A Huff, of South Boston, June 7, 1864

---

* He returned to Providence, R I , where he died October 27, 1867   He was killed by the accidental discharge of a pistol while taking it from his pocket.

[1966.]   JOSIAS L.[7] PECK, son of Robert,[6] married Nancy R. Wardwell, daughter of Joseph and Nancy Wardwell, of Bristol, R. I.

CHILDREN — EIGHTH GENERATION

2570   Emily Maxfield, b. Aug. 4, 1833   2571. James Alanson, b Mar 16, 1835. Died Dec. 23, 1836.

Emily M. married Allen Hoar, son of Joseph and Lucy Ann Hoar, of Warren, R I   Their children were *Jennie Linden,*[9] *Joseph Allen,*[9] and *Minerva Wheaton.*[9]

[1968.]   ROBERT A.[7] PECK, of Bristol, son of Robert, [6]married Sarah B. Bennett, daughter of Martin and Eliza Bennett. She was born August 18, 1820.

CHILDREN — EIGHTH GENERATION

2572   Frank H , b. April 11, 1847.   2574. Jane G , b July 12, 1855
2573. William H , b April 12, 1850   2575. William R., b. Feb. 3, 1859.
Died Jan. 22, 1855.

PART FOURTH.

THE DESCENDANTS OF SAMUEL² PECK,

FOURTH SON OF JOSEPH¹ THE ANCESTOR.

SAMUEL PECK was born at Hingham, Mass., and baptized there, February 3, 1638–9. He removed with his father to Seekonk, and remained upon the homestead after his decease. He was one of the deacons of the church. He also held various town and other offices. He was a Deputy to the General Court at Plymouth, in 1689 and 1692. He was the first representative from the town after the Colony of Plymouth and Massachusetts were united *

The following is a copy of his will, from the Records at Taunton, Mass , Book 2, p. 207:

I Samuel Peck of yᵉ town of Rehoboth in the county of Bristol in yᵉ Province of Massachusetts Bay Being in perfect health and of good and perfect memory thanks be unto God for the same do make & ordain this my last will & testament in manʳ & form following that is to say Item I give unto my only son Noah Peck my house barn orchard & house lot & all my land in the sᵈ division & in the great plain with my land lying easterly from Ebenezer Waltiers house and land with all my fresh meadow and salt meadow lying in Rehoboth or Swansey excepting the corn on the ground and I give unto my son Noah Peck one silver bowl

Item I give unto my daughter Sarah Sabin my feather bed on which I lie with the furniture belonging there unto one silver spoon &

---

* Plymouth Colony was annexed to Massachusetts by the charter of William and Mary, in 1692.

fifty acres of land lying & being in the north purchase with all my meadow in that purchase

Item   I give unto my son in law Samuel Paine fifty acres of Land lying on the east side of Palmers river and One hundred pounds commonage in the town of Rehoboth to be to his disposal of for any of my grand children at his discretion

Item   I give unto my grand daughter Anne Paine one feather bed with one coverled & two blankets

Item   I give unto my grand daughter Sarah Paine one silver spoon

Item   I give unto my son Noah Peck my wearing appearel my staf and my cart wheels and ploughs and chaines and if Joseph Paine serve him till his indenture be out then my son Noah is to fulfill all the indenture and then I give to said Joseph Paine forty acres of land which is to be layed out, the lot being drawn for it

Item   I give unto my son Noah Peck all my arms and amunition

Item   I do ordain & make my son Noah Peck Executor of this my last will and Testament   And my Will is that after my body be burried funeral charges & debts paid and the contract maid with my wife before marriage be fulfilled that then the remainder of my estate not particularly mentioned be equally devided between my son Noah & my daughter Sabin and my son in law Samuel Paine for the use of his children my grand children

Item   I give unto my son Noah Peck that piece of upland which lies joining to my salt meadow & all my interest in the undivided lands in the North purchase and the remaining part of my commonage in Rehoboth

In witness where of I now set my hand and seal the eleventh day of June Anno Domini one thousand seven hundred and five and in the fourth year of the Reign of Queen Ann

Signed Sealed & delivered in the presents of

JOHN BUTTERWORTH
SAMUEL SMITH   SAMUEL PECK
DANIEL CARPENTER

The will was presented to the court to be proved, June 2, 1708. In the reception of the inventory, he is called Deacon Samuel Peck.

The following deed is also upon record at Taunton, Book 8, p. 668:

To all christian people to whome these presents shall come — Deacon Samuel Peck of the town of Rehoboth in the County of Bristol in her Majiesties Province of the Massachusetts Bay in New England — Sendeth Greeting — Know ye that I the aforsaid Samuel Peck fo good consideration moveing me there unto — viz — the great and dear love and affection that I have to my son Noah Peck have freely given granted enfeaoffed and confirmed and by these presents do absolutely give grant enfeoff and confirm unto my said son Noah Peck his heirs executors administrators and assigns forever the westerly end of my dewelling house the end that he liveth in now — likewise five acres of my home lot the young orchard the said lot and the orchard at the easterly end of my house and as much land at the northerly end of my lot as will make up five acres my son allowing me free egress and regress into said home lott — likewise half the lot which was my fathers in the second division both for quantity and quality as it is bounded on the records of said second division of land — likewise half my land on the great plain both for quantity and quality as it is bounded in the records of said land — likewise half the land I bought of my brother Joseph Peck in the second division both for quantity and quality as it is bounded on the records of said land — likewise half the land I had of Stephen Pain adjoining to Joseph Bucklands land in said second division both for quantity and quality as it is bounded in the records for said land — and four acres of the lot I bought of Daniel Smith — and likewise all my two allotments lying on the easterly side of bushie meadow containing eighty six acres be it more or less as it is bounded on the records — Likewise my fresh meadow at the forty acres as it is bounded in the records — Likewise half my fresh meadow on the hill river both for quantity and quality as it is bounded upon the records for said meadow and likewise all my piece of salt marsh that lies by Benjamin Allens land butted and bounded as in the records may appear — and likewise the northerly piece of my salt marsh that lieth adjoining to Israel Barneys meadow and a hundred and twenty five pound commonage in said Rehoboth all of it lying and being in Rehoboth above said — To have and to hold the aforsaid housing, orchard upland and meadow ground before named with all and singular the timber wood underwood stone mines, minerals, waters, water courses, herbage, grass, feedings, rents profits hereditaments, immunities, privileges and appertanences there to belonging or in any manner of way appertaining, with the reversion and reversions remainder and remainders to him the said Noah Peck his heirs executors administrators and assigns forever — and as a good sure perfect and absolute Estate of inheritance in fee simple according to the tenor of her Majestyes Manour of East Greenwich in the County of Kent in the Realms of England by free and common Socage and not in but without any manner of Condition or retention title of Dower or Limetation of uses whatsoever as to alter change defeat or make void the same — And the said Noah Peck his heirs and assigns shall and may by fource and virtue of these presence from time to time and at all times forever hereafter lawfully peaceably and quietly have hold occupy possess and enjoy all the above given and granted premises and every part and parcel thereof free and clear and clearly acquited and fully discharged of and from all manor of other and former gifts grants bargains sales leases jointures dowries entails judgements executions extant and from all and all manner of other gifts grants titles troubles and incumbrances whatsoever

In witness whereof he the said Samuel Peck hath sit to his hand and seal this tenth day of march in the year of our Lord One thousand seven hundred four and five in the seventh year of her Majestys Reign Signed sealed and delivered in the presence of us

Witnesses GERSHAM TABER

DANIEL SMITH

SAMUEL PECK

He was twice married. His first wife, Sarah, was buried October 27, 1673. For his second wife, he married Rebecca Hunt, November 21, 1677, widow of Peter Hunt, and daughter of Stephen Paine. She died June 12, 1699.

CHILDREN — THIRD GENERATION

2576	Anne, b Dec 22, 1667	2580	Jaiel, b June 14, 1680 Buried July 6, 1680.
2577	Sarah, b Feb 2, 1669		
2578	Judith, b July 26, 1671 Buried Feb 2, 1681	2581	Rebecca, b Oct 22, 1681 Buried Nov 2, 1682
2579	+Noah, b Aug 21, 1678.		

Anne married Samuel Paine Her children were *Joseph,*[4] *Anne*[4] and *Sarah* [4]

Sarah married John Sabin, October 3, 1698.

[2579.] NOAH PECK[3] son of SAMUEL,[2] settled upon the homestead, given him by his father. He was a representative from his town to the General Court, in 1712. Upon the records he is called Lieut. Noah Peck.

I learn but little in relation to him, and find nothing in relation to his descendants.   He disposed of a portion of his lands soon after the decease of his father, and the remainder about 1719.

It is thought by some, that his sons all died young, or without issue; and by others, that he removed to Connecticut, or some distant place, where his descendants have not been distinguished from others of the name.   The former supposition is the most probable.

He married Hannah Winter, March 4, 1702.

CHILDREN — FOURTH GENERATION:

2582. Rebecca, b. Dec 1, 1702. Baptized Nov. 19, 1704

2583. Noah, b. June 8, 1705. Baptized July 8, 1705.

2584. Samuel, b. June 27, 1707. Died Feb. 15, 1710–11

2585 Hannah, b April 29, 1711.

2586. Sarah, b Dec 29, 1713

2587. Samuel, b. July 20, 1716.

PART FIFTH.

THE DESCENDANTS OF NATHANIEL[2] PECK,

THE FIFTH SON OF JOSEPH[1] THE ANCESTOR.

NATHANIEL PECK was born at Hingham, Mass., and baptized there October 31, 1641, and removed from there with his father and family to Seekonk, afterwards Rehoboth. He settled upon the lands given him and his brother Israel, in what is now Barrington, R. I., near the present residence of Ellis Peck, Esq. They were a part of the lands purchased by the proprietors of Osamequin and his son Wamsetta.

The record of the deed of these lands, known by the name of Poppanomscut, alias Phebe's Neck, Sowames or Sowamsit, is upon the proprietors' records now in the care of the Town Clerk at Warren, R. I., dated March 29, 1653, B. 1, pg 9, where their location and division into lots may be learned. They are now partly in Bristol, Warren, Swansey, Rehoboth, and Barrington.

The lands given to Nathaniel and Israel by their father remained undivided, the most of them at least, until after the son of Nathaniel became of age. They are referred to upon the proprietors' records, first after the decease of Nathaniel, as the lands of Israel and the heirs of Nathaniel; and afterwards, as the lands of Nathaniel and his uncle Israel.

Upon the proprietors' records, January 1698–9, B. 1, pg. 73, may be found the division of their lands, some lying at Kechmuet, Scamscammuck, Chachapoucoset, and other places.

Nathaniel and his wife died at an early age. He was buried August 12, 1676, and his wife Deliverance, May 1, 1675 (R. Rec. B. 1). He had three children, and left at his decease, — as appears by the Massachusetts Colonial records, — two, a son and a daughter.

The Court, as appears upon record, appointed Jonothan Bosworth and Samuel Peck, November 1, 1676, to administer upon the estate of Nathaniel Peck, there being " two children, a son and a daughter." The Court ordered that the son should have double that of the daughter, and that the estate remain undivided until they become of age, or until they choose their own guardians.

The births of two of his children are upon the records at Swansey. That of the daughter I could not find. A number of the first leaves of the first book of births at Swansey, have been destroyed or lost; it was without doubt upon them. She doubtless died young, as did her brother Elisha, as I find no mention of her name in the division of her father's estate.

CHILDREN — THIRD GENERATION

2588 +Nathaniel, b July 26, 1670.   2590. Elisha, b April 19, 1675 Died
2589.   ——, b.   April 30, 1675

[2588.] NATHANIEL[3] PECK, son of NATHANIEL,[2] settled upon the lands left him by his father. He was a prominent man, and held various public offices. He is called upon the records for several years Lieut. Nathaniel, and afterwards Deacon Nathaniel. He was twice married: first, to Christian Allen, of Swansey, March 8, 1695–6; second, to Judith Smith, of Rehoboth, July 18, 1705 (S. Rec. B 1). His first wife deceased June 8, 1702; his second wife November 10, 1743, he August 5, 1751.

The following is from his tombstone, which is in Barrington :

In Memory of Deacon Nathaniel Peck who departed this life on y[e] 5th day of August 1751 in y[e] 82[d] year of his Age
The righteous shall be had in everlasting remembrance

CHILDREN — FOURTH GENERATION

2591. Ebenezer, b April 24, 1697   April 17, 1709
       Baptized Sept 26, 1703   2596 Abigail, b Aug 12, 1709
2592 +Nathaniel, born July 10, 1699.   2597 Bathsheba, b Jan 15, 1710-11
       Baptized Sept 26, 1703   Died Dec 13, 1769
2593 +Thomas, b Oct 4, 1700 Bap-   2598 +Soloman, b Nov 11, 1712
       tized Sept 26, 1703.   2599 John, b July 1, 1714   Died
2594 Daniel, b July 28, 1706. By   July 23, 1714
       2d wife. Baptized April 13,   2600 John, b Feb 29, 1716   Died
       1707   May 14, 1716.
2595 +David, b Nov 1707 Baptized

Abigail married Mathew Piatt.

The graves of the two last children are in the burying-ground at Seekonk.

[2591.] EBENEZER[4] PECK, son of NATHANIEL,[3] resided in Barrington, near his father. He left no issue. His will is upon the records at Taunton, Mass., B. 4, p. 346, dated June 16, 1724.

He gives to his wife Mary, 250 Acres of Land in Ashford County, of Hartford, Conn., with his household stuff, one yoke of oxen, &c. To his brother Nathaniel, 100 acres of land in Ashford, and two bonds of 209 pounds, and his mare and sheep. He also gives his wife one bond of 33 pounds. He gives to his brother Thomas, 50 Acres of Land in Ashford, Conn. He gives to his brothers Nathaniel and Thomas a bond of 37 pounds and 16 shillings, and his wearing apparel, to be equally divided betwixt them. He appoints his honored father and Zachariah Bignell executors of his will.

[2592.] NATHANIEL[4] PECK, son of NATHANIEL,[3] settled in the south-easterly part of Seekonk, not far from what has since been known as Major Monroe's, upon the farm recently known as the Doct. Hutchins' place.

By his will, which is upon the Records at Taunton, Mass , B. 15, p. 107, dated May 8, 1756, he appears to have been a man of wealth. He is called upon the Records Lieut. Nathaniel.

He gives to his wife the use of the best room in his Mansion house, with a privilege in the kitchen. He gives her the privilege of keeping a cow and horse, winter and summer, and whatever else she may choose to keep so long as she remains his widow.

He also gives her 20 lbs. of flax and 15 lbs. of wool yearly; also all his indoor movables, one horse, and one cow. He requires his son Comfort to provide for her ten bushels of indian corn, five bushels of rye, two hundred weight of pork and one hundred weight of beef yearly, so long as she shall remain his widow. He also gives her his negro girl slave, named Rose.* He gives his daughter, Mary Jacobs,

---

* The names of slaves occasionally occur among these early settlers upon records and gravestones in the burial grounds.
The following is an instance .

Here lies the best of Slaves,
Now turning into dust
Ceasor the Ethiopian craves
A place among the just.

His faithful Soul is fled
To relms of Heavenly light,
And by the blood of Jesus shed
Is changed from black to white.
Jan 15 he quit the stage,
In the 77th year of his age. 1780.

wife of Allen Jacobs, 5 pounds 13 shillings and 4 pence ; to his daughter Abagail Barney, wife of Maitain Barney, 5 pounds 13 shillings and 4 pence. He gives five sheep to his beloved grandson Nathaniel Peck, and three to his granddaughter Mary Jacobs. He divides his lands and common rights among his three sons, Thomas, Comfort & Peleg ; giving Comfort the homestead. He makes Comfort and his wife his executor and executrix. His inventory, which is upon the records at Taunton, B. 15, P. 207, is lengthy. Among the property named is one negro man, about 70 or 80 years old, one negro woman, about 40 years old, appraised at 13 pounds 6 shillings and 8 pence. One negro girl, about 8 years old, appraised at 20 pounds. One mulatto boy, about 13 years old, bound as an apprentice until 21 years of age.

He died in the army at Fort Edward, August 5, 1756 (R. Rec. B. 1). His wife was Alce Fish, of Portsmouth, R. I.

CHILDREN — FIFTH GENERATION

2601 +Thomas, b Jan. 11, 1726–7.
2602 Mary, b Dec 1, 1728
2603 +Comfort, b. May 26, 1731.

2604 Christian, b Aug 25, 1733.
2605. Abigail, b Sept 11, 1735.
2606 +Peleg, b April 8, 1741.

Mary married Allen Jacobs
Abigail married Martin Barney.

[2593.] THOMAS[4] PECK, son of NATHANIEL,[3] lived and died in Seekonk, upon the farm since owned by and known as the Deacon Vial Medbery farm.

He married Deliverance May, of Swansey, January 1729. She was born December 5, 1712, and died January 3, 1791.

He died April 5, 1763. The division of his estate is recorded upon the Taunton Records, B. 18, p. 503, dated May 3, 1764. The estate was large. His son Ebenezer had a double portion.

CHILDREN — FIFTH GENERATION

2607 +Ebenezer, b Mar. 8, 1730
2608. Deliverance, b. Jan 8, 1732–3. Died Dec 23, 1775.
2609. Allen, b Aug 22, 1735. Died April 5, 1740.
2610. Gaius, b. Jan 17, 1737–8 Died in the army Oct 23, 1758.
2611. Lois, b. Aug. 1, 1741. Died Mai 25, 1812.
2612. Jemima, b. May 19, 1744. Died

Dec. 13, 1812.
2613 Bathsheba, b. Aug. 13, 1746. Died Sept. 19, 1789
2614. Huldah, b. May 8, 1749. Died Oct 24, 1770
2615 Chloe, b Aug 10, 1751. Died Oct. 1830
2616. Thomas, b May 18, 1755. Died on board a prison ship, Nov. 16, 1777.

Deliverance married Samuel Smith.
Lois married Daniel Thurber.

Jemima married John Bucklin
Bathsheba married Mathew Allen.
Huldah married Wilson Jacobs
Chloe married Asahel Wilmoth

[2595.] DAVID[4] PECK, son of NATHANIEL,[3] remained upon a part of the homestead where his grandson Sebea Peck was residing in 1863. He died March 4, 1771.

He married Sarah Humphrey, September 20, 1744.

CHILDREN — FIFTH GENERATION (Bar Rec B 1, p 23)

2617. David, b Aug 18, 1746.
2618. Sarah, b Mar 19, 1749-50. Died Mar. 31, 1752.
2619. John, b Mar 8, 1751-2. Died Oct 10, 1753
2620. Ezra, b July 3, 1748 Died April 12, 1752.
2621. Ezra, b. Oct 5, 1753. Died Jan 5, 1754.
2622. Rachel, b Oct 20, 1754.
2623. Lewis, b Oct. 18, 1757 Died young.
2624 +Joel, b Aug 28, 1759
2625 +Lewis, b Aug 30, 1761.
2626 John, b. May 12, 1763.
2627.+Noah, b Mar 31, 1765.
2628. Sarah, b Mar 7, 1767.

Rachel married Samuel Read, of Rehoboth.
John married Susan Jones, no issue
Sarah married Caleb Spencer, and settled in Clarendon, Vt.

[2598.] SOLOMON[4] PECK, son of NATHANIEL,[3] settled upon a part of the homestead.

He married Keziah Barnes, December 29, 1737. She died July 18, 1792. He died December 8, 1776. The following are the inscriptions upon their tombstones:

Here resteth all that was mortal of Solomon Peck Esq who died Dec[r] 8th 1776 in the 65th year of his Age

My flesh shall rest in hope to rise wak[d] by his powerful voice

All that was mortal of Kezia wife of Solomon Peck Esq[r] lieth here who died July 18th 1792 in the 75th year of her Age

A faithful wife and Mother dear Such she was who now lies here

CHILDREN — FIFTH GENERATION

2629.+Solomon, b Oct 29, 1738.
2630. Keziah, b Aug 3, 1740
2631. Hannah, b Feb 4, 1743. Died Aug 17 1752
2632. Samuel, b. Dec. 30, 1744. Died Aug. 3, 1814
2633. Benjamin, b. June 3, 1747. Died Oct 12, 1776.
2634. Amos, b. May 1, 1749. Died April 24, 1816.
2635 Esther, b May 18, 1751
2636. Daniel, b Mar 24, 1753. Died Sept 10, 1776
2637 Hannah, b Oct 17, 1755
2638 Nathaniel, b. Dec. 7, 1759 Died Oct. 9, 1776
2639.+Ebenezer, b. Dec. 11, 1762.

Kesiah married Comfort Peck, and died June 25, 1776.
Esther married John Vial, of Seekonk.
Hannah married Samuel Barns

[2601.]   THOMAS[5] PECK, son of NATHANIEL,[4] settled first in Providence, then in Scituate, R. I.

CHILDREN — SIXTH GENERATION

2640 +Nathaniel, b Sept. 24, 1751
    (R R B. 2, p 29).
2641 Abigail, b Oct 2, 1753.
2642 +Thomas, b Dec 27, 1757
By his second wife (2643) *Dorathy, his*

children were (*Scit. Rec*)
2644 +Peleg, b Sept 24, 1760.
2645 +Jacob, b May 31, 1764
2646 +Peter, b. Mar 27, 1767.
2647. Dorothy, b Mar 12, 1770.

   Dorothy married William Rutenber, and settled in Otsego County, N Y.

[2603]   COMFORT[5] PECK, son of NATHANIEL,[4] remained upon the homestead. He died May 29, 1814   He married, for his first wife, Hannah Barney; for his second, Kesiah Peck, (No. 2630), daughter of Solomon Peck, and for his third, Ruth Saunders, of Haverhill, Mass.

CHILDREN — SIXTH GENERATION

2648 Christian, b Feb 4, 1756.
    Died unm
2649 +Comfort, b Oct 17, 1760
2650 Kesiah, b Jan. 2, 1764.
2651 Hannah
2652 Ruth, b. Mar 15, 1770. Died

    June 10, 1780.
2653 +Nathaniel, b Feb. 20, 1774
2654 James, b Jan 28, 1776   Died
    July 11, 1799
2655 +Thomas, b April 17, 1779.
2656 Ruth.

   Kesiah married Levi Daggett, of Seekonk, where they lived and died   Their children were *Mary,*[7] *Kesiah,*[7] *John,*[7] *Levi,*[7] *Hannah,*[7] *Betsey,*[7] *Fanny*[7] and *Lydia*[7]
   Hannah married John M. Wood, of Swansey. Their children were *Seth,*[7] *Reuben*[7] and *Kinsley*[7]
   Ruth married Zedekiah Millard, of Rehoboth. Their child was *Elizabeth,*[7] who married John Martin, of East Providence, R I.

[2606.]   PELEG[5] PECK, son of NATHANIEL,[4] lived and died in Scituate, where I found his grandson Asahel Peck residing in 1860.

He married Esther Barney, November 27, 1760.

CHILDREN — SIXTH GENERATION

2657. Aaron   Died young
2658. Peleg   Died young
2659 +Barney.
2660 +Isaac
2661.+Ebenezer
2662. Hannah   Died young.

2663 Polly
2664 John   Died young
2665. Esther   Died Aug. 21, 1801,
    aged 27 years.
2666. Martha
2667. Welcome.

Polly married Wibor Williams.
Martha married Robert Strivner.

[2670.] EBENEZER[5] PECK, son of THOMAS,[4] remained upon the homestead. He died April 14, 1807.

He married, for his first wife, Sarah Carpenter; for his second, Sarah Brown; and for his third, Sybel Ormsbee.

CHILDREN — SIXTH GENERATION

2668. Hannah   Died unm. .Nov
      10, 1813, in her 59th year.
2669 +Gaius.
2670. Mehitable
2671 Sarah   Died young.

2672 Lucy.
2673. Jacinthia.
2674 Ruth
2675 +Ebenezer.
2676 +Thomas.

Mehitable married Isaac Martin, of St. Johnsbury, Vt Her children were *Sarah,[7] Isaac,[7] Hannah,[7] Hezekiah,[7] John,[7] Lucy,[7] Winthrop,[7] Huldah[7]* and *Ambrose* [7]

Lucy married Reuben Pierce. Her children were *Lucy,[7] Richard,[7] Rebecca[7]* and *George.[7]*

Jacinthia married, first, Samuel Barker; second, a Humphrey. Her children were *Samuel[7]* and *Lenea* [7]

Ruth married Barnabas Barker. Her children were *Sarah,[7] John,[7] Hannah,[7] Lucy,[7] Barnabas,[7] Almira,[7] Jacinthia[7]* and *Wallace* [7]

[2617.] DAVID[5] PECK, son of DAVID,[4] settled at first upon the paternal homestead, and afterwards in Seekonk, where he died. He married Elizabeth Bushee.

CHILDREN — SIXTH GENERATION

2677.+Aaron.
2678 Elihu
2679.+Ezra.
2680. Betsey

2681. Sally.
2682 Prudence.
2683. Judith.

Betsey married James French, of Seekonk.

Sally and *Prudence* married Nathaniel Carpenter. *Sally* left no issue. *Prudence* left children.

[2624.] JOEL[5] PECK, son of DAVID,[4] settled upon the homestead of his fathers. He married Lucy Fish, daughter of Daniel Fish, of Seekonk. He died November 11, 1833. She died March 2, 1864, in her 90th year.

CHILDREN — SIXTH GENERATION :

2684 +Horatio, b Dec 3, 1793.
2685 +Elnathan, b Jan 27, 1796.
2686 +Bela, b Jan 29, 1798
2687. Wealthy, b Sept. 22, 1800.
    18*

2688 +Sebea, b Jan 25, 1803.
2689 Fanny, b. Sept 6, 1805.
2690 Bethia, b Aug 4, 1808.
2691 Clarissa, b. Dec. 13, 1812.

Wealthy married Nathaniel Medbery, of Barrington.   Her children are :
Mathew,[7] *Lucy,*[7] *Andrew,*[7] *Theophilus,*[7] *Angeline*[7] and *James.*[7]

Fanny married Seth D. Clark, of East Providence.   Her children are ·
Clarissa,[7] *Augustus,*[7] *Julia,*[7] *Diana,*[7] *George*[7] and *William* [7]

Bethia married Benjamin B Medbery, of Barrington   Her children are :
Benjamin T ,[7] *Mary,*[7] *Horace*[7] and *Charles.*[7]

Clarissa married Robert T. Smith, no issue.

[2625]   LEWIS[5] PECK, son of DAVID,[4] left Barrington about
1786, and settled in Clarendon, Rutland County, Vt., where he
resided until a short time before his death, when he removed to the
town of Ira, where he died.   He was twice married : first, to Betty
Read, of Rehoboth, Mass. ; second, to Cynthia Green.   He died
January 1825.

CHILDREN — SIXTH GENERATION

2692.	Daniel, b Nov 1803.	2697	Jonathan. Died young.
2693.+	John, b. Oct. 28, 1787.	2698.	Salmon By 2d wife. Died
2694.	Rachel, b Feb 1792		young
2695.	Selina, b Oct 23, 1794.	2699.	Leland. Died young.
2696.	Samuel. Died young.	2700	Lydia. Died young.

Daniel was killed by the falling of a tree in the 19th year of his age.
Rachel married Charles Nichols.
Selina married Samuel Burrill.

[2627.]   NOAH[5] PECK, son of DAVID,[4] left Barrington in
1786, and settled at Clarendon, Vt.   He married, for his first wife,
Anna Spencer, in 1793.   For his second, he married Mehitable
You, March 1812.   His first wife died January 1, 1811.   His second wife died September 18, 1835.   He died August 19, 1842.

CHILDREN — SIXTH GENERATION .

2701.	Mary, b. Sept 16, 1794. Died April 13, 1835	2706 +	Noah, b. Jan 1807
2702.+	David, b. Nov 1, 1795.	2707.	Sarah, b Jan. 1809. Died Nov 7, 1823.
2703.	Annah, b Jan. 2, 1797. Died Nov. 1839.	2708.+	Lewis, b. Feb. 10, 1813. By 2d wife.
2704.	Hannah, b. Sept. 16, 1799. Died July 6, 1838.	2709.+	Daniel H , b. Jan. 29, 1815.
2705.	Betsey, b. Jan. 1803. Died May 16, 1836.	2710.	Alphonso C., b. Jan. 1, 1817.

Mary and *Annah* married Walter Rider, of Clarendon, Vt.
Hannah married Benjamin Bishop.
Betsey and *Sarah* died unmarried.
Alphonso C. was residing with his brother Lewis, unmarried, in 1863.

[2629.] SOLOMON[5] PECK, of Barrington, son of SOLOMON,[4] married widow Abigail Barney, formerly Abigail Peck (No. 2605), daughter of Nathaniel Peck, December 8, 1763. He resided where Asa Peck, his grandson, was residing in 1860. He died August 22, 1814. She died June 16, 1821.

CHILLDREN — SIXTH GENERATION :

2711. Abigail, b. May 12, 1764.
2712. Keziah, b Sept. 10, 1766.
2713.+Solomon, b. Feb 13, 1769.
2714.+Darius, b. June 25, 1772.

2715.+Ellis, b. Aug. 2, 1774.
2716. Bebee, b. June 1, 1777. Died April 19, 1781.

Abigail married Ebenezer Peck (No. 2661), son of Peleg.
Keziah married Joshua Read for her first husband, and David Hill for her second.

[2639.] EBENEZER[5] PECK, son of SOLOMON,[4] lived and died in Barrington. He lived near where Ellis Peck now resides. The house stood where Benjamin Medbery was residing in 1863. He married Huldah Brown, daughter of Amos Brown, of Rehoboth, December 2, 1785. She died April 22, 1816, in the 64th year of her age. He died April 20, 1816.

CHILDREN — SIXTH GENERATION :

2717.+Nathaniel, b. Jan 16, 1786.
2718.+Ebenezer, b Aug. 31, 1787.
2719. Huldah, b. Aug. 3, 1789.
2720. Bebee, b. June 18, 1791.

2721.+Benjamin, b. July 10, 1793.
2722 +Learned, b Oct 15, 1795.
2723. William H., b. June 5, 1798. Died April 22, 1816.

Huldah married Ebenezer Humphrey, and settled in Barrington. Her children are *Albert*,[7] *Samuel*,[7] *John*,[7] *Maria*,[7] *Nancy*,[7] and *Ann Eliza*.[7]

Bebee (from whom I received my information in relation to her father's family), married Benjamin Heath, September 13, 1812. Her children are . *Mary*,[7] *Benjamin*,[7] *Huldah*,[7] *William*[7] and *Clarissa*.[7]

[2640.] NATHANIEL[6] PECK, son of THOMAS,[5] married Sarah Paine, daughter of Nathaniel Paine. He resided in Providence. He was a caulker by trade. He and his wife died in Seekonk, at the residence of their daughter Hannah; he aged 76 years, and she 75.

CHILDREN — SEVENTH GENERATION

2724. Sebra, b Jan. 5, 1777. Died at sea, unm.

2725. Hannah, b. July 8, 1780.

Hannah married William Handy, of Seekonk. Mr. William Handy, of Seekonk, to whom I am indebted for my information, is her son.

[2642.] THOMAS[6] PECK, son of THOMAS,[5] left Rhode Island at an early date, and settled at what was known as the German Flats, N. Y., where he died about 1810. He married, for his first wife, as I am told, Lydia Knight; and for his second, Frances Davis, who died April 11, 1826.

CHILDREN — SEVENTH GENERATION

2726.+Philip, b. April 25, 1776.
2727.+Russell.
2728. Sally
2729. Ardilla. Suppose died unm.
2730. Charlotte.
2731. Barbary

2732 +Thomas, b. July 19, 1794.
2733 +Aı, b. Dec. 12, 1797.
2734 William F.
2735.+James.
2736 +Nathaniel.

Sally married Edward Davis, of Butternuts, N. Y.
Charlotte married a Hunt, and died soon after
Barbary married Richard Paddock, of Litchfield, N. Y.*
William F died young, in the town of Lorraine, N. Y.

[2644.] PELEG[6] PECK, son of THOMAS,[5] left Rhode Island about 1795, and settled in Otsego County, at or near Fly Creek. From there he removed to Richfield. He married Betsey Sweet, daughter of Jeremiah Sweet, August 13, 1779. He died November 4, 1849. She August 14, 1838.

CHILDREN — SEVENTH GENERATION

2737. Abner, b. Oct. 24, 1780.
2738. Joab, b March 12, 1782.
2739.+Pardon, b. Feb. 11, 1784.
2740. Freelove, b Nov 13, 1785.
2741. Lydia, b. June 7, 1787.
2742 +Thomas, b Aug 10, 1789.
2743. Betsy, b. May 4, 1791.

2744 +Alfred, b. Feb 20, 1793.
2745. Alfredia, b. Nov 29, 1794.
2746 Augustus, b Sept. 14, 1796.
2747. Hannah, b Jan 4, 1799.
2748 +Peleg, b. May 25, 1801.
2749 +Dorastus, b Aug. 23, 1803.

Abner settled in Lorraine, N. Y , where he and his wife died, leaving no children He married Joanna Dewey He died May 2, 1810
Joab died in Batavia, unm , December 30, 1841
Freelove married Ezıa Cary, and was residing with her son, Albert Cary, at Norwich, Chenango County, N. Y., in 1864.
Lydia married Eleazer Whipple, August 31, 1810, and settled in Richfield, Otsego County, N Y , where he died, October 30, 1830 She was residing in Orangeville, N Y , in 1864
Betsey married Thomas Leonard, and settled at first in Richfield, afterwards in Bethany, and then in Niagara County. She died October 13, 1860.

* Thomas Paddock, residing at Salmon River, Oswego County, N. Y., in 1865, is her son

Alfredia married Alfred Green. They were residing in Sturgis, Ill., in 1864.

Augustus died in the army of the United States, October 30, 1816, unm.

Hannah married Nathan Hawley, and was residing at Perry Centre, Mich., in 1864.

[2645]   JACOB[6] PECK, son of THOMAS,[5] moved from Rhode Island to Fly Creek, Otsego County, N. Y., where he died, March 1, 1813. He married Mercy Rutenber, born July 24, 1758. She died February 14, 1841.

CHILDREN — SEVENTH GENERATION.

2750   Celinda, b. May 25, 1785. Died Aug 31, 1851.
2751.   Cynthia, b Dec. 25, 1788. Died unm., May 11, 1819
2752   Daniel, b Feb 21, 1790. Died unm., Sept. 18, 1791.
2753.   Mercy, b Sept. 27, 1792. Died Nov 14, 1845.
2754.   Huldah, b Feb. 16, 1797.
2755.   Harris, b Dec 25, 1799. Died July 31, 1805.

Celinda married Benjamin Gallop, and settled at Fly Creek. Mr. Norman R. Stephens, to whose kindness I am indebted for my information, is her son.

Mercy married Alexander Lerow.

Huldah married Daniel J. Davidson. They settled at Richburgh, N. Y.

[2646.]   PETER[6] PECK, son of THOMAS,[5] left Rhode Island, and settled at Fly Creek, Otsego County, N. Y., about 1795. He died July 11, 1846. He married Sarah Ralph. She died September 3, 1843, in the 81st year of her age.

CHILDREN — SEVENTH GENERATION.

2756.   Zilpha.
2757.   Avis, b. Sept. 23, 1788.
2758   Susan, b July 5, 1793
2759.+William, b July 20, 1796.
2760.+Daniel, b. Nov. 5, 1799.
2761.   Sarah, b. Dec 3, 1801.
2762.   Amey, b. Sept. 11, 1804.
2763.   Peter.

Susan married Nathaniel Chapman, at Fly Creek, where she died, May 11, 1862, leaving seven children.

Avis and *Sarah* married Davis Brown, to whose kindness I am indebted for my information Avis died March 7, 1854, leaving four children. Sarah and Mr Brown were living at Richfield Springs in 1862 *

Amey was residing at Richfield Springs in 1862. She married Robert Souls.

Peter, I am told, married and settled in Michigan, and from there removed to Iowa. I have been unable to find him or his children.

[2649.]   COMFORT[6] PECK, son of COMFORT,[5] first settled near what has since been known as Leonard's Corners, in Seekonk,

---

* He died November 19, 1864, aged 68 years.

Mass. From here he removed into the State of New York. I have been unable to find any of his descendants. His relatives could tell me nothing in relation to them. He married Mary Saunders, of Swansey.

CHILDREN — SEVENTH GENERATION ·

2764. Ebenezer, b July 16, 1787. Died unm.
2765. Davis, b. Jan. 17, 1790.
2766. Comfort, b. May 13, 1793.
2767. Mary D , b Aug. 13, 1795
2768. Hannah, b. Nov. 17, 1797
2769. Almira S , b. Dec. 19, 1800.
2770. James.

[2653] NATHANIEL[6] PECK, son of COMFORT,[5] resided in Seekonk, Mass., near what is known as Leonard's Corners. He married Mary Wheeler, of Rehoboth, daughter of Aaron Wheeler. He died October 11, 1831 or 2. She died March 16, 1852.

CHILDREN — SEVENTH GENERATION

2771. Ann Eliza, b. Jan 1801. Died young.
2772. Mary W , b. Feb. 9, 1803.
2773. Lydia D , b. Nov. 18, 1805.
2774. Sophia L , b. July 21, 1808.
2775. Alice C , b Jan 11, 1811.
2776. Lois T., b Aug 22, 1813.
2777. Nathaniel, b. Nov. 5, 1825. Died young.

Mary married Brayton Read, of Fall River, Mass.
Lydia D. married Harvey French, of Seekonk, Mass.
Sophia L. married Elliott Holbrook, of Wrentham, Mass
Alice C. married George Blackman, of Charlton, Mass.
Lois T. married Bradford Walker, of Canandaigua, N. Y.

[2655.] THOMAS[6] PECK, son of COMFORT,[5] settled upon the homestead. He married Zenith Bullock, daughter of Barrett Bullock, of Rehoboth.

CHILDREN — SEVENTH GENERATION .

2778. Keziah, b. Sept. 21, 1802
2779. Sally, b. April 22, 1804.
2780. Thomas, b. May 15, 1806 , was unm. in 1864.
2781. James, b Oct 30, 1808
2782. Hannah, b June 8, 1811.
2783.+Comfort, b. May 16, 1814.

Keziah married Arnold Medbery, of Seekonk, died February 1845.
Sally married Joseph Allen, of Seekonk.
James was residing with his brother Comfort, unm., in 1863.
Hannah married Reuben Thurber, of Seekonk.

[2659.] BARNEY[6] PECK, son of PELEG,[5] left Rhode Island at an early date, and settled in Greensborough, Vt. From there he removed to Walcott, where he died, April 10, 1832. He married Elizabeth Colgrove, daughter of William Colgrove, December

1759. She was born January 1, 1768, and died March 1863, in her 96th year.

CHILDREN — SEVENTH GENERATION

2784 +Allen, b May 10, 1791.

2785. Charlotte, b June 1, 1793 Died June 29, 1836.

2786. Hannah. b Sept 5, 1795.

2787 +William, b Aug 5, 1797.

2788 Martha, b. Dec 5, 1799.

2789 +Welcome, b Feb 28, 1802.

2790 +Barney, b Feb 10, 1804.

2791 +Ira, b. Oct 28, 1805.

2792 Esther, b May 28, 1808.

2793.+Jeremiah, b Oct 13, 1812.

2794. Louisa, b. July 21, 1815.

Charlotte married Samuel Bastin.

Hannah married Rufus Bastin

Martha married William Read.

Esther married Orin Day, September 5, 1836, and was residing in Sharon, Vt , in 1863

Louisa married first, Garrettson Hunt, February 24, 1833, second, a Mr. Blackman, and was residing in Livingston, Clark County, Ill , in 1864.

[2660.] ISAAC[6] PECK, son of PELEG,[5] settled in Providence, R. I., where he lived and died, February 26, 1833, aged 67 years, 10 months and 23 days. He married Phebe Jencks, daughter of Ichabod Jencks, March 20, 1791. She died June 6, 1853, aged 83 years and 13 days.

CHILDREN — SEVENTH GENERATION

2795 Nancy J , b May 19, 1792.

2796 +John, b April 18, 1793.

2797 Rhoda, b Nov. 16, 1794.

2798 Phebe, b. Nov 23, 1797.

2799 Isaac, b. Feb. 13, 1800. Died unm.

2800 Joseph B , b Dec 5, 1801.

2801 +George H , b Jan 19, 1804.

2802 Almira, b Feb 16, 1806.

2803 William H , b May 28, 1808.

One b in 1797 Died in infancy.

Nancy married John Haradon, of Providence.

Joseph B married Bethiah Clark. He left no issue.

Rhoda married Enoch Steer, of Providence, R I

Phebe married William C Baker, of Providence, R I

Almira married William P Allen, of Providence, R I

[2661.] EBENEZER[6] PECK, son of PELEG,[5] resided in Scituate, R. I. He married, for his first wife, Abigail Peck (No. 2711), daughter of Solomon Peck, of Barrington, R. I.; for his second, Esther Barns; for his third, Sybel Searles; for his fourth, Phebe Walden. He died August 22, 1838.

CHILDREN — SEVENTH GENERATION .

2804. Abigail.

2805. Keziah.

2806. Hannah.

2807.+Barney.

2808 +Samuel

2809 Solomon Died young.

2810. Peleg Died young.

Abigail married John Stephens.
Keziah married Elisha Leach, and settled in Scituate, R I
Hannah married Samuel Bulas, of Providence.

[2667.] WELCOME[6] PECK, son of PELEG,[5] resided in Scituate, R. I., upon the homestead. He married Betsey Collins. He died December 28, 1828. She November 12, 1827, aged 41 years.

CHILDREN — SEVENTH GENERATION

2811 +Lewis, b Jan 8, 1804.
2812 +Stephen, b Feb. 14, 1805.
2813. Peleg, b Dec. 24, 1806.

2814. Sylvia, b Oct. 25, 1809.
2815.+Asahel, b. Jan 16, 1813.
2816 +Alfred O , b Oct 8, 1817.

Sylvia married Richard Searles, of Providence, where they were residing in 1864. To her I am indebted for a record of the family
Peleg was twice married first, to Bethiah Peck, widow of Joseph, formerly Bethiah Clark, second, to Phebe Brown. He left no issue

[2669] GAIEUS[6] PECK, son of EBENEZER,[5] lived and died in Lindon, Vt. He married. Hannah Peck (No. 217), daughter of Samuel Peck, of Rehoboth, Mass., May 19, 1782. They were married by her grandfather, Rev. Samuel Peck. She died February 4, 1832. He April 5, 1838.

CHILDREN — SEVENTH GENERATION .

2817. Lewis, b. Aug. 17, 1783.
2818. Delia, b Jan. 25, 1785. Died
         March 13, 1785.
2819. Sally, b May 7, 1787. Died
         July 27, 1787
2820. Lydia, b June 28, 1789 Died
         Feb 17, 1852
2821 +Hersa, b Dec 25, 1792.

2822. Henrietta, b April 12, 1794.
         Died unm
2823.+Samuel, b Nov 7, 1796.
2824. Clarissa, b May 16, 1799 Died
         June 20, 1804
2825 +William, b Nov. 2, 1802.
2826 +George C., b. July 24, 1805.

Lewis left no issue.

[2675.] EBENEZER[6] PECK, son of EBENEZER,[5] settled at first with his father, in Seekonk, Mass. From there he removed to Lindon, Vt., and from there to Derby, where he died, October 28, 1821. He married Elizabeth Winsor, daughter of William Winsor, of Seekonk, August 16, 1795.

CHILDREN — SEVENTH GENERATION

2827 Lucie, b. Oct. 1, 1796. Died
         June 3, 1798.
2828. Mary W , b May 21, 1798.
2829. Sarah, b. Oct 1, 1800.
2830. Abigail W , b. March 11, 1803.
2831. Eliza F., b. June 30, 1805.

2832. Ebenezer, b. Aug. 18, 1807.
2833. Nancy B., b Jan 28, 1810
2834. Susan H , b March 28, 1812.
2835. Lucy S , b. Jan. 1, 1815.
2836. Harriet N., b. June 24, 1817.

Mary W. married Mellen Benson, of Millville, Mass

Sarah married Lyman C Curtis, settled at Deer Park, Long Island.　She died August 22, 1855.

Eliza F. married Calvin Butler; settled at Summerville, N. J.

Nancy B. married Dan Hill, of Blackstone, Mass.

Lucy S. married Newton Darling, of Millville, for her first husband, and Jonathan Southwick, of Uxbridge, for her second

Harriet married William Jones, settled in Salsbury, Conn.

Ebenezer married Amanda Chase.　He died at sea, May 9, 1842

[2676.]　THOMAS[6] PECK, son of EBENEZER,[5] married ——.

CHILDREN — SEVENTH GENERATION :

2837 +Thomas.

2838.+Ebenezer.

2839.　Lucy

[2677.]　AARON[6] PECK, son of DAVID,[5] left Barrington, R. I., when eighteen years of age, and settled in Pittston, Rensselaer County, N. Y.　From here he removed to Otsego; from there to Burlington; and from there, in 1815, he removed to Ellicott, Chatauque County; and from there to Poland, where he was residing in 1864.　He married Dorcas Briggs, daughter of John Briggs, from Warwick, R. I., in 1803.　She was born December 25, 1778.

CHILDREN — SEVENTH GENERATION

2840.　Betsy, b. Sept. 6, 1805.

2841.+Ezra, b. July 8, 1808

2842.　Hannah, b. Sept. 14, 1810.

2843　Samuel, b. July 3, 1812.

2844　Sally, b Feb 3, 1815.

2845.　Ezekiel, b July 23, 1817.

Betsey was residing in Poland, with her parents, unm, in 1864.

Hannah married Ezra Smith, of Poland, N. Y.

Sally married Thomas Linkfield, and settled at French Creek, Chatauque County, N Y.

[2679.]　EZRA[6] PECK, son of DAVID,[5] settled first in Hubbardston, where he married Phebe Willard.　From there he removed to Barre, Mass., where his wife died, about 1815, and he about 1844.

CHILDREN — SEVENTH GENERATION

2846　Myra, b May 1, 1797.

2847 +Milton, b July 1, 1799.

2848.　Sumner, b. June 4, 1801.

2849　Sophina, b May 28, 1804.

2850.　Marinda, b Dec 10, 1810.

2851.　Chauncey, b Aug 1814. Died in 1816.

Myra married David Barnes, in 1824.　Her husband died in 1827.　She has two children *Lucy*,[8] b. March 21, 1825, and *David*,[8] b. October 28, 1827.　They were residing in Hubbardston, Mass., in 1864.

19

Sumner died unm , November 1862, in Templeton, Mass.

Sophina married Charles Austin, April 1857.   They reside in Hubbardston,

Marinda married Charles Austin, November 15, 1834.   Her children were *Tryphena*,[8] b. October 8, 1835, *Louisa*,[8] b. October 20, 1837, *Almina*,[8] b March 17, 1840; *Elvira*,[8] b March 4, 1844, *Harriet Sophina*,[8] b February 20, 1847   She died in Hubbardston, September 29, 1852.

[2684.]   HORATIO[6] PECK, son of JOEL,[5] resides in Swansey, Mass.   He married, for his first wife, Nancy Mathewson, daughter of Daniel Mathewson, of Barrington, R. I.; for his second, Martha Chase, daughter of Wanton Chase, of Pawtucket, R I.; and for his third, Martha Martin, daughter of James Martin, formerly of Newport, R. I.

CHILDREN — SEVENTH GENERATION

2852 +James B , b. March 29, 1822.

2853.+Henry C., b. Jan. 5, 1832.

2854. Martha Jane, b April 15, 1833.
        Died in infancy

2855. George E , b. Aug 8, 1835 ⎫
2856. Nancy Jane, b. Aug. 8, 1835. ⎬
        Twins. ⎭

2857   Hiram F , b Oct 1, 1837.

2858. John M , b May 30, 1840

2859. Albert S., b Jan 26, 1842

2860   Horatio W., b. Dec. 3, 1845

Hiram F married Sophia Tabor; no issue.

John M married Lydia Jane Smith, no issue.

Albert S married Mary C. Dunbar.   Died June 9, 1864, no issue.

Horatio W. was residing with his father, in 1863, unm.

[2685.]   ELNATHAN[6] PECK, son of JOEL,[5] resides in Seekonk.   He married Mercy Martin, daughter of Holden Martin, of Swansey, December 28, 1826.   She was born June 24, 1804.

CHILD — SEVENTH GENERATION ·

2861. Sarah A., b. Oct. 8, 1829

Sarah A. married Benjamin Walker, of Seekonk, June 8, 1855

[2686.]   BELA[6] PECK, son of JOEL,[5] resides in Barrington.   He married Lemyra A. Peck (No. 1899), daughter of Ambrose Peck, of Seekonk, March 18, 1821.

CHILDREN — SEVENTH GENERATION

2862   Alpheus M., b. Dec 20, 1821
        Died Sept. 14, 1822.

2863 +Edwin F., b. Dec. 8, 1823

2864. Albert H , b Jan 10, 1827.
        Died Feb. 13, 1833.

2865. Susan A , b. Aug 29, 1829

2866. Albert H , b. June 14, 1833.

2867. Horace M , b Mar 28, 1836
        Died March 15, 1839

2868. Horace T , b April 2, 1839

2869. Amie A. M , b. March 19, 1842.

Susan A. married George Bowen, of Barrington.

A bert H married Mary E Medbery, daughter of Benjamin Medbery, of Barrington, where they were residing in 1863

Horace T married Mary Humphrey, daughter of Samuel Humphrey, of Connecticut.

[2688.] SEBEA[6] PECK, son of ·JOEL,[5] resides upon the homestead. He married Rebecca Cooper, of Boston, September 14, 1834. She died December 5, 1854, in the 37th year of her age.

CHILDREN — SEVENTH GENERATION ·

2870   Ann Eliza, b. Aug. 30, 1835, unm in 1863.

2871   Emily F , b July 1, 1837.

2872   Seraphina M , b Sept. 15, 1840; unm in 1863.

2873   Horatio N , b. March 27, 1844.

2874.   Laura Elizabeth   Died Feb 21, 1851, aged 21 months.

Emily married Henry Fish, of Pawtucket, R. I.

[2690] REV. JOHN[6] PECK, son of LEWIS,[5] settled at Clarendon, Vt., where, I am told, he was pastor of the Baptist church. He removed, about 1837, to the town of Fowler, N. Y., and became the pastor of the church at Fullersville. He was residing at Black River in 1863. He was twice married: first, to Sabra Rounds; second, to Dolly Drummond (widow), formerly Dolly Graves.

CHILDREN — SEVENTH GENERATION

2875   Betsey C , b Sept. 26, 1810

2876 +Nathan R , b March 23, 1813

2877   Melissa, b Aug 18, 1814

2878   Lydia, b. March 12, 1817.

2879.   Lorain, b June 26, 1819.

2880 +Daniel, b. July 1, 1822

2881   Sarah, b Nov 12,1824.

2882.   Celinda, b. Feb. 21, 1827

[2702.] DAVID[6] PECK, son of NOAH,[5] settled at Clarendon, Vt., where he died, February 4, 1857. He married Harriet Freelove, daughter of David Freelove, of West Rutland. She was living in Ira, Vt., in 1864. She was born May 24, 1800.

CHILDREN — SEVENTH GENERATION

2883   Hannah M , b Aug 12, 1820.

2884   Harriet V , b Dec 20, 1821

2885   Loranda I , b. Dec 10, 1823.

2886   Sarah A., b Jan 28, 1826

2887 +George W , b Dec. 10, 1830.

2888.   Clarissa E , b Oct 5, 1836

2889.   Elsa A . b Aug 5, 1840

Hannah M. married J. C. Smith, September 5, 1842, resided in Ira, Vt , in 1864.

Harriet V married F. Freeman, March 20, 1844; resided in West Rutland, Vt., in 1864

Loranda I married H. Gorham, December 2, 1850; resided in West Rutland, Vt , in 1864.

Sarah A married J. S. Tuttle, October 1, 1845, resided in West Rutland, Vt , in 1864.

Clarissa E. married E. C. Fish, November 1, 1857, resided in Ira, Vt., in 1864

Elsa A married W. Wilkinson, February 1, 1860; resided in Ira, Vt., in 1864.

[2706.] NOAH[6] PECK, son of NOAH,[5] resides at Machias, Cattaraugus County, N. Y. He is a farmer. He married Melissa Smith, daughter of John Smith, of Wallingford, Vt., September 18, 1834.

CHILDREN — SEVENTH GENERATION

2890.	Marcellus, b Jan. 31, 1837.	2893	Helen, b July 1, 1844
2891.	Sophia, b Oct 25, 1839.	2894	Emory, b Dec 25, 1847.
2892	Henry, b Aug 2, 1840.	2895.	Warren, b May 18, 1852

Marcellus married Caroline Ellingwood, June 30, 1862.

Sophia married Anson Spencer, May 15, 1859. She died March 1, 1859, and he January 6, 1863.

[2708.] LEWIS[6] PECK, son of NOAH,[5] is settled upon the homestead, in the town of Ira, Rutland County, Vt. He married Harriet H. Brown, of Clarendon, June 11, 1837, daughter of John Brown.

CHILDREN — SEVENTH GENERATION ·

2896.	Harrison J , b Nov. 23, 1838.	2899.	Germont G , b. May 3, 1847.
2897.	Charles W , b Feb. 23, 1841.		Died Jan 8, 1850
2898.	Simon L , b Nov 29, 1844.	2900.	Mary Ann, b Aug 28, 1850.

The three sons were unmarried in 1863, and engaged in school teaching.

[2709.] DANIEL H.[6] PECK, son of NOAH,[5] settled at South Gibson, Susquehanna County, Pa., where he was residing in 1864, a farmer. He married Melissa B. Tower, daughter of Welcome Tower, September 9, 1838.

CHILDREN — SEVENTH GENERATION ·

2901.	Betsey, b July 28, 1839.	2905.	Frank Welcome, b. July 26, 1851.
2902.	Sarah Addie, b. June 19, 1842.		
2903.	Byron Eugene, b March 3, 1845 Died April 24, 1845.	2906.	Lewis William, b. Oct 8, 1854
2904.	Marianna Tower, b. Dec. 10, 1846.	2907.	Isabella Lavinia, b. April 22, 1859
		2908.	Blanche, b Sept. 21, 1862.

Sarah Addie married Dr E. W. Mason, December 11, 1860; resided at Honesdale, Wayne County, Pa.

[2713.] SOLOMON[6] PECK, of Seekonk, son of SOLOMON,[5] married Huldah Kent, December 10, 1795. She died October 29, 1817. He died December 7, 1857.

CHILDREN — SEVENTH GENERATION (Bar. Rec , B. 2, p 24)

290?. Huldah, b. Oct 3, 1796.
2910 Hannah, b. April 28, 1798.
    Died May 1, 1828.
2911. +Solomon, jr , b. Jan 22, 1800.
2912. Lydia, b. Dec. 28, 1801

2913 Betsey, b June 28, 1805. Died
    Dec. 22, 1805
2914. Esther, b. Feb 16, 1807 Died
    June 28, 1826
2915 Eliza W., b Sept 24, 1809
2916 Lemira W , b. Aug. 28, 1811.

Huldah married Joseph Armington, of Seekonk She died January 1850
Hannah married Deacon Vial Medbery She died May 1, 1828
Lydia also married Deacon Vial Medbery
Eliza W married Sanford Chase, of Connecticut.
Lemira W. married Herman A. Peck, of Providence (No. 2921). Died May 12, 1841.

[2714.] DARIUS[6] PECK, of Seekonk, son of SOLOMON,[5] married Lucy Peck, daughter of Deacon Charles Peck, January 24, 1799. Died September 1854.

CHILDREN — SEVENTH GENERATION

2917 Lucy Ann, b Jan 7, 1800.
2918 Keziah, b Sept 13, 1801
2919 +Calvin S , b May 22, 1803
2920 Rachel S., b March 12, 1805.

2921. +Hermon A , b. July 12, 1807 ⎫
2922 +Sylvester W , b July 12, 1807 ⎬
    Twins
2923 Julia Ann, b Feb 27, 1811.
    Died unm , March 1840

Lucy Ann married Job Luther, December 15, 1823
Keziah married Solomon Peck, jr , of Seekonk (No 2911), June 6, 1828
Rachel S. married Perry J. Chase, of Providence, December 1, 1831.

[2715.] ELLIS[6] PECK, of Barrington, son of SOLOMON,[5] married Sarah Hill, daughter of David Hill, December 10, 1801, for his first wife; and Lucy Bliss, daughter of Jacob Bliss, for his second wife, March 1818. His first wife died June 3, 1817. His second wife died December 9, 1853. He died July 27, 1854.

CHILDREN — SEVENTH GENERATION (Bar Rec , B. 2, p. 31)

2924. Sarah, b Sept 10, 1802 Died
    Jan 18, 1814
2925. Abigail, b March 29, 1804.
    Died Oct 23, 1846
2926. +Ellis, b. May 11, 1806.

2927. Hannah D , b June 17, 1810
    Died Dec 16, 1813.
2928 +Asa, b April 7, 1812
2929. Hannah, b. May 26, 1815
2930. William H , b. May 8, 1817
    Died June 29, 1817

19*

Abigail married George Bowen, of Barrington, for her first husband; and Benjamin Peck (No. 2721), for her second.

Hannah married Albert Medbery, of East Providence.

[2717.] NATHANIEL[6] PECK, son of EBENEZER,[5] settled, lived and died in Barrington, R. I., where his son Nathaniel was residing in 1864.

He married Cynthia Heath, May 29, 1808. She was born August 9, 1785, and died February 19, 1851. He died November 24, 1856.

CHILDREN — SEVENTH GENERATION ·

2931. Nathaniel, b. April 24, 1809.
2932. William B., b. June 4, 1812. Died Dec. 27, 1819.
2933. Samuel H., b. Oct. 6, 1814. Died Sept. 29, 1820.
2934.+Ebenezer, b. May 24, 1817.
2935. Joseph, b. Sept. 13, 1819. Died June 5, 1822.
2936. Cynthia H., b. Dec. 31, 1821.
2937. Wilmarth H., b. Dec. 15, 1825.

Nathaniel was residing upon the homestead, unm., in 1864.

Samuel was killed by the falling of a tree.

Ebenezer was killed by falling from a building. He was a carpenter.

Cynthia married Charles Campbell, of Providence, R. I.

Wilmarth H. married Abby A. Peck, widow of Ebenezer. He was residing in Providence, R. I., in 1863; no issue.

[2718.] EBENEZER[6] PECK, son of EBENEZER,[5] settled, lived and died in Barrington, September 22, 1828. He married Esther Vial, daughter of John Vial, of Seekonk.

CHILDREN — SEVENTH GENERATION

2938.+Daniel H., b. July 20, 1811.
2939.+John H., b. Aug. 15, 1813.
2940. Esther V., b. July 15, 1816.
2941. Huldah B., b. Jan. 19, 1820; unm. in 1863.
2942. Edwin H., b. Oct. 11, 1822. Died young.
2943. Ebenezer T., b. Nov 22, 1824.
2944. Elizabeth E., b. June 11, 1827, unm. in 1863.

Esther V. married George W. Johnston; were residing in Exeter, R. I., in 1863.

Ebenezer T. resided upon the homestead, in 1863, unm.

[2721.] BENJAMIN[6] PECK, son of EBENEZER,[5] was residing in Smithfield, R. I., in 1864. He married, for his first wife, Huldah Chaffee, daughter of Joseph Chaffee, of Seekonk, November 9, 1817; and for his second wife, Abigail Bowen, formerly Abigail Peck (No. 2925), daughter of Ellis Peck, of Barrington, R. I., December 24, 1837. His first wife died June 16, 1836. His second wife died October 23, 1846.

CHILDREN — SEVENTH GENERATION :

2945. Amanda M., b. Sept. 23, 1818.
Died Oct. 16, 1832.
2946. Benjamin B., b. July 28, 1820.
Died Dec. 15, 1820.
2947.+Benjamin W., b. Sept. 28, 1825.
2948. Mary Ellen, b. Jan. 22, 1829.
2949.+George S., b. Jan. 7, 1831.

2950. Emily Chaffee, b. Nov. 21, 1835;
unm. in 1863.
2951. Christopher, b. Nov. 9, 1839;
unknown.
2952. Rebecca, b. Feb. 4, 1846, unm.
in 1863.

Mary E. married Henry M. Horton.

[2722.] LEARNED[6] PECK, son of EBENEZER,[5] resided in Providence, R. I. He married Harriet C. Short, daughter of John Short, of Barrington, R. I., November 27, 1817. He died October 6, 1865.

CHILDREN — SEVENTH GENERATION ·

2953. Harriet N., b. May 8, 1820.
2954. William H., b. Oct. 10, 1822.
2955. Betsey S., b. Sept. 10, 1824.
2956. Sarah D., b. May 7, 1826.
2957. Julia M , b. Jan. 23, 1828.
2958. Charles C , b. Feb. 7, 1831.
2959. Rebecca D. K., b. Nov. 30, 1832.

2960. Amanda C., b. Jan. 18, 1834.
2961. Anna C., b. Dec. 5, 1835.
2962. Tristum B , b Jan. 7, 1838.
2963. James D , b. Sept. 3, 1839.
2964. Sarah U , b July 20, 1841.
2965. Milton L , b. March 24, 1843.
2966. George L., b. Feb 18, 1845.

[2726.] PHILIP[7] PECK, son of THOMAS,[6] first settled in Smithfield, R. I. In 1822, he removed to New Berlin, Chenango County, N. Y., where he died, February 17, 1856.

He married Avis Brown, daughter of Henry Brown. She was born May 23, 1776, and died August 5, 1862.

CHILDREN — EIGHTH GENERATION

2967. Philip, jr., b. Nov 18, 1797.
2968. Mary, b Oct 6, 1799.
2969. Jeremiah, b. Nov. 16, 1801.
2970. William R , b. Oct. 2, 1803.
2971. Albert B., b. May 10, 1805.

2972. Naomi, b. April 8, 1808.
2973. Julia Ann, b. Oct. 27, 1812.
2974. Thomas, b. Sept 14, 1814.
2975. Henry, b. July 7, 1817.

Philip settled in New Berlin, N. Y., where he was residing in 1864. He married Roby Patt, of Smithfield, R. I., August 9, 1827. She was born June 4, 1804. His children are (2976) *Elizabeth B* ,[9] b. October 10, 1828, died April 10, 1831, (2977) *Oren S.*,[9] b. May 5, 1830; (2978) *Sarah S.*,[9] b December 17, 1832, died June 19, 1849, (2979) *Richard B* ,[9] b. May 8, 1836, (2980) *Amey L* ,[9] b. August 3, 1837, died May 22, 1854, (2981) *William H.*,[9] b. September 16, 1840, was killed at the battle of Resaca, Ga , May 14, 1864, (2982) *Francis M.*,[9] b. May 23, 1844, died August 17, 1865, of the typhoid fever, contracted in the army.

Mary has been twice married · first, to Benjamin Handy, second, to Berry Eaton. Her children are *Allen,*[9] *Eliza,*[9] *Mary*[9] and *William R*[9]

Jeremiah was residing at Newton Corner, Mass., in 1867. He has been twice married first, to Reliance Hamlin, daughter of Capt. Zacheus Hamlin, of Hyannis, Mass.; second, to Lydia Richards. His children are (2983) *Erastus,*[9] b. June 8, 1824, and died February 27, 1826, (2984) *William R*,[9] b. January 18, 1826, (2985) *Adaline,*[9] b. January 25, 1828, (2986) *Lewin A*,[9] b. January 31, 1831,* (2987) *Mary,*[9] b. September 3, 1833, and died February 25, 1839; (2988) *Sarah J.,*[9] b. May 7, 1835. *By second wife* (2989) *Albert A. H.,*[9] b. December 5, 1842, *Alida S*,[9] b. April 3, 1844.

William R first settled at New Berlin, N. Y. From there he removed to Dundee, Kane County, Ill, where he resided in 1864. He married Mary Ann Hayze, September 2, 1827. Their first child was (2990) *William R., jr.,*[9] b. July 29, 1830, and died July 21, 1855. He married Mary Spofford, July 14, 1849. She survived him, and was residing in Pittsfield, Otsego County, N. Y, in 1864. His children are (2991) *Sarah M.,*[10] b. December 2, 1850; (2992) *Ruth M*,[10] b. December 4, 1831, and died February 12, 1852, (2993) *Celia L*,[10] b. March 3, 1854, (2994) *Charles E.,*[10] b March 3, 1855.

The second child of William R. was (2995) *Alonzo,*[9] b May 22, 1837. He married Elizabeth E Austin, July 11, 1857, and was residing in Dundee in 1864 His child was (2996) *Abbie Gertrude,*[10] b December 22, 1859.

The third child of William R was (2997) *George H*,[9] b September 21, 1839. He married Amanda Padelford, January 11, 1860; no issue. They reside in Dundee.

The fourth child of William R was (2998) *Adaliza L*,[9] b. December 8, 1841, and died April 7, 1857.

His fifth child was (2999) *Ruth M*,[9] b. January 14, 1844, and died October 12, 1849.

His sixth child was (3000) *Zara C*,[9] b. October 21, 1846.

His seventh was (3001) *Charles E.,*[9] b. May 28, 1850, and died February 11, 1853.

His eighth was (3002) *John W.,*[9] b. September 11, 1852.

Albert B settled in Providence, R I, where he was residing in 1864. He married Mary A. Lindsey, daughter of Benjamin Lindsey, of Attleborough, Mass, June 10, 1833. Their child, (3003) *Albert Lindsey,*[9] was born April 21, 1838, and died August 15, 1838

Naomi married Sidney Skinner, in 1826 Their children are *Emily,*[9] *Alonzo,*[9] *Albert,*[9] *Julia Ann,*[9] *Jira,*[9] *Abba*[9] and *Oliva.*[9] They reside in New Berlin, N. Y.

Julia Ann married Alba Ainsworth, in 1831. Their children were . *Mary*[9] and *Julia Ann*[9] They settled in New Berlin, N. Y

Thomas settled in Morocco, Newton County, Ind., where he was residing in 1864 He married Alsena Medbury, of New Berlin, N Y Their children are (3004) *Arlina,*[9] b. August 1839; (3005) *Maria,*[9] b. December 1840; (3006) *Helen,*[9] b. in 1843, (3007) *Mary,*[9] b in 1848) (3008) *Emma,*[9] b in 1850; (3009) *Amelia,*[9] b in 1856, and died in 1856

---

*He married H. D. Palmer, formerly H. D. Dexter, daughter of Freeman Dexter, of Winthrop, Me.

Henry settled at New Berlin, Chenango County, N. Y., where he was resid-ing in 1864. He married Matilda Adaline Dilley. She was born March 5, 1823. Their children are (3010) *Olive Elizabeth*,[9] b. July 30, 1840; (3011) *Julia Ann*,[9] b. May 28, 1844, (3012) *Albert D*,[9] b. June 7, 1845, (3013) *Luna A*,[9] b. November 13, 1848; (3014) *Ruth M.*,[9] b January 1, 1851, (3015) *John F*,[9] b. August 9, 1852, and (3016) *Matilda A*,[9] b. September 26, 1856.

[2727.] RUSSELL[7] PECK, son of THOMAS,[6] married Alice Madison, October 25, 1807. He settled in the town of Butternuts, N. Y.; from there removed to Richland County, Ohio; from there to Crawford County; from there to Cass County, Mich.; and from there to Kalamazoo. He afterwards settled about four miles north of Oskaloosa, Iowa, where he died, January 31, 1846. She died January 6, 1847.

CHILDREN — EIGHTH GENERATION ·

3017. Deliverance, b. the 9th of the 10th month, 1808.

3018. Thomas J , b the 24th of the 2d month, 1810.

3019. Daniel, b. the 21st of the 1st month, 1812.

3020. Susannah, b. the 9th of the 11th month, 1813

3021. Patience, b the 26th of the 1st month, 1816.

3022. Ebenezer M , b. the 29th of the 12th month, 1817.

3023. Sarah, b. the 27th of the 10th month, 1819.

3024. Job, b. the 16th of the 9th month, 1821.

3025. Hannah, b the 18th of the 8th month, 1823.

3026. Isabel, b. the 18th of the 10th month, 1825

3027 Deborah, b. the 27th of the 12th month, 1827

3028. Lucinda, b the 20th of the 4th month, 1830.

Deliverance married Henry Garver, for her first husband, and —— for her second. She settled in Jasper County, Mo , where she died. Her children were *Sarah*,[9] *William*,[9] *John*,[9] *Susannah*,[9] *Henry*,[9] *Edwin*,[9] *Edward*,[9] *George*,' *Andrew*[9] and *Charles*.[9]

Thomas died unm.

Daniel died in Otsego County, N. Y.

Susannah married Abel J McCleary, settled at Mitchelville, Polk County, Iowa Her children are *William R.*,[9] *Sarah A.*,[9] *Thomas J*,[9] *Abel J.*,[9] *Andrew J.*,[9] *Francis M.*,[9] *John W.*,[9] *Susannah*[9] and *Mary R*[9]

Patience married Roys H. Bristol; settled in Galesbury, Mich. Children are *Reuben R.*,[9] *Nancy A*,[9] *Russell*,[9] *Luther*[9] and *Ella*[9]

Ebenezer M married first, Jane Wortman, second, Polly D——. Children are * *Hannah A.*,[9] *Sarah R*,[9] *John W.*,[9] *William R.*,[9] *Amanda*,[9] *Laura L.*,[9] *Aeria A.*,[9] *Ebenezer M.*[9] and *Emma*.[9] He was residing at Oskaloosa, Iowa, in 1865.

Sarah married William D. Neely. Her children were: *William R. P.*,[9]

---

* The grandchildren of Russell were received too late to be numbered and entered in the index.

Finetta C ,[9] *Jane K P.,*[9] *Elvira,*[9] *Laura A ,*[9] *Napoleon B ,*[9] *Frank,*[9] *Elora A.*[9] and *Douglass* [9]

Job married Catharine J. Johnston, and died in Sacramento City, California. His children are *Russell,*[9] *Lucinda*[9] and *Job.*[9]

Hannah married first, George N Duncan, and second, Perry Windsor; was residing at Oskaloosa in 1865. Her children were *Thomas J ,*[9] *Dorotha A.,*[9] *Margaret A ,*[9] *George N* [9] and *Perry* [9]

Isabel was residing at Oskaloosa, in 1865, unm.

Deborah married John G. Laughland   Their child was · *Mary Alice* [9] Unknown where they are.

Lucinda married Jackson Windsor, and settled in California.

[2732.]   THOMAS[7] PECK, son of THOMAS,[6] resides in Bristol, Ontario County, N. Y.   He married Lucinda Pettis, daughter of David Pettis, of Herkimer, Herkimer County, N. Y., who died there, November 3, 1838.

CHILDREN — EIGHTH GENERATION

3029.	Sarah Ann, b. Dec. 17, 1817.	3033.	Lucinda, b April 17, 1828.
3030.	William F., b June 28, 1821.	3034.	Adelaide, b May 9, 1831.
3031.	Elizabeth, b. May 17, 1823.	3035	David, b March 22, 1834
3032	Thomas A , b. Aug 27, 1825.	3036.	James M , b Dec 22, 1837.

Sarah Ann married Enos B. Root, of Perinton, Monroe County, N Y , September 28, 1845

William F. married M L. Crego, April 28, 1860; resided in Auburn, Cayuga County, N Y , in 1864, no issue

Thomas A married Margaret Willet, January 8, 1861, settled in Perinton, Monroe County, N Y.

David married Charlotte Thompson, August 1, 1863, settled in Perinton. Their child is   (3037) *Alberta* [9]

[2733.]   AI[7] PECK, son of THOMAS,[6] settled at Watertown, Jefferson County, N. Y., where he died, December 30, 1829.   He married Sally Griswold, of Adams, Jefferson County, N. Y.   She was residing with her sons in 1865.

CHILDREN — EIGHTH GENERATION :

3038. Wyon, b Oct 12, 1819	3039 Ai, b Sept 4, 1823

Wyon married, for his first wife, Charlotte Lee; for his second, Mary Griff, and for his third, Sarah Ney. He was residing in Elgin, Ill , in 1865. His children were   (3040) *Mary J.,*[9] (3041) *Rose*[9] and (3042) *Sarah A.*[9]

Ai married Jane Ash. He was residing in Elgin, Ill , in 1865   His children were   (3043) *Josephine J ,*[9] (3044) *Edgar Ai*[9] and (3045) *Elizabeth* [9]

[2735.]   JAMES[7] PECK, son of THOMAS,[6] settled at East Cleveland, Ohio, where he died August 4, 1865.   He married Harriet Hamilton.

3046. Barbary P , b. Mar. 5, 1823
    Died Mar. 5, 1823.
3047 Harriet M., b Jan 9, 1826.
3048. Laura H , b Feb. 8, 1830.
3049. Mary H., b. May 11, 1834.

    Died August 1, 1835
3050. Samuel H , b. April 15, 1836.
3051. Mary E., b April 15, 1838.
    Died Oct 7, 1846

Harriet M. married Eddy McVay, of East Cleveland.
Laura H. married William McVay.

[2736.] NATHANIEL[7] PECK, son of THOMAS,[6] married, for his first wife, Sally Davis, daughter of John Davis; and for his second wife, Mahala Spicer, of Plainfield, N. Y. From there I am told he moved to Winfield, and from there to New Haven, Oswego County, and then to Sackett's Harbor; and that he afterwards died on his way to California as a missionary Methodist preacher. His widow and son Erastus were residing in Detroit in 1865. I wrote them several times, but could learn little from them in relation to the family.

3052 Sarah Melissa.
3053. Nathaniel
3054. Alanson
3055. Erastus
3056. Francis
3057. Hepsibeth.
3058. Amandana

3059 Woodhall.
3060. Ai.
3061. ——.
3062. ——. } Supposed died in in-
3063. ——. } fancy, unnamed
3064. ——. }

Amandana married William Killburn, and was residing in Redfield, N. Y., in 1865.

[2739.] PARDON[7] PECK, son of PELEG,[6] settled in Lorrain, Jefferson County, N. Y., where he and his wife both died. Her name was Sophia Burnham before marriage. She was born November 23, 1788. They were married January 14, 1808. He died July 4, 1829. She died March 31, 1825.

3065 ——, b Mar 7, 1809. Died
    Mar. 22, 1809.
3066. William, b. April 3, 1810. Died
    April 9, 1810.
3067. Sophronia, b April 1, 1811
    Died May 22, 1861
3068. Harriet, b Dec. 30, 1812. Died
    in 1858
3069 ——, b. Sept 22, 1814. Died

in infancy.
3070. Eliza, b May 23, 1817.
3071. ——, b April 26, 1819. Died
    May 1, 1819.
3072 Joseph B , b. June 29, 1820.
    Died Aug 18, 1820
3073. Sophia, b. Feb. 7, 1825. Died
    Mar 8, 1828.

* For my information in relation to this family, I am mostly indebted to the kindness of J. H. Corey, of Redfield, N. Y.

Sophronia married Dr. L. Bushnell, of Watertown, Jefferson County, N. Y. To him I am indebted for the record of the family.

Harriet married John Huson. They settled at Watertown, N. Y., where she died.

Eliza married George W. Hawes. They were living at Lafargeville, Jefferson County, N Y., in 1864.

[2742.] REV. THOMAS[7] PECK, son of PELEG,[6] was twice married; first, to Naomi Green, August 30, 1810, daughter of William Green, of Rhode Island; second, to Nancy A. Nichols, December 20, 1845, daughter of Jeremiah Nichols, of Connecticut. His first wife was born December 24, 1792, and died August 27, 1845. His second wife was born October 20, 1824, and was residing at Pierson, Mich., in 1864. To her kindness I am indebted for my information. He was a Methodist clergyman. He died March 6, 1862.

He commenced preaching in Naples, Ohio, in 1822. He was ordained Elder by Bishop Hedding, in 1839. He removed from Naples to Ohio, in hopes of benefiting his failing health, in 1854. From here, by the advice of his physicians, he removed to Wisconsin, where he remained four years without receiving any benefit, when it was thought advisable for him to return to the east of Lake Michigan. He removed to Pierson in 1859. He was a faithful minister, and I am told was much beloved by his people.

CHILDREN — EIGHTH GENERATION

3074. William T , b. June 29, 1811.
        Died Oct. 26, 1811.
3075. Nelson G , b Sept 10, 1812.
        Died July 20, 1836
3076. Merritt P., b. Oct. 13, 1814.
3077. Naomi A , b June 28, 1817.
3078. Freelove, b Aug 27, 1819
3079   Mary, b Mar 20, 1822. Died
        Mar 13, 1863
3080. Alfred, b Feb. 10, 1825. Died Mar 10, 1825.
3081. Alphronus, b. Feb. 10, 1825 Died Feb 14, 1825. } Twins.

3082. Thomas S , b July 23, 1827
3083. Nancy C , b Aug 23, 1830
3084. Polly M , b. Jan 7, 1834. Died
        Nov 1862.
        By second wife
3085. Naomi, b June 19, 1848.
3086. Dorastus, b Mar 15, 1850.
3087 Lydia C , b Nov 7, 1851.
3088 Mordaunt, b June 26, 1853
3089. William H , b July 3, 1859.

Merritt married Martha Polmantier, November 7, 1839 He was residing in North Chohocton, Steuben County, N. Y., in 1864 His children were (3090) *Emma*,[9] (3091) *Silsbee*,[9] (3092) *Newton*,[9] (3093) *Amenso*,[9] (3094) *Cerena*,[9] (3095) *Albert*[9] an (3096) *Alfredia*.

Naomi A married George M Pierson, July 31, 1842   She died March 26, 1848, leaving four children   *Theodore,*[9] *Florella J ,*[9] *George J* [9] and *Charles N* [9]

Nancy E married George M Pierson, the former husband of Naomi A , July 4, 1849   They were residing in Pierson, Mich , in 1864   Their children were . *Charles M ,*[9] *Thomas P ,*[9] *Mary Estella,*[9] *Albert Lewis*[9] and *Minnie Leuella* [9]

Freelove married Orison Pierson, of Pierson, Mich , where they were residing in 1864. Their children were . *Naomi,*[9] *Abellino,*[9] *Milford,*[9] *Freelove*[9] and *Emma.*[9]

Mary married William Polmantier, December 12, 1842. Their children were *Sydney,*[9] *Wallace,*[9] *Naomi*[9] and *Frances* [9]

Thomas S married Margaret Wheeler, September 7, 1849, and was residing in Fairbury, Livingston Co , Ill , in 1864   His children were   (3097) *Floyd,*[9] (3098) *Green,*[9] (3099) *Ford S.*[9] and (3100) *Frederick W* [9]

[2744] ALFRED[7] PECK, son of Peleg,[6] was a Universalist clergyman. He was ordained at Phelps, Ontario County, N. Y., October 3, 1822. He preached in western New York for many years. He also preached in Medina County, Ohio, where he was settled in 1838. He was preaching in Salisbury, Herkimer County, in 1850. He also preached in Marblehead and South Adams, Mass. In 1854 he removed to Iowa City, Iowa. He is said to have been a talented preacher, and much respected   He died March 4, 1860, at Stoughton, Wis. He was at the time, I am told, chaplain of the Wisconsin Legislature.

He was twice married; first, to Olive Knowles, October 10, 1822, daughter of Daniel Knowles, of Rye, Me.; second, to Matilda Nickerson, May 28, 1834, daughter of Hezekiah Nickerson, of Susquehanna County, Pa., formerly from Rhode Island. His first wife was born April 30, 1802, and died June 24, 1833. His second wife was born September 20, 1810. She survived him, and was again married, and residing in Leavenworth, Kansas, in 1864.

CHILDREN — EIGHTH GENERATION

3101. Maria Celina, b Sunday, Aug. 22, 1824. Died Sept 13, 1833

3102. Alfred Wallace, b. Saturday, Nov 22, 1828
By second wife

3103. Rollin George, b. Sunday, May 24, 1835. Died June 4, 1838

3104 Helen Ann, b. Sunday, June 4, 1837.

3105 Henry Clay, b Tuesday, July 23, 1839

3106 John Murray, b. Tuesday, June 29, 1841

3107 Marion Matilda, b. Jan 31, 1843

3108 Pardon E G , b Sept 17, 1853

Alfred W is a Baptist clergyman   He graduated at Madison University, N Y., August 15, 1858, and was ordained at Keysport, N. J., September 1, 1858.

He was settled at Superior, Wis , as a home missionary, three years, and at Rensselaerville, N Y , one year as pastor of the Baptist church there   He was residing in 1864 at Vallejo, Solano County, Cal , in the service of the American Baptist Home Missionary Society.

Helen A married George H Rushmore, March 12, 1856   They were residing at Leavenworth City, Kansas, in 1864.   Then children were   *Alfred J* ,[9] *Harry*,[9] *John*,[9] *George*[9] and *Edgar M.*[9]

Henry C enlisted in the United States Infantry   Was 1st Lieutenant, and a disbursing officer, at Elmira, N Y , for some time

John M , a Medical Student at St Louis, also entered the service   He was at the United States Marine Hospital at St Louis in 1864

Marion married S H Downie, of Leavenworth, November 1, 1865.

Pardon was residing at Leavenworth in 1864

[2748.]   PELEG[7] PECK, son of Peleg,[6] married Mary Bradley, in 1824, daughter of Ajuna Bradley.   She was born in 1808. They were residing at Perry Centre, Chiawassa County, Mich., in 1864.

CHILDREN — EIGHTH GENERATION

3109   Charles S , b Sept 27, 1825   3111.   Truman D , b Oct. 12, 1828
3110   Sarah A , b April 3, 1827

Charles S married S Martin   They resided in Cleveland, Ohio, in 1864 Their children were   (3112) *Lillie*,[9] (3113) *Clarence*,[9] (3114) *Herbert*[9] and (3115) *Ernest* [9]

Sarah A married V Demick

Truman D married A S Clark, daughter of Ezra Clark   Their children are   (3116) *Willie*,[9] (3117) *Eddie*,[9] (3118) *Charles*[9] and (3119) *Louisa* [9] They resided in East Cleveland, Ohio, in 1864

[2749.]   DOCT. DORASTUS[7] PECK, son of Peleg,[6] took his collegiate studies preparatory to the practice of medicine and surgery, at Fairfield, Herkimer County, N. Y.   He was twice married , first, to Rosilla Park, daughter of Doct Park, of Onondaga Co , N Y , January 2, 1825; second, to Mrs. Ellen F. Reed, formerly Miss Ellen F. Cooper, of St. Genevieve County, Mo., February 19, 1850.   He commenced the practice of medicine at the age of twenty-three years, and settled in Licking County, Ohio, in 1837. From there he removed, in 1841, to the then Territory of Iowa, and settled at Keosauqua, Van Buren County.   In 1859 he removed to Missouri, and settled in the town of Ironton, Iron County, where he continued to reside until his decease, June 18, 1868.*

Dr. Peck followed his profession more than forty years, and

---

* He was one of the Delegates to the Missouri Constitutional Convention, which convened January 6, 1865, at St Louis.

was a successful practitioner. Being naturally of a sympathetic temperament, he was eminently fitted to feel for the afflicted, and to become interested for their relief.

As a citizen he was respected, and called by the suffrages of his friends to fill many offices of responsibility; and while his general good character secured for him the respect and esteem of the public, his domestic and private virtues were such as to acquire the love and affection of his family.

CHILDREN — EIGHTH GENERATION

3120   Freelove Eliza, b Aug 15, 1827
3121   Lucy S , b Jan 6, 1830
3122   Carrol Romegn, b Dec 8, 1831
3123   Eliva Geraldyne, b Sept. 28, 1834
3124.   Caroline Lucinda, b May 24, 1837.
3125   Warren Elijah, b June 19, 1841
3126   Franklin Thomas, b Oct 23, 1843
3127.   Charles H , b Nov 19, 1850
3128   Leonard L., b Mar 23, 1855
3129   Manly D , b: Sept 14, 1857
3130   George Grant, b Mar 17, 1862

Freelove Eliza married Jacob Lane, May 6, 1846   He died of the cholera at Keokuk, Iowa, July 1854   She afterwards married Lewis E Bonney, of Keosauqua, Iowa, October 1858, and was residing at Ironton, Mo , in 1864

Lucy S married Thaddeus Robbins, at Keosauqua, Iowa, Dec 29, 1849   She died at Wiston, Mo , November 23, 1850

Carrol R married Emily Lindsey, at Arcadia, Mo , October 10, 1858   He was received in the United States Land Office, and engaged in mercantile business at Ironton, Mo , in 1864

Eliva G married James Lindsey, at Keokuk, Iowa, May 3, 1853   They were residing at Ironton, Mo , in 1864

Caroline L married Richard F. Trow, at Ironton, August 30, 1859, where they were residing in 1864

Warren E enlisted in the service of his country, was 2d Lieutenant in the 29th Missouri Volunteer Infantry   He was afterwards upon the Governor's Staff, — Aide-de-Camp, — with the rank of Colonel.

Franklin T was engaged in business with his father at Ironton in 1864

[2759.] WILLIAM[7] PECK, son of PETER,[6] married Julana Keyser, July 25, 1819, and settled at Richfield Springs, N. Y., where he died March 24, 1862.

CHILDREN — EIGHTH GENERATION

3131. Catharine, b Oct 15, 1821   3134. Charles, b Feb 2, 1830
3132 William, b Dec 10, 1823   3135. Lucina, b. April 13, 1834
3133 Margaret M , b. July 8, 1827

Catharine married Charles Jones, January 6, 1846, and settled at Fly Creek
Margaret married John W Kane, January 1, 1855, and settled at Oakville, Otsego County, N. Y.
William married Aurelia Conner, and was residing at West Burlington, Otsego County, N Y., in 1864 His child (3136) *George W*,[9] was born October 23, 1855, and died July 13, 1863
Charles married Adaline Robinson, October 9, 1859, and was residing at West Burlington, Otsego County, N Y , in 1864. His son (3137) *Willie C*[9] was born December 13, 1859
Lucina married Almond D Powers, February 12, 1854   They were residing in Bridgeport, Conn , in 1864.

[2760] DANIEL[7] PECK, son of PETER,[6] was residing at Hector, N. Y., in 1863.
He married Atalante Ann Winn, October 10, 1832.

CHILDREN — EIGHTH GENERATION

3138 Lydia Jane, b Oct 19, 1833.   3140 Roxana, b. Jan 29, 1848
3139 James, b. June 19, 1840.

[2783] COMFORT[7] PECK, son of THOMAS,[6] settled in Burlington, Iowa.
He married Mrs. Emily Anderson, formerly Miss Emily Goddard, in 1848.

CHILDREN — EIGHTH GENERATION

3141. Elizabeth Jane, b June 16,   3142 Hubbard Cavanaugh,
       1851   b Sept 22, 1855   } Twins
                                       3143. Thomas Edward, b.
                                              Sept 22, 1855.

[2784.] ALLEN[7] PECK, son of BARNEY,[6] settled in Wolcott, N. H.
He married Eunice Hubbell, December 1811. He died June 8, 1860. She died September 4, 1852.

CHILDREN — EIGHTH GENERATION

3144. Electa, b Sept. 16, 1812
3145. Rosanna H , b Oct 16, 1814
3146 Seth H , b. Feb 7, 1816
3147 Almira, b March 10, 1818
3148. Marinda, b April 6, 1820
3149 Emily L , b Sept 24, 1822
3150 C P Van Ness, b Jan 1, 1825
3151. Royal H , b May 22, 1827
3152 Salome B , b Dec 20, 1829
3153 Allen, b April 2, 1832 Died Aug 23, 1865

Electa married Duston C Nichols, of Charleston, N. H Their children are *Lucius,*[9] *Almira,*[9] *Alpheus,*[9] *Eunice,*[9] *Erastus,* [9]*John,*[9] *Emogene*[9] and *Charles* [9]

Rosanna H. married John Pickering, of Burlington Had one child *Mary,* in 1864

Seth H married Ann Palmer Their children are (3154) *Julius,*[9] (3155) *Melvin,*[9] (3156) *Albert,*[9] (3157) *Andrew*[9] and (3158) *Willie* [9]

Almira married Edmond Quimby, and settled in Oregon Their children in 1864 were *Eunice Jane,*[9] *Rosalinda,*[9] *Isabella,*[9] *Minnie,*[9] *Josephine*[9] and *Cornelia* [9] They buried two boys, each named *Isaiah* [9]

Marinda married Almond Fife, and have two children *Seth*[9] and *Mary* [9]

Emily married Orvis Taylor, and had one son (3159) *Julius* [9]

Van Ness married Jane Sweeny Their children are (3159) *Vernon,*[9] (3160) *Abby,*[9] (3161) *Ida,*[9] (3162) *Nellie,*[9] (3163) *James*[9] and (3164) *Mary* [9]

Royal H married Mrs Hannah D Twichell, October 1859, residing in Wolcott, in 1864, no children

Allen married Mis Eliza A. Tubbs, August 1859, residing in Wolcott in 1864, no children.

[2787] WILLIAM[7] PECK, of Calais, Vt., son of BARNEY,[6] married Hannah Haskill, daughter of Moses Haskill, in 1820 She was born September 13, 1800, and died December 7, 1863. He died July 1, 1864.

CHILDREN — EIGHTH GENERATION

3165 Sarah, b Sept 4, 1822
3166 Irena L , b. Nov 10, 1831
3167. William V , b Feb 9, 1834
3168 Wesley C , b Aug 8, 1836

Sarah married Otis Slayton, son of Jesse Slayton, no issue

Irene L married James P Land, in 1851 She died August 13, 1862, leaving one son *Wesley Elwin* [8]

William V. married Helen M Dudley, February 6, 1858, daughter of Willard and Polly Dudley His children are (3169) *Mary Evelina,*[9] born April 13, 1860, and (3170) *Mertella,*[9] born June 15, 1862

Wesley C. married Lenora Osgood, January 18, 1859, daughter of Curtis and Lucy Osgood His children are (3171) *Mary Emogene,*[9] born April 4, 1860, and (3172) *Alice Jane,*[9] b June 4, 1862

[2789.] WELCOME[7] PECK, son of BARNEY,[6] resided in Johnson, Vt., in 1863. He married Harriet G. Hayford, March 30, 1824, daughter of Jacob Hayford, of Johnson, Vt.

20*

3173. Hiram H , b March 15, 1827   1835.
3174. Thomas H , b Sept 26, 1829   3177 Lucia A , b. Nov 29, 1837
3175. Philo W , b February 29,   3178 Luella E , b Nov 4, 1840
       1832   Died June 13, 1861
3176. Marinda H , born April 4,   3179 Lyman B , b Mar 26, 1843.

Hiram married Alma M. Hill, and was residing in Wyoming, Jones County, Iowa, in 1864   His children were (3180) *Laforest H*,[9] (3181) *O H*,[9] (3182) *Harriet S*,[9] (3183) *Warren W.*,[9] (3184) *Charles M*[9] (3185) and *Franklin H*[9]

Thomas married Ann Bartrum, resided in Johnson, Vt , in 1864   His children were (3186) *Harvey B*[9] and (3187) *Luella*[9]

Philo married M Miller, and was residing in Bloomington. McLean County, Ill , in 1864   His children were (3188) *Harriet V*[9] and (3189) *Herbert A*[9]

Marinda H married G T Newman, and settled in Bloomington, McLean County, Ill

Lucia married Chester K Hill, and settled in Johnson, Vt.

Lyman was residing in Johnson, Vt., in 1864 , no children

[2790.]   BARNEY[7] PECK, son of BARNEY,[6] resides in Wolcott, Vt.   He married Cynthia Bugbee, daughter of Elisha Bugbee, of Morristown, Vt., January 18, 1824.

3190 Marquis D L , b July 8, 1826   3195 Madora A., b Oct 30, 1837.
3191 Orilla, b April 8, 1828   3196 Charles B , b Dec 30, 1839.
3192 William P , b Oct 10, 1830   3197 Luther B , b June 30, 1843
3193 Edmond B , b Jan 16, 1833   Died Feb 15, 1861
       Died Aug 22, 1862   3198. Sophronia, b June 1, 1846
3194 Esther P , b Sept 9, 1835.

Orrilla married Isaac D Nelson, of Montpelier, Vt , September 18, 1848, were residing in Walcott in 1864   Their children were   *Cynthia A* ,[9] *Philora L.*,[9] *Henry I*,[9] *Charles P*[9] and *George A*[9]

Marquis D L married Philora Ladd, December 18, 1853, and settled in Walcott, Vt . His children are (3199) *Almenia M*,[9] (3200) *Helen M*,[9] (3201) *Salina E*[9] and (3202) *Edmond V*[9]

William married Catharine Johnson, of Hardwick, Vt , October 15, 1854, resided in St Johnsbury, Vt , and had one child (3203) *Ellen H*,[9] in 1864

Esther P married Lindsey Nelson, of Mendon, Mass , February 28, 1850; resides in Wallcott, had one child *Willie L* ,[9] in 1864

Madora married Richard Downing, December 8, 1855, settled in Woodbury. Their children were   *Edgar G* ,[9] *Ida S* ,[9] *Adin A*[9] and *Flora J*[9]

[2791.]   IRA[7] PECK, son of BARNEY,[6] resides in Marshal, Clark County, Ill.   He has been twice married; first, to Mary Fuller, May 18, 1834: second, to Lucina F. Bailey, October 17, 1839.   His first wife died April 9, 1838.

3204. Calvin, b Oct 22, 1836, in Elmore, Vt

3205 Zeluca Z , b Dec. 2, 1840, in Elmore, Vt.

3206. Barney, b Oct 7, 1842 Died the same day.

3207. Ira, b April 11, 1844, in Elmore, Vt

3208 Horace D , b Dec 28, 1845. Died March 10, 1846

3209. John W , b. July 21, 1848, in Clark County, Ill

3210. Jervam D , b October 29, 1850, in Clark County, Ill

3211. Mary E , b June 9, 1854, in Clark County, Ill

Calvin married Sarah M McFarland, Sept 1, 1859, and was residing in Clark County, Ill., in 1863. Their son (3212) *William R* [9] was born September 24, 1862 *

The other children were residing at home in 1864.

[2793.] JEREMIAH[7] PECK, son of BARNEY,[6] resides in Walcott, Vt. He married Lucia Day, daughter of Orrin Day, of Sharon, Vt.

3213. Francis, b. April 20, 1834.

3214. Orin D , b. Sept 26, 1837

3215. Amelia R , b June 9, 1840.

3216 Horace D., b April 7, 1842

3217. Mary J , b July 30, 1844.

3218 Marcia L , b April 11, 1848

3219 Edmond E , b July 4, 1856. Died March 1857

Francis married Mahala B Paine, December 3, 1857 She died March 11, 1862 He was again married to Wealthy D. Loveland, November 24, 1863, and settled in Johnson, Vt.

Amelia R married Daniel Pearson, May 26, 1861, were residing in Wolcott in 1863 Their child was *Freddie F*,[9] b May 21, 1862

[2796.] JOHN[7] PECK, son of ISAAC,[6] married Elizabeth Clark, daughter of Thomas Clark. He died November 20, 1829.

3220. Charles, b 1812

[2801.] GEORGE H.[7] PECK, son of ISAAC,[6] resides in Providence, R. I. He is a merchant. He married, for his first wife, Nancy Sweet, June 12, 1823 ; for his second, Harriet M. Sweetland, August 27, 1837 ; for his third, Rebecca Stillwell, September 9, 1852. His first wife was born July 20, 1804, and died October 20, 1836. His second wife was born June 25, 1815, and died December 18, 1851. His third wife was born August 10, 1816.

---

* They have a son James[9] born since.

CHILDREN — EIGHTH GENERATION :

3221. Esther S , b April 16, 1824.
       Died Aug 20, 1825
3222 Ann F , b March 19, 1826.
3223 Isaac, b July 23, 1828

3224 George H jr , b May 6, 1832.
3225 John H , b. July 15, 1835
3226 Harriet A , b Dec 28, 1848.

Ann F married William F Andrews, of Providence, R I

Isaac married Sarah Burdick, daughter of Capt. George Burdick, of New-port, R I , October 30, 1851   They were residing in Providence in 1863   Their children were (3227) *George Augustus,*[9] b October 9, 1852, (3228) *Isaac Newton,*[9] b September 15, 1853 , (3229) *Stella May,*[9] b October 12, 1854 ; (3230) *Isaac Newton, 2d,*[9] b February 14, 1857 , (3231) *Mary Lizzie,*[9] b August 5, 1858 , (3232) *Nancy Sweet,*[9] b July 16, 1860 , (3233) *Frances Andrews,*[9] b December 30, 1861

George H , jr married Sophia Kinsley, of Newburyport, Mass , and was residing in Providence, R I , in 1863 , no issue.

[2807.] BARNEY[7] PECK, son of EBENEZER,[6] resides in Providence, R. I.   He married Mary A. Walling, daughter of John Walling, of Providence, R. I , October 14, 1839.

CHILDREN — EIGHTH GENERATION

3234. Ebenezer, b Nov. 17, 1840 }
3235. Mary Louisa, b. Nov.17, 1840 }
       Twins.

3236. Elizabeth Crawford, b Dec 14, 1849 Died Sept 1, 1850.
3237 William Henry, b March 4, 1853 Died March 22, 1858

[2808.] SAMUEL B.[7] PECK, son of EBENEZER,[6] resides in Providence, R. I.   He married Lydia Colvin, daughter of Holden Colvin, of Coventry, R. I.

CHILD — EIGHTH GENERATION

3238 Ethan

[2811] LEWIS[7] PECK, son of WELCOME,[6] settled first in Scituate, R I., but afterwards moved into Burrillville, where he was residing in 1863.   He has been twice married: first, to Sally Ann Colvin, daughter of James Colvin, of Johnston: second, to Lucy Vallett, daughter of Jonathan Vallett, of Gloucester.   His first wife died August 4, 1845.

CHILDREN — EIGHTH GENERATION

3239. Susan, b 1827
3240 Welcome, b July 30, 1829.
3241 Emily M , b. 1831.
3242. Nancy
3243. Peleg J , b. 1836.

3244 Mary F   Died Aug. 23, 1842.
3245 Phebe, b 1841
3246 Mary
3247 Emeline.

Susan married William Borden, of Scituate, R. I., and was residing in Bur-rillville, R. I , in 1866.

Welcome married Mary S. Trimm, daughter of William Trimm, March 9, 1850, and was residing in Burrillville, R I, in 1866

Emily M has been twice married first, to Stephen Pierce, second to Ezekiel Ralph, of Scituate, R I.

Peleg J married Jane Cooms, April 11, 1852, was residing in Burrillville, R I, in 1866

Phebe has been twice married · first, to Albert Philips, second, to George Fowles, of Burrillville, R. I.

[2812.] STEPHEN[7] PECK, son of WELCOME,[6] lived and died upon the homestead, in Scituate, R. I. He married Polly You, daughter of James You. He died August 14, 1829.

CHILDREN — EIGHTH GENERATION

3248   Betsey Ann.   3249   Lucinda Y.

[2815.] ASAHEL[7] PECK, son of WELCOME,[6] resides upon the homestead. He married Susan Colvin, daughter of James Colvin of Johnston, R. I.

CHILDREN — EIGHTH GENERATION

3250	Lizzie, b May 20, 1834	3254	Almira H , b Dec 3, 1840.
3251	Sarah M , b Jan 11, 1836	3255	Thomas W , b Nov 3, 1842
3252	Stephen P., b June 22, 1837.	3256	Lydia L , b Aug 4, 1844
3253	Asahel A , b. Jan 16, 1839	3257	Susan M , b. Oct 6, 1850

[2816] ALFRED O.[7] PECK, son of WELCOME,[6] resides in Scituate, R. I. He married Cordelia Colvin, daughter of James Colvin, of Johnston, R. I., April 21, 1836.

CHILDREN — EIGHTH GENERATION

3258.	William A., b. Nov. 30, 1839 Died May 5, 1855	3260	Mary E , b June 6, 1851 Died May 2, 1852
3259.	Ransom O , b Jan 9, 1842	3261.	Delia F , b. July 4, 1855
		3262.	Ella M., b. March 29, 1857.

Ransom O married Sarah A. Colvin, May 17, 1863

[2821.] HERSA[7] PECK, son of GAIEUS,[6] married a Widow Southworth. He died at Richford, Wis., November 1857.

CHILDREN — EIGHTH GENERATION ·

3263. Porter   3265. Albert.
3264. Page.

[2823.] SAMUEL[7] PECK, son of GAIEUS,[6] is settled at Barnet, Vt. He married Sophia Wood, of Barnet.

CHILDREN — EIGHTH GENERATION

3266. Geoige W , b Jan 14, 1827
           Died April 30, 1850
3267 Jane A., b July 17, 1829.
3268. Sophia, b June 24, 1831

3269 William E , b Maich 24, 1833
3270 Henry O , b Sept 11, 1835
3271. John H , b April 18, 1837

[2825.] WILLIAM[7] PECK, son of GAIEUS,[6] married Susan Eliza Dana, of Cabot, Vt. They resided in Chicago, Ill , in 1864.

CHILDREN — EIGHTH GENERATION

3272. Oscar Dana, b. Aug 23, 1832
3273. Eliza Dana, b Sept 30, 1834
3274. John William, b. Jan. 14, 1837.
3275. Catharine Dana, b Feb 15, 1839.

3276. Geoige Wesley, b May 9, 1841
3277 Chailes Edwaid, b. Sept. 1, 1844
3278 Wilber F , b Maich 6, 1846.
           Died Sept 23, 1859

Oscar D. was residing in California in 1864, was mailied, and had one child.

John William died at Little Rock, Mich., a soldier in the 29th Iowa Regiment. He left a wife and one child.

[2826.] GEORGE C.[7] PECK, son of GAIEUS,[6] resides at Lindon, Vt. He married Malinda Wing, June 20, 1838.

CHILDREN — EIGHTH GENERATION

3279 Ellen E , b Sept 16, 1839
3280 William H., b Jan. 3, 1841
3281. Julia M , b Dec. 5, 1842 Died Sept 30, 1843.

3282 Chailes C , b Sept 12, 1846.
           Died Jan 27, 1852
3283. Ida M , b. Oct. 16, 1854

[2837.] THOMAS[7] PECK, son of THOMAS,[6] married ——.

CHILD — EIGHTH GENERATION

3284.

[2838] EBENEZER[7] PECK, son of THOMAS,[6] married ——. He was in Washington, D. C., in 1866.

CHILDREN — EIGHTH GENERATION

3285.
3286.
3287.

3288
3289

[2841.] EZRA[7] PECK, son of AARON,[6] is a farmer, and resides in Jamestown, Chautauque County, N. Y. He married Harriet Perkins, daughter of Roswell Perkins, of Freehold, Warren County, Pa.

CHILDREN — EIGHTH GENERATION

3290 Marshall E , b Feb 1, 1836.
3291 Erastus P , b July 13, 1838
3292. Henry H , b Aug 11, 1840

3293 Julia A , b Nov 19, 1842.
3294 Mary J , b Feb 10, 1845.
3295 Ellen M , b. May 30, 1849.

Marshall E married Rhoda A Derby He was a soldier in the war, and was wounded

Erastus P married Lydia A Wares — His children are *Judson E* [9] and *Eliza A* [9] He was also in the army

Henry H was also in the army, and died at White House Landing, of the typhoid malaria, July 3, 1863

Julia A married Robert E Fuller He was also a soldier.

Mary J. married Horace A Willson He was also a soldier

[2843] SAMUEL[7] PECK, son of AARON,[6] resides at Ellicott, Chautauque County, N. Y., a farmer.

He married Almira Dunbar, daughter of Alvin Dunbar. of Ellicott, in 1850.

CHILDREN — EIGHTH GENERATION

3296 Annette, b May 16, 1851

3297 Charles, b Jan 11, 1859

[2845.] EZEKIEL[7] PECK, son of AARON,[6] resides at Carroll, Chautauque County, N. Y., a farmer.

He married Emeline Woodward, daughter of Reuben J. Woodward, of Ellicott, in 1850.

CHILD — EIGHTH GENERATION

3298 Lavern, b Sept 9, 1850.

[2847.] MILTON[7] PECK, son of EZRA,[6] first settled in Hubbardston. From there he removed to Hardwick, Mass , where he died, April 14, 1855. He married Mary Dexter.

CHILDREN — EIGHTH GENERATION

3299. Mary A , b Feb 23, 1824.
        Died in 1853.
3300. Jane R , b July 8, 1827.
3301 Horace M , b April 29, 1830
3302. Simon E W , b Aug 5, 1832.
3303 Sally B , b March 7, 1834
3304 Samuel D , b April 24, 1837.

3305 Cryton W , b Dec 10, 1838
        Died in 1838
3306. Luthera M , b. Dec. 10, 1840
        Died Dec 26, 1858
3307 William C , b. March 6, 1843
3308. Susan A , b Nov 3, 1847.
        Died July 31, 1848

Jane R married Francis Legate, June 2, 1847 Their children were *Francis Augustus,*[9] b February 14, 1854, *Lizzie J ,*[9] b November 23, 1857, and died November 29, 1859

Simon E W. married Almena Austin, and resided, in 1864, in Hardwick, Mass.

William C married Hannah N. Atwood, of Hardwick, Mass , March 11, 1862, and was residing in Greenwich in 1864.   Their child was   (3309) *Mary M.,*[9] b. May 12, 1863.

[2852.]   JAMES B.[7] PECK, son of HORATIO,[6] resided in Providence, R. I., in 1864.

He married Hannah R. Medbery, daughter of George Medbery, of East Providence, R I.

CHILDREN — EIGHTH GENERATION

3310.   Allen G , b March 14, 1846.   3313.   Nancy E., b April 23, 1853
3311.   Forrest A., b Oct 20, 1849.   Died April 16, 1855.
3312.   James M , b. June 4, 1851.

[2853.]   HENRY C.[7] PECK, son of HORATIO,[6] was residing at Whitinsville, Mass., in 1863.   He married Lydia S. Smith, daughter of Joseph Smith, of Somerset, Mass., October 9, 1853.

CHILDREN — EIGHTH GENERATION .

3314.   Leander Edwin, b May 6, 1861.   3315.   John Henry, b July 15, 1863.

[2863]   EDWIN F.[7] PECK, son of BELA,[6] married Abigail Bowen, daughter of Samuel Bowen, June 6, 1850.   They were residing in Barrington, R. I., in 1863.

CHILDREN — EIGHTH GENERATION

3316.   Alpheus F , b Sept 24, 1850.   3318.   Emma E , b. April 30, 1860.
3317   Maria B , b. July 24, 1852

[2876.]   REV. NATHAN R.[7] PECK, son of REV. JOHN,[6] married Mary Round, daughter of Joseph Round, of Monkton, Vt. He was residing in California in 1863.

CHILDREN — EIGHTH GENERATION :

3319.   Marritta, b. Jan 7, 1834.   3320.   Maria, b Sept 26, 1838.

Marritta married Rev Ralph Pierce, of the Black River Conference, N. Y. They went to India as missionaries, where she died, November 1862

Maria married Rev J. H Maddox, who was of the California Mission, in 1863.

[2880.]   DANIEL[7] PECK, son of REV. JOHN,[6] was residing at Fullerville, St. Lawrence County, N. Y., in 1864.   He married Martha Fuller, March 10, 1842.

CHILDREN — EIGHTH GENERATION:

3321. Anna, b. Dec. 25, 1845.   3323. Everett, b. Jan 11, 1860.
3322. Celinda, b. Feb 2, 1849.

[2887.] GEORGE W.[7] PECK, son of David,[6] was residing in East Rutland, Vt., in 1864. He married, for his first wife, Frances Howland, daughter of Sydney B Howland, January 9, 1854; and for his second, he married Helen Strong, daughter of Marvin Strong, February 8, 1860.

CHILD — EIGHTH GENERATION

3324. Merritt Emerson.

[2911.] SOLOMON[7] PECK, son of Solomon,[6] is settled upon the homestead. He married Keziah Peck (No. 2918), daughter of Darius Peck, January 6, 1828.

CHILDREN — EIGHTH GENERATION

3325 Solomon Augustus, b. Dec 8, 1828.
3326 Josephus Wales, b Aug. 12, 1831.
3327. Francis Wayland, b. March 20, 1834.
3328 Cornelius Carpenter, b Feb 16, 1836

Solomon A was residing with his father, in 1863, unm

Josephus W married Sarah I Peck (No 3346), daughter of Sylvester Peck, of Providence, R. I , July 2, 1857. He was residing in Providence in 1864. His children were (3329) Sarah Keziah,[9] b May 13, 1858 , and (3330) Julia Goddard,[9] b November 9, 1861

Francis W. married Mary Shed, of Providence, R I., and was residing in East Providence in 1864 She was the daughter of Ebenezer Shed. Their child was (3331) Marietta Frances,[9] b April 28, 1859

Cornelius C married Isabella Jane Anthony, daughter of David Anthony, of East Providence, R I , where they were residing in 1863 Their children were (3332) David Solomon,[9] b August 19, 1860; and (3333) Eliza Baker,[9] b. July 31, 1862.

[2919.] CALVIN S.[7] PECK, of Providence, R. I., son of Darius,[6] married Hannah Cooper, November 1, 1829, daughter of William Cooper.

CHILD — EIGHTH GENERATION

3334 Calvin Willson, b July 2, 1843 Died Sept. 19, 1845.

[2921.] HERMAN A.[7] PECK, of Providence, R. I., son of Darius,[6] married, for his first wife, Lemira Wheaton Peck (No. 2916), daughter of Solomon Peck, of Seekonk, April 23, 1834.

21

For his second wife, he married Mary Ann Fuller, daughter of Levi and Mary Fuller, January 19, 1843. His first wife died May 21, 1841.

CHILDREN — EIGHTH GENERATION.

By first wife

3335. Ellen Frances, b. Jan. 27, 1838.
3336. Lemira Wheaton, b May 15, 1841. Died May 26, 1841.

By second wife

3337. Herman Allen, b Oct 18, 1843. Died March 5, 1847
3338. John Flavel, b April 3, 1845.
3339. Mary Fry, b Jan 31, 1847.

3340 Ann Lemira, b Jan. 15, 1849.
3341. Lydia Keziah, b. Sept. 12, 1851.
3342. Lucy Ella, b. Feb. 8, 1854 Died Sept 30, 1859.
3343. Herman Sanford, b. April 14, 1856 Died May 7, 1864.
3344. Roxanna Fuller, b Sept. 15, 1858 Died May 12, 1864
3345. William Newton, b Feb. 10, 1862

[2922.] SYLVESTER W.[7] PECK, of Providence, R. I., son of Darius,[6] married Sarah L. Phinney, April 26, 1833, daughter of Edward Phinney, of Barnstable, Mass.

CHILDREN — EIGHTH GENERATION

3346. Sarah Ide, b June 9, 1834.
3347. Charles Henry, b. Oct. 22, 1837 Died June 11, 1839.
3348. Julia Ann, b July 9, 1840 Died Sept 9, 1858

3349 Jane Hudson, b Oct. 9, 1843.
3350. Francis Wheaton, b. July 7, 1846

[2926.] ELLIS[7] PECK, of Barrington, R. I., son of Ellis,[6] married Louisa Jones, daughter of William Jones, of Seekonk, February 28, 1830. He is a model farmer.

CHILDREN — EIGHTH GENERATION

3351. William Jones, b Dec 14, 1830 Died June 16, 1833
3352. William Jones, b. June 5, 1833
3353 Sarah Elizabeth, b Sept. 8, 1836.

3354. Leroy Ellis, b Dec 16, 1843 Died March 18, 1844.
3355. Arabella Louisa, b Sept. 4, 1845

William Jones married Virginia White, daughter of Thomas White, of Bristol, R I

Sarah Elizabeth married John White, of Bristol, R. I

[2928.] ASA[7] PECK, of Barrington, R. I., son of Ellis,[6] married Lucretia S. Remington, March 4, 1839, daughter of Enoch Remington, of Barrington. He is a drover and cattle broker.

CHILDREN — EIGHTH GENERATION

3356. Adelaide Eliza, b. March 22, 1840
3357. Leander R , b. Feb. 12, 1843.

3358. George Asa, b. Aug 22, 1846. Died Aug 28, 1846.
3359 Julietta L., b. Nov 7, 1848.

[2934.] EBENEZER[7] PECK, son of NATHANIEL,[6] settled in Providence, R. I., where he died, August 28, 1848. He married Abby A. Bump, daughter of Nathan Bump, of North Providence, June 8, 1843.

CHILDREN — EIGHTH GENERATION·

3360. Sarah E , b. May 1846. 3361. Edmond B., b. April 1847.

[2938.] DANIEL H.[7] PECK, son of EBENEZER,[6] resides in Barrington. He married Mary Ann Baker, of Lowell, Mass.

CHILDREN — EIGHTH GENERATION·

3362 Mary Esther. 3364. Edwin B. Died in the army.
3363. Daniel R. 3365. William S.

[2939.] JOHN H.[7] PECK, son of EBENEZER,[6] resides in Barrington. He married Charlotte Tanner, daughter of Daniel Tanner, of Warwick, R. I.

CHILDREN — EIGHTH GENERATION

3366. John H. 3367. William H. Died in infancy.

John H. resides in Barrington, R. I.

[2947.] BENJAMIN W.[7] PECK, son of BENJAMIN,[6] is settled in Providence, R. I.

He married Emily A. Gillmore, daughter of George Gillmore, of Providence, R. I., December 24, 1850.

CHILDREN — EIGHTH GENERATION :

3368. E. L., b Nov 4, 1851. 3370. Emily J., b. Dec. 31, 1858.
3369. Walter H , b. Jan. 20, 1857.

[2949.] GEORGE S.[7] PECK, son of BENJAMIN,[6] is settled in Providence, R. I.

He married Ellen C. Rhodes, May 10, 1855.

CHILDREN — EIGHTH GENERATION :

3371. Ellen Amanda, b. July 31, 1856. 3372. Emma Louisa, b. Jan. 11, 1859.
3373. George Albert, b. July 1, 1860.

PART SIXTH.

THE DESCENDANTS OF ISRAEL[2] PECK.

SIXTH SON OF JOSEPH[1] THE ANCESTOR.

ISRAEL was born at Hingham, Mass., and baptized there, March 4, 1644. He moved from there with his father and family to See-konk. He settled in what is now Barrington, upon the lands given him and his brother Nathaniel, near where is now the residence of Mr. Ellis Peck. For a description of these lands, see part 5th, in reference to the settlement of Nathaniel.

Israel Peck married Bethiah Bosworth, daughter of Jonathan Bosworth, July 15, 1670. They both lived to be aged. The following are the inscriptions upon their tombstones:

Here lieth the body of M[r] Israel Peck died Sept[r] y[e] 2[d] 1723 in y[e] 80th year of his Age

Here lyeth int[rd] the body of M[rs] Bethiah daughter of Jonathan Bosworth and wife of M[r] Israel Peck died Apr 4th 1718 Aged 75 years

He held various public offices. His will is recorded upon the records at Taunton, Mass., B. 4, p. 220. The following is a copy:

In the name of God Amen this eighth day of August Anno Domi 1718 and in the fifth year of the Reign of our Sovereign Lord George over Great Brittan & King I Israel Peck of Swansey alias Barring-ton in the county of Bristol within the Province of the Massachusetts Bay in New England yeoman being in the seventy sixth year of my age but retaining my memory and understanding as at other times thanks be given to god there fore remembering my own frailty do make and ordain this my last will & testament in manner following that is to say first and principally I commit my Soul unto the care of God that

21*

gave it me and my body to the earth to be decently intered at the discretion of my executor here after named and as touching such worldly
estate which it hath pleased God to bless me with in this life I give
and demise and despose of the same in the following manner and
form

Imp^{rs} It is my will that all my debts and funeral charges be well
and truly paid and satisfied in convenient time after my decease by
my executor here in after named

Item I give to my only son Nathaniel Peck having given to him
and to his heirs & assigns forever by a deed of gift under my hand
and seal bearing date the sixteenth day of July Anno Domi 1718 all
my housing Lands and meadows of any kind in Barrington in the
county of Bristol and also my stock and husbandry tools I do by
these presents ratify and confirm the same unto him the purpose and
true intent & meaning of said gift And farther I give and bequeath
unto my said son & his heirs and assigns forever all my rights in the
undivided lands in Rehoboth and any other lands which I shall not
other wise despose of in this my last will and testament my hunting
gun and silver spoons and what other movables I shall not particularly give to my daughters or their children

Item I give and bequeath unto my daughter the wife of Josiah
Dean and to my daughter the wife of Ephraim May and to the children of my daughter Mehetible Whitaker deceased equally to be
divided and to their heirs and assigns for ever all my lands in Rehoboth lying at or near the great meadow hill being two hundred &
thirty seven acres and forty acres more lying near to John Whitaker
in Rehoboth afor said only that land I formerly gave to the said John
Whitaker to be reckoned into and with my said grand children their
third part of the lands above given to my said daughter and grand
children the third part of the land given to my grand children. My
will is that it be equally devided between them or the survivors of
them Farther I give unto my said daughter & to my grand children
equally to be divided all my house hold goods, that is to say, my beds
& beding with the furniture and appurtances belonging to them table
lining and my pewter and brass vessels of all sorts and also I give to
my two daughters each of them a silver spoon and a silver spoon to
my grand daughter Mehetible she bearing her mothers name to gether
with the equall part of the house hold goods given to my grand children to be equally divided among them or the equal survivors of
them

Item I give and bequeath to my daughter Dean twenty pounds in stock at the market price to be paid by my said son to her heirs within three years after my decease

Item I give to my daughter Mary twenty pounds to be paid to her or her heirs by my said son Nathaniel Peck within three years after my decease in stock or cattle at the market price.

Item I give to the children of my daughter Mehetible twenty pounds in stock at the market price the value there of to be devided equally between them or the survivors of them to be paid by my son Nathaniel Peck within three years after my decease

And I do by these presents nominate and appoint my son Nathaniel Peck to be said executor to this my last will and testament disallowing and making null and void all other former Wills Testaments Legaces bequests & Executors by me in any way before this time named within and bequeathed ratifying & confirming this and none but this to be my last Will & testament In witness whereof I have set my hand & seal the day and year first above written.

Signed sealed and published and declared by the said Israel Peck to be his last will and testament in the presence of us the subscribers.

ZACHARIAH BICKNELL
ELISHA MAY
JOHN CARY.   ISRAEL PECK

CHILDREN — THIRD GENERATION

3374 Mehitable, b Aug 6, 1671.
3375. Israel, b Dec 18, 1673. Was drowned June 23, 1786
3376.+Nathaniel, b Sept 27, 1677

3377 Deliverance, b June 21, 1680.
3378 Israel, b Sept 3, 1686 Died Sept 6, 1686.
3379. Mary

Mehitable married John Whittaker.
Mary married Josiah Dean
Deliverance married Ephraim May, June 19, 1708

The following are the inscriptions from their tombstones :

Here liethe ye body of Mr Ephraim May died Sepr ye 25th—1721 in ye 51st year of his age

Here lieth ye body of Deliverance wife of Ephraim May & daugh^r of Israel Peck died Decm^r ye 9th 1727 in ye 48th year of her Age

[3376] NATHANIEL[3] PECK, son of ISRAEL,[2] settled upon the lands given him by his father, where he lived and died.

He appears to have been a prominent man in the town. His will may be found upon the early records of Warren, R. I., B. 1, p. 131. He had previously given away the most of his lands by deed.

He gives to his wife Sarah the improvement of his real and personal estate during her natural life.

He gives to his granddaughter, Sarah Mathews, 12 sheep with their lambs, two cows, 2 feather beds with the bedsteads & furniture belonging to them, and a high chest of draws to be delivered to her when she arrived to the age of 21 years, or on the day of her marriage.

He gives to his beloved son Israel and his eldest male heir, and to the heirs and assigns of the said male heir, a tract of land lying by Hunt's tree.

To Simeon and Nathaniel, his beloved sons, to be equally divided between them, he gives his husbandry, tools & tacklin.

He gives to his sons Israel, Simeon & Nathaniel, to be divided equally between them, his wearing apparel. He also makes his sons equal in his commonage rights in Rehoboth.

He gives to his beloved daughter Mary Bucklin, and his beloved granddaughter Sarah Mathews, all of his indoor and outdoor movables not in his will otherwise disposed of, to be equally divided between them after the decease of his wife.

He orders his sons Simeon & Nathaniel to pay the above legacies to Sarah Mathews, in consideration of which he gives to them, their heirs and assigns, to be divided according to quantity and quality after his wife's decease, all his land lying and being in Warren to be divided equally between them.

He appoints his wife Sarah his executrix. The will is dated Feb. 1st, 1755, and was proved Sept. 6, 1756.

Nathaniel married Sarah Field, of Hatfield, Mass., October 25, 1709. See Swansey Records.

CHILDREN — FOURTH GENERATION

3380	Mehitable, b Aug 18, 1711.	3383	Mary
3381.	+Israel, b July 21, 1713	3384	+Simeon
3382.	Sarah, b 1718	3385	+Nathaniel

Mehitable married the Rev. Peleg Heath.

The following is from the record of their publishment and marriage:

August 9th 1740 Then Rev Peleg Heath declared unto me the subscriber his and Mrs Bethiah Peck their intentions to be married to each other

Recorded by me   JOSIAH HUMPHREY *Town clerk*

August 26th 1740   Then Mr Peleg Heath and Bitihah Peck both of Barrington were lawfully married by me

SYLVESTER RICHMOND, *Justice of the Peace.*

Recorded by me   JOSIAH HUMPHREY *Town clerk*

Sarah married —— Mathews
Mary married James Bucklin, of Rehoboth, March 29, 1743.

[3381.]   ISRAEL[4] PECK, son of NATHANIEL,[3] settled upon the lands given him by his father.   These he afterwards disposed of, and settled at Winsor, Mass., where he remained about two years; and from there removed to Dalton, Mass., where he died March 16, 1800.

He married Sarah Adams, September 18, 1746.   The following is upon the Barrington Records:

PROVIDENCE Sept 18—1746.

These may certify that Israel Peck and Sarah Adams was lawfully married according to the laws of the colony of Rhode Island, pr me,

JABEZ BROWN *Justice of the Peace*

Recorded by me

JOSIAH HUMPHREY *Town clerk*

CHILDREN — FIFTH GENERATION

3386 +James, b. July 5, 1747	3389. Mehitable, b. July 1, 1752
3387. Israel, b. Feb. 20, 1748-9.	3390. Amy.
Died April 11, 1750	3391 Mary.
3388.+Israel, b Dec 6, 1750.	3392. Nancy

The first four children are recorded upon the records at Warren, R. I

Mehitable married, for her first husband, —— Sunderland. He left no children. For her second, —— Robinson, and settled in Lanesborough, where he died, leaving three children   For her third husband, she married a man by the name of Farnum, and settled at Litchfield, where she died

Amey married, for her first husband, Daniel Loomis, by whom she had four children. Mr Heman Loomis, of Rochester, N. Y, to whom I am indebted for my information, is her grandson. For her second husband, she married Isaac Johnston, and settled at Amsterdam, N Y., where she died in 1826 She was buried at Manney's corners.

Nancy married a Powel, of Lanesborough, where they settled and died

Mary married John Durfee, of Dalton, Mass., December 20, 1786   She died August 7, 1845   He died in 1843. They had twelve children. Rev. Calvin Durfee, of Williamstown, Mass., is their son. To his kindness and that of his sister, Mrs. Sarah Torry, of Berkshire, N. Y., I am indebted for my information.

[3384]   SIMEON[4] PECK, son of NATHANIEL,[3] settled upon
the land given him by his father.   He was a blacksmith by trade.
He deeded away his lands in 1758–9 and '60.   He afterwards settled at Amherst, Mass.   The records at Springfield, Mass., show
that he bought and sold lands in Amherst from 1773 to 1783.   He
died March 29, 1783.

He married Priscilla West, of Warren, R. I., November 24,
1748.

CHILDREN — FIFTH GENERATION ·

3393. Bethiah, b Oct 3, 1751.   3396   Mary, b April 17, 1758
3394 +Joseph Kelly, b Jan. 10, 1754.   3397   Nathaniel, b Aug 17, 1760
3395   Simeon, b. Feb. 6, 1756

I have been unable to learn what became of Bethiah, Simeon,
Mary and Nathaniel.

[3385.]   MAJ. NATHANIEL[4] PECK, son of NATHANIEL,[3]
settled upon the lands given him by his father.   These he disposed
of, and removed to Amherst, Mass., where he died November 27,
1807.   He kept a public house in Amherst for many years, and
seems to have been a very prominent and influential citizen.   He
bought and sold lands in Amherst and the adjoining towns.   In
these deeds, he is usually called Maj. Nathaniel, or gentleman,
instead of yeoman or laborer.   He was in the war of the Revolution, and I am told held a Major's commission.

His wife was Mary Peck, widow of Winchester Peck, formerly
Mary Mitchel, daughter of James Mitchel.   She was born August
20, 1731, and died May 15, 1814.

CHILDREN — FIFTH GENERATION (W. Rec. B 1)

3398. Sarah, b Feb. 2, 1754.   3402. Mary, b. Aug 3, 1768.
3399 +Winchester, b Feb 7, 1762.   3403. Mehitable, b. April 27, 1772.
3400. Jerusha, b. June 18, 1764.
3401. Nathaniel, b Nov. 17, 1765.
       Died in infancy.

This record is in the family bible, in the handwriting of Maj.
Nathaniel.   The births of the three first children are also upon
the records at Warren, R. I.   This bible, printed in London in
1728, was formerly the property of James Mitchel, the father of
Nathaniel's wife, and was in the possession of the granddaughter
of Nathaniel, Mrs. Elizabeth Moore, of Leverett, Mass., in 1864,
when I visited her for the purpose of examining this record.

Sarah, the eldest daughter of Nathaniel, married Elisha Warner, and settled in Amherst, Mass, where they died, leaving no issue. He died December 10, 1823, and she September 13, 1825

Mary married David Eaton, in 1787, and settled in Vermont. She died October 10, 1813, he August 20, 1823, leaving five children.

Jerusha married Samuel Miles, and settled in Williamsburg, Mass He died at an early age, she October 8, 1848 Their children were *Elizabeth*,[6] born April 5, 1789, and *James Michels*, born February 13, 1791, and died in 1792. *Elizabeth* married Lewis Moore, May 3, 1810, and was residing, a widow, in Leverett, Mass, in 1864 He died January 4, 1843 Their children are *Luther H*,[7] born May 10, 1811, *Jerusha P*,[7] born September 9, 1813. *Quartus K*,[7] born March 26, 1816, *George W*,[7] born March 5, 1818, *James M*,[7] born February 4, 1820; *William B*,[7] born November 11, 1821, *Mary S*,[7] born January 13, 1824, *Lewis*[7] and *Lucius*[7] (twins), born February 1, 1827, *Otis B*,[7] born September 5, 1830; and *Sarah E*[7], born February 21, 1832

Mehitable married Luther Henry. Their children were *Clarissa.*,[6] born December 20, 1794, *Margaret*,[6] born March 14, 1796, *Anna*,[6] born April 13, 1798, *a son*, born February 10, 1805, *John*,[6] born September 10, 1806, and *James*,[6] born September 30, 1808 The oldest daughter, Clarissa, married Gideon Stetson, March 26, 1816 They were residing in Shutesbury, Mass, in 1864 Margaret married Lewis L. Draper, and lived and died in Amherst, Mass. Mr Draper was residing in Northampton in 1864 Anna married Alvah Haskins, and settled in Shutesbury John married Ada Parks, and settled in Van Buren, Ark James married Sarah Raymond, and died in Shutesbury, Mass.

The following Deed is from the Records at Warren, R. I., B. 1, P. 258:

To all people to whom these presents shall come Greeting Know ye that I Nathaniel Peck jr of Warren in the county of Bristol in the colony of Rhode Island yeoman for and in consideration of the sum of One thousand pounds old Tenor have remised and released and by these presents for me and my heirs executors and administrators: do remise release and forever quitclaim unto Simeon Peck of Warren aforsaid blacksmith in full and peaceable possession and to the heirs and assigns of the said Simeon Peck: all the right tittle and interest use possession and demand which I the said Nathaniel Peck Jr now have or which I or my heirs or Executors can or may claim to have to of and in a certain piece or parcel of up land containing twelve acres which I the said Nathaniel and Simeon Peck bought to gether of our beloved brother Israel Peck the nineteeth day of Feb 1754 reference to said deed being had for the bounds said land lying and being in Warren aforsaid To have and to hold all and singular the premises with the appertenences unto the said Simeon Peck his heirs and assigns forever so that neither I the said Nathaniel Peck nor my heirs nor any other person or persons for me or them or in mine or their names right tittle or stead shall or may by any way or means hereafter chalange or demand any interest of us or to the premises and any of them shall be excluded and debared by these presents Furthermore I the said Nathaniel Peck and my heirs release the said premises with the appurtenances unto the said Simeon Peck and his heirs and assigns unto their own proper use against me and my heirs and all and every other person lawfully claiming by from or under me the said Nathaniel Peck Jr shall and will warrent and defend by these presents

In witness where of I have hereunto set my hand and seal this seventeenth day of April annoque Domini 1754

Signed sealed an delivered
in the presents of

JOHN KENNICUT   NATHANIEL PECK.
SOLOMON TOWNSEND

[3386.] JAMES[5] PECK, son of ISRAEL,[4] settled in Sheffield, Mass., where he and his wife died.

CHILDREN — SIXTH GENERATION

3404 James. Died young   3405 Martha.

Martha married James Austin, at Athens, N Y., August 8, 1804   They settled in Boston, Mass., where they resided about thirty years From Boston they removed to Jersey City, N J , where they both died   Mr. James Austin, a merchant, 85 Wall St., N. Y., is her son.

[3388.] ISRAEL[5] PECK, son of ISRAEL,[4] settled at Pittsfield, Mass. He married Sarah Marsh, of Dalton, Mass. She died March 1813. He died in Rochester, December 5, 1827, and I am told was buried at Brighton, Monroe County, and that upon his tombstone is the following :

" Isral Peck— died Dec 5 1827 aged 72* years. The deceased was from Pittsfield Mass and to his memory this monument is erected by one of his descendants"

CHILDREN — SIXTH GENERATION

3406. Laura, b. Oct 12, 1785. Died   3410 +Otis
        May 16, 1862.   3411 Eunice
3407.+Henry   3412. Elizabeth
3408 +Perez P.   3413 Harriet
3409. Julia.   3414. George A.

* An error. He was born December 6, 1750, and was 77 years old, lacking one day.

Laura married David Bush, of Pittsfield, April 7, 1807.

Julia married Theodore Hinsdale, of Pittsfield.

Eunice married Samuel Patterson, of Albany.

Elizabeth married, first, Leonard Monroe, second, William Holt, of Norwalk, Ohio

Harriet married Josiah Goodman, of Lafayette, Ind.

George A is unmarried

[3394.] JOSEPH KELLY[5] PECK, son of SIMEON,[4] settled at Amherst, Mass. He was drafted, and entered the army of the Revolution, where he died, November 1776. He married Sybel Hastings, of Amherst.

CHILD — SIXTH GENERATION :

3415. Joseph Kelly, b Nov. 4, 1776.

The widow married Timothy Green. Rufus Green, of Carroll, N Y., is a son.

[3399.] WINCHESTER[5] PECK, son of MAJ. NATHANIEL,[4] settled at Amherst, Mass. He was killed by the rolling of a log upon him, while superintending the building of a dam, at Montague Falls, August 18, 1797. He married Lydia Perkins. She died in 1850, in her 86th year.

CHILDREN — SIXTH GENERATION ·

3416 +Gustavus D., b in 1788
3417 Henry W , b April 1790
3418 Horace, b. 1791. Died the same year.

3419. Sarah, b June 1792
3420 Clarissa, b Sept 1794.
3421. Joseph, b. July 1796
3422.+Horace, b. Dec. 1797.

Henry W followed the seas, not known where he is

Sarah married Elisha Tilden, November 7, 1811, and settled in Chesterfield, Mass Their children are *Sally P* ,[7] *Clarissa H. P* ,[7] *Mary M* ,[7] *Henry W* ,[7] *Elisha W* ,[7] *Elijah B* ,[7] *Elisha W* ,[7] *Maria E* [7] and *Martha L* [7]

Joseph graduated at Amherst College, and died at Andover, while pursuing his theological studies, September 1827.

Clarissa married Joseph Tower; settled at Northampton no issue

[3407.] HENRY[6] PECK, son of ISRAEL,[5] was residing in York, N. Y., in 1864. He married, for his first wife, Lucy Miles, daughter of James Miles, in 1814; and for his second wife, Mary Baldwin, daughter of Joseph Baldwin. His first wife deceased in 1829.

22

CHILDREN — SEVENTH GENERATION ·

3423. Julia Elizabeth, b, Nov. 27,
1815

3424 +George Henry, b Feb. 5, 1819

3425 +Otis Lyman, b. April 15, 1822,
3426. Harriet Maria, b. June 18,
1825

Julia and *Harriet* are married and settled in Sandusky City, Ohio

[3408.] PEREZ P.[6] PECK, son of ISRAEL,[5] married Clarissa Goodman, daughter of Titus Goodman. They were residing at Sandusky, Ohio, in 1864.

CHILDREN — SEVENTH GENERATION

3427 Clarissa M , b July 31, 1817.
3428 Frederick, b May 20, 1819.
3429 Benjamin F., b Feb 8, 1821.
3430 Henry, b Oct 6, 1823.
3431 James S.

3432 Charles F
3433. Catharine C.
3434 Mary
3435 Ann Janette.
3436. Mary L *

Clarissa and *Catharine* married Angus Smith, of Milwaukee, Mich Clarissa died August 1858

Frederick was in the army and unmarried in 1864

James S. was residing in Milwaukee, and *Charles F.* at Toledo, in 1864, unm

Mary was residing in Milwaukee, unm , in 1864

[3410.] OTIS[6] PECK, of Pittsfield, Mass., son of ISRAEL,[5] married Martha C. Dickinson, daughter of Oliver P. Dickinson, of Pittsfield, October 30, 1824, where they were residing in 1864.

CHILDREN — SEVENTH GENERATION

3437. Maria E , b July 30, 1825
3438 Oliver D , b. July 15, 1827.
Died Feb. 17, 1831

3439 Frederick C , b Aug 30, 1829
3440 Martha A , b May 13, 1834.

Maria E was residing at home in 1864, unm.

Frederick C married Catharine M Goodrich, November 6, 1862, daughter of Milton Goodrich, of Pittsfield, where they were residing in 1864.

Martha A. was residing at home in 1864, unm.

[3415.] JOSEPH KELLY[6] PECK, son of JOSEPH KELLY.[5] He was a carpenter by trade. He died at the residence of his daughter, Mrs. Hannah Austin, of Perrysburgh, Pa., with whom he resided several years.

---

* I endeavored to obtain from Mr. Peck a better record of his family, but was unable to do so.

He married Isabella Hide, September 26, 1799. She died May 8, 1844, aged 69 years. He died September 18, 1859.

CHILDREN — SEVENTH GENERATION

3441. Mary, b Aug. 9, 1800
3442 +Samuel, b. Oct 18, 1801.
3443 +Joseph, b March 23, 1803.
3444. Hannah, b Feb 9, 1806
3445 +David B , b April 17, 1807.
3446 Emily, b Jan 31, 1809

3447 Parter, b 1810   Died, unm ,
    Oct 19, 1825
3448. Lurana, b June 11, 1813
3449 Eunice, b June 24, 1815.
3450 +Joel, b Aug 29, 1818

Mary married C—— Eldridge, was residing in Persia, N Y , in 1864

Emily married Charles Allen, and was residing in Persia, N Y , in 1864.

Lurana married a Johnston, and was residing in Raisonville, Monroe County, Mich , a widow, in 1864

Eunice was cast away on Lake Erie, and never found

Hannah married Hiram Austin, and was residing at Perrysburg, N Y , in 1864.

[3416] DR. GUSTAVUS D.[6] PECK, of Northampton, Mass , son of WINCHESTER,[5] graduated in his profession at the age of 21 years. He studied with Dr. Daniel Thurber, of Mendon, Mass. He first settled at Blackstone, Mass. From Blackstone he removed to Milford, Mass., where he remained in the practice of his profession until 1836, holding various public offices, acting also as councillor of the Massachusetts Medical Society. From Milford he removed to Sunderland, Mass., where he remained for ten years in practice. From there, in 1846, he removed to Northampton, Mass., where I found him still engaged in his profession in 1864. Although in his 77th year, he retained all his faculties to a remarkable degree for a man who had devoted fifty-six years to the practice of medicine. He has been, I am told, a very faithful, kind, and successful practitioner, much respected. He married Sally Perry, daughter of Elisha Perry, of Milford.

CHILDREN — SEVENTH GENERATION

3451 +Addison Sumner, b. July 19,
    1810, at Blackstone, Mass.
3452. Andrew Jackson, b April 9,
    1815, at Milford, Mass.

3453 +Albion Perry, b July 7, 1817,
    at Milford, Mass
3454. Sarah Annis, b Aug 29, 1819,
    at Milford, Mass.

Sarah Annis married Richard Chenery, August 1839, now (1864) United States Navy Agent at San Francisco, where she died, November 23, 1864 Her children are *Charles Eugene*,[8] b at Spring Prairie, Wis , June 16, 1841, and was, in 1864, Assistant Paymaster on board of the U S Steamer Narragansett, *James Perry*,[8] b. at Sunderland, Mass., May 9, 1843, and died at Northampton, March 22, 1864, of chronic diarrhœa, contracted in the Army of the Potomac He was a member of the 1st Company of Andrew's Massachusetts Sharpshooters *Leonard Edward,*[8] b. at Northampton March 11, 1846 He was a member of the graduating class of 1864 at the U S Naval Academy, at Newport, R I.

Andrew Jackson was drowned by the upsetting of a boat, in the harbor of St Augustine, Florida, April 19, 1836. He was a druggist by occupation, and was located there.

[3422.]   HORACE[6] PECK, son of WINCHESTER,[5] settled at West Brookfield, Mass., where he was residing in 1864. He has been twice married: first, to Sarah R. Fuller, of Hinsdale, N. H., June 29, 1816; second, to Climenia Wheeler, of Ashfield, Mass., March 5, 1834.

CHILDREN — SEVENTH GENERATION

3455.	Julia Ann	Died young.	3461.	Sarah R
3456	William.		3462	Chauncey.
3457.	Rachel	Died young.	3463.	Philo
3458	Mary Ann	Died young.	3464	Julia Ann, unm. in 1864
3459.	Joseph		3465	Lydia W., unm. in 1864
			3466.	Horace.

By second wife ·

3460   Albert.

William was a soldier in the army in 1864.
Joseph was a soldier in the army in 1864.
Albert was a soldier in the army in 1864
Sarah R married Joseph R. Knight, of Warren.
Chauncey was killed at the battle of Winchester.
Philo was killed at the battle of Gettysburg.
Horace was drowned February 3, 1857.

[3424.]   GEORGE HENRY[7] PECK, son of HENRY,[6] married Maria Cornelia Roberts, of Rochester, N. Y., September 19, 1848, and settled in Cleveland, Ohio, where they were residing in 1864.

CHILDREN — EIGHTH GENERATION ·

3467. Catharine Roberts, b. Sept. 10, 1849.   3468. George Henry, b. Sept. 30, 1858.

[3425.]   OTIS LYMAN[7] PECK, son of HENRY,[6] married Martha Clark, of Sandusky City, Ohio, November 12, 1849, where they were residing in 1864.

CHILDREN — EIGHTH GENERATION

3469. Harriet, b. Oct. 17, 1850
3470 Fanny, b Nov. 6, 1854. }
3471. Lizzie, b Nov. 6, 1854 }
    Twins.

3472. George Otis, b July 1858

[3442.] SAMUEL⁷ PECK, of Farmington, Pa., son of JOSEPH KELLY,⁶ married Clarissa Knapp, March 2, 1828.

CHILDREN — EIGHTH GENERATION

3473 George W , b Dec 18, 1829.
3474. Emily L., b, July 9, 1835.
3475 David B , b. March 1, 1839
3476 Comfort E , b Oct 10, 1846

[3443.] JOSEPH⁷ PECK, son of JOSEPH KELLY,⁶ settled in Spartansburg, Pa. He married Martha Hawkins, daughter of Duty Hawkins.

CHILDREN — EIGHTH GENERATION

3477. One, b March 4, 1826 Died in 1828
3478 Louisa, b March 24, 1828
3479. A son, b 1830 Died same year.
3480 A son, b 1831 Died in 1832.
3481 Mary Jane, b March 24, 1833.
3482. Emily H , b Sept 22, 1835
3483 Eunice L , b April 4, 1837
3484. Calista L , b Aug 21, 1839
3485 Mary Ann L , b July 21, 1842
3486 Joseph E , b July 27, 1848

Louisa married Green Alsdurf, in 1848, and settled in Sparta
Mary Jane married Frederick A Wise, in 1849, and settled in Bloomfield
Emily H married Henry Scouten, in 1852, and settled in Sparta
Calista L married Oscar N Dexter, in 1855, and settled at Spring Creek
Mary Ann L was residing in Canada, unm , in 1864
Joseph E was residing in Sparta, unm , in 1864

[3445.] DAVID⁷ PECK, son of JOSEPH KELLY,⁶ settled at Freedom, La Salle County, Ill. He married Luvilla Hawkins, daughter of Duty Hawkins.

CHILDREN — EIGHTH GENERATION

3487. Lucretia A , b 1829
3488 Porter, b 1832 Deceased.
3489. Joseph K , b 1834
3490 Joel, b 1836 Deceased.
3491. Jesse H , b. 1838 Deceased
3492 Martha, b 1841. Deceased
3493 Edward N , b 1844
3494. Mary Jane, b 1848
3495 Genilla, b. 1850
3496 David P., b 1855 Deceased.

Lucretia married David Jones They were residing in Meriden, La Salle County, Ill , in 1864. Their children were *Margaret E ,⁹ John D.,⁹ Indie L ,⁹ Delazon G ⁹* and *Ida M.⁹*

22*

[3450.] JOEL[7] PECK, son of JOSEPH KELLY,[6] settled in Gowanda, N. Y., where he was residing in 1864. He married Philena McIntyre, daughter of Royal T. McIntyre, December 17, 1838.

CHILDREN — EIGHTH GENERATION

3497. Alderson, b. Sept. 7, 1839.	3501. Melissa, b Nov 1, 1852
3498. Andrew, b. June 9, 1842	3502. Orson, b, Oct 14, 1856. }
3499 Lucretia, b Sept. 17, 1846.	3503. Aurilla, b. Oct. 14, 1856. }
3500. Isabel, b. Oct. 3, 1849.	Twins.

[3451.] ADDISON S.[7] PECK, son of DR. GUSTAVUS D.,[6] graduated at the Boston Medical School, in 1831. He read medicine with his father, and with Dr. Jabez Fisher, of Boston. He commenced the practice of medicine with his father, in Milford, Mass. In 1837, he removed to Hatfield, and from there to Holyoke, Mass. In 1862, he removed to Aurora, Esmeralda County, Nevada Territory, where he was appointed Judge of Probate. He died April 6, 1866.

He married Jane S. Whipple, daughter of Benjamin Whipple, of Dunbarton, N. H., November 1835. She died at Dunbarton, January 23, 1864.

CHILDREN — EIGHTH GENERATION

3504. Sarah Elizabeth, b. at Hatfield, Mass , in 1837.	3505. Benjamin Whipple, b. at Hatfield, Mass , in 1842.

Sarah Elizabeth married Lieut -Col William S. B Hopkins, of Northampton, Mass. They were residing in New Orleans in 1864

Benjamin Whipple was residing, in 1864, at Aurora, Nevada Territory, unm

[3453.] ALBION PERRY[7] PECK, son of DR. GUSTAVUS D.,[6] was residing at Northampton, Mass., in 1864. The early life of Mr. Peck, I learn, was passed as a teacher, previous to his settling at Northampton. He was elected teacher of the English School, at Worcester, Mass., June 22, 1828. He was also, I am told, principal of the school at Sunderland for some time.

The following extracts in relation to him were taken from the Northampton Business Directory :

Mr. Peck was appointed a Justice of the Peace in 1844. In 1855, he was appointed Register of Probate by Gov. Gardner. In 1856, he was chosen by the people to the same office, which he held until, by the act of the Legislature, the office was abolished, and its duties transferred to the Register of the new Court of Probate and Insolvency. In 1855, he was chosen a member of the General School Committee of Northampton.

In 1856, he was appointed Justice of the Quorum and Notary Public, and in 1860, a Trial Justice. In 1859, he was chosen Town Clerk. He has also been Treasurer of the Horticultural Club, and of the Hampshire, Franklin and Hampden Agricultural Society.

In addition to attending to his official duties, Mr. Peck has been engaged in other business.

In 1850, he was engaged in the grocery and druggist business. In 1853, he purchased the Lower Mills, so called, and carried on the flour and grain business until 1860, when he sold his interest.

I am told that he still holds the offices to which he has been elected to the very general satisfaction of the community, by whom he is not only honored but highly respected.

He married Sarah Ann Hibbon, daughter of James Hibbon, of Charleston, S. C., at Northampton, June 14, 1855.

CHILDREN — EIGHTH GENERATION

3506. Julia Emma, b. at Northampton, Dec. 23, 1857.

3507. Sarah Perry, b. at Northampton, Jan 30, 1860.

APPENDIX.

APPENDIX.

It was not at first designed to publish an account of any of the Pecks, aside from the descendants of Joseph Peck, the progenitor of the Massachusetts Pecks; but they were so mixed in their settlements throughout the country with other branches of the same patronymic descendants of other ancestors that it was unavoidable, and necessary to correspond with, and to collect much information in relation to others, before it could be determined to which branch of the name they belonged. As these correspondents and others seemed to expect that the information they had given was to be published, and desired to have it preserved, it was thought best to add an appendix, and publish it.

It was soon found that to render this intelligible, and of interest, it was necessary not only to add much more to it, but to follow out the different branches, trace them back to their ancestors, and separate their descendants from each other. This I have endeavored to do.

Although the descendants of neither of these ancestors have proved to be so numerous as those of Joseph, of Massachusetts, and his six sons, each of whom had families at an early date, yet their descendants have been found to be more numerous than was at first supposed. I have been fortunate in finding, though with much labor, all or nearly all of them. There are a few branches or families that I have been unable to carry through all the generations, owing to the imperfect manner in which early records were kept, and the want of interest felt in the subject, many refusing to assist me or to give me the information asked of them, or even to answer my letters or return my circulars. For these reasons there may be errors, — there doubtless will be, perhaps in assigning families or individuals to the wrong branch or ancestor, — if so, the arrangement of the work will enable those interested to find their proper places. There will doubtless be errors in names, dates and localities. For the correctness of these I have relied upon my correspondents and others who gave me the information, and have given it as it was given to me, where I had no means of knowing but that it was correct. There were a few records received which were not used for the want of others to complete the generations where they belonged, and render them intelligible.

The appendix has been the source of much loss as well as disappointment to me. It not only delayed the work much longer than was expected, but the subscriptions from the branches it contains amounted to but a small portion of its expense. The cost of its publication, and the collection of its material, was much more expensive, and required much more labor than was expected. To find and determine at this late day who were the children of Deacon Paul, Deacon William, Henry and Joseph, ancestors of the Connecticut Pecks, trace out their descendants to the present generations, and separate them from each other, required not only much of my time for two years, with a large correspondence, but also much travel, which was expensive.

I was obliged to make journeys into various towns, in different parts of the State, to examine town, church, probate and family records, and in but a few of them could I obtain any subscribers, and in no one of them enough to pay but a fraction of my expenses.

During my visits to Hartford, Wallingford, Stratford, Milford, Bridgeport and Norwalk, I obtained one subscriber towards paying my expenses, which with the town clerks' fees for copies, were over forty dollars. I was obliged to make other journeys, which were expensive. In Norwich, I obtained one subscriber; in Danbury, two; and in Newtown, where many of the early Pecks settled, and many of their descendants remain, four; and in the city of New Haven, to which place I made several journeys, and was obliged to spend much time in examining the town, church, probate records, and deeds, which was expensive, and where many of the descendants of Deacon Paul, Henry and Joseph reside, I obtained five. Where I sent my circulars, I obtained a few names; some not only gave me their own, but with much kindness obtained other names for me; while many refused even to return my circulars, although *each* contained, with the *return* postage, a *request* that they should do so.

Had I anticipated the want of interest in the subject, the coldness and indifference with which I have had to contend, among the Connecticut Pecks, I certainly never should have attempted to trace them out. Although some have lent me their aid, and treated me with a generosity and kindness which I shall long remember, some have treated me with a lack of generosity, if not a littleness and an unkindness which I shall try to forget.

Among the descendants of John, of Mendon, and among many of the descendants of the Connecticut Pecks, scattered through other States, I found more interest in the subject, and from them have received the most of my subscribers for the appendix.

Although I have had little to encourage me, I have done the best I could, and hope I shall have been the means of bringing much to the light in relation to the Connecticut Pecks, which would otherwise have been lost; and that the information I have collected will be of interest to many of them, and not only enable those of the different branches of the name to distinguish themselves from each other, but stimulate a desire to know more of their ancestry.

23

THE HINGHAM AND OTHER PECKS.

There were several bearing the surname of Peck who early emigrated from Old to New England and became progenitors, and died, leaving descendants. Some of these remained in Boston, while others settled in its vicinity, or removed to Connecticut. Mr. Savage says a (1) *Richard* Peck came over in the Defence, of London, in 1635, with (2) *Margery*, supposed to be his wife, and (3) *Israel* and (4) *Elizabeth*, his children, and is thought, by some, to have been the brother of (5) *Paul*, afterward Deacon Paul Peck, of Hartford, Conn.; but I have found no trace of him or his son.* Mr. Savage (see his excellent work, the Genealogical Dictionary) supposes his son Israel to have been the Israel of Rehoboth, Mass., who had Israel, b. Dec. 18, 1674 (should be 73), and Bethiah, Jan. 2, 1680; but in this supposition he is mistaken. This Israel was the youngest of the three sons of Joseph, ancestor of the Massachusetts Pecks, born, after his arrival in this country, at Hingham, Mass. Rev. Peter Hobart says, in his journal, that he was baptized March 4, 1644. For his family, see No. 3374. There was also a (6) *Nathaniel* Peck in Hingham, who, Daniel Cushing, the town clerk, says, arrived in 1635. Mr. Savage supposes him to have settled at Rehoboth, and to have been the Nathaniel who had a son Elisha by his wife Deliverance, born Aug. 25, 1676. But this Nathaniel was, also, the son of Joseph, the next older than Israel. His family is at No. 2588. Who the Nathaniel of 1635 was, or what became of him, is not known. He is supposed by some to have been the son of Robert, and to have returned to England. If so, he was about twenty-one years of age, being born, as may be seen by a reference to his father's family upon the chart, Sep. 13, 1614.

There was also a (7) *Simon* Peck in Hingham, in 1657, who, Mr Savage says, married Hannah Farnsworth. She d. April 16, 1659. He afterwards married Prudence Clap, of Dorchester, Feb. 13, 1660, daughter of Edward Clap. By Mr. Hobart's Journal, it appears that his children were, a *daughter*, b. Dec. 25, 1660; (8) *Joseph*, b. ——, d. Jan. 12, 1662, (9) *Joseph*, baptized Feb. 25,

---

* It will be seen that Mr Drake, in his list of the names of the founders of New England (Genealogical Register, Vol 14, p. 320), spells this name Perk instead of Peck, and the child's name Isabell, not Israel.

1663; (10) *John*, b. April 20, 1667; (11) *Joseph*, baptized Nov. 1, 1668; (12) *Sarah*, b. June 3, 1669; (13) *Joseph*, b. July 2, 1671, baptized the 9th, and died the 11th of same month. What became of Simon, or when he died, I did not learn. By an examination of the Hingham records, it will be seen that he sold his homestead in May, 1669. He drew four lots in the division of lands in Cohasset in 1670, but sold them in 1677. He was one of the selectmen.

THE BOSTON PECKS.

In relation to the Boston Pecks may be found, upon record there, many deeds, also wills, births, marriages and deaths. As I had occasion to examine and make memorandums of some of these while searching for lost ones of other branches, I give a few of such as were preserved, in hopes it may draw the attention of some one to the subject, who may trace out and publish a history of these Boston Pecks. Had I designed them at first for this use, I should have made the list more full and perfect.

Upon the Probate Records, B. 11, p. 259, may be found the appointment of Elizabeth Peck, widow, administratrix upon the estate of (14) *John* Peck, of Boston, mariner, deceased, dated Feb. 25, 1696–7.

On B. 14, p. 128, is the will of (15) *Thomas* Peck, sen., who was a shipwright, dated March 3, 1698. He seems to have been a man of wealth. He bought and sold much land in Boston and other places, and also vessels. In his will he bequeaths houses, lands, warehouses, wharves, docks, etc. He names his wife Elizabeth, sons (16) *John*, deceased, (17) *Benjamin*, (18) *Thomas*, jr., shopkeeper, and (19) *Nathaniel*; and daughters (20) *Faith* Waldo, (21) *Elizabeth* Fisher, and (22) *Rachel* Potter. John, deceased, and wife Elizabeth, had two daughters, if no more, (23) *Elizabeth* Gooch, and (24) *Mary*, and a son (25) *William*. Benjamin had two sons, (26) *Benjamin* and (27) *William*. Thomas J. and Nathaniel also had children not named in the will.

An administrator was appointed upon the estate of Martha Peck, widow, Jan. 1, 1750, B. 44, p. 27.

A guardian was appointed for (28) *Mary*, a minor daughter of (29) *Samuel* Peck, late of Boston, blacksmith, Oct. 1756, B. 51, p. 348.

An inventory of the estate of Samuel Peck was presented by (30) *Thomas Handasyde* Peck, Oct. 29, 1756, B. 51, p. 349. Martha Peck was appointed administratrix upon the estate of her husband, (31) *James* Peck, of Boston, mariner, Feb. 11, 1757, B. 52, p. 52. (32) *Samuel* Peck was appointed administrator upon the estate of his brother, (33) *William* Peck, of Boston, glazier, Jan. 4, 1760, B. 56, p. 207. He had a son (34) *John*, and (35) *William*, and an only daughter (36) *Mary*.

Mary Peck, widow, was appointed guardian of her son (37) *Benjamin*, under fourteen years of age, son of (38) *Nathaniel*, late of Boston, cordwainer, Feb. 13, 1761, B. 58, p. 70.

Thomas Handasyde Peck was appointed administrator upon the estate of his brother (39) *John*, late of Boston, glazier, Sept. 11, 1761, B. 59, p. 130. John had a son (40) *Robert Maynard* Peck. Thomas Handasyde's account as guardian of (41) *Mary* Peck was presented to the court July 6, 1763, B. 62, p. 106.

Thomas Handasyde Peck was appointed administrator upon the estate of his son (42) *John* Peck, March 18, 1768, B. 66, p. 188.

The will of (45) *Samuel* Peck,* cooper, of Boston, is upon B. 77, p. 57, dated May 8, 1777. He had children, (46) *Mary* and (47) *Sarah*, sisters, (48) *Mary*, and (49) *Hannah*, and brothers, (50) *Nathaniel*, and (51) *Benjamin*, and mother, Mary Peck, widow. His wife Sarah was executrix.

Sarah Peck, widow, was appointed administratrix upon the estate of Robert Maynard Peck, feltmaker, Jan. 28, 1782, B. 80, p. 438.

A guardian was appointed for (52) *Samuel*, son of (53) *Joseph*, late of Londonderry, N. H., Dec. 16, 1800, B. 89, p. 452.

The will of Moses Peck † is upon B. 99, p. 158, dated Oct. 12, 1799. Names his daughter *Sarah*, wife of Jonathan Stickney, and *Elizabeth*, wife of William Thurston, and son *Elijah*, who had a

* Mr Nathaniel Peck, of Lynn, Mass., is supposed to be a descendant from this branch of the name.

† Moses is a descendant of Henry, of New Haven, and is No. 60 with them.

son *Samuel,* who died, leaving a widow and sons, who were resid-ing in Roxbury, Mass., in 1863.

(54) *John* Peck was appointed guardian of (55) *William,* son of Robert Maynard Peck, July 17, 1792, B. 91, p. 230.

WILL OF THOMAS HANDASYDE PECK.

In the name of God, Amen; this thirty fiıst day of August, in the year of our, Lord One thousand seven hundred & seventy four, I, Thomas Handasyde Peck of Boston, in the county of Suffolk & Prov-ince of the Massachusetts Bay ın New England, Hatt Maker, being of sound Mind & Memory, Thanks be to God for it; & not knowing how short my Time in this World may be; Do make & ordaın, this my last Will & Testament, ın manner following.

First,— I do commit my soul ınto the Hands of God who gave it, & my body to the Earth, to be burried in a decent manner, by my Executors hereafter named, in Hope of a joyful Resserection by the Power, & thro' the Merits of my Lord & savior Jesus Christ. And, as to the worldly Goods God has been pleased to bestow on me, I do dispose ın the following manner.

First,— I do order, that all my just Debts & funeral Expenses be paid, after my Decease, as soon as may be.

Item.— I give unto my beloved Wife, Elizabeth Peck, Eighty Pounds lawful Money, to be paid her annually during her natural life by my Executor.

Item.— I give my said Wife, my Negro man, Solomon, durıng her natural life.

Item,— I give my said Wife my Horse & both my Chaise.

Item.— I gıve my said Wife, her living in my House where in I now live, with the Improvement of all the Land and Buildings belongıng there to, during her natuıal Life; the aforesaid House & Buildings to be kept ın Repair, out of my Estate.

Item.— I gıve my said wife, the improvement of all my Houshould Goods during her natural Lıfe.

Item.— I give to my Grandson Thomas Handasyde, son of my late son Doctor John Peck, & the Heirs of hıs Body, lawfully begotten, ıf he lives to the age of Twenty one years, all my Brıck Buildings ın Merchants Row; whıch I bought of Gillman Phillips Esq, with the land, & all the appurtenances there to belongıng; said Buildings to be kept ın good repair out of the Rent of saıd buildings, and my Executors to receive the rents of said buildings untill my Grand son

23*

arrives to the age of Twenty one years. But, if my said Grand son should die before he arrives to the age of Twenty One years, or he should leave no Heirs, lawfully begotten of his body ; then my will is, that my aforesaid Buildings go to the children of my daughter Elizabeth Perkins.

Item. — I give to my Grand son Tho⁵ Handasye Peck, thirty Pounds lawful money pr annum ; to be paid by his Guardian for his maintenance untill he arrives to the age of Twenty one years, and then, the said legacy to cease.

Item.— My Will is, that if my grand son, Thomas Handasyde Peck lives untill the age of Twenty one years, that my Executors pay him Two hundred and fifty Pounds lawfull money, out of my personal Estates ; also, if my said Grand son, (43) Thomas Handasyde Peck, should live to the age of Twenty four years, that then my Executors pay my aforesaid Grand son, Two hundred Pounds Lawful money, besides the aforegoing two hundred & fifty Pounds out of my personal Estate.

Item.— I give my four grand sons, viz, James Perkins, Tho⁵ Handasyde Perkins, Samuel Perkins and, Tho⁵ Handasyde Peck, all that Track or parcel of land which I bought of Mr Samuel Green of Boston Marriner, being one quarter Part of a full share of the Land called Muscongus, being on Ponobscut River, being two thousand two Hundred & fifty acres.

Item.— My Will is, that my Executor pay to my Honored Mother, Mrs Margaret Mitchel, Twenty six Pounds thirteen shillings & four Pence lawful Money, annually, during her natural life ; & if that is not enough to maintain her, then my Will is, that my Executor supply her out of my Estate, what may be sufficient for her, and at her death, to bury her handsomely out of my Estate. The above Twenty six Pounds thirteen shillings & foure pence is what I am obliged by Bond, to pay my said Mother.

Item.— I give to my Nephew Robert Maynard Peck, sixty six Pounds thirteen shillings & four pence, lawful Money, to be paid in one Month after my Decease ; & if he owes me any Debts on Book Note or otherwise, I release them.

Item.— I give unto Samuel Baley sixty six Pounds, thirteen shillings & four Pence, Lawful money, to be paid him in one Month after my Decease ; & if he owes me any Debts on Book, Note, or otherwise, I release them.

Item.— My Will is that Twenty six hundred & sixty six Pounds, thirteen shillings & four pence, Lawful Money, of my Personal Estate, be put to Interest by my Executors, on good land security, within this Province ; & the Interest of said money, with the rents of my Real Estate, to be appropriated towards paying my Mother, my wife, & my Grand son, annually, as above.

Item — My Will is, that my Executors pay out of the foregoing Money sixty pounds, thirteen shillings & four pence, Lawful Money, to each of my daughter Perkin's Children, when they arrive to the age of Twenty one years ; & when the above Legacies are paid, then I give all the Remainder of my personal Estate unto my Daughter (44) Elizabeth Perkins, & her Heirs.

Item. — I give to my Daughter Elizabeth Perkins, & the Heirs of her body, all the Remainder of my Real Estate, wherever it may be found, not before given away :

Item.— I do constitute my beloved Wife, Elizabeth Peck & my Daughter Elizabeth Perkins, to be my Executors, of this, my last Will ; here by revoking &, making void all Wills here to fore made by me.

In witness where of, I the said Thomas Handasyde Peck, the Testator, have here unto set my hand & seal this thirty first Day of August One thousand seven Hundred & seventy four.

Signed, sealed & published by the Testator, in Presence of us to be his last Will & Testament.

THOMAS HANDASYDE PECK

JOHN SYMMS
JON[A] W. EDES
BENJ[A] EDES

The will is recorded upon Book 76, page 101. He seems to have been a man of wealth. He was a merchant, and is said to have dealt largely in furs, and the importation of hats.

I regret that I have been able to learn so little in relation to him, his ancestors and descendants bearing the name. I found no one who could give me any information in relation to them ; or, who would take any interest in the subject.

His brother John died about 1761, leaving a son, Robert Maynard Peck, who died about 1782, leaving a son William.

The children of Mr. Peck were : Elizabeth, b. Feb. 14, 1735, and John, b. Aug. 24, 1743. The son, Doctor John Peck, died about 1768, leaving a son, Thomas Handasyde Peck. The daughter married James Perkins, a merchant of Boston, who died in middle age, leaving her a widow with eight children, three sons and five daugh-

ters. She was a woman of superior ability, energy and perseverance, and reared her family, giving them an education, and her sons
such advantages as fitted them for active business lives, which they
lived, occupying positions of honor and responsibility with credit
to themselves and to her.

She seems to have been a woman of excellent principles, generous, benevolent and charitable, and to have found time and means,
aside from the wants and cares of her family, to take an active
part with the charitable and benevolent associations of the time.

On her decease, which occurred in 1807, it was voted that the
officers of the Boston Female Asylum wear a badge of mourning
for the term of seventy-one days, corresponding to the number of
years she had lived.

Her descendants are numerous, many of them distinguished for
their wealth, intelligence and refinement. Her second son, Thomas
Handasyde Perkins, born Dec. 15, 1764, and named for his
grandfather Peck, to whom his mother was in part, at least,
indebted for her means of rearing her family, — became one of
the most eminent, successful and wealthy merchants of Boston.

A memoir of him was published by Thomas G. Cary, Esq., his
son-in-law, from which and other sources I have taken the liberty
to make a few extracts and draw for such facts in relation to him
as it was thought would be of interest to those of my readers who
might never see the excellent work of Mr. Cary.

His mother decided to give him a collegiate education; but, when
prepared for Cambridge, he was reluctant to enter upon the life of
a student, and was placed with the Messrs. Shattuck, then among
the most active merchants of Boston, where he remained until twenty-
one years of age. He then joined his elder brother James in form-
ing a house in St. Domingo. Finding that the climate there did
not agree with his health, he returned to Boston, his younger
brother, Samuel G., filling his place in the firm.

He soon after turned his attention to trade with China. During the revolution of 1792 in St. Domingo, his brothers returned
to Boston. He then formed a co-partnership with his elder brother
James, under the firm of J. & T. H. Perkins. This firm continued
until the death of the latter, in 1822. Their most important business
was the trade of their ships on the northwest coast and with China.

Your Obed Sev—
TWPickins

They finally established a house in Canton, under the firm of Perkins & Co., which became one of great importance, and was eminently successful.

Mr. Perkins found time, in addition to that required in his commercial pursuits, to devote to business of a public nature. About
1794, he was made commander of the military corps, which consti-
tuted the guard and escort on public occasions for the Governor,
with the rank of Lieutenant-Colonel, and was afterwards known as
Colonel Perkins. He was soon afterwards chosen President of the
Boston branch of the United States Bank. In 1805, he was elected
to the Senate of the State, and for many years afterwards was a
member of one branch or other of the State Legislature.

As the wealth of Col. Perkins accumulated, he expended a portion of it for charitable, public and benevolent purposes. He took
an active and very important part in measures for establishing the
Massachusetts General Hospital, with an asylum for the insane.
He and his elder brother James contributed five thousand dollars
each towards the fund. He also did much for the Boston Athe-
næum. He was one of the founders of the Bunker Hill Monument Association, and the originator of the statue of General
Warren, towards which he subscribed one thousand dollars. He
also took a deep interest in the completion of the national monument to the memory of Washington, and one of almost the last
acts of his life was an effort to raise funds in Massachusetts
towards insuring its completion. This noble act of his was pub-
licly alluded to by the Hon. Robert C. Winthrop, in a speech
before the Massachusetts Charitable Mechanic Association, at one
of their annual festivals. In alluding to this act of Col. Perkins,
he says:

I cannot forget the earnest and affectionate interest with which that
noble hearted old American gentleman devoted the last days, and I
had almost said the last hours, of his life to arranging the details and
the machinery for an appeal to the people of Massachusetts in behalf
of that still unfinished structure. He had seen Washington in his
boyhood, and had felt the inspiration of his majestic presence ; he had
known him in his manhood, and had spent two or three days with him,
by particular invitation, at Mount Vernon,—days never to be forgotten in any man's life ; his whole heart seemed to be imbued with the

warmest admiration and affection for his character and services; and it seemed as if he could not go down to his grave in peace until he had done something to aid in perpetuating the memory of his virtues and valor.

But perhaps no better description of the character of Col. Perkins can be given, or a more just tribute now paid to his memory, than is contained in a note by the Hon. Daniel Webster, written with his own hand on the blank leaf of a copy of his works, which he presented to him.

WASHINGTON, April 19, 1852.

MY DEAR SIR:—If I possessed anything which I might suppose likely to be more acceptable to you as a proof of my esteem than these, I should have sent it in their stead.

But I do not, and therefore ask your acceptance of a copy of this edition of my speeches.

I have long cherished, my dear sir, a profound, warm, affectionate, and, I may say, a filial regard for your person and character. I have looked upon you as one born to do good, and who has fulfilled his mission; as a man without spot or blemish; as a merchant, known and honored over the whole world; a most liberal supporter and promoter of science and the arts; always kind to scholars and literary men, and greatly beloved by them all; friendly to all the institutions of religion, morality and education; and an unwavering and determined supporter of the constitution of the country, and of those great principles of civil liberty which it is so well calculated to uphold and advance.

These sentiments I inscribe here in accordance with my best judgment and out of the fulness of my heart; and I wish here to record, also, my deep sense of the many personal obligations under which you have placed me in the course of our long acquaintance.

Your faithful friend,

DANIEL WEBSTER.

To the Hon. Thos. H. Perkins.

He died January 11, 1854, in the ninetieth year of his age.

The fine engraving which I give is from a portrait by Gambardella, an Italian artist, and, I am told, was a most excellent likeness of him at the age of 73 years. The expression, it will be seen, is indicative of the kind and noble heart he possessed.

Upon the early records of deeds in Boston are many conveyances to and from the Pecks, among which are the following: From Thomas Peck senior Shipwright and Elizabeth his wife of 20 Acres of land lying and being at muddy brook in the town ship of Boston (B. 12, p. 30) Jan 20–1680 consideration 30 pounds   Deed to Thomas Peck jr Shipwright of pasture land in Boston (B. 13 p. 239) in 1684.   Also, a deed from Thomas Peck of a vessel of 45.tons burden, then riding at anchor in the harbor of Boston dated Aug 24 –1760 B. 7 p. 33.

Upon the records in the office of the City Register may be found the following marriages, births and names of parents:

(56) *Elizabeth*, daughter of Thomas and Elizabeth, was born Jan. 19, 1652; (57) *Rachel*, daughter of Thomas and Elizabeth, b. Jan. 1, 1654; (58) *Joseph*, son of Thomas and Elizabeth, b. Dec. 11, 1656; (59) *Faith*, daughter of Thomas and Elizabeth, b. Dec. 8, 1658; (60) *Ebenezer* and (61) *Thankful*, children of Thomas and Elizabeth, b. July, 1665; (62) *Elizabeth*, daughter of Thomas, b. Feb. 6, 1672; (63) *Elizabeth*, daughter of Thomas, b. June 29, 1674; (64) *Elizabeth*, daughter of John and Elizabeth, b. Feb. 26, 1674; (65) *Thomas*, son of Thomas and Elizabeth, b. Sept. 12, 1678; (66) *Elizabeth*, daughter of Joseph and Sarah, b. Feb. 29, 1679; (67) *Mary*, daughter of (68) John and Elizabeth, b. July 5, 1680, (69) *John*, son of John and Elizabeth, b. Oct. 6, 1685; (70) *Joseph*, son of Joseph and Sarah, b. June 8, 1686; (71) *Benjamin*, son of (72) Benjamin and Mary, b. July 22, 1687; (73) *Samuel*, son of John and Elizabeth, b. Dec. 27, 1687; (74) *Tabitha*, daughter of (75) Nathan and Tabitha, b. March 14, 1687; (76) *Samuel*, son of Benjamin and Mary, b. Jan. 19, 1680; (77) *Jane*, daughter of Nathan and Tabitha, b. May 11, 1689; (78) *Rachel*, daughter of (79) Thomas and Hannah, b. Nov. 28, 1694; (80) *William*, son of John and Elizabeth, b. July 27, 1695; (81) *Ebenezer*, son of (82) Thomas and Joanna, b. May 8, 1696; (83) *Elizabeth*, daughter of (84) Ebenezer and Elizabeth, b. June 4, 1696; (85) *Joanna*, daughter of Thomas and Joanna, b. Oct. 20, 1698; (86) *Joseph*, son of Thomas and Joanna, b. Aug. 27, 1701; (87) *Elizabeth*, daughter of (88) Thomas and Elizabeth, b. Oct. 24, 1703; (89) *Joseph*, son of (90) Joseph and Mary, b. Sept. 16, 1711; (91) *William*, son of (92) James and Margaret, b. Aug. 29, 1712; (93) *Mary*, daughter of

(94) Samuel and Mary, b. Nov. 21, 1712; (95) *Thomas,* son of (96) Samuel and Elizabeth, b. Oct. 17, 1715; (97) *Samuel,* son of Samuel and Elizabeth, b. Sept. 9, 1717; (98) *Thomas* and (99) *Philip,* sons of (100) John and Sarah, b. Nov. 9, 1718; (101) *Mary,* daughter of Samuel and Elizabeth, b. Aug. 22, 1719; (102) *Thomas,* son of (103) Thomas and Sarah, b. March 6, 1720; (104) *John,* son of (105) John and Mary, b. July 23, 1721; (106) *John,* son of William and Mary, b. June 12, 1725; (107) *Samuel,* son of William and Mary, b. Oct. 25, 1727; (108) *Elizabeth,* daughter of Thomas Handasyde Peck and Elizabeth, b. Feb. 14, 1735; (109) *Abigail,* daughter of Moses and Elizabeth, b. Oct. 1744; (110) *Robert Maynard,* son of John and Hester, b. Oct. 1, 1747; (111) *Sarah,* daughter of Moses and Elizabeth, b. Nov. 24, 1752; (112) *Samuel,* son of Moses and Elizabeth, b. Oct. 30, 1758; (113) *Elizabeth,* daughter of Moses and Elizabeth, b. June 24, 1771; (114) *John,* son of Thomas Handasyde and ———, b. Aug. 24, 1743; (115) *Moses,* son of Moses and Elizabeth, b. July 4, 1766; (116) *Samuel,* son of Moses and Elizabeth, b. Sept. 21, 1768.

(117) *Mary* Peck and John Wells were married, Nov. 18, 1697; (118) *Thomas* and Elizabeth Sergeant, March 6, 1706; (119) *Benjamin* and Martha Clough, Nov. 2, 1710, (120) *James* and Hannah Baker, Jan. 25, 1710, (121) *Samuel* and Mildreth Willis, Jan. 20, 1711; (122) *Samuel* and Mary Penneman, Feb. 8, 1711; (123) *Mary* and William Lander, June 31, 1716, (124) *John* and Elizabeth Kelly, June 16, 1709; (125) *William* and Mary Gould, March 9, 1720, (126) *Samuel* and Elizabeth Parker, Sept. 22, 1714; (127) *John* and Sarah White, Nov. 11, 1714; (128) *Mary* and William Lamb, Jan. 31, 1716; (129) *Rachel* and Joseph Roberts, Nov. 29, 1716; (130) *Joanna* and John Rogers, Jan. 1, 1717, (131) *John* and Hannah Jackson, June 12, 1755, (132) *Samuel* and Abigail Mason, April 20, 1721; (133) *Nathaniel* and Lydia Claflin, Oct. 16, 1740; (134) *Mary* and Samuel Chandler, Sept. 18, 1735; (135) *Hannah* and John Mosley, Aug. 30, 1722; (136) *Margaret* and Thomas Mitchel, April 11, 1726; (137) *Sarah* and Thomas Odell, Nov. 9, 1727; (138) *Margaret* and James Hamilton, Aug. 24, 1736; (139) *Rebecca* and William Volencot, May 31, 1748; (140) *Elizabeth* and James Perkins, Dec. 29, 1755; (141) *Nathaniel* and Lydia Murrin, March 25, 1742; (142) *Mary* and John

Collins, Nov. 18, 1751; (143) *Elizabeth* and Edward Marshall, Oct. 11, 1752; (144) *Elijah* and Hannah Child, March 13, 1790; (145) *John* and Sarah Brewer, Nov. 11, 1764; (146) *Samuel* and Sarah Down, May 8, 1756.

(147) William Dandredge Peck, an eminent naturalist, and for several years Professor of Natural History at Harvard College, was a descendant of one of the Boston Pecks. He was born May 8, 1763. He was prepared for college by Mr. Ward, of Brookline. He was admitted Bachelor of Arts at Cambridge in 1782. In 1805, he was elected Professor of Natural History. He died at Cambridge, Oct. 3, 1822.* His father, John Peck, was said to have been one of the most successful shipbuilders and scientific naval architects that the United States had then produced.

THE MENDON PECKS.

When the Pecks of this branch were first found, they were supposed to be of the Rehoboth Pecks; and many of the families were traced out before it was discovered that they could not be connected with that branch of the name or with the Connecticut Pecks. After tracing them back to their ancestor, John Peck, of Mendon, Mass., he was supposed to be of the Boston branch, the son of Simon, of Hingham. As many of the branch desired that its descendants should be traced out, and their record preserved, and to reward those who furnished information, it was thought best to do so. It is hoped that some of them will now feel interest enough in the subject to trace their ancestor back, and learn whatever there may be of interest in relation to him.

---

* I was told that a son of his was residing in Sterling, Mass , and wrote him, but could get no response.

I should have been pleased to have published a more extended notice of his father and a history of his ancestry, if he would have furnished me with it.

DESCENDANTS OF JOHN PECK, OF MENDON, MASS.

John Peck settled in Mendon, Mass., where he died, Sept. 6, 1725. His son Simon was appointed administrator upon the estate. (Boston Records, B. 24, p. 174.)

CHILDREN — SECOND GENERATION

(1) Simon Peck, son of John and Milicent, his wife, was born March 27, 1693-4, (2) Hannah, b. ——; (3) John, b. March 8, 1698-9, (4) Mary, b March 28, 1702-3, (5) Elizabeth, b. July 16, 1709, (6) John again, b. March 27, 1714.

[1.] SIMON[2] PECK, son of JOHN,[1] being the eldest son, probably inherited his father's lands, and, as appears by the records at Worcester, Mass., soon began to dispose of them after his father's decease. He sold two full rights to Benjamin Taft, to be laid out in the eighth division, May 8, 1728. He also deeded, in 1736, seventy acres, lying at Magomisco hill, together with all the right, title and interest which his father had in the meadow known as Peck's meadow, to John Peck, Abijah Luther, and wife Prudence, and Elizabeth Peck, spinster, June 14, 1736. (B. 13, p. 340.) He deeded to Abraham Daniels, physician, a part of his homestead near the meeting-house, Dec. 8, 1739. He deeded to his son Ebenezer twenty acres of land in Uxbridge, Oct. 24, 1743, and to his sons Abraham and John all his home farm, March 6, 1750.

The following is a record of his family from the Uxbridge Records :

CHILDREN — THIRD GENERATION

(7)+Ebenezer, son of Simon Peck and Sarah his wife, was b. Nov. 28, 1720; (8)+Abraham, b. Jan 14, 1723-4 (9)+John, b. Dec 30, 1726; (10) Sarah, b. Oct. 18, 1729, (11) Anna, b. April 22, 1732, (12) Sarah, b Oct. 24, 1735, (13) Mary, b. Aug 7, 1738 She and Sarah both married, one a Whitney and the other a Lothrope.

[7.] EBENEZER[3] PECK, son of SIMON,[2] left Uxbridge about 1750, and settled in Ashford, Conn. By the records of Uxbridge, it appears that the intention of marriage between him and Sarah Allen, of Uxbridge, was made public April 2, 1739, and that they were married June 19, 1739.

CHILDREN — FOURTH GENERATION ·

(14) Samuel, b. March 5, 1740-1, (15) Hannah, b June 23, 1743, (16) Nathan, b Nov 7, 1745, (17) Rachel, b Feb. 17, 1747-8. He afterwards had, as I am told, (18) Ebenezer, (19) Simon, and (20) David, of whom I find no record.

[8.] ABRAHAM[3] PECK, son of Simon,[2] settled in Coleraine, Mass., where he died, July 18, 1798. He married Mary Stuart, of Londonderry, N. H., Dec. 21, 1724. She was born May 23, 1730, and died Jan. 19, 1801.

CHILDREN — FOURTH GENERATION

(21) Samuel, b Sept 18, 1755, d. Aug 23, 1771, (22) Sarah, b. May 7, 1757, d Sept 4, 1771, (23) Mary, b March 13, 1759, d Aug 5, 1767, (24) John, b Jan 17, 1761, d Aug 7, 1767, (25) Rachel, b Nov 11, 1767, d Aug 8, 1767, (26)+Abraham, b June 24, 1767, (27) Lydia, b Aug 8, 1770, d Aug. 9, 1775, (28) Margaret, b March 23, 1773, d. Aug. 13, 1775.

[9] JOHN[3] PECK, son of SIMON,[2] left Uxbridge about 1753. He removed to Ashford, Conn , where he lived until a short time prior to his decease, when he removed to Vermont to reside with his son, where he died in 1805. He was four times married. The intention of his marriage with his first wife, Mary Brown, of Rehoboth, Mass., was made public at Uxbridge, as appears by the records, Oct. 27, 1750. For his second wife, he married Elizabeth Dennison, of Hampton, who died June 1767. For his third wife, he married Jerusha Preston. For his fourth, he married a widow Hollis. His first wife and two children died in Rehoboth, Mass.

CHILDREN — FOURTH GENERATION

By his second wife were (29)+Joseph, (30) Polly, (31)+John, b Oct 7, 1759; (32) Rhoda, b Feb 3, 1761, (33)+David, b Sept 18, 1762, (34) Elizabeth, (35) Lydia, b Dec 26, 1766 By his third wife there were (36) John, b May 8, 1768; (37) Anna, b Sept. 10, 1769, (38) Eunice, b Sept 25, 1770; (39) Oliver, b. Aug 7, 1772, d young; (40) Levi, d young; (41) Elisha, b. March 25, 1777.

[26.] ABRAHAM[4] PECK, son of ABRAHAM,[3] settled in Coleraine, where he died, March 1, 1830. He married, for his first wife, Arathusa Bullard, February 3, 1790. She was born in Northampton, Mass., April 11, 1771, and died in Coleraine, August 23, 1824. For his second wife, he married a Mrs. Plympton, of Wardsboro', Vt. She died 1843.

CHILDREN — FIFTH GENERATION

(42)+Calvin, b. Nov. 1, 1791, (43) Samuel, b Jan 15, 1793, (44) John, b. May 27, 1794, (45) Jerry, b. Feb. 6, 1796, (46) Moses, b. May 2, 1798, d July 31, 1803, (47) Mary, b. Dec 19, 1799, d. July 28, 1803, (48) Arathusa, b Oct. 12, 1801, d. July 30, 1803, (49) Matilda, b. Nov. 27, 1804, m. Thomas Brown, of Coleraine, (50) Louisa, b. Dec. 21, 1806, m. William Johnson, (51)+Abia-ham, b. Nov. 2, 1808, (52) Lovella, b. May 7, 1811, m. Andrew H Marsy, of Coleraine, where they were residing in 1865, (53) Joanna, b Sept. 28, 1813, m. John C Browning, and was residing in Chicopee, Mass, in 1865, (54) Moses, b Sept 26, 1817, suppose d unm, (55) Harriet, by his second wife, b Aug 16, 1826, m. Joseph Hathaway, and was residing in Millbury, Mass., in 1865.

[29.] JOSEPH[4] PECK, son of JOHN,[3] resided in Monson, Mass., where he died, February 9, 1855, aged 99 years and 6 months. He married Eunice Jennings. She died July 16, 1832, aged 78 years.

CHILLDREN — FIFTH GENERATION ·

(56) Lemuel, (57) Lavinia, b in 1792, m Calvin Bowers, and settled in Newfield, Conn, (58) Roxanna, b in 1786, m Rodolphus Spaulding, d leaving seven children, (59)+Jason, b in 1788, (60)+Ira, (61) Hannah, b in 1797, m Joseph Walker, and had twelve children, (62)+Solomon, b. May 20, 1799.

[31.] JOHN[4] PECK, son of JOHN,[3] settled at first in Cavendish, Vt., and from there removed to Weston, where he died, Sept. 21, 1849. He was twice married: first, to Rebecca Badger; second, to Widow Hannah Austin, who died November 14, 1848. His first wife died about 1810.

CHILDREN — FIFTH GENERATION

(63) Olive, b 1792, m Joseph Baldwin, by whom she had five children, d. Nov. 8, 1840; (64) Palmer, d in the 23d year of his age; (65) Dolly, b Jan. 15, 1794, m Ephraim Kile, were residing in Weston in 1865, have sons and daughters, (66)+Oliver, b Jan 24, 1797, (67)+Oren, b in 1800, d Feb 18, 1840; (68)+Ezekiel, b in Cavendish, Vt, Jan 24, 1802, (69) Rhoda, b. in 1804, d. 1808, (70)+James I., b July 28, 1812, (71)+Daniel D., b. Feb. 14, 1817.

[33.] DANIEL[4] PECK, son of JOHN,[3] settled in Cavendish, Vt., where he died. He married Abigail ——.

CHILDREN — FIFTH GENERATION

(72) Jared, b. April 22, 1789, d young; (73)+Alva, b. Feb. 27, 1793, (74) Lucinda, b Sept. 25, 1795, (75) Bethiah, b. March 20, 1797, (76) Abigail, b. Nov. 13, 1798, (77) Charlotte, b. Sept. 21, 1800.

[41.] ELISHA[4] PECK, son of JOHN,[3] resided in Abington, Conn. He died September 26, 1866. He married Sarah Badger.

(78) Jerusha, b. May 2, 1795, (79) Betsey, b Dec 15, 1796, m Jared W. Snow, of Eastford, Conn , (80)+Alanson, b June 30, 1805, (81) Minerva, b April 19, 1809, m. Cyrel Kent, of Abington, Conn.

[42.] DR. CALVIN⁵ PECK, son of ABRAHAM,⁴ settled first in Castine, Me., and from there removed to Ellsworth, where he died, February 10, 1849. He married Susan Joy, May 24, 1815. She was born June 11, 1792.

(82) Mary S , b Feb. 11, 1816, m Emerson Googing; was residing at Mt Desert in 1865, (83) Ann C , b April 3, 1819, m Asa McAlister; was residing at Ellsworth in 1865, (84)+Calvin G , b Nov 1, 1817, (85)+Samuel J , b. Nov 5, 1820; (86) Arethusa, b. April 20, 1822, d Nov 16, 1839, (87) William D , b. Oct 10, 1823, was residing in California, unm , in 1865, (88)+Rowland H , b Oct 8, 1825, (89) Elizabeth, b June 27, 1827, m Byron G Pettingill, was residing in Ellsworth in 1865, (90) Sarah, b. April 7, 1829, d April 24, 1854, (91)+John M , b June 19, 1833.

[43.] SAMUEL⁵ PECK, son of ABRAHAM,⁴ settled in Blakeley, Pa , about 1829. where he died, July 7, 1864 By industry and perseverance, he became wealthy. He was a member of the church for many years. He took an active part in the cause of education, temperance, and the reforms of the day. He married Sarah Wilson, December 31, 1816, for his first wife; Susan Snidecor, June 28, 1845, for his second; and Sarah A. Bertholf, for his third, March 13, 1862. His first wife was born June 20, 1792; died July 17, 1842. His second wife died August 11, 1857.

(92)+Samuel L , b Nov 28, 1817, (93) Mary Ann, b April 4, 1819, m. George W Arnold, Feb 25, 1841, by whom she has children, was residing in Herrick, Pa , in 1865 (94) Sarah W., b June 25, 1821, m. Joseph M. Stephens, Sept. 12, 1841, by whom she has children, was residing in Madison, Luzerne County, in 1865, (95) Arathusa B , b Dec 29, 1823, m. Sidney P. Stevens, Sept 15, 1844, d. Oct. 20, 1860, leaving children, (96)+Jonathan W , b July 9, 1826, (97) Emeline O , b May 8, 1829, m R. S Benjamin, May 8, 1829, by whom she has children, was residing in Scranton, Pa , in 1865, (98) Elvira C , b May 8, 1829, m Andrew C Wise, Oct 18, 1854, was residing in Peckville * in 1865, has children, (99)+John D , b. April 26, 1831, (100)+Calvin

* So called from having been built up by the business carried on by Samuel Peck & Sons.

24*

F , b July 21, 1834 , (101) William W., by second wife, b. March 9, 1847; residing at Peckville in 1865 , (102) James E , by third wife, b. April 29, 1863.

[44]   JOHN[5] PECK, son of ABRAHAM,[4] was residing at Peckville in 1865. He had been twice married: first, to Elizabeth Champion; second, to Catharine Jordan. Had one child.

[45.]   JERRY[5] PECK, son of ABRAHAM,[4] settled in Blakeley, Pa. He married Henrietta Stratton.

CHILDREN — SIXTH GENERATION

(103) Adaline , (104) Eliphalet S , (105) Elizabeth , (106) Mary , (107) Charlotte and (108) Chauncey.*

[51.]   ABRAHAM[5] PECK, son of ABRAHAM,[4] married Julia Torry, daughter of Samuel Torry, of Berkshire, Tioga County, N. Y., August 31, 1837. He was residing at Coopersville, Ottawa County, Mich., in 1865.

CHILDREN — SIXTH GENERATION

(109) Malvina, b. Aug 20, 1838, d. Aug. 23, 1838 , (110) George T., b. Dec. 11, 1839 , (111) Frederick, b. Sept. 24, 1841, d. Oct. 1842 , (112) Albert V , b. Nov 8, 1842 , (113) Charles L., b. Sept. 19, 1841 , (114) Sarah A , b Jan 1, 1848 , (115) Thankful P., b. April 2, 1851 , (116) Lucius E , b June 6, 1853 , (117) Francis E , b Dec 31, 1855 , (118) Ernest H , b March 17, 1858 , (119) Isabella E., b. Aug 6, 1861.

[56]   LEMUEL[5] PECK, son of JOSEPH,[4] married Rhoda Cady, and settled in Belchertown, Mass., where he died, February 24, 1860. She March 22, 1862.

CHILDREN — SIXTH GENERATION

(120) Mary Ann, b Dec 21, 1808, m Lyman Waters , was residing in Somers, Conn , in 1865 , (121)+Robert J , b. March 14, 1811 , (122) Absalom C , b Jan. 9, 1814, m Adaline Cuttler, d May 5, 1855, no issue , (123)+John B , b July 6. 1816, d Feb 4, 1852, leaving three children, (124) Abner C , b May 31, 1819, d Feb 2, 1857 , (125) Sarah E., b Aug. 31, 1821, d Dec 12, 1840; (126) Lucy C , b. Aug. 16, 1824, d. Dec. 13, 1844 , (127) Joseph F., b July 25, 1830, d. in 1840.

[59.]   JASON[5] PECK, son of JOSEPH,[4] married Linda Cady. He was residing in West Stafford, Conn., in 1865.

* I wrote Mr. Peck for a more full record of his family, but could get no response.

(128) Minerva, (129) Eliza, (130) Mary Ann, (131) Rhoda; (132) Sophronia, and a son, who died in infancy.

[60.]   IRA[5] PECK, son of JOSEPH,[4] was residing in Stafford, Conn., in 1865.   He married Mary E. Bullard.

(133) Luther B , (134) Sarah E , who m Emor Smith, and was residing in Stafford, Conn , in 1865, (135) Ira, jr , (136) Mary B , (137) Martin L., who m. Sophia C. Smith, and was residing in Monson in 1865, and (138) Mary Ann, who d. aged 14 years.

[62.]   SOLOMON[5] PECK, son of JOSEPH,[4] settled upon the homestead, in Monson, Mass., where he died, July 22, 1864.   He married Olive Bowers, May 13, 1821.   She was residing with her son Levi in 1865.

(139) Harriet, b. April 9, 1822, m Abel Butler, Nov. 22, 1842, d Feb. 3, 1864, (140) Amos, b. Aug. 10, 1823, m Mercy Farrar, Nov. 26, 1856, (141) Amelia, b Oct 15, 1830, m Newell Taylor, Oct 1, 1854, and was residing in Palmer, Mass., in 1865, (142) Eunice J , b Aug. 3, 1833, m John Caughey, and was residing in East Bridgeport, Conn , in 1866, (143)+Levi, b. Aug 13, 1836, m. Minerva Colburn, Oct 7, 1857.

[66.]   OLIVER[5] PECK, son of JOHN,[4] married Lucy Austin, and was residing in Weston, Vt., in 1865.

(144)+John, b. Feb. 8, 1819, (145)+Almon, b May 28, 1821, (146)+Sceva, b. June 29, 1823, (147)+Alonzo C , b. Nov 13, 1825, (148) Lucena, b. May 25, 1828, m. Rev Ira Toggart, (149)+Oliver A , b Sept. 3, 1830; (150) Lucy A., b. May 29, 1832, m. L P Dean, (151) Hannah R., b Oct. 12, 1833, and was the Widow Hannah R Wilson, residing in Gaysville, Vt , in 1865, (152) Sylvia J , b Oct 13, 1835, m John H Fisher ; (153) Lucretia, b. July 28, 1840, m. George Metcalf, (154) Eugene K., b. Nov. 28, 1846, and was residing in Vermont in 1865, unm.

[67.]   OREN[5] PECK, son of JOHN,[4] married Sally Shattuck, December 4, 1823.   She was born January 29, 1777.   He died February 18, 1840.   She survived him, and married Lemuel Abbott, May 20, 1850.

(155) Oren H , b. June 25, 1825, d. April 27, 1828, (156)+James F., b. Jan. 20, 1827, (157) Sarah, b. Feb. 10, 1829, d. July 6, 1844, (158) Shattuck, b.

March 5, 1831. He was drafted, entered the army, and was killed April 2, 1865, at the taking of Richmond, (159) Lucy M , b Nov. 22, 1833, m Ora Abbott, d. March 15, 1863, (160) Oren A., b Feb 10, 1836, was residing in Rutland, Vt., in 1865, (161) Maiy E., b. May 28, 1840, m. Ransom Beckwith, Dec. 4, 1861, and settled in Weston, Vt.

[68.] EZEKIEL⁵ PECK, son of JOHN,⁴ settled first in Weston, Vt., where he resided until 1847, when he moved to North Richmond, N. H., where he was residing in 1865. He married Sina Fenn, of Weston, March 31, 1831. She was born in Ludlow, Vt., September 1, 1805.

CHILDREN — SIXTH GENERATION .

(162) Joel E , b Feb 12, 1832, d. Jan 2, 1849, (163)+Oren H , b Feb. 14, 1834, (164) H Annetta, b April 16, 1836, residing at home, unm., in 1865, (165) Melvina, b. Jan 20, 1838, residing at home, unm., in 1865.

[70.] JAMES F.⁵ PECK, son of JOHN,⁴ has been twice married: first, to Phebe B. Rhodes, daughter of Amasa and Olive Rhodes, April 29, 1841. She was born June 22, 1817, and died July 12, 1856. Second, to Mary B. Winship, daughter of John and Sally Winship, October 16, 1856. She was born June 27, 1828.

CHILDREN — SIXTH GENERATION

(166) Rhoda S., b. May 19, 1842, d. March 10, 1843; (167) Alvara F., b. April 23, 1846, (168) Angeline P., b. Feb. 26, 1850.

[71.] DANIEL D.⁵ PECK, son of JOHN,⁴ settled in Weston, Vt. He married Jane Stevens. He died in Iowa, where he was intending to settle, June 15, 1851. She survived him, and married John H. Congdon.

CHILDREN — SIXTH GENERATION

(169) Almeron D , b. Oct 6, 1843, (170) Philetus D., b. Dec. 27, 1847; (171) Edwina Jane, b. March 12, 1851.

[73.] ALVA⁵ PECK, son of DANIEL,⁴ married Charry Davis.

CHILDREN — SIXTH GENERATION :

(172) Otis W., b Nov. 27, 1822, d young; (173)+Christopher, b. Dec. 23, 1824, (174) Minerva, b June 14, 1826, (175) Annis, b. July 31, 1828, (176) Ira, b. June 25, 1830, m. Jenette Adams, no issue; (177) Sylvia, b. Aug. 7, 1832, (178) Isabel, b. June 16, 1834, (179) Alvira, b. Feb. 6, 1837.

[80.] ALANSON[5] PECK, son of ELISHA,[4] resides in Ashford, Conn. He married Abigail Carpenter, April 13, 1829.

CHILDREN — SIXTH GENERATION :

(180) Eliza A., b March 12, 1830, m Miner Grant, of Mansfield; (181) Julia C., b March 11, 1833, m James G Gaylord, of Ashford, Conn. He died for his country, Dec 22, 1864, in Salisbury prison. He was a young man very much respected (182) Andrew A , b March 4, 1835, m. Sarah Campbell, and was residing in Providence, R. I , in 1865; (183)+Joseph C., b. March 11, 1837, m Delia A Wilson, of Willimantic, Conn. He d Aug. 3, 1865 (184) Abigail I , b July 16, 1839, m. Rev. I. P. Bixby, of Boston, (185) Emily M., b. Aug 30, 1841 To Mr. Peck I am under many obligations for his kindness in answering my letters.

[84.] CALVIN G.[6] PECK, son of DR. CALVIN,[5] married Almira L. Marcy, and was residing in Ellsworth, Me., in 1865.

CHILDREN — SEVENTH GENERATION :

(186) Auritta A. , and (187) Roland M.

[85.] SAMUEL J.[6] PECK, son of DR. CALVIN,[5] married Nancy I. Conner, and was residing in New York in 1865.

CHILDREN — SEVENTH GENERATION .

(188) Calvin , and (189) Frederick W.

[88.] ROWLAND H.[6] PECK, son of DR. CALVIN,[5] married Helen A. Somerby, and was residing in Ellsworth, Me., in 1865.

CHILDREN — SEVENTH GENERATION ·

(190) Helen M. , (191) William , and (192) Florence C.

[91.] JOHN[6] PECK, son of DR. CALVIN,[5] married Ellen M. Frazier, and was residing in Ellsworth, Me., in 1863.

CHILDREN — SEVENTH GENERATION ·

(193) Agnes M.; (194) Frances E. , and (195) Mary E.

[92.] SAMUEL L.[6] PECK, son of SAMUEL,[5] married Harriet Wilson, October 16, 1848. She was born October 17, 1813; died January 1, 1865. He was residing in Peckville, Pa., in 1865. To his kindness I am indebted for my information in relation to his father and family.

CHILDREN — SEVENTH GENERATION .

(196) Charles W., b. Jan. 22, 1851, an infant son, b. June 10, 1854, d. Aug. 10, 1854, (197) Sarah E., b. Aug. 10, 1855, d. Aug. 15, 1859. ·

[96.]   JONATHAN W.[6] PECK, son of SAMUEL,[5] married Mercy E. Hall, May 26, 1853. She was born August 26, 1834. They were residing at Peckville, Pa., in 1865.

CHILDREN — SEVENTH GENERATION:

(198) Fenwick L., b. Sept. 18, 1854, (199) Francis L , b Oct. 28, 1856, (200) Myron E , b. March 5, 1861, d Aug. 12, 1861, (201) Edson S., b. Dec 8, 1862

[99.]   JOHN D.[6] PECK, son of SAMUEL,[5] married, for his first wife, Sarah C. Snidecor, August 26, 1852. She was born February 24, 1835, and died March 17, 1858. For his second, Dellona Stone, November 17, 1860. He was residing in Madison, Pa., in 1865.

CHILDREN — SEVENTH GENERATION

(202) George C., b July 17, 1853, (203) Sanford D , b. Feb. 28, 1857 , (204) Byron N., b. March 7, 1858 , (205) Herbert J , b. Sept. 15, 1863.

[100.]   CALVIN F.[6] PECK, son of SAMUEL,[5] married Phebe Ann T——, January 6, 1855. He was residing in Kent County, Del., in 1865.

CHILDREN — SEVENTH GENERATION

(206) Vira Isabel, b. Oct. 3, 1854 , (207) Eva Francelia, b Oct 12, 1857 ; (208) Dwight, b Nov. 7, 1859, d April 4, 1860 ; an infant son, b Feb. 3, 1862, d. Feb. 6, 1862 ; (209) Jenny, b. Jan. 10, 1863, d. Feb. 6, 1863 , (210) Freddy D., b. April 23, 1864.

[121.]   ROBERT J.[6] PECK, son of LEMUEL,[5] married Julia Ann Loomis, in 1834, and was residing upon the homestead, in Belchertown, Mass., in 1865.

CHILDREN — SEVENTH GENERATION

(211) Adelaide F., b in 1842 ; and (212) Alice J., b. in 1850.

[123.]   JOHN B.[6] PECK, son of LEMUEL,[5] married Caroline Easten.

CHILDREN — SEVENTH GENERATION

(213) Emma, b. in 1845 ; and (214) Abner and Absalom, twins, b in 1850.

[133.]   LUTHER B.[6] PECK, son of IRA,[5] married Lucinda Cross, and was residing in Monson in 1865.

CHILDREN — SEVENTH GENERATION .

(215) Ira L. ; (216) Martin L. ; (217) Charles L. ; and (218) F. B.

[135.]   IRA⁶ PECK, son of IRA,⁵ married, for his first wife, Laura Anderson; for his second, Harriet Hoar; and for his third, Charlotte Orcott.   He was residing in Wales in 1865.

CHILDREN — SEVENTH GENERATION ·

(219) Laura M ; (220) Willie M., (221) Albert, (222) Mary S.; and (223) Charles.

[140.]   AMOS⁶ PECK, son of SOLOMON,⁵ married Mercy F. Farrar.

CHILDREN — SEVENTH GENERATION

(224) Josephine, b Aug. 1858; (225) Albert, b. May 1862, and two died in infancy.

[143]   LEVI⁶ PECK, son of SOLOMON,⁵ married Minerva Colburn, October 7, 1857.   He was residing upon the homestead in Monson in 1865.

CHILDREN — SEVENTH GENERATION

(226) George S , b. Sept. 1860; (227) Frank A., b March 1864.

[144.]   JOHN⁶ PECK, son of OLIVER,⁵ was residing in East Somerville, Mass., in 1865.   He married Phebe Ann Barnard.

CHILDREN — SEVENTH GENERATION .

(228) John Arthur; (229) Ella Frances, (230) Henry Austin, and (231) Lucy Edith.

[145.]   ALMON⁶ PECK, son of OLIVER,⁵ married Rebecca W. Saunders, of Cavendish, Vt., and was residing in Proctorsville in 1865.

CHILD — SEVENTH GENERATION .

(232) Sidney A.

[146.]   SCEVA⁶ PECK, son of OLIVER,⁵ married Mrs. Sarah Bowen, formerly Miss Sarah Barnard.   He was residing in East Somerville in 1865.

CHILD — SEVENTH GENERATION :

(233) Walter Sceva.

[147.]   ALONZO⁶ PECK, son of OLIVER,⁵ was residing in Boston in 1865, and had been twice married: first, to Miss Catharine Hawley; second, to Mrs. Isabella Donnell.

CHILD — SEVENTH GENERATION :

(234) Emma Kate.

[149.]   OLIVER A.[6] PECK, son of OLIVER,[5] married Harriet
A. Clark, and was residing in Boston in 1865.

CHILDREN — SEVENTH GENERATION ·

(235) Hattie A., b. Nov. 20, 1857, (236) Elmer A., b. July 19, 1861.

[156.]   JAMES F.[6] PECK, son of OREN,[5] married Sylvia
White, March 20, 1852.   She was born May 21, 1821.   He was
residing in Weston, Vt., in 1865.

CHILDREN — SEVENTH GENERATION ·

(237) Filinda, b Oct. 21, 1852, (238) Sarah J., b. Dec. 20, 1853, d. Dec. 9,
1855, (239) Marion E., b. Oct. 4, 1855, (240) George O., b Oct. 9, 1857.

[163.]   OREN H.[6] PECK, son of EZEKIEL,[5] married Hattie A.
Cheney, June 5, 1861; born in Chesterfield, N. H., March 17,
1844.   They were residing in Swansey, N. H., in 1865.

CHILDREN — SEVENTH GENERATION .

(241) Etta A., b. March 11, 1863, and (242) Willie C., b. Sept. 1, 1864.

[173.]   CHRISTOPHER[6] PECK, son of ALVAH,[5] married
Mary H. Esty, and was residing in Cavendish, Vt., in 1865.

CHILD — SEVENTH GENERATION .

(243) Alvah C., b. Dec. 5, 1857.

[183.]   JOSEPH C.[6] PECK, son of ALANSON,[5] married Delia
A. Wilson.   She died March 29, 1865.

CHILD — SEVENTH GENERATION :

(244) Eugene B.

THE CONNECTICUT PECKS.

THE Connecticut Pecks are the descendants of Joseph, of Milford, Deacon William and Henry, of New Haven, and Deacon Paul, of Hartford. They were among the early settlers of the country. Each became the ancestor, or progenitor, of a numerous race. Their descendants are now scattered throughout most of the States and territories, mixed in their settlements with each other, and with the Massachusetts Pecks, requiring much labor to separate them.

What relationship existed between these ancestors has not been ascertained. None of the descendants, so far as I have learned, although many of them are men of wealth, and abundantly able, have ever attempted to trace them back to Europe, and learn the connection.

DESCENDANTS OF JOSEPH PECK, OF MILFORD, CONNECTICUT.

JOSEPH PECK resided at first at New Haven, Conn. His name does not appear upon the records until about 1643, although he is generally supposed to have resided there earlier, and to have been the brother of Henry, who settled there in 1638, with whom he seems to have resided, or associated, and with whom he probably came over to this country. Who his ancestors were has not been learned. I found none of his descendants who would take interest enough in the subject to assist in doing so. He left New Haven about 1649, and settled at Milford. He became a member of the church there in 1652. He was twice married: first, to Mrs. Alice Burwell, widow of John Burwell; second, to Miss Richards. The house in which he resided has but recently been taken down. It stood near the present residence of Capt. Cornelius B. Peck, a great-great-great-grandson, (who resides upon a portion of the ancient homestead,) and must have been more than two hundred years old. Its appearance was exceedingly unique and ancient, — two stories in front, in the lean-to style, sloping back to about six feet in rear, with a gable end to the street. He died in 1700-1. The

25

settlement of his estate is upon the Milford Records, Book of Deeds No. 3, pp. 75, 76 and 77. It is quite lengthy and specific. He deeds to his son Joseph his lands, upon the conditions that he shall provide for and support him during his life, reserving to himself the control of his house, and the right, if his son Joseph or his heirs should fail to provide sufficient comforts, to sell off lands from time to time for that purpose.

He gave legacies to his son-in-law, Thomas Hayes, Mary, wife of William Northrop, and his daughter Anna. These legacies and the debts were to be paid by Joseph; one-half of the legacies immediately after the decease of his father, and the balance within three years.

CHILDREN — SECOND GENERATION

(1) Elizabeth, bap in 1651, m Sergeant Thomas Hayes, Oct 29, 1677, (2) +Joseph, bap in 1653, (3)+John, bap March 4, 1655, (4) Mary, bap. April 29, 1670, m. William Northrop, (5) Ann, bap in 1672, (6) Hannah

[2.] JOSEPH[2] PECK, son of JOSEPH,[1] settled in Milford, where he died. He disposed of his estates by deeds to his sons, at different times, which appear upon record at Milford. He married Mary Camp, January 27, 1678–9.

CHILDREN — THIRD GENERATION

(7)+Joseph, b. Feb. 25, 1680–1, (8) Mary, b Dec. 15, 1682; (9) John, b Sept. 4, 1685, and d. Nov 27, 1709, (10)+Jeremiah, b 1687, (11)+Samuel, bap. 1690; (12)+Ephraim, bap 1692, (13)+Henry, bap 1695; (14) Elizabeth, bap 1697; (15) +Nathaniel, bap. 1699, (16) Abigail, b. Sept. 25, 1701, (17)+ Heth, b Oct 3, 1703.

[3.] JOHN[2] PECK, son of JOSEPH,[1] it is supposed, settled in Milford; but what became of him and his family is unknown. His father makes no mention of him or of his children in the settlement of his estate. They were probably deceased.

They are supposed to have been:

CHILDREN — THIRD GENERATION

(18)+Joseph, bap. in 1681, and (19) Rachel, b. in 1682

[7.] JOSEPH[3] PECK, son of JOSEPH,[2] at first settled in Milford, where he resided until about 1714, when he removed to Newtown, where he died. He was Town Clerk, and lived near what is now known as Newtown Street. He married Abigail Baldwin, of Milford, January 14, 1706–7.

CHILDREN — FOURTH GENERATION

(20)+Joseph, b. Oct 2, 1707, and bap 1710; (21) Abigail, b June 22, 1709, bap. in 1710, and d Dec. 3, 1720; (22)+John, b. March 28, 1713, (23) Mary, b. Oct 29, 1715, d Nov 19, 1718, (24) Elizabeth, b March 29, 1717, (25)+ Moses, b. Dec. 28, 1719; (26) Mary, b May 18, 1720; (27) Abigail, b. June 1722.

[10.] JEREMIAH³ PECK, son of JOSEPH,² resided in Milford. He married Hannah Fisk, daughter of Dr. John Fisk, of Rhode Island, August 20, 1713. His will is upon record at New Haven, B. 10, p. 491, dated October 5, 1765.

CHILDREN — FOURTH GENERATION

(28) Hannah, b May 6, 1716, m. David Clark, (29)+John, b. Dec. 9, 1718; (30)+Jeremiah, jr., b Jan. 12, 1720–1, (31)+Phineas, b. April 10, 1723, (32) Sarah, b May 25, 1726, (33) Sibbella, b. June 24, 1728, m. Jirah Bull, (34) Lucy, b. Oct. 23, 1730; (35) Comfort and (36) Content, twins, b April 1, 1734

[11.] SAMUEL³ PECK, son of JOSEPH,² resided in Milford. He married Martha Clark, May 5, 1714.

CHILDREN — FOURTH GENERATION ·

(37) Martha C , b Jan 31, 1714–15, (38)+Samuel, b May 21, 1716, (39) Mary, b July 30, 1718, (40)+Job, b. Sept. 15, 1720; (41) Abigail, b. in 1722; (42)+Nathan, b. in 1724.

[12.] EPHRAIM³ PECK, son of JOSEPH,² settled at first in Milford, and from there removed to Newtown, where he died, July 23, 1760. His will is upon record at Danbury, Conn., B. 1, p. 187, dated February 17, 1758, and proved August 18, 1760. He married Sarah Ford, of Milford, November 7, 1716.

CHILDREN — FOURTH GENERATION ·

(43) Sarah, b July 14, 1717, m. John Plat; (44) +Henry, b. April 14, 1719; (45)+Ephraim, b May 21, 1721, (46) Ruth, b. Jan. 28, 1723–4, (47)+Gideon, b. July 2, 1725, (48)+Ebenezer, b July 2, 1727, (49) Ann, b. Sept. 3, 1731, m. Caleb Malroy, (50) Damarias.

[13.] HENRY³ PECK, son of JOSEPH,² resided in Milford. He was a Deacon of the Congregational church. He died November 19, 1762. His will is upon record at New Haven, B. 10, p.

13, dated November 6, 1762. He was twice married: first, to Ann Ford, February 8, 1722–3, who died December 28, 1726; second, to Mary Northrop, widow of Amos Northrop, July 4, 1729.

CHILDREN — FOURTH GENERATION

(51)+Henry, b Dec 7, 1723, (52) Ann, b. Aug 15, 1725, m Jesse Lambert, Oct 28, 1748, d July 3, 1809, (53)+Benjamin, b Nov. 16, 1726, (54) Mehitable, b Oct 3, 1735, m Col. Allen.

[15.] NATHANIEL³ PECK, son of JOSEPH,² at first settled at Milford, and from there removed to Newtown, where he died. His will is upon record at Danbury, B. 3, p. 511, dated February 23, 1776, and proved the July following. He married Phebe ——.

CHILDREN — FOURTH GENERATION

(55) Phebe, b Feb 22, 1722–3, (56)+Nathaniel, b. Oct 9, 1734, (57) Ezra, (58) Elisha, (59) Eunice Foot.

[17.] HETH³ PECK, son of JOSEPH,² at first settled in Milford, and from there removed to Newtown, about 1740. He resided about one mile north of what is now known as Newtown Street. His will is upon record at Danbury, B. 7, p 132, dated April 24, 1781, and proved May 8, 1797. He died May 4, 1797. He married Hannah Camp, February 26, 1729–30.

CHILDREN — FOURTH GENERATION

(60)+Heth, b May 29, 1731, (61) Hannah, b July 5, 1733; (62) Mary, b. Dec 31, 1735, (63) Sarah, b April 14, 1738, (64)+ * Amiel, b July 24, 1740; (65) Hepzibeth, b July 23, 1742, (66)+Samuel, b Aug 20, 1744, (67)+Amos, b Jan. 12, 1746–7, (68) David, b Nov 17, 1748 was deceased at the date of his father's will, leaving a son (69) Zalmon, who married Rachel Peck (No. 574), and resided in Brookfield Their children were (70) *Sally Ann*⁵, (71) *Nicholas*⁵, (72) *Maria*⁵, (73) *William*⁵, (74) *Eliza*⁵, (75) *Garry*⁵, and (76) *Juliette* ⁵

[18.] JOSEPH³ PECK, son of JOHN,² is supposed to have resided in Milford, and that (77) Joseph⁴ and (78) Abigail, upon record, baptized in 1710, were his children.

[20.] JOSEPH⁴ PECK, son of JOSEPH,³ resided in Newtown. He married Rebecca Shepherd, June 20, 1732.

---

* He was appointed administrator upon the estate of his father, April 4, 1798.

CHILDREN — FIFTH GENERATION

(79)+Aaron, b. Jan 21, 1732-3, (80) Violet, b. April 28, 1735. m. Job Northrop, (81)+Daniel, b Dec 27, 1736, (82) Grace, b Nov. 28, 1738, m Jotham Sherman, (83) Rebecca, b June 6, 1742, and d. Jan 11, 1742, (84)+John, b. Jan. 29, 1744, (85)+David, b Sept 15, 1747, (86) Mathew, b. Jan 4, 1753. His will is recorded at Danbury, B. 3, p 466, dated Feb. 11, 1772, and proved April 6, 1780.

[22.] JOHN[4] PECK, son of JOSEPH,[3] I am told, settled at what is now Bridgeport. He died April 22, 1768. His will is upon the Danbury Records, B. 3, p. 42, dated March 19, 1768, and proved May 17, 1768. He married Bethiah Booth, November 8, 1739.

CHILDREN — FIFTH GENERATION

(87)+Jabez, b Sept 4, 1740; (88)+Joseph, b May 20, 1742, (89)+Asher, b July 6, 1744, (90) Abigail, b March 23, 1746, (91)+Israel, b June 14, 1748, (92) Elnathan, b Sept. 30, 1754, old style, d. Dec. 1767.

[25] MOSES[4] PECK, son of JOSEPH,[3] resided in Newtown. His will is upon record at Danbury, B. 9, p. 539, dated July 6, 1795. He married Elizabeth Baldwin, December 1, 1748. She died December 25, 1798.

CHILDREN — FIFTH GENERATION

(93) Ruth, b Oct 30, 1749, (94)+Abel, b Jan. 25, 1750-1, (95)+Enos, b July 27, 1752, (96) Ann, b Feb 6, 1754, (97) Mary, b. June 28, 1755, (98) Coziah, b. Aug 19, 1756; (99)+Hezekiah, b Aug 14, 1758, (100) Caleb, b. Aug 9, 1760; (101) Betty, b. Jan 11, 1762, (102)+Dan, b. June 10, 1763; (103) Lois, b Jan 26, 1765, (104) Esther, b Oct 26, 1766, (105) Sarah, b. April 26, 1768, (106) Nathan, b. Sept. 15, 1769, d Dec. 6, 1769, (107)+Nathan, again, b. Oct. 11, 1771

[29.] JOHN[4] PECK, son of JEREMIAH,[3] resided in Milford, where he died. His will is upon record at New Haven, B. 16, p. 623. He married Sarah Platt, February 15, 1750–1.

CHILDREN — FIFTH GENERATION

(108) Sarah, b. Oct 15, 1751, m. an Andrews, (109) Mehitable, b Feb, 15, 1753, m David Camp; (110)+John, b. June 26, 1755, (111)+Joseph, b. Aug. 26, 1757.

[30.] JEREMIAH[4] PECK, son of JEREMIAH,[3] settled at first in Milford, but from there removed to Watertown, about 1752,

25*

where he died. He married Frances Platt, daughter of Josiah Platt, October 26, 1743.

CHILDREN — FIFTH GENERATION

(112)+Jeremiah, b. Nov 4, 1744, (113) Content, b May 30, 1747, (114) Isaac, b Feb 9, 1748-9. He enlisted into the army of the Revolution, and was drowned while in the service. (115) Benjamin, b in 1750; also entered the army, and died of the camp distemper; (116)+Simeon, b Aug 30, 1752, (117) Comfort, and (118) Abigail, the dates of whose births I could not learn.

[31.]   PHINEAS[4] PECK, son of JEREMIAH,[3] settled in what was then known as Amity, now a part of Woodbridge, Conn. He left Milford about 1776. He was the first deacon of the first church in Woodbridge. His will may be found upon record at New Haven, B. 23, p. 147. He married Deborah Clark, February 18, 1745-6. She died January 1803.

CHILDREN — FIFTH GENERATION

(119)+Phineas, b. Jan. 1, 1746-7, (120)+Samuel F , b March 25, 1750; (121) Deborah, b Oct 3, 1752, m. Deacon Nathan Platt, (122)+Zenus, b. Jan 11, 1755, (123) Naomi, b May 8, 1758, m Stephen Hine, and settled in New Milford, (124) Bazeleel, b March 8, 1761, m Martha Bradley, of Woodbridge, and moved to Derby, Conn , where he died, aged about 75   His children were   (125) *Deborah[6]*, (126) *Harriet[6]*, and (127) *Patty [6]*—(128) Anon, b. Sept. 20, 1763, m a Beecher, and had one son, named (129) *Beecher [6]*

[38.]   SAMUEL[4] PECK, son of SAMUEL,[3] resided in Milford. He married Hannah Jennings, of Fairfield, Conn., August 18, 1735.

CHILDREN — FIFTH GENERATION

(130)+Samuel, b. Aug 22, 1736, (131)+Michael, b Aug 10, 1738; (132) Sarah, who m Mansfield Stone, and (133) Mehitable, who, I am told, m. Nehemiah Lewis, of South Britain, Conn.

[40.]   JOB[4] PECK, son of SAMUEL,[3] settled in Stratford. He married Betsey Judson, July 31, 1744. She was born September 25, 1725, and died December 21, 1780.

CHILDREN — FIFTH GENERATION

(134) Sarah, b. July 27, 1745, (135)+John, b April 2, 1747, (136)+Judson, b May 27, 1749, (137)+Josiah, b. Oct 15, 1751, (138)+Job, b Feb 7, 1753, (139) Beardsley, b June 7, 1756, (140) James, b March 17, 1759, d. Sept 1779, (141) Johanna, b. March 2, 1761, m. J Betts, and d Dec 24, 1782, (142) Phineas, b. July 25, 1764, d Sept. 1765, (143) Phebe, b. April 24, 1768, m E Wheeler, and d at Stratford.

[42.] NATHAN[4] PECK, son of SAMUEL,[3] resided in Stratford. He married Tabatha Bears, September 12, 1750.

CHILDREN — FIFTH GENERATION

(144) Josiah, b Oct 20, 1751, (145) Mary, b Sept 1, 1753, and perhaps others, whose births were not recorded.

[44.] HENRY[4] PECK, son of EPHRAIM,[3] resided in Newtown. His will is recorded at Danbury, B. 7, p. 1. He was twice married: first, to Ann Smith, December 23, 1755; second, to Hannah Leavenworth, August 6, 1765.

CHILDREN — FIFTH GENERATION

(146)+Zalmon, b May 10, 1758; (147) Lemuel, b. April 3, 1766, who was twice married His first wife was Amey Peck (No 251), daughter of Jabez Peck His second wife was Mary Griffen He resided in Newtown, where he died in 1839, leaving no issue (148) Mercy, b. Aug 10, 1767, m Levi Peck (No 164), (149) Hannah, b April 6, 1770, m Dan Peck (No 102), (150) +Andrew, b. May 21, 1773, (151)+Samuel, b July 2, 1775

[45.] EPHRAIM[4] PECK, son of EPHRAIM,[3] resided in Newtown, where he died, July 21, 1801.* His son Levirus was appointed administrator upon his estate, August 20, 1801, B. 8, p. 33. He married Sarah Porter.

CHILDREN — FIFTH GENERATION ·

(152)+Shadroch, b March 18, 1741, (153)+Enoch, b July 19, 1743, (154) Sarah, b July 24, 1746, (155)+Nathan, b Jan 10, 1749, (156)+Eli, b June 2, 1751, (157)+Levirus, b. Aug. 12, 1753, (158) Anna, b April 20, 1756; (159)+Isaac, b Aug. 2, 1758, (160) Mabel, b. Feb. 17, 1761, (161)+Ephraim, b. May 20, 1763

[47.] GIDEON[4] PECK, son of EPHRAIM,[3] married Abiah Smith, January 28, 1752, and settled in Newtown. His will is upon record at Danbury, B. 5, p. 507, dated January 6, 1790, and proved February 27, 1790.

CHILDREN — FIFTH GENERATION

(162)+George, b Dec 2, 1752, (163)+Oliver, b July 9, 1754; (164)+ Levi, b April 1, 1758, (165) Anna S., b March 16, 1760, m Samuel Beers, (166) Abiah, b March 31, 1762, m. a Bristol, (167)+Gideon, (168)+Abner; (169) Mary, m a Beers, (170) Currence; and (171) Amarillius.

---

* At his funeral, I am told, were his seven sons and three daughters, and many grandchildren

[48.] EBENEZER[4] PECK, son of Ephraim,[3] married Sarah Booth, March 13, 1757, and settled in Newtown, where he died, July 26, 1805. His will is upon record at Danbury, B. 9, p. 97, dated August 14, 1798, and proved August 19, 1805.

CHILDREN — FIFTH GENERATION

(172) Truman, b Jan. 13, 1758, d June 28, 1759, (173) Truman, again, b. Oct 22, 1759, (174) Eunice, b Dec 1, 1761, m. Philo Blackman, (175) Ebenezer, d. unm., (176) Ammon, d unm , (177) James, m Sarah Coborn, (178) Huldah, d. unm.

[51.] HENRY[4] PECK, son of Henry,[2] removed from Milford and settled in Brookfield, where he became a wealthy farmer for those days.

He was Deacon of the Congregational church for many years, of the old puritan cast, pious and conscientiously strict in all the requirements of his religious creed. He was noted for his kindness and benevolence, and the interest he took in the cause of truth and christianity. He was also a prominent public man. He was a Justice of the Peace for many years, and by his just and impartial decisions obtained the confidence of the public.

He was twice married: first, to Rachel Lambert, of Milford; second, to Mrs. Abia Peck, of Newtown (widow). His first wife died January 29, 1792. He died October 4, 1808. His second wife survived him.* His will may be found upon record at Danbury, B. 10, p. 32, dated May 20, 1802.

CHILDREN — FIFTH GENERATION

(179) Mary, b Dec. 25, 1752, m. David Jackson, by whom she had the following children *Lucy,*[6] b. Oct 15, 1773, m Zardis Skidmore, *Jesse,*[6] b May 10, 1775, m Lucy B Terrell and Fanny M Hawley, *Rachel,*[6] b Oct 1, 1776, d. young; *Amos,*[6] b June 8, 1778, *Henry,*[6] b March 21, 1780, m. Annis Skidmore, *John,*[6] b May 25, 1782, m. Sophia Lake, *Rachel,*[6] b Jan 16, 1784, m. Thomas Shute, *Patty,*[6] b Oct. 30, 1785, m. Morris Birdsell, *Clarry,*[6] b July 10, 1787, m first, John Segar; second, John Vantile, *Polly,*[6] b. Jan 12, 1789, m Daniel Stone, *Reuben,*[6] b Nov. 15, 1790; *Nirum,*[6] b, March 7, 1793 This large family, I am told, settled in Danbury, where they were wealthy, and among the most prominent citizens —(180)+David, b. March 21, 1755, (181) Jesse L , b May 31, 1757, d May 10, 1773, (182) John, b Dec 3, 1759, (183) Rachel, b. Feb. 7, 1762, d. Oct 3, 1796, unm. (184) Henry, b. March 3, 1766, (185)+Amos, b April 5, 1769.

---

* She was the widow of Gideon Peck, of Newtown (No. 47), and the mother of his son John's wife.

[53.] BENJAMIN⁴ PECK, son of Henry,³ resided in Milford. He was a prominent man. He was in the Revolutionary War, and was Captain of the company from Milford. He married Mary Smith, daughter of Jesse Smith, of Milford.

CHILDREN — FIFTH GENERATION

(186)+Abraham, b. June 29, 1761, (187)+Benjamin, b April 24, 1764; (188) Sarah, b. Nov. 25, 1765, m. Stephen Gunn, and settled in Milford, where she died, leaving the following children Sarah,⁶ who m. Abijah Carrington, Anna,⁶ who m. Rev. Benjamin Fenn, Stephen,⁶ who m. Pamelia Treat, Nathan,⁶ who m Lucretia Fenn, and Susan,⁶ who d unm —(189) Anna, b March 12, 1768, m John Strong, and settled in Milford, where she died. Her children were Nancy,⁶ who m. Joseph Pruden, settled in Georgia, and Selah⁶ Strong, town clerk of Milford in 1867.

[56.] NATHANIEL⁴ PECK, son of Nathaniel,³ resided at first in Newtown, and from there removed to Hinesburgh, Vt., where he died. He married Mary Foot, October 16, 1760.

CHILDREN — FIFTH GENERATION ·

(190)+Elijah, b. Sept 3, 1761; (191) Joel, b March 4, 1764, who was three times married, and left descendants, whom I was unable to trace out sufficiently to give a record of them, (192) Olla, b. March 25, 1765, (193) Ezra, b. April 20, 1770, and, I am told, settled at Hinesburgh, Vt , at first, and from there removed to Potsdam, N. Y , where he died, leaving four sons, who died young, and two daughters.

[60] HETH⁴ PECK, son of Heth,³ married Mary Skidmore, and settled in Newtown. He resided about one mile north of what is now known as Newtown Street.

CHILDREN — FIFTH GENERATION

(194) Amos, who d. unm., and (195)+Elnathan

[64.] AMIEL⁴ PECK, son of Heth,³ settled in Brookfield at an early date. and was, I am told, a Deacon, or Warden of the church for many years. He married Hepzibah Camp.

CHILDREN — FIFTH GENERATION

(196)+Julius, (197) Lemuel, m Amey Sherman; no issue He was the inventor of a corn sheller and fanning mill, which he manufactured quite extensively (198) Chloe, m Joseph Bassett, and settled in Canfield, Ohio, (199) Polly, m Azor Ruggles, and removed to Canfield, (200) Hannah, m. Cyrus Warner; (201) Alice, m. a Bennett.

[66.] SAMUEL[4] PECK, son of HETH,[3] was twice married:
first, to Sarah Skidmore; second, to Sarah Burrett (widow). He
resided in Newtown, where he died, May 12, 1832.

CHILDREN — FIFTH GENERATION

(202)+Isaac, b July 7, 1776; (203) Annis, who m Richard Botsford, (204)
Clarissa, in Benjamin C. Glover; (205)+David, and (206) Joanna, who m.
Gould Curtis.

[67.] AMOS[4] PECK, son of HETH,[3] married Sarah Lobdell,
and resided in Newtown.

CHILDREN — FIFTH GENERATION

(207) Amos, who resided in Newtown, where he died, leaving two daughters, (208) Hannah, d young; (209) Mary, m James B. Fairman, and d in
Newtown, leaving children, (210) Chloe, d young; (211) Andrew, d. young;
(212) Hannah, d. young.

[79.] AARON[5] PECK, son of JOSEPH,[4] resided in Newtown
at first, and from there removed to Sandgate, Vt.

CHILDREN — SIXTH GENERATION

(213)+Joshua, b Sept 9, 1756, (214) Rebecca, b Feb. 18, 1757, (215) Violet, b Feb 1, 1759, (216)+Elias, b Oct 23, 1760; (217) Adoniram, b Aug 1,
1762, (218) Joel, b. Sept 1, 1765, (219) Andrew, b Oct 27, 1769, m Lucinda
Booth His children were (220) *Orlando*[7], (221) *Joel*[7], (222) *Legrandison*[7],
(223) *Sabra*[7]; (224) *Marion*[7], and (225) *George B.*[7]—(226) Susannah, b. July
25, 1770.

[81.] DANIEL[5] PECK, son of JOSEPH,[4] resided in Newtown,
where he died April 3, 1776. His inventory was presented to the
Court of Probate, June 4, 1776 (Danbury Records, B. 3, p. 326).
He married Hannah B. Johnson, December 1, 1761.

CHILDREN — SIXTH GENERATION

(227) Lucy, b. Oct 17, 1762, d June 2, 1764, (228) Lucy, again, b July 23,
1764, (229) Ruana, b July 11, 1766, (230) Samuel, b. Aug. 12, 1768; (231)
Olive, b. March 18, 1771; Zadah, b. July 13, 1773, (232) Abigail, b. March 11,
1776.

[84.] JOHN[5] PECK, son of JOSEPH,[4] resided in Newtown, and
died there, July 21, 1820. He married Emily Burrett, September
3, 1767.

CHILDREN — SIXTH GENERATION

(233)+Rufus, b. March 6, 1768, (234) Grace, b. Feb 8, 1770, d June 1771;
(235) Comfort, b. March 11, 1772-3, m. Oliver Toucey, of Newtown; (236)

Grace, again, b. April 14, 1775, m. Ammon Hall, and settled in Vermont; (237) Lavinia, b March 29, 1780, m Joseph Burritt, (238) Clara, b. Dec 19, 1782, m John Johnson, of Newtown

[85.]   DAVID[5] PECK, son of JOSEPH,[4] married Mary Stillson, and resided in Newtown.

CHILDREN — SIXTH GENERATION

(239) David, m. Prudence Glover. His children are (240) *Winthrop*[7], (241) *Dillison*[7]; and (242) *Mary Ann.*[7]—(243) Hannah, m. Chauncey Botsford, (244) Daniel, m. Sally Ann Sherwood. His children are (245) *Eunice*[7]; (246) *David*[7], (247) *Chauncey B*,[7] the father of David J. Peck,[8] who is a lawyer residing in New Haven, Conn. (248) *Joseph*[7], (249) *Minot*[7], and (250) *Norman*[7], who settled in Monroe, Conn.

[87.]   JABEZ[5] PECK, son of JOHN,[4] resided in Newtown.   He was twice married; first, to Abiah Sanford, July 17, 1764; second, to Mabel Kimburly.*

CHILDREN — SIXTH GENERATION

(251) Amey, b Jan. 30, 1766, (252) Elnathan, b. Oct. 19, 1767, and d at Salsbury, N Y, March 1842, where his son (253) *Alonzo*[7] was residing in 1852, (254) John, b Aug. 1, 1769, (255) Phidema, b Sept 19, 1771, m. Eli Beers, (256) Anne, b May 19, 1773, (257) Daniel, b in 1776, settled in Durham, N Y., where he d in 1811, leaving children   He was a tanner and currier by trade and occupation, (258) Ira, b in 1784, was residing in Ripley, N. Y, in 1865, (259) Burwell, b in 1785, was residing in Durham in 1852. His sons (260) *Henry J*[7] and (261) *William*,[7] were doing business at Coxsackie, N. Y., in 1867; (262) Zenus, d. in Chautauque, N. Y., June 1851, (263) Abby; and (264) Maria.

[88.]   JOSEPH[5] PECK, son of JOHN,[4] resided in Newtown, where he died, May 6, 1796. He was a professor of religion, exemplary and respected. He married Mary Castle.

CHILDREN — SIXTH GENERATION

(265) Joseph, m. Anna Williams, and had ten children, (266) Anson, m. first, Anna Hubbell, second, Laura Sharp, and left three children, (267) Abner, d unm, (268) Sabra, m Dennis Nash, and was residing in Westport, Conn, in 1867, (269) Cyrus, settled in New Durham, N Y., where he d., leaving two children, (270) Abigail, m. Charles Avery, and was supposed to have been drowned while crossing the North River; (271) Russell, m Mary Ralyea His children are (272) *Emeline*[7], (273) *Eliza*[7], (274) *William B*,[7] who was residing at Napierville, Ill., in 1867, (275) *Russell C.*[7], (276) *Richard*[7];

---

* The house in which he resided was standing when I visited the town in 1867.

(277) *Sarah Jane*[7], and (278) *Sabra*.[7]—(279) Reuben, was residing in West-field, N. Y , in 1867, (280) Asahel, is a Methodist clergyman, and was residing in Portland, N Y., in 1867. To his kindness I am indebted for my information in relation to the family. He m. Celestia Tinkcom, and has six children.

[89.]   ASHER[5] PECK, son of JOHN,[4] resided in Newtown. He married Sarah Judson, November 17, 1768.

CHILDREN — SIXTH GENERATION ·

(281) Lemira, b Aug. 5, 1796, (282) Lucinda, b. Dec. 9, 1770; (283) Jeru-sha, b May 9, 1773, (284) John, b. Jan. 3, 1775, (285) Abel, b. June 26, 1776; (286) Judson, b. Jan. 10, 1778; (287) Edmond B , b. April 2, 1784.

[91.]   ISRAEL[5] PECK, son of JOHN,[4] resided in Newtown, where he died February 18, 1821.   He married Deborah Burr for his first wife, and Huldah Lake for his second.

CHILDREN — SIXTH GENERATION ·

(288) Turney, b. Oct. 1776, m. Rebecca Judson, and settled in Newtown. His children were · (289) *Burr*[7], (290) *Fairman*[7]; (291) *Nancy*[7], (292) *Rebecca*[7], (293) *Harry*[7], and (294) *Sylvia*.[7]—(295) Betsey, m James B Fair-man, (296) Oliver, m. Charity Raymon for his first wife, and Polly Sandford for his second.   He d. in Newtown, leaving no issue.

[94.]   ABEL[5] PECK, son of MOSES,[4] settled at Fishkill, N. Y., where he died.   He married Hannah Davis.

CHILDREN — SIXTH GENERATION ·

(297) Moses , (298) David; and (299) Betsey , all settled at Fishkill.

[95.]   ENOS[5] PECK, son of MOSES,[4] resided in Newtown. He was twice married : first, to Sibbel Griffen ; second, to a Mrs. Mar-shall.

CHILDREN — SIXTH GENERATION

(300) Wooster, m Betsey Marshall, and had   (301) *Elizabeth*[7], (302) *Elliott M.*[7], and *Henrietta M*,[7] who m. a Lathrop — (303) Abraham, set-tled in Zoar, a tailor by trade, (304) Arthur S., (305) Harvey, (306) Jerusha, (307) Sarah Ann, (308) Zuba, and (309) Esther, who m. Rufus Sumers, and was residing in Birmingham in 1867.

[99]   HEZEKIAH[5] PECK, son of MOSES,[4] settled at Fishkill, N. Y.

CHILDREN — SIXTH GENERATION ·

(310) Sally , (311) Miah , (312) Thomas and (313) Horace, twins; and (314) Caleb.

[102.]   DAN[5] PECK, son of Moses,[4] settled in Newtown, where he died March 25, 1833.   He married Hannah Peck, No. 149, daughter of Henry Peck.

CHILDREN — SIXTH GENERATION ·

(315) Marcia, (316) Charles, who m Freelove Nash, and had children (317) *Charles*[7], and (318) *Henry* [7] —(319) Hezekiah, d unm , (320) Herman, m. Maria Holly, and had children   (321) *Sylvia M* [7], (322) *Edward B* [7], (323) *Elizabeth*[7], and (324) *Herman H* [7] —(325) Lorin, m. Jane A Lawrence; had children   (326) *Arthur Q* [7], and *Marcia.*[7] —(327) Sylvia, d. unm.

[107.]   NATHAN[5] PECK, son of Moses,[4] settled in Sandgate, Vt., where he died.   He married Cynthia Terrell.

CHILDREN — SIXTH GENERATION

(328) Grandville; (329) Elvira; (330) Nelson, (331) Sally Ann, and (332) Orville.

[110.]   JOHN[5] PECK, son of John,[4] enlisted into the army of the Revolution, and served through the war.   He married Mary Camp, and settled in Litchfield, Conn., where he died December 1831.

CHILDREN — SIXTH GENERATION:

(333) Marquis De L , b Jan. 11, 1791, m. Hannah Judson   His children are (334) *George W* [7], (335) *Mary A.*[7], and (336) *Henry J* ,[7] who m Mary A. Squires, and has two children   (337) *Lottie B.*[9]; and (338) *Henry A* [8] —(339) Anna, b. Jan 12, 1794, m. Joseph Wells , (340) Sarah, b March 4, 1804, d. unm.

[111.]   JOSEPH[5] PECK, son of John,[4] married Hannah Lambert, of Milford, Feb. 16, 1778, and settled in Woodbury, where he resided until about 1814, when he removed to Onondaga, N. Y., where he died March 5, 1829.

CHILDREN — SIXTH GENERATION

(341) Nancy, b June 5, 1779, m. a Huntingdon, and settled at Onondaga, N. Y. , (342) Mehitable, b May 3, 1781, m. Judson Morris, and settled in Woodbury, Conn. , (343) Jeremiah, b. Aug 8, 1783, m. Polly Blois, Nov 8, 1804, and settled in Woodbury, where he d. Dec. 1863   His son (344) *Henry H* [7] was residing upon the homestead in 1866. (345) John, b. May 1, 1785 , was a physician, and settled in Burlington, Vt., where he died July 24, 1862   He married Almira C Keyse.   She died Oct. 16, 1842   His children are: (346) *Francis C* ,[7] b Nov 29, 1809, d. March 20, 1813, (347) *John H* ,[7] b Dec 24, 1810; resides in New York, (348) *Julian C P.*,[7] b Dec. 17, 1812, was residing in New York in 1867, (349) *Francis C* ,[7] b Nov. 28, 1814, d Aug 19, 1817; (350) *Samuel C.*,[7] b. May 29, 1816, d. Nov. 3, 1816, (351) *Theodore*

A.,[7] b. Aug 8, 1817; was residing in Watertown, N. Y., in 1867, (352) *George H*,[7] b. Nov. 4, 1819; was residing in San Francisco in 1867; (353) *William W*,[7] b. Jan. 17, 1821, was residing in Schenectady, N. Y., in 1867, (354) *Edward W*,[7] b Jan. 20, 1823, was residing in Burlington, Vt , in 1867, (355) *Henlen M. Y.*,[7] b. Aug. 19, 1825, d Feb. 23, 1827 —(356) Sarah, b. May 16, 1787, m. a Mr. Hooker, and was residing in Jersey City in 1866, a widow.

[112.] JEREMIAH[5] PECK, son of JEREMIAH,[4] resided in Watertown, Conn.   He was twice married; first, to Miss —— Scott, by whom he had three children, none of whom survived infancy; second, to Lois Bunnell.

CHILDREN — SIXTH GENERATION :

(356) Lois Ann, who d unm , and (357) Content, who m. Benoni Barney, and had by him eight children.

[116.] SIMEON[5] PECK, son of JEREMIAH,[4] married Sarah Merriman, and settled in Watertown, Conn.

CHILDREN — SIXTH GENERATION

(358) Isaac, b. in 1782, who was twice married first, to Roxy Bryan; second, to Mary Maltby, and had three sons (359) *Jeremiah*[7], (360) *Frederick*[7]*;* and (361) *Lemuel.*[7] —(362) Abigail, b. in 1783, m. John Seymore, and settled in Weymouth, Ohio; (363)+Benjamin, b Dec 27, 1785.

[119.] PHINEAS[5] PECK, son of PHINEAS,[4] settled in Woodbridge, Conn.   He entered the service in the war of the Revolution, and was taken prisoner and confined in the Old Sugar House in New York, where so many perished through the inhumanity of the British.   He was reduced, I am told, to a mere skeleton, but finally released and brought home by men upon a hand litter from New York.   He soon after died.

CHILDREN — SIXTH GENERATION ·

(364) Eunice, who m. Nicholas Beecher; (365) Elizabeth, who m. Dr. Jared Munson, and (366) Lucy, who m. Jerry Riggs.

[120] SAMUEL F.[5] PECK, son of PHINEAS,[4] married Elizabeth Platt, and settled in Woodbridge, where he died May 1834. She died June 1841, in her 93d year.

CHILDREN — SIXTH GENERATION ·

(367) Elizabeth, b Aug. 5, 1774, m Camp Newton, (368) Sarah, b. Feb 20, 1776, m. Edward Hine; (369)+Phineas, b Jan. 2, 1778 , (370) Huldah, b. Jan· 27, 1780; and (371)+Samuel, b. Feb 15, 1781.

[122.] ZENUS[5] PECK, son of PHINEAS,[4] married Hannah Treat, and resided in Woodbridge.

CHILDREN — SIXTH GENERATION

(372)+Jerre; (373) Mary, (374) Zenus, and (375) Hannah.

[130.] SAMUEL[5] PECK, son of SAMUEL,[4] married Mehitable Smith, July 7, 1762, and settled in Milford, where he died June 12, 1822. She died January 1826, aged 85 years. He was captain of a company from Milford in the war of the Revolution, and a very prominent man.

CHILDREN — SIXTH GENERATION

(376) Mehitable, b. Feb. 13, 1762-3, m Abraham Clark, of Milford, and d. Dec. 1851; (377) Samuel, b. Oct 19, 1764, d. Nov. 28, 1841. He was a shipmaster. (378) Ephraim, b. Nov 19, 1766. He was a draper and tailor. His children were (379) *Ephraim*[7], (380) *Egbert*[7]; (381) *Dumond*[7]; (382) *Catharine*[7]; and (383) *Rachel*[7] —(384) Hezekiah, b. Dec. 25, 1768, d. Jan. 13, 1846; was a farmer, and resided in Milford His children were (385) *Sarah*[7], (386) *Hezekiah*[7], and (387) *Benjamin B.*[7] —(388)+Nathan, b. March 20, 1771, (389)+Michael, b. Aug. 12, 1773, (390) Dan, b Nov. 28, 1775, resided in Milford. His children were (391) *Dan*[7]; (392) *Isaac*[7]; (393) *Hezekiah*[7], (394) *Samuel*[7]; (395) *Eliza*[7], and (396) *Hannah*[7], and perhaps others.

[131.] MICHAEL[5] PECK, son of SAMUEL,[4] resided in Milford.

CHILDREN — SIXTH GENERATION ·

(397) David, d. in Milford; (398) James, d. at sea, (399) Cole, d. at Oxford; (400) Anthony, d. at sea; (401) Michael, d. at Darien, Ga., (402) Henry, (403) Sybel, (404) Esther; and (405) Sarah.

[135.] JOHN[5] PECK, son of JOB,[4] married Mary Brooks, May 8, 1770, and settled in Stratford, Conn.

CHILDREN — SIXTH GENERATION ·

(406) David, b July 19, 1771, d Jan. 9, 1773; (407) Mary, b. Nov. 15, 1773; (408) John, b. Feb. 26, 1776, d Dec. 13, 1777; (409) John, b. Aug. 9, 1778, (410) Elizabeth, b. Dec. 22, 1781, d Jan. 30, 1785, (411) David B., b May 16, 1783, d. Feb. 4, 1785, (412) Betty, b. Nov. 13, 1785; (413) William, b. Feb. 25, 1788.

[136.] JUDSON[5] PECK, son of JOB,[4] resided in Stratford. He married Mary Blackman, December 20, 1775.

CHILDREN — SIXTH GENERATION :

(414) Sally, b. Sept. 19, 1776, (415) Dorotha, b. April 24, 1779; (416) Judson, b. Feb. 27, 1782, d. July 29, 1782, (417) Judson, again, b. Sept. 13, 1783; (418) Anna, b Aug. 13, 1786, and (419) Polly, b. Dec. 6, 1789.

[137.]   JOB[5] PECK, son of JOB,[4] resided in Stratford. He married Martha Wells, November 17, 1777. He died February 5, 1797; she September 15, 1798.

CHILDREN — SIXTH GENERATION ·

(420) James, b. June 21, 1778, m Abigail Sturges, and d. at Sullivan, N Y, Sept 22, 1832 His children are· (421) *Joel S*[7], (422) *Sophia*[7], (423) *Samuel*[7], (424) *James*[7], (425) *Martha Ann*[7], and (426) *Sarah P.*[7] —(427)+Phineas, b July 7, 1780; (428) Johanna, b Oct 9, 1782, (429) Lewis, b. June 24, 1785, m Hannah White, and lived and died in Stratford, (430) Joseph, b May 9, 1789 He was residing in New Lisbon, N Y, in 1866 His children are (431) *George F*[7], and (432) *Cornelius E.*[7] —(433) Charles, b Oct. 7, 1791, d. in Brooklyn, N Y, Dec 20, 1860, where his son (434) *Charles*[7] was residing in 1861 —(435)+John Wells, b. April 23, 1794, and Lewis, again, b. Oct. 3, 1796.

[138.]   JOSIAH[5] PECK, son of JOB,[4] resided in Stratford. He married Helen Birdseye, November 9, 1774.

CHILDREN — SIXTH GENERATION

(436) Thaddeus, b Aug 23, 1775, resided in Stratford, where he left descendants, (437) Josiah, b Nov 19, 1777, d Dec 26, 1785, (438) Helen, b. Jan 26, 1780, d Jan. 28, 1783, (439) Birdseye, b Jan. 23, 1784, m Francis Ann Gilbert, and d about 1813, leaving one son (440) *Nathan B*,[7] who was residing in Cincinnatus, N. Y, in 1866 —(441) Josiah, b. Feb 26, 1786, d in the West Indies, (442) Allis, b. Aug 9, 1788, m. Angus Curtis.

[146.]   CAPT. ZALMON[5] PECK, son of HENRY,[4] resided in Newtown, where he died April 21, 1812 He was twice married· first, to Zilpha Hard; second, to Mrs. Sarah Booth (widow).

CHILDREN — SIXTH GENERATION

(443)+Zera S, b Dec 18, 1752, (444)+Ezekiel, b. March 8, 1786.

[150.]   ANDREW[5] PECK, son of HENRY,[4] settled at first in Newtown, where he resided until 1813, when he removed to New Milford, since a part of Bridgewater, Conn. He married Lucinda Terrell. He died August 25, 1826; she September 5, 1848, aged 73 years.

CHILDREN — SIXTH GENERATION

(445) Mercy, b April, 25, 1795, m. Sylvester Sherman, and was residing in Bridgewater in 1867, (446)+Sherman, b March 8, 1797, (447) Amey, b Oct 4, 1799, m. Daniel Merwin Nov. 26, 1815. He d Nov 17, 1861, aged 73 years (448) George, b Nov. 5, 1802, resides in Southbury, (449) Sally, b Jan 17, 1807, m Hiram Keeler, Dec 1826, and settled in Bridgewater; (450) Minerva,

b June 3, 1810, m Daniel Keeler Jan 3, 1831, and settled in Bridgewater; (451) John, of New Milford, b April 15, 1813, and Maria, b Jan 19, 1816, m Andrew Weller, and resides in Roxbury, Conn.

[151.] SAMUEL⁵ PECK, son of HENRY,⁴ resided in Newtown. He married Nancy Malory. He was a joiner by trade.

CHILDREN — SIXTH GENERATION :

(452) Julia, m Philo Sample, and d in New Jersey, and (453) Philo, who settled in New Jersey, where he died, leaving two children

[152.] SHADRACH⁵ PECK, son of EPHRAIM,⁴ married Ruth Sharp, January 1, 1777, and resided in Newtown.

CHILDREN — SIXTH GENERATION

(454) Truman, b May 25, 1778, m Anna B Winton, and settled in Monroe, Conn His children were (455) *Polly*⁷, (456) *Emeline*⁷, and (457) *Preston* ⁷ — (458) Anna, b April 20, 1784, m Samuel Staples, (459) + John S., b March 5, 1787

[153] ENOCH⁵ PECK, son of EPHRAIM,⁴ married Mary Graves, and resided in Newtown. He died August 7, 1814.

CHILDREN — SIXTH GENERATION

(460) Ethel, who became a clergyman, settled at Vergennes, Vt , (461) Amos, (462) Cyrenus, (463) William, (464) Enoch, (465) Mabel, (466) Annis, and (467) Mary Ann.

[155] NATHAN⁵ PECK, son of EPHRAIM,⁴ married Huldah Fabrique, and settled in Newtown, where she died October 29, 1812. He died May 1, 1816.*

CHILDREN — SIXTH GENERATION

(468) John B., b Sept 15, 1776, settled at Wilmington, N C , where he died Nov 1808, leaving a daughter (469) *Polly* ⁷ — (470) Lewis, b July 26, 1778, d in childhood, (471) Charles, b Oct 26, 1780, d unm , (472) Sarah, b. March 18, 1783, m Daniel Morehouse, (473) Louis F , b Aug. 21, 1785, settled and died in North Carolina, where he was a celebrated physician, (474) Jared B , b Feb 15, 1788, m Maria A Northrop. He also removed to North Carolina about 1810, but returned in 1815, and settled in New York City, where he was superintendent of the Orphan Asylum. He was a member of the Sunday School committee for visiting the Sabbath schools of the city, and also an Elder in the Church He was residing in New Haven in 1867, a Deacon in the Chapel Street Congregational Church. His children are (475)

---

* The house in which he resided is now gone, and a new one occupies its place

Matilda[7], (476) *Angouleme*[7]; and (477) *Emeline* [7] — (478) Martha, b. April 23, 1791, m Lewis Beecher; (479) Anna, b Jan. 15, 1794, a son, b. Aug 23, 1797, d in infancy

[156.]   ELI[5] PECK, son of EPHRAIM,[4] settled at first in Newtown, but removed from there to Derby, where he died.   He married Hannah Lacy.

CHILDREN — SIXTH GENERATION

(480) Lacy, (481) Eleazer; (482) Daniel L.; and others.

[157.]   LEVIRUS[5] PECK, son of EPHRAIM,[4] married Anna Wheeler, June 24, 1778.   He resided in Newtown, where he died June 14, 1810.*

CHILDREN — SIXTH GENERATION

(483) + Thomas W., b Sept 9, 1779; (484) Polly, b Nov. 18, 1781, m. Jeremiah Beers, (485) Richard, b July 28, 1786, d June 1851, unm.

[159.]   ISAAC[5] PECK, son of EPHRAIM,[4] resided in Newtown, where he died, February 1855.   He married Lucy Ferris.   She died August 1834, aged 73 years.

CHILDREN — SIXTH GENERATION :

(486) Peter F , b July 24, 1779, d. Dec 20, 1855, (487) Polly Ann, b. Oct. 17, 1780, m. Ebenezer Griffin, and d. July 10, 1830; (488) Louisa, b Feb 16, 1782, d Jan 25, 1807, (489) Fanny, b Jan. 22, 1784, m David Blackman; (490) Philo, b. July 7, 1787, d. Oct 12, 1822, (491) Isaac, b May 17, 1788, d. May 23, 1788, (492) Levi, b April 25, 1790, d Jan 15, 1795, (493) Isaac, again, b March 24, 1793, d. April 6, 1793, (494) Lucy, b. Aug. 28, 1794, m. Gershom Dimon, (495) Levi, again, b April 29, 1797, (496) Isaac, again, b. June 22, 1800.

[161.]   EPHRAIM[5] PECK, son of EPHRAIM,[4] at first settled in Newtown, but from there removed to Woodbury about 1792, where he died.   He was twice married: first, to Elizabeth B. Hall, October 5, 1785; second, to Susan Tuttle, February 16, 1825.

CHILDREN — SIXTH GENERATION

(497) Benjamin C , b May 29, 1786   He was residing in Woodbury in 1867 his children are   (498) *Eleazar*[7], (499) *Preston D.*[7], (500) *Charles B* [7], (501) *Sally Jane*[7], (502) *Marietta*[7], (503) *Fanny*[7], (504) *Betsey*[7], and (505) *David*[7] — (506) Ephraim B , b. May 30, 1790, lived and died in Woodbury   His children are   (507) *Henry W* [7], (508) *Alfred C.*[7], (509) *Robert*[7], (510) *Betsey Ann*[7],

---

* The house in which he resided was occupied by his son Thomas W when I visited him in 1867

and (511) *George H*[7] —(512) Eliza, b Aug. 13, 1804, (513) George, b. May 20, 1809, was residing at Greenwich, Ohio, 1866

[162.] GEORGE[5] PECK, son of GIDEON,[4] removed from Newtown to Sandgate, Vt., where he died March 23, 1831. He married Ann Peck, No. 96, daughter of Moses. She died March 9, 1844.

CHILDREN — SIXTH GENERATION

(514)+Clark, b May 15, 1778, (515) Seth, b Oct 24, 1779, m Anna Northrop, and removed to Hampton, N. Y, where he died Dec. 5, 1858, (516) Betty, b. March 21, 1781, d Aug. 15, 1849, (517) Hezekiah, b June 15, 1782, m. and settled at Marietta, Ohio, (518) Thomas, b April 1, 1786, m Mindwell Lacy, and settled in Wisconsin, where he died July 14, 1865, (519) Amarillis, b March 23, 1789, m William Lakin, settled in Ohio, and d Oct 1865, (520) Mary Ann, b March 7, 1784, d Feb 17, 1790; (521) Josiah, b. July 29, 1791, d. Aug 16, 1791, (522) Eli, b March 6, 1794, d. July 19, 1798, (523) Smith, b. Feb 15, 1797, d. July 14, 1798.

[163.] OLIVER[5] PECK, son of GIDEON,[4] married Lucy Sickles, and resided in Newtown. He died April 21, 1810; she died February 1860, aged 94 years. His will is recorded at Danbury, B. 10, p. 336.

CHILDREN — SIXTH GENERATION

(524) Oliver, supposed to have settled at Bethel, N Y, (525) Mary, d. young; (526) Amarillis, d. unm., (527) Abiah, m Joseph Crowfoot, (528) Zachariah W, d unm, (529) Lucy Ann, m Rufus Shepherd, (530) Joseph S., m. Sarah Brownell, (531) Mary Ann, d unm; (532) Carloss, m Abigail Clark, and settled in Bloomingdale, Mich, (533) Carlton, d young; (534) Betsey Ann, b July 13, 1808, m Joseph (No. 248), son of David, for her first husband, and Grandville P. Glover for her second, (535) Currence, b. July 30, 1810, m. Nathan Burr

[164.] LEVI[5] PECK, son of GIDEON,[4] settled in Southbury, Conn, where he died, August 8, 1836. He married, first, Mercy Peck (No. 148), daughter of Henry; second, Eunice Erwin.

CHILDREN — SIXTH GENERATION

(536) Henry, b Jan 27, 1793, m. Polly Ann Percival, and d. in Newtown, July 17, 1843, leaving two children (537) *George*[7], and (538) *Edwin*[7] —(539) Mercy, b. Nov. 30, 1795, m. Cyrus Sherman, and was residing in Woodbury in 1867, (540) Samuel B, b June 11, 1800, d. July 15, 1856, m Julia E Fairweather, of Newtown, where she was residing in 1867 His children were (541) *George B.*[7], (542) *Sarah J.*[7], (543) *Julia E*[7], and (544) *Edward S.*[7] —(545) Nancy, b. Nov 15, 1803, (546) Russell, b. Sept. 6, 1805, d. March 10, 1807, (547) Mary, b. July 19, 1808, d. Sept. 6, 1808, (548) George S., b. Nov. 28, 1814, d. Dec. 22, 1828.

[167.]   GIDEON[5] PECK, son of GIDEON,[4] resided in New-town, where he died, March 2, 1824.   He married Betsey Brisco, daughter of John Brisco.   She was living in 1867, being in her 90th year.

CHILDREN — SIXTH GENERATION:

(549) George, who m. Polly Peck (No. 455), daughter of Shadrach Peck, and d in California, from injuries received by being thrown from a wagon, (550) Henry, m Emily Sherman, and settled in Seymour, Conn , (551) Le-grand, m. Laura Dimon, and was residing in Newtown in 1867, (552) Clark, d. in Rio de Janeiro, unm , (553) Polly, m Harmon Parmalee; (554) Ann S., m. Russell Crowfoot, (555) Betsey, m Andrew Northrop, (556). Laura, m a Gilbert, (557) Gideon S , was residing in California in 1867, (558) Lois, m. Edmond Fairchild, (559) Charles, settled in Bethel, Conn , where he still resides   His children are   (560) *Sidney S.*[7] , (561) *Horace*[7], (562) *Samuel T*[7]*;* and (563) *Gideon* [7]

[168.]   ABNER[5] PECK, son of GIDEON,[4] married Jane Bots-ford, and resided in Newtown, where he died, August 16, 1844.

CHILDREN — SIXTH GENERATION:

(564) Polly, d unm ; (565) George C., m. Ann Tomlinson.   His children are   (566) *John F.*[7], (567) *Gideon*[7], (568) *Homer*[7], (569) *Cornelius*[7], (570) *Abby*[7], and (571) *Harriet*.[7] —(572) Jane Ann, m. Lewis Booth

[180.]   DAVID[5] PECK, son of HENRY,[4] settled in Brookfield, where he died, April 23, 1843.   He was a soldier in the war of the Revolution, and served under Washington.   Although the hard-ships and privations he suffered impaired his health, he was an in-dustrious and prosperous farmer, and lived for many years to enjoy the fruits of the freedom and independence of his country, for which he fought.   He married Isabella Nichols, of Newfield.

CHILDREN — SIXTH GENERATION:

(573) Jesse L., b. Oct 31, 1777, m. Annis Sherman, and d. at an early age, leaving one child, (574) Rachel, b Dec. 8, 1779, m. Zalmon Peck (No. 69); (575) Ira, b. April 7, 1782, m. Sally Kirtland, of Bridgeport, Conn , where he died.   He had three children   (576) *Olivia*[7]*;* (577) *David*[7], and (578) *Sarah Ann.*[7] —(579) Sarah, b. Oct 20, 1787, m. first, Dr. Levi Beardslee, second, Andrew S Darrow, and was residing in Watertown, Conn , in 1866.   (580)+ Michael, b. July 3, 1789; (581) Fowler, b. Aug 29, 1791, d. in infancy, (582) Fowler, again, b. March 2, 1793, m. Mary Turner, and settled in Brookfield, where he resided until about 1855, when he removed to Dement, Ill , where he was living in 1866.   His daughter (583) *Janette A* ,[7] to whose kindness I am indebted for my information, m. George Payne, and was also residing in Dement in 1866.   (584) Amarillis, b. Dec. 25, 1795, m. John T. Hawley, of

Monroe, Conn., no issue; (585) Marshall G., b. March 3, 1798. He was twice married first, to Jenette A. Jones, second, to Narcissa Benedict, by whom he had children

[182] JOHN⁵ PECK, son of HENRY,⁴ resided in Brookfield, where he was an extensive farmer. He was an excellent citizen, a worthy member of the church, generous and benevolent. He was twice married: first, to Amarillis Peck (No. 171), daughter of Gideon; second, to Clarina Wheeler. His first wife died December 16, 1785. His second, November 7, 1835. He died February 9, 1839.

CHILDREN — SIXTH GENERATION

(586)+John A., b. Dec. 9, 1785, and (587) Amarillis, b. Dec. 4, 1787, d. Jan. 11, 1794.

[184.] HENRY⁵ PECK, son of HENRY,⁴ resided in Brookfield. He was an excellent farmer, enterprising and industrious. He was a prominent man in the town, holding various public offices. He took a leading interest in education and in the improvement of society generally, and was highly esteemed in the community in which he resided for his social qualities, benevolence and kindness. He married Hannah Northrop, May 26, 1791. He died August 29, 1834. She July 26, 1827.

Henry Peck

CHILDREN — SIXTH GENERATION ·

(588) Hannah, b March 24, 1792, m. Elias Sturdivant, of Bridgeport, March 19, 1812, by whom she had five children *Henry L Sturdivant*, of Bridgeport, is her son She d May 5, 1860. Her husband, Nov. 13, 1861 (589) Henry L., b. May 4, 1797, was a merchant in New York City for some time From

Henry L Peck

there he returned to Brookfield, where he continued in the mercantile business for over thirty years, and became wealthy He was an influential citizen, a member of the Congregational church, and one of the leading temperance men of the town He m. Elizabeth Smith, of Brookfield, Oct 19, 1828. His children were. (590) *Henry,*⁷ who d. young; (591) *Harriet E*⁷, and (592)

Henry S,[7] who succeeds him in business —(593) Hermon V., b Dec 22, 1800. He d. a Christian, in 1831, unm., (594) Hiram N , b Oct. 19, 1804 , was a successful merchant in New York, of the firm of H. N. Peck & Co , importers of Russian goods He was a member of the church, and a Sabbath-school teacher, and Superintendent for many years. (595) Harriet, b. Jan. 16, 1807,

m. William G. Smith, of Newtown, Aug. 30, 1830. Mr. Smith d. May 20, 1835. She was residing in Brooklyn, N. Y., in 1867. Her children are *Henry B*[7] and *William P.*,[7] commission merchants, of New York, and *George B.*,[7] who d. June 25, 1835. — (596) Henrietta, b. Dec 4, 1809, m. Benjamin M. Starr, of Brookfield, Sept. 9, 1832, where they were residing in 1867. Their daughter *Elizabeth H*,[7] m. Aaron Williams, of Hartford, Conn. (597) Hetta Ann, b. March 22, 1814, d. unm.

To Mrs. Starr, and her sister, Mrs. Smith, I am under many obligations for their kindness and assistance.

[185.]   AMOS[5] PECK, son of Henry,[4] resided in Brookfield. Although of feeble health from his youth, he was an industrious and good farmer, kind and obliging, and much respected. He married Lucy Blackman, of Newtown, November 27, 1792. He died March 23, 1835. She October 24, 1855.

CHILDREN — SIXTH GENERATION

(598) Betsey, b. March 1, 1795, m. Benjamin Hawley, by whom she has nine children, (599) Maria, b. July 6, 1797, d. Jan. 29, 1864, (600) Amos G., b. April 5, 1800; was residing in Brookfield, unm., in 1866.

[186.]   ABRAHAM[5] PECK, son of Benjamin,[4] resided in Milford.

CHILDREN — SIXTH GENERATION ·

(601)+Abraham, b. Jan 2, 1786, (602) Amey, who m. David Curtis; and (603) Sally, who m. David Camp.

[187.]   BENJAMIN[5] PECK, son of Benjamin,[4] resided in Milford. He married Nancy Buckingham, daughter of Enoch Buckingham, of Huntington, Conn.

CHILDREN — SIXTH GENERATION :

(604)+Cornelius B., b. Jan. 31, 1800; (605) Benjamin, b. Aug. 1, 1803, m. Abigail Fowler, daughter of Joseph Fowler, of Milford. His children are: (606) *Sarah A*,[7] m Albert Baldwin, and (607) *Susan*,[7] unm. in 1866. —(608) Nancy, m. Erastus Clark, of Milford; no issue.

[190.] ELIJAH[5] PECK, son of NATHANIEL,[4] removed from Newtown to Hinesburgh, Vt., where he died, September 29, 1843. He was twice married: first, to Mehitable Hurlburt; second, to Sally Morgan. His first wife was born March 11, 1757, and died April 5, 1810. His second wife was born April 12, 1772, and died April 22, 1850.

CHILDREN — SIXTH GENERATION

(609)+Eli, b. May 25, 1782; (610)+Zera, b. Oct. 29, 1784; (611) Mary Ann, b. Jan. 17, 1787, m. John Eldridge, and settled in Hinesburgh, where she d. June 1, 1852, leaving five children; (612) Hannah, b. Sept. 2, 1790, m. George Dudley, settled in Hinesburgh, where she d. Nov. 1, 1860, leaving one child, a daughter; (613) Olly, b. Oct. 9, 1792, m. Lyman Clark, settled in Hinesburgh, and d. June 1, 1824, leaving no issue; (614) Mabel, to whom I am indebted for my information, was b. in 1813, and was residing in Charlotte, Vt., in 1867, unm.

[195.] ELNATHAN[5] PECK, son of HETH,[4] settled upon the homestead, where he died in 1821. He was twice married: first, to Jerusha Blackman; second, to Sarah Merwin, formerly Sarah Beers.

CHILDREN — SIXTH GENERATION :

(615) Amos G., b. in 1793, m. Eunice Botsford, of Newtown, where he was residing in 1867. His only child, (616) *Charlotte J.*,[7] b April 2, 1829, d. May 22, 1856, unm.

[196] JULIUS[5] PECK, son of AMIEL,[4] married Sarah Dunning, of Warren, Conn., and settled in Sharon. He died in 1823, aged 58 years. She died August 28, 1842, aged 72 years.

CHILDREN — SIXTH GENERATION .

(617) —— ——; (618) Polly, b. March 5, 1796, m. a Mr. Cathcart, and d. in Michigan, (619) Amiel, b. Dec. 16, 1798, m. Rebecca Dunbar, and was residing in Johnsonville, Ohio, in 1867. He had two daughters (620) *Sarah*[7]; and (621) *Mary*.[7] —(622) Betsey, b April 27, 1800; was unm. in 1867, and residing in Sharon, Conn ;(623) Lemuel, b. July 26, 1802, was unm., and residing in Sharon in 1867, (624) Sally, b. Sept. 17, 1804; was residing in Sharon, and unm , in 1867, (625) Amanda, b Nov. 24, 1806, m. Lyman Warner, of Brookfield, and d March 29, 1832; (626) Harriet, b. Jan. 10, 1809, m. and d. leaving

children; (627) Julius B., b. Dec 7, 1811; settled in Waverly, Ill , (628) Cyrenus H , b March 2, 1814, and was residing in Brookfield in 1867. He m. Abigail Blake His children are (629) *Sarah J.*[7], (630) *Edgar*[7], (631) *Charles L*[7], (632) *Carrie L*[7], and (633) *Lemuel*,[7] who d. at Chantillary, Va , in the United States Service.

[202.] ISAAC[5] PECK, son of SAMUEL,[4] lived and died in Newtown. He married Aurelia Botsford.

CHILDREN — SIXTH GENERATION

(634) Jabez, b. Dec 10, 1804, m. Henrietta Jarvis. His children are (635) *Charles A*[7], (636) *Elizabeth J.*[7]; (637) *Albert W.*[7], and (638) *Nelson J.*,[7] who died in the service of his country. —(639) Harriet, b. Feb. 4, 1807, (640) Robert S , b. March 1, 1814, was three times married first, to Abigail Booth; second, to Mary Lake , third, to Elizabeth Curtis. He d. in Newtown. (641) Sarah E., b. Dec. 24, 1827.

[205] DAVID[5] PECK, son of SAMUEL,[4] resided in Newtown. He married, first, Rebecca Beers; second, Harriet Booth.

CHILD — SIXTH GENERATION

(642) Simeon B ; resides in Newtown. He m , for his first wife, Caroline Curtis , and for his second, Elizabeth Peck, widow of Robert S His children are (643) *Abner B* ,[7] of Montgomery, Ala.; (644) *Henry J.*,[7] deceased , and (645) *David C* ,[7] who resides in Newtown.

[213] JOSHUA[6] PECK, son of AARON,[5] settled in Jay, N. Y., where he died, in the 93d year of his age. He married Rachel M. Mallory.

CHILDREN — SEVENTH GENERATION

(646) Parrilla, b Oct 14, 1782; (647) Philo, b Sept 14, 1784, (648) Phodima, b Feb 8, 1786, (649) David, b Nov 26, 1788, m Ruth Hamlin, and resides in Jay, N. Y His children are . (650) *Norman*[8], (651) *Nelson*[8], (652) *Almira*[8], (653) *Alvira*[8], (654) *Mary A*[8], (655) *Violet A*[8], (656) *Polly*[8], and (657) *Armenia.*[8] —(658) Joel, b. Feb 14, 1791, (659) Lyman, b Feb 27, 1793, (660) Andrew, b April 16, 1795, (661) Thomas, b June 27, 1798, m Louisa Arnold, and resides in Wilmington, N Y. His children are (662) *Louisa*[8], (663) *Chester*[8], (664) *Scott*[8], (665) *Caroline*[8], (666) *Harriet*[8], (667) *Jane*[8], (668) *Levi*[8], (669) *Martha*[8], (670) *Phebe*[8], (671) *Esther*[8], and (672) *Joel*[8] —(673) Alvah, b. April 2, 1801, m Dorothy Hathaway, and resides in Jay, N. Y. His children are (674) *Dillavan*[8]; (675) *Sybil*[8], (676) *Joshua*[8], (677) *Ebenezer*[8]; (678) *Lyman*[8], (679) *Esther*[8], (680) *Phodima*[8], (681) *Gibbs*[8], (682) *Marinda*[8], (683) *Caroline*[8], and (684) *Daniel.*[8] —(685) Polly, b Jan 8, 1804.

[216.] ELIAS[6] PECK, son of AARON,[5] settled at Shandaken, N. Y., where he died, December 1846. He married, for his first

wife, Patience Sanford; for his second, Obedience Sanford; and for his third, Rachel Winey.

CHILDREN — SEVENTH GENERATION:

(686) Betsey; (687) Serenus, (688) John; (689) Polly, (690) Peter; (691) Jacob, (692) Garret, (693) Sally, (694) Daniel, (695) Abigail; (696) Abraham, and (697) John, 2d. Abigail, to whom I am indebted for my information, m. Jeremiah Shaw, and resides in Shandaken.

[233.] RUFUS[6] PECK, son of JOHN,[5] married Sally Hall, of Newtown, Conn., and removed to Streetsborough, Ohio, where he died, March 6, 1848.

CHILDREN — SEVENTH GENERATION:

(698) Chloe, b. March 1800, m. Abel Dibble; (699) Lyman W., b Dec. 26, 1801, m Eliza Cummings, Dec. 26, 1826, and d. in Streetsborough, Aug. 9, 1865. His children are (700) *Rufus H*[8], (701) *William*[8], (702) *Ann Eliza*[8]; (703) *Emma J*[8], and (704) *Lyman L.*[8] —(705) William H., b. July 23, 1803, m. Lydia Bradey, of Lee, Mass, April 10, 1828. His children are (706) *Sarah Ann*,[8] m E S. Bradley, and settled at Cleveland, Ohio; (707) *William S*,[8] m. Elvira V. Gifford, and settled at Wickliffe, Ohio; (708) *Edward R.*,[8] m. Myra A. Talcott, of Starr, Ohio, and (709) *Joseph H.*,[8] of Hudson, Ohio, to whose kindness and assistance I am indebted. He married Miss Nancy W. Gardner, of Cambridge, Mass, July 17, 1867. —(710) John N, b March 15, 1805, m. Sophia Garfield His children are (711) *John B*[8], (712) *William H*[8], (713) *Mary A*[8], and (714) *Sophia*[8] —(715) Eli, b Feb 14, 1808, m. Eliza Judd His children are (716) *Buel*[8], (717) *Julia A.*[8], (718) *Charles*[8], and (719) *Cyrus.*[8] — (720) Nancy P, b July 20, 1809, m. George Bradley, (721) Clara, b. March 1, 1810, m first, Jacob Mayherr; second, John Foster; (722) Sarah Ann, b. May 31, 1812, d unm., (723) Russell, b Oct. 7, 1814, m. Dency Gillett, for his first wife, and Adeline Judd, for his second. His children are (724) *Franklin*[8]; (725) *Andrew*[8], (726) *Mary A*[8], and (727) *Joseph P.*[8] —(728) Henry, b June 17, 1817, m Emeline Jenkins. His children are (729) *Sophia*[8], (730) *Norman*[8], (731) *Arthur*[8], (732) *Helen*[8], (733) *Effie*[8], (734) *Elsie*[8], and (735) *Cora*[8] —(736) Nathan, b July 17, 1819, m Betsey Mellen. His children are (737) *Lydia Ann*[8], (738) *John*[8], (739) *Chloe*[8], (740) *Eugene F.*[8], and (741) *Ida E.*[8] —(742) Horace, b. March 2, 1822, m. Ann Rich His children are. (743) *Leroy*[8], (744) *Amanzo*[8], (745) *Wilbier*[8], and (746) *Albert.*[8]

[363.] BENJAMIN[6] PECK, son of SIMEON,[5] resided in Watertown, where he died, February 1, 1867. He was a very prominent man, and much respected. He was Deacon of the Congregational church for about fifty years. He married Selima Atwood.

CHILDREN — SEVENTH GENERATION:

(747) Elmer N, b Oct. 29, 1810, m Lurena Scovill, and settled in Richland, Mich. His children are. (748) *Ellen L.*[8], (749) *Edgar M.*[8], (750) *Charles S.*[8];

27

(751) *Elmer J*[8]*;* and (752) *Frederic B*[8] —(753) Horace M., b. Aug. 7, 1814,
m Emeline Barrus, and settled in Richland. His children are (754) *Susan
C*[8], (755) *Horace B*[8], (756) *Frances S.*[8], (757) *Herbert N.*[8]*;* (758) *Charles
A*[8], and (759) *Benjamin M.*[8] —(760) Samuel M., of Watertown, Conn , b.
Sept. 22, 1821, m. Marietta Hurd. His children are (761) *Samuel H.*[8], and
(762) *Anna M.*[8]

[369.] PHINEAS[6] PECK, son of SAMUEL,[5] married Anna
Smith, and resided in Woodbridge, Conn., where he died, November 20, 1856. She survived him, and was still living in 1867, in
her 91st year.

(763) Louisa, b. Nov. 1, 1779, m. Lewis Thompson, (764) Phineas E., b.
Nov 3, 1801, m. first, Nancy Beecher; second, Mrs Electa Mood. He resides
in Colebrook, Conn , and has had the following children (765) *Charles E*[8],
(766) *Ann L*[8], (767) *John F.*[8]*;* (768) *Robert D.*[8], (769) *Jerome B*[8], (770)
Robert J[8], (771) *Lewis T*[8], (772) *Nancy E.*[8], (773) *Phineas E.*[8], and (774)
Charles E[8] —(775) William, b Sept. 8, 1803, to whom I am indebted for my
information in relation to his branch of the name, resides in Woodbridge.
He m Elizabeth Tolles, of Bethany. His children are (776) *George C.*[8]*;*
(777) *William W.*[8], (778) *Leonard E.*[8], and (779) *Jane E*[8] —(780) Sidney W.,
b. Aug 30, 1805, d. unm , (781) Silas J , b Feb. 1, 1808, m Adaline M. Bald-
win He resided in Woodbridge. His children are (782) *Phineas E.*[8], (783)
Martha A.,[8] who m. Marcus E. Baldwin, of Woodbridge, now Town Clerk;
and (784) *Henry C*[8] —(785) John, b. Oct. 20, 1810; resides in Woodbridge.
He formerly resided in New Haven, where he was a master builder, doing an
extensive business. He m. first, Jenette Baldwin, second, Louisa Baldwin.
His daughter (786) *Helen F.*,[8] m. Walter B. Peck (No. 584), a descendant of
Henry, of New Haven.

[371.] SAMUEL[6] PECK, son of SAMUEL,[5] married Rebecca
Beecher, and resided in Woodbridge, where he died, February 20,
1865. His wife October 6, 1851, aged 67.

(787) Bennett B , who is a cattle broker of extensive business. His children are (788) *Caroline*[8], (789) *Ruth*[8], (790) *Frances*[8], and (791) *Ella.*[8] —
(792) Caroline E., m. Zalmon Sperry, of Bethany.

[372.] JERRY[6] PECK, son of ZENAS,[5] married Amelia Ford,
and died April 14, 1854.

(793) Aurelius, who m. Ruth Osborn His children are · (794) *Mary M.*[8],
(795) *Jane A.*[8], (796) *Edwin F.*[8], (797) *Eleazer J.*[8]*;* (798) *John T*[8], (799)
Nathan J.[8], (800) *Frederic L*[8]*;* (801) *Sarah A*[8], (802) *Helen O.*[8], (803)
Hiram O.[8], (804) *William J.*[8], and (805) *Daniel A.*[8] —(806) Edwin J., resides

at Indianapolis; is a man of wealth and influence, (807) Mary A., m Nathan P Thomas, (808) Maria, m George Bates, (809) Julia, m. William Fairchild, of Oxford, Conn ; (810) Eunice, m. and d. about 1850.

[388.] NATHAN[6] PECK, son of SAMUEL,[5] lived and died in New Haven. He married Mehitable Tibbats, daughter of Capt. Samuel Tibbats, of Milford, Conn , and granddaughter of Jesse Lambert, who married Ann, daughter of Capt. Henry Peck.

CHILDREN — SEVENTH GENERATION

(811) Wyllys, b July 15, 1797, resides in New Haven, and has been twice married first, to Jennett Alling, daughter of Capt Stephen Alling; second, to Sarah, daughter of Rev Moses Gillett His children are (812) *Elizabeth A*[8], (813) *Harriet E*,[8] d in 1828, (814) *Jenette A*[8], (815) *Harriet E*,[8] again, and (816) *Lucy C*[8] —(817) Nathan, b Sept 2, 1799, d April 27, 1802, (818) Nathan, again, b. Feb 6, 1802. He resides in New Haven, a wealthy and prominent man He is President of the Merchants' National Bank To his kindness I am indebted for much of my information in relation to the New Haven Pecks He m Mary Ann, daughter of Eli Townsend, Esq , of New Haven. His children are (819) *Julia C*,[8] d March 7, 1847, (820) *Robert,*[8] who graduated at Yale College, (821) *Marietta,*[8] d March 13, 1854, (822) *Margaret T*,[8] who m. Dr. Robert Stone, of New York, and (823) *Ellen W*,[8] who d Feb. 23, 1835 —(824) Henry E , b March 18, 1805, graduated at Yale College, in 1823, and was admitted to the bar as a lawyer He afterwards purchased the *Connecticut Journal,* and the *New Haven Chronicle,* which he published for several years He afterwards entered into the West India trade, with his brothers He was a Representative from New Haven for several years He was also in the Senate, of which body he was President, in 1851 and 1852 He m Elizabeth Sheldon, daughter of Dr Elisha Sheldon, of Troy, N Y He d May 6, 1858 His children were (825) *Mary H*[8], (826) *Samuel S*[8], (827) *Phebe W*[8], and (828) *Henry E*,[8] who d in the Confederate prison at Millens, Nov. 1863 —(829) Caroline, m Rev John Churchill, of Woodbury, Conn

[389] MICHAEL[6] PECK, son of SAMUEL,[5] resided in Milford, and was a carpenter and joiner by trade. He married Mary Marshall, January 1, 1797. He died December 27, 1861.

CHILDREN — SEVENTH GENERATION .

(830) Jonathan M , b Oct. 12, 1799, settled at Augusta, Ga His children are (831) *Julia*[8], (832) *Cordelia H*[8], (833) *Martha A*[8], (834) *Abigail*[8], and (835) *James*[8] —(836) Maria, b. Oct 12, 1801, (837) Elnathan, b Aug 11, 1803. He settled in New Britain, where he was one of the first to engage in the manufactory of hardware. He continued in the business until his decease He removed to New Haven about 1860, where his sons are still engaged in business. He d Dec 28, 1865. His children are (838) *Henry F*[8], (839) *Charles,*[8] of New Britain, a deacon of the church, (840) *Abigail*[8], (841) *Mary J.*[8], (842) *Martha*[8], (843) *John M*[8], (844) *Ann E*[8], and (845) *Oliver D*[8] —

(846) Susan, b. April 23, 1805, (847) Julia, b. Oct 23, 1807; (848) Elisha T., b. Oct 22, 1810; resides in Milford, Conn. His children are (849) *Catharine*[8], (850) *Jonathan*[8], (851) *Catharine*,[8] again, (852) *George T.*[8], (853) *Julia A.*[8], and (854) *Emma L.*[8] —(855) Abigail, b. June 5, 1813.

[427.] PHINEAS[6] PECK, son of Job,[5] was a distinguished clergyman of the Methodist Episcopal church. He died at Watertown, N. Y., April 19, 1836. He married Sallie Pettegrew.

CHILDREN — SEVENTH GENERATION

(856) Augustus J., b. Sept 29, 1805, (857) Betsey A, b June 29, 1807; (858) John P, b Dec. 3, 1809, (859) Warren M, b April 6, 1812, (860) Mary N, b. April 22, 1814, (861) Hannah F., b April 26, 1816, (862) Joseph W, b. April 20, 1818, (863) Sarah, b. April 25, 1820; (864) Phineas, b. April 24, 1823, (865) Phebe S., b. Nov. 16, 1824

[435.] JOHN WELLS[6] PECK, son of Job,[5] settled in Manlius, N. Y., where he was engaged for many years in mercantile pursuits. He was a member of the Methodist Episcopal church, and noted for the interest he felt in the cause of truth and Christianity. He was largely instrumental in the erection of the church at Manlius, and by his exertions and liberal contributions promoted its continued advancement and prosperity. He held the office of steward and class-leader for many years, and was noted for his zeal, prudence and fidelity. The Sunday-school was his peculiar delight. He held the office of Superintendent during the greater part of his life.

All benevolent enterprises found in him a friend. He also took a deep interest in the cause of education. He was for many years trustee and agent of the Oneida Conference Seminary, at Cazenovia. The Genesee Seminary, at Lima, and the Middletown College, were objects of his special interest.

He married Miss Phebe Raynor, daughter of James Raynor, Esq., of Cazenovia, N. Y., November 3, 1819. He died at Manlius, September 3, 1847. She November 13, 1854.

CHILDREN — SEVENTH GENERATION

(866) John J, now a Major General, b. Jan 4, 1821; (867) C Lewis, b June 26, 1822, d. July 30, 1823, (868) Phebe A, to whom I am indebted for my information in relation to the family, b. Feb 12, 1825, (869) Charles H., b. March 30, 1835. He was a merchant, and d. at Newbern, N. C, Oct. 9, 1864.

Gen. John J. entered the United States Military Academy in 1839, and graduated eighth in the large class of 1843, a brevet 2d Lieutenant of Artillery. His life has been an active one, and his military career brilliant and honorable.

In 1845, he entered the army of Gen. Taylor, with Duncan's Flying Artillery, and continued in the service through the Mexican war.

The part he acted, and the estimation in which his services were held, may be learned in the following extract from a letter of Gen. Worth to the Hon. Erastus Corning, John Van Buren, and others, dated City of Mexico, December 8, 1847:

"I have desired my young and gallant friend, Lieut. Peck, to hand you this, and beg to commend him to your consideration and kind attention. You will find the name and services of this officer in an official account of every battle, save one, from the commencement of this war to the conquest of the basin, as the associate of Duncan or Smith. He is of our State, and worthy of it."

For his gallant and meritorious conduct, he was honored with the brevet rank of Captain and Major.

On his return from the war, his fellow-citizens tendered him a public dinner, and presented him a sword, with the following inscription upon it:

Presented to

MAJOR J J PECK,

By the citizens of Manlius, as a testimonial of respect for his gallant and
meritorious conduct in the battles of Palo Alto, Resaca de la Palma,
Monterey, Vera Cruz, Cerro Gordo, Contreras, Churubusco,
Molino del Rey, Chepultepec, Causeway and Gate
of San Cosme and City of Mexico.

This was a record that a young man surely might well feel proud of.

He continued in the United States service until 1853, when he resigned his commission, and retired from the army, to enjoy a less arduous and more quiet life. He became one of the first movers of the Syracuse and New York Railroad, to which he devoted some time. He was for several years President of the Board of Education. The Hamilton College conferred upon him the honorary degree of A. M.

27*

In 1856, he was the democratic nominee for Congress, and was tendered a renomination in 1858.

On the breaking out of the rebellion, he tendered his service to the government, and the President made him a Brigadier, August 11, 1867. Gen. McClellan asked for his services, and he was with him through the Peninsular campaign, participating in the battles, and rendering important service. His timely arrival at the battle of Williamsburg was said to have saved the day. He assumed the command of the centre, and recovered the battery and ground lost by Hooker. He is highly complimented by Gen. Keyes (Off. Rep., May 14, 1862) for his coolness, excellent judgment, and the admirable dispositions of his forces.

He was promoted, June 24, to the command of Gen. Casey's Division, and July 4, made a Major-General, for his services in the field and his gallant conduct with his commands when under fire. At the battle of Fair Oaks, he had two horses shot under him.

Headley, in reference to one of these, in speaking of him (Vol. 1, p. 428), says: "Peck's horse, while dashing through the fire, received a ball through the neck; the next instant another pierced his flank. Still unhurt, this gallant commander was spurring on, when a cannon ball took off both of the hind legs of his steed; he sank to the ground. Mounting another, he cheered on the troops by his dauntless bearing." At the battle of Malvern Hill, his division occupied the extreme right of the line. In that memorable march to Harrison's Landing, the rear-guard of the whole army fell to his care, and in spite of the enemy he saved the entire trains.

In September, he assumed command of the forces south of the James. His duties here were very arduous, but he performed them with signal ability, meeting with but few losses, and preserving all the great interests intrusted to him.

During his command here, Longstreet besieged Suffolk, with from 30,000 to 40,000 men; but after continuing it from April 10 to May 3, and constructing from eight to ten miles of covered ways and field works, with such noted West Pointers as Hill, Hood, Picket, French and Gannett, to advise with, found himself out-manœuvred, outgeneralled, and foiled in all his operations, and raised the siege in the night, with heavy losses of men and material.

The following extract from a letter written him by Gen. Meade shows the estimation in which his generalship and services were held by men qualified to judge of and appreciate them:

"That, with the limited force under your command, you should have held in check and defeated the designs of such superior numbers, is a fact of which you may well be proud, and is the most practical proof of your own skill and the gallantry of your troops."

In September, 1863, he took command of the Army of North Carolina. Here, it will be remembered, his troops were not idle, and the only disaster which occurred was that at Plymouth (surrender of Gen. Wessels to an overwhelming force), and for this Gen. Peck was never blamed. Had his requests been acceded to when he reported the ram "Albemarle" upon the stocks, the position of things would have been different.

His administration was excellent, saving large sums to the government, breaking up contraband trade, etc. He established a system of schools for whites and blacks, and pushed the colony at Roanoke Island to a success. He did much for the colored race, thrown upon his hands in vast numbers

He was released from his duties here April 25, 1864, and repaired to his home for health. In July, Gen. Dix asked for his assistance, and he was assigned as second in command in the Department of the East, and was for some time upon the Canadian frontier. At the time of the assassination of the President, he was in command of the department, and issued the orders to the military, etc. At the great meeting in Wall Street, N. Y., he paid a high tribute to the memory of the late chief magistrate. At the commemoration of the raising of the flag by Gen. Anderson over Fort Sumter, he was President of the day, and delivered an address at the Academy of Music.

At the conclusion of the war, he returned again to the pursuits of civil life. His residence is at Syracuse, N. Y.

He has been a communicant of the Protestant Episcopal Church many years, and served as Vestryman and Warden of St. Paul's.

He was a delegate to the National Democratic Convention of 1856, and to the Charleston and Baltimore Convention of 1860; and Delegate at Large to the Cleveland Convention of Soldiers and Sailors in 1866. He was tendered a professorship in the Virginia Military Institute in 1850.

He m. Miss Robie H. Loomis, of Syracuse.

His children are   (870) *Loomis Wells*[3] ,   (871) *Duncan Worth*[8] ;   (872) *James*[8] *Kendrick*[8] ,   (873) *Ida Virginia*[8] ,   (874) *Robie Loomis*[8] ,   and (875) *Eunice Mabel* [8]

[443.]   ZERA[6] PECK, son of ZALMON,[5] resided in Brookfield. He was a prominent public man, member of the Legislature, etc. He married Clary Smith, September 10, 1805.

CHILDREN — SEVENTH GENERATION

(876) Ralph B , b in 1866, m. Caroline Merwin, of Brookfield, and settled at Montgomery, Ala , (877) Harriet, b Sept 1, 1810, m William Glover; (878) Sophia, b Jan. 11, 1816, m John Cornwell, and settled in Bridgeport

[444.]   EZEKIEL[6] PECK, son of ZALMON,[5] resides in Newtown.   He has been twice married : first, to Miss Sarah Ann Johnson, March 1802 ; second, to Mrs. Betsey Briscoe, December 29, 1818.

CHILDREN — SEVENTH GENERATION

(879) Zilpha, b. Nov. 10, 1809, m. Alva B Beach, of Newtown, (880) Zalmon S , b May 22, 1812   He resides in Newtown, where he is a prominent public man, and has been Postmaster for many years   To his kindness I am indebted for much of my information in relation to the Newtown Pecks   He m Miss Polly J Lum, April 6, 1833   His children are   (881) *Sarah Ann*,[8] b Dec 24, 1834, d July 17, 1836 , (882) *Henry S* ,[8] b Sept 1, 1838, m Isabella Barton , (883) *Austin L* ,[8] b June 3, 1844, m Susan M Root , and (884) *Mary Frances*,[8] b June 19, 1850 — (885) John B , settled at Cleveland, Ohio , (886) Zera, who also settled at Cleveland.

[446.]   SHERMAN[6] PECK, son of ANDREW,[5] resides in Bridgewater, Conn   He is a prominent man.   He has been a member of the Legislature, and held various public offices.   I am indebted to his kindness and assistance.   He has been twice married : first, to Electa Young, who died November 13, 1835, aged 29 years ; second, to Lois Livingston, April 10, 1836.

CHILDREN — SEVENTH GENERATION

(887) Henry S , b May 30, 1834, and d Nov. 30, 1859 , (888) Edgar L , b Jan. 9, 1837, m Martha Keeler, Nov. 13, 1861 , (889) Edwin Y , b April 28, 1838   He was drowned May 22, 1863.   (890) Ann Maria, b Aug 25, 1839, m Frederick Jones, Dec 30, 1862 , (891) Frederick A , b Jan 29, 1841, was residing at home, unm , in 1867 , (892) Ophelia L , b Aug 12, 1843, m Daniel Canfield, Sept 7, 1862

[459.]   JOHN S.[6] PECK, son of SHADRACH,[5] resides in Naugatuck, Conn. He married Betsey Sherman.

CHILDREN — SEVENTH GENERATION:

(893) Eliza, m Andrew Clark; (894) Brownson; resides in New York City. His children are (895) *Edgar*[8], (896) *Isaac*[8], (897) *Brownson*[8], and (898) *Anna*[8] —(899) Charles, d. in 1849, leaving two children; (900) John A., m. Eunice Cauder, and resides in Naugatuck. His children are· (901) *Lela A.*[8]; (902) *Charles B*[8], (903) *Mary E.*[8]; (904) *John H*[8]; and (905) *E. Louisa.*[8]

[483.]   THOMAS W.[6] PECK, son of LEVIRUS,[5] was residing upon the homestead in 1867. He has been twice married: first, to Sarah Ann Toucey; second, to Theodocia Coe. His first wife died June 21, 1821. His second, February 18, 1846.

CHILDREN — SEVENTH GENERATION:

(906) Fanny, b. July 29, 1804, m Noah B Smith, and settled in Northfield; (907) Alosia, b. July 25, 1809, m. Harley Sandford, (908) Richard W , b May 10, 1812, m. Sarah Cadwelder. He was residing in Hillsville, Pa., in 1867, and had one daughter (909) *Alosia R.*[8] —(910) Abel T., b. March 7, 1815, was residing in Newtown in 1867. He represented the town in the Legislature in 1857. He m Huldah Hawley. His son (911) *Richard W,*[8] b. Jan. 29, 1852, d. Sept 27, 1855 —(912) John B , b Jan 24, 1817, was residing in Newtown in 1867. He was a Senator in 1862 He m Charlotte C Colt. His children are: (913) *Fanny C ,*[8] b Sept 5, 1854, and (914) *John R.,*[8] b. April 2, 1863. —(915) Charles A., b. Oct 30, 1823, d Sept. 3, 1826.

[514.]   CLARK[6] PECK, son of GEORGE,[5] settled at Sandgate, Vt., where he died, May 8, 1865. He married Polly Ann Baldwin. She was born October 29, 1786, and died November 9, 1860.

CHILDREN — SEVENTH GENERATION:

(916) Louisa, b June 21, 1807; (917) Levi, b. July 23, 1808, to whose kindness I am indebted for my information; (918) Smith, b. Nov. 18, 1809; (919) Amanda, b March 19, 1811, (920) Baldwin, b. May 1, 1813, (921) Amey, b. Sept. 3, 1815, (922) Ann, b. Feb. 10, 1817, (923) Laura, b. Sept. 28, 1825.

[580.]   MICHAEL[6] PECK, son of DAVID,[5] resided in Brookfield. He married Polly Trainer. He died May 5, 1859. She died January 18, 1863.

CHILDREN — SEVENTH GENERATION:

(924) Mary A., b. Oct. 11, 1823, m. Leonard L. Wilkinson; (925) David N., b March 1, 1824, m. Lucinda Lent. His children are: (926) *Charlotte G.*;[8] (927) *Harriet*[8], (928) *Polly*[8], (929) *Edgar*[8], (930) *Jane*[8], and (931) *Agnes.*[8] — (932) Charles, b. March 29, 1825, m. Amelia Devan. His children are. (933)

George[8]*;* (934) *Charles*[8]*;* and (935) *Anna B.*[8] —(936) Harriet E , b. April 4,
1829, m. Reuben B. Bailey; (937) John H , b Feb 2, 1831, (938) Sarah J , b.
Sept. 13, 1833, m Charles C. Sherman, (939) William S , b. May 14, 1836, m.
Abby Smith. His children are · (940) *Charles*[8]*;* and (941) *Edgar.*[8]

[586.] JOHN A.[6] PECK, son of JOHN,[5] was twice married:
first, to Huldah Keeler, February 17, 1811; second, to Sally H.
Payne, July 1, 1847. His first wife died October 20, 1842. His
second August 29, 1860. He died August 22, 1864.

CHILDREN — SEVENTH GENERATION

(942) Henry W., b. May 1, 1812, m. Joanna W. Platt His children are (943)
Franklin K[8], (944) *Isabel C*[8], (945) *Henry W.*[8], and (946) *Ella J*[8] —(947)
George W., b. Sept. 22, 1813, m. Mary Andrews, and had one daughter. (948)
Adaline M[8] —(949) Amerillis, b. Oct. 21, 1815, m. Medad R Kellog; (950)
Clareny, b Aug 2, 1817, m. Sherman Foot, (951) John L , b April 12, 1820,
m. Sarah T. Law, (952) Aiza C , b June 8, 1822, m. Jennie Bodes. His chil-
dren are (953) *John A.*[8], and (954) *William H*[8] —(955) Lucy Ann, b Oct.
31, 1824, m Edwin Smith; (956) Adaline, b. Jan. 30, 1827, (957) Alfred A., b.
Oct. 27, 1830.

[601.] ABRAHAM[6] PECK, son of ABRAHAM,[5] was residing
in Milford in 1867. He married Dolla Tibbetts.

CHILDREN — SEVENTH GENERATION

(958) Charles H., b May 7, 1808; (959) David, b Dec. 20,1809, (960) Sarah,
b. Jan 14, 1812; (961) Julia, b Dec 22, 1813, (962) Wyllis, b. Jan 18, 1816,
(963) Mary E , b. May 7, 1818, (964) Benedict, b July 2, 1820; (965) Treat,
b. Jan. 13, 1823, (966) Rosanna, b Feb 15, 1825, (967) Abraham, b July 14,
1827, (968) Elizabeth, b. Sept. 7, 1831, (969) Margaret, b. March 7, 1838.

[604.] CORNELIUS B.[6] PECK, son of BENJAMIN,[5] married
Mary Ann Perry, daughter of Abner Perry, of Huntington, Conn.,
October 19, 1823. He resides in Milford, Conn., where his great-
grandfather Henry lived and died, being a portion of the original
estate of the ancestor Joseph. He is a prominent public man.
To his kindness I am indebted for many facts of interest in relation to his ancestors.

CHILDREN — SEVENTH GENERATION ·

(970) Mary Ann, b June 3, 1825, m. Capt. Ebenezer W. Ruggles, of Bridge-
port, Conn ; (971) Sarah Frances, m Ebenezer W. Beckwith, of Cromwell,
Conn.; (972) Henry C., b. in 1829, was residing at home until in 1867, (973)
John, b Dec. 1831, m Adelaide Morse. His children are: (974) *Fannie,*[8] b.
Aug. 1865, and (975) *Cornelius H.,*[8] b. Jan 2, 1867.

[609.]　ELI[6] PECK, son of ELIJAH,[5] settled in Jericho, Vt., where he lived and died.　He married Amanda Bartlett.

CHILDREN — SEVENTH GENERATION:

(976) Eli, d. young; (977) Moses, settled in Jericho.　His children were: (978) *Eli*[9]; (979) *William*[8]; (980) *Sarah*[8], and (981) *Charlotte.*[8] —(982) Mabel, m. Norman Wright.

[610.]　ZERAH[6] PECK, son of ELIJAH,[5] settled in Hinesburgh, Vt.　He married Abbie Blackman.

CHILDREN — SEVENTH GENERATION:

(983) Charles; (984) Myron; and (985) Betsey.

DESCENDANTS OF HENRY PECK, OF NEW HAVEN, CONNECTICUT.

Henry Peck early settled at New Haven. He was among the first settlers there in the spring of 1638. He and Deacon William Peck, who also settled there in 1638, were doubtless relatives, and may have been brothers. They are supposed to have emigrated to this country in the company of Gov. Eaton, with the Rev. John Davenport and others, who arrived at Boston, June 26, 1637, in the ship "Hector."

Who his progenitors were has not yet been ascertained. I have found none of the descendants to second any efforts of mine to do so, although many of them are abundantly able. He signed the fundamental agreement or compact of the settlers, made June 4, 1639, and took an active interest in the management and affairs of the settlement. His home lot was in that part of the town now the city. A portion of it, on what is now George Street, continues in the possession of his descendants. He died in 1651. His will is dated October 30, 1651.

CHILDREN — SECOND GENERATION :

(1)+Eleazer, bap. March 13, 1643, (2)+Joseph, bap. Sept. 5,1647, (3)+Benjamin, bap Sept. 5, 1647, (4) Elizabeth, b. March 16, 1649, and bap. March 24, 1650. She m. John Hotchkiss, Dec. 4, 1672.

These baptisms are upon the church records. The birth of Elizabeth is upon the town records.

Mr. Savage says, in his Genealogical Dictionary, that there were two sons by the name of Eleazer, one dying young There may have been, but I found but one name on record. Mr. Savage and others also say that Joseph and Benjamin were twins, but if there is any evidence of it upon the records, I failed to find it.

The following is the entry as it stands upon the record, with the two preceding entries, which I give to show its relation to them.

"Mary Hooker daughter of Mr William Hooker bap 5–7*–1647
Susannah & John Brasy ye same day
Joseph & Benjamin Peck ye same day"

They were both baptized the same day that Mary Hooker was, Sept. 5, 1647, but I see nothing in the record which indicates that they were twins.

---

* The 7th month Old Style was September.

[1.]   ELEAZER² PECK, son of HENRY,¹ married Mary Bunnell, of New Haven, daughter of William Bunnell, October 31, 1671, and settled in Wallingford, Conn , where they lived and died. She was born May 4, 1650, and died July 20, 1724, in her 75th year. He died in 1734, in his 91st year.   His will is upon record at New Haven, B. 6, p. 179, dated May 4, 1735, and proved March 1, 1735–6.

CHILDREN — THIRD GENERATION:

(5) Samuel, b. March 3, 1672–3, d. March 12, 1672–3 , (6) Abigail, b March 6, 1673–4 , (7) Samuel, again, b in 1675 , (8) Mary, b July 14, 1677, m. a Mr. Ebenetha, (9) Martha, b July 2, 1679, (10)+Stephen, b Aug 4, 1681; (11) +Eleazer, b Feb. 19, 1683, d in 1684, (12) Eleazer, again, b. June 1685 , (13) +Nathaniel, and (14) Elizabeth, who m. William Hough, are named in the will, but not found upon the records of births *

[2.]   JOSEPH² PECK, son of HENRY,¹ lived and died in New Haven.   He resided upon the homestead.   He married Sarah, daughter of Roger Alling, of New Haven, November 28, 1672. His widow was appointed to administer upon his estate, September 5, 1720, and returned the inventory September 30, 1720.   The court ordered a division of the estate among the heirs, October 6, 1720, New Haven Rec , B. 5, pp. 38, 39 and 48.   The widow was still residing upon the estate in 1729 when her grandson Joseph sold his interest in it.

CHILDREN — THIRD GENERATION

(15) Sarah, b Sept 11, 1673, m. Thomas Gilbert, March 31, 1698 , (16)+ Joseph, b Oct 9, 1675 , (17)+Samuel, b. Dec 29, 1677 , (18)+James, b Feb. 17, 1679–80; (19)+John, b Oct 6, 1682 , (20) Eliphalet, b May 12, 1685, not named in the settlement of the estate, was probably then deceased, (21) Abigail, b. May 2, 1686, m Robert Talmadge; (22) Mary, b. Oct. 6, 1689, m a Mr. Roe , (23) Ebenezer, b. May 2, 1693, not named in the settlement of the estate, probably died without issue.

[3.]   BENJAMIN² PECK, son of HENRY,¹ settled in New Haven, where he died.   He resided in the second division, at the place then known as the Sperry farms, afterwards Amity Society, now a part of Woodbridge.   His will is dated March 3, 1730, and

* It was with great difficulty and much labor that I was able to find what became of this family, and trace out their descendants   Much in relation to their early history yet remains in the dark   It seems to have been unknown to Mr. Savage and others, that Eleazer had a family or left any descendants.

28

proved April 5, B. 5, p. 560.   He married Mary Sperry, daughter of Richard Sperry, March 29, 1670.

CHILDREN — THIRD GENERATION ·

(24)+Benjamin, b. Jan. 4, 1670; (25) Mary, b. Sept 3, 1672, m. John Brownson, and was residing in Farmington, Conn , June 3, 1730; (26) Joseph, b. Feb 26, 1676, who is supposed to have d. without issue, as his property was divided among his brothers and sisters,—New Haven Rec., B. 4, p. 436; (27) Esther, b in 1679, m. Eliphalet Bristol, (28) Ebenezer, b April 24, 1681, d. in infancy, (29)+Ebenezer, again, b. Jan 5, 1684; (30) Desire, b. Aug. 26, 1687, m. Nathaniel Burnett, May 10, 1709, and settled in that part of Wallingford, now Cheshire, (31) John, probably d without issue, as no account of his descendants is found, (32) Lydia, m Solomon Terry, and settled in Danbury, Conn., (33) Mehitable, m. Ebenezer Stevens, and resided in Danbury.

[10.]   STEPHEN[3] PECK, son of ELEAZER,[2] resided in Wallingford.   He married Susannah Collier, April 10, 1706.

CHILDREN — FOURTH GENERATION .

(34)+Jonathan, b. Dec 14, 1706, (35) Abel, b. Feb 25, 1709; (36) John, b. Sept. 16, 1713; (37) Susannah, b. Sept. 3, 1717; and probably others.

[11.]   ELEAZER[3] PECK, son of ELEAZER,[2] at first settled in Wallingford, where he resided until about 1726, when he removed to Southington, Conn.   He was twice married: first, to Ann —— ; second, to Elizabeth Culver, October 30, 1726.

CHILDREN — FOURTH GENERATION ·

(38) Hannah, b. Jan 20, 1717, (39) Mehitable, b July 19, 1719; (40)+Eliakim, b Oct. 24, 1721; (41) Benajah, b Feb 8, 1724, (42) Gideon, b. —— ; (43) Charles, b. Nov 8, 1727, (44)+Eleazer, b. July 2, 1730; (45) Zebulon, b. Dec. 9, 1733.

[13.]   NATHANIEL[3] PECK, son of ELEAZER,[2] resided in Wallingford.   His wife was Sarah ——, who died February 14, 1780.   He died March 26, 1752.   His will is upon record at New Haven, B. 8, p. 143, dated September 3, 1751, and presented to the court for approval April 4, 1752, from which his eldest son Joseph appealed.   His son Phineas and Abel Munson were the executors.

CHILDREN — FOURTH GENERATION ·

(46) Sarah, b. March 21, 1713, m. Abel Munson, Nov. 7, 1728; (47) Joseph, b. July 19, 1716, (48)+Phineas, b Aug 4, 1719, (49) Barnabas, b Dec. 2, 1723, (50) Mary, b. June 1, 1725, m. John Sharp, Nov. 10, 1743, (51) Daniel, b. April 30, 1731, d. July 26, 1751.

[16.]　JOSEPH³ PECK, son of JOSEPH,² settled in Newark, N. J. He disposed of the lands set to him from his father's estate to his brother James and Samuel. He was a blacksmith by trade and occupation. He married Lydia, daughter of Edward Ball, of N. J. She died August 22, 1742. He died January 9, 1746.

CHILDREN — FOURTH GENERATION

(52)+Joseph, b in 1702, and (53)+Timothy, b. in 1709.

[17.]　SAMUEL³ PECK, son of JOSEPH,² settled in New Haven, where he died. His will is upon record there, dated January 14, 1728–9, and was presented to the court for approval November 16, 1739, B. 6, p. 286. He married Abigail, daughter of Nathaniel Hitchcock, December 30, 1703.

CHILDREN — FOURTH GENERATION·

(54) Sarah, b. March 21, 1705, m Anthony Thompson, April 20, 1727, (55) Samuel, b Oct 9, 1708, (56)+Timothy, b April 6, 1711, (57)+Amos, b Jan. 29, 1712-3, (58) Elizabeth, b Oct 27, 1714, (59) Mary, b. Feb. 2, 1715-16, (60)+Moses, b Nov 19, 1717, (61) Abigail, b Nov 2, 1719; (62) Roger, b. June 13, 1721, supposed to have been lost at sea. Administration upon his estate was granted to his brother Timothy in 1753 This ancient document is in the possession of Charles Peck, Esq, of New Haven, neatly preserved in a frame under glass.

[18.]　JAMES³ PECK, son of JOSEPH,² settled in New Haven, where he died in 1760. His will is upon record there, dated February 11, 1760. He was twice married: first, to Abigail Morris, February 4, 1705–6; second, to Hannah Leek, July 10, 1729.

CHILDREN — FOURTH GENERATION

(63) Ebenezer, b Jan 20, 1706-7, supposed d. unm; (64)+James, b. Aug. 4, 1708, (65) Hannah, b Aug 10, 1710, m James Heaton, Oct 29, 1730; (66) Abigail, b July 1, 1713, m Thomas Potter; (67) Sarah, m Timothy Howell, Aug. 7. 1755, (68) John, b June 30, 1718, supposed d young; (69) Morris, a twin to John, supposed also d young; (70)+Stephen, by 2d wife, b. June 5, 1730. He was the executor of his father's will, and administered upon his mother's estate.

[19.]　JOHN³ PECK, son of JOSEPH,² lived and died in New Haven upon the paternal homestead, located on what is now George, below Church Street, (still occupied by the descendants of Henry, now more than two hundred years since his decease.) He married Esther Morris, January 30, 1706–7.

(71)+Joseph, b. Jan 27, 1707-8, (72)+Eliphalet, b. March 4, 1710; (73)
John, b. Aug 30, 1712, d young. The widow m. John Mix She was ap-
pointed guardian of the children, Jan 5, 1720-1. Joseph chose his uncle
Samuel his guardian, and James was afterwards appointed guardian for
Eliphalet Samuel was appointed to administer upon the estate, June 6, 1720,
New Haven Records, B 5, p 28. The court ordered the property divided.
One-third was set to the widow. The remainder was divided into four parts,
of which Joseph, the eldest son, had two, and Eliphalet and John each one.
To Joseph was set a right in the dwelling-house and homestead To Eliphalet,
a part of the old and new house and a part of the orchard To John, a part
of the old and new house, with the barn and a part of the orchard Where
the original boundaries of this lot were, and where the orchard was located,
might now be of interest to the antiquarian, or the curious, among the
descendants, to learn A gentleman, Mr Nathan Peck, to whom I am
indebted for much of my information upon the subject, informs me that he
well remembers when there were ancient fruit trees standing there, one of
which was removed some fifty years since, then supposed to have been more
than one hundred years old The estate was purchased of the widow and
heirs of John by his brother James, and by him conveyed to James, jr , and
by him to Stephen and others.

[24.] BENJAMIN[3] PECK, son of BENJAMIN,[2] at first settled
in New Haven, and from there removed to Norwich, West Farms,
now Franklin, Conn. He was admitted a freeman there in 1700.
He was a man of wealth and distinction. His wife Mary died
March 3, 1728. He died May 31, 1742.

(74) Dinah, b Nov 30, 1700, m Jacob Willis, (75) Elizabeth, b. Aug 16,
1704, d Aug 4, 1720; (76)+Joseph, b Nov 14, 1706, (77) Mary, b Feb 19,
1708-9, (78) Benjamin, b. Dec 4, 1710, resided in Norwich, where he died.
His children were (79) *Reuben*[5], (80) *Benjamin*[5], (81) *Susannah*[5], and (82)
Benjamin, 2d [5] —(83) John, b May 7, 1712-13, resided in Norwich, where he
died in 1743, leaving a son (84) *John*,[5] who died young —(85) Ebenezer, b.
Feb 15, 1715-16, resided in Norwich His children were (86) *Ebenezer, jr* [5],
(87) *Abihu*[5], (88) *Sarah*[5], (89) *Elizabeth*[5], and (90) *Seril* [5] —(91)+Jonathan,
b. March 1, 1717-18, (92) Daniel, b May 9, 1719, settled in Scipio, N Y ,
where he died. His children were (93) *Elizabeth*[5], (94) *Mary*[5], (95) *Anna*[5],
(96) *Anna, 2d*[5]; (97) *Jedediah*[5], (98) *Esther*[5], and (99) *Sperry*,[5] whose son
(100) *Asa*,[6] died at Spring Green, Wis , in 1867, leaving children as follows
(101) *Eunice*[7], (102) *Olney*[7], (103) *Elisha F* [7], (104) *Stephen A* [7], (105)
Thomas[7], (106) *Lester N* [7], (107) *Charles S* [7], and (108) *Theodore*[7], who
resides there, and to whom I am indebted for my information —(109) Submit,
b. Aug 1, 1722, (110) Phebe, whose name appears upon the deed, but is not
found upon the records of births.

[2).] EBENEZER[3] PECK, son of BENJAMIN,[2] settled in New Haven, and it is supposed in that part known as Amity Society, now a part of Woodbridge. He was twice married: first, to Hannah Hotchkiss; second, to Elizabeth Wilmott. His will was presented to the court to be proved May 1768, but was not approved of. The court ordered the estate divided among the heirs, B. 10, p. 509.

CHILDREN — FOURTH GENERATION ·

(111)+Ebenezer, b March 12, 1710; (112) Hannah, b Feb 15, 1711-12, m. a Sperry; (113) Mary, b. Nov 2, 1714, m a Perkins, (114)+Joseph, b. March 28, 1718, (115) Rachel, b Aug 1, 1721, m a Perkins, (116) Ambrose, b March 5, 1725, (117) Lydia, b. Dec 11, 1728, (118) Eunice, b Aug 6, 1730, d young; (119) Bathsheba, b. Sept 27, 1732, (120)+Benajah, b June 1, 1735, (121) Benjamin, b Aug 14, 1737, d young; (122)+Stephen, b Aug 5, 1742, (123) Eunice, 2d; b Sept. 28, 1744, m Jesse Ford, and d March 26, 1730; (124) Benjamin, 2d, b March 10, 1746-7. He was a blacksmith, and resided in Woodbridge. He m. Thankful Russell, and had several daughters.

[34.] JONATHAN[4] PECK, son of STEPHEN,[3] resided in Wallingford, where he died, December 14, 1752. His will is dated October 4, 1752. He married Thankful Benham, January 31, 1733.

CHILDREN — FIFTH GENERATION

(125) Sarah, b Nov. 16, 1733, (126) Susannah, b. Nov 8, 1735, (127) Eunice, b Jan 13, 1739, d. Oct 12, 1752, (128) Martha, b. Feb 2, 1741, (129) Thankful, b Aug 15, 1743, (130) Ruth, b Dec 22, 1745, (131)+Samuel, b. April 26, 1752, and probably others, whose births were not recorded.

[40.] ELIAKIM[4] PECK, son of ELEAZAR,[3] resided in Southington, Conn. He was twice married. His first wife was Sarah Woodruff. His second was ———. His first wife died March 9, 1768. His second wife died of the dropsy, September 28, 1809. He died of the palsy, May 7, 1801.

CHILDREN — FIFTH GENERATION :

(132) Thomas, bap Oct 15, 1752, m Mrs. Mary Judd, d Dec. 23, 1800. He was found dead in the highway, supposed to have died in a fit, (133) Abigail, bap July 25, 1754. (134)+Eliakim, bap. Nov 1759, (135) Phebe, bap. Sept. 9, 1764, m Hemingway Bradley, and d Oct. 30, 1842.

[44.] ELEAZAR[4] PECK, son of ELEAZAR,[3] settled at first in Farmington, and from there removed to Sand Lake, N. Y., about 1791, where he died about 1813. He married Elizabeth Woodruff, December 6, 1755.

28*

(136)+Isaac, b Aug 21, 1756, (137) Reuben, b. Nov. 5, 1757, m. Sarah Gridley, of Berlin, (138) Gemima, b. May 1, 1760, m Benjamin Brunson, (139) Lucy, b Oct 7, 1763, m John Belknap, (140) Samuel, b. Dec. 16, 1766, (141)+Selah, b Feb. 16, 1771.

[48.]   PHINEAS[4] PECK, son of Nathaniel,[3] resided in Wallingford, Conn.   He was twice married: first, to Phebe Munson; second, to Leah Cook.

(142) Lydia, b Oct 13, 1745, d Dec 20, 1745, (143) Susannah, b. Sept. 28, 1748, (144) Rebecca, b. March 4, 1751, m first, Amos Williams, second, a Pearsons, and d in Middletown, (145) Nathaniel, b May 2, 1753, d in Wallingford, unm , (146)+Phineas C., b Jan 9, 1756, (147) Barnabas, b Sept. 25, 1758, d in the Revolutionary war, unm , (148) Joseph, b. Oct 4, 1761, also d in the war, unm., (149) Lydia, b. Jan 2, 1764, m first, Nathan Mathews, second, Samuel Thurber; (150) Daniel, b. June 28, 1769, d on board a prison ship, unm.

[52.]   JOSEPH[4] PECK, son of Joseph,[3] settled in Newark, N. J., now East Orange, where he died, July 12, 1772.   He was a farmer, a prominent man, for many years deacon of the Presbyterian church.   He married Jemima Lindsey.

(151)+David, b in 1727, (152)+Jesse, b in 1730; (153)+John, b in 1732, (154) Joseph, b Jan 2, 1735, (155) Moses, b Oct. 6, 1740; (156) Abigail, b. about 1743, (157) Ruth, who m Stephen Dodd, and settled in Tioga County, N. Y., and (158) Elizabeth, b. in 1747, m John Wright, and d. in 1819.

[53.]   TIMOTHY[4] PECK, son of Joseph,[3] settled in Morristown, N. J., where he died, October 17, 1797.   He was twice married: first, to Phebe ——; second, to Mrs. Hannah Ball, widow.

(159) Nathaniel, b in 1742, m. Mary Condit, by whom he had daughters, but no sons, (160) Sarah, who m. Nathaniel Beach, (161) Lydia, who m Jonathan Hedden, (162) Phebe, who m. Ezekiel Gable; and (163) Abigail, who m. a Gardner.

[56.]   TIMOTHY[4] PECK, son of Samuel,[3] married Lydia Lines, September 23, 1736, and removed to Bethany, where he died.   He was a deacon in the church for many years.   His will is dated April 5, 1784.   The following is from his tombstone:

"In memory of Deacon Timothy Peck, who after he had served his own Generation, by the will of God fell on sleep, Jan. 1784, in the 73d year of his age."

CHILDREN — FIFTH GENERATION:

(164) Timothy, b July 5, 1737, (165) Lydia, b March 13, 1738-9, m. Samuel Hotchkiss, (166) Peninah, b. Aug. 5, 1740, m. first, Charles Todd, second, David Hotchkiss, (167) Titus, b. April 7, 1742; was a Lieutenant in the Revolutionary war, and died of the camp distemper The following is from his tombstone "In memory of Lieut Titus Peck, who lived beloved, and died lamented by all his acquaintances, Oct 29, 1776, in his 39th year." (168)+ Roger; (169) Caleb, (170) Mary, m. Samuel Hotchkiss, (171) Martha, m. Joel Hotchkiss, (172)+Samuel, b. in 1753.

[57.] AMOS[4] PECK, son of SAMUEL,[3] settled at first in New Haven. He was one of the founders of the Congregational Church, now known as the second or North Church. From New Haven he removed to Mount Carmel, Conn., where he died January 28, 1783. He married Elizabeth Leek. He was a Deacon of the church.

CHILDREN — FIFTH GENERATION ·

(173) Abigail, b. Oct. 30, 1742, (174) Elizabeth, b June 22, 1744, (175) Sarah, b Feb 21, 1745-6, (176) Mary, b. Sept 30, 1747, (177)+Amos, b July 29, 1749, (178) Phebe, b May 13, 1751, (179) Moses, b. March 13, 1753, (180) Elijah, b. April 12, 1755, (181) Hannah, b May 21, 1757, (182) Jesse, b. Aug. 29, 1760; (183)+Joseph, b. July 5, 1762.

[60.] MOSES[4] PECK, son of SAMUEL,[3] was a watchmaker by trade, and settled in Boston, Mass. His will is on record there, B. 99, p. 158, dated October 12, 1799.

CHILDREN — FIFTH GENERATION:

(184) Abigail, b Oct 1744, (185) Sarah, b Nov. 24, 1752, m. Jonathan Stickney; (186) Samuel, b Oct 30, 1758, d. young; (187) Moses, b July 4, 1776, d. young; (188) Samuel, again, b. Sept. 21, 1768, d young; (189) Elizabeth, b. June 24, 1771, m. William Thurston, (190)+Elijah.

[64] JAMES[4] PECK, son of JAMES,[3] called upon the records James, jr., Lieut. and Capt. James, resided in New Haven. He married Mary Hitchcock. He was the keeper of a tavern, the location of which is given on Wadsworth's Map of New Haven, 1748.

CHILDREN — FIFTH GENERATION

(191) Eunice, b Feb. 14, 1731-2, (192) Ebenezer, b. Jan 1, 1733-4, (193) William, b. July 12, 1736; (194) Abiah, b. Nov. 22, 1738, (195) Thankful, b.

April 9, 1741; (196) James, b. Jan. 14, 1742-3, settled at first in New Haven, where he was a shipmaster; from there removed to Canaan, Conn., where he died, leaving two sons (197) *William*[6], and (198) *Sheldon.*[6] —(199) Mary, b. Feb. 25, 1744-5, (200) Hannah, b. Feb. 15, 1746-7, (201) Abigail, b. March 6, 1748-9; (202)+Ebenezer, second, b. Jan 14, 1750-1.

[70] STEPHEN[4] PECK, son of JAMES,[3] settled in New Haven, upon the George Street estate, so called, purchased by his father of the widow and heirs of John, grandson of Henry the Ancestor. The house in which Stephen resided I am told stood upon the northeast side of the street, and was large for those days. It was doubtless the new house alluded to and set to Eliphalet and John, the great-grand-children of Henry, in the division of their father's estate. It was taken down some fifty years since, having the appearance of being very old.

Stephen married, first, Esther Munson; second, Lydia Miles.

CHILDREN — FIFTH GENERATION.

(203) Esther, b. July 1, 1753, m. Nathan Oaks. The house in which she resided, and which is upon this estate, is still standing in a good state of preservation, occupied by the widow of her son, Charles H Oaks, and her grand-daughter, the wife of Professor George E. Day, of Yale Theological Seminary. (204)+Henry, b. Aug 20, 1755; (205) Elisha, b Oct 11, 1757, d. young; (206)+John, b. Dec. 12, 1759, (207) Stephen, b. Feb. 2, 1765, d. in the West Indies, unm ; (208) Sarah, b. April 24, 1766, m. Thomas Trowbridge; (209) Lucy, b. July 20, 1768, m William Trowbridge.

[71.] JOSEPH[4] PECK, son of JOHN,[3] left New Haven at an early date, and settled at Norwalk, Conn., and from there it is supposed removed to what is now Bethel.

CHILDREN — FIFTH GENERATION

(210)+Joseph, b. in 1734, (211)+Abijah, (212) Ezra, d. in 1826, leaving no sons, (213)+Levi, (214) Mary, and (215) Rebecca.

[72.] ELIPHALET[4] PECK, son of JOHN,[3] settled in Danbury. He left New Haven at an early date. It was with much labor and difficulty that I was able to trace out and find what became of him and his brother Joseph. It was supposed that they, as well as their brother John, might have died without issue; and had it not been for the information given me, and the generous kindness shown me by Rev. George Peck, of Providence, Penn., a descendant of Eliphalet, and his earnest desire that his branch of the name might be traced back and connected with its proper ancestor, I, perhaps, never should have traced them out, and should thus have left out of the history their descendants, who, it will be seen, are a very important branch of the name. I had found Mr. Peck and his brothers, and learned the distinguished positions they occupied, but was unable to connect them either with the Connecticut or Massachusetts Pecks, or to tell to what branch of the name they belonged, until he gave me the name of his great grand-father, and assured me he was of Danbury, Conn. After a careful examination of my manuscripts and papers, I came to the conclusion that his branch could be no other than the descendants of the Joseph or Eliphalet whom I had been unable to follow beyond their youth, and the appointment of their guardians, and determined to settle the matter, if possible, beyond any doubt upon the subject. I visited Danbury, and the adjoining towns, but could learn from none of the records, or aged persons I found, where the Danbury Pecks were from, or who the Ancestor was. I had already examined the town, Church, Probate and Land Records, at New Haven, but a more protracted examination afterwards enabled me, with other evidence, to decide the matter, and there is now no question but that Joseph and Eliphalet were the Ancestors of the Danbury Pecks, and the descendants of Henry, of New Haven.

Eliphalet lived and died in Danbury, at an advanced age. The Church Records at Bethel show that he and his wife Rebecca and son Jesse became members at its organization.

CHILDREN — FIFTH GENERATION.

(216) Jesse, (217) Phineas, (218) Elkanah, (219) John; (220) Stephen; (221) Esther, who m Stephen Curtis, and (222) Rebecca, who m. Aaron Stone

[76.] JOSEPH[4] PECK, son of BENJAMIN,[3] resided in Norwich. He was a prominent man. He kept a public house for many years. He was three times married: first, to Hannah Carrier, of Colchester, March 5, 1729; second, to Elizabeth Edgarton, of Norwich, October 19, 1742; third, to Elizabeth Carpenter, of Norwich, December 22, 1754. His first wife died February 2, 1741–2; his second wife died September 1, 1753; his third wife died December 26, 1817. He died September 9, 1776. His will is upon record at Norwich, B. 6, p. 87, dated January 9, 1776.

CHILDREN — FIFTH GENERATION ·

(223) Simeon, b. April 21, 1730, d. July 22, 1731, (224) Joseph, b. May 21, 1731, resided in Norwich, now Franklin, where he died. The division of his estate is upon record at Norwich, B. 11, p 35. He m., for his first wife, Joanna Rudd, of Norwich, June 9, 1752, for his second, Susanna Brokway, of Lime, Oct. 12, 1756; for his third, Rachel Fitch, of New London, Feb. 2, 1763, and for his fourth, Mrs. Zeiviah Hastings, Dec .20, 1764. His children were: (225) *Joanna*[6], (226) *Asa*[6], (227) *Luna*[6], (228) *Susannah*[6], and (229) *Roxana* [6] —(230) Simeon, again, b. Jan. 21, 1732-3, resided in Norwich, where he died. He m. Ruth Willis, Jan. 29, 1755. His children were (231) *Rose Anna*[6], (232) *Walter*[6], (233) *Ebbee*[6], (234) *Jabez*[6], (235) *Jathleel*[6], (236) *Simeon*[6], (237) *Eliel*[6], (238) *Ruth*[6], (239) *Lydia*[6], and (240) *Joseph.*[6] —(241) Jathleel, b. June 23, 1734, (242) Gideon, b. Nov. 10, 1736, d Oct. 19, 1740; (243) Hannah, b. July 19, 1739, (244) Gideon, again, b. Jan 25, 1741-2, resided in Norwich. He m. first, Irena Tracy, of Norwich, April 18, 1763, second, Sarah Edgcomb, March 1, 1769. His children were (245) *Azel*[6], (246) *Wealthy*[6], (247) *Eleanor*[6], and (248) *Irene.*[6] —(249)+Bela, b. July 10, 1758, (250) Cynthia, b. Aug. 14, 1761.

[91.]   JONATHAN[4] PECK, son of BENJAMIN,[3] resided in Norwich. He married Bethiah Bingham, January 14, 1741-2. The division of his estate is on record, B. 7, p. 36, dated September 5, 1780.

CHILDREN — FIFTH GENERATION

(251)+Phineas, b. July 28, 1743, (252) Bethiah, b. March 6, 1745, m. Hezekiah Edgerton, (253) Lucy, b May 20, 1747, m. Jason Gager; (254)+Darius, b March 14, 1749-50; (255) Sybel, b. March 16, 1752, m Elijah Edgerton; (256) Eunice, b. Oct. 1754; (257) John, b. Nov 14, 1756; was lost at sea, (258) Jonathan, b. Nov. 9, 1758; d. Dec. 14, 1758, (259)+Jathleel, b Jan 1, 1760.

[111.]   EBENEZER[4] PECK, son of EBENEZER,[3] settled in New Haven. He married Mary Johnson, January 20, 1736-7.

CHILDREN — FIFTH GENERATION ·

(260) Hannah, b. Jan. 8, 1737-8, (261) Mary, b. Sept. 24, 1739, (262) Ebenezer, b. Sept. 27, 1741, (263) Noah, b. Dec. 3, 1743, (264) Hannah, again, b. Dec. 7, 1745; (265) Rachel, b. June 10, 1748; (266) Jane, b. April 22, 1753.

[114.]   JOSEPH[4] PECK, son of EBENEZER,[3] settled at Amity, now a part of Woodbridge. He married Anna Perkins, January 12, 1743-4. His will is at New Haven, B. 16, p. 622.

CHILDREN — FIFTH GENERATION .

(267) Seth, settled in Bristol, Conn.; (268) Joseph, who was a jail-keeper, and had children, viz (269) *Joseph*[6], (270) *Bela*[6], (271) *Nancy*[6], and (272) *Sarah.*[6] —(273) Dan, settled in Bristol, (274) John, who m. Lois Osborn, and had children, viz (275) *Osborn*[6], (276) *Francis*[6], (277) *John*[6], (278) *Eliza*[6]; and (279) *Charlotte,*[6] now the widow Ceveit, residing at New Haven. —(280) Henry, who settled at Bristol; (281) Amey, (282) Dorcas, (283) Bathsheba; (284) Asenath; and (285) Electa, who m. Roger Alling.

[120.] BENAJAH[4] PECK, son of EBENEZER,[3] resided in Woodbridge, where he died May 19, 1785. The distribution of his estate is on record at New Haven, B. 18, p. 51. He married Sarah Mansfield.

CHILDREN — FIFTH GENERATION .

(286) Eunice, who m. Asahel Brooks; and (287)+Jonathan Mansfield Peck, b. in 1857, and probably others not on record.

[122.] STEPHEN[4] PECK, son of EBENEZER,[3] married Eunice Bradley, daughter of Timothy Bradley, and resided in Woodbridge, where he died, June 13, 1830. His will is upon record at New Haven, B. 40, p. 293.

CHILDREN — FIFTH GENERATION :

(288)+Silas, b. May 23, 1765, (289)+Hezekiah, b. July 7, 1767; (290)+ Stephen, b. Dec 30, 1774, (291) Edward, b. Oct. 23, 1778, d. unm., June 24, 1841, (292) Eunice, b April 3, 1781, m. Deacon David Smith; (293) Sally, b. Dec 5, 1783, m. John Hubbard, (294) Polly B., b. July 17, 1787, m. David Perkins.

[131.] SAMUEL[5] PECK, son of JONATHAN,[4] is supposed to have married Anna Hall, and at first settled in Wallingford, and from there removed to Manheim, N. Y., about 1800, where he died, November 20, 1824.

CHILDREN — SIXTH GENERATION :

(295)+John; (296) Elihu, d. unm.; (297)+Isaac; (298) Augustus, d. unm.; (299) Eunice, m. a Gillett; (300) Anna, b. Sept. 5, 1780, m Thomas Sherwood; (301) Martha, b. Jan. 22, 1784, (302) Thankful, b. June 27, 1790.

[134.] ELIAKIM[5] PECK, son of ELIAKIM,[4] settled in Southington, and from there is said to have removed to Colebrook, Conn.

(303) James, m. a Miner; (304) Erastus, m. Lucretia, daughter of Jesse Carrington, (305) Huldah, m. a Miner; (306) Josiah, (307) Jeremiah, (308) Raymond, (309) Sally, and (310) Asenath. Jeremiah, and Raymond who m. Fanny Woodruff, settled at the West.

[136.] ISAAC⁵ PECK, son of ELEAZAR,⁴ settled at Sand Lake, N. Y., where he died in 1838. He married Hannah Munson. She died February 28, 1846, aged 85 years.

(311) Nabby, d. aged about 25 years, without issue, (312)+Marcus; (313) Candace, m. Herman Griffen, and left children, (314) Hannah, m Pearce Horton, and d in 1840, leaving children, (315)+Lucus, (316) Betsey, m Gideon Butts, and d in 1824, leaving children, (317) Isaac, enlisted into the United States service, and was drowned at St. Augustine by the upsetting of a boat, Feb. 1825.

[141.] SELAH⁵ PECK, son of ELEAZAR,⁴ settled in Greenbush, N. Y., and from there removed to Camden. He died in Athens, Mich., in 1859. He married Temperance, daughter of Benjamin Wilcox, of Bristol, Conn.

(318) Eleazar, b. Jan. 6, 1793, settled at Camden, N Y. His children were. (319) *Polly*⁷, (320) *George S*⁷; (321) *Daniel*⁷, (322) *Catharine*⁷, (323) *Amey L.*⁷, (324) *William J*⁷, (325) *Temperance L.*⁷, (326) *John S*⁷, (327) *Fannie A.*⁷, (328) *Eleazar G*⁷, (329) *Sidney M*⁷, and (330) *Hannah D.*⁷ —(331) Van Rensselaer, b in 1800, settled in Camden, N. Y. His children were (332) *Norman*⁷, (333) *Lyman B*⁷, and (334) *Reuben V.*⁷ —(335) Harriet, m. Isham Simons, and resides in Athens, Mich.; (336) Amey, m David Hitchcock, of York, Mich., (337) Caroline, m. Joel Hitchcock, (338) Sophia, m. Smith White.

[146.] PHINEAS C.⁵ PECK, son of PHINEAS,⁴ resided in that part of Wallingford, Conn., now Prospect. He died August 15, 1809. He married Elizabeth Doolittle. She died December 20, 1843, in her 92d year.

(339) Benjamin, b. in 1776, (340) Samuel, b. in 1780, and d. in Green, N. Y, in 1860 His children are (341) *Horace*,⁷ resides in German, N. Y , (342) *Clarissa*⁷, (343) *Daniel*⁷; (344) *Samuel S*⁷, (345) *Asahel P.*⁷, (346) *Philo N*⁷, (347) *Levi H.*⁷; and (348) *Betsey M.*⁷ —(349) Nathaniel, b. in 1784, resides in Camden, Ind. His children are. (350) *Elizabeth*⁷, (351) *Joseph F.*⁷, (352)

John C[7], and (353) *George W.*[7]—(354) Esther, b in 1787, m. a Mr Huff, and resides, a widow, in Middletown, Conn , (355) Elizabeth, b in 1790, and d in 1864, unm.

[151.]   DAVID[5] PECK, son of JOSEPH,[4] was a farmer, and resided in East Orange, N. J., where he died April 5, 1796.   He married Mary Williams.

CHILDREN — SIXTH GENERATION

(356) Daniel, d in 1827, no issue, (357)+James, (358) Abiel, m Phebe Canfield, no issue; and (359) Ruth, who also d without issue.

[152.]   JESSE[5] PECK, son of JOSEPH,[4] settled in East Orange, where he died September 17, 1771.   He was a farmer.

CHILDREN — SIXTH GENERATION

(360) Moses, b in 1757, d in 1783, no issue, (361) David, b in 1762, d in 1815, no issue, (362) Jeremiah, d in 1797, no issue

[153.]   JOHN[5] PECK, son of JOSEPH,[4] settled in East Orange, where he died December 28, 1811.   He was a prominent man; Judge of the County Court, a member of the Legislature, etc.   He was twice married: first, to Elizabeth Dodd; second, to Mary Harrison.

CHILDREN — SIXTH GENERATION

(363) Joseph, b Nov 27, 1758, m Mary Hedden, resided in East Orange His children were   (364) *Phebe*[7], (365) *Betsey*[7], (366) *Lydia*, (367) *Mary Ann*[7], (368) *Aaron*[7], (369) *Sarah*[7], (370) *Fanny*[7], and (371) *Deborah*[7] —(372) +Stephen, b in 1760; (373) Jared, joined the Revolutionary Army, and was supposed to have been killed, (374) Aaron, b in 1771, m Esther Canfield His children were   (375) *Lewis*[7], and (376) *Nancy*[7] (377)+John, b Nov 28, 1773, (378) Rhoda, m Caleb Hedden, (379) Betsey, m Ezekiel Ball, (380) Sarah, m Stephen Hedden   Her descendants reside in New Albany, Ind

[168]   ROGER[5] PECK, son of TIMOTHY,[4] settled at first in Bethany, Conn., and from there removed to Waterbury, where he died about 1809.   He was a prominent man; a member of the Legislature, etc.   He was twice married: first, to Philena Hine; second, to Mary Atwater.

CHILDREN — SIXTH GENERATION

(381) Betsey, m Edward Perkins, and d in Medina, Ohio, leaving children (382) Roger, m a Miss Camp, and d in Bethany, leaving two children (383) *Sidney*[7], and (384) *Susan*,[7] who were twins. —(385) Lydia, m Lyman Sperry,

and settled in Summit County, Ohio, and has children, (386) Levi, b Oct. 8, 1780, m Polly Sperry, and d in 1850 His children were (387) *Mary*,[7] d in infancy, (388) *Lucius G*,[7] who resides in New Haven, a lawyer of extensive practice, to whom I am indebted for my information in relation to the family, and (389) *Juliette*,[7] who d in infancy. —(390) Virus, was lost at sea, (391) Salome, d in infancy, (392) Mary P, living and unm. in 1866, (393) Charles, d. in 1854, (394) John A., m Ann Ruggles

[172] SAMUEL[5] PECK, son of Timothy,[4] was a soldier in the Revolution. He settled in Bethany, Conn., where he was killed August 9, 1796, in removing hay from the field. He married Mary Beach.

CHILDREN — SIXTH GENERATION

(395)+Samuel, b in 1776, (396) Isaac, b July 25, 1779, m Catharine Tator, and settled in Ledyard, N Y. His children were (397) *Catharine*[7], (398) *Frederick H*[7], and (399) *Cynthia*[7] —(400) Polly, m Daniel Willmarth, d in 1861, leaving 11 children, (401) Truman, (402)+Titus, (403)+Abel, b May 15, 1789, (404) Martha, b July 20, 1791, m first, Merritt Kimball, second, Gideon Willcox, and resides in New Haven, (405)+Jeremiah, b Oct 17, 1793.

[177.] AMOS[5] PECK, son of Amos,[4] resided in Hamden, where he died October 23, 1838. He married Lois Chatterton, January 2, 1772. She died September 22, 1852, aged 100 years, 8 months and 6 days.

CHILDREN — SIXTH GENERATION :

(406)+Jeremiah, b Dec 18, 1773, (407) Benjamin, b March 13, 1776, (408) Mary, b, Jan 28, 1779, m Deacon Jesse Bradley, (409) Lois, b Jan 27, 1782, m Samuel Dickerman, (410) Chloe, b March 13, 1786, m Seymore Tuttle, (411)+Amos, b. Nov 14, 1794.

[183.] JOSEPH[5] PECK, son of Amos,[4] resided in Hamden, Conn. He died August 9, 1845. He married Olive Chatterton.

CHILDREN — SIXTH GENERATION

(412) Sarah, m a Morse, (413) Olive, m Seymore Goodyear; (414) Julia, d unm, (415) Hannah, m a Roe, (416) Fanny, m a Hall, and (417) Zeri, whose children were (418) *Elizabeth*[7], (419) *Lorenzo*[7], (420) *Andrew*[7], (421) *Cornelius*[7], (422) *Mehitable*[7], (423) *Marinda*[7], (424) *Catharine*[7], and (425) *Friend.*[7]

[190] ELIJAH[5] PECK, son of Moses,[4] settled, lived and died in Boston, Mass.

CHILDREN — SIXTH GENERATION

(426)+Samuel, b. June 4, 1778, (427) Sarah, (428) Abigail, who m. a Mr Leach, and Mary, who m. Benjamin Stickney.

[202.] EBENEZER[5] PECK, son of JAMES,[4] called upon the records Captain, resided at New Haven. He was an enterprising merchant. Prior to the embargo of 1807, was said to have been the largest ship-owner of that collection district. He married Rebecca Dickerman.

CHILDREN — SIXTH GENERATION

(429) Ebenezer, b Aug 23, 1791, was lost at sea, (430)+James, b March 6, 1793, (431) Rebecca, b Jan 5, 1795, d April 1863, unm , (432) Mary, b. Jan 30, 1797, d in 1806, (433). Martha, b Sept 15, 1799, m Cornelius Hogeborn, (434) Grace, b Sept 1, 1801, m William C Butler; (435) Emily, b Oct 24, 1803, m Rev Judson A Root, for many years pastor of the Congregational church, at Branford She resides at New Haven, (436) Harriet, b. Jan. 4, 1806, is unm.

[204.] HENRY[5] PECK, son of STEPHEN,[4] resided in New Haven upon the George Street Estate. The house which he built is occupied by Lewis Mix. He married Hannah Lewis.

CHILDREN — SIXTH GENERATION

(437) Esther, b Dec 19, 1783, m first, Capt David G Phipps, second, Capt Solomon Phipps, (438) Mary, b Feb 5, 1785, m Thomas Dugal, and d in Georgetown, D C , (439) Grace, b Dec 2, 1786, m Eli Mix, had a large family Charles E Mix, her eldest son, has been chief clerk in the Indian Department at Washington for many years, (440) Elisha, b May 27, 1788, d. Oct. 18, 1789, (441)+Elisha, again, b May 5, 1790.

[206] JOHN[5] PECK, son of STEPHEN,[4] married Mary Lewis, and resided near his brother Henry They were spar and block-makers, their shop was upon the same lot near their dwelling. He died October 12, 1805.

CHILDREN — SIXTH GENERATION

(442) Nehemiah L , b. Aug 4, 1789, resided at the South, d Feb 2, 1821, unm , (443) Nancy, b Sept 9, 1791, d Jan 10, 1858, unm , (444) Betsey E , b Jan 29, 1793, d July 27, 1847, unm , (445) Mary, b Dec 19, 1798, d Nov. 4, 1859, unm , the sale and division of her estate among the heirs at law who were very numerous, was procured by Henry White, Esq , of New Haven. the distinguished antiquarian, as well as lawyer, to whose kindness I am indebted for information upon the subject.

[210] JOSEPH[5] PECK, son of JOSEPH,[4] was a Presbyterian clergyman, and preached at Bethel, Conn. He commenced his labors there in 1786. He died May 19, 1791, and was buried there. His ministration seems to have been very acceptable to

his people. From the Church records, it appears that he came there from an adjoining Presbytery.

CHILD — SIXTH GENERATION

(446)+Joseph, settled in New Milford, Conn

[211]   ABIJAH[5] PECK, son of JOSEPH,[4] settled in Danbury, Conn., where he died. His will is upon record there, B. 8, p. 401. He married Rachel Stevens.

CHILDREN — SIXTH GENERATION

(447)+Eliakim, (448)+Abijah, (449) Annie, who m. Peter Benedict, and (450) Rachel, who m Edward Eli

[213]   LEVI[5] PECK, son of JOSEPH,[4] resided in Danbury, where he died March 4, 1815. He was twice married. first, to Jerusha Starr, of Danbury; second, to Sarah Booth, of Stratford.

CHILDREN — SIXTH GENERATION .

(451) Noah, who d in Northeast New York, and left children, viz (452) *Hiram*[7], (453) *Lavinia*[7], (454) *Harmon*[7], (455) *Albert*[7], (456) *Edward*[7], (457) *James*[7], and (458) *Levi*[7] —(459)+Eli, b Aug 23, 1778, (460)+David, b Feb 18, 1781, (461) Anah, b May 29, 1783, m Ezra G Knapp, and settled in Westmoreland, N Y Her sons, O P,[7] and *William*,[7] reside at Fondulac, Wis — (462) Daniel, b June 29, 1787, d April 25, 1865, unm, (463)+William, b, Dec. 12, 1789, (464) Jerusha, b Jan 29, 1792, d Feb 24, 1816, (465) Joseph, b, Jan 21, 1796, d Oct 14, 1849, unm , (466) Rebecca, b. Feb. 15, 1800, resides in Danbury, a widow.

[216]   JESSE[5] PECK, son of ELIPHALET,[4] settled in the south part of Danbury, now Bethel, upon new lands where he made himself a farm. The house in which he resided has been torn down, but the one erected near it by his son is still standing, and was occupied by Samuel Judd in 1867.

He and four sons entered the army in the Revolutionary war. He and his sons Nathaniel and Eliphalet were taken prisoners and confined in New York until they took the small-pox, when they were released, and came home on foot. His son Eliphalet recovered from the disease, and returned to the army, but he and his son Nathaniel died. He was a member of the Church at Bethel, with which he United at its organization with his father and mother, in 1760. He married Ruth Hoyt. She was born February 26, 1738, and died February 2, 1809. He died January 28, 1777.

Belu Peck

(467) Nathaniel, b Dec 12, 1757, d Feb 1, 1777, (468)+Eliphalet, b March 19, 1758, (469)+Jesse, b Dec 22, 1759, (470) Benjamin, b Sept 24, 1761, (471) Lois, b Oct 28, 1763, m Israel Nickerson, lived to be aged, left no issue, (472)+Calvin, b Sept 3, 1765, (473)+Luther, b June 12, 1767, (474) +Daniel, b Aug 21, 1769, (475) Mercy, b Oct 29, 1771, d Nov. 30, 1776, (476) Esther, b Aug. 13, 1773, d Dec 25, 1776

[249.] CAPT. BELA[5] PECK, of Revolutionary memory, son of JOSEPH,[4] resided at Norwich, Conn, where he died, December 15, 1850, in the 93d year of his age. During a long life, industry, energy, prudence, firmness and integrity, were the leading traits of his character. He had strong common sense, and great practical wisdom.

He was twice married first, to Miss Betsey Billings, daughter of Capt. William Billings, October 20, 1787, second, to Mrs. Lydia Spaulding, widow of Asa Spaulding, August 18, 1819. His first wife died November 24, 1818, aged 54 years. His second wife died August 18, 1835, aged 68 years.

(477) William Billings, b Nov 30, 1788 He d Dec 18, 1805, while a student at Yale College, (478) Charlotte, b Oct 21, 1790 She m Ebenezer Learned, Esq, of New London, Oct 10, 1808 She d in 1819, leaving three children *Betsey P*,[7] *Ebenezer, jr*,[7] and *Billings P*[7] *Learned* — Betsey P, b. Nov 1809, m Rev Robert McEnen, and resides in New London, Conn Ebenezer, b Nov 1811, is a graduate of Yale College, and resides in Norwich, where he studied and practised law, and is now President of Norwich Fire Insurance Company. Billings P, b June 1813, is a graduate of Yale College, resides in Albany, N Y, and is President of the Union Bank (479) Harriet, the youngest daughter of Capt Bela Peck, was b March 17, 1795 At the age of 12 years, she was taken by her father to Bethlehem, Pa, and placed in the celebrated Moravian School at that place She remained there during 1807–8, and finished her school studies at Hartford, in 1809

On May 11, 1812, at the early age of 17 years, she was married to William Williams, of Norwich, Conn She accompanied her husband to Europe in 1823, and resided one year in France Since that time, her home has been in Norwich, in which city she has, for the past quarter of a century, exerted an influence as marked as it has been beneficent

Mrs. Williams inherited from her father those distinguishing characteristics to which his success in life was due, — a clear, active mind, a discriminating judgment, unusual business tact, and untiring energy Her generous impulses are continually prompting her to well directed acts of kindness and benevolence

In 1856, Mrs Williams founded and liberally endowed the "Peck Library,"

29*

in the Norwich Free Academy, which will remain a permanent and lasting memorial of her own generosity, and her father's name.

Gen Williams, her husband, was born in Stonington, Conn., March 12, 1788 At an early age he was employed in a shipping house in New York City, where he received a thorough mercantile training For several years after their marriage he was engaged in manufacturing, at Norwich Falls

From 1821 to 1827, he performed a number of successful commercial voyages to Europe and South America.

In 1828, he engaged in the whaling business, in New London, where he established the house of Williams & Bains. Though residing in Norwich, he has continued to be interested in, and connected with this business, up to the present time

In 1833, he was instrumental in establishing the Merchants Bank, of Norwich, of which institution he was chosen first President. This office he held for twenty-five years, resigning the same at the age of 70.

In 1858, he, with a few other public spirited gentlemen, organized and endowed the Norwich Free Academy, which has proved one of the model high schools of New England. He is now President of the Board of Trustees of this institution

He united with the Congregational church in 1820, and has ever been active in good works He is a corporate member of the American Board of Commissioners for Foreign Missions, and Vice-President of the Bible, Seaman's Friend, and Home Missionary Societies.

For a score of years, Gen. Williams has devoted a large portion of his time to the promotion of the cause of education in Eastern Connecticut During many seasons he visited annually nearly every district school within twenty miles of his house, distributing among them useful books and papers, and encouraging both teachers and pupils by his words of advice and the interest he evinced in their welfare.

He has always manifested an especial interest in the moral and religious condition of the Mohegan Indians, living on a government reservation a few miles from Norwich, and by his personal effort, and weekly visits, the church situated in their midst has in a great measure been sustained

He still continues active, promoting by his means and influence every benevolent enterprise, at home or abroad, which commends itself to his judgment

Their children are *William Peck[7] Williams*, b May 1813, d Feb 1815, *Thomas Wheeler[7] Williams*, b June 1815, d Sept 12, 1855, aged 40 years His early training was for the mercantile profession, which he received in the counting-house of Messrs Grinnell, Minturn & Co, New York From there, at the age of 20, he entered the counting-house of Messrs Williams & Bains, New London, who were in the whaling business He soon became a partner, and during the last fifteen years of his life was extensively engaged in the commerce of New London He was an honorable, practical, successful merchant *Bela Peck[7] Williams*, their youngest son, b April 12, 1817, d July 6, 1831, of brain fever, from too severe application to his studies, in preparation for college He was a youth of much promise.

Truly Yours
Wm Williams

[251.] PHINEAS[5] PECK, son of JONATHAN,[4] settled in Norwich, now Franklin. He married Elizabeth Barstow, December 22, 1768. She died in 1823. He died September 15, 1813.

CHILDREN — SIXTH GENERATION

(480)+Jonathan, b Sept. 13, 1769; (481) Elizabeth, b. July 16, 1772, (482) Phineas, b Oct 14, 1774, (483)+Gates, b Feb. 27, 1778; (484) Jathleel, b. June 30, 1780; (485)+Ambrose, b. July 10, 1782, (486) Phebe, b. Oct. 8, 1785, m. Daniel Gager, March 22, 1805.

[254.] DARIUS[5] PECK, son of JONATHAN,[4] resided in Norwich. He was twice married: first, to Hannah Warner, of Windham, November 5, 1772; second, to Mary Frances. His inventory was presented to the court April 30, 1804 (B. 10, p. 281).

CHILDREN — SIXTH GENERATION

(487) Bradford, b Nov. 5, 1773, d in the U. S. service, (488) Darius, b. Oct 11, 1775, d at sea; (489) John, b May 6, 1778, d in the West Indies, (490)+Joseph, b. Jan. 21, 1782; (491) Henry, d in Charleston, S C , (492) Warner, d on Staten Island, (493) Hannah, m Gerdon Fitch, and settled in Cleveland, Ohio, (494)+Elisha, b June 20, 1796, (495) Anna, m Henry Parks, (496) Lucy, m. Alfred Young, and was residing in New Haven, a widow, in 1866

[259] JATHLEEL[5] PECK, son of JONATHAN,[4] resided in Norwich, where he married Olive Hyde.

CHILDREN — SIXTH GENERATION

(497) John, b. Oct 22, 1782, and (498) Lucretia, b. Sept 12, 1784.

[287] JONATHAN MANSFIELD[5] PECK, son of BENAJAH,[4] resided in Woodbridge. He married Elizabeth Andrews. The following is from his tombstone:

" In memory of Lieut. Jonathan Mansfield Peck, who, at his daily labor, by a falling tree was instantly deprived of life, on the 21 of April, 1788, in the 30th year of his age.

" As a husband a father and a friend, he was a pattern of imitation."

CHILDREN — SIXTH GENERATION .

(499)+George F , b. Jan 5, 1781, (500) Rosannah, m Jacob Tolles, (501) Amarita, m Reed Bosworth, (502) Benajah, and (503) Betsey, who m Jesse Byington.

[288.]   SILAS[5] PECK, son of STEPHEN,[4] resided in the north-easterly part of Woodbridge, where his son Lewis has since lived and died, and where his grandson, Stephen Miland Peck, now resides.   He died April 6, 1841.   He married Electa Carrington.

CHILDREN — SIXTH GENERATION

(504) Almira, m. Simeon Sperry; (505) Ansel, settled in Vermont, (506) Lauren, settled in Vermont, (507) Amanda, (508)+Lewis, (509) Eunice, (510) Electa, (511) Garra, and (512) Sebia.

[289.]   HEZEKIAH[5] PECK, son of STEPHEN,[4] lived and died in Woodbridge, upon the same farm where his father and brothers Stephen and Edward also lived and died.   He married Sarah Downs, daughter of Seth Downs.   He died May 2, 1840.

CHILDREN — SIXTH GENERATION

(513)+Horace, b. Jan. 26, 1791, and (514) Polly, b Jan. 5, 1796

[290.]   STEPHEN[5] PECK, son of STEPHEN,[4] resided in Woodbridge, where he died, June 28, 1832.   He married Eunice Perkins.   She died December 17, 1831, aged 86 years.

CHILDREN — SIXTH GENERATION

(515) Lydia, m David R Baldwin, (516) Abiah, m Abner Bradley; (517) Maria, m Treat Clark, (518) Eliza, m first, William Bradley, second, Dennis Carrington, and (519) Betsey, who m first, John Newton, second, Nelson Newton.

[295.]   JOHN[6] PECK, son of SAMUEL,[5] resided in Manheim, N. Y., where he died.   He was killed by being thrown from a load drawn by a frightened team.   He married Polly Smith.

CHILDREN — SEVENTH GENERATION

(520)+Reuben, b Aug. 23, 1802, (521) Chauncey, b. Nov. 16, 1805, (522)+Elihu, b April 14, 1809, (523)+Amaziah, b. Sept 16, 1812, (524) John, b March 25, 1815, resides at Port Jackson, N Y. His children are *James W.,*[8] *Rosetta E ,*[8] *Reuben,*[8] *Abigail B ,*[8] *Hiram,*[8] *Eliza Ann,*[8] and *Clarissa* [8] They were received too late to be numbered and entered in the index

[296]   ISAAC[6] PECK, son of SAMUEL,[5] died in Danube, N. Y.

CHILDREN — SEVENTH GENERATION

(525) William, (526) Lucy, (527) Isaac, (528) Lydia, (529) Mathew, (530) Eli, (531) Cornelius, (532) Lyman, (533) James, (534) Henry, and (535) Lucinda.

[312.] MARCUS[6] PECK, son of ISAAC,[5] resided at Sand Lake, N. Y., where he died, March 19, 1851. He was a farmer, and a prominent public man, Town Clerk, Supervisor, and a Justice of the Peace for many years. He married Margaret Garner, in 1806.

CHILDREN — SEVENTH GENERATION

(536) Mary Ann, b March 23, 1807, (537)+Joel B., b. April 1, 1809; (538) Lucretia, b July 11, 1811, (539) Louisa, b Jan. 25, 1816, and (540) Margaret, b Nov. 2, 1819.

[315] LUCAS[6] PECK, son of ISAAC,[5] resided at Sand Lake, N. Y., where he died, in 1844. He married Catharine Miller.

CHILDREN — SEVENTH GENERATION

(541) John; (542) Betsey, (543) Hannah, (544) Silas; and (545) Hiram, who d leaving a wife and two children at Sand Lake.

[357] JAMES[6] PECK, son of DAVID,[5] settled upon the homestead, where he died. He was a farmer. He married Hannah Canfield.

CHILDREN — SEVENTH GENERATION

(546)+William, b Sept 13, 1790; (547)+Aaron, b March 2, 1798, (548) Phebe, b June 17, 1801, d. March 29, 1848 She m Samuel Condit, of Orange, N. J, by whom she had twelve children. The youngest, *Edward A.*[8] *Condit, Esq.*, b Feb 22, 1845, graduated at Nassau Hall, Princeton, N J. To him I am indebted for much of my information in relation to the New Jersey Pecks.

[372.] STEPHEN[6] PECK, son of JOHN,[5] resided in North Orange, where he died. He married Naomi, daughter of Timothy Condit.

CHILDREN — SEVENTH GENERATION

(549)+Peter, b Jan 4, 1784, d Jan 5, 1865, (550) Eunice, b. July 22, 1790, d Feb 21, 1844, (551) Maria, b. Sept 22, 1794, and (552) Moses, who d. in 1806, unm.

[377.] JOHN[6] PECK, son of JOHN,[5] resided in East Orange, where he died, April 1863. He married Phebe Mathews.

CHILDREN — SEVENTH GENERATION.

(553) Mary, b Aug 31, 1795, m Moses Sayers, d. Aug 15, 1829, (554) Eliza, b Aug 22, 1798, m Cyrus J Lyon, of East Orange, (555)+Stephen M, b. April 2, 1801, (556)+John, b April 18, 1805, (557) Nancy, b May 2, 1808, m. James W Tickenor, and was residing in Newark in 1866, (558) Lydia, b. Sept. 23, 1811, m first, Alanson C Munn, second, Christian Reynor, and was residing in Newark in 1866, (559) Phebe M, b Sept. 25, 1815, m. William F. Baldwin, and was residing in West Orange in 1866.

[395.] SAMUEL[6] PECK, son of SAMUEL,[5] married Esther Judd, of Waterbury, Conn., and removed to Homer, N. Y., where he died, April 1816. She died in 1856.

CHILDREN — SEVENTH GENERATION ·

(560) Minersa, b. Nov. 11, 1802, (561) Minerva, b June 1, 1804; (562)+Ira, b Dec 5, 1805, m Sarah A Simmons, had children, viz (563) *George S*[8]; (564) *Miles G*[8], (565) *Jerome T*[8], (566) *Sarah A*[8]; (567) *William I*[8]; (568) *John S*[8], (569) *Mary E.*[8], and (570) *Martha E*[8] — (571) Polly, b June 22, 1807; (572) Anna, b March 6, 1809, (573) Samuel, b July 12, 1811, (574) Maria, b. April 12, 1813, (575) Laura, b. April 6, 1815, and (576) Roswell J., b. Nov. 1, 1816.

[402] TITUS[6] PECK, son of SAMUEL,[5] resided in Bethany, where he died, July 27, 1855. He married Sybel Nettleton. She died March 25, 1834.

CHILDREN — SEVENTH GENERATION ·

(577) Mary M , b April 30, 1816, (578)+Ephraim, b April 3, 1819; (579)+ Isaac L , b. March 14, 1821; (580) Laura A., (581)+Titus D., b. March 3, 1832.

[403.] ABEL[6] PECK, son of SAMUEL,[5] settled in Mattewan, N. Y. From there he removed to Monticello, Ill., and from there returned to New Haven, Conn. He was twice married first, to Sarah Camp; second, to Louisa Hicks. He died October 22, 1859.

CHILDREN — SEVENTH GENERATION

(582) Samuel, b. March 7, 1813, m. Mary S Bryan, and had (583) *Mary Frances*[8], and (584) *Walter B.,*[8] who m. Helen F , daughter of John Peck (No 785), a descendant of Joseph, of Milford — (585) Sarah Ann, b in 1815, (586) Harriet, b in 1817, (587) Martha, b in 1819; (588) Eliza, b in 1821, (589) Abel, b in 1826, (590) Hannah, (591) Clark, b in 1828, (592) Lyman, b. in 1830; and (593) Lucy, b. in 1832.

[405.] JEREMIAH[6] PECK, son of SAMUEL,[5] married Julia, daughter of Amasa Roberts, January, 1822. She died October 30, 1866. He was residing in New Haven in 1867.

CHILDREN — SEVENTH GENERATION

(594)+Robert, b Nov 23, 1822, (595)+Milo, b May 28, 1824, (596)+ Charles, b April 27, 1826, (597) Jane, b March 12, 1828, m first, Henry Dyer, Sept 9, 1849, second, Charles Morris, and resides in New Haven, (598) Abigail, b Nov 25, 1830, m Royal Lewis, and resides in Thompson, Ill , (599) Emily, b March 4, 1833, d Dec 2, 1835, (600) Sarah, b. Feb. 29, 1836, was residing in New Haven, unm., in 1867.

[406.]   JEREMIAH⁶ PECK, son of AMOS,⁵ resided at first in Hamden, Conn., and from there removed to Brunswick, Ohio, about 1835, where he died, September 14, 1853.   His widow was still living there in 1866.

CHILDREN — SEVENTH GENERATION ·

(601) Miles, m Eunice Bradley. His children are   (602) *Mary*,⁸ who resides in Woodbridge, Conn , unm , and (603) *Willis*,⁸ a carpenter and joiner, who m Ellen Dayton, and resides in Meriden, Conn. — (604) Otis, d. young; (605)+Willis, (606)+Lucius, and (607) Eliza.

[411.]   AMOS⁶ PECK, son of AMOS,⁵ resided in Hamden, Conn.   He married Louisa Todd, February 19, 1817.   She died November 23, 1865, aged 68 years.   He died April 26, 1866.

CHILDREN — SEVENTH GENERATION

(608) Louisa J., b Dec 24, 1818, m Bayed Munson, April 1, 1838, (609) Amos B., b. Feb 1, 1820; and (610)+John B , b. Feb 18, 1825.

[426.]   SAMUEL⁶ PECK, son of ELIJAH,⁵ resided in Roxbury, Mass.   He married Hannah, daughter of David Baker.   He died September 3, 1849.   She was residing in Roxbury in 1866.

CHILDREN — SEVENTH GENERATION .

(611) Sarah, b Nov 13, 1809, (612) William, b Feb. 17, 1812, (613) Mary Ann, b March 2, 1814, (614) Samuel, b Oct 30, 1816, (615) Moses, b. June 26, 1819, (616) George, b Jan 11, 1822, (617) Hannah, b March 14, 1824, (618) Lucy, b Sept 18, 1826, and (619) Luke, b Feb 18, 1830.

[430]   JAMES⁶ PECK, son of EBENEZER,⁵ married Ann Atwater, and removed to Jeffersonville, Ind., where he died, in 1865.

CHILDREN — SEVENTH GENERATION

(620) Mary A , (621) William A., (622) Elizabeth H , (623) Ebenezer; (624) James C , (625) Henry H., (626) Edward H. R , (627) Anna H , and (628) Edwin P   Henry H , to whom I am indebted for my information, is a school teacher, and resides at Post Creek, N Y. He married Zilpha Wetherell, of Norwich, Conn   His children, in 1867, were (629) *Mary H* ⁸, (630) *Louisa H* ⁸, (631) *Frank M* ⁸, (632) *Hattie E.*⁸, and (633) *Ida J.*⁸

[441.]   ELISHA⁶ PECK, son of HENRY,⁵ was a Captain in the U. S. Navy.   He was in the service more than fifty years.   He died June 11, 1866.   He married Grace Bonticon.

(634) Evelina, b in 1836, m Capt William W. Low, of the U S. Navy; (635) Henry L., b in 1839; (636) Joanna B., m. Maj James Whittemore, June 24, 1863. He graduated at West Point in 1860, and is an engineer in the U. S. service

[446]   JOSEPH[6] PECK, son of REV. JOSEPH,[5] settled in New Milford, where he died.   The following is from the town records;

" Joseph Peck, of New Milford, & Prescilla Starr, of Danbury, was joined in lawful marriage by y[e] Rev. Mr. Joseph Peck, on y[e] first day of Nov., A. D. 1787.   Prescilla, wife to Joseph Peck, deceased on y[e] 20th of Nov., A. D. 1788.   Joseph Peck and Uraina Bennett was joined in marriage on y[e] 20th day of Dec., 1790."

(637) Prescilla, b. Oct 8, 1788, m Herbert Canfield, and settled in Bridgewater, Conn , (638) Joseph, b Aug 28, 1792, m Fanny Warren, and removed to Montgomery, N Y , where he died   His children are (639) *James*[8], (640) *Frederick*[8], (641) *Joseph*[8], and (642) *Webb* [8] —(643) Bennett, b May 21, 1795, settled in New Milford, where he died. He m Miranda Stone. His children are (644) *Walter B.*,[8] who resides in Bridgewater; (645) *Catharine L* [8], (646) *John B* [8], and (647) *Henry A* [8] — (648) James M , b. Oct 12, 1801, d in New Milford, leaving two children   His widow m. Edward Murry, and resides in Honesdale, Penn.

[447.]   ELIAKIM[6] PECK, son of ABIJAH,[5] resided in Danbury, where he died.   He married Polly Starr.

(649) Charles, b Sept 4, 1787, (650) Beulah, b Oct 15, 1789, (651) Sally, b March 21, 1792, (652) Starr, b April 2, 1795, (653) Amarillas, b Nov 26, 1797, (654) George, b Aug 11, 1800; (655) Lucy, b in 1803, (656) Rachel, b. in 1806, (657) Stephen S , b. Oct 27, 1809

[448.]   ABIJAH[6] PECK, son of ABIJAH,[5] removed with his family to Alabama.   He married Clarissa Stedman.

(658) Henry, b Nov 21, 1791, (659) Frederick, b Sept 18, 1793, (660) Sophia, b Jan 16, 1796, (661) Edwin, b March 18, 1798, (662) Abijah, b March 9, 1800; (663) James S , b April 19, 1802, (664) Thomas, and (665) Clarissa, who m a Mr. Gale (Genealogical Register, vol. 14, p. 73).

[459.]   ELI[6] PECK, son of LEVI,[5] removed from Danbury to the town of Westmoreland, N. Y.   He was twice married: first, to

Martha Rogers, of Northford, Conn.; second, to Mrs. Ruth Hart, formerly Miss Ruth Stebbins. His first wife died July 1, 1835. He died December 17, 1852. His second wife survived him, and was residing in Clinton, N. Y, in 1867.

CHILDREN — SEVENTH GENERATION

(666) Angeline, b Nov 12, 1804, m Samuel Patterson, and resides in Clinton, (667)+William S, b Oct 30, 1806, (668) Laura, b April 20, 1809, m. John Park, of Clinton, (669) Frederick Rogers, b June 11, 1811, was killed Aug 22, 1814, by falling into the flume of a paper mill, and passing through the wheel, (670) Madelia, b Nov 3, 1812, d April 4, 1813, (671)+Frederick B, b. Nov 25, 1815

[460] DAVID[6] PECK, son of LEVI,[5] removed from Danbury, Conn, to Thompson, Ulster County, N. Y He was twice married first, to Lucy Rogers; second, to Mrs. Anna Russell, whose maiden name was Gilbert. His first wife died June 20, 1831; his second, January 21, 1859. He died at Cortland, N. Y., December 28, 1866.

CHILDREN — SEVENTH GENERATION

(672) Caroline, m, Dr Marcus Merrick, and d leaving one child, who d in June 1833, (673) Philander, m Clarissa C Brink, and d at Chicago in 1852 His sons (674) *Henry*[8] and (675) *George*,[8] d, one aged 24 and the other 22. His widow resides in Chicago — (676) George E, m first, B N Hibbard, second, Minerva Brink His children all d in infancy He d in 1843

Thus it will be seen that the name becomes extinct in the family of David He outlived all his children and grandchildren.

[463] WILLIAM[6] PECK, son of LEVI,[5] resided in Danbury, Conn, where he died June 11, 1858. He married Sarah Starr, October 8, 1811.

CHILDREN — SEVENTH GENERATION

(677) William S, b Dec 31, 1813, and (678) Elizabeth A, b Dec 21, 1819. William S resides in Danbury, where he is a prominent public man, one of the principal selectmen, etc, transacting most of the business of the town He married Eliza Mallory His children are (679) *Harriet E*,[8] b May 26, 1835, (680) *Levi M*,[8] b Oct 1, 1840, m Harriet Jennings His child, (681) *Lillian*,[9] was b. Jan 18, 1867

[468] ELIPHALET[6] PECK, son of JESS,[5] removed from Danbury to Providence, Saratoga County, N. Y, in 1795, and from there to Alexander, Genesee County, about 1824, where he died in 1842. He married Abigail Hawley.

CHILDREN — SEVENTH GENERATION ·

(682) Nathaniel, b in 1782, resides at Brownsville, N. Y, m Abigail Starr, and has the following children (683) *Samuel S*,[8] d in 1858, (684) *Laurentina*,[8] m a McDonald, and resides at Brownsville, N Y, (685) *Louisa*,[8] m. Cyrus Allen, and resides at Peach River, N. Y, (686) *Caroline*,[8] m. Almerin Wilson, and resides at Brownsville, N Y, (687) *Sarah*,[8] is deceased, (688) *Andrew*,[8] is deceased, (689) *Riley W*,[8] resides in Brooklyn, N. Y, to whose kindness I am indebted He m Delia A, daughter of the late Rufus Green, M. D, of New York City, and has two children (690) *Francis S*[9], and (691) *Caroline W*[9]—(692) *Minerva*,[8] m John W. Collins, of Toledo, Ohio, (693) *Chauncey A*,[8] of Los Angelos, Cal, and (694) *Myron H*,[8] of Dexter, N Y — (695) Samuel, b in 1784, resides in Brownsville, N Y, (696) Eliphalet, b in 1786, resides at Stone Mills, N. Y, (697) Abigail, b in 1789, m Jacob Conklin, and resides, a widow, at Greenfield, N Y, (698) Benjamin, b in 1791, d in Orangeville, N Y., where some of his family reside, (699)+Eli, b in 1793, (700) Asa, b in 1795, d unm, (701) Rebecca, b in 1798, m Clark Tabor, and is deceased, (702) Sally, b in 1801, d unm, (703) Ruth, b. in 1805, m. Cherick Vande Bogart, and is deceased.

[469.] JESSE[6] PECK, son of JESSE,[5] settled in the Southern part of Danbury, now Bethel, upon the homestead with his brother Benjamin. The house in which he resided and reared his family is still standing, now occupied by Samuel Judd. He was in the Revolutionary war five years. He died May 5, 1808. He was a member of the Presbyterian church. He married Anna Nickerson.

CHILDREN — SEVENTH GENERATION

(704)+William, b Nov 26, 1783, (705)+Jesse, b Oct. 11, 1784, (706)+Levi, b April 30, 1791, (707) Joseph bap in 1794, (708) Anna, b March 17, 1794, resides in Danbury, Conn, (709) Zillah, bap. in 1796, is also residing in Danbury.

[470] BENJAMIN[6] PECK, son of JESSE,[5] resided upon the homestead which he occupied with his brother Jesse. He was a Presbyterian deacon. He was twice married. first, to Elizabeth Nickerson; second, to Mary Osborn. His first wife died without issue

CHILDREN — SEVENTH GENERATION *

(710) John C. resides in Fairfield, Conn, has been three times married first, to Eunice Northrop, second, to Emeline Morgan, third, to Mary C Couch His children are (711) *George N*[8], and (712) *Mary E*[8]—(713) Benjamin H. resides in or near the town of North East, N Y He m Susan Northrop His children are (714) *Calvin*[8], (715) *Elizabeth*[8], and (716) *Emma*[8]

---

* The full record of the family was received too late for insertion There was one child that died in infancy.

[472]   CALVIN[6] PECK. son of Jesse,[5] settled at first in Danbury; from there he moved, in 1796, to Greenfield, Saratoga County, where he resided until 1806, when he removed to Pompey, Onondaga County, where he died July 19, 1841. He was a Baptist deacon. He married, first, Mindwell Taylor; second, Martha Abbott.

CHILDREN — SEVENTH GENERATION

(717) Mindwell, b July 17, 1785, m Stephen Thomas, and d in Illinois, (718) Mercy, b Jan 4, 1787, d unm , (719) Calvin L , b June 25, 1788 , (720) +Daniel C , b Feb 4, 1794, (721) Polly, b Jan 4, 1797, m Abraham Thomas, and resides in Fabius, N Y. To her I am indebted for my information

[473.]   LUTHER[6] PECK, son of Jesse,[5] resided at first in Danbury, Conn. He afterwards settled at Middletown, N Y. He was married to Annis Coller, by Rev. Joseph Peck, (No. 210), September 27, 1787. She died October 23, 1839; he September 30, 1848. They were both honored members of the church, and devoted Christians.

He was for many years a class leader, and distinguished for the zeal and fidelity with which he discharged his duties, and the interest which he took in the cause of Christianity.

CHILDREN — SEVENTH GENERATION

(722) Rachel, b Nov 8, 1788, m John Bennett, Dec 26. 1804, and settled at Broklestraw, Penn , (723) Martha, b July 31, 1790, m Joshua Jaquays, March 15, 1810, and settled in Broklestraw, Penn , (724) Elizabeth, b July 22, 1792, d Nov 30, 1822 , (725)+Luther H , b Nov 3, 1793 , (726)+George, b Aug 8, 1797, (727) +Andrew, b April 29, 1800 , (728) Mary, b Nov 8, 1801, d Nov. 14, 1822 , (729) William, b Dec 7, 1802 He is a Methodist clergyman, and itinerates He m Charlotte Wallen, Jan 1, 1828, no issue , (730) Anna, b March 9, 1806, m Solomon Crowell, Feb 23, 1824, and settled in Chatauque County, N Y , (731) Susanna, b Aug 26, 1808, m Royal Blanding, Aug 5, 1827, settled in Chatauque County, N Y , (732)+Jesse T , b April 4, 1811

The above family is a very remarkable one The sons, all of them, five in number, are distinguished clergymen of the Methodist Episcopal church, and two of them eminent authors Five of the grandchildren, it will also be seen, are distinguished clergymen of the same denomination of Christians

[474]   DANIEL[6] PECK, son of Jesse,[5] resided at first in Danbury, but afterwards settled in the city of New York, where he was a merchant. He was an Episcopalian, a church warden for many years. He married Phebe Whitlock. He died June 21, 1829; she April 21, 1857.

(733) Benjamin W , b Nov. 20, 1791, (734) Laura E , b Dec 26, 1797, m a Mi Fox, and d May 22, 1829, (735) Phebe U , b July 6, 1804, m a Townsend, and d April 1857, (736) Daniel S , b June 24, 1806, d. Dec 7, 1834 , (737) George H , b July 30, 1809, resides in New York City.

[480]   JONATHAN[6] PECK, son of PHINEAS,[5] settled at first in Franklin, Conn , and from there removed to Pembroke, N. Y. He was twice married · first, to Martha Willis , second, to Lois Crocker. His first wife died July 17, 1805. His second wife died in Ravenna, Ohio. He died in Parma, N Y., October 12, 1846.

(738) Eunice, b Dec 4, 1791, m Stephen Armstrong; is a widow, and resides at Pierpont, Ohio, (739) Martha, b Aug 12, 1794, m a Wilson, and d at Parma, N Y , (740)+Lucius, b Nov 9, 1797, (741)+Jonathan H , b. July 15, 1801, (742) Joshua W , b Aug 19,1803 , (743) Dyer S and (744)+ Asa C , twins, b Oct 25, 1806   Dyer S d Nov 13, 1806

[483]   GATES[6] PECK, son of PHINEAS,[5] resided at Delta, N. Y., where he died, September 11, 1865. He married Lurena Rudd. She died July 17, 1867, aged 83 3-4 years.

(745) Franklin, b April 21, 1805, resides in Leighton, Mich , (746) Eliza Ann, b April 14, 1807, resides at Delta, (747) Marietta, b Aug 18, 1809, m Samuel Savery, and removed to Provo City, Utah , (748) Cornelia M., b Jan. 24, 1812, d Sept 9, 1814 , (749) Charles R , b Aug 1, 1814, d Aug 20, 1814 , (750) Benjamin R , b Oct 9, 1815, m Fanny Bailey   He was drowned July 3, 1861   (751) Eloise C., b Nov 9, 1818, m Israel Williams. He d in 1860. She resides at Delta   (752) Cleore F , b Nov 7, 1822, to whom I am indebted for my information in relation to the family, m Daniel Smith, jr , and resides at Delta.

[485]   AMBROSE[6] PECK, son of PHINEAS,[5] resided in Franklin, Conn., where he died, February 25, 1855. He married Eunice Hazen, September 9, 1810. She died March 1, 1843.

(753)+John H , b July 10, 1811; (754) William B , b May 12, 1816   He went South, and has not been heard from for years , is supposed to be dead.

[490]   JOSEPH[6] PECK, son of DARIAS,[5] resided for some time in Columbia, Tolland County, Conn , and from there removed to South Harford, Penn., where he still resides. He is a wheel-

wright by trade, which occupation he has followed in co..nection with farming.   He married Polly Collins.

CHILDREN — SEVENTH GENERATION

(755) Philura, b June 14, 1817, m J C Powers, (756) Hannah M , b May 8, 1819, m Joseph Powers, (757)+Darias, b Jan 25, 1822, (758) Mary M , b July 22, 1826, resides at home, (759) Eleazar C , b Sept 23, 1828, also resides at home.

[494.]   ELISHA[6] PECK, son of Darias,[5] resided at Waterville, N. Y.   He married Lucy Hinchly, August 20, 1817.   He died June 18, 1868.

CHILDREN — SEVENTH GENERATION

(760) Timothy H , b Sept 8, 1818, resides at West Brookfield, N Y , (761) Jirah H , b April 30, 1822, d Oct, 8, 1834, (762) Mary H , b May 8, 1824, m Hermon T Greenslit, resides at Marshall, N Y , (763) Edwin S , b March 16, 1827, settled at Waterville, N Y , (764) Frances E , b Feb 1, 1830, d April 26, 1859, (765) John L , b April 2, 1832, resides at Bloomington, Ill , (766) Ellen L , b. Aug. 31, 1835, m. Silas B Greenman, Jan 7, 1856, resides at Westerly, R I.

[499]   GEORGE F[6] PECK, son of Jonathan M ,[5] resided in Woodbridge, where he died, March 25, 1860.   He married Fanny Ball, October 19, 1800.

CHILDREN — SEVENTH GENERATION

(767) Stiles, b April 17, 1802, d Feb 4, 1850; (768) Jonathan M , b Jan. 29, 1804, d Oct 6, 1822, (769) George, b May 16, 1806, m Sylvia Tuttle, and had (770) *George F H*[8], (771) *Bennett W*[8], and (772) *Henry S*[8] — (773) Henry, b July 25, 1808, d Sept 7, 1815, (774) William B , b Aug 12, 1810, d Sept 15, 1866, (775) Milo, b Jan 3, 1813, d Aug 31, 1815, (776) Lucius W , b Dec 28, 1814, m Mary E Smith   His son, (777) *Willie*,[8] was b June 30, 1850 — (778) Fanny L , b Oct 1, 1817, m Nathan N. Sperry.

[503.]   LEWIS[6] PECK, son of Silas,[5] married Ann Beecher, and resided in Woodbridge.

CHILDREN — SEVENTH GENERATION

(779) Ephraim R , (780) Eliza Ann , (781) Minerva , (782) Irom , (783) Silas E , (784) Henry , and (785) Stephen M

[513]   HORACE[6] PECK, son of Hezekiah,[5] resides in Woodbridge, upon the paternal homestead, about four miles from New Haven, upon the road to Waterbury, where his father and grandfather lived and died.   He is a deacon of the church and a promi-

30*

nent man. To his kindness I am indebted for my information in relation to his branch of the name He married Sarah Stevens, May 9, 1813. She died June 21, 1855.

CHILDREN — SEVENTH GENERATION

(786) Sarah, b Feb 21, 1814, d young; (787) Emily, b Feb 21, 1817, m. Edward S Rowland, a merchant, of New Haven, (788) Horace E , b Jan 27, 1819, d March 1, 1845, (789)+Stephen A , b Nov 20, 1822, (790)+William S , b May 4, 1826

[520] REUBEN[7] PECK, son of JOHN,[6] resided at Little Falls, N Y., where he died, November 16, 1842. He married Marall Chase, February 24, 1825.

CHILDREN — EIGHTH GENERATION

(791) Julia Ann, b Dec 27, 1825, m Phillips Michael, a wealthy farmer of Lassallsville, N Y , by whom she has four children, (792)+Francis B , b May 14, 1827, (793) Matilda, b July 6, 1828, m Abraham Michael, of Lassallsville, a brother of Phillips, and also a wealthy farmer He d April 5, 1866, leaving one son, who resides upon the homestead with his mother. (794)+Fayette S , b April 19, 1830

[522] ELIHU[7] PECK, son of JOHN,[6] resided in Florida, N. Y., where he died, March 8, 1867. He married Permelia Brown, who died June 5, 1867.

CHILDREN — EIGHTH GENERATION

(795) Alfred, b Jan 15, 1833 He is the proprietor of a cheese factory at Millers corners, Florida, N Y He m Martha A Failing; has three children (796) *May A*[9], (797) *Charley*[9], and (798) *Amanda*[9] — (799) Elmina, b. Aug 7, 1834, m William E Van Allen, of St Johnsville, N Y , (800) Asa, b April 12, 1836, m Libbe Koons, and resides at Fonda, N Y , (801) Polly A , b April 22, 1838, m William J Merry, and resides in Florida, (802) James, b April 20, 1841, served three years in the war against the rebels, by which his constitution was ruined, he d Jan 27, 1867, leaving a wife and one child, (803) Malvin, b Aug 29, 1844, also served three years in the war ; m Prudence Frisbee, and resides in Florida, (804) Elery E , b Aug 22, 1849, is unm , and resides in Florida

[523] AMAZIAH[7] PECK, son of JOHN,[6] resided in St. Johnsville, N Y., where he died, December 3, 1847. He married Mary Bellinger.

CHILDREN — EIGHTH GENERATION

(805) Lucy, b May 28, 1839, d March 12, 1842, (806) Elizabeth, b Nov 11, 1840, m Jeremiah E Smith, (807) Helen, b Jan 12, 1842, m Pardee Yoran, (808) Alonzo, b Jan 17, 1844, d Nov 7, 1865, (809) Albert, b Feb 8, 1846, m Emily House, resides in Avoca, N Y , (810) Amzi, b Jan 31, 1848, resides in St Johnsville

[537]   JOEL B [7] PECK, son of MARCUS,[6] resides in the town of Sand Lake, N. Y.   He is a prominent man; has been supervisor of the town, etc.   During the rebellion, he had charge of raising the town's quota of men, disbursing the money, etc., for that purpose.   He is a farmer, and also carries on the lumbering business.   He married Pamelia Horton, June 9, 1832.

CHILDREN — EIGHTH GENERATION

(811) Charles H , b. March 30, 1833, graduated at Union College, Schenectady, and is a teacher of a school at Albany , (812) Mary L , b Oct 18, 1834, is m , and is settled in Sand Lake , (813) Amanda B , b June 13, 1837, resides in Sand Lake , (814) Marcus, b June 6, 1839 , enlisted in Company H, 169 V Reg , and d at Army Hospital, Washington, D C , March 19, 1863, of typhoid fever ; (815) Emma, b May 6, 1841, is m , and resides in Sand Lake , (816) George H , b July 27, 1844, d April 20, 1853 , (817) Arthur M , b Feb 2, 1848, resides at home , (818) Alice, b May 30, 1851, resides at home , (819) G Munson, b April 3, 1855, also resides at home.

[546]   WILLIAM[7] PECK, son of JAMES,[6] settled in East Orange, N. J., where he died, May 4, 1849.   He married Fanny Canfield.

CHILDREN — EIGHTH GENERATION

(820) Ira, b March 26, 1822, (821) James, b Jan 30, 1825 , (822) Phebe E , b June 19, 1814, m. John M Crowell, (823) Rhoda, b April 14, 1816, m. Linus Pierson, (824) Margaret E , b Nov 26, 1819, m Alford Jones, (825) Mary Ann, b May 20, 1827 , (826) Harriet, b Dec 4, 1831, m Elias O Doremus, (827) William, b March 26, 1834, and d Aug 20, 1836

[547]   AARON[7] PECK, son of JAMES,[6] settled in East Orange, N. J , where he died.   Mr Peck was, for many years, an enterprising business man.   He was President, and at one time principal owner, of the Sussex Railroad, and also the proprietor and chief owner of the village of Roseville, now a part of the city of Newark.   His disease was pneumonia.   Its fatal character became apparent several days before his decease.   He prepared for the event with a calmness of one about to enter upon a journey, and was conscious to the last.   He died April 8, 1865, in well-directed hopes of a future life beyond the grave.   His wife was Miranda, daughter of Bethuel Pierson, of Orange, N. J.   She died December 1863.

CHILDREN — EIGHTH GENERATION

(828) Caroline, b Sept 1, 1821, m Rev David H Pierson , (829) Mary Jane, b Oct 29, 1831 , (830) George, b July 9, 1826, a surgeon in the U S Navy,

m Eliza A , daughter of Dr Stephen S Brewster; (831) Cyrus, b Nov. 1, 1829 He is Secretary of the Continental Insurance Co , N Y , m Mary P , daughter of Rev John T Halsey His children are (832) *Helen O ,*[9] b Nov. 20, 1853 , (833) *Edward H ,*[9] b Dec 17, 1857 , (834) *William H ,*[9] b Feb 16, 1860; and (835) *Edith M ,*[9] b March 2, 1865 — (836) Aaron, b June 6, 1836, graduated at Nassau Hall, Princeton, N. J , m Julia, daughter of Stella Manning, Esq He was licensed to preach in 1864, and ordained in Cleveland, Ohio, in 1866 His child, *Julia May,*[9] was b · Jan 1, 1865, and d July 9, 1865.

[549]   PETER[7] PECK, son of STEPHEN,[6] was a farmer, and resided in South Orange, N. J., where he died, January 5, 1865. He married Ruth Quimby for his first wife, and Rhoda Harrison for his second.

CHILDREN — EIGHTH GENERATION

(837) Margaret, b Feb 9, 1806, (838) Naomi, b Nov 9, 1808, (839) Phebe, b Dec 20, 1811, (840) Maria, b July 4, 1814 , (841) Ruth, b July 15, 1817 , (842) Moses, b March 24, 1824, and (843) Margaret, again, b Feb 8, 1826

[555]   STEPHEN M.[7] PECK, son of JOHN,[6] resides in Livingston, N. J , a farmer. He has been twice married : first, to Martha Baldwin ; second, to Margaret Pierson.

CHILDREN — EIGHTH GENERATION

(844) Emeline L , b April 25, 1827, m William Williams, of East Orange , (845) Mary, b Aug 29, 1829, is unm , (846) Malinda, b March 28, 1832, d. Dec. 4, 1834 , (847) Elizabeth, b Sept 17, 1834, is unm , (848) Theodore M , b April 25, 1837, (849) Sarah B , b Sept 1, 1839, m William Jaffrage, of Roseville, N J , (850) Martha and (851) Henry, twins, b Aug 16, 1843 , Martha m Benjamin Simpson, Henry d in 1860; (852) Emma, b March 9, 1845, d April 21, 1847, (853) Stephen A , b Sept. 18, 1846, d Aug. 22, 1849 , (854) Emma, again, b March 30, 1849.

[556.]   JOHN[7] PECK, son of JOHN,[6] resides in East Orange, N. J., a farmer. He married Charlotte Tickenor.

CHILDREN — EIGHTH GENERATION

(855) Henry H and (856) Abby H , twins, b March 30, 1834 , (857) Charlotte F., b May 19, 1838 , (858) Alvin T , b Sept. 25, 1840

[562.]   IRA[7] PECK, son of SAMUEL,[6] married Sarah A. Simmons.

CHILDREN — EIGHTH GENERATION :

(859) George S , b Sept 21, 1833 , (860) Miles G , b Jan 8, 1835 , (861) Jerome T , b March 4, 1837 , (862) Sarah A , b. June 1, 1838 , (863) William Ira, b. Sept 11, 1843 , (864) John S , b. March 1, 1847 , (865) Mary E. and (866) Martha E , twins, b April 17, 1850.

[578] EPHRAIM N.[7] PECK, son of Titus,[6] resides in Bethany; is a joiner and carpenter by trade. He has been twice married: first, to Caroline M. Flagg; second, to Sarah H. Wilcox.

CHILDREN — EIGHTH GENERATION

(867) Eugene A ; (868) George I , b Dec 4, 1850; and (869) Charlie E , b. Nov 14, 1856.

[579.] ISAAC L [7] PECK, son of Titus,[6] resides in Bethany; is a joiner and carpenter. He has been twice married: first, to Mary Ann Hunt; second, to Mahala A. Church.

CHILDREN — EIGHTH GENERATION .

(870) Henry L., b. June 27, 1848, (871) Eugene H , b. Aug. 27, 1851, and (872) Mary A

[581.] TITUS D.[7] PECK, son of Titus,[6] resided in Bethany. He married Louisa Brainard. She died September 4, 1866.

CHILDREN — EIGHTH GENERATION

(873) Frank, (874) Mary, (875) Jane; (876) Bird, (877) Minnie; and (878) Lillie.

[594.] ROBERT[7] PECK, son of Jeremiah,[6] resided in New Haven, where he died, October 13, 1851. He married Lucena G. Hamlin, of Plainville, Conn.

CHILDREN — EIGHTH GENERATION ·

(879) Ava R , b Jan 19, 1844 He was a Lieutenant in the N Y Vol Infantry, in the early part of the Rebellion, and afterwards joined the cavalry, was taken prisoner, and died in the military prison, at Salisbury, N C , Dec 5, 1864 , (880) Charles W., b April 17, 1847, d Sept. 13, 1850; (881) Charles H., b June 29, 1851.

[595] MILO[7] PECK, son of Jeremiah,[6] resides in New Haven. He is a manufacturer of machinery, in connection with his brother Charles, under the firm of Milo Peck & Co. He married Susan DeWolf, of Conway, Mass.

CHILDREN — EIGHTH GENERATION

(882) Mary Helen, b Sept 17, 1856, (883) George William, b Sept. 14, 1858 , (884) Julia Rebecca, b Oct. 3, 1860; (885) John Ledyard, b. July 4, 1863.

[596] CHARLES[7] PECK, son of Jeremiah,[6] resides in New Haven, where he is a prominent man, a member of the Common

Council, etc. To his kindness I am indebted for much of my information in relation to his branch of the name. He married Mary Elizabeth, daughter of Harvey Munson, of New Haven.

CHILDREN — EIGHTH GENERATION.

(886) Emily Frances, b May 27, 1854, (887) Charles Harvey, b July 22, 1857, d Oct. 26, 1858, (888) Willie Frank, b Sept. 26, 1859, d Feb 4, 1860; (889) Robert Jeremiah, b. April 22, 1862.

[605.] WILLIS⁷ PECK, son of JEREMIAH,⁶ settled in Brunswick, Ohio, where he died, January 13, 1840. He married Sarah M. Potter, September 3, 1828.

CHILDREN — EIGHTH GENERATION ·

(890) Jeremiah W., b. Feb. 12, 1830; (891) Mary C., b. March 11, 1832, (892) Louisa O., b. Aug. 7, 1834.

[606.] LUCIUS⁷ PECK, son of JEREMIAH,⁶ settled in Brunswick, Ohio, where he died, October 24, 1859. He married Fanny Scranton. She died July 12, 1836.

CHILDREN — EIGHTH GENERATION.

(893) Lewis W., b. April 12, 1837, d. at the battle of Resaca, Ga , (894) N. E , b in 1839, m. Sarah Ayloid, and resides in Brunswick His children are, (895) *Mary A.*⁹; and (896) *Lewis E.*⁹ — (897) Eliza M., b. Sept. 25, 1841, (898) Wyllys M., b Dec. 24, 1843, d. in 1863, at Bleat Lick, Ky , a soldier; (899) Oliva A , b Sept 1, 1846, d Dec. 25, 1847; (900) George H , b Oct 20, 1849, d. Jan. 1864, (901) Frederick, b. March 3, 1854, resides in Brunswick

[610.] JOHN B.⁷ PECK, son of AMOS,⁶ resides at Mount Carmel, Conn. He married Adaline A. Bradley. To him I am indebted for my information in relation to his branch of the name.

CHILDREN — EIGHTH GENERATION

(902) Leander B., b. May 26, 1848, (903) Adaline, b. Sept. 12, 1854.

[667.] WILLIAM S.⁷ PECK, son of ELI,⁶ married, for his first wife, Urana Park; for his second, Lydia Stebbins; and for his third, Mary A. Neville. He died at Palmyra, Jefferson County, Wis., May 13, 1849.

CHILDREN — EIGHTH GENERATION

Clement L., who d aged about 3 years, and (904) Clement S , who resides in Berlin, Wis., is married, and has one child.

[671.] FREDERICK B.[7] PECK, son of ELI,[6] resides in Berlin, Wis., where he is of the firm of "Peck, Warner & Peck," dealers in hardware, cordage, stoves, glass, etc. He married Hannah Park, October 4, 1837.

CHILD — EIGHTH GENERATION

(905) Covell A , b Sept 16, 1839, is a partner in business with his father. He m Dora C. Russell, and has two children. (906) *Fred R* [9], and (907) *Minnie* [9]

[699.] ELI[7] PECK, son of ELIPHALET,[6] resides in Alexander, N. Y. He married Nancy Smith.

CHILDREN — EIGHTH GENERATION

(908) Walter, resides at Rockford, Ill , is a manufacturer of wind-mill pumps He has been twice married first, to Mary E Simmonds, second, to Amelia C Cady, has one daughter, who m. Samuel G Saunders, and resides at Rockford, (909) Asa, (910) Mary, m first, Lucius Lincoln, second, Peter G Bulkley, (911) Priscilla, m Edwin E Hoising; (912) Adelia, m. Charles Griswold, (913) Lois, in Jones Smith.

[704] WILLIAM[7] PECK, son of JESSE,[6] was a farmer, and resided in New Fairfield, Conn., where he died, April 3, 1847. He married Polly Ann Dickinson.

CHILDREN — EIGHTH GENERATION ·

(914) Dennis H , b Feb 19, 1805, has six children (915) *Augustus*[9], (916) *Franklin*[9], (917) *Hiram*[9], (918) *William*[9], (919) *Sarah F*[9], and (920) *Phebe S.*[9] — (921) Eliza A., b Aug 18, 1807, (922) Sylvia S , b April 2, 1810; (923) Polly Ann, b. Aug 2, 1812, (924) William, b March 12, 1815, has one child (925) *Eliza J*[9] — (926) Jesse, b Jan 29, 1818, (927) Annie, and (928) Fannie, b. Feb 27, 1821.

[705.] JESSE[7] PECK, son of JESSE,[6] resided in Danbury, where he died, May 8, 1832. He married Anna Taylor, daughter of Timothy Taylor.

CHILDREN — EIGHTH GENERATION

(929) Silliman B , b Nov 10, 1806, and has three children (930) *Ezra*[9], (931) *Egbert*[9], and (932) *Jeannette* [9] — (933) Ammon T , b Feb 23, 1815, resides in Danbury, has two children (934) *Coradova B* [9], and (935) *Cola S* [9] — (936) Timothy T , b. April 21, 1819, has one son (937) *Timothy S*[9]

[706] LEVI[7] PECK, son of JESSE,[6] is a Baptist clergyman, and resides in Sanford, N. Y. He married Naomi, daughter of Deacon Ira Benedict.

(938) Ira S , b May 28, 1813 , (939) Harriet N , b. March 27, 1815 , (940) Emeline B , b July 17, 1817, m John E Bowers, of Oxford, N Y , (941) Henry E , b. Feb 21, 1831, (942) Mary E C , b Sept 28, 1834   Henry E. resides in Sanford He m Augusta E King, daughter of Deacon Eli King, Esq , and has three children (943) *Ella R* ,[9] b Sept 21, 1856 , (944) *Achsa E* ,[9] b July 22, 1858 , and (945) *Herbert B* ,[9] b. Aug 2, 1862.

[720.] DANIEL[7] PECK, son of CALVIN,[6] married Samantha Curtis. They both died in Hastings, Oswego County, N. Y., in 1842.

(946) Laura S , b Dec 16, 1817 , (947) Bethiah E , b Dec. 10, 1819 , (948) Mille E , b Dec 16, 1821, m William Rich, and resides at Central Square, N Y , (949) Calvin, b Dec 1, 1823 , (950) Tirzah H , b May 22, 1826 , (951) Daniel E , b Aug 11, 1829 , (952) Martha A , b July 3, 1837.

[725.] LUTHER H.[7] PECK, son of LUTHER,[6] is a clergyman of the Methodist Episcopal church, and resides at Pitcher, N. Y. He has been twice married: first, to Mary Kenyon, of Little Rest, R. I, September 16, 1816; second, to Dorcas Carpenter, December 2, 1866. His first wife died May 23, 1865.

(953) George W , b May 31, 1818, m Abigail Bennett , resides near Portage City, Wis , and has the following children (954) *Mary*,[9] b Feb 23, 1842 , (955) *Andrew*,[9] b Sept 17, 1843, d Oct 18, 1863, a soldier in the war against the Rebellion , (956) *Thomas*,[9] b Jan 8, 1845, d Sept 25, 1863, also a soldier in the service of his country , (957) *Abbie*,[9] b Dec 10, 1846 , (958) *George W*,[9] b. Feb 7, 1849, and (959) *Luther H* ,[9] b June 21, 1851 — (960) Mary Ann, b Jan 6, 1820, m. George Atwell , (961) Martha, b May 13, 1822, m. Benjamin L. Corning ; (962) Jonathan K , b Dec 31, 1824   He graduated at Dickinson College, Penn , in 1852, was licensed to preach, and joined the Wyoming Conference in 1853, and is now Presiding Elder of the Honesdale District He married Mary Searle, and has the following children (963) *Carrie A* ,[9] b Feb 28, 1858 , (964) *James S* ,[9] b Dec 27, 1859 , (965) *Mary A* ,[9] b. Nov 28, 1861, and (966) *Jesse L* ,[9] b March 28, 1864 — (967) Luther, b March 9, 1827, is also a clergyman , in Lucy Lyman, and at present itinerates , (968) Elias B , b July 18, 1832, m Elizabeth McLane, and resides in Pitcher, N Y   His children are (969) *Ophelia M* ,[9] b May 10, 1855 , (970) *Addie M* ,[9] b. July 20, 1859 , (971) *Jennie*,[9] b Oct 16, 1861, d Jan 21, 1864, and (972) *Cordelia C* ,[9] b July 4, 1865 — (973) Andrew, b April 16, 1835, m Lucy A West, Aug 23, 1865, resides in Pitcher, and has one child (974) *Mary E* ,[9] b Sept 28, 1866 — (975) Eliza M , b April 15, 1838, d Oct 21, 1840

[726]   GEORGE[7] PECK, son of LUTHER,[6] resides at Scranton, Penn.   He is a clergyman of the Methodist Episcopal church. He commenced his labors in 1816, being then 19 years of age.   In 1821, he had charge of the church at Paris, N. Y., and during the two following years was stationed at Utica.   In 1824, he was appointed Presiding Elder on the Susquehanna District.   He was also a member of the General Conference which met that year, and he has been elected a delegate to every General Conference since that time, making in all twelve.   He was also a member of the Evangelical Alliance, which met in London in 1846.

As a scholar and student, he ranks high.   Endowed with cool, strong sense, and possessed of great logical acumen, his keenest weapons were early called into use for the defence of the faith. In 1825, he was challenged to a public debate, by a Unitarian, at Kingston, Penn., and won an acknowledged victory.   The following year he accepted a challenge to write in a Universalist magazine, which led to the publication of his first work, which was entitled "Universalism Examined."   In 1835, he received the degree of Master of Arts, from the Wesleyan University; and in the fall of that year was elected Principal of the Oneida Conference Seminary at Cazenovia, where he remained four years, being then appointed Presiding Elder on the Susquehanna District, for the second time.   In 1840, he received the degree of Doctor of Divinity, from the college at Augusta, Ky ; and the same year was elected editor of the *Methodist Quarterly Review*, which post he occupied eight years, during which time the *Review* rose to a high literary standard   In 1848, he was elected editor of the *Christian Advocate and Journal*, in which capacity he served four years.   In 1852, at the solicitation of numerous friends, he returned to the Wyoming Conference, the scene of his early labors; and since then he has been six years a Pastor, and eight years a Presiding Elder.

As an author, Dr. Peck stands deservedly high.   The following are his principal works: "Universalism Examined"; "History of the Apostles and Evangelists", "Christian Perfection"; "Rule of Faith"; "Reply to Dr Bascom's Defence of American Slavery"; "Manly Character"; "History of Wyoming"; "Early Methodism"; "Our Country; its Trials and its Triumphs."

Dr. Peck ranks high as a preacher.   His style is clear, logical and convincing. In his discourses, the argument rises in massive proportions, his soul seems to glow with religious fervor; and when the theme calls forth all his strength, the truth sways the audience with resistless power. In church legislation and discipline, he has frequently been called to occupy positions of responsibility, demanding the highest qualifications of judgment, fidelity, and sometimes courage, and he has always acquitted himself with honor. As a patriot, his volume of sermons on the country and the Rebellion, his numerous addresses, delivered in times of national disaster and gloom, are a noble record of steadfast faith and devotion to the right.

As a man, Dr. Peck is loved by all who know him, and most by those who know him best; a judicious counsellor, a sympathizing friend, an affectionate husband and father, a noble hearted man. Thus holding on his way through a long and useful life, he carries in his remembrance the records of half a century of stirring history, in which he has acted a part, and still remains vigorous and active, enjoying a serene, cheerful, Christian old age. He married Mary Myers, daughter of Philip Myers, Esq., of Kingston, Penn., June 10, 1819.

CHILDREN — EIGHTH GENERATION

(976) George M., b April 17, 1820. He was educated at the Oneida Conference Seminary, and is a clergyman of the Methodist Episcopal church, and now Presiding Elder of the Lackawanna District of the Wyoming Conference He resides at Providence, Pa He married Sarah Louisa Butler, July 18, 1839 His children are (977) *Merit B* [9], (978) *George,*[9] deceased, (979) *Luther W*[9], (980) *Josiah E*,[9] deceased, and (981) *William H*[9] — (982) Luther W , b June 14, 1825, graduated at the University of New York, and is Pastor of the Methodist Episcopal church at Hyde Park, Penn. He m Sarah Maria Gibbon, Jan 18, 1847. His children are (983) *Helen*[9], (984) *Mary E.*[9], (985) *Emma D*[9], (986) *Francis A*,[9] d Dec 20, 1859, (987) *Sarah M*[9], (988) *Susan U G*[9], (989) *Jesse T*[9], and (990) *Fanny M*[9] — (991) Mary H , b April 10, 1827, was educated at Rutger's Institute, New York City, m Rev. J T. Crane, Jan 18, 1847, by whom she has nine children Mr. Crane is a graduate of Princeton College, New Jersey, and is Presiding Elder of Newark District (992) William F , b Sept. 17, 1828, d April 17, 1829, (993) Wilbur F , b Sept 11, 1833, graduated in the Medical Department of the University of New York, and is practising medicine at Waymart, Penn. He married Sarah Jane Dean, Jan 20, 1857 His children are (994) *George*[9], (995) *Louisa*[9], (996) *Luther*[9], (997) *Mary Catharine*[9], and (998) *Wilbur*[9] George and Louisa only are living

JESSE T. PECK, D.D.

[727.] ANDREW[7] PECK, son of LUTHER,[6] is a clergyman of the Methodist Episcopal church, and resides at Cortland, N. Y. To him I am indebted for much of my information in relation to his father's family. He married, for his first wife, Polly Hudson, June 23, 1824; for his second, Electa Gunn, June 9, 1833; and for his third wife, Betsey Fenn, September 22, 1858. His first wife was born in Scituate, R I., February 3, 1804, where she was also baptized. She died November 29, 1832. His second wife was born October 9, 1805, in Salem, N. Y., and baptized in Guilford, September 1829. She died August 29, 1857. His third wife was born in Brookfield, N. Y, June 17, 1809, and baptized in infancy.

CHILDREN — EIGHTH GENERATION

(999) Betsey, b Feb 9, 1826, and bap June 8, 1828, m George Willson, and resides in Elgin, Minn, (1000) Ursula, b April 9, 1827, bap June 8, 1828, m Fields Place, and settled in Guilford, N Y, where she d Sept. 6, 1863, (1001) Sylvia, b Aug 26, 1829, bap Sept 23, 1833, m Peter Kessler, and resides at Dayton, Ohio, (1002) Wesley, b Sept 25, 1831, bap Sept 23, 1833 He is a Methodist clergyman, belongs to the California Conference, where he resides, and now itinerates He m Harriet C Stiles His children are (1003) *Ellen H*,[9] b Nov 2, 1853, (1004) *Charles W*,[9] b May 31, 1857; and (1005) *Anna B*,[9] who was b April 3, 1862, and d May 2, 1862 — (1006) An infant son, b. Nov 1, 1832, d Nov 2, 1832, (1007) Mary S, b Dec 12, 1834, bap Feb 21, 1835, m James Atkinson, and resides at Cazenovia, N Y, (1008) Emory, b. May 26, 1836, bap Nov 8, 1836, m Francis Fisk, and resides in Brownsville, Nebraska, (1009) Ellen N, b Aug 17, 1838, bap July 21, 1839, and d at Madison, N Y, Aug 14, 1839, (1010) William G, b Aug 25, 1841, bap June 12, 1842, d Dec 7, 1854, (1011) Elbert A, b. July 4, 1846, bap. in 1847, resides at Woodstock, N. Y.

[732] JESSE T.[7] PECK, son of LUTHER,[6] is a clergyman of the Methodist Episcopal church, with which he united in 1827. In 1829, he was licensed as a local preacher, and July 12, 1832, he was received into the Oneida Conference, and stationed successively at Dryden, Newark Valley, Skaneateles and Potsdam. By a division of the territory, he became a member of the Black River Conference. He was subsequently elected Principal of the Gouveneur Wesleyan Seminary, in St. Lawrence County, where he remained four years. He then became Principal of the Troy Conference Academy, in West Poultney, Vt., where he labored very successfully in the cause of education for seven years, being a member of the Troy Conference during this period. In 1848,

he resigned the principalship at the Conference Academy, to accept the Presidency of Dickinson College, at Carlisle, Penn., one of the oldest colleges in the United States, where he remained four years. During this latter period, he was a member of the Baltimore Conference. He then became pastor of the Foundry Church in Washington, D. C., where he remained two years. After this, he was appointed Secretary and Editor of the Tract Society of the M. E. church, and performed the duties of this office with great zeal and ability. Subsequently to this, he became pastor of Green Street Church in the city of New York. He was then transferred by the Board of Bishops to California, where he labored as pastor of important churches and Presiding Elder, for nearly eight years. On returning East, on account of the state of Mrs. Peck's health, he served for a time as pastor of St. Paul's church in Peekskill, N. Y., whence he was transferred to the Troy Conference, and stationed at Hudson Street church in Albany, where he now resides.

As will be seen by the preceding outline of his labor, Dr. Peck has thus far led a very busy life, and has had many important interests intrusted to his hands by the church and the community. It may be added, that while in preaching and teaching he has been "in labors abundant," his pen has not been idle. Contributing largely to certain leading periodicals, he has also found time to write several volumes of permanent value. He is the author of the works entitled "The Central Idea of Christianity"; "The True Women", "What must I do to be Saved?" and "The History of the Great Republic, considered from a Christian Standpoint" He has also been four times a member of the General Conference, and at the election of Bishops, in 1864, Dr. Peck received the highest number of votes among the candidates not elected. He was afterwards elected editor of the *Northern Christian Advocate;* but, deeming it his duty to return to California, he declined this important office. He married Persis Wing, October 13, 1831, daughter of Capt. David Wing, of West Dennis, Barnstable Co., Mass. They have no children.

[740] LUCIUS[7] PECK, son of JONATHAN,[6] resides at Bayzetta, Ohio. He married Abby, daughter of Abraham Crowley, of Norwich, Conn.

(1012) Lucius W , b June 4, 1824, resides at Austinsburg, Ohio, m Charlotte I Tuttle His children are (1013) *Eliza C* [9], (1014) *Laura H* [9], (1015) *Anna A* [9], and (1016) *Frederick G* [9] — (1017) Henry C , b May 15, 1826, m. Ellen E Sanford His children are (1018) *Frank H* [9], (1019) *Willie A* [9], (1020) *Florrie E* [9], (1021) *Linus A* [9], (1022) *Carrie E* [9], and (1023) *Minnie A* [9] — (1024) Eunice R , b. May 14, 1828, m Stoughton Davis, (1025) Eliza C , b June 9, 1831, m first, Linus H. Webb, second, A D Martin, (1026) Phineas F , b. Aug. 8, 1834, d Oct 16, 1850; (1027) Mary A., b May 7, 1839, m. first, Elisha G. Tew, and second, Joseph L Tew.

[741] JONATHAN H.[7] PECK, son of JONATHAN,[6] settled in Parma, N. Y. He was twice married: first, to Polly Scott; second, to Mary Ann Pitcher.

(1028) Willis, b Oct 21, 1825, m Polly E Harrington His children were (1029) *Phebe*[9], (1030) *Alfred L.*[9], (1031) *Almon H* [9], (1032) *Edward*[9], and (1033) *Washington P* [9] — (1034) Almon, b May 21, 1828, m Amey E Miner; (1035) Edward, b March 21, 1832, m first, Harriet Simmons, second, Orlynthia Timmer; d Aug 30, 1862, leaving two children (1036) *Morton*[9], and (1037) *Clarissa* [9] — (1038) Ephraim E , b Oct 20, 1833, (1039) Jonathan P , b June 6, 1836, d Nov 19, 1857, (1040) Alfred L , b. Dec. 13, 1841, d Sept. 3, 1854, (1041) Theron P., b Dec 30, 1845.

[744.] ASA C.[7] PECK, son of JONATHAN,[6] resides in Kingsville, Ohio. He married Marietta Fulton, a descendant of Robert Fulton. She died September 7, 1855.

(1042) Anson S , b Aug 8, 1834, resides in Charleston, Ohio, m. Ellen L. Loomis, and has one son (1043) *Charles M* [9] — (1044) Frances E , b Sept 2, 1837, d Sept 23, 1846, (1045) Eliza J , b Aug. 5, 1842, who m Lucius W. Hubbell, July 3, 1826, and (1046) Lois J , b Oct. 30, 1849.

[753.] JOHN H.[7] PECK, son of AMBROSE,[6] resides at Yantic, Conn. He is a merchant, doing business at Norwich. He married Abby Ann Hyde, eldest daughter of Amasa Hyde, Esq., January 29, 1834.

(1047) Eunice H., b. Feb 25, 1835, d Nov. 7, 1835, (1048) John H , b Sept. 7, 1838, graduated at Yale College in 1863, and is Principal of the High School at New Britain, Conn He m Hattie B Dibble, and has had two children (1049) *John H ,*[9] who d Sept 28, 1865, and (1050) *Frederick D* [9] — (1051) Jennie A., b Aug 21, 1840, m James C. Pratt, and resides at Hartford, Conn ,

31*

(1052) William H , b May 12, 1842, m. Susan A Gates, of Stowe, Mass , where he resides, (1053) James H , b April 2, 1844, d. Sept. 1, 1844, (1054) Annie H , b July 12, 1846, resides with her parents, (1055) Samuel N , b Feb. 12, 1848, and resides at Toledo, Ohio.

[757]   DARIUS[7] PECK, son of JOSEPH,[6] resides in Mishicot, Wis.   He married Christian Birdsall, December 24, 1825.

CHILDREN — EIGHTH GENERATION

(1056) George L , b Jan 5, 1847, (1057) Henry J , b Sept 17, 1848, (1058) Caroline A., b May 27, 1850; (1059) Mary E , b July 25, 1854, (1060) Charles B., b. April 10, 1857, (1061) Martha A., b. June 23, 1865.

[789]   STEPHEN A.[7] PECK, son of Deacon HORACE,[6] resides in New Haven, Conn.   He married Maria A. Newhall, April 26, 1849.

CHILDREN — EIGHTH GENERATION

(1062) Sarah M , b Jan 15, 1850; and (1063) Stephen A., b Jan 29, 1855.

[790]   WILLIAM S.[7] PECK, son of Deacon HORACE,[6] resides in Woodbridge.   He married Hannah T. Newhall, September 10, 1850.

CHILDREN — EIGHTH GENERATION

(1064) Fanny J , b Sept 7, 1851, (1065) Mary A , b July 7, 1854; (1066) Alice E , b June 23, 1857, (1067) William H , b Jan 10, 1862, d Nov. 19, 1864, (1068) Frank H , b June 8, 1869.

[792.]   FRANCIS B.[7] PECK, son of REUBEN,[6] is a Universalist clergyman, and resides at Oxford, Chenango County, N. Y. He married Miss Betsey Snell, of Ephratah, Fulton County, January 27, 1848.

CHILDREN — EIGHTH GENERATION

(1069) Clinton R , b May 9, 1850; (1070) Mary E , b Oct 20, 1857, (1071) Frank, b. March 1, 1860.

[794.]   FAYETTE S.[7] PECK, son of REUBEN,[6] resides at Burtonsville, Montgomery County, N. Y.   He is a farmer, engaged in the dairying business, and in fruit and hop growing. He married Miss Sarah Wright, daughter of Mr. Ralph Wright, of Oppenheim, Fulton County, September 8, 1850.

CHILDREN — EIGHTH GENERATION

(1072) Murray R , b Oct 12, 1851, (1073) Lucinda, b. July 27, 1856, and (1074) Emma, b Oct. 23, 1861.

DESCENDANTS OF DEACON PAUL PECK,

OF HARTFORD, CONNECTICUT.

DEACON PAUL PECK is supposed to have been born in Essex County, England, in 1608, and to have come to this country in the ship "Defence," in 1635; and remained in Boston, Mass., or its vicinity, until 1636, and then removed to Hartford with the Rev. Thomas Hooker and his friends. His name is in the list of the proprietors of Hartford in 1639. From the records of the town, it appears that he became one of its leading men. His residence is said to have been upon what is now Washington Street, not far from Trinity College, the site of which being still known by aged persons as the "Peck lot."

I regret to have found so little interest felt in relation to him, or in my endeavors to trace out and give a history of his descendants. A very few have offered their assistance; many have refused to answer my letters, or give the information asked of them.

He was Deacon of the Congregationalist Church from 1681 until his decease, December 23, 1695. His will is upon the Probate Records, B. 5, pp. 217-18-19, dated June 25, 1695, and proved January 15, 1695-6. It is quite lengthy, and is of interest in its details and descriptions of his property. His inventory amounted to £536 and 5s.

He makes bequests to his wife Martha, sons Paul and Joseph; his daughters Martha Cornwell, Mary Andrew, Sarah Clark and Elizabeth How; his grandsons Paul and Samuel; and his son-in-law John Shepherd.

He also names his granddaughter Ruth Beach, and son-in-law Joseph Bonton, to whom Samuel was required to pay legacies.

CHILDREN — SECOND GENERATION

(1)+Paul, b in 1639, (2) Martha, b in 1641, m John Cornwell, June 8, 1665, of Middletown, where she died March 1, 1708-9 Her children were *Mary[3]*, *Martha[3]*, *John[3]*, *William[3]*, *Paul[3]*, *Hannah[3]*, *Joseph[3]*, *Thankful[3]*, *Thankful, 2d[3]*, and *Benjamin[3]* (3) Elizabeth, b in 1643, m —— How, of Wallingford, (4)+John, b. Dec 22, 1645, (5)+Samuel, b in 1647, (6)+Joseph, bap Dec 22, 1650; (7) Sarah, b. in 1653, m. Thomas Clark, of Hartford, (8)

Hannah, b. in 1656, m. John Shepherd, of Hartford, May 12, 1680; (9) **Mary**, b. in 1662, m. John Andrew, of Hartford, and d. in 1752 *

[1.]   PAUL² PECK, son of Deacon PAUL,¹ resided in West Hartford, where he died in 1725.   He married Elizabeth Baisey, daughter of John Baisey.

CHILDREN — THIRD GENERATION :

(10)+Paul, b in 1666, (11)+John, b in 1672, (12) Martha, b in 1676, m. Samuel Hubbard, of Middletown, now Berlin, Conn , (13) Samuel, b in 1680, also settled in Berlin, (14) Hannah, b in 1681, m first, Joseph Hopkins, April 27, 1699 , and second, John Porter, Dec. 13, 1713   She resided in Waterbury. (15)+William, b in 1686 , (16) Ruth, b in 1688, m Samuel Sedgwick, jr , Feb. 1, 1711, for her first husband, and Samuel Culver, of Wallingford, Jan. 3, 1728, for her second.

[4.]   JOHN² PECK, son of Deacon PAUL,¹ became a member of the church at Hartford in 1696.

CHILDREN — THIRD GENERATION

(17) John, jr , b May 1, 1661, (18) Elizabeth, b Oct 7, 1664 , (19) Sarah, b June 20, 1668 , (20) Joseph, b March 6, 1671, (21) Ruth, b Dec 21, 1677 , (22) Susannah, b. Oct 16, 1680; (23) Jonathan, b. Oct 6, 1683.

[5.]   SAMUEL² PECK, son of Deacon PAUL,¹ resided in West Hartford, where he died, January 10, 1696.   He married Elizabeth ————.

CHILD — THIRD GENERATION :

(24)+Samuel, b. in West Hartford, in 1672.

[6.]   JOSEPH² PECK, son of Deacon PAUL,¹ settled in Windsor, where he died, June 26, 1698.   He married Ruth ————. She was appointed administratrix upon his estate, April 1698.

CHILDREN — THIRD GENERATION

(25) Elizabeth, b in 1686, d young; (26) Ruth, b. in 1692, d young; (27) Joseph, b. in 1694, and settled in Tolland County, where he died, leaving an infant son, John. An administrator was appointed upon his estate in 1741; (28) Ruth, m. a Mr. Mason.

[10.]   PAUL³ PECK, son of PAUL,² removed to Litchfield at an early date.   He was one of the first settlers there.   He and his

---

* It would appear from the will, that there were two other daughters, whose names were not upon record, one who married Joseph Bonton, and the other the mother of Ruth Beach, unless one married a second husband.

brother John both took an active part in the Indian war.   He married Leah Muzzy,* of Hartford, August 20, 1701. He died December 21, 1751; his widow died June 5, 1767.

CHILDREN — FOURTH GENERATION

(29) Paul, b April 27, 1702   He was known as a great hunter and trapper, a kind of "Kit Carson," I should suppose, from what I learn of him.   He was killed in the Revolutionary war at the time the British burned our military stores at Danbury, Conn   He was in his 75th year, unm , † (30) Elizabeth, m Benjamin Webster; (31) Leah, m Benjamin Bissell, (32)+Elisha, (33) +Thomas, (34) Rachel, m Reuben Hibbard; (35)+Cornelius, b. in Hartford, Feb. 24, 1713, (36)+Benjamin.

[11.]   JOHN³ PECK, son of PAUL,² married Mehitable Reeve, of Hartford, November 9, 1707, and removed to Litchfield about 1720.

CHILDREN — FOURTH GENERATION:

(37) John, b Nov. 3, 1708, settled in Vermont at an early date; (38)+Abraham. (39) Isaac, m Ruth Tomlinson, of Litchfield, May 20, 1736, and removed to Canaan, (40) Jacob, d in early life, (41) a daughter, who died in infancy; (42)+Reeve, b March 3, 1723, (43) Lydia, m Elisha Peck (No 58), son of Samuel. She died at the residence of her son Asa, in Litchfield, aged 96 years.

[15.]   WILLIAM³ PECK, son of PAUL,² removed to Litchfield, in 1727.   He married Lois Webster.

CHILDREN — FOURTH GENERATION ·

(44) Jerusha, b. Sept 1727, m. Joseph Vaill, (45)+Timothy, b. March 6, 1730; (46) Lois, b Sept 1732, m John Osborn, (47) Eunice, b Sept 1736, (48) Margaret, m Capt Harris Hopkins, (49) Abigail, m. James Stodard, (50) Sarah, m. Abel Brown.

[24.]   SAMUEL³ PECK, son of SAMUEL,² settled in Middletown, now Berlin. He married Abigail Collier, daughter of Joseph

---

* It is difficult to tell upon the records at Hartford whether this name is Muzzy, Mowry, or Merry

† He is said to have been killed by a British officer, who was so exasperated at the deadly aim of Paul's gun among his men, that he seized it and bent it over the wall behind which he had fought.   This gun, I am told by Benjamin Peck, of Palenville, N Y., grandson of the brother of Paul, was recovered, straightened and repaired, and always known by the name of Paul's hunting gun

Paul and his brothers, he tells me, were the first to carry guns into Litchfield, and that he now has in his possession the two owned by his brothers.

Collier, March 6, 1701. He died December 9, 1765; she died October 28, 1742.

CHILDREN — FOURTH GENERATION:

(51)+Samuel, b. at Kensington, Jan. 6, 1701, (52)+Moses, b April 1703, (53)+Isaac, b. at Simsbury, Nov 28, 1706; (54)+Abijah, b. Dec 28, 1709, (55)+Zebulon, b in Middletown, Sept 1, 1712, (56)+Amos, b. in Kensington, March 3, 1715, (57) Abel, b in Kensington, Dec. 28, 1717, and d. Sept. 19, 1742, unm. He was a physician (58)+Elisha, b. at Kensington, March 11, 1720; (59) Elijah, b in Lyme, July 23, 1723, m. Mary Strong, daughter of Hewett Strong. His children were (60) *Jabez*,[5] b in 1755, and (61) *Daniel*,[5] b in 1758, and probably others, (62) Lucy, b Dec 19, 1727, (63) Lois, who is named in the will of her father, but not recorded with the family

[32.] ELISHA[4] PECK, son of PAUL,[3] married Sarah Grant, January 1730-1, and settled in Litchfield.

CHILDREN — FIFTH GENERATION ·

(64) Elisha, b July 10, 1731, (65) Abijah, b. Oct 1733, m first, Keturah ———, who d Sept. 1772, in her 44th year; second, Rhoda Fitch (widow), June 1773, formerly Rhoda Collins His children were (66) *Keturah*,[6] b. Jan 22, 1774, (67) *Abijah*,[6] b Feb 5, 1776, and probably others not on record. — (68) Dille, b. June 25, 1735-6, m. William Graves, (69) Abiah, b. Sept. 20, 1738.

[33.] THOMAS[4] PECK, son of PAUL,[3] settled in Litchfield. He married Sarah Smith, August 17, 1733.

CHILDREN — FIFTH GENERATION ·

(70) Ann, b. Feb 7, 1734-5, (71) Mindwell, b Oct 26, 1737, (72) Thomas, b. April 24, 1740; (73) Sarah, b Aug 18, 1742, (74) Amey, b. April 12, 1745, (75) Levi, b June 23, 1745, d in 1802, (76) Rachel, b. Oct 7, 1752, (77) Elijah, b Oct 27, 1754; resided in Litchfield, where he m Hannah Harrison His children were (78) *Almon*,[6] (79) *Freeman*,[6] (80) *Elijah*,[6] (81) *Rhoda*,[6] (82) *Clarissa*,[6] (83) *Mahala*,[6] and (84) *Lucy*.[6] He d in 1794.

[35.] CORNELIUS[4] PECK, son of PAUL,[3] settled in Litchfield, where he died, October 31, 1801. He married Bethiah Beebe, February 5, 1748-9.

CHILDREN — FIFTH GENERATION ·

(85) Elizabeth, b. May 9, 1750, m Abel Atwater; (86) Cornelius, b March 26, 1753, (87) Mary, b. July 27, 1754, and probably others not recorded.

[36.] BENJAMIN[4] PECK, son of PAUL,[3] married Mary Frisbie, October 22, 1755, and resided in that part of Litchfield known as Chestnut Hill.

(88)+Benjamin, b. Dec 28, 1756, (89) Mary, b. July 12, 1759, m. Richard Wallace, and resided in Litchfield, where she d Feb. 18, 1835, aged about 75 years, leaving a large family, (90) Anna, m James Stone, (91) Rachel, b. Oct. 8, 1766, m. Norman Buel, and resided in Litchfield, (92)+Eliada, b. July 16, 1770.

[38.] ABRAHAM[4] PECK, son of PAUL,[3] resided in Litchfield, where he died, August 1801, in the 91st year of his age. He married Hannah ——.

(93)+Abraham, b. Nov. 15, 1763, (94) Sybel, b. Aug 9, 1765, and probably others not upon record

[42.] REEVE[4] PECK, son of JOHN,[3] married Rachel Granger, of Granbury, Conn., and settled in Litchfield, where he died, aged about 80. His wife died 1817, aged 96.

(95) Moses, b Jan. 19, 1754, d unm, (96)+Reeve, (97) Ann, b Jan. 27, 1757, m Richard Wallace, (98)+Reuben, b Jan 24, 1760; (99)+Asahel, b Aug. 13, 1762, (100) George, b. Nov 17, 1765, and I am told settled in Cornwall, Vt., (101) Rachel, b. Feb. 18, 1769, m. David Vaill.

[45.] TIMOTHY[4] PECK, son of WILLIAM[3], married Sarah Plumb. He died November 20, 1772.

(102)+Philo or Philosibbius, b Oct 3, 1752, (103) Anna, b. March 29, 1755; (104) Rhoda, b. March 21, 1758, m Lot Chase, (105) Sarah, b Jan 3, 1762, (106)+Timothy, b Aug. 26, 1765, (107)+Virgil, b. Sept. 4, 1769, (108) Rachel, b Feb. 18, 1770.

[51.] SAMUEL[4] PECK, son of SAMUEL,[3] resided in Berlin, Conn., where he died, August 25, 1784. He married Thankful Winchel, January 10, 1725. She died January 6, 1762.

(109) Sybel, b June 4, 1726, d. Aug. 16, 1736, (110) Eldad, b June 4, 1728, d Aug 22, 1736, (111) Thankful, b April 30, 1732, d. Aug 31, 1736, (112)+ Samuel, b. May 2, 1734, (113) Eldad, b. in 1738, (114)+Eldad, again, b. in 1740.

[52.] MOSES[4] PECK, son of SAMUEL,[3] married Sarah Kellogg, August 14, 1732, and resided in Kensington, where he died, December 30, 1759. His wife died June 12, 1770.

(115) Oliver, b March 13, 1737, d Nov 4, 1810, m Patience Clark, March 24, 1757 She d Jan. 20, 1808, (116) Rhoda, b Dec 15, 1733, d April 18, 1734, (117) Rhoda, a twin sister, b April 18, 1734, m. Reuben Clark, Dec 21, 1759, d March 24, 1801, (118) Moses, b June 24, 1735, m. Rosanna ——, d in 1810; (119) Sarah, born April 11, 1741, m Timothy Clark in 1759; (120)+Abel, b. May 5, 1743.

[53.] ISAAC[4] PECK, son of Samuel,[3] married Lois Porter, of Farmington, December 1729, and died in Kensington, October 27, 1748.

(121)+Freeman, b Oct 9, 1732, (122) Jabez, b Sept 16, 1734, (123) Lois, b. Oct. 14, 1739, d Sept 22, 1743, (124)+Joseph, b Aug. 14, 1744

[54] ABIJAH[4] PECK, son of Samuel,[3] resided in Berlin, where he died, March 13, 1797. He married Abigail Galpen, of Middletown, June 10, 1742. She died July 21, 1775.

(125) Abigail, b Feb. 2, 1744, m Ozias Bronson, of Winchester, where she died at an advanced age, (126)+Abijah, b July 11, 1747, (127) Joseph, b July 6, 1749, d Dec. 1822, no issue, (128) Anna, b Jan 21, 1752, m Thomas Thompson, d July 24, 1790, leaving four sons and three daughters, (129)+ Jesse, b March 3, 1754, (130) Mercy, b March 29, 1756, m a Thompson She d. July 6, 1790

[55.] ZEBULON[4] PECK, son of Samuel,[3] married Mary Edwards, daughter of Josiah Edwards, of East Hampton, L. I., July 10, 1735. He died in Bristol, Conn., January 13, 1795. His wife died May 23, 1790.

(131) Abigail, b. May 20, 1736, m Hezekiah Gridley, removed to Clinton, N Y, where she d April 21, 1826, (132)+Justus, b Nov 14, 1737, (133) Elizabeth, b Sept 30, 1739, d Nov 16, 1741, (134) Mary, b Aug 12, 1741, m Israel Fuller, July 23, 1761 She d Oct 11, 1785, (135)+Zebulon, b in Meriden, April 15, 1743, (136)+Abel, b in Meriden, 1745, (137)+David, b in Bristol, May 13, 1749, (138)+Lament, b. May 8, 1751, in Farmington, now Bristol, (138) Elizabeth, b in Bristol, in 1753, m Abel Hawley, Dec 16, 1772, and d in Clinton, N Y, March 12, 1816, (139)+Josiah, b. Jan 19, 1755.

[56.] AMOS[4] PECK, son of Samuel,[3] married Mary Hart, July 26, 1750, and settled in Middletown. where he died, April 6, 1802. She died June 22, 1771.

CHILDREN — FIFTH GENERATION

(140) Mathew, b July 16, 1751, m Huldah Rice, (141)+Amos, jr, b Jan.
25, 1754, (142) Ruth, b. Nov 28, 1756, m Benjamin Hopkins, and d March 5,
1824, (143) Mary, b March 9, 1760, m Elisha Hart, (144) Huldah, b Sept.
13, 1762 She was twice married. She d March 28, 1847, (145)+Lemuel, b
March 28, 1765, (146) Lucy, b Dec 2, 1767, m Asahel Dickinson. She d.
Dec. 1, 1853.

[58.] ELISHA[4] PECK, son of SAMUEL,[3] settled in Middletown,
now Berlin, where he died, May 29, 1762. He married Lydia
Peck, No. 43, daughter of John Peck, May 17, 1743, both being
the great-grandchildren of Deacon Paul.

CHILDREN — FIFTH GENERATION.

(147)+Asa, (148)+Ariel, (149)+Elisha, b Feb 25, 1757, (150) Amey, m.
William Gibbs, (151) Lydia, m John Buel, (152) Sybil, m Lemuel Orton.

[88.] BENJAMIN[5] PECK, son of BENJAMIN,[4] settled at first
in Litchfield, where he resided until about 1798, when he removed
to Palenville, N. Y., where he died in 1820. He married Mary
Buel.

CHILDREN — SIXTH GENERATION

(153) Orman, d in 1804, aged about 22 years, (154) Benjamin, m. Jane
Bret, and was residing upon the homestead in 1865 His children are (155)
Benjamin[7], (156) *Orman*[7], (157) *William*[7], (158) *Laura*[7], (159) *Margaret*[7],
(160) *Cornelia*[7], (161) *Minerva*[7], (162) *Calista*[7], and *Jane*[7] —(163) Clarissa,
m John Burnham, and settled at Cairo, (164) Polly, m John Palmer, and
also settled at Cairo.

[92.] ELIADA[5] PECK, son of BENJAMIN,[4] settled upon the
homestead, where he died. He was three times married: 1st, to
Sally Beckwith, October 28, 1798, 2d. to Abigail Whittlesey, June
4, 1806; 3d, to Julia Sherman, May 7, 1826.

CHILDREN — SIXTH GENERATION

(165) Benjamin, b Nov 7, 1799, (166) Henry D, b May 23, 1807, (167)
Sheldon W, b. Aug. 31, 1809, (168) James, and perhaps others, not upon
record

[93.] ABRAHAM[5] PECK, son of ABRAHAM,[4] married Honor
De Wolf. He removed from Litchfield to Cornwall, Vt., about
1802.

CHILDREN — SIXTH GENERATION

(169) Hannah, b April 22, 1788, (170) Alanson A, b Feb 4, 1790, m Nancy
De Lano. His children are. (171) *Benjamin R.,*[7] residing at Cohoes, N. Y., in
32

1867, (172) *Mary V* [7], (173) *Henry G* [7], and (174) *Lydia* [7] —(175) Epaphroditus, b July 6, 1791, (176) David, b Dec 8, 1794, d Feb 18, 1796, (177) Mary, b March 6, 1796, (178) Lucretia, b April 22, 1798, (179) Isaac, b July 27, 1800; (180) Frederick, b March 12, 1803, (181) Sybil, b Dec. 14, 1805; (182) Electa, b Aug 22, 1807

[96] REEVE[5] PECK, son of REEVE,[4] married Sarah Butler, April 14, 1774, and settled at first in Litchfield, and from there is supposed to have removed to Cornwall, Vt.

CHILDREN — SIXTH GENERATION

(183) Eleazar, b Feb 24, 1776, (184) Samuel, b March 20, 1778, (185) Sarah, b Sept 22, 1780; (186) Reeve, b Nov 4, 1782; (187) Horatio, b Sept. 23, 1799, (188) Sarah and Rachel, by a 2d wife

[98.] REUBEN[5] PECK, son of REEVE,[4] married Sarah Churchel, and settled in Cornwall, Vt.

CHILDREN — SIXTH GENERATION

(189) Darius, settled in Cornwall, where he died June 28, 1867, leaving no issue, (190) Romeo, m Sarah Chatterdon, and was residing in Cornwall in 1867 His children were (191) *Reuben O* [7], (192) *Jennie L* [7], (193) *Romeo R* [7], (194) *John C* [7], (195) *Aretus C* [7], (196) *Rachel A* [7], and (197) *Ellery H* [7] —(198) Julius, m 1st, Sally Lampher; 2d, Augustine Van Guilder His children were (199) *George* [7], (200) *Reuben* [7], (201) *Julius* [7], (202) *Celor* [7]; (203) *Celio.* [7] —(204) Sally.

[99.] ASAHEL[5] PECK, son of REEVE,[4] married Anna Marsh, February 1789, and remained in Litchfield.

CHILDREN — SIXTH GENERATION

(205) Chauncey, b Aug 25, 1789, m Minerva Bidwell, April 23, 1812 He d Feb 18, 1867 His children were (206) *Harriet C* ,[7] b Dec 9, 1814, (207) *Hiram W* ,[7] b. April 9, 1818, (208) *Stephen B* ,[7] b June 2, 1820; *Frances S* ,[7] b April 27, 1825, and (209) *James B* ,[7] b in 1828 — (210) Horace, b June 10, 1791, m 1st, Lydia Orton, 2d, Amelia Doolittle His children were (211) *Charles J* [7], (212) *Burr O* [7], (213) *Louis* [7], and (214) *Harriet* [7] —(215) Asahel, b April 29, 1792, m Abigail Catlin His children were (216) *Henry C* [7]; (217) *Maria E* [7], (218) *Helen* [7], (219) *Newton* [7], and (220) *Julia* [7] —(221) Elijah M , b Oct 29, 1794, m. Harriet Turner His children are (221) *Edward O* ,[7] residing in Litchfield, Conn , in 1867, (222) *Mary Ann* [7], (223) *Emeline A* [7]; (224) *Adaline* [7]; and (225) *Angeline* [7], twins — (226) Ozias, b May 17, 1797, m 1st, Mahala Hubbard, 2d, Harriet Ann Pond His children were (227) *Martha J* [7], (228) *Lemon O* [7], and (229) *Ozias W* ,[7] who is a physician, and resides in New Haven —(230) Edmond, b Aug 14, 1799, m Ann Perkins, had one son :

---

* This name was received too late to be numbered with the others.

(231) *Edmond P* [7] —(232) Anna, b. April 18, 1801, m. Herman Bissell, (233) Julius, b July 29, 1804, m. Eunice Warner *, (234) Harriet, b June 10, 1806, (235) William, b March 14, 1808, m. 1st, Emeline Loveland, 2d, Cordelia Mc-Donald He died in Wisconsin in 1866 His children were. (236) *Aaron*[7], (237) *Edmond*[7], and (238) *Caroline*[7], and perhaps others.

[102.] PHILO[5] PECK, son of TIMOTHY,[4] married Hannah Hicks, of East Hampton, L. I.

CHILDREN — SIXTH GENERATION

(239)+Alfred, b Feb 26 1779, (240) Rhoda, b Sept. 25, 1782, m Virgil Walter; (241) Polly, b. April 29, 1785, (242) Mary Ann, b. Nov. 20, 1795, m Jeremiah Norton.

[106.] TIMOTHY[5] PECK, son of TIMOTHY,[4] married a Joy.

CHILDREN — SIXTH GENERATION

(243) Luther, who d. in London, England, unm , (244) Clara, (245) Sarah, (246) Virgil, and (247) Mary.

[107.] VIRGIL[5] PECK, son of TIMOTHY,[4] married Mary Wallace, granddaughter of Benjamin Peck (No. 36), November 28, 1799. He died October 15, 1804. She survived him, and married Dr. Abel Catlin, March 20, 1808. She was born October 13, 1781, and died December 21, 1860.

CHILDREN — SIXTH GENERATION :

(248) Mary W , b Sept 11, 1800, m Edward D Mansfield, April 25, 1827, d. March 10, 1837, (249) Helen, b. July 26, 1802, died unm May 27, 1822, (250)+William V , b. April 16, 1804.

[112.] SAMUEL[5] PECK, son of SAMUEL,[4] resided in Berlin, where he died, July 18, 1802. He married, for his first wife, Ruth Hopkins, March 3, 1757; for his second, Sarah ——, March 31, 1773; and for his third, Abigail Lattimer, December 7, 1775.

CHILDREN — SIXTH GENERATION

(251) Thankful, b. Feb 3, 1758, (252) Elizabeth, b. Oct. 7, 1761, (253) La-vinia, b. April 25, 1766, (254) Solomon, b June 22, 1767, (255)+Samuel, b. Sept 25, 1768, (256)+Edward, b Nov. 21, 1776.

[114.] ELDAD[5] PECK, son of SAMUEL,[4] married Mary Foster, February 9, 1764; died September 14, 1824.

---

* He had a son Cornelius, who died in Bristol, Conn.

CHILDREN — SIXTH GENERATION

(257) Submit, b. Dec 30, 1764, (258) Seth, b May 4, 1767, (259) Philema, b. Oct 14, 1771, m Mathew Judd, Jan 20, 1800; (260) Eldad, b Nov. 5, 1774, (261) Erastus, b June 29, 1779.

[120.] ABEL⁵ PECK, son of Moses,⁴ married Deborah Curtis in 1768. He died July 16, 1822. She died December 30, 1824.

CHILDREN — SIXTH GENERATION

(262) Billy K , b in 1772, d April 13, 1811, (263) Major B , b in 1774, m. Lucy Lewis, (264) Rhoda B , b in 1776, m. Gideon Huntley, and d April 28, 1819, (265) Sally B , b in 1779, (266) Sylvester, b. in 1784, d July 31, 1858. There were other children, who died young.

[121.] FREEMAN⁵ PECK, son of Isaac,⁴ married Lois Lindley, June 4, 1753; died July 24, 1762.

CHILDREN — SIXTH GENERATION

(267) Isaac, b Aug 14, 1753, (268) Lois, b Dec. 24, 1754, (269) Olive, b. April 9, 1757; (270) Freeman, b. May 31, 1760.

[124.] JOSEPH⁵ PECK, son of Isaac,⁴ settled, lived and died in Berlin.

CHILDREN — SIXTH GENERATION

(271) Sarah, b April 8, 1770; (272) Hannah, b Dec 24, 1771, (273) Lucretia, b Aug. 16, 1774, (274) Lydia, b Dec 19, 1776, (275) Joseph, b April 13, 1779, d. April 17, 1823, (276) Asenath, b. July 22, 1781.

[126.] ABIJAH⁵ PECK, son of Abijah,⁴ removed with his family to the State of New York, about 1812, and died at the residence of his grandson, Joseph L , in Cayuga County, May 18, 1828. He was three times married; first, to Lucy Percival; second, to Huldah Boardman; third, to Mrs. Abigail Owen.

CHILDREN — SIXTH GENERATION

(277)+Warren, b. Dec 30, 1786, (278) Joseph, d unm , (279) Lucy, (280) Abijah, was residing in Norwalk, N. Y , in 1866, m. Polly Reynolds, (281) Anise, (282) Sally, m. John Nichols, and was residing, a widow, in Peru, Ohio, in 1866.

[129.] JESSE⁵ PECK, son of Abijah,⁴ married Philoma Cook, daughter of Rev. Samuel Cook, November 15, 1785. She was born July 14, 1761, and died March 16, 1815. He died at Rochester, N. Y., April 29, 1823.

(283) Emily, d in infancy, (284)+Everard, b Nov 6, 1792, (285)+Henry, b Jan 3, 1795, (286)+Jesse, b Jan 19, 1798, and Emily 2d, b March 31, 1802, m. Thomas Kempshall.

[132.] JUSTUS⁵ PECK, son of ZEBULON,⁴ resided in Walcott, Conn., where he died, November 23, 1813. He married Lucy Frisbee, September 6, 1759. She died December 11, 1823, aged 83 years. He was a deacon of the Congregationalist Church for many years, and held various public offices.

(287) Lucy, b March 10, 1761, m and d in New Hampshire, leaving children, (288)+Elisha, b Sept 9 1763, (289) Mary, b Sept 23, 1766, m Joshua Cook, of Rutland, Vt, Jan 20, 1789, (290) Sarah, b June 10, 1768, d March 30, 1773, (291) Rachel, b Nov 13. 1771, m Rev Asa Talmadge, of Southington, Conn, Oct 17, 1801, d June 5, 1845, (292) Justus, b June 28, 1774, d Sept 2, 1777, (293) Sarah, 2d, b. June 28, 1779, m and d April 23, 1850; (294) Lowley, b Dec 15, 1782, m Stephen Carter, jr, of Walcott, Nov 15, 1804, d Dec 14, 1861, (295) Rhoda, b Jan 4, 1786, d March 30, 1792, (296) Justus L, b April 29, 1788, m Sarah Merriman, of Southington, d April 15, 1812, no issue.

[135.] ZEBULON⁵ PECK, son of ZEBULON,⁴ removed from Bristol, Conn, to Clinton, N. Y., in 1801, and died in Marshall, N. Y., January 23, 1820. During his residence in Bristol, he was one of the leading public men, and very popular. He was a Justice of the Peace many years, and a member of the Connecticut Legislature for fourteen sessions. He was a delegate in the Convention to act upon the adoption of the United States Constitution, voting yea. He was a Deacon of the Congregationalist Church. He was three times married; first, to Esther Hart, November 2. 1769; second, to Mrs. Mary Watson, June 11, 1778; third, to Mrs. Mindwell Chubb.

(297) Roxanna, b April 14, 1770, d Jan 5, 1849, (298)+Isaac, b Nov 23, 1771, (299) Beulah, b March 12, 1774, d Dec. 1, 1786, (300)+Silas, b March 30, 1776, (301)+Zebulon, b March 24, 1779, (302) Esther, b April 7, 1781, m. Salmon Barns, of Bristol, Conn, and d in Wisconsin, Dec 1860; (303) Sylvia, b July 23, 1782, d March 12, 1794, (304) Lorena, b June 4, 1784, d Nov 1805, (305)+Anthony, b March 19, 1786, (306) Beulah, b. March 23, 1789, m Daniel Northrop, March 2, 1815, and d at Fayetteville, Onondaga County, N Y., Nov. 10, 1865, leaving children and grandchildren.

32*

[136]   ABEL[5] PECK, son of ZEBULON,[4] married Abigail Gay-lord, of Bristol, Feb. 11, 1768.   He was drafted in the war of the Revolution, and died on his way home from Valley Forge, January 26, 1778.   His widow married Deacon James Wells, of Newington, September 4, 1785.

CHILDREN — SIXTH GENERATION

(307)+Samuel, b Jan 5, 1769, (308) Candace, b Jan 16, 1771, m Jonathan Stodard, and d in 1826, (309) Abel, b Jan 12, 1774, m Huldah Abernethy, (310) Abigail, b May 13, 1776, m Timothy Stedman.

[137]   DAVID[5] PECK, son of ZEBULON,[4] settled in Southington, where he became a prominent man, holding various public offices.   He married Huldah Coggswell.   He died September 30, 1821.

CHILDREN — SIXTH GENERATION

(311) Mary, b Jan 25, 1773, d Nov 12, 1849, (312) Huldah, b July 8, 1775, m Riley Smith, of Southington, d March 10, 1838, (313) Asahel, b July 19, 1777, m Diadema Dunham, of Southington, d Jan 18, 1856   She died Jan 14, 1849, (314) Seth, b July 7, 1781, m Salome Lewis, of Walcot, Conn, and resided in Southington, where he d March 29, 1843, she d April 15, 1853, no issue, (315) Sally, b Oct 2, 1783, m S Judd, d July 14, 1824, (316) Oren, b Aug 26, 1785, m Ann Seward, d March 11, 1852, she Jan 18, 1853, no issue, (317) Phila, b Aug 31, 1787, m. Edward Converse, Dec 4 1811, (318) Leuina, b May 13, 1790, m Joel Carrington, d. May 5, 1847

[138]   LAMENT[5] PECK, son of ZEBULON,[4] resided in Bristol, where he died, May 5, 1823.   He held various town and church offices.   He married Rachel Tracy.

CHILDREN — SIXTH GENERATION

(319) Sally, b Feb. 7, 1784, m Capt A Bunnell, of Plymouth, Oct 3, 1822, he d July 20, 1860; she survived him, and was residing in Bristol in 1865, no issue, (320)+Tracy, b April 5, 1785, (321)+Richard, b Dec 15, 1786, (322) Susannah, b Aug 31, 1788, m Sylvester Rich, Jan 5, 1812, and was residing in Croton, N Y, in 1865, (323) an infant, b Sept 21, 1790, d Oct 8, 1790, unnamed, (324) Ephroditus, b Oct 26, 1791, d in South Carolina, Nov 16, 1811, unm, (325)+Nehemiah, b Sept 26, 1793, (326)+Neuman, b Nov 25, 1795, (327) Rachel, b Dec 25, 1797, m Israel Russell, he d in 1851, she was residing in Cromwell, Conn, a widow, in 1865, (328) James G, b June 24, 1800, m first, Marcia Crane, Jan 1, 1840; second, Sarah Smith, and was residing upon the old homestead in 1865, and has had two children   (329) James G,[7] b Sept 29, 1840, d July 11, 1844, and (330) Mary E,[7] b. March 10, 1844, was residing at home in 1865.

[139] JOSIAH[5] PECK, son of ZEBULON,[4] married Jemima Rogers, January 26, 1782. He died April 26, 1811. His wife died August 30, 1850. They were buried in the South burial-ground, at Bristol, where their tombstones may still be seen.

CHILDREN — SIXTH GENERATION

(331) Isabinda, b Jan 5, 1782. m Miles Lewis, of Bristol, Nov 26, 1801, d. April 20, 1847, no issue, (332)+Wooster, b. March 7, 1784, (333) Mary, b in 1786, m Sylvester Woodruff, of Southington, Conn, Jan 1, 1806, d May 23, 1810, (334) Catharine, b Oct 12, 1788, m Elias Foot, settled in New York City, where she d Dec 16, 1858, leaving children, (335) Lyman, b in 1790, d April 4, 1794, (336) Harry, b in 1795, d at Buffalo, N Y, in 1814, a soldier in the United States army, (337) Fanny, b May 25, 1801, m. Noble Jerome, Dec 11, 1823, was residing in Waterbury, Conn, a widow, in 1865, (338) Almira, b Aug 4, 1798, d. Nov 19, 1844, (339) an infant, b April 4, 1804, lived but a few days.

[141] AMOS[5] PECK, son of AMOS,[4] married Anna Scoville, December 4, 1781. He died March 18, 1826.

CHILDREN — SIXTH GENERATION

(340) Polly, b Sept 29, 1782, m Dr Josiah M Ward, Oct 10, 1815, d in Berlin, May 20, 1853, (341) Nancy, b Nov 7, 1784, m William Dunham, Feb 27, 1812, d in Berlin, April 15, 1853, (342) Desire, b Oct 29, 1786, (343) Noah, b in 1788, m Millicent Oliver, d in New Orleans, May 1826, leaving a family in Tennessee, (344) Norman, b Feb 15, 1791, m Mary E Hibbard, of England, Oct 4, 1823, d in Berlin, Sept 13, 1861, (345) Mathew, b Aug. 3, 1793, m Sarah Ellsworth, Oct 13, 1824, d June 6, 1834, (346) Norris, b Dec. 9, 1795, m Eliza Langdon, and settled in Berlin, (347) Lucy, b July 19, 1798, d April 23, 1832, unm

[145.] LEMUEL[5] PECK, son of Amos,[4] married Lydia Dickinson. He died in Berlin, February 22, 1821; she died April 15, 1826.

CHILDREN — SIXTH GENERATION

(348)+Seldon, b Jan. 25, 1794, (349) Harriet, b. Feb. 14, 1796, d. Nov. 11, 1828, (350)+Sherman, b. Dec. 28, 1800.

[147] ASA[5] PECK, son of ELISHA,[4] left Berlin about 1784, and settled in Litchfield. He died at South Farms in 1818. He volunteered in the war of the Revolution during one of the alarms, and was in the service for some time. He married Hannah Farnum, June 15, 1786.

CHILDREN — SIXTH GENERATION.

(351) John M , his only child, was b in Litchfield, Conn , Oct, 31, 1789 He became a distinguished Baptist clergyman   He was ordained to the Ministry in 1813, and became Pastor of the church at Amenia, Dutchess Co , N Y., in 1814   In 1817, he was appointed a Missionary, under the Baptist General Convention, and moved to St Louis   He afterwards settled at Rock Spring, Ill , where he died, March 15, 1858   He was mainly instrumental in establishing the Theological Seminary there.   Shurtleff's College, at Upper Alton, was established through his instrumentality.   Harvard College conferred the degree of D D upon him in 1852

His wife, before marriage, was Sally Paine   She died Oct 24, 1856. His children were   (352) *Eli P ,*[7] b July 28, 1810; (353) *Hannah,*[7] b June 10, 1812, (354) *Harvey J ,*[7] b. Sept 28, 1814, (355) *William C ,*[7] b Feb 11, 1818, (356) *Mary Ann,*[7] b Sept 18, 1820; (357) *William S ,*[7] b Nov. 13, 1823, (358) *John Q. A ,*[7] b Aug. 27, 1825, a *son,*[7] b. Dec 10, 1827, d in infancy

[148]   ARIEL[5] PECK, son of ELISHA,[4] after the war of the Revolution, in which he served, settled in Montgomery County, and died at Ellesburgh, Jefferson County, N. Y.   He married ——— Higby.

CHILDREN — SIXTH GENERATION

(359) Lucy, m Isaiah Byington, and settled in Stockbridge, Mass , (360)+ Lumon, b May 7, 1769 , (361)+Elisha, b March 7, 1774 , and (362) Sarah, who was twice married   first, to John Hall , second, to a Mr. Benedict.

[149]   ELISHA[5] PECK, son of ELISHA,[4] settled in Lenox, Mass., where he lived and died.   He married Lucretia Patterson.

CHILDREN — SIXTH GENERATION

(363) John, b March 7, 1779, and d Feb 1851, leaving three sons and one daughter ; (364) Jabez, b Nov 2, 1780, to whom I am indebted for my information, was residing in Lenox, Mass , in 1866 * (365) His son Henry M Peck, resides at Haverstraw, N Y., where he has an extensive brick manufactory , (366) Betsey, b Oct. 27, 1782, m a Mr Judd, and d in Lenox, leaving children , (367) Oliver, b Aug 22, 1786, and d in Lenox, in 1856, leaving two sons and one daughter; (368) Elisha, b March 4, 1789 , was of the firm of Phelps, Peck & Co , extensive importers and manufacturers of copper, tin and sheet iron ware, in New York, where he died in 1851, leaving children , (369) Elijah, b Oct 1, 1791, settled in Lenox, and has two sons and one daughter; (370) Roxanna, b Jan 16, 1796, resided in Lenox, where she d in 1832, leaving one son, (371) Lura, b in 1801, m a Mr. Phelps, of Lenox, and had two daughters

---

* Died March 10, 1867.

[239]   ALFRED[6] PECK, son of PHILO,[5] lived and died in Litchfield, upon the ancestral homestead.   He married Susan Baldwin, of Litchfield.

CHILDREN — SEVENTH GENERATION ·

(372) James B , b Jan 28, 1808, m Amanda Kibbon. His children were (372) *Ellen A* [8], and (374) *Walter K.*[8] —(375) Walter, b Jan 10, 1810, d Nov 8, 1834, (376) Edmond, b June 5, 1812, d April 10, 1844, unm. , (377) Alvin, b. Feb 16, 1815, d Feb 9, 1838, unm. , (378) William G , b. Oct 16, 1820; he is a professor in Columbia College, N Y. , he married, first, Elizabeth M Davis, second, Ida Dayton His children are   (379) *Henry S* [8], (380) *Guy D* [8], and (381) *Ida J* [8] — (382) Andrew, b. April 14, 1824, d Nov 22, 1847, unm.

[250]   Judge WILLIAM V.[6] PECK, son of VIRGIL,[5] was residing at Portsmouth, Ohio, in 1865, where he has been one of the Judges of the Supreme Court.   To his kindness, I am indebted for letters of interest in relation to his branch of the name.   He is a descendant from Deacon Paul Peck, both on his father's and mother's side, his great-great paternal grandfather and his great-great-great maternal grandfather being one and the same person. He married Mary Ann Cook, July 8, 1830.

CHILDREN — SEVENTH GENERATION

(383) Mary C., b Jan 29, 1832, m L C Damain, Dec 27, 1852 , (384) William V . b Dec 2, 1836, m Harriet E McCollister, April 1858   His children in 1865 were   (385) *William V*,[8] b March 9, 1859 , (386) *Mary Ann*,[8] b Aug 13, 1861 , (387) and *Helen*,[8] b. Aug 16, 1863 , John H , b Aug 11, 1842 , Ellen L., b. Dec. 30, 1846   There were other children who died young.

[255]   Deacon SAMUEL[6] PECK, son of SAMUEL,[5] resided in Berlin, where he was a deacon of the Congregationalist Church. He married Polly M. Upson, November 27, 1794.   She was born July 13, 1776, and died December 15, 1853 ; he died March 19, 1833.

CHILDREN — SEVENTH GENERATION

(388) Warren, b. July 4, 1796, d. Nov 27, 1802 , (389) Samuel H , b Dec 14, 1798, d. in New Orleans, Sept. 12, 1862.   He married, first, Sarah Ann de Pate , second, Maryette Kellog   His children were (390) *Samuel H.*[8], (391) *William H* [8], (392) *Marcus M* [8], (393) *Ossian G* [8], (394) *Leroy M* [8], (395) *Mertis V* [8], (396) *Milton A* [8], (397) *DeWitt C* [8], (398) *Marius K* [8], (399) *Anthony A* [8]*;* and *Augustus.*[8] —(400) Russell U., b. April 28, 1804, resides in Southington, Conn   He married, first, Lydia Botsford, second, Susan Curtis , third, Eunice C Woodruff.   His children are (401) *George B* [8], (402) *Sarah Ann*[8], (403) *Samuel H* [8], (404) *Betsey L* [8], (405) *Susan Amelia*[8], (406) *Celinda A* [8] and (407) *Susan A.*,[8] *twins.* — (408) Henry P., b. Aug. 6, 1812, (409) Sally M , b. Sept. 14, 1814.

[256]   EDWARD[6] PECK, son of SAMUEL,[5] resided in Berlin, where he died, March 11, 1834.   He was a joiner and carpenter by trade.   He was twice married; 1st, to Saiah Langdon, March 23, 1802; 2d, to Polly Williams, August 8, 1816.

CHILDREN — SEVENTH GENERATION

(410) Warren, (411) Asahel, (412) Everlin, (413) Aldin, b Dec 19, 1817, m 1st, Jane E Webster; 2d, Elizabeth W Stewart, resides in Meriden, Conn. His children are   (414) *Emma E* [8], (415) *Augusta A* [8], (416) *Grace A* [8], (417) *Charles A* [8], and (418) *Carlton C W* [8] —(419) Cornelius W., b Feb 22, 1820, m Lucy Ann Hale, March 22, 1848, and resides in Berlin, Conn   His children are   (420) *Ellen M* [8], and (421) *Edward J.* [8] —(422) Jehiel, b. Oct 3, 1823, (423) Edward A , b March 2, 1829.

[277]   WARREN[6] PECK, son of ABIJAH,[5] resided in Lock, N. Y., where he died, February 2, 1836.   He was three times married; 1st, to Abigail Owen; 2d, to Roxy Standish; 3d, to Hannah Pearsons.

CHILDREN — SEVENTH GENERATION

(424) Phylinda, b Aug 15, 1806, m Stephen Birdsell, and d March 15, 1843, (425) Joseph L , b April 18, 1809, to whom I am indebted for my information, resides in Lock, N Y. He m Mary Jones, Oct 28, 1832, and has two sons (426) *Charles,* [8] b Feb 20, 1836, and (427) *Corydon,* [8] b Oct 6, 1838 —(428) Susannah, b. Feb. 22, 1814 , (429) Warren, b May 15, 1816, m. Mary Birdsell, has two children   (430) *George W.* [8], and (431) *Carrie* [8]—(432) Caroline Matilda, b. Nov 9, 1818

[284]   EVERARD[6] PECK, son of JESSE,[5] resided at Rochester, N. Y., where he died, February 9, 1854.   He was editor and proprietor of the Rochester *Telegraph*.   He married, 1st, Chloe Poiter; 2d, Martha Farlee; 3d, Mrs. Alice Walker (widow).

CHILDREN — SEVENTH GENERATION

(433) Norman, d June 1849, leaving one son   (434) *Benjamin,* [8] who was residing at Springfield, Mass , in 1866 —(435) Emily, m Horace Turner, d. Nov. 29, 1856, (436) Charles, d Aug 12, 1857, (437) Henry, was residing at Oberlin, Ohio, in 1863, (438) William F., and (439) Edward W , at Rochester.

[285.]   HENRY[6] PECK, son of JESSE,[5] settled at New Haven, Conn., where he died, March 1, 1867.   He was Mayor of the city for several years.   He married Jerusha Clark, of Hartford.

CHILDREN — SEVENTH GENERATION

(440) Horace C., b. Jan. 10, 1820; (441) Henry J , b July 10, 1822, d. Sept. 3, 1822, (442) Emily C., b. Jan. 16, 1824, d. Sept 4, 1824, (443) Henry, b. Aug. 31, 1827, (444) William C., b. Oct. 23, 1830; (445) Lorenzo B., b. Dec. 24, 1835.

[286]   JESSE[6] PECK, son of JESSE,[5] resides in New Haven. He was bred a printer, which occupation he followed for many years.   He was subseqently Clerk of the Probate Court, Justice of the Peace, and Public Notary for several years; also, Surveyor of Customs, and since, Inspector and Clerk of the Customs, which last position he was occupying in 1867.   He married Evelina Hayes, daughter of Col. Stephen Hayes, of Newark, N. J.

CHILDREN — SEVENTH GENERATION

(446) Everard, b Feb 24, 1835, d July 24, 1836, (447) Eveline H , b July 29, 1838, d Nov 24, 1851, (448) Everard H , b Nov 7, 1845   He entered the army in 1864, in the 1st Connecticut Cavalry, and served under General Sheridan, and was honorably discharged at the close of the war

[288.]   ELISHA[6] PECK, son of JUSTUS,[5] left Connecticut in 1817, and settled in New Berlin, N. Y., where he resided about ten years   From there he removed to Howard, Steuben County, N. Y., where he died, February 28, 1843.   He married Huldah Ford, November 24, 1785.

CHILDREN — SEVENTH GENERATION

(449) Moses, settled at Fabius, Onondaga County, N Y , where he died His widow was residing at Apulia, in 1866   His children were (450) *Elisha*,[8] of Apulia, (451) *William M*,[8] of Fabius, (452) *Eliza*,[8] who m John R. Robertson; (453) *Lucia*[8], (454) *Harriet*[9] and (455) *Mary* [8] —(456) James, d. leaving children   His son, *Lucius*,[8] a physician, was residing at Java, N Y , in 1866 —(457) Justus, settled in New Berlin, N Y , and from there removed to Ohio, and was residing at Richmond Centre in 1866   His children are . (458) *Huldah*[8], (459) *Edwin O*[8], (460) *James W*[8], and (461) *Austin* [8] —The children of Edwin O are   (462) *Sarah A*[9], (463) *Edwin O*[9], (464) *Darius B*[9], (465) *Lemuel A*[9], (466) *Justus L*[9], (467) *Milo C*[9], (468) *Luella R*[9], (469) *Charlie E*[9], (470) *Archie*[9], and (471) *Dudley A*[9] —The children of James W are   (472) *Janette*[9], (473) *Mary J*[9]; (474) *Aurilla*[9], (475) *James W*[9], (476) *Cynthia*[9], (477) *Huldah L*[9], (478) *Estella*[9], and *Verona* [9] —(479) William was residing at Wallace Station, N Y , in 1864, (480) Polly, m Augustus Simonds, (481) Marcus, was residing at Goshen, Ind , in 1865   His children are (482) *Almira*[8], (483) *Ripley C*,[8] of Chohocton, N Y , (484) *Adaline*[8]; (485) *David S*,[8] of Goshen, Ind , (486) *Eunice*[8], (487) *Marcus A.,*[8] of Goshen , (488) *Hester M*[8], and (489) *George A*,[8] also of Goshen —(490) Elisha A , m Emily Westcott, and d. about 1834, (491) *Henry A*,[8] his only son, was residing at Baraboo, Wis , in 1864 * —(492) Austin J , m the widow of Elisha A   She d. in 1862   He was residing in 1864 at Leoni, Mich , with his daughter, Mis C M Dipple

---

* He died, June 27, 1867, in the 37th year of his age.   His children are Cora, Randall, and Jay Irwin.

[298.] ISAAC[6] PECK, son of ZEBULON,[5] married Luena Candee, February 12, 1800, and died in Marshall, N. Y., April 30, 1851.

CHILDREN — SEVENTH GENERATION:

(493) Eliza, b Dec 12, 1800, m Chester Gaylord, May 22, 1833, and was residing in Marshall, N Y., in 1865, (494) Almira, b Jan. 18, 1803, m David Barton, Jan. 17, 1820; (495) John C , b Nov 3, 1805, m Anna Whitney, Oct 12, 1823, d Feb 14, 1865, (496) George B , b Nov 22, 1807, m Charlotte Lumbard, March 16, 1831, for his first wife, and Harriet Buckingham, Feb 18, 1852, for his second His children are. (497) *Almira*[8], (498) *Charlotte*[8], and (499) *Dwight B* [8] — (500) Mary, b. May 10, 1810, m Frederick B Nichols, Sept. 26, 1832, d Nov. 26, 1833, (501) James I , b June 29, 1812, m Louisa Atkinson His children are (502) *Charlotte*[8], (503) *John*,[8] who d. in the army, (504) *Wayne*[8], (505) *Mark*[8], (506) *Edward*[8], and (507) *Isaac*,[8] who d young. — (508) Harriet R , b Aug 15, 1815, m John Dean, Oct 10, 1838. He held an office in the Treasury Department at Washington, where he died Oct. 16, 1863.

[300.] SILAS[6] PECK, son of ZEBULON,[5] was twice married: first, to Betsey Chubb, January 23, 1800, and second, to Mrs. Mary Coe, March 24, 1807. He died October 31, 1839.

CHILDREN — SEVENTH GENERATION

(509) Edward, b in 1801, m first, Mary Eastman; second, Alvira Page; d. in 1837 His children are (510) *Esther L* [8], (511) *John E* [8], and (512) *Sarah* [8] — (513) Betsey L , b in 1803, d in 1818, (514) Amzi C , b in 1808, m Margaret Lumbard in 1833. His children were (515) *Edward*[8], and (516) *Adelaide*[8], and three who d young. — (517) Lydia A., b in 1810, m. S A Hitchcock; (518) Sarah P , b in 1813, m Thomas Murry; (519) Esther H , b in 1815, m Charles Trobridge, (520) George A , b in 1820, m. Edith M Brown. His children are (521) *Hugh T* [8], (522) *Helen M* [8]; (523) *Julia A*,[8], (524) *Willis P*.[8], (525) *Fred C*.[8], and one d in infancy. He resides upon the homestead.

[301.] ZEBULON[6] PECK. son of ZEBULON,[5] married Susan Bartholomew, March 31, 1807, and died in Deansville, Oneida County, N. Y., November 15, 1865.

CHILDREN — SEVENTH GENERATION ·

(526) Caroline S., b Feb 5, 1808, d Nov. 21, 1812, (527) Mary Ann, b. June 8, 1809, d Nov 24, 1812, (528) Evaline, b July 12, 1811, d Feb. 23, 1840; (529) Susan B , b Sept 21, 1813, (530) Charles B , b July 8, 1815, m Lucina Miller, d March 26, 1857 His children are (531) *Lucy M* ,[8] b Nov. 4, 1839; (532) *Susan J* ,[8] b. March 16, 1843, (533) *Eva E* ,[8] b July 25, 1845, (534) *Franklin J* ,[8] b Aug 11, 1855. — (535) Mary Ann, b April 15, 1821, (536) Hawley Z , b. Jan 5, 1824, m Sarah A Stone, Oct 31, 1854, and was residing in Deansville, N. Y , in 1864 His children are. (537) *Charles*,[8] b. Sept. 26, 1857, (538) *Ella A* ,[8] b. Dec. 13, 1862.

Helen Sophie Peek

[305] ANTHONY[6] PECK, son of ZEBULON,[5] was twice married· first, to Mary Greenlist, April 5, 1814; second, to Cynthia Moor, February 26, 1829. He died at Marshall, April 19, 1845.

CHILDREN — SEVENTH GENERATION

(539) Mary, m Ansel D Hancheet, and was residing in Marshall, N Y , in 1865, (540) Malissa, m Warren Kellogg, and was residing at Chittenango in 1865, (541) Anthony, m Delia E Gates His children in 1865 were (542) *Anthony*[8], and (543) *Edward S*[8] — (544) Maria, m John B Barton, and was residing in Rome in 1865, (545) William, m Lydia Moor He enlisted in the 7th Pennsylvania Cavalry, and d of a wound received during a charge into Shelbyville, Tenn He held a lieutenant's commission He left two children (546) *Minnie*[3], and (547) *Willie* [8] — (548) DeWitt C , m Mary Barton, and was residing at Mexico, N Y , in 1865 He is a lawyer His children were (549) *Fayette H*[8], and (550) *Carrie A* [8] —(551) Fayette, m Clara M Norton, and was residing at Marshall, N Y , upon the homestead, in 1864, and had one child *Helen N*[8] —(552) Juliette, d young; (553) Harriet N , was residing at home in 1864 unm

[307.] SAMUEL[6] PECK, son of ABEL,[5] settled in Bristol, where he died April 1, 1826. He married Hannah Manross, June 9, 1791. She died May 5, 1855.

CHILDREN — SEVENTH GENERATION

(554) Sylvester, b in Bristol, Conn , Aug 12, 1794, m Miss Fanny Roberts, of Bristol, May 28, 1818 She was b Sept 24, 1792 He resided in West Haven, Conn He was a man much respected in the community in which he resided, kind and obliging; honorable in his dealings, whose word and promise were held inviolate He was a man of talents, fond of reading, and conversant with the passing events of the day He had travelled through many of the States, and become well acquainted with human nature To him I am indebted for his kindness, and the interest he took in the history of his branch of the name He d at West Haven, May 11, 1868 His widow, an amiable and intelligent lady, still resides there His children are (555) *LaFayette M* ,[8] b Jan 22, 1822, d July 18, 1830; (556) *Sylvester B* ,[8] b Jan 25, 1827, d Aug 27, 1828, (557) *Mary Jane*,[8] b Feb 10, 1829, m Charles N Shumway, of Oxford, N Y They reside in the town of Phelps, where she is much respected by her friends and acquaintances. They have one child *Fannie Gertrude* [9] —(558) *Angeline C* ,[8] b Feb 13, 1832, d June 21, 1856 She was, I am told, possessed of fine talents, and pleasing in her appearance and manner (559) *Helen Sophie*,[8] b July 19, 1834 She is a lady well educated, and from her correspondence seems possessed of an excellent mind, cultivated and refined She is an admirer of the fine arts, poetry, music, painting, etc , in some of which she is said to excel, an excellent and chaste writer, and I am told an occasional contributor of a poem to some of the magazines and papers. — (560) Emily, b April 21, 1797, d April 3, 1803 , (561) Angeline, b May 28, 1799, m Oren Ives, Dec 23, 1824 , (562) Samuel, b May 3, 1803, m Harriet

Bartholomew, March 14, 1827, and settled in Virginia, (563) Emily, b March 9, 1805, m Anson Beckwith, July 25, 1825, d July 16, 1851, (564) Abel G , b Jan 8, 1807, m first, Lydia H Read, second, Eliza Ann Boles. He was residing in Boston in 1864 His children were (565) *Morganna L.*[8], (566) *Persis A* [8], (567) *William*[8], (568) *Angie M* [8], and (569) *John,*[8] who d in infancy — (570) William, b. Dec 27, 1809, d in Boston, Sept 12, 1846, no issue

[320.]   JUDGE TRACY[6] PECK, son of Lament,[5] resided in Bristol, Conn.   He was for many years a prominent public man. He was repeatedly a member of both branches of the Connecticut Legislature; was several years Judge of Probate, Justice of the Peace, Canal Commissioner, County Surveyor, etc., and without intermission for more than half a century held different and important offices in the town.   He was much interested in the genealogy and history of his branch of the name.   I called his attention to the subject in 1851.   I am indebted through the kindness of his daughter, Miss Kezia A. Peck, for many facts and much information from his manuscripts since his disease, in relation to his branch.

He married Sally Adams, of Litchfield, February 3, 1812.   He died February 12, 1862.

CHILDREN — SEVENTH GENERATION

(571) Epaphroditus, b Nov 13, 1812. He was the pioneer of the American clock business in Europe He d in Liverpool, Eng , Sept 20, 1857, (572) Sally H , b March 17, 1815, d Dec 9, 1815, (573) Sarah T , b Nov 5, 1816, m Charles E Smith, of Plymouth, Sept 26, 1839 He d Jan 9, 1854 She was residing in Bristol, a widow, in 1865, (574) Rachel R , b Sept 27, 1818 m Charles Bronson, of Waterbury, July 25, 1848, where they were residing in 1865, (575) Joseph A , b Oct 9, 1820, d Dec 4, 1822, (576) an infant, b July 6, 1822, d July 12, 1822, (577) Joseph A., 2d, b Feb 18, 1824, m Mary E. Thorp, Sept 1, 1846, and settled in New Haven, no issue, (578) Josiah T , b Aug 3, 1826, m Ellen L Barnard, Nov 23, 1847 He was residing in Bristol in 1866, where he was Deputy Collector of Internal Revenue His children were (579) *Miles L* [8], (580) *Eliza J* [8], (581) *Theodore B* [8], (582) *Epaphroditus*[8], and (583) *Edson M* [8] — (584) Eliza J., b. Aug 19, 1828, d July 17, 1847, (585) Henry A , b July 26, 1832 He enlisted into the 10th Regiment of Connecticut Volunteers, Oct 1861, was promoted, and returned with the regiment a captain, in 1865 He was in twenty-three battles   (586) Kezia A , b. Nov 25, 1834 She graduated at the State Normal School in 1859. She was residing in Bristol in 1865, (587) Tracy, b May 24, 1838 He graduated at Yale College, where he held an honorable position, ranking high as a scholar He afterwards visited Paris, Rome, and Germany, where he completed his studies   After his return from Europe, he was offered and accepted a position in Yale College, which he was occupying in 1866.

[321] RICHARD[6] PECK, son of Lament,[5] settled in Bristol. He married Sophia Miller, of Burlington, June 28, 1815.

CHILDREN — SEVENTH GENERATION

(588) Elizabeth G , b Nov 14, 1816, (589) Abby M., b Dec 12, 1818, d June 28, 1836, (590) Sophia M , b March 24, 1821, m Charles Root, Dec 20, 1843, was residing in New Haven in 1865, a widow, (591) Richard L , b Feb 19, 1824, d April 13, 1824, (592) Richard L , 2d, b July 13, 1826, served nine months in the 25th Regiment Connecticut Volunteers, and was residing in Bristol in 1866, (593) Jonathan M , b. Nov. 1, 1829, settled in Plymouth

[325] NEHEMIAH[6] PECK, son of Lament,[5] was twice married first, to Martha Scoville, November 6, 1824; second, to widow Lydia Roberts, January 22, 1851. He died at Burlington, Vt., March 30, 1861.

CHILDREN — SEVENTH GENERATION

(594) James, b Sept 20, 1825, d July 19, 1830; (595) Mary S , b April 20, 1827, m Charles Shumway, Oct 16, 1849, d Aug 21, 1855, leaving one child, (596) Nehemiah, b May 2, 1829 He was for some time a merchant in Burlington, Vt He d at New Britain, Conn , in 1863, (597) James G , b May 28, 1831, m Rebecca S Clark, of New Britain, Dec. 14, 1854, where they were residing in 1865 His children are (598) *Charles S* [8], (599) *Martha*[8], and (600) *James S* [8] — (601) David B , b March 15, 1833. m Frances A Brainard, of Keene, N H., May 31, 1859 He was for some time associated with his brother in business at Burlington He enlisted in 1861 He was in the Vermont 7th Regiment. He at first held a captain's commission, and afterwards that of Lieut -Colonel, (602) Susan R , b May 11, 1855, d Oct 15, 1853, (603) Sarah B , b Feb 7, 1838, m Percy Rice, of Cleveland, Ohio, in 1864, where they settled, (604) William Henry Harrison, b Feb 1, 1841, enlisted for the war; was severely wounded before Richmond, and was transferred to the Veteran Corps, with the rank of captain

[326] NEUMAN[6] PECK, son of Lament,[5] moved to Wisconsin in 1841, and settled at Mount Pleasant, now Caledonia. From there he removed, in 1856, to Delona, now Excelsior, Sauk County, where he was residing in 1865 He has been a prominent man, holding various public offices. He has been twice married · first, to Achsah Bailey, May 15, 1822; second, to Sarah Cone, October 27, 1829.

CHILDREN — SEVENTH GENERATION

(605) Francis N , b July 21, 1830, m. Eliza J Montgomery, Nov 3, 1853; was residing in Excelsior, Wis , in 1865, (606) James and (607) John, twins, b May 13, 1831 They were merchants, residing at Burlington, Vt , in 1865. James m. Mrs Grace A Dyer, widow of Lieut. Dyer of the United States

Navy. John m Louisa W Terrell   (608) Charles, b May 27, 1833, m Catharine A Weidman, Jan 27, 1859, and settled in Caledonia, Wis , (609) Achsah,
b May 9, 1836, m Lyman B Montgomery They settled in Windfield, Wis ,
(610) An infant son, b Sept 10, 1834, lived but a few days (611) Erastus C ,
b Nov. 2, 1837, m Helen M Sears, of Caledonia, Wis , where they were
residing in 1865 , (612) Abby R , b Nov 14, 1838 , was residing with her parents, unm , in 1865 She was a school teacher.

[332.] WOOSTER[6] PECK, son of JOSIAH,[5] settled in Castleton, Vt , where he died May 10, 1844. He married Sarah Davis,
November 23, 1809.

CHILDREN — SEVENTH GENERATION

(613) Josiah, b in 1812, m Lucy Cole, of Johnsbury, N Y , (614) Mary, b
in 1814, m Lewis Minor, of Castleton , (615) Henry, b in 1816, m Elizabeth
Whitehouse His children are (616) *Albert*,[8] b in 1852, (617) *Carlos*,[8] b in
1860; and (618) *Robert*,[8] b in 1862 — (619) Noah, b in 1818, d young; (620)
Martha, b. in 1820, m William Adams , (621) Almira, b in 1822, m Burk
Couch , (622) Ruth Ann, b in 1828 , (623) Sylvia, b in 1830, d. in 1856 , (624)
Lyman, b in 1832, d in 1834, (625) Aldin, b in 1836, was killed at the battle
of the Wilderness, May 5, 1864 , (626) Emeline, b in 1839

[348.] SELDEN[6] PECK, son of LEMUEL,[5] resides in Berlin.
He married Lucy H. Hart, November 1, 1826. To him I am
indebted for his kindness, and the interest he has taken in the
history.

CHILDREN — SEVENTH GENERATION ·

(627) Sherman H , b March 17, 1829 , (628) Hattie E , b April 16, 1835, m
Nathaniel L Bradley, Oct 25, 1859 , (629) Henry H , b Dec 25, 1837 He is
of the firm of Miller & Peck, Waterbury, Conn , (630) George S , b. May 9,
1840, d in 1865 , (631) Lucy Ann, b. Oct. 17, 1844

[350.] SHERMAN[6] PECK, son of LEMUEL,[5] was residing at
Honolulu, Sandwich Islands, in 1866. He married Emily Hopkins,
September 12, 1838.

CHILDREN — SEVENTH GENERATION

(632) Lucia E., b in 1839 , (633) Emma W , b in 1841 , (634) Charles S., b
in 1846, d May 9, 1847 , (635) Francis S , b in 1848, d. in 1850

[360.] LUMON[6] PECK, son of ARIEL,[5] resided at Cold Spring,
Wis., where he died April 1844. He married Eunice Bell.

CHILDREN — SEVENTH GENERATION

(636) Elisha , (637) Sally, m a Mr. Bishop, and was a widow in 1846, (638)
Ariel, deceased , (639) Daniel H., deceased , (640) Chester, residing at North

Brookfield in 1866, (641) David B, residing at Fort Atkinson, Wis, in 1866, (642) Alanson, deceased, (643) Harriet, deceased, and (644) Diadema, who m a Lawrence, and was a widow in 1866.

[361.] ELISHA[6] PECK, son of ARIEL,[5] settled in Stockbridge, Mass., where he resided until 1818, when he moved to what is now Brownhelm, Ohio, where he died January 7, 1859. He married Meliscent Byington, September 10, 1797.

CHILDREN — SEVENTH GENERATION ·

(645) Joseph, b. Aug. 13, 1798, d Oct. 22, 1823, (646) Julius, b. Oct 22, 1799, d Nov 29, 1829, (647) Chauncey, b March 14, 1801, m Abby Lewis, d. Aug 27, 1848 His children were, (648) *Mary*[8], (649) *Xenophon*[8], (650) *Julius*[8], and (651) *Chauncy* [8] — (652) Amelia, b. Jan 14, 1803, m Rodney Andrews, (653) Elisha F, b. May 25, 1806, m Sally Ann Morse, July 3, 1833. He was residing in Brownhelm, Ohio, in 1866. His children are (654) *Ann M*,[8] b April 21, 1834, m Henry O Allen, (655) *Lydia M.*,[8] b Sept 23, 1835, (656) *Henry F*,[8] b. April 1837, d Feb 4, 1864, and (657) *William E.*,[8] b Aug. 5, 1841 — (658) Jane M, b Aug 25, 1808, m Moses B Crosby, May 21, 1829, (659) Caroline, b Oct 28, 1810, m Oren Cable (660) Mary, b. Oct. 20, 1812, m John C Bacon, Jan. 1, 1837, (661) Lydia, b Nov 29, 1814, d Oct 9, 1835, (662) Delia, b Jan 7, 1817, m Dr John Davis, d May 5, 1844, (663) Enos H., b. April 22, 1819 He was the second child born in the town of Brownhelm. He m Ivan C. T Shotten, no issue.

33*

DESCENDANTS OF DEACON WILLIAM PECK,

OF NEW HAVEN, CONNECTICUT.

The following account of some of the male descendants of Deacon WILLIAM PECK, of New Haven, Conn., intended to present sufficient of the genealogy of his descendants to identify and distinguish them from those of other branches of the same patronymic, was furnished me by Judge Darius Peck, of Hudson, N. Y. He informed me that he was preparing a history of them himself, which makes it improper and unnecessary for me to give a more extended one.

[1.]   WILLIAM PECK was born in London, England, in 1601. His progenitors are unknown. With his wife Elizabeth and his then only child Jeremiah, he emigrated to this country in the ship " Hector," arriving at Boston, June 26, 1637, in the company of Gov. Eaton, Rev. John Davenport, and others, and was one of the founders of the New Haven Colony in the spring of 1638. He was a merchant by occupation, a man of high standing in the Colony, and a deacon of the church in New Haven from 1659 until his decease, October 4, 1694, at the advanced age of 93 years. His tombstone is still standing in the cemetery of New Haven.

His sons were: (2) *Jeremiah ;* (3) *John ;* and (4) *Joseph.*

Jeremiah was the first teacher of the Colony Collegiate School, in New Haven, in 1660–1661; the first settled minister in Saybrook, Conn., in the fall of 1661; in Elizabethtown, N. J., in 1669 or 1670; in Greenwich, Conn., in 1678; and in Waterbury, Conn., in 1690, where he died, June 7, 1699, in his 77th year

[3.]   *John* settled in Wallingford, Conn., in 1672, and died there in 1724, aged 86 years.

[4.]   *Joseph* settled about 1662, in Lyme, Conn., where he was a Justice of the Peace and Deacon of the Church, and died in 1718, in the 78th year of his age.

DESCENDANTS OF REV. JEREMIAH PECK, SON OF DEACON WILLIAM PECK.

[2]   Rev. JEREMIAH PECK had four sons: (5) *Samuel;* (6) *Caleb;* (7) *Jeremiah, jr.;* and (8) *Joshua.*

Caleb and *Joshua* had no descendants.

[7.]   *Jeremiah, jr.*, settled in Waterbury, Conn., in 1790; was a deacon of the Northbury church in that town, and a deputy to the General Court of Connecticut. He died in Waterbury, in 1751, aged 84 years. He had but one son: (9) Jeremiah, 3d, who died there in 1750, aged 44 years, leaving but one son, (10) Lemuel, born 1748, by whose death, in 1758, the descendants in the male line of Jeremiah, jr., became extinct, and his brother Samuel became the common ancestor of all the male descendants then living of Rev. Jeremiah Peck.

[5.]   *Samuel*, son of Rev. Jeremiah, settled in Greenwich, in 1678, and died there in 1746, in his 88th year. He was a man of large wealth and influence. He was a Justice of the Peace, in Greenwich, for about fifty years, and held many important positions in that town. He had nine sons born in Greenwich, from 1687 to 1706, viz (11) *Samuel, jr.;* (12) *Jeremiah;* (13) *Joseph;* (14) *David;* (15) *Nathaniel;* (16) *Eliphalet;* (17) *Theophilus;* (18) *Peter;* and (19) *Robert;* all of whom lived and died in Greenwich except David, who died in the adjoining town of North Castle, N. Y. They died from 1733 to 1783. The other eight sons have a numerous and widely scattered posterity, mostly farmers in their various localities. Many have been deacons and civil magistrates, and several of them ministers of different religious denominations.

[11.]   *Samuel, jr.*, had two sons: (20) John; and (21) Samuel, 3d. The latter was a deacon of the church in Greenwich, Conn., dying there in 1793; and his son (22) Calvin was a deacon in Sharon, Conn., dying there in 1837, both aged 73 years. (23) Augustus L., a grandson of Calvin, resides* in Sharon, Conn. John,

---

*Some of these persons may have changed their residence since the communication was written.

son of Samuel, jr., had four sons born in Greenwich from 1742 to 1758, viz: (24) John, jr.; (25) Heath; (26) Nathan; and (27) Abijah. John, jr., was a soldier in the French war until the peace of 1763, and died in Smyrna, N. Y., in 1819, aged 77. Heath and Nathan died while in service, during the Revolutionary war, through which Abijah also served as a soldier, and afterwards became a Baptist minister in Clifton Park, N. Y., where he died in 1848, in the 91st year of his age. His son (28) Abijah, jr., was, in 1841, a member of the Legislature of the State of New York. Another son, (29) Solomon C., and a grandson (30) John, are living in Clifton Park, N. Y. (31) Nathan, and (32) John, sons of John, jr., were Baptist ministers. The latter was somewhat distinguished as such, and died in 1849, in the 70th year of his age. His three sons · (33) Darius, (34) Philetus B., and (35) Linus M., were liberally educated, the first being a lawyer, residing in Hudson, N. Y., and the last two Baptist ministers, who died in early life in 1847. Another son of John, jr., (36) Stephen N., resides in Solon, N. Y., in the 89th year of his age.

[15.] *Nathaniel* was for several years a Justice of the Peace, in Greenwich, Conn., where he died, in 1765, aged 68 years. His grandson, (37) Jonathan Richard, settled in Flushing, Long Island, N. Y., in 1790, and became the progenitor of the numerous families of his surname in that locality. He was a man of great sagacity and enterprise, and died there in 1822, aged 54 years. His son (38) Richard was an Episcopal clergyman, in Sheldon, Vt., where he died in 1846, aged 46 years. His grandson, George W., resides in New York City. (39) George W., son of (40) Walter, who was the great-grandson of the above-named Nathaniel, has been a member of Congress from the State of Michigan, and resides in Lansing, in that State.

[17] *Theophilus* had a grandson (41) David, who was a Baptist minister in Greenwich, and died there in 1835, aged 81 years. His grandson (42) David graduated at Yale College, in 1849; is a Congregational minister, and resides in Barre, Mass. (43) Isaac, another grandson of Theophilus, was a member of the Legislature of Connecticut; resided at Round Hill, in Greenwich, Conn., and died there in 1860, aged 83 years. His only son (44) Isaac, a graduate of Yale College, in 1821, is an

Episcopal clergyman, and resides in Greenwich, Conn. (45) Whitman, a great-grandson of Theophilus, a graduate of Yale College, in 1838, is a Congregational minister, and resides in Ridgefield, Conn. Of his other great-grandsons, (46) Jared V. has been a member of the Legislature and member of Congress from Westchester County, N. Y.; (47) John, a graduate of Western Reserve College, in 1842, is a Presbyterian minister in the State of Minnesota; (48) William J., has been President of the Board of Aldermen, in New York City, where he resides; and (49) Elias, is a physician, in Newburgh, N. Y. (50) Edward M. is an Episcopalian clergyman, in Riverdale, N. Y.

[19] *Robert* had a son (51) Robert, who was a deacon of the church in Greenwich, and died there in 1828, aged 85 years.

DESCENDANTS OF JOHN PECK, SON OF DEACON WILLIAM PECK.

[3] JOHN PECK had but one son, (52) *John, jr.*, who survived infancy. He was a deacon of the church in Wallingford, Conn., and died there in 1771, at the advanced age of 97 years. Some of his descendants still reside upon the premises which were the ancestral homestead nearly two hundred years ago. He had only one son, (53) Samuel, a prominent man, who resided in Wallingford, and died there in 1755, aged 51 years. Samuel had six sons born in Wallingford, from 1727 to 1750, viz· (54) *John;* (55) *Samuel, jr.;* (56) *Charles;* (57) *Jesse;* (58) *Nicholas;* and (59) *Joel.*

[54.] *John* settled in Cheshire, Conn., and died there in 1799, aged 72 years. His sons were: (60) Samuel, 1st; (61) John; (62) Asa; (63) Levi; and (64) Samuel, 2d, all born in Cheshire, Conn., from 1756 to 1777, and died there, except Samuel, 1st, who died in the Revolutionary army, and Samuel, 2d, who died in East Bloomfield, N. Y., in 1848, to which place he had removed in 1835. While the latter resided in Connecticut, he held prominent military positions; was several years a Justice of the Peace, deacon of the church, and member of the Legislature

of Connecticut. Many of his descendants reside in East Bloomfield, and in the State of Michigan.

[55] *Samuel, jr.*, settled in Wallingford, Conn., and died
there in 1815, aged 81 years. He had sons: (65) Theophilus;
(66) Samuel; (67) John; (68) Isaac; and (69) Amos, born
there from 1764 to 1777.

Theophilus and Samuel in 1789, and Amos a few years later,
emigrated from Wallingford to Lexington (now Jewett), N. Y.,
where Theophilus died in 1839, aged 75; Samuel in 1834, and
Amos in 1845, each aged 68 years. The descendants of these
three brothers are very numerous there, and in other parts of the
country. Theophilus had a son (70) Charles, who died there in
1866, in the 77th year of his age, leaving a son (71) Alfred, who
is postmaster in Jewett, N. Y. John lived in Farmington, Conn.,
and died there in 1811, aged 42. Two of his six sons, (72) Ira
and (73) Chauncey, are living, the former in Hartford, Conn , and
the latter in Windham, N. Y. (74) Henry K., a son of the former,
resides in New York City. Isaac lived on the old homestead of
his ancestors, in Wallingford, and died there in 1847, aged 76
years. His sons (75) Samuel and (76) Joel reside in Wallingford.

[56.] *Charles* died at West Point, N. Y., in 1780, while in active service in the Revolutionary army, aged 44 years. His sons
who survived infancy were: (77) Jehiel; (78) Jesse; (79) Benjamin, (80) Charles, jr.; (81) Joel; and (82) John, born from
1757 to 1780. Jehiel and Benjamin were both in the Revolutionary army; the former died in Rockville, Md., about 1830, aged 73
years, and the latter in Fall River, Mass , in 1854, aged 84 years.
Jesse died in Farmington, Ohio, in 1832, aged 71 years. Charles,
jr., died in Shaftsbury, Vt., in 1857, aged 85 years. Joel died in
Scott, N. Y., in 1851, aged 77 years, and John is said to be living
in Bristol, Conn., aged 86 years.

[57] *Jesse* was unmarried, and died at Lake George, N. Y.,
in 1758, while a soldier in the French war.

[58] *Nicholas* lived in Wallingford, and died there in 1821,
aged 77 years. His son (83) Jesse S. died in Buffalo, N. Y., in
1845, aged 76 years, where his son, (84) Jesse, now resides.

[59.]   *Joel* settled in Farmington, Conn., where he died in 1842, aged 92 years. His only son (85) Jesse resided and died there in 1856, aged 78 years. His only grandson, (86) Joel, and his only great-grandson, (87) Joel W., resided there in 1865.

DESCENDANTS OF JOSEPH PECK, SON OF DEACON WILLIAM PECK.

The male descendants of Joseph Peck are far more numerous and widely extended than those of his brothers John and Jeremiah. On and soon after the close of the Revolutionary war, many of them migrated in almost every direction from the home of their common ancestor.

[4]   JOSEPH had only two sons who survived infancy · (88) *Samuel,* and (89) *Joseph J.*   The sons of *Samuel* were . (90) Samuel, jr.; (91) William; (92) Benjamin; (93) Elijah; (94) Jedediah; (95) Daniel; and (96) Silas, all born in Lyme, Conn., from 1707 to 1724.   The sons of *Joseph, jr.,* who survived infancy, were : (97) Jasper; (98) John; (99) David; and (100) Nathaniel. The sons of Samuel and Joseph, jr., all died in Lyme.   (101) Richard, a grandson of Samuel, jr., and, soon after, his brother (102) Jason, emigrated from Lyme and settled in Lexington, N Y., or its immediate neighborhood. The former died in Durham, N. Y., in 1837, aged 84 years, and the latter in Reading, N Y., in 1845, aged about 77 years.   Another brother, (103) Abner, settled in Shelburne, Mass , where he died in 1842, aged 82 years. (104) Jedediah and (105) Elisha, sons of the above-named (93) Elijah, emigrated from Lyme, the former in 1790, the latter about 1800, and settled in Burlington, Otsego County, N. Y.   The former was a man of great native ability and influence. For ten consecutive years he was a member of the Legislature of the State of New York, six years in the Assembly, and four years in the Senate, and for many years a County Judge of Otsego County, N. Y.   He died in 1821, aged 73 years. (106) Jasper J., a son of (97) Jasper above-named. was a military officer in the French war, and also in service in the

Revolutionary war, and died in Lyme, in 1821, aged 84 years His son (107) Richard S. was a physician, and died in Chatham, N. Y., in 1827, where his son (108) Oliver J., a physician, now resides. (109) Oliver, a grandson of Jasper, jr., is a physician in Sheffield, Mass. (110) Reynold, jr., a grandson of Jasper, jr., was a member of the Legislature of the State of New York, in 1840, from Ontario County. Several of the descendants of Jasper, jr., and of his brother (111) Reynold, settled in West Bloomfield, N. Y., and its vicinity. (112) Charles L, a grandson of (98) John, resided in Lyme, Conn., on the homestead of the ancestor Joseph, two centuries ago. (113) William, a son of (100) Nathaniel, graduated at Yale College, in 1775. He soon after entered the Revolutionary army, in which he held the rank of Colonel, and served until October 1781. He was U. S Marshal, of Rhode Island, from 1790 for about twenty years. He resided in Providence, R. I., where he died in 1832, in the 76th year of his age, leaving no male descendants. (114) Mather, jr., (115) David H., and (116) Richard, grandsons of Nathaniel, emigrated from Lyme; Mather, jr., and Richard to Bethany, N. Y., the former in 1806 and the latter in 1808, and David H. in 1812. In 1864, David H. was living in Middletown, Butler County, Ohio, aged 77 years, and Mather, jr., in Bethany, N. Y., aged about 79 years. Mather, jr , has a son (117) Gilbert M., residing in Bethany, N. Y.; David H. a son (118) Orandos X., residing in New York City; and Richard, jr., a son (119) Israel M., in Stafford, N. Y. (120) John M., a grandson of David, resides in Schenectady, N. Y., and (121) Charles C., a greatgrandson of David, in New York City.

ADDITIONS, ALTERATIONS AND CORRECTIONS.

I HAVE endeavored to give all the additions and make all the alterations and corrections which I have been asked to make, or which have been found necessary. Many of these were received while the work was in the press, *too late* to be made elsewhere, and many of them even after it was printed, while the index was being prepared It was found impossible to collect so many names, — about eleven thousand, with as many dates, — and carry them through the press without the necessity of alterations and corrections

After the arrangement of the work, it was carefully read through, and compared with the letters, records and documents from which it had been compiled. Where different dates of the same events, and different names of the same individuals and children, were given by different persons and by the same person at different times, or where errors of any kind were suspected, letters of inquiry were written After the work was printed, it was again read through, and all typographical errors found, however small or unimportant, pointed out, instead of leaving them to the query and conjecture of the reader as is sometimes done in such works.

Israel H. Peck, of Johnstown, Ohio, informs me, in relation to his branch of the name, that his grandfather, Benjamin, and Cyrus, the brother of his grandfather, lived and died in King's County, Nova Scotia. Cyrus kept a public house at Kentsville After his grandfather, Benjamin, died, his father, whose name was also Benjamin, came to the States, and settled at Johnstown, Ohio, in 1817, where he died in 1819, leaving eight children, — four sons and four daughters. One of the sons, Samuel, was residing at Marquette, Mich , in 1864 He supposes that his grandfather came from England to Nova Scotia.

Joseph Peck was born in Bolton, Conn , in 1761, and died in Irasburgh Vt , in 1850. His brother Jonathan died leaving a family of fourteen children His widow and son, Russell, were residing in Keene, N H , in 1863 Joseph was a Methodist clergyman. His sons were *John, Joseph, Joel S* , and *Jared.* *Jared* was residing in Potton, Canada East, in 1863. *John* died in Irasburgh, Vt., in 1852 His children are Joel, Charlotte, Ann, Freeman S , of Salem, Mass , Melissa K , Dyer H., of Boston, Mass , Abigail L , Margaret G., John; Alonzo D , a merchant of Boston; William F., and Elisha S , who resides in Salem *Joel S* resides in Worcester, Mass His children are John M., Joel J , of Worcester, Cyrus F , Maria J ; Tyler S , who was killed on the Norwich and Worcester Railroad, June 18, 1866, Mary E , Almira and Charlotte.

Page 34, nine lines from top, for Sept 20, 1697, read Apr 20, 1697. Page 42, eighteen lines from bottom, for March read May Page 48, eleven lines from top, for fifth generation read sixth , and, seventeen lines from top, for Gilnore read Gilmore

34

Add, page 52, in relation to Mrs. Rebecca Baker, formerly Rebecca Peck — She died Nov. 19, 1868, in the 84th year of her age Page 53, thirteen lines from top, for July 21 read Jan 26. Page 62, eighteen lines from top, for Learned read Lorinda. Page 80, twenty lines from top, for James Chappell read Richard. Page 84, eleven lines from bottom, for Oliver O read Oliver D Page 86, four lines from bottom, for 1862 read 1832. Page 90, seventeen lines from top, for Dec. 20 read Dec 2 Page 91, fourteen lines from top, for 1810 read 1816, and, thirteen lines from bottom, for Nov. 17 read 19.

Add to the family of Sanford Wilcox, page 99, ten lines from top, Sylvanus, b Dec 19, 1867. Page 103, eleven lines from top, for Arnold read Arnold J. Page 107, nine lines from bottom, for Hannah W. read Hannah H. Page 108, five lines from top, for Lorinda read Lucinda. Page 113, seventeen lines from bottom, for Chauncey P. read Chauncey C. Page 114, eleven lines from top, for Jan 22 read Jan 19, and, sixteen lines from top, for George G. read George C., and, six lines from bottom, for June 23 read June 25 Page 115, twelve lines from bottom, for Oct 1830 read Nov 1830 Page 124, fourteen lines from top, for April 11, 1763, read April 13, and, eight lines from bottom, for Sept. 1775 read 1777 Page 133, nineteen lines from bottom, for 1650 read 1657 Page 141, three lines from top, for P Rec. read R Rec

Add, in relation to Joseph Peck [1558], page 141, the following — After leaving Massachusetts he resided for some time in New Hampshire. From there he removed to Clinton, N. Y, afterwards Bainbridge. He remained here until 1812, when he removed to Lisle, N Y. His first wife died, and he married for his second wife a Mrs Norton He died in 1818; she, in 1839. His children, after he left Attleborough, were *Joseph*, whose children are Enos, of Farmersville, N Y., Jonathan, of Syracuse, Cyrus, Harvey, Laura Ann, and Harriet — *Nicholas*, d unm , — *Bethana*, d unm , — *John*, whose children are John D , of Whitney's Point, N. Y., Walter L., of Lisle; Huldah, Anna and Catharine, — *Hezekiah*, whose children are Diana, Elizabeth, Reed, of Cortland, N. Y., to whose kindness I am indebted for my information, Malvina, Mary, George W., of Auburn, N. Y , editor of the *Auburn Journal*, Martha L., and Mark, — *Noah*, who settled in Michigan, — *Ezekiel*, who died in Illinois, — *Benjamin*, who died in Bainbridge, — *Polly*, *Esther*, *Elizabeth*, and *Anna*, each of whom were married and had issue. Page 144, four lines from bottom, for 1788 read 1778 Page 150, seven lines from bottom, for Elioenoi read Elioenai Page 153, eight lines from top, for Sept. 20 read 22. Page 154, twenty lines from bottom, for 1821 read 1829 Page 158, eleven lines from top, for Bucon read Bacon. Page 160, ten and eleven lines from top, for Autill read Antile. Page 164, five lines from top, for Gardiner read Gardner. Page 173, nineteen lines from top, for July 11 read Jan 11 Page 176, seven lines from top, for 1837 read 1842, and, nineteen lines from top, for July 5 read 25

Add to the family of Thomas [1795], page 176, John, b Feb 6, 1853 Page 177, eleven and nineteen lines from top, for Hollan read Hollon, and, twenty-two lines from top, for Franklin read Friend Page 178, seven lines from top, for 1834 read 1838. Page 180, nine lines from top, for Brookline read Brooklyn Page 184, four lines from bottom, for Jan 7 read Jan 13. Page 185, nineteen lines from bottom, after daughter of, and before Jerusha, add Timothy and. Page 188, six lines from bottom, for 1864 read 1838 Page 192, six lines from bottom, for Nov 17 read 7. Page 193, six lines from top, for Hannah read Lydia E. Page 200, twelve lines from bottom, for Feb. 2 read 20.

Add, page 201, eleven lines from top, to the family of Noah [2579], Abigail, b Nov. 29, 1711

Add with the Pecks of Seekonk, Mass , Israel, who married the widow of Nathaniel Hunt, and resided for some time on the plain, so called, where is now the depot of the Boston and Providence Railroad   Who his father was I did not learn.   He probably belonged to some one of the Rehoboth families, where his name was not recorded   His son Cyril settled at Pawtucket, in Mass   He married, first, Millicent Clay, daughter of James Clay, and, second, widow Clarissa Wheeler.   He died in 1830, aged 80 years.   His children were *Zelinda,* who married Ephraim Walker and Dan Robinson, *James, Cyril, Friendly,* and *Israel,* who settled at Savannah, where they died, *Joseph,* who d in Pawtucket, *William,* d. in one of the Western States, *Amey,* who m. William Hovey, and was residing at Fort Atkinson, Wis , in 1863, *Hannah* and *Millicent,* who was residing in Providence, R. I , unm. in 1863   Page 208, eighteen and twenty-one lines from bottom, for Kesiah read Keziah.   Page 209, three lines from top, for [2670] read [2607].   Page 213, eleven lines from bottom, for July 20 read July 25.   Page 220, seventeen lines from bottom, for June 11 read June 1   Page 221, at top, for Mason read Maxon.   Page 224, fourteen lines from top, for July 14 read July 4 , and, eighteen lines from top, for Charles[10] E , b. Mar 3, 1855, read Charles[10] W., b Oct. 22, 1855 , and, ten lines from bottom, for Abba read Alba.   Page 225, four lines from top, for 1844 read 1842   Page 227, four lines from bottom, for Mar. 8, 1828, read Mar. 8, 1825.

Add, in relation to Warren E. Peck, page 231, at bottom, — He was drowned on the 12th of Sept., 1868, while attempting to cross a stream in the Belleview Valley, Mo , swollen by a flood.

He was assessor and deputy sheriff, and, at the time of the melancholy event, was returning home from the performance of his official duties   The following is among the resolutions passed at a meeting of Camp Willson, Post No 7, G A R , Ironton, Mo., where he was Junior Vice-Commander —

" Resolved, that in the death of our comrade our society has sustained an irreparable loss, our community been deprived of a good citizen, our country of a true patriot, our county of a faithful official, his wife a kind and affectionate husband, and his children an indulgent father."

The Ironton paper said of him   "As a friend, neighbor, and officer, his loss is deeply felt, as a soldier he made himself an enviable record , and as a citizen and public officer he was universally liked."

Page 232, three lines from bottom, for N H. read Vt.   Page 233, eight lines from bottom, for Mary Evelina read May Eveline   Page 237, fourteen lines from bottom, for Apr. 21 read Apr 24   Page 241, three lines from bottom, for Herman read Hermon

Add to the family of Hermon A. Peck, [2921], page 242, five lines from top, Lucy Ann, b. June 29, 1835, d Oct 1, 1839 , and, ten lines from top, for Herman read Hermon.   Add, page 271, five lines from top, after sixty and before pounds, six.   Page 253, fifteen lines from bottom, for 1788 read b July 28, 1787.   Page 278, three lines from bottom, for June 23 read June 2 , and, two lines from bottom, for Feb 17 read 11.   Page 279, three lines from top, for 1724 read 1754 , and, eleven lines from bottom, for 1830 read 1831.   Page 280, at top, for Nov. 2 read Nov. 7, and for Marsy read Marcy.   Page 282, seventeen lines from bottom, for Thankful read Franklin. Page 283, seven lines from top, for Emor read Eber W., and, seventeen lines from top, for 1823 read 1825 Page 285, sixteen lines from top, for Auritta read Aurilla, and, two lines from bottom, for June 10 read June 23. Page 291, six lines from top, for 1718 read 1715. Page 300, eight lines from top, for 1796 read 1769.

Add to the family of Asher Peck [89], page 300, ten lines from top, Joanna, b Oct 28, 1788, Lucy, b. May 10, 1790. His 1st wife d. Nov. 2, 1812. He married for his 2d wife Jane Morrison, March 21, 1813. She died July 25, 1822. He died July 7, 1822. Page 301, nine lines from top, for Arthur Q read Arthur L, and, eleven lines from top, for Cynthia read Diantha, and, two and four lines from bottom, for Nov. read Oct.

Add to the family of Michael Peck [131], page 303. Fenn. He married Sarah Treat. He died at Guadaloupe, W. I., of yellow fever, about 1803 His widow married Elijah Bryan, and lies buried in the cemetery at Milford, Conn. His children were Treat Fenn and Anthony Treat Fenn Peck was born Sept 2, 1801 He married Maria Bradley, of New Haven, Conn, and removed to Wilmington, N. C., about 1820, where he still resides. His children are *Sarah M*, *Mary B*, unm., *Caroline A*, d. young; *Emily T.*, unm, *George A.*, a merchant of Wilmington, married a daughter of O G Paisley, *William M.*, d in 1865, and *Caroline A.*, 2d, who d. in 1867. Sarah M, to whom I am indebted for my information, married Levi A. Hart. Mr. Hart is a native of Southington, Conn, an enterprising business man, engaged in carrying on a foundry, machine-shop, etc. Their children are Harriet, Mary Anna, Maria Treat, Millie, Annetta, Sarah L., Frederic Levi, and Leila Austin.

Add for the family of Anthony Peck, the brother of Treat Fenn — He married Harriet Clark, of Milford, Conn., and removed to Talmadge, Ohio, where he died, about 1840; his death being the result of injuries received by a fall from his haymow. His widow and son, H A Peck, still reside there.

Add to the family of Joseph, (430), page 304, eleven lines from top, Martha M., twelve lines from bottom, for 1752 read 1782

Add for the family of Levi, No (495), page 306 — He married Marcia Beers Feb 9, 1825 She d July 13, 1850. He was residing in Newtown in 1867 His children were *Cornelia*, b. July 26, 1828, d. July 28, 1833, *Cornelia* again, b. Feb 14,1835, married John Judson, and d Mar. 4, 1859 Page 310, two lines from top, for Oct. 19 read 29. Page 313, fourteen lines from bottom, for Joseph P. read Josephine; and, seventeen lines from top, for Bradley read Beardsley. Page 314, twelve lines from top, for Thompson read Thomas

Add in relation to Wyllys Peck (811) page 315. He died April 22, 1869. Mr Peck was one of the prominent men of New Haven, highly esteemed as a citizen, as a business man, and for his faithful performance of the duties intrusted to him by the public He was for many years of the firm of Bryan & Peck, and subsequently engaged with his brothers in the West India trade. He was for several years one of the Aldermen of the city and held various public trusts. Page 321, fourteen lines from bottom, for 1860 read 1864. Page 322, fifteen lines from bottom, for Rosanna read Roxana. Page 325, six lines from top, for May 4 read May 24. Page 326, four lines from top, for Sept. 3 read Sept 23, and, eight lines from bottom, for Apr 4 read Apr. 9.

Add to the family of James, page 327, after Morris and before Stephen — Eunice, b. June 2, 1721. Page 328, thirteen lines from bottom, for May read

March. Page 330, first line at bottom, for Apr. 5, 1784, read Apr. 24, 1775. Page 334, six lines from bottom, for Jan. 8 read Jan 18.

Add for the family of Benjamin Peck, page 338, No. (407) — He resided in Hamden, Conn. His children were *Sophia, Lewis, Rebecca, Henry,* of Hamden, *Francis,* of Jackson, Ill ; *Frederic,* of New Haven, *Lois A* , *Edson,* of Watertown, Conn , *Chloe A.* and *Silvia C* Lois A., to whom I am indebted for my information, married Lewis Perkins, and resides in Hamden. Page 340, seventeen lines from top, for Levi read Lewis. Page 341, twenty lines from bottom, for McEnen read McEwen

Add for the family of Phineas, page 343, No (482) . — He settled in Warren, N. Y., where he was wounded by a cannon discharge, July 4, 1810, and died from its effects He married Edna Rogers His children were *Gates,* residing in Deansville, N Y , until in 1867 , and *Calista,* who m. E. D. Robinson, and was residing at White Pigeon, Mich , in 1867.

Add for the family of Jathleel, page 343, No (484) — He settled at Warren, N Y , where he died in 1860. He married Almenia White His children were *Louisa E* , m Jefferson Lyman and resides at Jordonsville, N Y , *Ralph S* , m. Marion Marquises, resides in Brooklyn, L I , *Alfred P* , m. N Tenny, and resides in New York city.

Add to the family of Jathleel, page 343 [259], Lydia, Arad, Olive, Sophia, Jared, Asenath, Almira, and Burleigh. Lydia married Ebenezer Huntington, of Windham, Conn. Their daughter, Diana, to whom I am indebted for my information, was born in Windham, Conn , June 14, 1811, married Horace Cobb, of Windham, Vt., Apr. 22, 1835, and was residing at Spring Mills, N Y., a widow with her family, in 1867.

Add to the family of Jeremiah [405], page 346, at bottom, after 1867, married Dec 24, 1868, Rufus Aggett, of New Haven, Conn Page 347, eleven lines from top, for Louisa read Lovisa. Page 350, four lines from bottom, for North read South. Page 351, nine lines from top, for Jan. 4 read Feb 4 Page 353, nine lines from top, for Hinchly read Hinckley. Page 354, twelve lines from bottom, for Malvin read Melvin.

Add to the family of Milo Peck [595], page 357, three lines from bottom, *Jeremiah A* , b Sept. 26, 1867. Page 359, fifteen lines from top, for Hosing read Hosington Page 363, thirteen lines from bottom, for Woodstock read Cortland Page 365, eleven lines from bottom, for 1826 read 1862. Page 368, twelve lines from bottom, for June read Jan Page 370, five lines from bottom, for May read Mar. Page 371, four lines from top, for Rachel read Rhoda, and, six lines from top, for Paul read John, and, six lines from bottom, for June 4, 1726, read Mar 12, 1726.

Isaac Peck, supposed to be the son of Abraham, moved from Litchfield, Conn , to near Hudson, N Y , and from there to Onondaga His brother Jacob removed to Cornwall, Vt , where he died. He had a family of ten children Some of them have large families His son, *Doct. Jacob Peck,* was residing at Norfolk, St Lawrence County, in 1866.

Add to the family of Abijah Peck, page 376, No (280), after Reynolds His children were *Sarah A* , *Angeline B* , *Harriet, Charlotte, Lucy, Polly, John B* , and *Clara.* Harriet, from whom I received my information, married William Page, and was residing in Norwalk, Ohio, in 1866. Page 389, six lines from bottom, for Crosby read Cooley.

34*

INDEX.

A general index of the names of all the Pecks in the work was at first prepared, but it was found to contain so large a number of such names as Mary, John, William, and other common names, as to make it the work of too much labor and perplexity for a person to find their own name or that of the person sought for among them. It was therefore thought best to not only reduce its size by making a separate index for the appendix, but by dividing that into separate ones for each branch of the name which it contains.

To still further facilitate finding the name and identifying the persons, a local index of the parents in the several branches of the name, with their residence,* has been given. By this a person will be able to find their own or the name of their parents with much more ease and facility. To find them by the former might have been the work of hours, by this it is comparatively but the work of a moment.

DIRECTIONS.

To find the name of a female, or of a child, or of a person who has no family, look for the name of the father † with his family, and you not only find their name, but the names of their brothers and sisters.

To find the father with his family, look for the same number in brackets which stands against his name in the index.

When there is a star against the name in the index, look for it in the numerals or consecutive numbers, and you will find the person and whatever is said of him or his children, in connection with or immediately following his father's family.

In the appendix, the numerals or consecutive numbers are inclosed in parentheses.

When the name of the father is found, he may be readily traced back and his ancestors learned or traced forward, and his descendants found.

Take as an example the name of Thomas Peck, whose number in the index and in brackets, with his family, is 2642. Turn back to this number in the numerals or consecutive numbers, and you find him and his father, Thomas, and all the family. Look at the left of his father's name, and you have in brackets the number 2601. Turn back to that number in the numerals, and

---

* Some of these residences may have been incorrectly given me, or may have been changed, but as it would so much help to identify the persons and facilitate tracing out their descendants it was thought best to give them. It was preferred rather than the plan of giving the dates of births

† The general index may be referred to when the parents are unknown.

you find the family of his grandfather, Nathaniel, — who are his uncles* and aunts Look at the left of his grandfather's name, and you have the number 2592, look for that number in the numerals, and you find the family of his great-grandfather, Nathaniel. Look at the left of his name, and you have the number 2588 Look for that number in the numerals, and you have the family of his great-great-grandfather Nathaniel, who was born at Hingham, Mass, after his father came over to this country.

To trace Thomas forward and find his descendants, turn to his number 2642 in brackets, and you find this + sign before the names of his sons, indicating that they became parents, and are carried forward to the same number in brackets which is here against their names, where *they* and *their* families may be found.

Take Philip as an example Turn forward to *his* number, 2726 in brackets, and you find him and his family of nine children As the families are not carried forward beyond this generation, the grandchildren immediately follow the children, and it will be seen that you have before you the names of nine[8] children, fifty[9] grandchildren, and five[10] great-grandchildren, who are of the tenth generation,† being the grandchildren, the great-grandchildren, and the great-great-grandchildren of Thomas, his descendants, through his son Philip.

EX·PLANATIONS.

In the arrangement of the work, the numerals or consecutive numbers at the left of the names represent the number of each person individually from the ancestor.

This + sign placed before a name indicates that the person becomes a parent, and refers forward to the number of that person, inclosed in brackets, where he and his family may be found.

When the name is not carried forward to another place in the book, whatever is said of the person is said in connection with or immediately following the father's family.

The figures in brackets at the left of the name refer back to the numerals or consecutive numbers where that person and his father's family may be found

The small figures over the names and above the line represent the number of the generation to which the person belongs.

* It will be seen that this sign + is placed before the names of his uncles; which indicates that they became parents, and are carried forward to the same number in brackets, which here stands against their names, where *they* and *their* families may be found without again turning to the index; each may also be traced back through their ancestry, or forward through their descendants, without turning to the index

† It will be seen by the chart or pedigree that the ancestor Joseph is traced back in England through his ancestors, by authentic records certified to by the Heralds, twenty generations; which, added to the ten in this country, makes thirty generations through which the name is traced.

LOCAL INDEX.

	No
Horace,[7] of Dellona, Wis.	1827
Horace,[7] of Providence, R I	1963
*Horace G ,[8] of Alexandria, N Y	2221
*Horace,[8] of Chateaugay, N Y.	2441
Horace,[6] of West Brookfield, Mass.	3422
Horatio,[7] of Rehoboth, Mass.	399
Horatio N ,[7] of Rochester, N Y	444
Horatio N.,[7] Kansas	579
*Horatio G ,[8] sup. of Saratoga, N Y.	888
*Horatio A.,[8] of Grand Rapids, Mich.	2323
Horatio,[6] of Swanzey, Mass	2684

I.

	No
Ichabod,[4] of Cumberland, R I.	10
Ichabod,[5] of Cumberland, R I.	33
Ichabod,[6] of Fulton County, N Y.	98
Ichabod,[6] of Montpelier, Vt	182
Ira,[6] of Owassa, Mich	114
Ira B.,[7] Woonsocket, R I.	302
Ira, of Half Moon, N Y	325
Ira L ,[7] of Farm Ridge, Ill.	345
Ira R.,[7] of East Bloomfield,;N Y.	442
Ira,[7] of Marshall, Ill.	2791
Isaac,[7] of Coventry, R.I.	655
Isaac L ,[7] of Warren, R.I	1964
*Isaac,[8] of Huntington, C.W.	2479
Isaac,[6] of Providence, R.I.	2660
*Isaac,[8] of Providence, R I.	3223
Israel,[7] of Swanzey, Mass.	1728
Israel,[3] of Dalton, Mass	3381
Israel, of Pittsfield, Mass.	3388

J.

	No
Jacob,[6] of Fly Creek, N Y.	2645
Jacob,[7] of Mobile, Ala.	361
James,[6] of Glenville, N.Y	119
James,[6] of Rehoboth, Mass	127
James,[6] of Montpelier, Vt.	147
James W ,[6] of Topsham, Vt.	198
James M ,[7] of Kentucky	458
James W ,[7] of Boston, Mass.	587
James C ,[7] of Providence, R I.	1472
James,[6] of Seekonk, Mass.	1610
James,[7] of Hopewell, N.B.	1777
James M ,[7] of Warren, R I,	1917
James,[7] of East Cleveland, Ohio	2735
James B ,[7] of Providence	2852
James,[5] of Sheffield, Mass	3386
Jathniel,[3] of Rehoboth, Mass.	4
Jathniel,[4] of Rehoboth, Mass	13
Jathniel,[5] of Rehoboth, Mass	44
Jathniel,[7] of Rehoboth, Mass.	385
*Jathniel,[8] of Taunton, Mass.	998
Jeremiah,[6] of Attleborough, Mass	99
Jeremiah,[7] of Adrian, Mich	323
Jeremiah,[7] of Taunton, Mass	402
*Jeremiah,[8] of Newton Corner, Mass.	2969
*Jeremiah,[8] of Adrian, Mich	883
Jeremiah,[7] of Wolcott, Vt.	2793
Jerome B ,[7] of Medway, Mass	552
Jesse F ,[6] of Pelham, Mass	108
*Job,[8] of Sacramento City, Cal	3024
Joel,[6] of Cumberland, R I	103
Joel F.,[7] of Wrentham. Mass	301
*Joel C.,[8] of Troy, N.Y.	659
Joel,[7] of Gowanda, N.Y.	3450
Joel,[7] of Poestenkill, N Y	272
Joel,[5] of Seekonk, Mass	2624
John,[6] of Montpelier, Vt	65
John,[6] of Waterbury, Vt.	168
John Suppose,[7] of Sand Lake, N Y	275
John,[7] of New York city	321
John W.,[7] of Cynthiana, Ky.	500
John Q A ,[7] of Montpelier, Vt	538
John C ,[7] of Waukegan, Ill	558
John N ,[7] of Gorham, N.Y.	571
*John,[8] of Johnstown, N.Y	710
*John A.,[8] of Newton, Mass.	778
John,[6] of Seekonk, Mass.	1411

	No
John,[4] of Attleborough, Mass	1517
John,[5] of Attleborough, Mass	1562
John,[6] of Bristol, R.I	1640
John,[7] of New Bedford, Mass.	1732
John T.,[7] of Troy, Pa.	1824
*John E ,[8] of New Bedford, Mass	1991
*John,[8] of Hopewell, N B.	2119
*John M ,[8] Rev , of Claremont, N H	2307
*John B , sup ,[8] of Xenia, Iowa	2510
John, Rev.,[6] of Black River, N Y.	2690
John,[7] of Providence, R I.	2796
John H.,[7] of Barrington, R.I.	2939
*John W ,[8] of Little Rock, Mich.	3274
Johiel,[7] of Hopewell, N.B	1786
Jonathan J.,[7] of Barre, Vt	450
Jonathan,[3] of Bristol, R I	1500
Jonathan,[4] of Bristol, R I	1520
Jonathan,[5] of Bristol, R I	1568
Jonathan,[6] of Rehoboth, Mass	1662
Jonathan,[5] of Rehoboth, Mass.	1582
Jonathan,[6] of Attleborough, Mass	1618
Jonathan,[6] of Alexandria, N Y.	1638
Jonathan,[7] of Alexandria, N Y.	1800
Jonathan,[7] of Columbia, Pa	1822
Jonathan,[7] of Bristol, R.I.	1876
*Jonathan,[8] Hammond, Wis	2215
*Rev Jonas O.,[8] of Chelsea, Mass	1152
Joseph,[4] of Rehoboth, Mass.	71
Joseph,[6] of Middletown, N Y	111
Joseph,[6] of Charlton, Mass	227
Joseph,[7] of Kalamazoo, Mich	329
Joseph S ,[7] of Rehoboth, Mass !	463
Joseph,[3] of Seekonk, Mass	1496
Joseph,[4] of Rehoboth, Mass.	1505
Joseph,[5] of Rehoboth, Mass	1558
Joseph,[5] of Providence, R I	1604
Joseph,[6] of Bristol, R.I	1612
Joseph,[7] Fair Haven, Mass	1735
Joseph,[7] of Hopewell, N B	1791
*Joseph B ,[8] of Dorchester, Mass.	2141
Joseph K ,[6] of Amherst, Mass	3394
Joseph,[7] of Spartinsburgh, Pa	3443
Josiah,[5] of Rehoboth, Mass	79
Josiah,[6] of Eaton, Mass	231
Josiah,[7] of Washington, Ind	640
Josias L ,[7] of Bristol, R.I.	1966
Joshua,[6] of Montpelier, Vt	163
Joshua,[6] of Smithfield, R I	1613
Josephus,[7] of Northbridge, Mass	1911
Josephus,[7] sup. of Rehoboth, Mass.	447
*Josephus W ,[8] of Providence, R I.	3326
*Judson N ,[8] of Hopewell, N B.	2144

K.

	No
Dr. Kelly,[7] of Cumberland, R I.	816

L.

	No
Learned,[6] of Providence, R I	2722
Lemuel,[6] of Rehoboth, Mass.	144
*Leonard G ,[8] of Carthage, N Y.	2280
Levi,[6] of Westminster, Vt	101
Levi,[7] of Huron, Ohio	363
Levi,[7] Chelsea, Mass.	586
*Levi S ,[8] Fulton, Wis	783
Lewis,[5] Providence, R.I	81
Lewis,[6] of Ellenville, N Y.	115
Lewis,[7] of Mount Tabor, Vt	288
Lewis,[7] of Cumberland, R I	306
Lewis,[7] of New York	482
Lewis,[6] of Ira, Vt	2708
Lewis,[7] Burrillville, R I.	2811
Lewis,[6] Ira, Vt	2625
Libbeus,[7] of Providence, R.I.	410
Loring,[5] Lake Pleasant, N.Y	1578
Lucius W ,[7] of Salt Lake City	461
Lucius B ,[7] of Montpelier, Vt.	514
Luther B ,[7] of Providence, R I.	1475
Lyman,[7] of Rehoboth, Mass	395
Lyman,[7] of Royalston, Mass.	528

OTHER NAMES.

The small figures placed over or at the right of the number of the page denote the number of times the name occurs upon that page.

A.

Abel, 31, 96[2]
— Abigail, 85
Adams, 18, 194,[2] 249.
Ainsworth, 224.[3]
Akerly, 152, 153, 176
Aldrich, 63[5], 79, 98.
Alexander, 38, 58, 77[2]
Allen, 18, 43, 44, 45,[2] 53, 89[2], 95, 96, 118, 199, 204, 207; cht 214, 215, 127, 255.
Allers, 194[2]
Algiers, 52.
Alsdurf, 257
Alston, 99
Anderson, 232
Andrews, 63,[6] 236
Angel, 63
Anthony, 241,[2] 184.
Armington, 149,[2] 124, 221
Armstrong, 93,[6] 101.
Arnold, 56, 88,[2] 90, 92,[2] 123,[2] 147[2]
Ash, 226
Atwood, 240.
Ann, 198
Anne, cht
Austin, 80,[4] 218,[6] 224, 239, 252,[2] 254, 255.
Ayers, 84[2]

B.

Babbs, 21.[2]
Babb, 23[2]
Babbett, 154.
Babcock, 182.
Bacon, 26,[2] 178
Bagley, 69
Bailey, 62, 55, 164, 234.
Baird, 102
Baker, 52, 82, 87, 191, 215, 243.
Baldwin, 52, 80, 253[2]
Ballard, 193[2]
Ballou, 55,[2] 57,[2] 58,[3] 59, 91,[2] 89, 92
Barber, 95.
Barker, 156, 209.[11]
Barns, 74, 90, 96, 179, 207, 208, 215, 217[3]
Barnard, 167
Barney, 45, 100, 108, 119,[2] 126,[4] 206,[2] 208,[2] 149,[3] 162, 165,[2] 169,[2] 199, 211.
Barrus, 50,[3] 65.
Bard, 61.
Bartlet, 47
Barton, 74, 79[2]

Bartrum, 234
Bardshaw, 98
Bastin, 215.[2]
Batchelor, 73, 69[2]
Beckwith, 177.
Bellows, 70, 116[2]
Bellinger, 179.
Bennett, 152, 158,[4] 183, 191, 195.[3]
Benson, 217
Benedict, 63, 72
Bicknell, 136,[2] 247.
Bickford, 184
Bignell, 205
Birdsell, 60.
Bishop, 38, 58, 75, 92, 153,[2] 210
Blackinton, 90.[3]
Blacket, 93[2]
Blake, 135.
Blaisdale, 169.[3]
Blackman, 214, 215.
Blandin, 32.
Blaxton, cht
Blood, 115.
Bliss, 16, 36, 42, 52, 53,[3] 67, 64, 65, 73, 99,[2] 101,[2] 103, 107,[2] 125,[3] 167, 189, 221[2]
Booth, 61
Bonney, 170, 231.
Borden, 236.
Bosworth, 53, 139, 149, 156, 245,[2] 204
Bourn, 115[2]
Bowen, 33, 64, 97,[2] 137, 128, 149, 177, 180,[2] 191, 219, 222,[2] 240[2]
Bowers, 34
Bowler, 70
Boyce, 52
Boice, 158[5]
Bradford, 15, 18, 19, 154,[4] 179.[2]
Bradley, cht, 230[2]
Brady, 189.
Brambles, 67.
Bray, 70, 176
Brayton, 120.
Brewster, 152, 173, 174.
Brigham, 164
Briggs, 74, 149, 154,[4] 168, 173, 190, 217[2]
Bristol, 225.[5]
Brindle, 183
Broderick, 93.
Broadshaw, 179, 182
Broddast, 180
Brown, 38,[2] 46,[2] 80, 115, 136.[2] 159,[7] 161, 177,[2] 182,[2] 186,[2] 209, 211,[2] 213, 216, 220,[2] 223,[2] 249.

Broughton, cht.
Brooks, cht
Bruning, cht.
Bryant, cht
Buck, 153
Buckland, 199.
Bucklin, 31, 207, 249.
Bacon, 158
Budd, 179
Buel, 61
Buffam, 75
Bugbee, 234[2]
Bulas, 216.
Bullock, 36, 51, 159,[2] 214[2]
Bump, 243[2]
Bunker, 110.
Burr, 92, 184[2]
Burk, 144
Burt, 106.
Burrill, 194,[2] 210.
Burns, 87.
Burgen, 167.
Burbank, 177.[2]
Burlingame, 55[2]
Burnett, 113
Burdick, 236.[2]
Burnham, 227.
Bushnell, 228.
Bush, 112,[2] 253
Bushee, 209
Butts, 150
Butler, 78, 186, 217.
Butterfield, 118.
Butterworth, 48, 61 122, 134, 198, 133.

C

Calder, 70
Calhoun, 143,[2] 174,[3] 175
Caldwell, 178
Calkins, 151.
Campbell, 57, 222.
Cameron, 104.
Capron, 65, 151[2]
Carr, 118.[2]
Carder, 137.
Carmitte, 56.
Carpenter, 31, 51, 64, 66,[2] 71, 78,[2] 90,[2] 115, 123, 124, 167,[2] 198, 209,[3] 140
Carr, cht.
Carrier, 116.
Carson, 189.
Caruthers, 187.
Cary, 212,[2] 247.
Casey, 70, 192
Cass, 74[2]
Caswell, 148
Cave, cht.

Ceasar, 34, 205
Chadwick, 150.
Chafee, 54, 125, 126,[2] 222[2]
Chamberlayne, 178
Chapman, 38, 213
Chappel, 169,[2] 80.
Chase, 52, 53, 62,[3] 147, 160,[3] 164, 217, 218,[2] 221[2]
Chenery, 255[4]
Cheeney, 188.
Chickering, 128
Childs, 54,[2] 164
Chipman, 87
Christy, 71.
Christie, 127.
Christyan, 84.
Church, 188,[7] 161.
Clark, 14. 61, 48, 75, 113, 119,[2] 162, 174, 210,[7] 215, 230,[2] 235,[2] 256
Clapp, 171.[2]
Clayton, cht
Clement, 104
Clifford, 71
Clough, 106
Cobb, 172.[2]
Codding, 66.[3]
Coggshall, 101,[2] 181.[2]
Colby, 67, 105,[2] 188.[7]
Cole, 59,[2] 104,[2] 128,[2] 142, 164, 181,[2] 187.
Coleman, 111[2]
Colegrove, 214.[2]
Collins, 189, 216.
Colopy, 113.
Colvin, 236,[4] 237[3]
Congor, 93,[7] 158.[2]
Cooms, 237.
Connor, 232.
Corey, 117, 227
Cooper, 19, 60,[2] 177,[2] 122, 134, 210, 230, 241,[2] 20, 29.
Cowles, 159[8]
Cornell, 184
Covel, 30, 35, 53.
Couch, 192
Cowel, 194
Craig, 183
Cram, 172.
Crego, 226.
Crocker, 75.
Crompton, 24.
Cronk, 60
Cross, 179
Crossman, 65, 176.
Crosby, 73.
Crowningshield, 89
Curtis, 84, 115,[2] 217.
Cumstock, 91.

APPENDIX.

BOSTON AND HINGHAM PECKS.

A.
Abigail . . 109

B
Benjamin . . 17
Benjamin . . . 26
Benjamin . . . 37
Benjamin . . . 51
Benjamin . . . 71
Benjamin . . . 72
Benjamin . . . 119

E.
Ebenezer . . . 81
Ebenezer . . . 60
Ebenezer . . . 84
Elizabeth . . 4
Elizabeth . . . 21
Elizabeth . . 23
Elizabeth . *44
Elizabeth . . 56
Elizabeth . . . 62
Elizabeth . . . 63
Elizabeth . . . 64
Elizabeth . . . 66
Elizabeth . . . 83
Elizabeth . . . 87
Elizabeth . . . 108
Elizabeth . 113
Elizabeth . 140
Elizabeth . . 143
Elijah . . . 144

F.
Faith 20
Faith 59

H.
Hannah 49
Hannah 135

I.
Israel 3

J
James 31
James 92
James 120
Jane 77
Joanna 85
Joanna . . 130
John 10
John 14
John 16
John 34
John . 39
John 42
John 54
John 68
John 69
John 100
John 104
John 105
John 106
John 114
John 124
John 127
John 131
John 145
Joseph . . 8
Joseph . . . 9
Joseph . . . 11
Joseph . . . 13
Joseph . . . 53
Joseph . . . 58
Joseph . . 70
Joseph . . 86
Joseph . . . 89
Joseph . . . 90

M.
Mary 24
Mary 28
Mary 36
Mary 41
Mary 46
Mary 48

Mary 67
Mary . . . 93
Mary 101
Mary . . . 117
Mary 123
Mary 128
Mary . . . 134
Mary 142
Margaret . . 136
Margaret . . 138
Margery . . . 3
Moses 115

N.
Nathaniel . . . 6
Nathaniel . . 19
Nathaniel . 38
Nathaniel . 50
Nathaniel . . 133
Nathaniel . . . 141
Nathan . . 75

P.
Paul 5
Philip 99

R
Rachel 22
Rachel . . . 57
Rachel . . . 78
Rachel . . . 129
Rebecca 139
Richard 1
Robert . . . 110
Robert M. 40

S.
Samuel 29
Samuel . . . 32
Samuel . . 45
Samuel . . . 52
Samuel . . . 73
Samuel . . 76
Samuel 94

Samuel . . 96
Samuel . 97
Samuel 107
Samuel . 112
Samuel 116
Samuel . . 121
Samuel . 122
Samuel 126
Samuel . 132
Samuel 146
Sarah . 12
Sarah . . 47
Sarah . 111
Sarah . 137
Simon . . . 7

T.
Tabatha . . . 74
Thankful . . 61
Thomas II . . 30
Thomas H . †43
Thomas . 15
Thomas, jr 18
Thomas . 65
Thomas . 79
Thomas . 82
Thomas . 88
Thomas . . . 95
Thomas . 98
Thomas . 102
Thomas . 103
Thomas . 118

W
William . . . 25
William . 27
William . 33
William . 35
William . . . 55
William . 80
William . 91
William . . . 125
William Dan-
dredge 147

* See the will of Thomas Handasyde Peck, page 271, for this name.
† See his will, page 271, for the name.

OTHER NAMES.

B.
Baker, 276.
Baley, 270.
Brewer, 277.

C
Cary, 272
Chandler, 276.
Child, 277.
Claflin, 276.
Clap, 266.[2]
Clough, 276.
Collins, 277.

D.
Down, 277.

E.
Edes, 271 [2]

F.
Fisher, 267
Farnsworth, 266.
35*

G.
Gambardella, 274.
Gooch, 267.
Gould, 276.
Green, 270.

H.
Hamilton, 276.

J.
Jackson, 276.

K.
Kelly, 276.

L.
Lander, 276.
Lamb, 276.

M.
Marshall, 277.
Mason, 276.

Mitchel, 270, 276.
Mosley, 276.
Murrin, 276.

O.
Odell, 276.

P
Parker, 276
Penneman, 276.
Perkins, 270,[3] 271, 272, 276
Philips, 269.
Potter, 267

R.
Rogers, 276.
Roberts, 276.

S.
Savage, 266.

Sergeant, 276
Shattuck, 272.
Stickney, 268.
Soloman, 269.
Symms, 271

T
Thurston, 268.

V
Valincott, 276.

W
Washington, 273.
Waldo, 267
White, 276.
Webster, 274.
Wells, 276
Willis, 276.
Winthrope, 273.

DESCENDANTS OF JOHN PECK, OF MENDON, MASS.

A

Abraham,[3] of Coleraine, Mass 8
Abraham,[4] of Coleraine, Mass. 26
Abraham,[5] of Coopersville, Mich. 51
Alanson,[5] of Ashford, Conn 80
Almon,[6] of Proctorsville, Vt 145
Alonzo C ,[6] of Boston, Mass 147
Alva,[5] of Cavendish, Vt 73
Amos,[6] of Monson, Mass. 140

C

Calvin,[5] of Ellsworth, Maine 42
Calvin G ,[6] of Ellsworth, Maine 84
Calvin F.,[6] Kent County, Del. 100
Christopher,[6] of Cavendish, Vt. 173

D.

Daniel,[4] of Cavendish, Vt 33
Daniel D ,[5] of Weston, Vt 71

E

Ebenezer,[3] of Ashford, Conn. 7
Elisha,[4] of Abington, Conn , ... 41
Ezekiel,[6] of North Richmond, N H. . . . 68

I

Ira,[5] of Stafford, Conn 60
Ira, jr ,[6] of Wales, Mass 135

J

James,[5] of Weston, Vt. 70
James F ,[6] of Weston, Vt 157
Jason,[5] of West Stafford, Conn 59
Jerry,[6] of Blakely, Pa 45

John,[3] of Ashford, Conn 9
John,[4] of Weston, Vt 31
John,[5] of Peckville, Pa 44
John,[6] of Ellsworth, Maine 91
John D ,[6] of Madison, Pa 99
John B ,[6] d in Palmer, Mass 123
John,[6] of Somerville, Mass 144
Jonathan W ,[6] of Peckville, Pa 96
Joseph,[4] of Monson, Mass 29
Joseph,[6] d Aug 3, 1865 183

L.

Lemuel,[5] of Belchertown, Mass 56
Levi,[6] of Monson, Mass. 143
Luther B.,[6] of Monson, Mass. 133

O.

Oliver,[5] of Weston, Vt 66
Oliver A ,[6] of Boston, Mass 149
Oren,[5] d Feb. 18, 1840 67
Oren H ,[6] of Swanzey, N.H. 163

R.

Robert,[6] of Belchertown, Mass 121
Rowland H ,[6] of Ellsworth, Maine 88

S.

Samuel,[5] of Blakeley, Pa 43
Samuel J ,[6] of New York 85
Samuel L ,[6] of Peckville, Pa 92
Sceava,[6] of East Somerville, Mass 146
Simon,[2] of Mendon, Mass 1
Solomon,[5] of Monson, Mass 62

OTHER NAMES.

A.
Abbott, 283, 284.
— Abigail, 280.
Adams, 284.
Anderson, 287.
Allen, 278.
Arnold, 281
Austin, 280, 283.

B.
Badger, 280 [2]
Baldwin, 280.
Barnard, 287 [2]
Beckwith, 284.
Benjamin, 281
Bertholp, 281.
Bowers, 280, 283.
Bowen, 287
Brown, 279.
Browning, 280
Bixby, 285.
Bullard, 279, 283.
Butler, 283.

C.
Cady, 282 [2]
Campbell, 285.
Carpenter, 285.
Caughey, 283.
Champion, 282.
Cheney, 288.
Clark, 288
Colburn, 283, 287.

Congdon, 284.
Conner, 285
Cross, 286
Cuttler, 282.

D.
Daniels, 278.
Davis, 284
Dean, 283
Dennison, 279.
Donnell, 287

E.
Easten, 286.
Esty, 288

F.
Farrar, 283, 287.
Fenn, 284.
Fisher, 283.
Frazier, 285.

G.
Gaylord, 285.
Googing, 281.
Grant, 285

H
Hathaway, 280.
Hall, 286
Hawley, 287.

Hoar, 287.
Hollis, 279

J.
Jennings, 280.
Johnson, 279.
Jordon, 282.
Joy, 281.

K.
Kent, 281
Kile, 280.

L.
Loomis, 286.
Lothrop, 278.
Luther, 278

M.
Marcy, 280, 285.
McAlster, 281
Metcalf, 283.
— Millicent, 278.

O.
Orcott, 287.

P.
Pettingill, 281.
— Phebe Ann T , 286.
Plympton, 279.
Preston, 279.

R.
Rhodes, 284.[2]

S
Saunders, 287.
Shattuck, 283
Smith, 283.[2]
Snidecor, 281, 286
Snow, 281
Somerby, 285.
Spaulding, 280.
Stephens, 281.
Stevens, 281, 284.
Stone, 286.
Stratton, 282
Stuart, 279.

T.
Taft, 278.
Taylor, 283.
Toggart, 283
Torry, 282 [2]

W.
Walker, 280
Waters, 282
White, 288.
Whitney, 278.
Wilson, 281, 283, 285, 288.
Winship, 284 [3]
Wise, 281.

DESCENDANTS OF JOSEPH PECK, OF MILFORD, CT.

OTHER NAMES.

DESCENDANTS OF HENRY PECK, OF NEW HAVEN, CT.

OTHER NAMES.

DESCENDANTS OF DEACON PAUL PECK, OF HARTFORD, CONN.

A

	No
Abel,[5] of Bristol, Conn.	136
*Abel G ,[7] of Boston, Mass	564
Abijah,[4] of Berlin, Conn	54
Abijah,[5] of Cayuga County, N Y	126
*Abijah,[5] of Litchfield, Conn	65
*Abijah,[6] of Norwalk, N Y	280
Abraham,[4] of Litchfield, Conn	38
Abraham,[5] of Cornwall, Vt.	93
*Alanson A.,[6] of Cornwall, Vt	170
*Aldin,[7] of Meriden, Conn	413
Alfred,[6] of Litchfield, Conn	239
Amos,[4] of Middletown, Conn	56
Amos,[5] of Berlin, Conn	141
*Amzi C ,[7] of Marshall, N.Y	514
Anthony,[6] of Marshall, N Y	305
*Anthony,[7] of Clinton, N.Y	541
Ariel,[5] of Ellesburgh, N Y	148
Asa,[5] of Litchfield, Conn	147
Asahel,[5] of Litchfield, Conn	99
*Asahel,[6] of Farmington, Conn	215
*Austin J ,[7] of Leoni, Mich	492

B

	No
Benjamin,[4] of Litchfield, Conn	36
Benjamin,[5] of Litchfield, Conn	88
*Benjamin,[6] Palenville, N Y	154

C

	No
*Chauncey,[6] of Litchfield, Conn	205
*Chauncey,[7] of Brownhelm, Ohio	647
Cornelius,[4] of Litchfield, Conn	35
*Cornelius W ,[7] Berlin, Conn	419

D

	No
David,[5] of Southington, Conn.	137
*De Witt C ,[7] of Mexico, N Y	548

E

	No
Edward,[6] of Berlin, Conn	256
*Edward,[7] of Marshall, N Y	509
*Edwin O.,[7] of Richmond Centre, Ohio	459
Elinda,[5] of Litchfield, Conn	92
Eldad,[5] of Berlin, Conn	114
*Elijah M ,[6] of Litchfield, Conn	221
*Elijah,[5] of Litchfield, Conn	77
*Elijah,[4] of Berlin, Conn	59
*Elijah,[6] of Lenox, Mass	369
Elisha,[4] of Litchfield, Conn	32
Elisha,[6] of Brownhelm, Ohio	361
Elisha,[5] of Lenox, Mass.	149
*Elisha A ,[7] of Eagle, N.Y	490
*Elisha,[6] of New York city	368
*Elisha F.,[7] of Brownhelm, Ohio	653
Elisha,[6] of Howard, N Y	288
Elish,[4] of Middletown, Conn.	58
Everard,[6] of Rochester, N Y	284

F

	No
*Fayette,[7] of Marshall, N Y	551
Freeman,[5] of Berlin, Conn	121

G

	No
*George B ,[7] of Marshall, N.Y.	496
*George A ,[7] of Marshall, N Y	520

H

	No
Henry,[6] of New Haven, Conn.	285
*Henry M ,[6] of Haverstraw, N Y	365
*Henry,[7] of Castleton, Vt	615
*Horace,[6] of Litchfield, Conn	210

I

	No
Isaac,[4] of Kensington, Conn	53
Isaac,[6] of Marshall, N Y.	298

J

	No
*Jabez,[6] of Lenox, Mass	364
*James B ,[7] of Litchfield, Conn	372
*James,[7] of Howard, N Y.	456
*James W.,[7] of Richmond, Ohio	460
*James I ,[7] of Deansville, N Y.	501

	No
*James G ,[7] of New Britain, Conn	597
Jesse,[5] of Rochester, N.Y	129
Jesse,[6] of New Haven, Conn	286
John,[2] of Hartford, Conn	4
John,[3] of Litchfield, Conn	11
*John M ,[6] of Rockspring, Ill.	351
Joseph,[5] of Berlin, Conn.	124
*Joseph L.,[7] of Lock, N Y	420
Joseph,[2] of Windsor, Conn	6
*Josiah T.,[7] of Bristol, Conn	578
Josiah,[5] of Bristol, Conn	139
*Julius,[6] of Cornwall, Vt	198
Justus,[5] of Walcott, Conn	132
*Justus,[7] of Richmond Centre, Ohio	457

L

	No
Lament,[5] of Bristol, Conn	138
Lemuel,[5] of Berlin, Conn.	145
Lumon,[6] of Cold Spring, Wis	360

M

	No
*Marcus,[7] of Goshen, Ind	481
Moses,[4] of Kensington, Conn	52
*Moses,[7] of Fabius, N Y	449

N

	No
Nehemiah,[6] of Burlington, Vt	325
Neuman,[6] of Excelsior, Wis.	326
*Norman,[7] of Rochester, N Y	433

O

	No
*Oliver,[6] of Lenox, Mass	367
*Ozias,[6] of Plymouth, Conn	226
*Ozias W , of New Haven, Conn	229

P

	No
Paul,[2] of Hartford, Conn	1
Paul,[3] of Litchfield, Conn	10
Philo,[5] of Litchfield, Conn	102

R

	No
Reeve,[4] of Litchfield, Conn	42
Reeve,[5] of Cornwall, Vt.	96
Reuben,[5] of Cornwall, Vt	98
Richard,[6] of Bristol, Conn	321
*Romeo,[6] of Cornwall, Vt	190
*Russell U ,[7] of Southington, Conn.	400

S

	No
Samuel,[2] of West Hartford, Conn	5
Samuel,[3] of Middletown, Conn	24
Samuel,[5] of Berlin, Conn	112
Samuel,[4] of Berlin, Conn	51
Deacon Samuel,[6] of Berlin, Conn	255
Samuel,[6] of Bristol, Conn	307
*Samuel H ,[7] of New Orleans	389
Selden,[6] of Berlin, Conn	348
Silas,[6] of Marshall, N.Y	300
*Sylvester,[7] of West Haven, Conn	554

T

	No
Thomas,[4] of Litchfield, Conn	33
Timothy,[4] of Litchfield, Conn	45
Timothy,[5] of Litchfield, Conn	106
Judge Tracy,[6] of Bristol, Conn	320

V

	No
Virgil,[5] of Litchfield, Conn	107

W

	No
Warren,[6] of Lock, N Y.	277
*Warren,[7] of Moravia, N.Y	429
William,[3] of Litchfield, Conn	15
*William,[6] d. in Wisconsin	235
*William G ,[7] of New York	378
*William,[7] of Marshall, N Y	545
Wooster,[6] of Castleton, Vt	332

Z

	No
Zebulon,[4] of Bristol, Conn.	55
Zebulon,[5] of Marshall, N.Y.	135
Zebulon,[6] of Deansville, N Y.	301

OTHER NAMES.

GENERAL INDEX.

The following index contains the names of all the Pecks in the work, excepting those in the local index and pedigree.

The names will be found in the consecutive numbers

Name	No	Name	No	Name	No	Name	No
Jonathan M	2087	Kezia	2650	Lois T	2776	Lydia	191
Jonathan W	2385	Kezia	2712	Lois	2611	Lydia	220
Jonathan	2415	Kezia	2778	Lloyd G	2019	Lydia	281
Jonathan	2697	Kezia	2805	Lorinda R	1185	Lydia	293
Jonas G	513	Kezia	2918	Loranda I	2885	Lydia	481
Jonas O	1152	Kirk	795	Loring	1656	Lydia	582
Joseph	36	**L**		Loring D	1859	Lydia B	638
Joseph	55	Laforest H	3180	Loring	2345	Lydia	647
Joseph	100	Lattimer	1768	Loram	2879	Lydia H	652
Joseph C	486	Laura	438	Lorenzo	2242	Lydia J	677
Joseph W	633	Laura J	503	Louisa A	348	Lydia A	714
Joseph	752	Laura J	805	Louisa	541	Lydia M	745
Joseph W	1255	Laura A	859	Louisa	636	Lydia	769
Joseph J	1302	Laura	952	Louisa	742	Lydia	882
Joseph	1504	Laura J	1313	Louisa	878	Lydia J	938
Joseph	1540	Laura M	2021	Louisa	1430	Lydia A	1029
Joseph	1546	Laura	2050	Louisa	951	Lydia W	1232
Joseph	1716	Laura R	2549	Louisa A	1493	Lydia W	1227
Joseph B	2000	Laura W	2551	Louisa	2027	Lydia E	1355
Joseph S	2004	Laura	2874	Louisa	2357	Lydia	1417
Joseph C	2086	Laura H	3048	Louisa	2794	Lydia	1455
Joseph	2492	Laura	3406	Louisa	3119	Lydia	1510
Joseph	2509	Laura	3448	Louisa	3478	Lydia	1548
Joseph B	2800	Lavonia	318	Louis W	2406	Lydia	1575
Joseph	2935	Lavinia	554	Lowell H	1257	Lydia	1644
Joseph B	3072	Lavinia	2117	Lucy	173	Lydia	1697
Joseph K	3415	Lavinia A	2147	Lucy	308	Lydia	1725
Joseph	3421	Lavinia	2195	Lucy Ann	412	Lydia	1798
Joseph	3459	Lavinia	2257	Lucy	357	Lydia B	1891
Joseph E	3486	Lavinia	2352	Lucy	494	Lydia	1929
Joseph K	3489	Lavern	3208	Lucy Ann	1072	Lydia N	1979
Josiah	499	Leander E	3314	Lucy A	1086	Lydia D	2088
Josiah	508	Leander R	3357	Lucy A	1093	Lydia D	2095
Josiah E	1374	Lebarron	1933	Lucy H	1147	Lydia	2177
Joshua V	2113	Lelia	2046	Lucy W	1226	Lydia	2209
Josephus F	1980	Leland	2699	Lucy L	1304	Lydia A	2366
Josephine B	1039	Leland T	849	Lucy A	1381	Lydia	2507
Josephine M	1192	Lemira	1899	Lucy	1416	Lydia A	2553
Josephine E	1488	Lemira M	2486	Lucy	1880	Lydia	2700
Josephine	1490	Lemira W	2916	Lucy	2056	Lydia	2741
Josephine C	1060	Lemira W	3337	Lucy	2057	Lydia D	2773
Josephine	2270	Lena C	961	Lucy	2097	Lydia	2820
Josephine A	2538	Leonora B	797	Lucy E	2363	Lydia	2878
Josephine J	3043	Leonora	1309	Lucy	2672	Lydia L	2912
Judith	32	Leonard	2417	Lucy S	2835	Lydia C	3087
Judith A	749	Leonard L	3128	Lucy	2839	Lydia J	3138
Judith	1513	Lepha	1335	Lucy A	2917	Lydia L	3256
Judith	2578	Lepha	209	Lucy S	3121	Lydia K	3341
Judith	2683	Lepha	215	Lucy E	3342	Lydia W	3465
Julianna C	414	Leroy E	3354	Lucie	2827	Lyman	317
Julia E	940	Lewis	372	Lucia A	3177	Lyman	480
Julia M	1076	Lewis R	1148	Lucinda	336	Lyman	564
Julia A	1162	Lewis J	904	Lucinda B	1973	Lyman B	3179
Julia A	2219	Lewis	1216	Lucinda	3033	Lyman	1262
Julia A	2258	Lewis	839	Lucinda T	3249	**M**	
Julia	2346	Lewis	1219	Lucius	1160	Madora A	3195
Julia A	2370	Lewis J	1375	Lucena	836	Mahala	576
Julia A	2375	Lewis	2519	Lucina E	1361	Mahala D	656
Julia M	2440	Lewis	2623	Lucina S	2024	Mahala	741
Julia A	2923	Lewis	2625	Lucina S	2236	Mahala A	860
Julia M	2957	Lewis	2817	Lucina	3135	Mahala	2005
Julia A	2973	Lewis W	2906	Lucretia	3028	Malinda	2211
Julia A	3011	Lewin	2086	Lucretia A	3487	Manly D	3129
Julia M	3281	Lilly K	1293	Lucretia	3499	Mary	5
Julia A	3293	Lilly	2464	Luella E	3178	Mary	35
Julia G	3330	Lillie	3112	Luella	3187	Mary	42
Julia A	3348	Lilis	1482	Luna A	3013	Mary	52
Julia	3409	Linda	397	Lucilla J	2065	Mary	94
Julia A	3455	Lizzie	615	Lury	2432	Mary	161
Julia A	3464	Lizzie	3250	Lurana	3448	Mary	170
Julia E	3423	Lizzie	3471	Luther F	1495	Mary	179
Julia E	3546	Lodence	2268	Luther B	3197	Mary	250
Julius	3154	Lois	304	Luthera M	3306	Mary	278
Julietta L	3359	Lois	105	Luvertia	1161	Mary	330
Justin A	1037	Lois	1632	Lydia	62	Mary	339
K		Lois	1772	Lydia	72	Mary	342
Kate	1290	Lois	2030	Lydia	75	Mary	413
Kezia	2630	Lois K	2063	Lydia	97	Mary Ann	424
				Lydia	155		

Name	No.	Name	No	Name	No	Name	No
William W	975	William	2120	William H	2573	Willie B	1292
William A	992	William R	2123	William R	2575	Willie	2276
William H	1018	William F	2135	William H	2723	Willie	3116
William F	1042	William L	2150	William F	2734	Willie C	3137
William E	1057	William R	2216	William B	2932	Willie	3158
William C	1089	William W	2225	William H	2954	Willaid H	1134
William M	1149	William R	2238	William	2981	Willaid	1252
William H	1182	William H	2803	William R	2984	Willaid	1766
William H	1201	William H	2930	William	3066	Willaid	2031
William T	1210	William L	2273	William T	3074	Willaid	2460
William F	1321	William A	2281	William H	3089	Willis R	1322
William H	1465	William De Wolf	2294	William R	3212	Wilbeit F	2239
William H	1466	William S	2319	William H	3237	Wilmaith H	2954
William	1643	William H	2322	William A	3258	Wolcott	289
William	1674	William B	2331	William E	3269	Wolfoid	2461
William	1720	William	2354	William H	3280	Woolsey	2214
William	1722	William M	2379	William W	3285	Woodhall	3059
William	1807	William M	2380	William N	3345		
William	1825	William M	2389	William J	3351	Z	
William L	1845	William F	2407	William S	3665	Zack	972
William K	1901	William H	2421	William H	3367	Zara C	3000
William E	1959	William	2444	William	4456	Zeluca Z	3205
William F	1984	William	2524	Wilbor M	864	Zilpha G	912
William J	2016	William	2542	Wilbor F	3278	Zilpha	2753
William	2110	William H	2557	Willie	1078		

DESCENDANTS OF JOHN PECK OF MENDON, MASS.

Name	No	Name	No	Name	No	Name	No
A		Dolly	65	**H**		Lydia	27
Abigail I	184	Dwight	208	H Annetta	164	Lydia	35
Abigail	76			Hattie A	235		
Abner C	124	**E**		Hannah	2	**M**	
Abner and Absa-		Ebenezer	18	Hannah	15	Malvina	109
lom	214	Edson S	201	Hannah	61	Mary	4
Absalom C	122	Edwina Jane	171	Hannah R	151	Mary	13
Absalom	214	Elizabeth	5	Harriet	55	Mary	23
Adaline	103	Elizabeth	34	Harriet	139	Mary	47
Adelaid F	211	Elizabeth	89	Helen M	190	Mary	82
Agness M	193	Elizabeth	105	Henry A	230	Mary Ann	93
Albert V	112	Eliphalet S	104	Herbert J	205	Mary	106
Albert	221	Eliza	129			Mary Ann	120
Albert	225	Eliza	180	**I**		Mary Ann	138
Alice J	212	Ella F	229	Ira	176	Mary B	136
Almeron	160	Elmer A	236	Ira L	215	Mary Ann	130
Alva C	243	Elvira C	98	Isabella E	119	Mary E	161
Alvara F	167	Emeline O	97	Isabella	178	Mary E	195
Alvira	179	Emily M	185			Mary S	222
Amelia	141	Emma	213	**J**		Margaret	28
Andrew	182	Emma K	234	James E	102	Martin L	137
Angelina P	168	Ernest H	118	Jared	72	Martin L	216
Anna	11	Etta A	241	Jerush	78	Marion E	239
Ann C	83	Eugena B	244	Joanna	53	Matilda	49
Anna	37	Eugena K	154	Joel E	162	Minerva	81
Annis	175	Eunice	38	John	3	Minerva	128
Arathusa	48	Eunice	142	John	6	Minerva	174
Arathusa	86	Eva F	207	John	24	Moses	46
Arathusa B	95			John	36	Moses	54
Aurilla A	186	**F**		John A	228	Myron E	200
		F—— B	218	Joseph F	127		
B		Fenwick L	198	Josephene	224	**N**	
Bethia	75	Filinda	237	Julia C	181	Nathan	16
Betsey	79	Florence C	192				
Byron N	204	Francis E	117	**L**		**O**	
		Frances E	194	Laura M	219	Oliver	89
C		Francis L	199	Lavinia	57	Olive	63
Calvin	188	Frank A	227	Levi	40	Oren H	155
Charlott	77	Freddy D	210	Lovella	52	Oren A	160
Charlott	107	Frederick	111	Loisa	50	Otis W	172
Chauncey	108	Frederick W	189	Lucina	148		
Charles L	113			Lucina	74	**P**	
Charles W	196	**G**		Lucius E	116	Palmer	64
Charles L	217	Genny	209	Lucy A	150	Philetus D	170
Charles	223	George T	110	Lucy C	126	Polly	30
		George C	202	Lucy M	159		
D		George S	226	Lucy E	231	**R**	
David	20	George O	240	Lucretia	153	Rachel	17

DESCENDANTS OF JOSEPH PECK, OF MILFORD, CONN.

DESCENDANTS OF HENRY PECK, OF NEW HAVEN, CONN.

DESCENDANTS OF DEACON PAUL PECK OF HARTFORD, CT.

DESCENDANTS OF DEACON WILLIAM PECK, OF NEW HAVEN, CONN.

NAMES RECEIVED TOO LATE TO BE NUMBERED.

NAMES OF PECKS IN THE ADDITIONS AND ALTERATIONS.